Death, Mourning, and Caring

Robert Marrone
California State University

BROOKS/COLE PUBLISHING COMPANY

I(T)P® An International Thomson Publishing Company

Pacific Grove • Albany • Bonn • Boston • Cincinnati • Detroit • London • Madrid • Melbourne
Mexico City • New York • Paris • San Francisco • Singapore • Tokyo • Toronto • Washington

Sponsoring Editor: *Steve Schonebaum*
Developmental Editor: *Betsy Friedman*
Marketing Team: *Lauren Harp*
Production Editors: *Debra A. Meyer*
Nancy Roth
Brenda Owens
Manuscript Editor: *Elliot Simon*

Interior Design: *Lois Stanfield/LightSource Images*
Cover Design: *Lois Stanfield/LightSource Images*
Cover Photo: *PhotoDisc*
Photo Researcher: *Jeanne Hallquist*
Typesetting: *Carlisle Communications*
Cover Printing: *West Publishing Company*
Printing and Binding: *West Publishing Company*

COPYRIGHT© 1997 by Brooks/Cole Publishing Company
A Division of International Thomson Publishing Inc.
I(T)P® The ITP logo is a registered trademark under license.
For more information, contact:

BROOKS/COLE PUBLISHING COMPANY
511 Forest Lodge Road
Pacific Grove, CA 93950
USA

International Thomson Publishing Europe
Berkshire House 168–173
High Holborn
London WC1V 7AA
England

Thomas Nelson Australia
102 Dodds Street
South Melbourne, 3205
Victoria, Australia

Nelson Canada
1120 Birchmount Road
Scarborough, Ontario
Canada M1K 5G4

International Thomson Editores
Seneca 53
Col. Polanco 11560
México D. F. México
C. P. 11560

International Thomson Publishing GmbH
Königswinterer Strasse 418
53227 Bonn
Germany

International Thomson Publishing Asia
221 Henderson Road
#05–10 Henderson Building
Singapore 0315

International Thomson Publishing Japan
Hirakawacho Kyowa Building, 3F
2-2-1 Hirakawacho
Chiyoda-ku, Tokyo 102
Japan

Printed in the United States of America.

10 9 8 7 6 5 4 3 2 1

Library of Congress Cataloging-in-Publication Data
Marrone, Robert L.
    Death, Mourning and Caring / Robert Marrone
        p.   cm.
    Includes bibliographical references and index.
    ISBN 0-314-09979-4 (hardcover : alk. paper)
    1. Death—Social aspects.   2. Death—Psychological aspects.
3. Bereavement.   4. Thanatology.   I. Title.
HQ1073.M365 1997   96-32070
393—dc20   CIP

To my parents, Ernest and Joan Marrone,
for the gift of their love and caring

In Memory
of

"Gammy"
Hazel Elaine Freitas
June 8, 1917 ~ June 8, 1995

The dignity with which you lived your life
is the dignity with which you died.
We miss you.

Brief Contents

Contents

Preface

Thanatology is the interdisciplinary study of death and dying. Despite the classic Greek origins of the word "thanatology," the field came into being in the mid-twentieth century—in the wake of World War II. It is a relatively young, but well-established field of study with roots in psychology, sociology, anthropology, philosophy, theology, biology, medicine, social work, ethics, law and other disciplines as well. My hope is that *Death, Mourning and Caring* has truly captured the contributions of these various disciplines and that this book is given added meaning within the rich interdisciplinary context that has defined the field of thanatology over the past 50 years.

Death, Mourning and Caring is organized into three major parts: Part One: Death and Dying; Part Two: Grieving and Mourning: A Life Span Perspective; and Part Three: Caring and Preparing.

In Part One, Chapter 1, we examine how attitudes toward death have changed over recorded time—and how current interest in death, dying and caring is affecting contemporary society. In Chapter 2, we review when and how Americans die. In Chapter 3, our focus is on the psychological processes connected with dying and the near-death experience and, finally, in Chapter 4, Part One is completed with a review of the stages, phases, and tasks of mourning.

In Part Two: Grieving and Mourning, we review the literature on death and dying from a lifespan perspective. In Chapter 5, we focus on the child's understanding of death and mourning. We concentrate on adolescent conceptions of death and the crisis of adolescent suicide in Chapter 6 and in Chapter 7, we review adult conceptions of death and the high-intensity grieving and mourning of parents. Finally, in Chapter 8, we close this section with a review of the aging process, spousal mourning, and the search for meaning in old age.

In Part Three: Caring and Preparing, we focus on caring for the terminally ill and those in mourning, as well as preparations for our own death and dying. In Chapter 9, we review the treatment of the dying in hospitals, in home-care, and in hospice programs. In Chapter 10, we consider the anxieties connected to death as well as preparations for dying and death, from simple tasks to highly complex right-to-die and death-with-dignity issues. In Chapter 11, we review body disposal and funeral rituals from around the world with an emphasis on their role in honoring the dead and in comforting loved ones. Finally, in Chapter 12, a rich array of death-, and dying-related resources is presented.

Supplementary Material

The Instructor's Manual with Test Bank contains information helpful to the busy instructor, including lecture outlines, classroom exercises, and additional resources, prepared by Robert Deaton at The University of Montana. The Test

Bank, written by Pam Schaeffer of Marquette University, is a high-quality collection of at least 30 multiple-choice and essay questions for each chapter.

Acknowledgments

I am deeply appreciative of the many friends, students and professional colleagues who assisted me in the creation and development of *Death, Mourning and Caring*. I would like to thank a few by name.

Special thanks to Elena Marie Azevedo, my spouse and all-time best friend, for her help in editing this work, as well as her emotional and intellectual support during the three years I worked on this project; and to my son, Jason, for always being there with kind words.

Thanks to JoAnn Ferrigno, R.N. of Roseville Community Hospital, Roseville, California, for her helpful review of chapter 9. She is truly my sister; and to Rita McGhee of Hospice of Auburn, California, for her wisdom and compassion; and to Marie Mastracco for her help in reviewing rock 'n' roll music and video material. To Patricia Dickson for supporting this project when it was merely a twinkle in the author's eye.

Thanks to my editor, Steve Schonebaum of West Publishing, for keeping this project creative, challenging, and on course; and to Debra Meyer, Nancy Roth, Brenda Owens, and Betsy Friedman of West Publishing for their help in producing this text. I would like to acknowledge my associates at Brooks/Cole/ITP, Vicki Knight, Jim Brace-Thompson, and Lionel Yang, for their kind welcome.

Among the many reviewers listed below, I would especially like to thank Joseph Heller, Professor Emeritus, California State University, Sacramento, for his multiple reviews of the manuscript, for his unwavering personal support throughout the writing of this text and, for requesting that I teach a course in the Psychological Aspects of Death and Dying many years ago. I extend my gratitude to all the reviewers of this work, with special thanks to Robert Wrenn, University of Arizona; Pamela M. Schaefer, Marquette University; Robert L. Deaton, University of Montana; and Bruce Horacek, University of Nebraska for their many contributions.

Annette Marie Allen
Alabama State University

Ronald K. Barrett
Loyola Marymount University

Thomas E. Bruce
Sacramento City College

Cecelia H. Cantrell
Georgia State University

Robert L. Deaton
The University of Montana

Emanuel Gale
California State University, Sacramento

Joseph R. Heller
California State University, Sacramento

Rosemary P. Holland
Colorado State University

Bruce J. Horacek
University of Nebraska at Omaha

Wayne E. Meeker
Mesa State College

Pamela M. Schaefer
Marquette University

Jennifer Solomon
Winthrop University

David Welch
University of Northern Colorado

Alban L. Wheeler
Morehead State University

Harold A. Widdison
Northern Arizona University

Robert L. Wrenn
The University of Arizona

PART ONE

Death and Dying

American Attitudes Toward Death and Dying

Countless changes have surrounded death over recent centuries, from how and when we die to where we die. And yet the grief and sorrow we feel in mourning the loss of someone deeply loved remain a human constant, cutting across time, culture, and national boundary. Our grief is experienced in very concrete and obvious ways: the shock, disbelief, and physical weakness, the puddle of tears behind the eyes, the tightness in the throat, the shortness of breath, the need to sigh repeatedly, and the emptiness in the pit of the stomach that has nothing to do with any need for food. Waves of sadness continue to ebb and flow in our experience, sometimes violently, sometimes gently, draining our energy and ability to concentrate. At night, though the body seems to sleep, the heart seems hardly to rest at all. Sometimes, awakened by our own weeping, we reach out to the darkness, cursing the night. And then we awake to the challenge of healing—and of transforming the sorrow of the moment into hope for the future.

The Pattern of Invisible Death

Beyond the universally shared elements of the grieving process, there are ways of thinking, feeling, and behaving in the face of death that are the result of growing up in a particular culture. As Americans, we are a truly multiethnic society, and our ways of dealing with death and dying reflect a vast array of attitudes, beliefs, and rituals. Nevertheless, the pattern of attitudes and funeral practices adopted by European Americans, called the pattern of *invisible death,* continues to eclipse all other views (Aries, 1974). The sorrow and pain connected with death and loss may indeed be visceral and universal, but the pattern of attitudes called invisible death, in which feelings and thoughts are kept private to the mourner, has changed—and is changing—the faces we put on the mourning after.

People have mourned in different ways during different historical periods. French social historian Philippe Aries (1974) provides fascinating insights into the changing attitudes and beliefs about death, dying, and mourning among Europeans and European Americans. Aries reveals how Western attitudes toward dying and the dead have evolved historically from a *visible,* naive acceptance of death in the Middle Ages to an ambivalent, *filtered* relationship with death and dying in the early nineteenth century, and finally, during the twentieth century, to *invisible death*—a complex of attitudes toward death and dying characterized by cognitive denial, emotional repression, and behavioral passivity.

VISIBLE DEATH

Dying was different in days gone by. For example, consider the thoughts, feelings, and activities connected with the dying and death of the old coachman in Tolstoy's classic short story "Three Deaths" (Aries, 1974). The old man lies on his back, searching for breath, dying on the kitchen floor, near the warmth radiating from the brick oven. He knows he is dying—there is no doubt about it, no denying the inescapable—pretense is absent from the moment. When the old woman asks him tenderly how he feels, he replies, "It hurts me all over. My death is at hand, that's what it is."

Over the centuries, this is how death often occurred—recognized and orchestrated by the dying person, who, knowing that the end was near, prepared for dying. Lying on the back so that the face could be turned eastward, toward heaven, the dying person carried out a series of ritualized steps linked with the ceremony of visible death. In fact, in the period between 1100 and 1400, these ritualized steps were laid out in little manuals, called *ars moriendi,* or "the art of dying." The manuals, essentially little "how to" books, contained instructions on how to achieve a peaceful and graceful death (Copenhaver, 1978).

Ars Moriendi

The "art of dying" defined the final days for most people in times past. In the epic poem *Chanson de Roland,* the legendary medieval French hero Roland, in the midst of his dying, expresses sorrow over the end of his fascinating life (Aries, 1974). He becomes sad as he recalls the beloved persons and things he has come to know in his life. He weeps and cannot keep himself from sighing.

Friends and loved ones surround Roland's deathbed because death is a public ritual, and Roland's bedroom is a public place to be entered freely. It is crucial that friends, family, and neighbors, including children, be nearby in the final moments of Roland's life. Family and friends visited the dying, cried, sobbed, prayed, or meditated at their bedside, chatted with them, and prepared their favorite foods. When a fever intensified, a cool cloth was offered and placed on the forehead. And when the dying person became frightened or saddened or reactive to the pain, friends and family offered kind words and a hand to hold. When death was near, so were loved ones (Hallam, 1996).

One by one, family by family, they approach him, sharing kind words and recollections, and they ask Roland's forgiveness for old slights and hurts. Oliver, his best friend, asks for forgiveness for any harm he might have unintentionally done him over the years. "I pardon you here and before God," Roland replies softly. And the two old friends bow to each other in faint smiles. As the next loved one moves toward Roland's bedside, Oliver retreats, his eyes filled with tears. And so the ritual moment of Roland's death slowly unfolds, until it is time for him to forget the world and begin meditating on the afterlife and the prayers of forgiveness.

The final prayer said, all that remained was to wait for death and the closing of the final chapter. Should the death occur slowly, the dying, as well as everyone in attendance, waited in hushed silence. The last prayer had been said, the last chapter was nearing completion, and another word was never uttered (Aries, 1975). For the dying as well as for those in attendance, the presence of death was accepted as inevitable, producing what Levine (1991:68) calls "conscious dying." Death was the last chapter in a private drama, and the dying person was to be master over his or her death, creating an appropriate final scene (Morgan, 1995).

Last Rites

Following death, the body would sometimes be left in bed. While some family members and friends might weep, others would speak to the deceased, sharing final thoughts, feelings, and memories in the last moments of what may have been a long, heartfelt tragedy. Immediate family and close friends would then clean and clothe the body while others prepared the wooden coffin. The body would then be gently placed in it, and laid out in the parlor for a visitation or *wake* (night vigil).

During the funeral, death was celebrated by a solemn ceremony whose main purpose was to honor the deceased and his or her connectedness with family and community. The body would be carried to the burial ground, to be lowered by neighbors and family into a grave they had dug at the family plot or at a nearby churchyard. In honor of the deceased, spouse, children, immediate family, extended family, best friends, and neighbors, in turn, would fill the grave with flowers, mementos and, finally, fresh earth. Following final services, all the participants would return to the deceased's home to comfort one another, to honor the memory of the departed, and to sit together sharing food, drink, and conversation.

FILTERED DEATH IN EARLY AMERICA

Between 1600 and 1830, death was a vital part of the American experience. Death still had presence. In many American towns, even if people were untouched by death in their own families, they still heard the funeral bell tolling in the distance and might encounter the funeral procession as it wound its way

Family members cherish this post-mortem photograph of Grandmother Esther who died at home of cancer in 1917 at age 39. She called each of her four children to her bedside individually to say goodbye before she died.

from the local church, through town, to the local graveyard (Leming and Dickinson, 1994). Death occupied space and time. Death still embraced meaning and summoned spiritual yearning in those it touched.

In her review of the writings on parental grief in European American history, social scientist Laura Smart (1993–94) discovered that parents in the 1600s through the mid-1700s strove to keep their emotions in check when their children died. The rise of emotion-stirring religions, beginning in the 1700s, brought a norm of increased expressiveness to the colonies. By the early 1800s, women had begun to leave records of their grieving and mourning in letters and diaries. Emotional expressiveness following infant death reached its peak during the nineteenth century, according to Smart, but decreased toward the end of the century and became all but taboo by the middle of the twentieth century.

Paul Rosenblatt (1983) has captured this high point of emotional expressiveness in a compelling analysis of how people mourned the dead in the United States in the nineteenth century. While examining hundreds of diaries written by Americans—some who were left behind by loved ones venturing west in search of riches and others who had lost loved ones to disease at an early age—he discovered a process of mourning characterized by a great outpouring of emotion and yearning, tempered with an acceptance of death as a natural and inevitable life event (Harvey, 1995).

Most people in this primarily agricultural period were well acquainted with death. For example, in nineteenth century America, postmortem photography was a socially acceptable, publicly acknowledged form of honoring the dead. Photos of the deceased were publicly displayed in albums and in frames on parlor walls or on fireplace mantels. Initially, death pictures were portraits that attempted to soften death by displaying the body as if asleep or even conscious. By the turn of the century, however, the deceased were being displayed in a casket, with an increasing emphasis on the funeral (Ruby, 1988–89).

By the mid-nineteenth century, the attitude toward death had changed slowly and imperceptibly in most Western industrialized nations. During the eighteenth and nineteenth centuries, family ties and affection played so central a role in life that the death of a loved one meant the loss of a relationship. The surviving family member had, according to Morgan (1995:34) "*literally* lost a part of him- or herself. Persons are composed not only of body parts, but also of history and relationships. The bereaved person is wounded as truly as if blood were dripping from torn flesh. This loss of the other was first reflected in the 19th century."

As a consequence of this shift to placing increased value and meaning on relationship and family ties, the initiative concerning death passed from the dying person to the immediate family. The wishes of the dying person were now filtered through the wishes and desires of family members and, in turn, to undertakers, morticians, funeral directors, and their assistants. Death had slowly changed from a personal, psychological event to a collective, sociocultural event, with the family playing a central role in their loved one's dying and death.

At first, the family sought to spare the dying person from the painful gravity of the ensuing death, and their efforts were aimed at softening the stark finality of it. This attitude was soon overtaken by a different one, however—one that has come to typify our contemporary attitude toward death and dying. From now on, we must deny the messy painfulness of death and loss, and repress the disturbingly painful emotions caused by the presence of death in an otherwise joyful life.

Sociologists Michael Leming and George Dickinson (1994:413) connect these changes with the rise of the American middle class and its attempt to distinguish itself from both American common people and European aristocracy. They note that between 1830 and 1945, the ideas and institutions with which Americans approached death changed in a process that some have called "the dying of death." This process brought about "the practical disappearance of the thought of death as an influence upon practical life, and the tactical appearance of funeral institutions designed to keep death out of sight and out of mind." According to Philipe Aries (1974), the attempt to hide death and make it invisible was done, not for the sake of the dying person, but for the sake of loved ones and society in general.

INVISIBLE DEATH

During the first half of the twentieth century, an attitudinal sea change overtook the Western world. This was due to important societal changes brought on by the revolution in modern medicine, the resultant increase in life expectancy, and changes in our view of ourselves and our place in nature. At the same time, in the relative blink of an eye, the family retreated from the center of the death scene to the periphery, as medical professionals took over the tasks of caring for the dying and mortuary professionals took over the tasks of performing funeral and burial rites. The site of the deathbed scene also changed. Beginning in the 1950s, we were less and less likely to die at home, near loved ones and the warmth of the hearth and the familiar. Instead, we died in sterile, fluorescent-lighted hospital complexes among the hard, shiny medical devices and busy medical personnel, not because death was destined or natural or inevitable, but rather because the physician had not succeeded in healing the patient.

THE DISAPPEARANCE OF DEATH

"In our day, in approximately a third of a century, we have witnessed a brutal revolution in traditional ideas and feelings, a revolution so brutal that social observers have not failed to be struck by it. It is really an absolutely unheard-of phenomenon. Death, so omnipresent in the past that it was familiar, would be effaced, would disappear. It would become shameful and forbidden."

Source: Aries (1974), p. 85.

Today, the art of dying has been replaced with a mostly technical phenomenon, a medical event determined by a team of doctors, nurses, and technicians with the help of printouts from heart, brain, and respiratory monitors, and dissected into tiny steps by machines and medical personnel. It is impossible now to know which of these little digitized steps is real death: Is it the one in which consciousness is lost, or the one in which breathing or the heart stops, or the one in which electrical recordings of brain activity flat-line? These are the little "invisible deaths" that have replaced the dramatic deaths and ritual moments of old.

And so it goes. . . . The event of death, followed by a simple telephone call, casts the funeral director, clergy, organist, florist, printer, casket maker, cosmetician, embalmer, tombstone carver, cemetery crew, and grief counselor into their respective roles. Together, it is they who will orchestrate the tasks of preparing the dead for burial and loved ones for coping with the mourning after.

Sociologists Lynne Ann DeSpelder and Albert Lee Strickland (1992:13) part the curtain for us on our contemporary rituals of invisible death. Today, walking into the "slumber room" of a typical European or American mortuary, we might admire the elaborate, shiny metal casket that has replaced the wooden coffin of old. The corpse, with circulatory system bathed in tinted, lanolin-laced embalming fluid, shows all the signs of the mortician's skill in cosmetic "restoration," or what DeSpelder and Strickland (1992:13) call "the stark appearance of death diminished."

At the funeral or memorial service, things may seem more familiar as friends and relatives rise, in turn, to eulogize their loved one. But where is the deceased during this ritual of honoring him or her with kind words and salty tears? Off to the side of things, the casket lid locked shut, death tastefully hidden from view.

Finally, at graveside, where family and friends might appear more as passive observers than active participants, the funeral services conclude. Amazingly, family and friends turn and begin walking toward their cars—leaving the casket sitting on its foldaway gurney, unburied. The cemetery crew will complete the actual burial only after the limos have departed.

The deceased and the family are no longer at the center of the death event for most Americans. Prayers, meditations, and words of forgiveness may play no part in the final chapter. Strong emotions are to be avoided so as not to disturb the other hospital patients or the children. Powerful displays of sadness or anger or fear no longer inspire piety but rather, repugnance—a sign of emotional

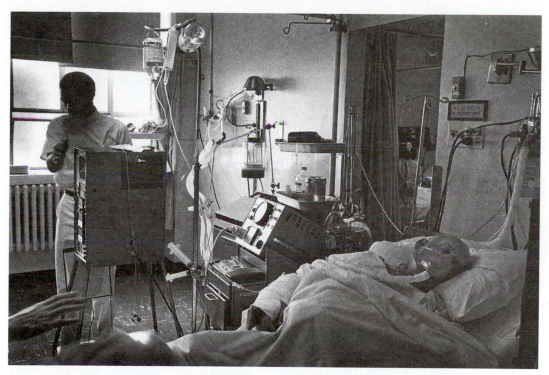

A terminally ill patient lies dying in a rural hospital room surrounded by scanners, tubes, and other life-support equipment while a technician wheels in one more electronic device.
© *George Gardiner/Stock, Boston*

instability, or of bad manners. Within the family, one is restrained from letting go of these deep feelings for fear of unsettling others. One may cry, but only in a quiet and solitary way.

FACTORS INFLUENCING INVISIBLE DEATH

The term *death system* was coined by Kastenbaum and Aisenberg (1972) to describe a society's total pattern of attitudes and practices concerning death, dying, and mourning at any given time, including the persons, places, and things that represent death or that deal with death. The European American death system has undergone quick and powerful changes in the last century. In fact, the pattern of invisible death has been adopted so quickly, so pervasively, by so many people in Western societies, that it is often seen as natural and typical of all peoples, everywhere and always. And yet, despite our attempts to hide death and make it invisible, death refuses to die. According to Canadian philosopher and thanatologist John D. Morgan (1995:40–42), "Our North American death system, . . . is the result of our limited exposure, which is a result of our high life expectancy, . . . but in many ways, our life is no different from that of the peasant in the 14th century. The peasant missed a fully human life because he or she was inundated with death. We do not live fully because we reject death."

MODERN TIMES

"In our Western society, grief has become a hidden emotion. Death is often an anonymous happening, occurring in a hospital or nursing home, where the dying person is surrounded by medical technology. In many instances death is announced by telephone, and the family member is advised to make funeral arrangements and have the body removed from the hospital morgue at his or her earliest convenience. Brief 'viewing' hours at a funeral home confront us with a body that appears to have little relationship to the person we knew. We are expected to return quickly to the demands of our daily life and cope effectively with the burdens of an often radically changed life. We have become efficient in doing away with widow's veils, wailing women, long tearful wakes, dramatic scenes at the grave site."

Source: Seeland (1990), p. 53.

Many factors have contributed to our pattern of invisible death during the past century. Industrialization, advances in medical science and technology, improved living conditions, declining infant mortality rates, increases in average life expectancy, smaller family units, geographic mobility, and influences of the media all have played a role in shaping our contemporary death system.

Industrialization

Industrialization was the earliest and most pervasive factor influencing modern attitudes toward death and dying. Moving toward full throttle in the early twentieth century, this powerful economic and social phenomenon had several direct consequences. Increased food production, better housing, expanding public education, improved water and sewage facilities, quicker methods of communication and transportation, taken together, improved the general standard of living so quickly that death became a less familiar visitor in people's lives. Now, if crops failed in one community or one part of the country, this knowledge could be communicated to other communities, surplus food from somewhere else could easily be transported to meet the demand, and malnutrition or starvation could be alleviated or eliminated.

Changes in public health, falling on the heels of changes in our understanding of communicable diseases, led to quarantine procedures, separation of drinking water from sewage, mosquito abatement, and the control of other disease vectors, such as mice and rats. Altogether, the fruits of industrialization created slow but steady improvements in basic living conditions that contributed greatly to dramatic declines in infant mortality rates and steady increases in life expectancy. In the second quarter of the century, another phenomenon would move to center stage whose effects on mortality rates and life expectancy would know no equal in the history of humankind: the revolution in medicine (Azevedo, 1996).

Modern Medicine

Between the 1930s and the 1950s, the biomedical model of disease, with its emphasis on cure over prevention, was becoming dominant and the physician and hospital were moving to center stage. New medical technologies, immunization programs, and sterile treatment facilities were localized in particular places, namely, hospitals. Instead of bringing medicine to the sick person, changes in transportation and communication allowed the sick person to be brought to the hospital center for treatment.

HOSPITAL SCENE

"I remember her as she lay in her hospital bed in July. Unable finally to deny the pain. And for the first time in our relationship of 21 years was forced to allow someone else to take care of her. My father could not stand the sight so he stayed outside, pacing up and down the hallways. I could not help staring at her. Disbelief that this person with tubes running in and out like entrances and exits to a freeway was the same person who just six months before had laughed gaily and danced at my wedding."

Source: Ruth Kramer Ziony, "Scream of Consciousness," quoted in DeSpelder & Strickland (1992:166).

This period saw the development, in rapid succession, of serums, vaccines, antitoxins, and toxoids to combat many deadly infectious diseases. John F. Enders cultivated live polio viruses that resulted in the polio vaccines of Jonas E. Salk and Albert B. Sabin. Elie Metchnikoff discovered the principle of phagocytosis, the process by which white blood cells engulf and destroy bacteria, and William M. Bayliss and Ernest H. Starling found that chemicals they called hormones are vital to the control of many bodily functions. Typhoid fever, diphtheria, tetanus, spotted fever, whooping cough, polio, cholera, bubonic plague, and measles were among the diseases brought under control. By the end of World War II, general mortality rates had dropped significantly, especially following the introduction of antibiotics, and average life expectancy had increased by more than twenty years. Beginning in the 1950s, breakthroughs in neonatal care began dramatically to affect the infant mortality rate—from 29.2 per 1,000 live births in 1950 to 26 in 1960, 20 in 1970, and 8.5 in 1992 (NCHS, 1995a).

Diagnostic devices were developed and their use became more reliable. Willem Einthoven invented the mechanism for the electrocardiograph, which detects and records heart irregularities. Beginning with the invention of the kidney machine in 1954, ever-increasing arrays of biomedical technologies and drugs have extended our lives and affected both our attitudes and our expectations about dying and death (Compton's, 1995). Karl Landsteiner's research on human blood uncovered the ABO system and the Rh factor. August von Wassermann developed a test for syphilis.

Many advances in surgery also occurred. Beginning with the earlier discovery of anesthesia, means were found to maintain lung inflation and breathing rhythm when the vacuum inside the chest is disturbed by surgery. This made possible heart operations and the removal of diseased portions of lungs. Surgical transplantations of kidneys, livers, and hearts would soon follow. Today, the replacement or repair of dysfunctional organs is an accepted, even expected, part of medical practice. Highly sophisticated machinery monitors biological functions, including heart and brain rhythms, body temperature, and blood chemistry, providing on-the-spot computer readouts and printouts that often make a crucial difference in life-and-death situations.

Since the early 1970s, major technological advances have improved physicians' ability to see inside the human body for the purpose of disease detection and diagnosis. Invasive and sometimes

PERCENTAGE OF DEATHS IN U.S. HOSPITALS, NURSING HOMES: 1900–1994

Year	Percentage
1900	20%
1949	49%
1988	60%
1994	80%

Sources: NCHS (1995a); Nuland (1993).

painful or even dangerous techniques have beenreplaced by safer, noninvasive methods. The familiar X-ray machine, joined by innovative imaging systems such as computerized axial topographic (CAT) scanning, provide images of plane sections through a patient's body, allowing medical personnel to see organ dysfunction, such as tumor growth, without cutting into the body. These methods include new uses for conventional X rays, detection of radioactive materials within the body, and techniques such as positron emission tomography (PET), ultrasound, and magnetic resonance imaging (MRI).

In concert with advances in electronics, engineering, nuclear physics, immunology, pharmacology, biochemistry, and cellular biology, medical science is now developing recombinant-DNA technologies that are yielding new clues to aid in the treatment of some of the world's most troubling diseases. High-tech medical advances continue to raise many moral, ethical, and economic questions about the limits of their use, the social and economic costs, and right-to-die issues. But there can be little doubt that advances in medical science have had profound effects on our expectations of when, how, and where we die.

DRUGS AND LIFE EXPECTANCY

Country	Drug Expenditures per Capita	Life Expectancy at Birth
Japan	$94.18	76
Switzerland	78.73	73
France	77.80	73
United States	70.88	73
Argentina	58.67	69
Brazil	10.57	64
India	1.30	52

Adapted from: K. Long and T. Reim (1985). *Fatal Facts.* Crown, New York, p. 50.

Life Expectancy and the Family

High death rates at the turn of the century, especially among infants and young people, made death a frequent and expected part of the human experience. A typical household contained an extended family, including aged parents, aunts, uncles, grandparents, and children of varying ages. In this setting, the chances of experiencing death firsthand were much greater than in today's smaller, nuclear families.

Because of shrinking family size, members of the typical family in western Europe, the United States, and Canada today can expect to live nearly 20 years without experiencing the death of another family member (Fulton, 1970). How unlike the past, when mothers died during childbirth in great numbers, and many babies were stillborn, or one or both parents might die before their children had grown to adolescence, or siblings or cousins died during early childhood from a variety of communicable diseases. The trajectory of a typical death a century ago was more likely to be rapid and sudden. In 1900, for example, brief-trajectory microbial diseases accounted for about 40% of the deaths in the United States, while today they account for only 4%. The result has been a lessened incidence of firsthand experience with death and a tendency on our part to assume that death is an event that happens in old age.

Of course, expectations that a newborn infant will survive or live to a ripe old age are not shared by all Americans or by those in other parts of the world where

HEART TRANSPLANTATION AND GRIEVING

Researchers have discovered a form of paradoxical behavior in heart transplant recipients including depression and failure to take necessary immunosuppressant medication. Many of the transplant patients experience various phases of grief reaction connected to their loss, including the loss of their heart, which impacts not only the patient but also the physician (Fertziger, 1991). Social workers Julia Rauch and Kyle Kneen (1989) found that heart transplant recipients confront several adaptive tasks following transplantation, including dealing with the loss of the old heart, psychological acceptance of the new heart, fear of physiological rejection of the new heart and death, and spiritual concerns related to themes of resurrection and rebirth. These theorists suggest that the metaphoric meaning of the "heart" in general, and its meaning to the heart transplant recipient in particular, may aid in thinking about, understanding, and facilitating the heart transplantation process and its psychological impact on the recipient, the surgeon, and loved ones.

poverty, poor living conditions, and high rates of mortality during infancy and childhood still prevail. In fact, poor or poorly educated persons in the United States and Canada today have higher death rates than wealthy or better-educated persons, and these differences increased between 1960 and 1986 (Morgan, 1995).

Geographic Mobility

Trains, planes, and automobiles have revolutionized human mobility. Every year in the United States, about 20% of the population pack their belongings, pull up stakes, say goodbye to relatives and friends, and move elsewhere (NCHS, 1992). Distance separates family and friends as changes of employment and lifestyle require moving on, while in previous times relationships were closely tied to a sense of place and to kinship relationships. Children, once grown, are now likely to move to other cities and towns in search of work and change, and rarely live in the same house with parents or brothers and sisters for extended periods of time. Suburban tract homes, senior citizen subdivisions, and trailer parks tend to discourage close intermingling with neighbors or between different generations. Taken together, the decline of continuity and personal contact in extended families and nuclear families and our ever-quickening mobility has tended to rip the fabric of the old family structure, and to segregate the young from the old and the living from the dying (Deaton, 1995).

Death and Language

The revolution in communication (telephone, radio, TV, movies, tape, CDs, Internet, e-mail, etc.) has not only brought massive amounts of information to our homes and workplaces, it has also tended to bring the same information to all of us. Although some regional, ethnic, and generational differences exist in the information we access, the commonalities are much greater than the differences. In this light, the language we use and the images we create and are exposed to regarding dying and death reveal a great deal about our cultural attitudes toward death. In general, we are highly ambivalent about death and dying—immersed, as it were, in an ongoing approach–avoidance conflict. We appear to have tremendous difficulty talking about death honestly and forthrightly in our day-to-day world; at the same time, we reveal an almost obsessive fascination with death and dying in literature, nursery rhymes, TV, film, and even humor.

JACK IN THE BOX

You are cautioned to drive slowly as you enter the Gatling Funeral Home in Chicago. Stopping at a speaker phone, you press the button for service and an attendant in a control room asks whom you'd like to see. The computerized system of switches, relays and timers allows the attendant to accommodate requests to see as many as a dozen different bodies. "I would like to see the remains of Jack Doe," you might say over the speaker phone. "You may proceed" the attendant replies, using controls to turn on the lights and cameras over the body of the deceased lying in one of the "slumber rooms."

You sign the register, conveniently placed under the speaker phone, drive a few feet to the viewing area, where a head shot of the loved one in a coffin instantaneously appears on a 31-inch color TV screen. Dirge muzak creates a somber ambiance. The picture lasts only three seconds, but you can push the button over and over again for as long as you like. Some visitors will stare at the screen, clicking the button every three seconds for a half-hour on occasion. When you're finished, you drive through and another car takes your place.

Lafayette Gatling, the owner, is seeking a patent for the system and is planning bigger and better things for his funeral home, which already sells flowers and sympathy cards for mourners who forgot theirs and holds weddings in the main chapel on weekends. In addition to adding slumber rooms, Mr. Gatling plans to make videotapes of the remains and the funeral services, which he hopes to sell to the bereaved.

Carloads of people, pressed for time, as well as busloads of senior citizens, some confined to wheelchairs, have paraded through the drive-in to see the images of embalmed friends and relatives.

Adapted from an article by Isabel Wilkerson, *New York Times,* February 23, 1989, p. 10.

As long as death is out there somewhere, in print or broadcast, glamorized in song or on screen, or trivialized through humor, we seem to be fascinated by it. Bring it home, however, to our everyday conversations—have death touch our lives in real ways—and we become almost obsessed with denying it, softening it, or spouting euphemisms to hide it from ourselves and from each other. Consider the paradoxical use of death-related language. Americans go to great length to avoid saying the words *dead* and *dying* in situations actually having to do with death and dying. Instead, we replace direct language with *euphemisms*—words that are comparatively softer, less offensive, or more frivolous than those that designate more precisely what is intended. Expressions like "passed away," "laid to rest," "kicked the bucket," "bit the dust," "checked out," "gone to their reward," "bought the farm," "on her last leg," "whacked" and "no longer with us" are substitutes for more direct words such as *died, buried, terminally ill,* and *killed.*

On the other hand, if you think Americans have difficulty with death-related words in nondeath-related situations, you'd be "dead wrong." We have words like "dead battery," "dead end," "dead quiet," "deadline," "deadbeat dad," "dead giveaway," and "deadhead". We say, "I'm dying to do that" or "that outfit is to die for" or "I could have died laughing." We appear to use death-related words to dramatize or intensify a word or expression, relying on the emotional intensity connected with death and dying to heighten the feeling tone of our everyday language. The use of death-related language is inversely proportional to how much we refer to death: We tend to employ it more often when we are not speaking about death and less often when we are (Neaman & Silver, 1983; Partridge, 1966).

Death and the Media

It is ironic that death appears to be more abstract and invisible for children to-day even though media experts report that the average American 15–year-old has seen tens of thousands of murders on television, witnessed an endless array of bloody wars and mayhem in the news, experienced countless exploding bodies and interminable rivers of blood in the movies (Bordewich, 1988:34). Because we are unlikely to know personally the murdered or maimed individuals in these media presentations, however, the effect of this "death overload" is probably minimal.

Fulton and Owen (1987–88:381) note that for the baby boom generation, which constitutes nearly one-third of the American population, the television experience only superficially portrays grief and the ruptured lives that death can leave in its wake. Television's way of dealing with death revolves around a few basic messages: Death is fun and reversible; death is brutal but fast; death is horrible but distant.

1. *Death is fun and revocable.* Cartoon characters such as Tom and Jerry, Popeye, Bugs Bunny, Road Runner, and Roger Rabbit, among a host of others, are routinely annihilated by other cartoon characters, in a variety of ways: cut into pieces, exploded, smashed, pushed from cliffs, shot, etc, only to reappear in the next frame or after the commercial break as alive, reconstituted, and ready for the next "fun" killing. Electronic computer games such as "Doom" offer similar stomach-churning blood and gore, but in three-dimensional, interactive, multimedia presentations. Up to 7 million copies of the game have been downloaded to IBM-compatible computers, and its success has already spawned several spinoffs and competitors. "Doom" add-ons now allow players to change the identity of the grotesque assembly-line villains and instead blast monsters that look like Barney the Dinosaur, Star Wars characters, Beavis and Butt-head, or even the American president and first lady.

2. *Death is brutal but fast.* Television shows such as *Homicide: Life on the Street, Law and Order,* and *Murder One* and movies aired on TV such as *The Terminator, Die Hard, Natural Born Killers, Pulp Fiction,* and an endless stream of "hack-and-slash" horror movies all present the predominant message that young males are violent killers and are killed in graphically horrific ways. The long-standing Hollywood and TV tradition of associating violence and death with the young male has recently added young females, such as seen in *Thelma and Louise* and *Fatal Attraction,* to the list of those who wantonly shoot, hack, and slash. From

> **WOODY ALLEN ON DEATH:**
>
> "I believe in sex and death: Two experiences that come once in a lifetime."
>
> "The only difference between sex and death is that you don't get nauseous after death."
>
> "I don't mind dying, I just don't want to be there when it happens."

nightly newscasts and magazine shows to made-for-TV movies, the message is transmitted that dying, death, grieving, and mourning are resolved in a specific time span, ranging from approximately 30 seconds to 90 minutes.

3. *Death is horrible but distant.* Predominant in global newspaper and TV news coverage is the message that death, when it does occur, usually happens elsewhere and mostly to people who are alien to ourselves. For example, before the World Trade Center bombing in New York in 1993 and the truck bombing of the Federal Building in Oklahoma City in 1995, virtually all multiple-casualty terrorist killings and war deaths occurred outside the continental United States, in such countries as England, Ireland, Bosnia, Lebanon, Somalia, and Haiti.

Taken together, industrialization, high-tech medicine, longevity, mobility, and the portrayal of death in our language and the media have created and reinforced a predominant European American attitude based on distancing ourselves from death and dying. For the majority of Americans, and for most inhabitants of the Western world, direct experience with all the facets of natural human death has been dramatically diminished. Care for the dying and care of the dead have been moved away from the family and out of the home, so many of us have little experience with the moment immediately before, at the time of, or immediately after the death of someone we love. Gerontologist Georgia Barrow (1996:304) writes,

> Since people now typically die in hospitals, the final moments of life are seldom observed, even by the family. Of the nearly 2 million patients currently residing in nursing homes, only 20% will ever return home. . . . Health professionals, rather than family, care for the dying. Dying in institutions is depersonalized, and it serves to dissociate society from death and dying. The body goes to a funeral parlor rather than home. We no longer stay after the graveside service to see the earth shoveled back into the grave, let alone do it ourselves. Serving a meal to all who attend the rites or holding a wake is becoming less common.

DEATH-DENYING ATTITUDES

Among the first studies to focus directly on the variety of death-related attitudes among diverse groups of Americans was a study conducted by Richard Kalish and David Reynolds (1981). The information was obtained by at-home interviews of 434 persons, conducted by professional interviewers. The study's participants were approximately equally divided among four ethnic groups (African Americans, Asian Americans, Hispanic Americans, and European Americans), three age groups (20–39, 40–59, and 60+), and men and women. The number of studies of American attitudes toward death and dying since this breakthrough investigation has increased (Irish, 1993; J. Brown, 1990; Perry, 1993; Blackhall et al., 1995), and though it would be impossible to make definitive statements about how all persons in any ethnic group deal with death and mourning, the various results do reveal thematic differences unique to each ethnic group.

Kalish and Reynolds's multiethnic study (1981), for example, revealed that European Americans had less contact with death and dying than African Americans, Hispanic Americans, or Asian Americans and were least likely to

The children of Captain John J. Drennan of the New York Fire Department, a fire captain who had battled for 40 days to survive burns suffered in a fiery Manhattan brownstone, grieve beside the casket at the burial in Staten Island May 11, 1994, in New York.
AP/Wide World Photos

participate in funerals and memorial rituals. They were, in general, more death-avoidant or death-denying than any other group, although they did not admit to a greater fear of death. Three-quarters of the sample of European Americans said they "would try very hard to control the way they showed their emotions in public" and more than half said they would not worry if they could not cry during the process of grieving. Nearly one-half the sample said they would not touch a corpse, and two-thirds said they would not kiss a corpse at a funeral. Nearly half of the European Americans sampled said that death crossed their minds "never," "hardly ever," or about "once per year."

ATTITUDINAL DIMENSIONS OF INVISIBLE DEATH

Attitudes are relatively lasting patterns of thinking, feeling, and behaving toward a concrete or abstract thing, person, or idea. European American attitudes toward death and dying, which have been described as death-denying or death-avoiding

(Kalish, 1985a; Kastenbaum, 1992; Barrow, 1996), can best be understood as a combination of three particular attitudinal dimensions: cognitive denial, emotional repression, and behavioral passivity.

Cognitive Denial

Sometimes when we are threatened, frustrated, or in conflict, we choose ways of coping that meet the situation directly. We can *confront* the situation head-on, fighting against the change in our lives and the feelings connected to the change, and behave in ways that intensify our efforts to overcome the unexpected or unwanted. We can *compromise* by giving up some part of what we wanted or expected and balance the sense of loss by persuading others to forfeit some of their wants or desires for the sake of compromise. Or we can admit defeat and loss, stop fighting, and *surrender* to change.

According to sociologists and social psychologists, following an initial period of shock and denial of a traumatic event, we are likely to search for reasons and explanations of the event as a way of coping cognitively (Hewstone, 1989).

EMOTIONAL INSULATION

"Why does denial occur? Because—for some persons and under some conditions—death is too stressful to contemplate. Since we can't fully obliterate the knowledge that death is real, we unconsciously find ways to insulate ourselves from the emotional impact of this knowledge, and these may require us to avoid contact with or mention of death. If I don't talk about it or read it, then it isn't there, and it can't happen to me."

Source: Richard Kalish (1985b:86).

Faced with a stressful life change, such as divorce, loss of job, death of a loved one, or a serious disease, we are likely to create an *account,* or storylike narrative, that attempts to explain what caused the loss and how it has affected our thoughts, feelings, actions, and relationships (Harvey, Weber, and Orbuch, 1990; Walter, 1996). This is part of our attempt to assimilate the traumatic event into our assumptions about the world and to tell our story to others (Morris, 1993:659). In the course of such account-making and confiding, we restructure our cognitions, cope with our grief, test reality, and strengthen our continuing relationships with others.

Other times, however, we are so devastated and so severely threatened by our own thoughts and emotions that we protect ourselves from the reality by refusing to perceive or think about it. This defense mechanism, termed *cognitive denial,* has become an integral part of our contemporary attitude toward dying and death.

For many of us, finding out that we are terminally ill and have only a few weeks to live or that a loved one has died unexpectedly during the night would be emotionally devastating, placing us under tremendous stress. Denial, one of the most common and most indirect defense mechanisms, is a refusal to acknowledge the emotion-arousing aspects of an event or memory through active forgetting of the event itself. Psychologist R. S. Lazarus (1969) cites the dramatic example of a woman who was near death from severe burns over much of her body. At first she was depressed and frightened, but after a few days she began to feel sure she would soon be able to return home and care for her children, although all medical indications were to the contrary. By denying the extent of her injuries this woman was able to stay calm and cheerful. She was not merely putting on an act for relatives and friends—she believed she would recover. She was in denial of the reality of her imminent death. She died a few days later.

Short-term denial of a traumatic event is a natural coping mechanism that allows us to prepare for the waves of emotion building within us. *E-motion* implies motion outward, and many of the mammals studied so far appear to react with shock and numbness in the face of separation and loss, followed by a stream of emotions and corresponding behaviors. On the other hand, long-term denial, which functions not to prepare us for grieving and mourning but to repress emotions because they are too painful or too threatening, is often destructive to the individual in the long run. Numerous studies have revealed that denial and repression of anger, hostility, fear, sadness, or depression weakens the immune system's responsiveness, making us more prone to disease (Eysenck, 1988; Marrone, 1990).

Deathbed denial is a form of cognitive denial. Robert Kastenbaum, a research pioneer in the field of thanatology, offers some insight into the role of denial in the face of death. His research project involved college students who were instructed to envision their own deathbed scene *as it was most likely to occur.* Participants, asked to imagine the deathbed scene with as much detail as possible, were then instructed to write detailed descriptions of these scenes (Kastenbaum and Normand, 1990). After describing the scene, the respondents were asked to make one change that would result in a happier scenario and another change that would result in a more distressing deathbed scene.

The gap between what one can realistically expect to experience while dying in America these days and the death scenes imagined by these participants suggests just how powerful the role of denial may be in forming our attitudes toward death and dying. For instance, although nearly 80% of Americans now die in hospitals and nursing homes, the overwhelming majority of respondents expected to die at home, and almost all (96%) expected to be alert, lucid, and aware right up to the moment of death. Except for those respondents who expected to die in an accident, respondents almost invariably expected to be surrounded by loving, supporting, even cheerful loved ones. In fact, 20% of respondents imagined their deathbed scene would be at a large family reunion. Spring and sunshine were the conditions most often specified by female respondents, and almost all respondents expected to die within a very short time interval: a few minutes, hours, or, at most, days. Most respondents imagined their deathbed scenes in old age or very old age (more than 100 years old).

Equally interesting findings had to do with possible events that were not mentioned by the participants. There were very few deathbed scenes in which last words or parting gifts were exchanged. Shifts in thinking regarding the meaning of life and death, which often result from *life reviews,* the active remembering of the sequence of events in our lives, were seldom mentioned. References to an afterlife were rare, and most respondents did not mention having any thoughts or insights about the loved ones around them, about what they had shared or not shared with family and friends, or about what was left unfinished in their love relationship with other persons in their lives. Many did not report on their emotional state at all.

For the most part, respondents substituted disembodied fantasy for embodied reality in imagining their actual deathbed scene. In describing the responses of participants in his study, Kastenbaum (1992) observed that in most cases they forgot that the dying person's body is no longer a source of pleasure and joy.

Denial is, of course, a matter of degree. We can use fantasy to substitute for reality in many ways. We may deny that we are truly dying. We may deny that a loved one has died, believing the news to be inaccurate or mistaken. Or we may deny our true feelings and emotions in the face of loss. Perhaps, at the very extreme, we may even deny death itself, and hold to the belief that death's finality and irrevocability are merely technical glitches to be overcome through high-tech medical intervention and cryoengineering.

Emotional Repression

The most common defense mechanism for blocking out painful feelings and emotions is *repression*. Sigmund Freud called it the cornerstone on which psychoanalysis is built. Like other defense mechanisms, repression is directed at both external dangers, such as fear-arousing events, and internal dangers, such as emotions and memories that cry out for gratification but arouse anxiety or guilt at the same time.

Many psychologists believe that repression is a sign of struggle against feelings and impulses that conflict with conscious values. For instance, most of us are taught that losing control of our emotions is wrong, that crying is a sign of weakness, or that displays of anger or fear are signs of immaturity. But it is only human to feel deep sadness, fright, or anger, at least sometimes. The conflict between our feelings and our values can create anxiety, and one way of coping defensively with the anxiety is to repress our feelings, to block out, to some degree, awareness of our underlying fear, anger, sadness, or disgust. In cognitive denial, we block out or distort perceptions and thoughts of a reality with which we won't cope. In emotional repression, we muscularly block out or mute either unacceptable bodily feelings and emotions that are painfully connected to an event in our lives or memories of those events.

Kastenbaum's deathbed studies (1992:30) revealed that for most respondents, the dying process was not only brief but almost completely free of emotional distress. Very few respondents reported any anxiety, fear, sadness, disgust, or anger. Very few expected to have pain or other symptoms. In fact, nearly 80% imagined their deathbed scene as painless, and only 6% actually imagined themselves experiencing pain. Male respondents never mentioned weakness, loss of consciousness, bleeding, numbness, or head-throbbing; these symptoms were mentioned occasionally by female respondents. Certain physical symptoms, such as nausea, diarrhea, and constipation, were never mentioned in the total sample.

This is not how we are likely to die. Direct studies of dying people and their experiences reveal marked differences from the anticipated deathbed scenes studied by Kastenbaum and colleagues (Levy, 1987–88; Mor, Greer, and Kastenbaum, 1988; Nuland, 1993). Dying people experience a variety of emotions and symptoms; dying may take weeks, months, or even years; and the exhaustion, after a long struggle with illness and disability, often evokes emotional breakdown and confusion of thought and memory. Bodily functions,

FAHRENHEIT −320°

Stephen Bridge sits in his sterile office in a Phoenix airport industrial park surveying the new home of Alcor Life Extension Institute, the world's largest and most prominent cryonics group. Cryonics is the controversial practice of freezing the remains of people and pets whom doctors and the rest of the world consider dead, in the hope of reviving them when medical technology can cure what ails them. Alcor's twenty-seven human "neuropatients" each signed over large amounts of money to have their blood drained and glycerol and other similar cryoprotectant chemicals circulated through their remains before being cooled in liquid nitrogen to −320° Fahrenheit.

Tired of the hassles in California, the crowding and the earthquakes, Bridge moved the entire operation, including ten frozen human bodies, seventeen preserved human heads and assorted pet heads and bodies—all kept in giant steel vats in the back room—to Phoenix.

"When an earthquake hits, our patients can't exactly get up and run out of the building," Bridge said with a smile.

Note: There are two types of cryonics: Full-body cryonics, which involves freezing of the entire body, and neuro-cryonics, which involves freezing only the head or brain. The cost to sign up and be placed on a waiting list by the Alcor Life Extension Foundation is $4,100, plus $288 a year to keep the name on the list. Neuro freezing costs $41,000 and full-body freezing is $120,000. The cost of yearly maintenance can reach up to $10,000 a year.

Sources: Adapted from George de Lama, Frozen-body capital of U.S., *Chicago Tribune*, May 29, 1994, p a-4. The note is adapted from Robert Kastenbaum (1995). Cryonic Suspensions, *Omega*, April, p. 159.

pain control, and bleeding may not always be taken care of by others. The dying person may experience waves of despair, terror, and rage. And yet the respondents in the deathbed-scene study had difficulty integrating these facts into their deathbed expectations and imaginings.

Psychotherapist Alexander Jasnow (1985) maintains that emotional repression and cognitive denial of death have become necessary in chaotic modern society in order for individuals to maintain the illusion of normal life. Death represents a loss of continuity and a potential threat to the individual's psychological survival. Denial, repression, and the promise of immortality, Jasnow suggests, allows the individual to avoid the intense despair and depression associated with loss.

According to Lendrum and Syme (1992:11–12),

The denial of the existence of feelings is a way of separating and thus "protecting" ourselves from too frightening or too painful feelings. In this way we can come to convince ourselves that we are unaffected by the loss and in turn convince others of this make-believe. When this happens, grief may seem to disappear, but signs of locked-in feelings such as coldness and uninvolvement signal that grief has gone "underground" or become blocked.

Others suggest that cognitive denial and emotional repression, together, create the context for complicated, pathological mourning reactions, including chronic depression and suicide. Horowitz, Bonanno, and Holen (1993), for example, building on a personality-based theory of pathological grief, suggest that two major factors, in combination, may predict complicated, pathological mourning reactions. Individuals who harbor highly ambivalent thoughts of and feelings for the deceased, and who also exhibit tendencies toward excessive control to repress unwanted feelings and emotions, are more likely to experience chronic depression and other symptoms of complicated mourning.

CARING INSIGHTS

Unhelpful Responses

Unhelpful remarks made to persons in mourning often originate in our unconscious attempt to deny our own fear of death or may be a reflection of society's difficulty in accepting death and the strong feelings connected with death and dying. Unhelpful remarks include the following:

- It's God's will.
- Don't cry—crying only upsets you.
- It was meant to be.
- They're better off.
- Don't be morbid.
- There are other fish in the sea.
- Never speak ill of the dead.
- Isn't it time you got back to normal?
- You can always . . . [have another baby or get married again]

Behavioral Passivity

he behavioral dimension of an attitude involves the observable responses we make in reaction to events and experiences in our lives. These reactions are, to some degree, built up out of the learning process and the role of reinforcers in our lives. A *reinforcer* is an event whose occurrence increases the probability of a certain response. A positive reinforcer works by giving the individual something pleasant. A negative reinforcer works by taking away something that is unpleasant or threatening.

Imagine yourself in past times dealing with the final moments of pain of a loved one as he or she slowly dies, then digging the grave, cleaning the body, setting out favorite clothing, and throwing earth on the casket, all the time filled with a combination of anger, anxiety, fear, sadness, and pain. Now consider a typical contemporary death scene—the final moments in an antiseptic hospital room, monitors beeping, loved one sedated by drugs; a funeral director to retrieve and prepare the body; a cemetery crew to bury the deceased—all in place as negative reinforcement of our passivity, to remove the "unpleasantness" of the mourning process.

Together, cognitive denial and emotional repression have come to define our dominant cultural attitudes toward death and dying to such an extent that we have become passive observers to our own dying and to the mourning after. We leave the behavioral orchestration to physicians, funeral directors, and other "doctors of grief" (Aries, 1975). Findings from the deathbed-scene study (Kastenbaum, 1992) reveal that in imagining their dying as they believed it would actually occur, respondents experienced virtually no pain, loved ones were there to support and cheer them on, and they were alert and lucid throughout the scene. Everything is being taken care of in these scenes, every need—whether physical, social, psychological or spiritual—is being taken care of by

LET'S PRETEND

"Ordinary life in today's society is marked by heavy repression of death-related anxiety. . . . This takes a toll on us. This is why we become conformists. We seek the security that is promised by tying into a system that will meet our dependency needs and help us deny our intrinsic vulnerability. Certain events and experiences may disrupt this "let's pretend" arrangement. We are then faced with the challenge of either restoring the tenuous system of mutual (illusionary) support, or confronting death as aware and vulnerable individuals."

Source: Kastenbaum (1992), p. 138.

others. Interestingly, when asked to revise their deathbed scenes, subjects in this study found it much easier to create a more disturbing scene than a happier one. The commonest additions were degree of pain, amount of time before dying, and being alone. In creating a happier deathbed scenario, the denial, repression, and pacification of elements of reality were so complete for many respondents that they could not think of a deathbed scene that was more comforting or satisfying than the original. The most popular additions were the presence of a particular person, sharing feelings with a loved one, and a lessening in the time it took to die. Many said that they could not really improve on the first version. As one person put it, "I guess I imagined it as I wanted it to be—even though I was supposed to imagine it as it would be" (Kastenbaum, 1992).

For many European Americans, dying, death, and the mourning after have become morbid states to be orchestrated, shortened, or even erased, whenever possible. Except among some Mormons, orthodox Jews, Amish, and some other minority groups, we have become increasingly comfortable with the actions of medical personnel, funeral directors, and others, both to isolate and to orchestrate the events of our dying and death. We have become reluctant to speak truly about death, to acknowledge the anonymous, depersonalized treatment of death in our everyday lives, and truly to feel and participate in our own dying. Consequently, we tend to become passive observers when we actually have to cope with our own death or the death of a loved one. Why? Psychologists have spent decades studying obedience, compliance, conformity, groupthink, and other social phenomena and, although we do not have all the answers, we can offer a number of hypotheses (Rathus, 1993:701): socialization, conformity, lack of social comparison, perception of legitimate authority, and inaccessibility of values.

Socialization. Despite the expressed American ideal of independence, we are socialized to conform and to obey others (such as parents and teachers) from the time we are little children. Faced with the novelty and stress of dealing with death and dying, we are more likely to engage in authority-bound behavior and conformity-seeking cues from parents, funeral directors, physicians, and the like as to how we are expected to behave.

Conformity. Conformity has been shown to vary in degree with the ambiguity of the situation. When the task or situation is poorly defined, conformity tends to be higher. In an ambiguous situation, individuals are less sure of their own view and are more willing to conform to that of the majority. The more an individual is attracted to the group, expects to interact with it in the future, is of

CARING INSIGHTS

Death and Empowerment

There is a point in each of our lives when we can ignore our parent's wishes and society's wishes and control every facet of our lives by ourselves. We can decide where and when to eat, whether we will go to school or to work; whether we will marry, have children, or remain single. In essence, we come of age as mature and responsible adults and take control of our lives. Part of the work of empowering ourselves involves overcoming our fear of death and the powerful pressures to conform, comply, repress, and deny.

relatively low status in the group, and does not feel completely accepted by the group, the more he or she tends to conform (Morris, 1993:646–647). Studies in conformity by sociologists and social psychologists consistently reveal that individuals are more likely to conform to group behavior when there is a lack of social support for nonconforming behavior (Morris, 1993).

Lack of Social Comparison. Because death and dying have become such unfamiliar experiences to many Americans and because they are not generally talked about in our day-to-day interaction, we often lack opportunity to compare our ideas and feeling states with those of people in the same situation. In personally dealing with death and dying, we might tend to conclude that our experience is unique or isolated, believing that no one could possibly feel the pain and confusion we feel. We are thus less likely to have a clear impression as to what to do in dealing with dying and death and are more likely to become authority-bound and conforming in our behavior.

Perception of Legitimate Authority. Psychological research has consistently revealed that most of us remain willing to engage in many acts, even morally reprehensible acts, at the behest of a legitimate-looking authority (Milgram, 1974). Acquiescence to authority figures, including clergy, funeral directors, physicians, and nurses, is a powerful motivator of various behaviors, especially when we are confused and under the stress of dealing with death and dying.

Being immersed in a particular way of dealing with death and dying throughout one's life makes it progressively more difficult to extricate oneself from those ways. By the time we are expected to observe death and dying passively because we ourselves are about to die or because a loved one has just died, we are already in collusion with the behavioral orchestration and already have a "foot-in-the-door" (Freedman and Fraser, 1966).

Inaccessibility of Values. People are more likely to act in accord with their attitudes and values when those values are readily available and accessible and they themselves are not under severe stress. Many people would probably agree that it is wrong to engage in cognitive denial, emotional repression, or behavioral passivity in the face of death. But when we are distressed by the sadness, despair, and pain connected with death and dying, these very attitudes and beliefs may become less accessible to us. As a consequence, it could become more and more difficult for us to behave in ways that are consistent with them.

DEATH AVOIDANCE AND DEATH DENIAL

In reviewing the dominant American death system, psychiatrist Elisabeth Kubler-Ross (1969:2), one of the founders of the field of thanatology, concludes that European Americans have a problem coping with death because they fear and deny it. "We are reluctant to reveal our age," she states. "We spend fortunes to hide our wrinkles; and we prefer to send our old people to nursing homes" (1975:28). We also shelter children from death and dying and, by so doing, we may actually make them more fearful of those events. She believes that we tend to depersonalize dying people because relating to them can be very painful for family and friends, and for nurses, doctors, and mental health professionals as well. Often, dying people are separated from familiar faces and are segregated with other sick and dying folks in a hospital or nursing home. Because we do not believe that we could possibly die of natural causes, we associate death with "a bad act, a frightening happening." She observes that while some other cultures are *death affirming,* American culture is *death denying.*

In recent years, thanatologists have noted that dominant American attitudes are undergoing a dramatic change toward greater openness and acknowledgment of death, dying, and the mourning after. The rise of the death education movement in the United States, the aging American population, the increasing ethnic diversity of the American populace, the establishment of more than 2,000 hospice programs to care for the terminally ill, as well as the public debate about assisted suicide, the right to die and death-with-dignity are often cited as some of the factors associated with these changes. The pattern of invisible death that defined European American attitudes for decades would appear, to some observers, to be undergoing slow but steady change toward increasing openness and acceptance of death and dying.

DEATH AS AN APPROACH–AVOIDANCE CONFLICT

Robert Kastenbaum (Kalish and Reynolds, 1985) offers an alternative way of viewing present-day American attitudes toward death and dying. Rather than describing contemporary American attitudes toward death as merely death-denying or death-avoiding, he suggests applying the idea of the *approach–avoidance conflict* as a way to understand them.

Neal Miller (1944, 1959), one of the first psychologists to describe and quantify conflict situations, developed a number of hypotheses about how animals, including human beings, behave in situations that have both positive and negative aspects. The approach–avoidance conflict results from having to choose an alternative or goal that has both attractive and repellent aspects. For example, consider the difficult decision of attending the funeral of a friend. We would like to avoid our own sadness, as well as the expressions of sorrow and loss by family members. On the other hand, we want to honor our friend's memory and to be there to comfort family and other loved ones (Lefton, 1994). According to Miller, the desire to approach a goal grows stronger as we get nearer to it, but so does the desire to avoid it. The avoidance tendency usually increases in strength faster than does the approach tendency. In an approach–avoidance conflict, therefore, we approach the goal until we reach the point at which the tendency to approach equals the tendency to avoid the goal. Afraid to go any closer, we stop, fall back, and approach again, vacillating until we have to make a decision or until the situation changes.

Applying this idea to the study of attitudes toward death and dying allows us to view their complexity as a result of the interaction between the motivation to approach and the motivation to avoid, or as a conflict between societal goals (e.g., honoring the dead and comforting the living) and personal needs (e.g., avoiding or minimizing unpleasant feelings). Not visiting graves or attending funerals could then be interpreted as having a low approach value rather than a high avoidance value. Richard Kalish (1985a:28), in commenting on the approach–avoidance conflict hypothesis, considers it "an important refinement [that] may help avoid some nonparsimonious assumptions about motivation when the root of the behavior (or lack of behavior) can be viewed as an absence of felt need." Thanatologist John D. Morgan (1995:40) describes the approach–avoidance conflict as "a tension between our pragmatism and our religiosity, between our conviction that we can do anything and our respect for life as a unique gift."

The approach–avoidance concept offers a less categorical, less judgmental, more balanced way of viewing the panoply of American attitudes toward death and dying, but it is only a beginning. As Robert Kastenbaum (1993) has noted, thanatology has set for itself the unenviable task of bringing knowledge and understanding to the dynamic, contradictory, and occasionally opposing attitudes we hold toward death, dying, and the mourning after.

Ethnic Variations and Change

As Americans, we inhabit what is for the most part a nation of immigrants, an ever-changing rainbow of ethnic, racial, and religious hues. The most recent U.S. census reveals that the dominant European American culture accounts for about three-quarters of the U.S. population. African Americans, with a population of 30 million, account for 12.1% of the total U.S. population, followed by Hispanic Americans (9.1%), Asian Americans (2.9%), and American Indians (0.8%). In fact, as a nation, we are in a state of significant demographic change. In the past decade, the racial/ethnic/religious composition of the United States has changed to a greater degree than in any other decade in this century. One in five Americans were members of ethnic minorities in 1980, compared with one in four in 1990. The fastest population growth was recorded for people whose origin was Vietnamese (135%), East Indian (126%), Korean (125%), and Laotian-Hmong (1,500%), and immigrants accounted for more than a third of the growth in both the Hispanic American and Asian American communities

Our flag is red, white and blue, but our nation is a rainbow—red, yellow, brown, black and white—and we're all precious in God's sight.

—Jesse Jackson (1984)

Church members assist a grieving woman during a funeral service honoring her loved one.
© *Nicholas Sapieha/Stock, Boston*

(Irish, 1993:191). The U.S. Census Bureau reported that, in 1994, 22.6 million Americans (about 8.7% of the population) were born in other countries, the country's highest immigrant population level since 1940.

We are a nation rich in ethnic, racial, and religious diversity. The logic of different languages, religious traditions, and customs mirrors differences in our views of the world. Looking at the world through a blue-tinted lens reveals a world different from that seen through a lens of amber, red, or green. In the final analysis, loss, grieving, and the mourning process are intensely personal; and yet these profound experiences cannot be separated from who we are as members of the ethnic culture that nourished us.

AFRICAN AMERICAN ATTITUDES

Juan Turner (1993: 201) observed that among African Americans, the single largest minority group in the United States, "death in general is an awesome state. The spirit is extremely important, and the body houses the spirit. We believe that life is a bridge, a transition, and that death brings us to a better place. Most African Americans believe in life after death: immortality is a given. We may fear death and not want it to come; but also at times it is welcomed."

AT A PENTECOSTAL FUNERAL

"After many admonitions to 'sinners' and much praise of Sister Backler, the pastor ended his sermon, the last soloist sang, and the church prepared to see Sister Backler for the last time. Two assistants to the funeral director went to the casket, arranged the interior lace in its appropriate place. Then they stood on either end of the casket while two other assistants, accompanied by a church nurse, took each member of the immediate family to view the body. . . . After all the family had viewed the body, leaving the members distraught by their emotional outbursts, all the rest of the congregation stood and formed a line and marched around to view Sister Backler. They touched her, kissed her, embraced her, and frequently had to be restrained in their emotions."

Source: Williams (1974), p. 100.

In contrasting Southern Baptists, northern Unitarians, and African American Catholics, there appears to be no single pattern of African American attitudes toward death and dying, although many American burial and funeral practices can be traced back to Africa. For example, the act of throwing earth into the grave, though not exclusively African, was brought to the American continent by African slaves. The custom of decorating graves with broken earthenware, still common in certain areas of the South, has been traced back to Angola (Genovese, 1976: 201). Broken earthenware placed on the grave is meant to symbolize that, although the body is broken, the spirit lives on.

According to sociologist Hosea Perry (1993:55), "One thinks of funerals in the white culture as more formal and less emotional than within black death rituals. Pentecostal and Southern Baptist funerals, with long emotional sermons and wailing and sobbing in response from the mourners, have become stereotypes for all black funerals." Based on his interviews with more than 115 middle-class and upper-lower-class African Americans, primarily in Alabama, Florida, Georgia, Kentucky, Mississippi, and North and South Carolina, Perry (1993) found significant differences in the amount of emotional expression at funerals and during the period of mourning. Based on his analysis, Perry (1993:64) concluded that, although some interviewees spoke about the positive effects of being emotional at funerals, "such rituals are more common among those in the rural South, among the more evangelical religious (e.g., Church of God, Missionary Baptist, Pentecostal), and within population segments having less educational and fewer economic resources." Among African Americans in urban areas, in the North, within the upper economic and social classes with more education, and among Roman Catholic and mainstream Protestant congregations, "the trend to less emotional funerals, shorter sermons, and less wailing is evidence that the black funeral customs are becoming more like those in the white community."

J. A. Brown (1990) also reported that middle-class African Americans have, to a great extent, taken over attitudes closer to those of the dominant society than are those of other African Americans. Among African Americans interviewed in the Kalish and Reynolds multiethnic study (1985a), three-fourths reported they would "try very hard to control the ways they showed their emotions in public" during the mourning period. Sixty-four percent said they would "let themselves go and cry themselves out" in either private or public, as compared to 70% of European Americans, 71% of Asian Americans, and 88% of Hispanic Americans. More than half (51%) said they would touch a corpse at a funeral, while an

AFFIRMING THE ESSENCE

"Death in the black community is perceived as a celebration of life, a testament to the fact that a life has been lived, that the earthly journey is completed. Those who serve as witnesses in the presence of death, extended family, friends, and church members, to affirm the essence of the person's existence, are ready to testify to the fact that the deceased has fought the battle, borne the burden, and finished the course; they are ready to understand and say well done."

Source: White (1984), p. 46.

overwhelming majority said they would not kiss a corpse at a funeral. African Americans also reported relying on friends, neighbors, and church associates for support when dealing with death and mourning. Among African Americans, family relationships were not as important for support as they were among Asian Americans and Hispanic Americans, but they were slightly more important than among European Americans.

Two-thirds of African Americans in the Kalish and Reynolds investigation said they would carry out spouses' dying wishes even if they were felt to be senseless and inconvenient, and 62% said it was unimportant to wear black clothing during the mourning period. African Americans preferred burial over cremation by a 20:1 ratio. Juan L. Turner (1993:202) observes that the preferred method of body disposal among African Americans is to have the deceased buried "back home. Because we believe in the sanctity of the body and spirit, there is a common resistance to cremation. Costly funerals, unfortunately, often are a norm for African Americans, regardless of economic level, some believing that they show how much they care for the loved one in that way."

Of the four ethnic groups studied, African Americans had highest (88%) agreement with the statement that "people can hasten or slow their own death through a will-to-live or a will-to-die." Statistical analysis revealed significant differences between African Americans and the other ethnic groups, with African Americans expecting to live much longer than the others. Bengtson, Cuellar, and Ragan (1976), in their study of ethnicity and aging, also found that African Americans had longer subjective life expectancy than Hispanic Americans or European Americans. Ninety percent of the sample predicted they would die a natural death at an old age, while 2% of the African American sample said they would prefer to die by suicide. These varied results suggest that the attitudes of African Americans are as influenced by socioeconomic class, geographical location, and historical heritage as are those of members of other groups, so their attitudes are varied and personal.

In a study of terminally ill persons in an African American community, J. A. Brown (1990) reported that African American families are reluctant to place terminally ill loved ones in a hospital or nursing home, preferring instead to keep them at home. In a recent ethnic-attitudes study by Blackhall et al. (1995), 89% of African Americans believed a patient should be told of a diagnosis of metastatic cancer and 69% believed a loved one should be told of a terminal prognosis, closely paralleling European American attitudes.

HISPANIC AMERICAN ATTITUDES

Hispanic Americans are the second largest minority group in the United States. Within this group, 63% are Mexican Americans, 13% are Puerto Rican Americans, 5% are Cuban Americans, and some 18% have origins mostly in South American and Central American countries (Soto and Villa, 1990).

Younoszai (1993:69–76) observes that

> death is different in Mexico. Not biologically different, and not emotionally less stressful. . . . People do not celebrate death joyfully, nor with less pain or suffering, but with more acceptance and more understanding. . . . Death is present everywhere in Mexico. It is in the literature, on murals, in cutout paper figures, and on the streets. . . . Death is seen as a companion, or sometimes as a lover. Death is omnipresent and a part of life. Sometimes death is viewed as a woman, and sometimes it is a man. There is no gender preference. Death is death. And it must always be included as a part of the Mexican reality.

A young woman displays death masks during El Dia de Los Muertas festivities. On November 1 and 2, vendors outside cemeteries sell food, sugar skulls, bread of the dead (pan de muerto) and brightly painted toys in the shape of caskets, skeletons, and skulls. © *Sergio Dorantes*

According to Younoszai (1993:76), among Hispanic Americans, "an openly emotional response to death is expected. No one is ashamed to cry and to freely express grief. Children are socialized early to accept death in a very informal way."

Grabowski and Frantz (1992–93) compared Hispanic Americans and European Americans on their grief intensity following both sudden and expected death. They found that following sudden death, Hispanic Americans had a significantly greater grief intensity than they did for expected death, and that in either kind of death the intensity of emotional expression among Hispanic Americans greatly exceeded that of European Americans. Among participants, neither funeral attendance, time since death, nor closeness of relationship had significant effect on grief intensity. Among Latinos, neither participation in a Novena nor acculturation had a significant effect on grief intensity.

Hispanic Americans in the Kalish and Reynolds study (1981) were least likely to "try hard to control their emotions" during a funeral as compared to African Americans, Asian Americans, and European Americans. Hispanic Americans were alert to the bereaved's underreacting, i.e., not

THE DAY OF THE DEAD

El Dia de Los Muertos, or The Day of the Dead, is a unique holiday that is celebrated annually on November 1 and 2 in Mexico, Guatemala, Spain, Peru, and other Latin American countries. It is also celebrated in U.S. cities that have a large Hispanic American population, including San Francisco, Sacramento, Los Angeles, Houston, Dallas, and New York.

November 1, All Saints' Day, is a day to honor the souls of children (i.e., "little angels") who die before they ever have a chance to sin and therefore are believed to go directly to heaven. November 2, All Souls' Day, is the day to honor the souls of deceased adults. During these two days, people gather to celebrate with feasts, parades, music, and laughter.

On the morning of November 1, the family goes to the local cemetery where their loved ones are buried. Outside the cemeteries, vendors sell food, drinks, candles, sugar skulls, *pan de muerto* (bread of the dead), and a variety of brightly painted toys in the shape of skulls and skeletons. The family scrubs down the tombstones and decorates them with marigolds, called the flower of the dead. Then the family spreads marigold petals from the cemetery to their front doors so the dead might find their way back home. At night, families return to the cemeteries with food and drink and candles, to eat and socialize in a festive mood.

Festivities continue into All Souls' Day, when people partake of parades in which a coffin, with someone pretending to be dead, is carried through the streets while people dressed as skeletons wave and laugh. Death is poked fun of and everyone accepts the humor. Special foods are prepared by the family, including chicken smothered in chocolate sauce, tamales, enchiladas, and pan de muerto. Food is also placed on the altar, along with other things the deceased may have liked particularly. Finally, the family joins together, for it is believed the dead return to become part of the family again, sharing in the meal.

showing any overt signs of grief or, as one respondent said, "when they can't cry" (34% compared to under 10% for the other ethnic groups). More than one in three (37%) admitted to thinking of their own death once a week, while 38% never or hardly ever thought of their own death. Kalish and Reynolds (1981) also reported that Hispanic Americans in their study visited grave sites more frequently than other groups, spent more time at the cemetery during burial, and wore black clothing for the longest time. Seventy-six percent of Hispanic Americans in the Kalish study said touching the body at the wake was acceptable, and over half said they would kiss the corpse at the funeral. Hispanic Americans preferred burial over cremation by a ratio of 20:1.

Hispanic Americans had the lowest agreement (37%) with the statement that others should be told of terminal illness, and only 19% believed they could tell a loved one they were dying, as compared to 50% of other groups. In the Blackhall et al. multiethnic study (1995), less than half (48%) of Mexican Americans believed a loved one should be told of a terminal prognosis. While only 41% believed a patient should decide about the use of life-support systems, nearly nine of ten Mexican Americans agreed that the family should be told the truth about their loved one's illness.

Ninety percent of the Mexican Americans in the Kalish and Reynolds multiethnic study were Roman Catholics with a strong locus of emotional support in the family unit. Accordingly, when a member is dying, the family typically arranges shifts of visitors. Kalish and Reynolds (1981) found Mexican American families more likely than other groups to call a priest when someone is dying, and may have last rites performed several times. Nearly 90% of Hispanic Americans would call for clergy if nearing death themselves, as compared to about 50% for the other ethnic groups. Based on her studies of Hispanic American attitudes toward death and dying, Stephanie Siefken (1993), stresses the importance in Hispanic American culture of having a doctor who is considered one of the family, who focuses on the inner importance of the person, and who exhibits respect for the patient. She found that these concerns have a bearing on decisions regarding hospitalization versus home care for the terminally ill in the Hispanic American community.

Garcia-Preto (1986:33–34), based on her study of terminally ill persons in a Puerto Rican community in New York, wrote that, for Puerto Ricans "not being able to be present during illness or time of death of someone close to them makes the loss more difficult to accept." Eisenbruch (1984:335) reported that an accepted grief reaction among Puerto Rican women in a New York City community includes *el ataque,* consisting of "seizure-like patterns with a hyper-kinetic episode, a display of histrionics or aggression, and sometimes the climax of stupor." In the Puerto Rican American community, *el ataque* is considered normal for women; following a code of *machismo,* the men show little or no grieving behavior.

There are vast differences among Hispanic Americans in their attitudes toward death and dying. Marcial Vasquez (1993:204) observes that for Christian Hispanic Americans, there is no finality in death. Death is seen not as an end but as a beginning, a door passing from one state to another. For those of Catholic background, death brings passage to heaven if their actions have warranted that, if their sins have been forgiven, or if they have received last rites. Protestants focus more on resurrection, especially those who are Pentecostals. When a Hispanic American dies, Vasquez (1993:204–205) notes, "many of the same traditions apply now as in Euro-American or Canadian funerals, whether Catholic or Protestant, because some customs have been lost through acculturation."

ASIAN AMERICAN ATTITUDES

In 1988, an estimated 6.9 million residents of the United States could trace their origins back to Asia or the Pacific Islands (Corr, Nabe, and Corr, 1994). Together, Chinese Americans, Filipino Americans, and Japanese Americans account for nearly two-thirds of this population.

Kalish and Reynolds (1976) found that communication is so tightly controlled within the community of Japanese Americans that even when members of the community are dying and in distress, health care providers may have difficulty determining this because such persons are highly restrained in communicating their feelings. Eisenbruch (1984) made similar findings among Chinese Americans, who were described as "stoic" in the face of death and had a strong tendency not to question authority. This stoicism regarding death found some support in that only 10% of Asian Americans in the Kalish and Reynolds study admitted thinking about their own death once a week while nearly 70% admitted thinking about their own death never or rarely.

HAWAIIAN VISIONS

A six-year study of case reports on hallucinations and visions of Native Hawaiians from the Cultural Committee Report of the Queen Lili'uokalani Childrens' Center in Honolulu (1972) revealed that Hawaiian Americans experience frequent visions of the dead. Visions are usually of a known, identified person who, in life, had been close to the visionary—a vision of a living person is rarely reported. The voice, which may not be experienced as the voice of the deceased, is thought to be an *aumakua,* or ancestor God. Visions of deceased grandparents or grandchildren are reported slightly more often than those of parents or children, and such a vision is seen as an almost real presence. Clothing, appearance, and mannerisms are described in detail. The phrases "I saw grandma" and "Kimo appeared" are used more often than "I saw a vision of grandma" and "Kimo's spirit appeared."

The reaction to the vision or mystic voice follows a rather typical pattern: The vision or voice itself seldom frightens, although the message may do so. Anxiety is more apt to be present when the message is misunderstood. For example, in one account from a Hawaiian American woman who frequently visited her dead son's grave, she recalled being upset upon seeing her son, and wondered what was wrong and what her son was trying to tell her. In other cases in which the vision does not convey a specific message, the recipient is likely to interpret the vision as an attempt by the deceased to send his or her love through to them. Psychologists and social workers use a number of criteria to determine whether the person is psychotic, seriously neurotic, or simply following his or her cultural heritage. Mary Kawena Pukui, for example, points out that when one person in a group sees a vision or hears a voice but nobody else in the group experiences or senses the vision, then it is probably not a true vision, or *ulaleo,* but one that came from within the person's mind completely. A vision that leads to disappointment, such as when strange lights lead a fisherman to a place where there are no fish, or when a voice tells a person to climb a cliff and the person gets hurt in the process, is not a true vision. In these cases, the person simply imagined the voice or the lights. A true vision, according to Pukui, does not harm or confuse but rather guides and advises us.

Source: Mary Kawena Pukui, E. W. Haertig, and Catherine A. Lee. (1976). *Nanal Ke Kumu,* Vols. 1, 2. Hui Hanai, Honolulu.

Lee, Lieh-Mak, and Hung (1983−84) found that Chinese American children with uncontrolled leukemia were more tense, detached, and guarded than children hospitalized with nonlife-threatening problems. The authors observed that Chinese American parents are especially reluctant to discuss death with their children. Death is a taboo subject in general, and particularly when children are involved. The child, even the fatally ill child, is left to develop and test death concepts with little or no adult guidance (Kastenbaum, 1986).

Japanese Americans (Kalish and Reynolds, 1981; Hirayama, 1990), Cambodian Americans (Lang, 1990), and Korean Americans (Blackhall et al., 1995) have been found to be unlikely to tell a seriously ill loved one that they are dying. In the study by Blackhall et al. (1995), only 35% of Korean Americans believed a loved one should be told of a terminal prognosis, as compared to 63% of African Americans and 69% of European Americans.

Funerals and other memorials are regarded as very important social events among many Asian Americans because the death of a loved one allows for a continued relationship between the deceased and the survivors. In the Kalish and Reynolds research (1981), nearly all of the Japanese American respondents believed that those who died watched over those who remain alive on earth. Kalish and Reynolds (1981) found that only 31% of Asian Americans said they would touch the body of a loved one at a funeral (as compared to a majority for other ethnic groups), and few said they would kiss the deceased at a funeral service. Three-fourths of Asian Americans said they would constrain themselves from public displays of grief, while an almost equal number (71%) agreed that they would "let themselves go and cry themselves out" in private. They were also reported to have very conservative mourning traditions, with few members believing that remarriage or even dating after the death of a spouse was appropriate. These same respondents also had the highest expectations for family support (74%) and the lowest expectations for support from friends, neighbors, and community members (9%). In general, Asian Americans prefer to die at home.

NATIVE AMERICAN INDIAN ATTITUDES

There are approximately 350 distinct American Indian tribes in the United States and 596 different bands among the "First Nations" of Canada. Attitudes and values differ greatly from tribe to tribe. For example, the Apache regard a dead person's body as an empty shell, while the Lakota speak to the body of the deceased and understand it to be sacred. The Navajo do not believe in an afterlife, while most other American Indian nations do. Brokenleg and Middleton (1993:103), based on their studies of tribal nations, state, "It may aid in understanding the significance of tribal distinctions to note that the Cherokees, for example, are as culturally different from the Crows as the English are from the Chinese."

The Lakota (Sioux), the second largest nation in the United States and the largest in the upper Midwest, believe in a balanced universe where death is considered a natural counterpart of life. According to Brokenleg and Middleton (1993:104), "the afterlife begins at some point after death, when the soul journeys south until it comes

GOLDEN WINGS AGAINST THE SKY

"Many of the American Indian experiences prior to death seem fantastic to people from a Western cultural and philosophical heritage. . . . Death is often forecast by unusual spiritual or physical events, which are understood to be natural and in the order of things. For example, at the time of a person's death another family member will often see the ghost of the person and be told of the death soon afterward. Another relatively common sign that a family member has died is that a blue light will be seen coming from the direction of the dead relative's home or room. An accepted sign that a person will die soon is that she or he will report being visited in dreams by dead relatives.

In the Spring of 1990, four children died in a trailer fire on the Rosebud reservation. Earlier that day, the children had seen four eagles circling overhead and had pointed them out to their mother. The importance of this was not understood until after the children had died. The significance of this event is the rarity of four eagles circling together, along with the fact that eagles are messengers from the spirit world."

Source: Brokenleg and Middleton (1993), p. 107.

to the Ghost Road, also known as the Milky Way. The Ghost Road leads to *Wanagi Makoce,* the Spirit Land. This is the place where all dead go, whether human or animal."

There is an enormous reverence for the body among the Lakota because it is seen as the residence of the person's essence. According to Brokenleg and Middleton (1993:105) unrestrained grief is appropriate and is regarded as a good thing among men and women. Women typically wail loudly during the mourning process, and men will often sing mournful, emotional songs. "Lakota philosophy differs fundamentally from Western culture. Likewise, the Lakota grief model differs from current Western models, because denial and anger are minimal. This is a function of the acceptance of the natural order of things as opposed to the cognitive inquiry of Western culture" (Brokenleg and Middleton, 1993:105).

The strong cohesiveness of the Lakota family requires that relatives of a dead person go to any lengths to be present at the wake and funeral. To the Lakota, a person's death is understood as a very sacred thing. Carr and Lee (1978:280) reported that, in contrast to the Lakota Sioux, among the Navajo, death taboos "favor bringing the sick into the hospital to die rather than permitting them to die at home" so that the home will not be polluted by the experience of death. Carrese and Rhodes (1995) found that once in the hospital, however, policies complying with the Patient Self-determination Act, which are intended to expose all hospitalized patients to advance medical care planning, are ethically troublesome to the Navajo. During interviews, thirty-four Navajo informants, including patients, health care providers, and traditional healers explained that patients and providers should think and speak in a positive way and avoid thinking or speaking negatively; 86% of those questioned considered advance care planning a dangerous violation of traditional Navajo values. These findings are consistent with the most important concept in traditional Navajo culture, which combines the concepts of beauty, goodness, order, harmony, and everything that is positive or ideal. Discussing negative information or negative medical outcomes conflicts with the Navajo concept and was viewed as potentially harmful by these Navajo informants.

NO SMOKING ALLOWED

"A Chippewa woman accused a county hospital of denying her the right to practice her religion. Hospital guards had stopped her from burning sage in her room. (In some American Indian ceremonies sage is burned and the smoke is fanned with an eagle feather to purify people or objects.) She was praying for strength to deal with the possibility that she might not be able to walk again. The guards forced the woman to her knees, although she had recently had spinal fusion and was under physician's orders to remain prone. Hospital officials contended that the issue was not one of religion but of fire hazard. Further, the hospital had a firm no-smoking policy. The patient said her religious ceremony did not fit that policy, and she filed suit in district court. At another hospital in the same city, staff members had permitted tribal medicine as long as health and safety were not endangered."

Source: Irish (1993), p. 5.

DEATH, DYING, AND ACCULTURATION

On some of the most fundamental issues of death and dying, some American ethnic groups hold vastly different views from the American mainstream. As in the case of the Navajo (Carrese and Rhodes, 1995), these ethnic differences can pose difficult questions for hospitals as well as for physicians, nurses, and other medical personnel. For example, there are an estimated 120,000 (Laotian) Hmong refugees now living in various cities in the United States and Canada (Irish, Lundquist, and Nelsen, 1993). The Hmong believe that a spiritual world coexists with the physical world, which is inhabited by a wide variety of spirits, many of which can influence human life. Bruce Thowpaou Bilatout (1993:79–100), in his study of 15,000 Hmong immigrants in the Minneapolis–St. Paul area, found that modern medicine conflicts with these spiritual convictions. Many traditional Hmong families continue to rely on shamans, or spiritual leaders, to diagnose and cure illness. One shaman explained that "every human being has twelve spirits. The spirits represent the eye, the mouth, the nose, the hand, the body parts. If those spirits wander around and go into another body, it can cause a person to get sick, and then they would call a shaman. The shaman would come in and perform a ritual ceremony to barricade the road so the spirits can't wander around. That way they have nowhere to go, so they have to go back to the body and the person can get better." (Irish, 1993:7).

Such beliefs lead many Hmong to refuse, or to hesitate to accept, certain medical practices. Surgery and blood tests can release one's spirits, which then must be located and lured back. Removing an organ can prevent a person from reincarnating, because reincarnation requires an intact body. Autopsies on elders are taboo for the same reason.

In a study of 800 elderly patients by the University of California, it was found that immigrants from Mexico and Korea were far less willing to let patients make decisions about medical care than were either European Americans or African Americans (Blackhall et al., 1995; Mydans, 1995). Should a patient with terminal illness be told the truth that he or she is dying? Should seriously ill patients make decisions about their hospital care, including the use of life-support systems? In all four groups studied (African American, European American, Korean American, and Mexican American), nine out of ten participants agreed that the family should be told the truth about the patient's illness, but only 35% of immigrant Korean Americans and 48% of immigrant Mexican Americans said the patient should be told the truth. European Americans and African Americans were about twice as likely as Korean immigrants to answer "yes" to these questions, and about one-and-one-half times as likely as Mexican immigrants. For many ethnic Americans, from numerous countries, the role of the family looms larger and that of the individual patient smaller than is generally the case with mainstream American society. Leslie Blackhall, a bioethicist, states, "With the American emphasis on patient autonomy, we may have lost sight of the fact that, for many cultures, the family unit is more important than the individual in decision making" (Mydans, 1995:A13).

Reviewing the extensive research on the variation of ethnic attitudes toward death and dying, sociologist Donald P. Irish (Irish, Lundquist, and Nelsen, 1993:187) concludes that acculturation has had varying impact on these American groups. He notes that "Each of the ethnic groups . . . has had to modify its ways of dealing with dying, death, and grieving within North American society." In the study of ethnic attitudes toward death and dying by Blackhall et al. (1995), for example, there was some evidence in the study that acculturation to American society by Korean and Mexican immigrants affected these views.

Using standard tests to measure factors such as proficiency in English, the study found that acculturated Korean Americans and Mexican Americans were somewhat more likely to favor telling a loved one the truth about a terminal prognosis than those not acculturated (Mydans, 1995). African Americans, Mexican Americans, and Native Americans, to a greater or lesser degree, have been able to retain many traditional ways. They have remained nearer to their "indigenous sources," the deep South, the Southwest, and Indian reservations, than have recent immigrant groups. The Hmong and others with small and scattered populations have had much more difficulty in maintaining their traditional ways (Irish, Lundquist, and Nelsen, 1993:187).

Is America a Death-Denying Culture?

As extreme as some of the purely American death-avoiding and death-denying rituals are, including the earlier-described drive-through mourning scene at the Gatling Funeral Home and the frozen heads and bodies at the cryonics firm, the assumption that Americans deny death and dying has become highly complex and questionable. The variety of attitudes toward death in America's ethnic communities, along with changes in European American attitudes in recent decades, begins to suggest that the American tendency to deny or avoid death and dying may not be as extreme as other, less diverse Western societies.

American social psychologist Richard Kalish (1985:86), for one, points out that "although we do use euphemisms, keep children from knowledge of death and remove dead patients from their hospital rooms without telling their roommates why, we nonetheless accept death in other instances. For example, cemeteries are kept open to public view, and newspapers run obituaries and death notices." The wake, too, increasingly avoided in industrialized Europe, persists in the United States as 'viewing the remains,' or the 'visitation.' " The English model, on the other hand, involves an almost total suppression of anything connected or suggesting death. In England, as Jessica Mitford (1963) has observed, they don't *view* bodies.

The funeral, the cemetery, and veneration in regard to the tombstone or marker have persisted in modern American society. Burials are not shameful, and they are not as hidden as in Western European countries. In fact, in many cases, our funeral rituals reveal a mixture of commercialism and idealism, becoming occasions of showy exhibitionism reflecting the family's power, status, and caring. Somewhat surprisingly, death and dying were very much a part of the experience of participants in Kalish and Reynolds multiethnic study (1985). During the two-year period preceding the in-depth interviews, over two-thirds of respondents had attended at least one funeral and over 40% of the entire sample had visited or talked with at least one dying person. Most of the deaths the researchers encountered were from natural causes, but nearly one-third of the respondents had known at least one accident victim. A handful had known people who died by suicide or homicide. Commenting on these findings, Richard Kalish wrote, "Perhaps—and only perhaps—we have denial mechanisms that exclude the affective [emotional, felt] impact of death and dying, but we most certainly do not escape continuing contacts with the ultimate reality of life" (Kalish and Reynolds, 1985:26).

Although the overwhelming majority of respondents in the multiethnic study were committed to controlling their public expression of emotion, more than half the respondents believed that a dying person should be told that he or she is dying, with 75% wishing to be informed of their own terminal illness. These results are comparable to four previous American studies reviewed by Hinton (1967) in which patients and their loved ones were asked whether a terminal cancer patient should be told about his or her condition. The results were overwhelmingly affirmative (66–89%). Vernon, in a study of primarily youthful Americans (1970), found that 71% believed in informing the dying, while the Blackhall et al. survey of elderly African Americans and European Americans (1995) found that nearly 90% believed a loved one should be told of a diagnosis of metastatic cancer, and almost two-thirds believed a loved one should be told of a terminal prognosis. On the other hand, as regards their own death and funeral, fewer than 15% of respondents in the Kalish and Reynolds multiethnic study (1985) had made funeral arrangements and only 25% were paying on a funeral plot.

Are we a predominantly death-denying, death-avoiding society, or do we reveal a complex mixture of positive and negative attitudes toward death, dying, and the mourning after? Critical of some aspects of the American death-education movement, Walter (1995:246–247) suggests that the idea that we are a "death-denying society" rests with our tendency to romanticize primitive and traditional cultures. He questions the assumptions that traditional or preliterate cultures view death as "natural" and are more accepting of death and dying than we are. Citing evidence from the fields of cultural anthropology and sociology, he suggests that our tendency to see our own society's response to death as "denying," "avoidant," or in some other way "unnatural" stems from the myth of the noble savage. He says that if the notion of "natural" death is simply meant to remind us (p. 247) that

> death is a part of the human condition which we cannot and should not run away from, all is well and good. But as soon as the concept gets caught up with nostalgic readings of how people die and grieve in traditional societies, we are in a world of myth. . . . Humane approaches to dying and grieving today should be grounded not in mythical notions of the natural, but in the on-going project to develop ways of dying and grieving appropriate to our time and place.

Changing Attitudes and Death Education

Perhaps because the taboo against death has never really been a total taboo in the United States, we have been both a leader in the establishment of a new and critical perspective on death and dying as well as the birthplace of thanatology, death education, and grief counseling as fields of research, study, and practice.

The birth of thanatology as a modern field of study occurred in the 1950s, although the topic of death and dying did not come into its own until the 1970s. Psychology's first organized approach to death was a 1956 symposium entitled "The Concept of Death and Its Relation to Behavior," which was presented at the annual meeting of the American Psychological Association and chaired by Herman Feifel (Feifel, 1990). The symposium served as the basis for the 1959 book, *The*

Meaning of Death, edited by Feifel, and generally viewed as a seminal work that brought concerns for death and dying to the American scholarly community.

Succeeding years saw a slow building of activity until interest burst in the late 1960s and early '70s. Like sex, death was not a new event; but like sex, it was rarely discussed. Sex came out of the closet in the 1960s; death came out of the closet in the 1970s. Pioneering books by Fulton (1965), Hinton (1967), Kubler-Ross (1969), Kastenbaum and Aisenberg (1972), Weisman (1972), Parkes (1972), and others brought focus to the growing number of death-and-dying workshops and courses being offered in various universities and professional schools, as well as to the increasing number of journal articles being published. Newly established journals included *Omega* (1969), *The Journal of Thanatology* (1973), and *Death Education* (1977), now called *Death Studies.* According to Leviton (1977), the number of death-education college courses increased from 20 in 1970 to 1,100 in a 4-year period. A survey of 1,251 American colleges and universities reported more than a decade ago revealed that 75% were offering courses in death and dying and that these courses were offered in many different departments. The majority of such courses were offered through sociology and social work departments, followed by psychology, religious studies, philosophy, and health education departments (Cummins, 1978).

In its brief life, the death-education movement has turned into a major force in broadening our grasp of the phenomena of death and dying. It has familiarized professionals and students with the needs and issues surrounding death and dying. It has increased our knowledge of the professionals involved with death: funeral directors, medical personnel, and governmental organizations. It has stimulated debate, study, and understanding of the legal, moral, and ethical issues concerning death. It has helped students and professionals learn to cope with the death of significant others. And it has taught others the techniques of counseling and caring for the dying and the bereaved.

Few would doubt that the death-education movement has greatly facilitated a change in our attitudes toward death and has worked to bring death back into our consciousness. As a result, death is becoming more human and dying is becoming more humane. And yet, the emotional aspect of death still seems beyond our grasp. According to philosopher John D. Morgan (1995:400), "we do not have an *affective consciousness* of death. We do not seem to take seriously that death is the end of our possibilities, the collapse of our space and time."

Philippe Aries (1974) described our orientation to death as **invisible death** and as **death-denied.** Elisabeth Kubler-Ross (1969) and others have referred to our culture as **death-denying.** At the same time, more deaths have occurred in our lifetimes than in the history of the human race, we have lived under the ominous shadow of potential nuclear holocaust for five decades, we have seen thousands of death abstractions on TV and in movies and computer games, and we have heard the sounds of grief and mourning in music throughout the ages (Morgan, 1995). Still, rather than viewing death as a transformation, as a natural ending of life, many of us continue to view death as a waste and as a barrier to life's meaning. Perhaps, as Morgan (1995:40) has noted, death in America is no longer so much denied as simply rejected. Perhaps our emerging pattern of attitudes toward death and dying is better called *death-rejected*.

In this sense, the work of the death education movement has just begun. Wass (1990), in her sample of death education and grief/suicide intervention in 423 public schools around the United States, from prekindergarten through twelfth grade, found that only 11% of schools offer a course or unit on death education, only 17% offer a grief-support program, and just 25% have a suicide-prevention/ intervention program. In a sample of fifty-three U.S. universities and colleges, Wrenn (1991a, 1994) found that only 38% had a written policy for dealing with the death of a student or faculty member and 30% had training available for counseling survivors. Social worker Robert L. Deaton (Deaton and Morgan, 1992; Deaton and Berkan, 1995) has drawn particular attention to the need for administrative, faculty, and student guidelines and educational programs for dealing with death occurring at schools, especially death by suicide.

Robert Wrenn (1991a, 1991b, 1992, 1994), a contemporary leader in the death-education movement, maintains that students are often more eager and willing to learn about death and to discuss and ask questions than their teachers are to teach about death and dying. In advising students and teachers, he says (1994:6), "I would encourage you to find people of vision and compassion within your school system with whom you can share some of these ideas. Together, you might be able to try some things that will make your school a more humane place to be in times of crisis."

Death education is helping us to cope with dying and death and is opening up new pathways to thanatological research and practices. But above and beyond these contributions, death education can actually improve the quality of our living by motivating us to strive to make each day count in a positive way. Dickinson (1986), for example, studied the effect of death-and-dying courses in pre- and posttests of attitudes of students enrolled in college courses. The results revealed less fear of death and death-related events at the end of the course. Results of a similar high school study of pre/post comparisons of adolescents showed that their level of anxiety decreased significantly as a result of an 18-week death-education course (N. Rosenthal, 1980). Other research studies have shown that college courses on death and dying can have differential effects on individuals, with some students reporting an increase in death anxiety while others report a decrease in death anxiety (Knight and Elfenbein, 1993). Elisabeth Kubler-Ross (1969), one of the founders of modern thanatology, notes that years of studying the psychology of death and of tending to the sick and dying does not make her particularly depressed or anxious, but does make her appreciate each day of life and to be thankful each morning she awakes for the potential of another day.

Herman Feifel (1990:36), in his Distinguished Professional Contributions award address to the 1988 annual convention of the American Psychological Association, reflected on the changes he'd seen in the death-education movement since he chaired the first psychology symposium on the subject 32 years previously. Among the many insights offered, he noted that

> the movement has been a major force in broadening our grasp of the phenomenology of illness, in helping humanize medical relationships and health care, and in advancing the rights of the dying. It is highpointing values that undergird the vitality of human response to catastrophe and loss. Furthermore, it is contributing to reconstituting the integrity of our splintered wholeness . . . sensitizing us to our common humanity. . . . I believe that how we regard and how we treat the dying and survivors are prime indications of a civilization's intention and target. . . . [I]n emphasizing awareness of death, we sharpen and intensify our appreciation of the uniqueness and preciousness of life.

Chapter Summary

American ways of dealing with death and dying reflect a vast array of attitudes, beliefs, and rituals. In this chapter, we have reviewed the dominant European American pattern of attitudes called *invisible death,* in which feelings and thoughts are kept private to the mourner, in contrast to African American, Hispanic American, Asian American, and Native American attitudes.

We have studied the pattern of invisible death in terms of its history, sociological factors (industrialization, medical revolution, shrinking family size, etc.), psychological factors (cognitive denial, emotional repression, and behavioral passivity), as well as the changes it is undergoing as a result of increasing ethnic diversity, an aging population, and the American death-education movement.

The description of America as a death-denying culture has been questioned. We have concluded that this description is too simple. We are, in a sense, a culture immersed in an approach–avoidance conflict about death and dying. This gives the field of thanatology the unenviable task of bringing knowledge and understanding to the dynamic, contradictory, and occasionally opposing attitudes we hold toward death, dying, and the mourning after.

FURTHER READINGS

Aries, Phillipe (1974). *Western Attitudes Toward Death: From the Middle Ages to the Present,* Johns Hopkins University Press, Baltimore/London.

Feifel, H. (ed.) (1959). *The Meaning of Death.* McGraw-Hill, New York.

Irish, D. P., Lundquist, K. F., and Nelsen, V. J. (eds.) (1993). *Ethnic Variations in Dying, Death, and Grief.* Taylor and Francis, Washington, D.C.

Kalish, Richard A. (ed.) (1985). *The Final Transition.* Baywood, Farmingdale, New York.

Kubler-Ross, Elisabeth (1969). *On Death and Dying.* Macmillan, New York.

Leming, Michael, R., and Dickinson, George E. (1994). *Understanding Dying, Death and Bereavement.* Harcourt Brace, New York.

Wass, H., and Niemeyer, R. A. (eds.) (1995). *Dying: Facing the Facts.* Taylor and Francis, Washington, D.C.

Death in America: When and How We Die

We are one species among many, inhabiting a small, blue planet spinning in a cosmic sea, and we live and die on this little outpost in the universe. There is no question that we will all die. However, questions of how we will die and when we will die have been of grave concern to us over recorded time. Some of us will die young and some will die old; others will die in midlife. We will die in strange and unexpected ways, and in ways predictable and straightforward. We will die slowly, aware of each breath in the chest, and we will die suddenly, instantaneously, and without warning. Yet, for each of us, the final chapter of our lives will be distinctly our own. Though countless others have passed this way before us, the way we die will be as unique and as curious as the way we have lived.

Transitions

Because of historical declines in infant mortality and childhood infectious diseases during the past century, dying in the United States is now more characteristic of the very old than of the young or middle aged. This dramatic historical shift in the distribution of American deaths, from dying young to dying old, is termed an *epidemiologic transition.*

Ravaged primarily by infectious diseases—such as cholera, influenza, pneumonia, and tuberculosis—and high infant mortality rates, humanity had an average life expectancy at birth of only 22 years during the Roman Empire, 33 years in Europe during the Middle Ages, and 36 years around the time of the American Revolution. In 1900, according to the National Center for Health Statistics (NCHS) (1995b), average life expectancy in America was only about 47 years. In contrast, a person living in the United States today can expect to live to 78.9 years if female, and 72.1 years if male. In fact, 39% of women alive today, and 21% of men, can expect to reach their eighty-fifth birthday and the trend toward increased life expectancy is expected to continue into the twenty-first century. In its latest projection of life tables, the National Center for Health Statistics (1995b) predicts that average life expectancy at birth may reach 82.6 years in the year 2050—85.6 years for women and 79.7 years for men. The age group 85 and older is expected to be seven times its present size by the year 2050 (NCHS, 1995b).

Potential Life Lost in America

With the epidemiologic transition from dying young to dying old, infectious diseases have given way to chronic conditions, such as heart disease and cancer, as major killers of Americans. Of the more than 2 million people who die in the

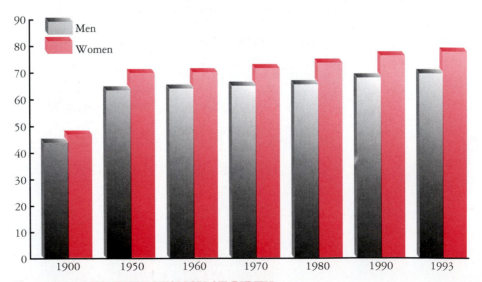

Figure 2.1   LIFE EXPECTANCY AT BIRTH
Source: NCHS, 1995b

United States in any given year, the most common cause of death is heart disease, followed in frequency by cancer, stroke, and lung disease. In addition to the actual number of deaths due to particular causes, or the rate of deaths per 100,000, another set of figures calculates the number of years of *potential life* lost by Americans as a result of particular causes. According to the National Center for Health Statistics (1995a), "years of potential life lost" is calculated as the years these persons would have lived if they had lived to be age 65. Based on years of potential life lost in the United States today, cancer turns out to be the number one killer, followed by heart disease, accidents, suicide, birth defects, murder, and AIDS.

Dying Trajectories

The cause of death, whether by cancer, heart disease, accident or birth defect, is associated with a particular pattern of dying. These patterns of dying, the duration and shape of the terminal course through time, are called **dying trajectories** (Glaser & Strauss, 1966, 1968). The **duration** of a death refers to the time between the onset of dying and the actual arrival of death, while the **shape** of death refers to the course of the dying process, whether it is predictable or not, whether death is expected or unexpected, or whether the death involves remissions and relapses or involves no forewarning at all. Death can be sudden or, to varying degrees, expected.

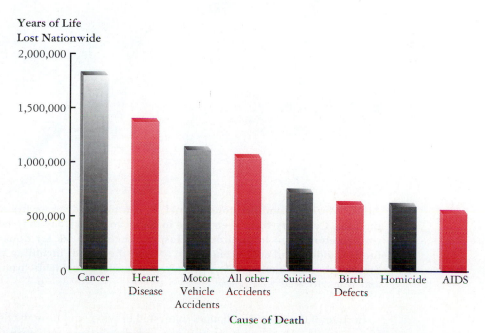

Figure 2.2   THE EIGHT LEADING CAUSES OF DEATH IN THE UNITED STATES DEFINED BY YEARS OF POTENTIAL LIFE LOST BEFORE AGE 65
Source: NCHS, 1995a.

Amela Moric, 10 and her cousin Amel, 8, run to avoid sniper fire as they cross the Lion Cemetery from their home in Sarajevo. Every day they have to cross the cemetery to go to the Kosevo Hospital kitchen to ask for donations of food. Children and adolescents from around the world, including the United States, are more likely to die suddenly as a result of accidents, murder, suicide and war. *AP/Wide World Photos*

In spite of the dramatic changes witnessed in when and how we die, one thing has remained true throughout history—infants, children, adolescents and young adults are more prone to die by a **brief trajectory,** by more sudden means

**LEADING CAUSES OF DEATH
BY AGE IN THE U.S.**

- *Infancy (0–1 years):* birth defects, accidents, heart disease, pneumonia and influenza, diabetes, homicide

- *Childhood (1–14 years):* accidents, cancer, congenital anomalies, homicide, heart disease, suicide

- *Adolescence and Early Adulthood (15–24 years):* accidents, homicide, suicide

- *Adulthood (25–64 years):* cancer, heart disease, accidents, pulmonary diseases, AIDS, pneumonia, diabetes

- *Old Age (65 years and older):* heart disease, cancer, stroke, accidents, pulmonary diseases, pneumonia, influenza, diabetes, suicide

Source: NCHS, 1995a.

involving fatal accidents, homicide, suicide, and war. The death of American infants, for example, especially non-white infants, continues to provoke concern. Sociologist Michael C. Kearl (1995:9) notes that, despite the fact that between 1915 and 1990, the U.S. infant mortality rate dropped from 99.9 to 9.1 deaths for every 1,000 births, ". . . by the early 1990s, the United States ranked behind 22 other nations in preventing infant deaths."

Stress and Life

The dramatic rise in life expectancy in the past hundred years, from 47 years to over 76 years, is attributable not only to the medical and municipal control of infectious diseases, but to nutritional, shelter, and lifestyle improvements brought about by industrialization. Taken together, technologically-advanced production, distribution, transportation, education, and communication systems, along with the revolution in high-tech medicine, have created a world our ancestors could have barely imagined.

There is a downside to these innovations, however, that now includes global warming, epidemics of infectious disease; the effects of air, water and ground pollution on the environment; and the effects of physical and psychological **stress** on the health of human beings and other animals. In a sense, we have made a swap on the questions of *how* and *when* we die, choosing a later death from cancer or heart disease instead of an early death from infectious diseases. And yet, as thanatologist Lewis Aiken (1994:14) notes, ". . . it is doubtful that anyone who suffered through the epidemics of bubonic plague, cholera, influenza, poliomyelitis, and mass starvation of former times would view the exchange as an unfavorable one."

How We Die

In the following sections we review some of the most common causes of death in the United States, along with contributions researchers are making to a deeper understanding of *how and when we die.*

HEART DISEASE

The human heart is the central player in an unending loop of vessels called the circulatory system. Beating about 100,000 times per day, or about 3 billion beats per lifetime, the heart delivers the equivalent of 4,300 gallons of blood per day to every outpost of our bodies. The development of lesions on the coronary arteries, the arteries that circulate blood within the heart itself, is the principal cause of heart disease.

The arterial lesions are caused by deposits called *plaques,* which thicken the arterial walls until they are partially or totally obstructed. When the coronary arteries become rigid and narrow as a result of these plaque deposits, a condition called *atheroschlerosis* results in which the supply of blood to portions of the heart muscle is temporarily or permanently choked off. This results in a variety of symptoms, from periodic chest pains caused by an insufficient supply of blood to the heart, called *angina pectoris,* to a more serious *myocardial infarction,* or heart attack, involving an all-but-complete blocking off of the heart's blood supply. Like the pain of a charley horse, caused by the seizure of muscle tissue in the leg, the muscle fibers that make up the heart seize, causing a heart attack.

Heart disease, hypertension, stroke, atheroschlerosis, and other cardiovascular diseases are, as a group, the primary cause of death in the entire world. During 1992, an estimated 722,770 people in the United States alone died from heart disease (NCHS, 1992).

Heart disease was, until recently, considered a man's disease, and most of the research essentially ignored women. Men, ages 35 to 64, are still the leading candidates for heart attacks. They suffer them 4.5 times more often than women the same age. Today, in fact, about 10 million American women also suffer from heart disease, 10% of women ages 45–64 have some form of it, and each year almost a quarter of a million women die from it, making heart disease the number-one killer of American women. One in five of us will develop some form of heart disease before our sixtieth birthday (American Heart Association, 1996).

The yearly death rate from heart disease is declining, according to the American Heart Association (1996): overall death rates from heart attack declined 31.4% from 1982 to 1992; in 1950 the death rate per 100,000 from heart attack was 226.4, but in 1991 it had dropped to 108.0; decreases in heart disease death were greatest in the Northeast and least in the South. Two possible reasons for these significant decreases

BEDSIDE ENCOUNTER

Surgeon Sherwin B. Nuland (1993) describes a myocardial infarction witnessed while he was a third-year medical student. The patient, James McCarty, married and employed as a construction executive, was 52 years old at the time.

> As I sat down at his bedside, he suddenly threw his head back and bellowed out a wordless roar that seemed to rise up out of his throat from somewhere deep within his stricken heart. He hit his balled fists with startling force up against the front of his chest in a single synchronous thump, just as his face and neck, in the flash of an instant, turned swollen and purple. His eyes seemed to have pushed themselves forward in one bulging thrust, as though they were trying to leap out of his head. He took one immensely long, gurgling breath, and died.

Source: Quote from Nuland (1993), p. 5

in cardiovascular diseases are improved medical care and decreased smoking and cholesterol levels.

Emotions and Afflictions of the Heart

The risk of developing heart disease has been linked to high blood pressure, or *hypertension,* and to a history of heart disease in close relatives, indicating a possible genetic predisposition. Heart disease is also linked to cigarette smoking, extreme overweight, and a high level of cholesterol in the diet (American Heart Association, 1996). But researchers have discovered that emotional *stress* can also play a significant role in the development of heart disease.

People who are continually subject to a great deal of stress—and who lack the skills to cope with it—are at significantly greater risk for heart disease than are people who experience less stress or who have the skill to manage it (Cottington & House, 1987). For example, it has been found that jobs that are psychologically demanding, or jobs that offer little opportunity to control your own working conditions (i.e., low "job decision latitude"), such as cook, waiter, and hospital orderly, seem to breed heart disease (Karasek et al., 1981). On the other hand, certain people seem to make heavy psychological demands on themselves, regardless of their work situation, and, as a result, run a greater-than-average risk of developing heart disease. These "coronary-prone" individuals engage in a particular configuration of cognition, feelings and behaviors called the ***Type A behavior pattern*** (Friedman & Rosenman, 1974).

Interestingly, Friedman and Rosenman, the cardiologists who discovered the Type A pattern, first became interested in the role stress was playing in their patients' lives when they noticed that the front of the seats in their waiting room were excessively worn, suggesting that their patients were, literally, sitting on the edge of their seats. Subsequent research led to the discovery of a behavior pattern typified by people who are hard-driving, competitive, and aggressive and who experience great time-urgency in almost everything they do. Type A individuals regularly try to do more than one thing at a time, are likely to speak in a fast, loud, explosive style, and, often, display clenched fists and aggressive facial expressions (Rosenman, Swan, & Carmelli, 1988).

More recent research findings reveal that a specific feature of the Type A behavior pattern that appears to be most harmful to the Type A person is *hostility* (Eysenck, 1988; Suarez, 1990). Labora-

STROKE

A stroke occurs when a blood vessel bringing oxygen and nutrients to the brain bursts or is clogged by a blood clot or some other obstruction. Deprived of oxygen, nerve cells in the affected part of the brain die, causing paralysis or diminished function in parts of the body controlled by these nerves.

The condition hits more than 500,000 Americans each year, causing death in 150,000, according to the American Heart Association (1995). The incidence is strongly related to age, with more than 70% of cases in people 65 years of age or older.

More than 3 million Americans are living with varying degrees of disability caused by stroke, which costs the nation $33 billion a year, about a quarter of it going for rehabilitation. The National Stroke Association (1995) estimates that with good rehabilitation, 70% of stroke survivors can regain independence in daily activities.

tory studies have shown that hostile people react to stressful situations with greater increases in heart rate and blood pressure than do people who are lower in hostility, and that it is these short-fused people who are most likely to have heart attacks (T. W. Smith & Pope, 1990; Suarez & Williams, 1989; Marrone, 1990).

The behaviors associated with the Type A behavior pattern place both men and women at risk for heart disease, but because of apparent gender stereotyping, the risks connected to psychological stress may be greater for Type A women. In one psychological survey, it was found that Type A men are admired as hard-driving go-getters by their wives, while Type A women are devalued as too independent and not nurturing enough by their husbands. Men married to Type A women were found to be less satisfied with the marriage than women married to Type A men; and in marriages in which the woman is Type A, both husband and wife were more likely to want a divorce (Sullaway & Morell, 1990).

The biologic path by which hostility and anger contribute to heart disease appears to involve changes in blood pressure levels. A favored hypothesis is that abnormally large rises in blood pressure caused by emotionally stressful events can lead to injury of the endothelium, the inner lining of the arteries. Once injury occurs in the endothelium, plaque begins to form at this site, narrowing the artery and thus creating an increased risk for a heart attack (Suarez, 1990).

HIDDEN KILLERS

Heart disease, cancer, stroke, accidents, and diseases ranging from diabetes to AIDS are some of the leading causes of death in America, according to death certificates. But death certificates say nothing about what caused the illness or accident in the first place. According to the American Medical Association, here is what really kills Americans.

CAUSE	DEATHS IN 1990
Tobacco	400,000
Poor diet/inactivity	300,000
Alcohol	100,000
Microbial infections	90,000
Toxic agents	60,000
Firearms	35,000
Sexual behavior	30,000
Motor vehicles	25,000
Drug abuse	20,000

Source: Journal of the American Medical Association, November 10, 1993, p. 1,022.

The intimate association between the heart and our emotional and mental life has been alluded to throughout human history and will likely continue to be of interest to psychological researchers. In this light, it is interesting to note that more than 350 years ago, William Harvey, the English physician who first discovered the circulation of the blood and the role of the heart in propelling it, wrote, "Every affliction of the mind that is attended with either pain or pleasure, hope or fear, is the cause of an agitation whose influence extends to the heart."

CANCER

To distinguish certain ulcerations from ordinary body swellings, ancient Greek physicians gave the name ***karkinos*** ("hard") to the rough and stony swellings they observed in the breast or protruding from the rectum or vagina of their

A CANCER GLOSSARY

Cancer: A broad term used to describe more than 100 different malignant tumors; 95 percent of all cancers take the form of solid tumors.

Benign tumor: Does not invade other tissues and is therefore not cancerous. A benign tumor is rarely a threat to life, usually can be surgically removed, and usually does not recur.

Malignant tumor: Characterized by uncontrolled cell growth and the ability to spread (*metastasize*) to other tissues.

Carcinomas: One of three groups of cancer cells, classified by the type of cell in which they originate. Carcinomas arise from epithelial tissue, the tissue that covers or lines organs of the body. Examples include the skin and the lining of the lungs.

Sarcomas: Another classification of cancer cells that arise from connective tissue, such as bone, cartilage, and muscle. Sarcomas also affect the liver, lungs, spleen, kidneys, and bladder.

Lymphomas, leukemias, myelomas: Arise in the vascular tissues of the body. Lymphomas are tumors of the lymphatic system; leukemias are tumors of the blood system; and myelomas form in the tissues that give rise to blood cells.

Carcinogen: A substance or agent that increases the risk of cancer by damaging DNA, the molecule that stores genetic information in cells. When carcinogens cause mutations in genes that control cell growth, it can lead to cancer. Carcinogens can be chemical, physical, or viral.

patients. In the second century, A.D., Galen, Greek philosopher and physician, described the appearance of a creeping jagged mass of tissue, ulcerated at its middle, as "just like a crab's legs extending outward from every part of the body" (Nuland, 1993:206). Centuries later, the Latin word for crab, *cancer,* came into common usage.

As a disease process, cancer is characterized by uncontrolled cell growth resulting in a *tumor,* or *neoplasm.* The tumor is *benign* if it is restricted to a particular clump of cells. But many tumors are *malignant,* or *metastatic,* and spread not only to the surrounding tissue but also to distant parts of the body. Cancer is not a single disease, but is, rather, a general term for more than 100 diseases, found in 69 different anatomical sites.

Because most cancers take from 10 to 40 years to develop, the risk of cancer increases as we age. Cancer is responsible for over 500,000 deaths per year in the United States, or about 1,400 deaths per day. Following decades of study, medical researchers are beginning to understand the biological mechanisms of cell behavior that underlie the onset and development of cancer. Survival rates are improving, dramatically in the case of some cancers, but in many cases the eventual outcome is death.

Cancer is mainly a disease of the elderly. In 1990, about 12% of Americans 65 and older accounted for two-thirds (67.7%) of all cancer deaths nationwide. By contrast, Americans 19 and younger, who constitute about 30% of the population, contributed less than 1% of cancer deaths. Cancer mortality rates among Americans 65 and older rose nearly 1% a year between 1973 and 1990, mainly due to a greater number of lung cancer deaths from smoking (National Cancer Institute, 1996).

Cancer, Stress, and the Immune System

Psychological researchers, as well as physicians and nurses, have noted associations between significant losses, like a death in the family, and subsequent illness,

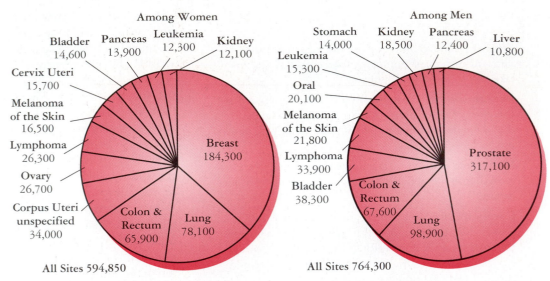

Figure 2.3   UNITED STATES COMMON CANCER DEATHS, 1995
Source: American Cancer Society (ACS), 1996.

including cancer. The association seems greatest when the person experiencing loss is in cognitive denial, emotionally repressed, or clinically depressed. In one dramatic study of over 2,000 men, Richard Shekelle et al. (1981) found that those men whose responses to a psychological test showed them to be extremely depressed were twice as likely as other men to have died of cancer 17 years later. In another study, Persky, Kempthorne-Rawson, and Shekelle (1987) studied a group of women with breast cancer for about 2 years and found that those who expressed their anger and fear outwardly rather than keeping it to themselves were more likely to recover. The spread of cancer was greatest among women who dealt with fear, anger, and sadness by ignoring them. Hans Eysenck (1988:32), following a review of psychological studies of the cancer-prone personality, writes,

> The type of personality often ascribed to the cancer-prone individual combines two major features. One is an inability to express emotions, such as anger, fear and anxiety; the other is an inability to cope with stress and a tendency to develop feelings of hopelessness, helplessness and, finally, depression. In general, more recent studies characterized the cancer-prone person as unassertive, overly patient, avoiding conflict and failing to express negative emotions.

Other research suggests that the grieving process and the experience of loneliness may also have a negative impact on the immune system (Sarason & Sarason, 1989). Researchers have found that prolonged stress, and the negative emotions that usually accompany it, can inhibit the functioning of the immune system, preventing it from producing cells that fight off cancer cells (Zautra et al., 1989; Marrone, 1990). When individuals repress their negative feelings and deny the conditions that produced them, they can become depressed, and depression can suppress the immune system.

STEPS TO A HEALTHIER SELF: BEHAVIOR MODIFICATION AND BREAST CANCER

"Katarina Kolb loved her married boyfriend, but he seemed to be much more concerned about his wife than he was about her. Katarina, a 38-year-old German woman, also felt rejected by her father but could not speak to him about it. And she had breast cancer.

Katarina—not her real name—felt depressed and hopeless. According to psychologists Ronald Grossarth-Maticek and Hans Eysenck, she had the classic personality traits of a person vulnerable to cancer. She repressed her anger and anxiety, and felt helpless to find ways to solve her problems.

To change this disease-prone behavior, Katarina took a course of treatment that Grossarth-Maticek and Eysenck call 'autonomy training.' During either individual or group sessions, therapists explain the difference between the healthy and disease-prone personalities and use relaxation methods, coping techniques, and desensitization to help patients move toward the healthy personality style. Grossarth-Maticek and Eysenck use this approach with both cancer-prone and heart-disease-prone people. Individuals susceptible to heart disease learn to abandon the tendencies toward hostility and aggression that the researchers say put them at risk. The key change for cancer-prone people is to stop being overly passive.

Cancer-prone personality types often believe that they are incapable of meeting their needs on their own and depend on another person, job, or institution to enhance their sense of self. Katarina, for example, could not get the support she longed for from her married boyfriend but felt she couldn't get along without him. Her feelings of helplessness and anxiety led to passive acceptance of the situation.

When the therapist asked Katarina to explain her behavior, she gained a sense of perspective on herself for the first time. "I've never really thought about this, but it's very destructive, really. Every time I get rejected I get depressed." At her therapist's request, she began to write down ways to get rid of self-defeating behavior.

Her first step was to avoid confrontations with her father in which she knew she would end up feeling rejected. 'I won't make demands on him, because when I do, I usually lose and I find that difficult to bear.' The therapist helped her use imagery to picture several situations involving her father in which she had no expectations and did not need to make any demands.

Katarina reported success at her next session and said she was beginning to like and value herself. She was becoming less dependent on her father and boyfriend and wanted to find new, interesting activities to take her mind off her illness. 'I will call up my girlfriend and ask her to go for a walk with me every day, and I will ask my old

ALZHEIMER'S DISEASE

Alzheimer's disease strikes about 10% of people over 65 and nearly half of those 85 or older (Alzheimer's Association, 1996). Memory loss, especially for recent events, is usually the first sign, followed by more profound and debilitating mental, behavioral, and bodily control impairments. If no other cause intervenes, Alzheimer's patients usually die after having infections, such as pneumonia, or other complications 3 to 20 years after the first signs appear. Although Alzheimer's disease is rare in persons under age 50, it is now being classified as "early onset" for persons as young as 30 to 40 years of age, and "late onset" for persons 65 years of age or older (C. Miller, 1995; Allen, 1995). Based on a recent review of the relevant research, Carol Miller (1995) speculates that Alzheimer's tennis partner whether he would like to come and have a game with me,' she added.

By the next session. Katarina had gone for several walks and had found three new tennis partners. She told her therapist that she wanted to be more relaxed; she wanted 'a state in which inner inhibitions and fears are reduced, in which I believe in myself, trust myself and think I am doing the right thing.' The therapist put her into a state of deep hypnosis and repeated some suggestions, created by Katarina herself: 'I've become more relaxed, happier and happier, and find myself in a wonderful landscape near the sea. I am at one with nature and free of all inhibitions. At the same time I can believe in myself and the success of all my wishes.'

Eventually, Katarina sought ways to change her relationship with her boyfriend. He usually visited her once a day, promising to stay for a long visit, but always left after only a short time. 'Such behavior I will not tolerate any more!' she decided. Again, she used mental imagery, picturing unfulfilling moments in the relationship, and soon she had little desire to see her boyfriend again.

Mental imagery is also used to help other cancer patients combat their disease. Patients visualize white blood cells conquering a malignancy, and by doing so begin to feel some mastery over the illness, while also learning to release anger and resentment.

Autonomy training emphasizes avoiding behavior that leads to short-term solutions, such as escaping a personal rejection, but has long-term negative effects, such as an overall sense of helplessness. And Katarina had clearly reached a new level of autonomy. By ending her relationship with her boyfriend she chose long-term independence over the short-term goal of having some of her boyfriend's attention.

Grossarth-Maticek and Eysenck have found that the patients who succeed in changing their behavior in this way become more self-reliant, less demanding, and less rigid than those who don't learn to make these changes. And for those who make the changes, Grossarth-Maticek and Eysenck's research shows that chances of getting cancer are greatly reduced. If they already have the disease, their lives should be prolonged by several years. While Katarina still had some self-doubts at the end of her therapy, she also had learned coping skills to deal with her problems.

'I have experienced the negative consequences from putting one's self second.' she said. 'I shall always keep these consequences in my thoughts, act accordingly and feel good about myself.' "

Source: Mia Adessa, in Eysenck (1988), pp. 28–32, 34–35.

disease may run in families, suggesting a common linkage, perhaps genetic in nature.

Studies in the mid-1970s suggested that 2.5 million Americans had Alzheimer's. Now the Alzheimer's Association (1996) reports as many as 4 million people in the United States may be afflicted. Although not officially recognized in government mortality statistics as a cause of death, the Alzheimer's Association estimates that more than 100,000 Americans die of Alzheimer's each year, which would make it the fourth-leading cause of death among adults in the United States, after heart disease, cancer, and stroke. National experts believe that Alzheimer's deaths are probably substantially underreported—attributed to pneumonia or cardiac arrest—when in fact Alzheimer's disease is the underlying cause of death (Alzheimer's Association, 1996).

CARING INSIGHTS

Symptoms of Alzheimer's Disease

If you notice several of the following symptoms (compiled by the Alzheimer's Association) in an elderly person, schedule an appointment with a physician.

- Memory loss that interferes with everyday activities
- Repeatedly asking the same questions or forgetting appointments
- Difficulty performing familiar tasks, such as forgetting how to serve a meal
- Language problems, such as forgetting simple words
- Disorientation, such as getting lost on a familiar street
- Poor judgment such as forgetting about a child in his or her care or leaving the stove on
- Problems with abstract thinking, such as no longer being able to follow simple directions
- Continually misplacing items or putting them in odd places
- Significant mood swings or significant changes in personality or behavior
- Loss of initiative

The Alzheimer's Association calculates the cost of care for Alzheimer's patients in the United States at between $80 billion and $90 billion a year. The National Institute on Aging estimates that the number of Americans afflicted by the disease may more than triple by the year 2050 if no way is found to prevent or cure the disease. Similar increases in Alzheimer's death rates have been predicted for England, Australia, Norway, and Canada (Alzheimer's Association 1996).

HOMICIDE AND SUICIDE

Suicide and homicide result in more premature loss of life for Americans each year than anything but accidents, AIDS, cancer, and heart disease. The United States reported 19,796 homicides and 29,286 suicides in 1991 (Leming & Dickinson, 1994:330). The average U.S. suicide occurred at age 43, while the average homicide killed a 34-year-old. European American males had the highest rate of life lost to suicide, while African American males had the highest rate of life lost to murder (NCHS 1995c). Firearms were the method of choice for most of the life lost to both suicide (57%) and homicide (61%), and took from their victims more than 1.2 million "years of potential life." According to the National Center for Health Statistics (1995c), guns were the fourth-leading cause of premature deaths in the United States after nonfirearm-related injuries, cancer, and heart disease.

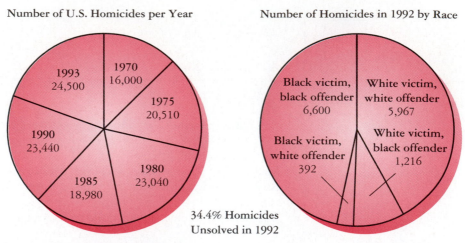

Figure 2.4   **BODY COUNT**
Source: FBI, May, 1996
Source: J. A. Fox, & G. Pierce. (1993). Northeastern University, National Crime Analysis.

Homicide

The United States has the highest firearm-related homicide rates of any industrialized nation, by a wide and ever-growing margin. In 1992, for example, handguns were used in the murders of 13,220 people in the United States. That compares to thirteen such killings in Australia, thirty-three in Britain, thirty-six in Sweden, sixty in Japan, eighty-seven in Switzerland, and 128 in Canada, all countries with strict regulation of firearms (FBI, 1996). In 1992, according to the National Center for Health Statistics (1995a), homicide was the tenth-leading cause of death in the United States. After accidents, homicide was the second-leading cause of death for Americans in the workplace in 1995. (U.S. Department of Labor, 1996).

In terms of age, the highest rates of homicide are in the 15–24-year-old group, with the 25–34-year-old group running a close second. Together, these two age groups account for nearly 60% of the homicide victims in the United States. The National Center for Health Statistics (1995c) reports that in the years 1985–1991, arrests for criminal homicide increased 140% among 13- and 14-year-old boys and 217% among 15-year-old boys. The numbers were equally high for older teenagers. The homicide rate among African Americans is more than six times that of European Americans; in the total population, the murder rate for American males is more than three times higher than for females. For young, male African Americans, homicide is the number-one cause of death.

ALZHEIMER'S DISEASE

"At first he couldn't remember things—where he'd left his book, what day it was, the names of people and things, even something he'd just said. Then it got worse.

He would just wander off. Sometimes I'd find him in the neighborhood, as though he'd gone for a walk and got lost. Other times I'd get a phone call from a total stranger saying my husband was clear across town and would I please come and take him home."

Source: Food and Drug Administration (1996).

SERIAL KILLERS/REPTILE BRAINS

Almost exclusively male, a serial killer is someone who murders two or more victims over a period of time, with breaks or "cooling-off" periods between some victims. The lengths of time may range from a few days to several years, with the crimes often being sexually motivated (Dehart & Mahoney, 1994). John Wayne Gacy, for example, killed 33 young men over a 7-year period. Between 1950 and 1970, only two cases of murders of ten or more are known in the United States, in contrast to 39 known multiple-murder cases since 1970 (Jenkins, 1988).

Unlike other motivations for murder, including jealousy, material gain, revenge, and ideological conviction (Egger, 1984), the serial killer's behavioral orientation, according to DeHart and Mahoney (1984:31) "is expressive, rather than instrumental, with the murderer seeking enhancement of a personal psychological state rather than material gain."

A number of theories, including psychophysiological, psychological, and sociological models, have been proposed as possible explanations of the serial killing phenomenon, though the issue remains unresolved. A recent and controversial model from the field of paleopsychology postulates that human aggression reflects the consequences of neurologically regressed patterns of behavior. According to this triune brain theory (MacLean, 1970), the human brain consists of three distinct structural components: the most primitive neural chasis, or Reptilian-complex, which controls maintenance functions of the body; the second-order, limbic structures, or Mammalian-complex, which control the emotions, hunger, pain avoidance, and pleasure seeking; and the highest-level, cerebral cortex, or Human-complex, which contributes to rational thought and logical analysis. According to Bailey (1987), the human neocortex acts as an inhibitory filter for powerful impulses from the lowest brain and that aggression results from deficient or failed neocortical inhibition of basal impulses. The serial killer's behavior, from this perspective, arises from a basic reliance upon the functioning of the repetitive and unemotional processes of the Reptilian-complex and on the emotion-oriented limbic system. The serial killer acts as a reptilelike predator who fails to respond to behavioral constraints imposed by more advanced neocortical functions.

Survivors of Murder   A murder typically involves a brief dying trajectory: It is usually sudden and unexpected and often involves a short duration from the act of violence to the death of the victim. As a result, homicides often present special problems for survivors. Not only is the murder itself likely to be shocking and unclear, but the murder victim is likely to be young, and may be related to the killer. Nearly 50% of victims are murdered by a relative, friend, or acquaintance. In these cases, the survivors must deal with both the murder of one loved one and the arrest of another.

Murders that are random, or "drive-by" shootings, are particularly vicious, and often leave the survivors psychologically devastated. If the murderer is apprehended, the survivors must then deal with an often-lengthy court trial, impressions of injustice (Redmond, 1989), and accompanying feelings of anger, rage, and depression. Harvey (1996:93) observes that "one of the worst types of losses to violence occurs when the perpetrator is never found. Grieving cannot be completed when a killer is not found—or when a family never learns exactly what happened when their loved one died."

Young Americans are fifteen to twenty times more likely to die from homicide than their counterparts in other industrialized nations. Homicide is the number one cause of death for young, male African Americans (NCHS, 1995c). © *Mark Costantini*

Suicide

The concept of suicide derives from the Latin *sui* ("of oneself") and *cede* ("a killing") and is widely defined as "a conscious act of self-induced annihilation" (Shneidman, 1985). Suicide is among the ten leading causes of death in the Western world. In a survey of sixty-two countries conducted by the World Health Organization (WHO) for the years 1980–1986, the United States ranked near the middle (#24) in terms of suicide rates.

Gender differences in suicide rates have remained steady since the end of World War II. According to the National Center for Health Statistics (1995a), three times as many women as men attempt to kill themselves, but four times as many men as women actually die by their own hand. This fact may have something to do with the way they choose to commit suicide. While firearms are the predominant method of killing oneself in America, among both men (64%) and women (39.8%), more women (25%) try to overdose on drugs, especially barbiturates, than men (5.2%). And men are more likely to choose hanging than women (13.5% to 9.4%), while women are more likely to choose carbon monoxide than men (12.6% to 9.6%). The more lethal means chosen by males may, in itself, account for the gender differences in completed suicides, although the question of why males choose more lethal and more violent means of killing themselves has suggested other theories associated with male depression, as well as lower serotonin levels and higher testosterone levels in males (D. C. Clark, 1993; Stillion and McDowell, 1995).

The most likely candidates for suicide are elderly, white, alcoholic men, but for white males, in general, the frequency of suicide increases across the life span. For women, the frequency rates are highest in middle age. As compared to adolescents, the suicide rate for the elderly is higher all over the world. However, in recent years there has been an enormous (200–300%) increase in the number of adolescents and young adults, 15–24 years of age, who have both attempted and completed suicide, so that, today, in the United States, suicide ranks as the third-most frequent killer of 15–24-year-olds. A 1991 psychological survey conducted by The National Centers for Health Statistics found that 27% of 11,631 high school students had "thought seriously" about killing themselves in the previous year, and that one in twelve had actually tried to kill themselves (NCHS, 1992).

Suicide researchers, called **suicidologists,** agree that many suicides result from an underlying psychological disorder, primarily depression, often coupled with alcoholism and drug abuse. In fact, clinically depressed individuals are at a 50% greater risk of killing themselves, and the neurotransmitter serotonin may play a significant role. The National Institutes of Mental Health, for example, recently reported that twenty-two of twenty-two autopsies of brain and body fluid have

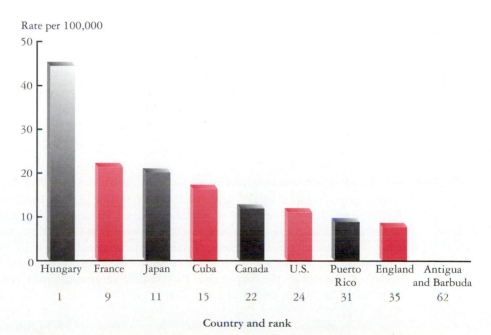

Rate per 100,000

Country and rank

Figure 2.5   SUICIDE RATES (PER 100,000 POPULATION), 1980–1986
Source: Encyclopedia of Sociology. (1992). Macmillan, NY, pp. 2111–2119.

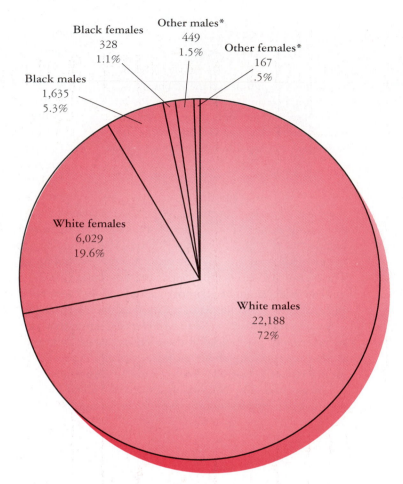

Black females
328
1.1%

Other males*
449
1.5%

Other females*
167
.5%

Black males
1,635
5.3%

White females
6,029
19.6%

White males
22,188
72%

*Includes American Indian, Chinese, Hawaiian, Japanese, Filipino,
Other Asian, Pacific Islander, and Other

Figure 2.6   RATES OF U.S. SUICIDE BY RACE AND GENDER
Source: National Center for Health Statistics (1992).
Source: ★Includes American Indian, Chinese, Hawaiian, Japanese, Filipino, other Asian,
Pacific Islander, and other.

correlated low levels of serotonin with suicide; and that about 20% of depressives
with low serotonin levels committed suicide within 1 year, while in another
group, with normal levels of serotonin, between 1% and 2% killed themselves.
Not surprisingly, research has consistently shown that, on average, men tend to
have lower serotonin levels than women. By raising serotonin levels with newer
forms of antidepressants, such as Prozac and Zoloft, psychopharmacologists are
beginning tests of the hypothesis that raising serotonin levels can raise the
threshold for acting on suicidal impulses.

Survivors of Suicide   Suicide is a relatively rare event: 99.9% of Americans don't
commit suicide. But for the nearly 30,000 a year who do, suicide takes it full toll

CHEATED BY DEATH

To gain some feel for and some insight into the personal experience of a person preparing to make an attempt at suicide, we turn to this excerpted description of his attempt at killing himself offered by Al Alvarez (1974).

"*I built up to the act carefully and for a long time. . . . It was the one constant focus of my life, making everything else irrelevant, a diversion. . . .*

I see now that I had been incubating this death far longer than I recognized at the time. When I was a child, both my parents had half-heartedly put their heads in the gas-oven. Or so they claimed. . . .

Maybe this is why, when I grew up and things went particularly badly, I used to say to myself, over and over, 'I wish I were dead.'. . .

Then one day I understood what I was saying. I was walking along the edge of Hampstead Heath after some standard domestic squabble, and suddenly I heard the phrase as though for the first time. I stood still to attend the words. I repeated them slowly, listening. And realized that I meant it. . . .

My life felt so cluttered and obstructed that I could hardly breathe. I inhabited a closed, concentrated world, airless and without exits. I doubt if any of this was noticeable socially. . . . I simply was tenser, more nervous than usual. . . . But underneath I was going a bit mad. I had entered the closed world of suicide and my life was being lived for me by forces I couldn't control. . . .

I remember that Christmas standing at the front door, joking with the guests as they left. 'Happy Christmas,' we call to each other. I closed the door and turned back to my wife.

As I reconstruct it, I went upstairs to the bathroom and swallowed forty-five sleeping pills. . . . I [had] stopped taking the things and began hoarding them in preparation for the time I knew was coming. When it finally arrived, a box was waiting stuffed with pills in all colors, like M&M's. I gobbled the lot. . . .

After that, I remember nothing at all until I woke up in the hospital. . . . But that was three days later, three days of oblivion, a hole in my head. . . .

Somehow, I felt death had let me down; I had expected more of it. I had looked for something overwhelming, an experience which would clarify all my confusions. . . . But all I got was oblivion. For all intents and purposes, I had died: my face had been blue, my pulse erratic, my breathing ineffectual; the doctors had given me up. I went to the edge and most of the way over; then gradually, unwillingly and despite everything, I inched my way back. And now I knew nothing at all about it. I felt cheated.

Months later. . . . Once I had accepted that there weren't ever going to be any answers, even in death, I found to my surprise that I didn't much care whether I was happy or unhappy; 'problems' and the 'problem of problems' no longer existed. And that in itself is already the beginning of happiness."

Source: A. Alvarez. (1974). *The Savage God: A Study of Suicide.* Random House, New York, pp. 291–306.

on those left behind. In most instances, suicide seems an enormously selfish act that has enormous impact on the survivors in the form of anger, guilt, and grief. Suicides arouse intense emotions in the survivors because the act of intentional self-killing is often seen as an act of desertion that threatens our own, sometimes tenuous, defenses against experiences of nothingness and emptiness.

ACCIDENTS, WAR, AND NATURAL DISASTERS

A traumatic incident—whether an accident, a natural disaster, or the result of war, combat, or terrorism—can, of course, happen to anyone. And whether we are directly involved or know someone who is involved, such incidents exert a powerful influence on the survivors.

Accidents

Accidents, especially automobile accidents, are the fourth-most common cause of death among Americans and the leading cause of death among persons ages 34 and younger. Although the percentage of young people involved in alcohol-related motor vehicle accidents has declined in recent years, alcohol continues to be a factor in about one in five fatal vehicular crashes involving young people ages 16 and 17 and more than a third of the fatal crashes involving young people between the ages of 18 and 21 (Statistical Abstracts of the United States, 1990). In fact, accidents are the leading cause of *premature* deaths in the United States and account for about 2.2 million years of potential life lost each year (NCHS, 1992). The U.S. Department of Labor (1994) reported that highway accidents were the number-one cause of on-the-job deaths in 1992 and 1993. Ninety-two percent of those killed on the job were men.

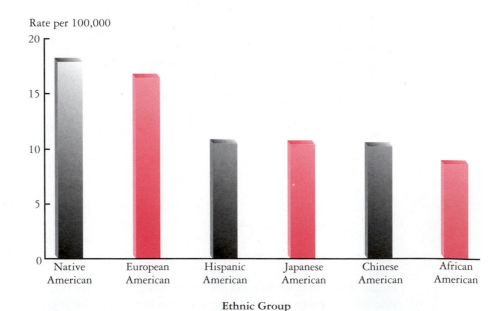

Figure 2.7   ETHNICITY AND SUICIDE
Source: John L. McIntosh. (1995). Epidemiology of Suicide in the United States. In *Death: Current Perspectives,* 4th ed., J.B. Williamson & E.S. Shneidman (eds.) Mayfield, Mountain View, CA, p. 334.

American deaths from head injury since 1977 exceed the total of war dead from all U.S. battles, including the Revolutionary War. Yearly, head injury creates 5,000 cases of seizure disorders, leaves up to 90,000 victims permanently disabled, and claims as many as 100,000 lives, including 10 of every 100,000 children. And in the 15 seconds it took to read those statistics, another head injury occurred (NCHS 1995c). Most likely it was a young man, for his risk is more than twice that of a woman. Mishaps involving cars, motorcycles, and other vehicles account for half of all head injuries.

The annual tally of head injuries is conservatively estimated to be over 2 million, with 500,000 requiring hospital admission. The survivors' cognitive (perceiving, thinking, remembering), behavioral, and physical disabilities can mean years of hopelessness and anguish, for neither medical science nor rehabilitation offers complete cure. The person is often profoundly changed. Personality alteration, lack of inhibition, poor judgment, and impaired social perception can drive loved ones and their needed support from the patient, even to the point of family breakup. John Harvey (1996:107) observes that "many people suffer brain injuries that transform their lives and the lives of their loved ones into something that is akin to constant sorrow. It is never the same as it was and will never be the same, even though the patient may look normal and be in otherwise fine health. The adjustment process for all people concerned in these situations can be very difficult, and divorce is common."

The effects of fatal farm accidents on the surviving families can be especially devastating. For example, Rosenblatt and Karis (1993–94) studied 21 farm families after a fatal accident for factors involved in bereaved family members becoming more distant from one another after the death. A number of factors were found to influence "family distancing," including blaming and fear of being blamed for the death, possible economic crises following the death, differing ideas about expressions of grief, and preoccupation, depression, and low energy caused by the grieving process itself. Living and working at the scene of the accidental death, replacing the labors of the deceased person, and deciding other work-related matters provided special problems for two-thirds of these families. These problems prolonged grieving and further complicated family matters.

Natural Disasters

Worldwide, deaths due to natural disasters are said to constitute up to 4% of the total deaths in the world each year (Pijawka, Cuthbertson, & Olson, 1987–88).

HIGH-TECH DEATH

A Michigan man who died last summer was the first worker killed by a robot in this country, and his death suggests the need for new approaches to factory safety, a federal safety expert said today.

The 34-year-old victim, working with automated die-casting machinery last July, was pinned between the back of a robot and a steel pole, the National Centers for Disease Control and Prevention reported today. The worker suffered a heart attack, lapsed into a coma and died five days later.

The Atlanta-based federal health agency noted that more than 6,200 robots were in use nationwide.

Source: Adapted from *New York Times*. (1985). Death By Robot Brings Call for Improved Safety, March 22, p. 8.

Disasters, be they natural (such as floods, volcanos, earthquakes, and fires), or technological (such as airplane crashes, chemical spills, and nuclear contamination), can be defined as life-threatening events that affect many people within a relatively brief period of time, bringing sudden and great misfortune. People are injured or killed, others are missing, and homeless survivors are likely to be in shock (DeSpelder & Strickland, 1992).

Those who come to the aid of survivors of a disaster may also become "survivors" in that their work of *postvention*—that is, help given in the aftermath of a disaster—involves an intense emotional encounter with human suffering and pain. Psychologists, working with paramedics, emergency medical team personnel, rescue teams, as well as police and fire units, now engage these workers in *critical incident stress debriefing* sessions in which they are counseled to express their thoughts and feelings following a disaster and, thereby, prevent many of the symptoms of post-traumatic stress disorder (PTSD).

A RECORD OF MASS KILLINGS (IN MILLIONS)	
China: Mao's cultural revolution, 1966–1976	20 million
U.S.S.R.: Stalin's reign of terror (W.W. II)	20 million
Europe: the Holocaust, 1933–1945	11 million
Indonesia: killings of 1965–66	500,000
Cambodia: the Khmer Rouge killing fields, 1975–79	1.6 million
Bosnia: "ethnic cleansing," 1992–94	200,000
Rwanda: Tutsis, 3 months in 1994	1+ million

Source: Newsweek, August 1, 1994, p. 37.

War

Worldwide, wars and other military actions have accounted for at least 110 million deaths in this century alone (Elliot, 1972). Sixty-two million of those deaths occurred in cities under siege, concentration camps, prisoner of war camps, economic blockades, and the aftermath of "scorched earth" tactics. Forty-six million deaths were caused by big guns, aerial bombs, and small arms fire, while another 1–2 million deaths were caused by germ and gas warfare. In April of 1994, for example, it was reported that more than 250,000 Rwandans were shot or hacked to death within a 3-week period while many others died fleeing the bloodshed in a 2-day mass migration numbering 250,000 to 500,000 people (Weiner, 1994).

Human-induced violence, accidents, and natural disasters create situations that typically evoke high levels of stress and may result in post-traumatic stress disorders in survivors. The psychological impact of these events comes from actual physical injury or threat of injury and from the possibility of loss of life. Military personnel in combat, for instance, must deal with the constant fear of capture, mutilation, and death. Physical exhaustion, loss of sleep, constant hyperstimulation, and concern about the killing and maiming going on around them only heightens the stress of war.

Post-Traumatic Stress Disorder

With few exceptions, people exposed to war, plane crashes, automobile accidents, explosions, fires, earthquakes, tornadoes, sexual assaults, or other terrifying

COPING WITH THE BODIES: OKLAHOMA CITY, 1995

It was a little after 9 A.M. on a typical workday in downtown Oklahoma City when an explosion took down the Federal Building and 168 lives with it in America's most devastating terrorist attack. Fire and police personnel, rescue workers, hospital workers, and volunteers rushed to the scene to search for the wounded and the dead. Hours stretched into days and days into weeks as they painstakingly searched mounds of rubble for the bodies of children and adults. How does one cope with such an experience? Beyond the commitment to professionalism and human compassion, what strategies are adopted to deal with these living nightmares? Studies of other disasters have revealed some of the reactions experienced and the coping strategies used by rescue workers.

Before exposure to bodies, workers responding to disasters often report feelings of anticipation of their own reactions to the bodies. The lack of information about the nature of the disaster or their specific task was also reported as a stressor. To cope with these stressors it was found that practice drills and briefing as to the nature of the disaster was very helpful for rescue workers.

During exposure, workers reported extreme sensory stimuli as a stressor. The sight of mangled bodies, the smell of decomposing flesh, and the actual touching of the bodies or body parts can be described as sensory overload. Often workers would wear gloves to reduce the sensation of touch. They would smoke cigars, burn coffee, or place fragrances, such as peppermint oil, inside surgical masks to avoid the smell. They would also purposely avert their gaze from the bodies as much as possible. Another stressor present during exposure to the bodies occurs with the handling of personal effects. This seemed to increase the emotional involvement with the victim and increase stress. Supervisors suggest increasing emotional distance by not thinking of them as bodies but as just part of the job. "Gallows" humor was also used to distance oneself from the victim, as were frequent breaks, adequate sleep, and food.

After exposure, workers reported a need for something to help the transition back to regular life. Postevent debriefing sessions were found to be helpful in reducing stressors and aiding in the transition. Also, support from the fellow workers and the families of the workers was important after an event. Those that could do so found comfort in discussing the situation with their spouses. Some did not wish to burden their spouses with the stress and needed to discuss the incident with fellow workers or professional mental health workers. Many workers reported not feeling the need for professional counseling after a disaster, and some stated they feared they would be ridiculed or fired for seeking professional help.

Source: Adapted from McCarroll et al. (1993), pp. 209–214.

experiences show psychological shock reactions—transient personality decompensation (R. C. Carson & Butcher, 1992). The symptoms may vary greatly, depending on the nature and severity of the terrifying experience, the degree of surprise, and the personality makeup of the individual.

A disaster syndrome appears to characterize the reactions of many victims of such catastrophes. A victim's initial responses following a disaster typically involve three stages: (a) the *shock stage,* in which the victim is stunned, dazed, and apathetic; (b) the *suggestible stage,* in which the victim tends to be passive, suggestible, and willing to take directions from rescue workers or others; and (c) the *recovery stage,* in which the individual may be tense and apprehensive and show generalized anxiety, but gradually regains psychological equilibrium. Victims often show a need to repetitively give an account of the catastrophic event. It is in the third stage that post-traumatic stress disorder may develop (R. C. Carson & Butcher, 1992).

These three stages are well illustrated in the Andrea Doria disaster, in which fifty-two persons died and over 1,600 were rescued (P. Freidman & Linn, 1957, p. 426):

> On July 25, 1956, at 11:05 P.M., the Swedish liner Stockholm smashed into the starboard side of the Italian liner Andrea Doria a few miles off Nantucket Island. . . . During the phase of initial shock the survivors acted as if they had been sedated,. . . as though nature provided a sedation mechanism which went into operation automatically. During the phase of suggestibility the survivors presented themselves for the most part as an amorphous mass of people tending to act passively and compliantly. They displayed psychomotor retardation, flattening of affect, somnolence, and, in some instances, amnesia for data of personal identification. They were nonchalant and easily suggestible. During the stage of recovery, after the initial shock had worn off and the survivors had received aid, they showed . . . an apparently compulsive need to tell the story again and again, with identical detail and emphasis.

In some cases, the clinical picture may be complicated by intense grief and depression. When an individual feels that his or her own personal inadequacy contributed to the loss of loved ones in a disaster, the picture may be further complicated by strong feelings of guilt, and the post-traumatic stress may last for months (R. C. Carson & Butcher, 1992). This pattern is well illustrated in the case of a husband who failed to save his wife in the jet crash at Tenerife in 1977 (see nearby box).

In some instances, the guilt of the survivors seems to center around the belief that they deserved to survive no more or perhaps even less than those who died. Sometimes individuals who undergo terrifying experiences exhibit symptoms of stress that may endure for weeks, months, or even years. In a recent review and comparison of all published disaster research in which estimates of postdisaster psychopathology were included, the average effect was that 17% of individuals showed psychological adjustment problems in the aftermath of the disaster (Ru-

FIRE AND PAIN

"Martin's story is quite tragic. He lost his beloved wife of 37 years and blames himself for her death, because he sat stunned and motionless for some 25 seconds after the [other plane] hit. He saw nothing but fire and smoke in the aisles, but he roused himself and led his wife to a jagged hole above and behind his seat. Martin climbed out onto the wing and reached down and took hold of his wife's hand, but 'an explosion from within literally blew her out of my hands and pushed me back and down onto the wing.' He reached the runway, turned to go back after her, but the plane blew up seconds later. . . .

[Five months later] Martin was depressed and bored, had "wild dreams," a short temper and became easily confused and irritated. 'What I saw there will terrify me forever,' he says. He told [the psychologist who interviewed him] that he avoided television and movies, because he couldn't know when a frightening scene would appear."

Source: Perlberg, M. (1979, April). Trauma at Tenerife: The psychic aftershocks of a jet disaster, *Human Behavior*, 49–50.

bonis & Bickman, 1991). Shore, Vollmer, and Tatum (1989) studied the prevalence rates of post-traumatic stress disorder in two northeastern communities and found a *lifetime prevalence* rate of post-traumatic stress reaction, according to DSM-IV diagnostic criteria, to be about 3% for both men and women.

Recurrent nightmares and the compelling need to tell the same story about the disaster again and again appear to be mechanisms for reducing anxiety and desensitizing the self to the traumatic experience. Tension, apprehensiveness, and hypersensitivity appear to be residual effects of the shock reaction and to reflect the person's realization that the world can become overwhelmingly dangerous and threatening (Harvey, 1996). *Survivor's guilt*—that is, feelings of guilt about having failed to protect loved ones who perished—may be quite intense, especially in situations where some responsibility can be directly assigned (Egendorf, 1986; Okura, 1975).

Victims may also experience an "anniversary syndrome"—intense symptoms experienced on the anniversary of the disaster, including death anxiety, exaggerated reactions to ordinary life events, nightmares, death guilt, psychological numbing, flashbacks, impaired social relationships, and a search for meaning (Sarason and Sarason, 1989:124). These types of symptoms have been widely observed in veterans returning from combat. In one study, 43% of a sample of Vietnam veterans experienced the disorder (Frye & Stockton, 1982). That study and others indicated that soldiers who experienced more intense combat or saw their friends killed in action were more likely to suffer from post-traumatic stress disorder (Breslau & Davis, 1987).

Psychologist Edwin Parson (1986), based on his work with Vietnam veterans in Veteran Administration hospitals, proposes that a pervasive readjustment problem that cuts across all diagnostic categories with Vietnam veterans can be referred to as *post-traumatic death syndrome.* The syndrome and its components were analyzed in their relationship to major symptoms of post-traumatic stress disorder and found to exist in veterans with and without PTSD. The "death" syndrome is a complex configuration of chronic fears, chronic grief states, pronounced death anxiety, and a profound attraction to death themes, with a paradoxical fear of death and dying in reference to self and others. According to Parsons, those individuals with post-traumatic death syndrome also exhibit symptoms and conditions that contribute to the veteran's "functional disability" in affirming and fully participating in life.

AIDS

Acquired immune-deficiency syndrome (AIDS) is a communicable disease caused by the *human immunodeficiency virus (HIV)* and spread by the exchange of bodily fluids, which can occur during sex, the sharing of needles, blood transfusions, or across the placenta during pregnancy. The virus attacks the immune system's lymphocyte cells directly, compromising the immune system of those who contract it, making them susceptible to infections they could easily have fought off otherwise. The virus also attacks the central nervous system indirectly by causing the release of proteins that, in large amounts, are toxic to neurons, causing inflammation and ultimately death to the neurons. Up to 20% of people diagnosed with AIDS suffer memory loss, confusion, uncontrollably jerky movements, and staggering gait in the later stages of the disease. Children

**YOUNG AMERICANS
INFECTED WITH AIDS**

- One of every ninety-two young American men
- One of every thirty-three young African American men
- One of every sixty Hispanic American men
- One in every 1,667 European American women
- One in every ninety-eight African American women
- One in every 222 Hispanic American women

Source: CDC (1996)

diagnosed with AIDS suffer severe learning defects as their disease develops (Lau & Allan, 1994).

Anyone can contract AIDS, and it is spreading into the U.S. heterosexual community in greater numbers, so that AIDS now ranks eighth among the leading causes of death in the United States. According to the Centers for Disease Control and Prevention (1996), AIDS is now the leading cause of death among Americans between the ages of 25 and 44 years. Deaths among this group increased from 37,000 in 1993 to 42,000 in 1994 and caused one of every three deaths of African American men and one of every five deaths of African American women (Ring, 1996). Almost half of the HIV cases tracked by the CDC have been reported since 1993, with the fastest increase in cases among adolescents, young adults, injection drug users, women and non-whites (Ring, 1996). The National Cancer Institute estimates that ". . . 100,000 to 400,000 people either do not know they are infected or have not had the HIV status reported—making for a very disturbing future." (Ring, 1996:1)

The rise in AIDS-related deaths has effectively stalled the nation's century-long increase in life expectancy, wiping out the longevity benefits from a continuing decline in infant mortality and the conquering of infectious diseases with antibiotics. After reaching a peak of 75.8 years in 1992, life expectancy at birth fell slightly to 75.5 years in 1993 and did not budge from there in 1994, preliminary data from the National Center for Health Statistics (1995a) show.

Worldwide, nearly 22 million people have been infected with HIV, and 6,842,000 have AIDS itself, including 1,566,000 children and 2,451,000 women. The Centers for Disease Control and Prevention (1996) reports that, each day, approximately 6,000 people around the world are infected with HIV. In sub-Saharan Africa, where 85% of all AIDS cases have occurred, at least 40% of the epidemic's victims are women and the pandemic is now sweeping through Asia so fast that no one can count its victims. Significant new levels of HIV infection have been detected in Vietnam, Malaysia, Laos, Cambodia, Burma, and China's Yunnan province, according to the World Health Organization (WHO, 1996). By the most conservative estimates, WHO epedemiologists predict that 40 million people—10 million in Asia alone—will be infected with HIV by the year 2000.

AIDS and Psychological Stress

AIDS first appeared in the United States in the homosexual community and then in the intravenous drug community, making them both high behavioral risk groups. Bisexual men and hemophiliacs are also considered high risk. All of these groups may be more psychologically stressed because of societal pressures, or may be placed under great stress and become depressed after it is discovered that they are infected with the AIDS virus (Marrone, 1990:94). Two studies in the *Journal of the American Medical Association* (1994) offer conflicting reports on whether psychological depression does affect the functioning of the immune system in this population. One study by researchers at the University of California at San Francisco found that the rate of decline in certain helper T-cells of the immune system among fifty men with HIV who were classified as depressed on a self-administered questionnaire was 38% greater than the decline in 227 HIV-infected men who were not depressed. But a multicenter study led by researchers at Johns Hopkins University found no significant difference in T-cell decline among 365 depressed men with AIDS compared with 1,353 who weren't depressed.

There are, as of this writing, no cures for AIDS, although promising treatments that can slow the virus growth are both in use and under further development. Single-drug antiviral treatments, such as AZT, nevirapine, and L-524, are showing progress in retarding the multiplication of the virus. In the case of AZT, recent research has found it useful in preventing transmission from mother to child. Combination-drug treatments have been approved for use, and two new drugs will add up to fifty-six possible three-drug combinations that could be tested and used for treatment. It is hoped that three-drug combinations will work better than two-drug combinations, which failed to combat the constantly mutating HIV. Other forms of intervention include specific opportunistic-infection treatments, gene therapy, and therapeutic vaccines, such as the Jonas Salk Immunogen. But behavioral prevention is the main tool we have against this global epidemic. And since prevention involves avoiding high-risk behaviors, psychological techniques for modifying behaviors, attitudes, opinions, and beliefs have a major role to play in a variety of situations.

Communicable Diseases and a New Epidemiologic Transition

There are newer statistical indicators that suggest that a second epidemiologic transition may be developing (Garrett, 1994). In fact, in early 1996 the American Medical Association reported that **infectious disease has become the third-leading cause of death in the United States,** exceeded in number only by cancer and heart disease. In addition to AIDS, infectious disease threats include tuberculosis, *E. coli,* drug-resistant pneumonia, hepatitis, hantavirus, and ebola.

In the United States the death rate from infectious diseases that were once thought to be virtually conquered rose by 58% from 1980 to 1992. Infectious disease mortality increased 25% among those age 65 years and older and 630% among 25–44-year-olds (Pinner et al., 1996). Respiratory tract infections, particularly dangerous for older people, were responsible for nearly half the deaths from infectious diseases in 1992. Medical experts have concluded that global warming, drug resistance, and evolution itself are combining to create new health threats based on the spread of communicable diseases. In a collaborative effort involving twenty-one countries, thirty-six scientific and medical journals are producing special reports on microbial health threats to be published in the coming years.

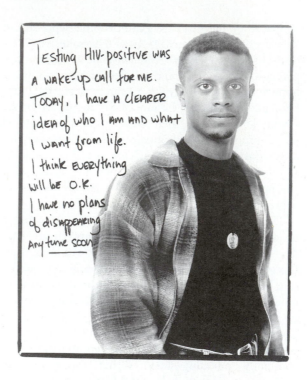

Testing HIV-positive was a wake-up call for me. Today, I have a clearer idea of who I am and what I want from life. I think everything will be O.K. I have no plans of disappearing anytime soon.

Be Here for The Cure. Get Early Treatment for HIV.
Call 1 800-367-2437

Photograph by Annie Liebovitz/San Francisco AIDS Foundation

Additional research on communicable *nosocomial infections* (hospital-acquired illnesses caused by bacteria, viruses, protozoans, and fungi) indicates that they affect nearly one of every twenty hospital patients in the United States each year (roughly 2 million people) and directly caused 19,000 deaths and indirectly contributed to 58,000 deaths, according to the U.S. Centers for Disease Control and Prevention (1995a). A number of factors are to blame, including resistance to antimicrobial drugs and medical advances that require more invasive procedures. The most worrisome trend is the rise in disease-causing microbes that are unfazed by current drugs, such as antibiotics, and are actually strengthened by the widespread use of antibiotics. By destroying or inhibiting the growth of weaker microbes, these medications allow drug-resistant germs to multiply and flourish.

In 1995, the National Center for Health Statistics (1995a) reported that emerging new diseases, such as AIDS, as well as re-emerging familiar ones—including malaria, pneumonia, and tuberculosis—pose public health threats that require more vigorous, comprehensive, and systematic efforts to monitor and combat them. In the meantime, multidrug-resistant tuberculosis has broken out

"It's a race between the human species and microbial predators. We must use our social intelligence, our wits, to stay a step ahead of the genetic evolution of microbes."

–Joshua Lederberg, Rockefeller University, 1996

in several U.S. cities; a recent cholera epidemic ravaged Peru and is spreading northward; malaria is on a rampage throughout parts of Africa, Asia, and South America; and AIDS is virtually everywhere.

A variety of factors contribute to the emergence of communicable disease. In moving both people and goods from one place to another, people may unknowingly transport a disease vector. Land development may situate people close to animals living in the wild, such as deer, that serve as hosts to the ticks that carry Lyme disease, and deer mice that spread the hantavirus. And global warming could result in a wider range for disease vectors such as mosquitoes, rats, and mice (Azevedo, 1996).

At the same time, the World Health Organization (1996) estimates that AIDS, a communicable disease, will cut 30 years off the life of the average resident of Thailand by the year 2010 and that in thirteen other developing nations, the death rates will be two and one-half times higher than they would have been without AIDS. In Zambia, for instance, the average life expectancy would be 66 years in 2010. Because of the AIDS epidemic, it is expected to be just 33 years. WHO estimates that AIDS may cost 121 million lives by the year 2020.

The worldwide plague of AIDS and, potentially, other fluid-borne and airborne viral and microbial diseases might lead us to speculate that we are entering a new global epidemiologic transition where communicable diseases once again determine how and when many of us will die.

Chapter Summary

Because of the historical declines in infant mortality and childhood infectious diseases, dying in the United States is now more characteristic of the very old than of the young or middle-aged. This dramatic historical shift in the distribution of American deaths, from dying young to dying old, is termed an epidemiologic transition. In the past 20 years, the older population in America has grown twice as quickly as all other age groups.

With the epidemiologic transition from dying young to dying old, infectious diseases have given way to chronic conditions, such as heart disease and cancer, as major killers. Of the more than 2 million people who die in the United States in any given year, the most common cause of death is heart disease, followed in frequency by cancer, stroke, and lung disease. Based on years of potential life lost in the United States today, cancer turns out to be the number-one killer, followed by heart disease, accidents, suicide, birth defects, murder, and AIDS.

Suicide and homicide result in more premature loss of life for Americans each year than anything but accidents, AIDS, cancer, and heart disease. Accidents, especially automobile accidents, are the fourth-most common cause of death among Americans and the leading cause of death among persons age thirty-four and younger. Worldwide, deaths due to natural disasters are said to constitute up to 4% of the total deaths in the world each year. Wars and other military actions have accounted for at least 110 million deaths in this century alone. A traumatic incident—whether an accident, a natural disaster, or the result of war, combat, or terrorism—can exert a powerful influence on the survivors in the form of post-traumatic stress disorders.

AIDS is spreading into the U.S. heterosexual community in greater numbers, so that AIDS now ranks eighth among the leading causes of death in the United States. The Centers for Disease Control and Prevention reports that, each day, approximately 6,000 people around the world are infected with HIV. By the most conservative estimates, World Health Organization epedemiologists predict that 40 million people—10 million in Asia alone—will be infected with HIV by the year 2000.

There are newer statistical indicators that suggest that a second epidemiologic transition may be developing. The worldwide plague of AIDS and, potentially, other fluid-borne and airborne viral and microbial diseases might lead us to speculate that we are entering a new global epidemiologic transition where communicable diseases once again determine how and when many of us will die.

FURTHER READINGS

Friedman, M., & Rosenman, R. H. (1974). *Type A Behavior and Your Heart*. Knopf, New York.

Glaser, B. G., & Strauss, A. (1966). *Awareness of Dying*. Aldine, Chicago.

Garrett, Laurie. (1994). *The Coming Plague*. Farrar, Straus & Giroux, New York.

Marrone, R. (1990). *Body of Knowledge: An Introduction to Body/Mind Psychology*. State University of New York Press, Albany, NY.

Nuland, Sherwin. B. (1993). *How We Die,* Knopf, New York.

Shilts, R. (1987). *And the Band Played On: Politics, People, and the AIDS Epidemic*. St. Martins Press, New York.

Solzhenitsyn, A. (1969). *Cancer Ward*. Bantam, New York.

Trumbo, D. (1972). *Johnny Got His Gun*. Bantam, New York.

THREE

Dying and the Near-Death Experience

Human beings have seldom found death easy. Since the beginning of recorded history, the literature of eastern and western civilizations reveals just how difficult it has been for us to accept death and dying. Philosophies and religions have always provided some sense of meaning to our living and dying. And yet, for most, coming eye-to-eye with the final moments of life remains life's most terrifying and mysterious experience. We spend our lifetimes growing, changing, ordering, structuring, and becoming who we are and who we are challenged to be. And then, in what seems a cruel twist of fate, we come face-to-face with the process of dying.

Our dying might take less than a minute, or be drawn out for days, months or years. In sudden death, there is barely enough time to react with surprise and shock at the event of our death before our organs collapse and our brain rhythms become erratic and then, flat-line. In extended dying, as our cells and organs draw to a slower close, we have time to float from one phase of dying to another and back again, until final termination arrives. And in between, when death involves weeks and months, we float along our own dying trajectory, left to confront and surrender to the inevitability of death while keeping the flames of hope alive (Kubler-Ross, 1969).

Dying: Stages, Phases, and Tasks

One of the most important and popular psychological studies of the dying process was conducted by psychiatrist Elisabeth Kubler-Ross (1969). Much of her work, inspired by a group of theological students seeking her advice on how to research the question of dying, involved in-depth interviews with dying patients. Kubler-Ross found that the only way to go about this exploration was to talk with dying people and to ask them to be our teachers.

Talking to a dying person seemed a relatively straightforward research technique and yet, as Kubler-Ross quickly discovered, it was quite difficult to accomplish—not because dying patients resisted talking with her, but because her colleagues hindered access to the them. When she approached her fellow physicians and asked them to tell her which of their patients were terminally ill, she found, to her amazement, that there wasn't "one dying patient in the whole 600-bed hospital" in which she worked (1969: 23). Probing further, she discovered that physicians refused to allow her access to dying patients because, in their estimation, the patient was "too weak," "too sick," or "too tired" or "the patient didn't feel like talking." When she did locate her first dying patient, however, she found that he was quite willing and able to talk to her about his experiences (Pollio, 1982). It became evident to Kubler-Ross in that moment that talking about death was off-limits only for the physicians with whom she worked, not for the dying patients. She writes

> With few exceptions, the patients were surprised, amazed, and grateful. Some were plain curious and others expressed their disbelief that a young, healthy doctor would sit with a dying old woman and really care to know what it is like. In the majority of cases the initial outcome was similar to opening floodgates. It was hard to stop them once the conversation was initiated and the patients responded with great relief to sharing some of their last concerns, expressing their feelings without fear of repercussions (Kubler-Ross, 1969:157–158).

KUBLER-ROSS' STAGE MODEL

Based on her interviews with more than 400 dying persons over a ten-year period, Kubler-Ross published her popular and ground-breaking book, *On Death and Dying* (1969). What she concluded about dying is relevant not only for the dying person, but also for family and healthcare providers who tend to the terminally ill and dying. Her model presented the idea that the dying process, and the experience of profound loss, in general, proceeded as a series of stages through which we pass. These stages of dying include: shock/denial, anger, bargaining, depression, and acceptance.

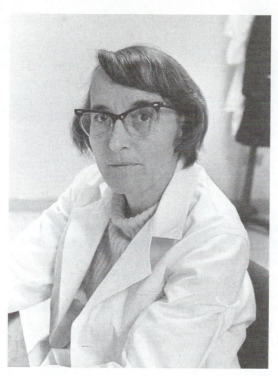

Elisabeth Kubler-Ross, one of the founders of modern thanatology, states that studying death and tending to the dying makes her appreciate each day of her life. © *AP/Wide World Photos*

Shock/Denial

Informed of a terminal illness or of impending death, our first reaction is typically numbness, shock and withdrawal. Our pupils dilate, our breath catches high in the chest, and our muscles tense in fear, freezing us to the spot. Our shock reaction shortly merges with cognitive denial. We are likely to think, "It couldn't be true, it couldn't be me, not me." We might insist that an error has been made and demand a second diagnosis. Kubler-Ross contends that the reactions of shock and denial are necessary in order to give us time to come to terms with the reality of the event of our dying.

This shock/denial stage of the process may last from a few seconds to a few months, but as Kubler-Ross found, it is usually short-lived. In fact, she discovered that fewer than 1% of the more than 400 terminally ill people whom she interviewed persisted in denying their illness until they died. The denial stage typically ended when the individual came to recognize and accept that the event of dying was true and imminent.

Anger

Following recognition of the reality of the situation, we are likely to experience anger, which we often express as envy and resentment of those whose lives will continue after we are gone, and whose plans and dreams may yet be fulfilled. In this stage, according to Kubler-Ross, dying individuals express anger to almost everyone they encounter because they often believe they are losing their life unjustly. The question typically arises: "Why? Why me? Why not somebody else? Why?" The anger, according to Pollio (1982:416) ". . . often takes the form of complaining about things, "My sheets are dirty and wrinkled; don't you care about me?" Or it may take the form of constantly asking for things that cannot be given and then complaining about not getting them. What we really want to scream at this stage can be phrased as "Hey, I'm still alive, don't you forget that. You can hear my voice, you can see me, I still have rights, I'm not dead yet."

Kubler-Ross observed that the expression of anger tended to bring fears, frustrations, sadness, hatred, and a variety of other emotional states to expression as well. For this reason, the patience and understanding of other people is particularly important at this stage of dying because anger is an important emotional expression for the dying person to complete. Otherwise, an individual will die with repressed anger, fears, sorrows, and feelings of guilt concerning the way they have lived their lives and dealt with others.

Physicians, nurses, and loved ones have a particularly difficult time with the dying person during the anger stage, for they tend to feel that the person is screaming at and criticizing them when in fact he or she is screaming at no one in particular and everyone in general. The dying person is easier to deal with when seen as a unique person engaged in the process of grieving the imminent loss of life rather than as a threatening or defective medical product (i.e. a "patient"). Although the patient is angry and difficult to deal with, being angry does not make the patient any less vulnerable or any less afraid (Pollio, 1982).

Bargaining

As our anger diminishes, we will try to bargain our way out of dying by exchanging something, anything, for a longer life. It is as if the dying person "learning that s/he cannot get what s/he wants by demanding it (in anger), now turns to asking nicely and tries to strike a bargain" (Kimmel, 1974:424). We may bargain with God, promising to give our lives to God, or do good works for the benefit of humankind in exchange for a bit more time to live. We might offer to donate our organs to others so that they might live, if only we too can have a little more time to live. Most dying persons bargain for a specific amount of time: a day, a month, a year, until a child graduates from college or a spouse's next birthday. If we somehow live out the bargained amount of time, we most likely will rebargain for more time. These bargaining sessions with doctors, family members, clergy, Mother Nature, or God are natural and healthy attempts to cope with the reality and realization of our approaching death (Kubler-Ross, 1969).

Depression

As bargaining fails and time begins to run out, the dying individual often surrenders to acute depression, regretting past failures and mistakes that can no longer be corrected, and grieving over lost time than can never be recaptured. Struggling to accommodate the event of our dying and all its ramifications, we eventually come to the profound recognition that our condition is to terminate in death, and there is nothing we or anyone else can do about it.

Kubler-Ross observed two different types of dying-related depression in her patients: one that has do with what we have already lost (reactive); and one that has to do with what we are about to lose (preparatory). A *reactive depression* may occur, for example, in an individual who has a loss of physical function due to surgery or whose freedom has been limited by illness or chronic pain. A preparatory depression may occur when a dying individual thinks about forth-coming losses, such as inability to walk or talk, or an inability to care for loved ones or oneself. Kubler-Ross (1969:87) observes that ". . . The patient is in the process of losing everything and everybody he loves. If he is allowed to express his sorrow he will find a final acceptance much easier, and will be grateful to those who can sit with him during this stage of depression without constantly telling him not to be sad."

Acceptance

Tired and weak, we at last enter a state of "quiet expectation," submitting to our fate. Many dying persons arrive at the last stage of acceptance when they are no longer angry or depressed about dying. Their feelings have been expressed to those around them and their questions have been answered. When the final stage of acceptance is reached, the person emerges from depression and withdrawal and once again asks to be with his or her family, perhaps for the last time. One particularly predictable phenomenon at this stage is the tendency of the dying person to want to be with only one other special person as he or she approaches the final stage of the process (Kubler-Ross: 1969).

Typically, dying individuals in this stage are drowsy, withdrawn, drugged, and asleep much of the time. Talking seems superfluous in this twilight state of consciousness, and all they want is to be with the one special person who will be there with them, to sit with them, perhaps to read to them, and maybe to hold them. Ebbing in capacity, withdrawing from the world, they may not engage in much or any conversation. And yet, according to Kubler-Ross, it is most important that they be visited, engaged and embraced because it tells them that others care; that they matter in the lives of others; and that dying and death need not be lonely, frightening experiences.

Kubler-Ross maintains that acceptance is not the same as resignation. Resignation, Kubler-Ross points out, is more like defeat or disappointment. Acceptance, on the other hand, is perhaps best captured by the attitude that "it's my time now, and it's all right." The acceptance stage is not a happy time or a depressing time but is, rather, a period essentially devoid of feeling. "The final struggle for survival is over," and the dying person seems to be taking "a final rest before the long journey," as one of Kubler-Ross's patients put it. At this final stage in the dying process, the person feels a profound sense of closure—that unfinished business has been concluded in a mindful and responsible way, and the final chapter of life is nearing completion. Kubler-Ross maintains that coming to an acceptance of our own death is an active choice we must make. In so doing, we affirm the limitations of being human for the last time and, by doing so, we reaffirm our connectedness to all living/dying beings in times past and in times yet to be.

Kubler-Ross's groundbreaking work brought death and dying out of the closet, making healthcare providers and society in general more aware that death is a part of life and a legitimate part of clinical care—and that with sensitivity and understanding it can be faced openly and honestly (Gentile and Fello, 1990:97). According to thanatologist Charles Corr (1993), Kubler-Ross taught three main lessons: that the dying are still alive and have unfinished needs which they want to bring to closure; that to become effective caregivers, we must listen actively to those who are coping with dying and learn to view the world through their eyes; and that in learning from those who are facing the final moments of life we learn more about ourselves, our values, and our own search for meaning.

CRITICISMS OF THE STAGE MODEL

Kubler-Ross' theory of the stages of dying has not gone without criticism over the years. These criticisms were based, for the most part, on a lack of empirical support in the research literature, as well as the restrictive nature of the stage theory itself (Shibles, 1974; Schulz and Aderman, 1974; Shneidman, 1973; Weisman, 1974). Robert Kastenbaum (1977), for one, argued that there is no evidence that every person moves through all five stages. Weisman (1974) also found limited support for the stage theory, arguing that there is an ongoing interaction among emotional expressions throughout the dying process. Dying persons have a continual ebb and flow of emotions which are not as linear and entirely predictable as the stage model would assume.

Another criticism of Kubler-Ross' stage theory concerned the way healthcare professionals have applied the model. They may become annoyed with dying people who do not move neatly through the expected stages. As Rhodes and Vedder (1983:75) point out, "Kubler-Ross did not intend these stages of dying to be an inevitable or normative process, as we can see by case studies and examples in her book, where all the stages were not present in each dying person." In contrast, according to Heller (1996), ". . . individuals flip-flopped from stage to stage in defiance of the proposed orderly progression." And yet, the popularity and simplicity of the stage model sometimes results in subtle and not-so-subtle pressures to be exerted on dying patients by physicians, nurses, and family members to conform to the model—or be labeled "in denial."

PATTISON'S PHASE MODEL

E. Mansell Pattison (1977), a pioneer in thanatological theory and research, offers a phase model of the dying process. The model portrays the dying person as displaying a variety of emotional expressions in the dying process that increase or decrease in intensity just as the person has reacted to challenges, crises, and conflicts throughout life. He recommends that caregiving efforts be directed at locating the stresses and crises that arise at a particular phase in the person's dying trajectory; tracking and empathizing with the emotional reactions produced by the moment-to-moment experience of dying; and learning to respond to the dying person's particular needs, especially the need to die with dignity and grace.

In his book *The Experience of Dying* (1977), Pattison proposes a three phase model as a strategy to gain an understanding of the dying process. These phases of the dying process include an acute phase, a chronic living/dying phase, and a terminal phase. He emphasizes that phases are only meant to be a helpful way of dividing up the living/dying experience so as to assist clinical practice and caregiving by loved ones. They are not meant to be viewed as an inevitable and immutable linear process.

The Acute Phase

During the acute phase, which corresponds to Kubler-Ross's denial, anger, and bargaining stages, the individual experiences an ever-rising anxiety created by the critical awareness of impending death. At times, the sense of crisis increases until a point is reached where the individual becomes frozen in fear and cannot function. At this juncture, the dying person will either have to use psychological defense mechanisms, such as cognitive denial and emotional repression, to reduce the anxiety and stress of the situation, or psychologically disintegrate. Pattison and others (Corr, 1992; Harvey, 1995) stress that loved ones should assist the dying person in reducing the numbing anxiety generated during this phase by emphasizing reality issues connected with dying and providing emotional support throughout the process. Then, in time, the dying individual will probably show signs of the emotional turmoil typical of the chronic living/dying phase of the dying process.

The Chronic Living/Dying Phase

Pattison portrays the dying person in this second phase as confronting a number of fears surrounding dying and death while continually questioning the unknown: "What will happen to my body, myself, my family and friends while I am dying and after I am dead?" The fears to be confronted include those that fall into typical areas of concern for the dying (Simpson, 1979; Lonetto and Templer, 1986; Niemeyer, et al., 1986):

- fears related to the dying process itself (for example, fear of pain and suffering, or of dependence on others)
- fears related to death itself and its meaning (for example, fear of nonbeing, or fear of loss of identity)
- and fears related to the consequences of death, such as fear of the unknown and fear of judgment or punishment in the afterlife.

If fears surrounding death and dying are resolved, the dying person is more likely to begin to accept death gracefully during this phase. These fears include the fear of (1) abandonment, (2) loss of self-control, (3) suffering and pain, (4) loss of personal identity, (5) the unknown, and (6) regression into self.

1. Fear of Abandonment.   About 80% of American deaths now occur in isolated hospital rooms and convalescent homes, where the individual has little human contact. The fear of facing the moment of dying without a loved one nearby, without a hand to hold and without an advocate to deal with doctors and nurses and other health professionals, can sometimes overwhelm the dying person. We might include within the fear of abandonment *fear of loneliness, fear of social death,* and *fear of loss of family and friends.*

2. Fear of Loss of Self Control.   According to Pattison, dying persons often feel a sense of dependency on others and a fear of weakness about controlling their own lives. Encouraging them to keep some sense of power and authority over their day-to-day lives and some ongoing role in family matters can often counter these mounting fears. *Fear of loss of body function* may also play a role in the fear of loss of control. With increased weakening, loss of weight or bodily disfigurement, the dying person may fear rejection by loved ones (Rhodes and Vedder, 1983). Pattison states (1977:52) that external disfigurement may provoke a sense of being ugly and unacceptable. The dying person may despise his or her distorted body image ". . . and may try to hide his or her unlovely self from loved ones, for fear that the family will also despise the ugly body, reject him or her and leave him or her alone." Physical touch by loved ones and medical personnel may act to counter this fear of bodily disfigurement—but the touch *must* be initiated by the dying person whenever possible. Even an attempt to hold the hand of a dying person should be accomplished by sliding the hand under his or her hand so that the person may take the initiative to stroke or hold the hand that is offered (McGee, 1995).

3. Fear of Suffering and Pain.   Medication may provide relief from pain and reduce discomfort for some dying patients, but a recent study suggests that 50% of dying patients in American hospitals spend their final days in what they describe as moderate to severe pain (Knauss and Lynn, 1995). Pattison suggests that advances in pain management techniques can greatly impact this growing fear.

In addition, he contends that the reduction of pain and suffering may also depend on helping the dying person to reframe his or her attitudes to view the pain as part of the disease process and not as a punishment or the result of being abandoned by loved ones. *Fear of sorrow,* like preparatory depression, is a form of psychological pain which emerges when a person thinks about what is to be lost upon dying, including the care and security of loved ones. The dying person is sometimes overwhelmed with catastrophic fantasies regarding these losses and changes.

4. Fear of Loss of Personal Identity.   The fear of loss of loved ones, body functions, consciousness, and control over life threatens the maintenance of a sense of self. Pattison believes that self-esteem, dignity, and integrity of the self are maintained in the process of dying when the dying person is encouraged to keep in touch with loved ones and maintain contact with work and community whenever possible. The maintenance of these contacts insures that the dying person will continue to perceive himself or herself as the same person he or she has always been, inhabiting the same familiar world.

5. Fear of the Unknown.   With this fear, the dying person is often swept into repetitious questions about the unknown—from questions of an afterlife to questions of what will happen to his or her family. The crisis of facing terminal illness appears to blur distinctions between what is known and what is not; between what can be known and what cannot. The resultant emotional confusion and spiritual crisis can sometimes plunge the dying person into a deepening depression. Dugan (1987:23), for example, speculates that dying patients contemplating suicide may be using their suicidal ideas as ". . . a form of symbolic communication, conveying emotional and spiritual pain and attempting to make sense of inner experiences."

6. Fear of Regression into Self.   Pattison describes the fear produced as the dying person progresses to the terminal phase in which he or she faces the experience of being pulled away from the external world ". . . into a primordial sense of being where there is no awareness of time or space or boundaries between self and others. (Pattison, 1977:55). As he or she enters the terminal phase of living/dying, "the fear of regression begins to loom. With the diminution of physical capacity and the clouding of consciousness, the sense of regression may be frightening . . . and the dying person may fight against the regression. This may produce the so-called death agonies, the struggle against regression of the self."

Interestingly, in a study by Davidson (1979:169) in which terminally ill patients were asked to rank their major fears, the overwhelming majority ranked *fear of abandonment* as their major concern, with *fear of loss of control* and *intractable pain* as their next greatest problems. *Fear of death,* itself, ranked ninth on the list. Davidson found that, by resolving these fears, the dying person gains increased feelings of self-esteem, personal dignity, and psychological integrity and will face dying with increased hope and courage.

Terminal Phase

During the third and final phase of the dying process, the person still wants to live but now accepts the fact that death is not going to go away. One sign of entrance into the final phase of dying involves a cognitive shift from expectational hope to desirable hope. A person will now feel it is desirable not to want to die but not expectable as a hope (Stotland, 1969). Functioning at a low energy level, this shift may reflect a reaction to bodily signals that indicate energies must be conserved.

In the terminal phase, the dying person begins the process of withdrawing from the outside world and immersing awareness in the internal self. As dying persons proceed through this final phase, they may fight against regression into self. Loved ones and caregivers can help by facilitating their turning away from this world's reality and accepting surrender to the internal self so that regression and withdrawal will occur (Rhodes & Vedder, 1983:78).

An important part of Pattison's outline of the terminal phase of dying is his presentation of various definitions of death, including physiological, biological, psychological, and social death. *Social death,* for example, occurs when the dying person is forced to withdraw from the social world by physical separation, isolation from communication with family and loved ones, and depersonalization by medical personnel. This may happen long before the patient enters the terminal phase of the dying process. Illustrations abound where families virtually abandon an aged parent to die in a nursing home.

Scottish thanatologists Helen Sweeting and Mary Gilhooly (1991–92) note that three groups of patients often experience social death: those in the final stages of terminal illness, the frail elderly, and those suffering from loss of their essential personhood because of coma, Alzheimer's disease, or senile dementia.

Social death occurs when the dying person is forced to withdraw from the social world by physical separation, isolation from meaningful communication with family members and depersonalization by medical personnel. © *Lonny Shavelson/Impact Visuals*

They maintain that the dehumanization and depersonalization connected with long periods of institutionalization provide the opportunity for social death by the medical establishment's practice of transforming dying human beings into medical "cases."

Psychological death, according to Pattison, typically appears when a person's physiological functions have greatly deteriorated, social withdrawal is all but complete, and the individual regresses deep into the self by way of various states of consciousness, including sleep, dreaming, and coma. *Biological death* occurs when there is no longer any consciousness or purposeful activity, as seen in various vegetative states, such as irreversible coma. Finally, *physiological death* represents the condition where vital organs no longer operate and the person is declared "dead."

CARING INSIGHTS

A Dying Person's Bill of Rights

I have the right to be treated as a living human being until I die.

I have the right to maintain a sense of hopefulness, however changing its focus may be.

I have the right to be cared for by those who can maintain a sense of hopefulness, however changing this might be.

I have the right to express my feelings and emotions about my approaching death in my own way.

I have the right to participate in decisions concerning my care.

I have the right to expect continuing medical and nursing attention even though "cure" goals must be changed to "comfort" goals.

I have the right not to die alone, to be free from pain.

I have the right to have my questions answered honestly, not to be deceived.

I have the right to have help from and for my family in accepting my death and the right to die in peace and dignity.

I have the right to retain my individuality and not be judged for my decisions which may be contrary to the beliefs of others.

I have the right to expect that the sanctity of the human body will be respected after my death.

I have the right to be cared for by caring, sensitive, and knowledgeable people who will attempt to understand my needs and will be able to gain some satisfaction in helping me face my death.

Source: Karen C. Sorenson and Joan Luckmann. (1979). *Medical-Surgical Nursing: A Psychophysiologic Approach* (3rd ed.). W.B. Saunders, New York, as quoted in Aiken, 1994, p. 302.

The beginning of the terminal phase can be viewed by the dying person as the start of giving up and withdrawing from the social and psychological worlds they once inhabited. Both psychological and social death are sometimes hastened when the dying person is forced to exist outside of the social circle of friends, family, and medical personnel and is isolated from psychologically meaningful input. This may lead to psychological death, as the dying individual psychologically withdraws from the world, which is followed in turn by biological and, finally, physiological death.

TASK MODELS

Our culture does not prepare us to cope with our own dying or the dying of others. The dying have needs above and beyond the physical treatment of their medical illness, needs requiring emotional, social, psychological, and spiritual support. But how many doctors recognize a patient's emotions? How many of us, in caring for a dying friend, child, or spouse, can create and maintain an environment filled with compassion and balance? What socialization do we receive for managing this most terrifying, and most challenging, of experiences? How many of us are willing to overcome our cognitive denial, emotional repression, and behavioral passivity to engage the final task of living our dying?

"You cannot prevent the birds of sorrow from flying over your head, but you can prevent them from building nests in your hair."

– Old Chinese proverb

Living Our Dying

When one listens to a dying person, or reads the accounts of terminally ill people, it is clear that it is not the fear of death itself that is the central concern. Rather, it is the fear of abandonment, the fear of loss of personal control, and the fear of loss of meaning (Davidson, 1979). Perhaps we cannot imagine what it will be like to not exist, but we can easily imagine what it might be like to no longer cope, to feel vulnerable and helpless, to be dependent on others to meet our everyday physical needs, and no longer to feel like we are in charge of our own lives. We know what happens when we are admitted to hospitals. We are literally stripped of almost everything familiar—clothing and routine, personal objects—and told when to eat and sleep. Even if we are treated in a courteous manner, there is still an undeniable sense of dependence and vulnerability.

For the patient hospitalized for a short stay, and a cure, the feeling of loss of control may be fleeting and masked by the visits of family and friends—and by the good news of a successful treatment. The terminal patient, however, is in a much more vulnerable and tenuous position and much more likely to be overwhelmed with the loss of integrity and control (Larson, 1993). Because we are essentially order-seeking creatures, the reality of dying presents a powerful and chaotic shake-up in our sense of self and a powerful challenge to participate responsibly in our own dying.

To participate truly in our own dying, we must not only overcome our cognitive denial and the tendency to repress our feelings of anger, fear, and sadness, but we must surmount our behavioral passivity as well. To do so, we must take responsibility, acknowledge our ability to respond to the degree possible, and act to satisfy the needs that arise as we cope with our dying. Humanistic psychologists believe that satisfying many of our needs involves conscious choices, and that beyond the elemental needs for food and comfort, human beings strive for loftier goals, such as fulfilling our potential, discovering a sense of personal and spiritual meaning, and dying with dignity, wholeness, and grace.

Needs of the Dying/Tasks of the Living

Psychologist Abraham Maslow (1943, 1971, 1973) initiated a view of human beings as active, responsible, and creative decision makers. He viewed human motivation as consisting of needs ranging from those related to basic survival, such as needs for food, water, and freedom from pain, to "higher" psychological needs, such as needs for love, knowledge, order, self-fulfillment, and "something bigger than we are to be awed by" (1971:105).

An important feature of this theory is the idea that some needs are more fundamental than others and have to be at least partly satisfied before other, higher needs become active. Thus, in living our dying, we must first satisfy our basic physiological needs (such as hunger, thirst, and pain control), and safety needs (such as living in a secure, nurturing environment) before we will be motivated to satisfy needs higher up the pyramid. Once physiological and safety needs are met, people begin striving to satisfy love or belongingness needs (the need to receive affection from others and to feel part of a group) and self-esteem needs (the need to feel positively about one self and to be esteemed by others). Finally, at the top of the pyramid, is the need for self-actualization, the desire to attain the full use of our potential in acceptance of self, of others, of nature, and of our spiritual yearnings.

In an interesting study of the role of spirituality in persons with acquired immune deficiency syndrome (AIDS), researchers found that it is not uncommon for persons with AIDS to be drawn even closer to their spiritual beliefs. These included beliefs in a caring, higher power, the value of life, the importance of support from religious laypersons and close friends, living an ethical life, the importance of facing death, and the presence of an inner peace (Warner, Carment, & Christiana, 1989).

Based on Maslow's humanistic model, psychotherapist Carl Rogers (1902–1987) developed a systematic formulation of the humanistic perspective based

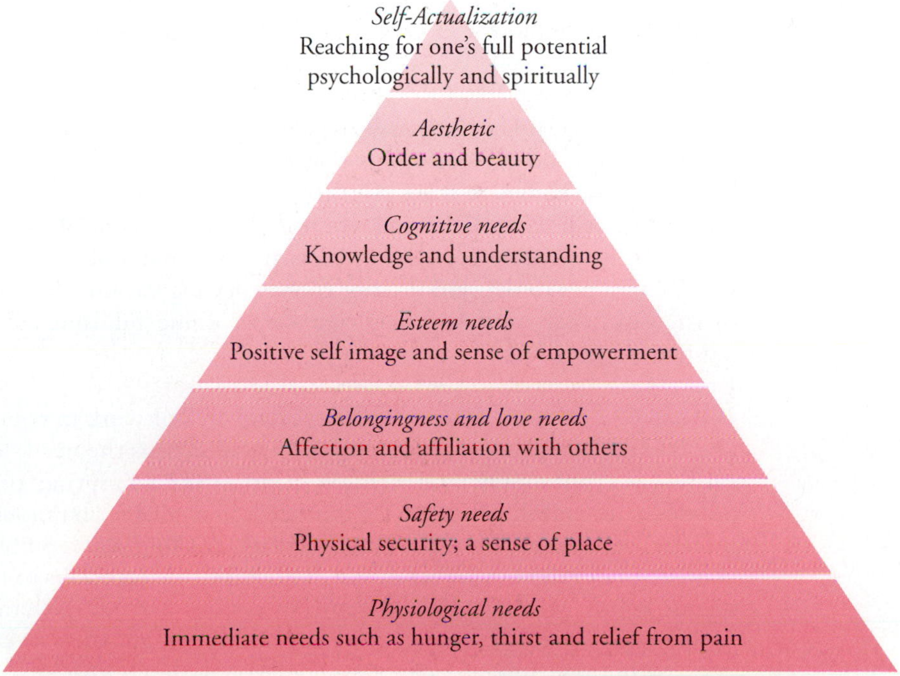

Self-Actualization
Reaching for one's full potential
psychologically and spiritually

Aesthetic
Order and beauty

Cognitive needs
Knowledge and understanding

Esteem needs
Positive self image and sense of empowerment

Belongingness and love needs
Affection and affiliation with others

Safety needs
Physical security; a sense of place

Physiological needs
Immediate needs such as hunger, thirst and relief from pain

Figure 3.1   MASLOW'S HEIRARCHY OF HUMAN NEEDS

largely on his pioneering research into the nature of the psychotherapeutic process. Rogers (1951, 1959) stated his views in a series of propositions that bear directly on the task of living our dying. These propositions can be summarized as follows.

- Each individual exists in a private world of experience of which the I, me, or myself is the center.
- The most basic striving of an individual is toward the maintenance, enhancement, and actualization of the self.
- An individual reacts to situations, such as coping with dying, in terms of the way he or she perceives them and in ways consistent with his or her sense of self and view of the world.
- A perceived threat to the self, such as coping with a terminal illness or imminent death, is followed by a defense—including a tightening of perception and behavior and the introduction of self-defense mechanisms, such as denial, repression, and passivity.
- An individual's inner tendencies are toward wholeness, and, in living our dying, we can choose to behave in rational and constructive ways, individually choosing pathways toward personal dignity and spiritual insight.

Corr's Task-based Coping Model

Based on Maslow's hierarchy of needs and Roger's therapeutic insights, Charles Corr (1992) has developed a task-based coping model that involves active participation in living our dying. Rather than stages or phases of dying, the task-based model offers a fuller range of challenges while supporting greater empowerment of the dying person in dealing with physical, psychological, social, and spiritual needs. In addition, this model provides guidance for loved ones and health care professionals in recognizing the tasks of coping with the process of dying.

Physical Needs.   The first task to be mastered in living our dying is to acknowledge basic physical needs that remain unsatisfied, and then to identify tasks we must complete to satisfy these needs, such as achieving nutrition, full hydration, pain control, bowel control/regularity, control of vomiting, and normal sleep patterns. Identifying these needs, communicating them to family and medical personnel, and making choices among various alternatives are some of the tasks that must be completed before these fundamental needs can be satisfied (Corr, 1992).

Psychological Needs.   The second important area of work in coping with dying involves the satisfaction of psychological needs, such as the needs for psychological security, autonomy, and richness (Corr, 1992). Ensuring that health care providers are indeed providing for our needs in a reliable and timely manner will increase our sense of psychological security. Making active choices about the conduct of our lives, whether directly or by designating others to make decisions in our behalf, will increase our sense of control and self-government. Finally, with a sense of security and control in place, we might then seek to enrich our lives with those unique activities and favored things that give psychological meaning to our lives. For example, D. Smith and Maher (1993), in an investigation of attitudes that may be psychologically beneficial to the dying, their families, and their caregivers, administered the Omega Attitudes Inventory to 327 hospice coordinators. Caregivers were asked to identify one particular patient each that they believed died a healthy death and the attitudes of that person that were associated with that healthy death. Results revealed that the most facilitative attitudes and activities were having control over one's life, discussing the practical implications of dying with others, exploring an afterlife, reviewing the past, and examining the painful truths of life and death with both seriousness and humor. Also important were talking about religious/spiritual issues, appearance and personal cleanliness, the presence of significant others in one's life, and participating in physical and emotional expressions of caring.

Social Needs. The third task area concerns two interrelated aspects of social needs, namely, sustaining and enhancing the interpersonal attachments that we value, and tending to the social "business" surrounding our demise. In the first instance, Corr (1992) notes, it must be the dying person who decides which of these love relationships he or she values and wishes to strengthen during the terminal phase of life, and these choices may change as one lives through the process of dying. The second set of social tasks has to do with finishing unfinished business involving advance directives for health care, funeral and burial arrangements, organ donation, hospital charges and payments, willing belongings to heirs, dealing with insurance, and other investments and relationships.

Spiritual Needs A fourth and final set of tasks in coping with dying concerns the satisfaction of spiritual needs—seeking sources of spiritual nurturance and meaning. German thanatologist David Aldridge (1993) contends that issues of abandonment, suffering, loss of hope and meaning, and the transitions from living to dying are essentially spiritual, not solely physiological, psychological, or social, and that, in many instances, all of these contexts are interlinked. He suggests that the principle benefits of tending to the spiritual needs are a lessening of state anxiety, improved feelings of general well-being, and an increasing spiritual awareness for the dying person.

Canadians Diane Stephenson and Janice Leroux (1994), for example, report the case of a creatively gifted 11-year-old boy, dying of cancer, who applied creative skills from the love of his life, music, to totally new areas, including controlling pain and writing. His understanding of his own dying, and the meaning he attached to it, brought him to conclude that lethargy and pain were obstacles to be overcome if he was to live out his short life in meaningful and creative ways.

Meeting our creativity and spiritual needs in the process of dying is an integral part of any holistic, task-oriented approach, because many people facing death are actively searching for meaning in life as well as in death. We may find meaning in a personal god, in the grandness of nature, in certain religious rituals and practices, or in an individual value system. Doka and Morgan (1993:2–3) have identified the following three principal spiritual tasks for those who are dying.

1. *The need to find meaning in or the ultimate significance of life.* Answers do not necessarily have to be found in religious beliefs, but an inability to find meaning can create a deep sense of spiritual pain. The dying person's belief system can give a sense of purpose in life and help sustain personal values.
2. *The need to die an appropriate death.* People who are dying need to accept their death within a framework that is congruent with their values and lifestyle. In some cases, individuals may need help in making decisions about the way in which they will die. Guidance from a special friend or from someone they recognize as a spiritual leader may be helpful.
3. *The need to transcend death.* Transcendence can be achieved through reassurance of immortality in religious doctrine, or through the acknowledgment of future generations that their deeds will live long after they die.

To find meaning in the final moments of life, to die appropriately, consistent with our own self–identity, and to find hope that extends beyond the grave, to our loved ones and, perhaps, to humankind, may be among the most important accomplishments in truly living our dying.

Final Moments and Near-Death Experiences

The physical changes that unfold during the process of dying are paralleled by certain psychological changes that appear to occur just before a person dies. These alterations develop in the individual's cognitive abilities, emotional state, and experiences of altered states of consciousness. Lieberman (1966), for example, found that elderly persons in a "death imminent" group experienced increasing levels of cognitive disorganization and distortion. Nearing the moment of death, they psychologically withdrew from the world in an attempt to deal with this experience of personal fragmentation. Commenting on these observations, Lieberman (1965:189) states that "individuals approaching death pull away from those around them not because of a preoccupation with themselves but because they are preoccupied . . . with an attempt to hold themselves together."

Clarissa Pinkola Estes (1994:15), a psychoanalyst who was close to nearly 100 terminally ill clients in her 22 years of practice, describes the transformative moment that occurs when a person enters the part of life that is dying:

> I have seen something rise in the dying person, something I can only imagine as the terminally ill person's life force, their soul rising to the top of their body, starting to tap at their bones, beginning to rattle at their lungs, looking for the way out of the shell. Over time, everything about the very ill person deflates; the skin, the bones, even the personality begins to fade. But at the same time, another pulse seems to grow ever larger and stronger, a something, a someone, who knows it is time and who wants to let loose. Anyone with open eyes and heart who has been close to the dying sees this.

HYPNOS AND THANATOS

Beyond the state of cognitive disorganization experienced in the final moments of dying, we must also deal with the fears produced as the sense of self dissolves

CARING INSIGHTS

On Visiting with the Dying

1. Often, dying people do not say what they want or mean, and the people close to them do not know what to say and do.
2. The first step is to relax any tension in the atmosphere in whatever way comes easily and naturally.
3. Don't think anything extraordinary is supposed to happen—just be yourself. As Tibetan scholar Sogyal Rinpoche has observed, the most essential thing in life is to establish an unafraid, heartfelt communication with others, and this is never more important than with the dying person.
4. Encourage the dying person warmly to feel as free as possible to express thoughts, feelings, fears, and emotions about dying and death.
5. You must give the person complete freedom and permission to say and do whatever he or she wants.
6. When the dying person is finally communicating, do not interrupt, deny, or diminish what is being communicated. It will take all your skill, sensitivity, and compassion to enable them just to be themselves.
7. Sit there with your dying friend, relative, or patient as if you had nothing more important or enjoyable to do. As Sogyal Rinpoche reminded us, as in all grave situations of life, two things are most useful: a commonsense approach and a sense of humor.
8. If the dying person targets you for blame, anger, rage, or guilt extraction, do not take anything too personally. Dying creates vulnerability and dissolves ego defenses. When you least expect it, you may become the target for spontaneous emotional expression.
9. Avoid, at all cost, preaching to the dying or giving them your spiritual formula for life—unless they ask.
10. Don't be surprised or distressed if your visit seems to have very little effect and the dying person does not respond. People will die just as they have lived, and we can never know the deeper effects of our caring.

Source: Adapted from: Rinpoche (1992).

and we are pulled away from the external world into a primordial sense of being where there is no awareness of time or space and no boundaries between self and others. Pattison (1977) speculates that this terminal state of consciousness, termed *regression into self,* is similar to the state of consciousness we experience just before we fall off to sleep each night, or when we are awakened by an alarm clock in the early morning and feel the weight of sleep pulling us back into a drowsy slumber. This parallel between the dying moment and the experience of sleep may be traced back to the Greeks, who believed that death (Thanatos) was a twin brother to sleep (Hypnos). Euphemisms for *death* that involve sleep or rest (e.g., "grandma has gone to sleep," "rest in peace") are common, as are terms such as "slumber rooms" for casket-viewing rooms in mortuaries and "final resting place" for cemetery plots.

Thanatologist and Tibetan scholar Sogyal Rinpoche (1992:344) draws a similar parallel between dying and the drowsy state of slumber preceding sleep. He says, "When we fall asleep, the senses and grosser layers of consciousness dissolve. . . . Next, there is a dimension of consciousness which is so subtle we are normally completely unaware of its very existence. . . . For most of us, all we are aware of is the next stage, when the mind becomes yet again active, and we find ourselves in a dream-world—all of which we believe to be solid and real, without ever realizing that we are dreaming." This drowsy, altered state of consciousness between wakefulness and sleep is called the *hypnogogic state of consciousness*. Records of electrical brain rhythms and verbal reports of individuals during the hypnogogic state of consciousness reveal a progression of events that may give us some clues to the final experience of dying and some insight into numerous published reports of near-death experiences.

Entering the hypnogogic state of sleep, we at first appear to lose volitional control over our mental processes and become so focused on internal events that we are carried along by them and become uninterested in the external world. We then lose awareness of surroundings and withdraw further into sleep because we are not only uninterested in the external world at this point, but are rapidly losing awareness of immediate surroundings. The final event, following increasing degrees of ego dissolution and loss of contact with the external world, is a break with reality and an immersion in a dream world in which we now believe that our internal experiences are actually happening in the external world. At this point, according to Vogel, Foulkes, & Trosman (1966), there is disorientation in time and place brought about by a regressed ego state in which the sleeping subject appears to be hallucinating. Other researchers report the frequent occurrence of thinking and memory processes during the hypnogogic state with content that appears to be more plausible, more concerned with everyday life, and more pleasant. (Rechtschaffen, 1976; Barber, 1976; Tart, 1989)

Generally, these drowsy periods also are characterized by brief and discontinuous regressive dream content and fragmented hallucination-like experiences. Examples include single, isolated images, meaningless patterns, an incomplete scene or bits and pieces of a scene, bizarre images, dissociation of mind and body, and magical thinking. Physiological psychologist N. P. Carlson (1977:408) points out that, for some people, these "hypnogogic hallucinations are often alarming or even terrifying." Foulkes (1966) notes that subjects often report heightened awareness of bodily sensations, bodily positions, and states of muscular fatigue and relaxation during the hypnogogic state of consciousness. Bodily sensations include shrinkage or swelling of limbs, feelings of constriction about the waist, and floating sensations.

One of the more interesting findings is the relationship of personality to the amount of dreamlike fantasy reported in the hypnogogic sleep state. Persons who showed lesser amounts of such fantasy material during the hypnogogic state

FINAL MOMENTS: THE EYES OF KATIE MASON

Consider the abrupt death of Katie Mason as seen through the eyes of her mother, Joan. The knife attack on her nine-year-old daughter was played out at a county fair in a small Connecticut city. The unprovoked assault on the young girl, who was repeatedly stabbed in the neck, face, and upper torso, was made by a male stranger, later determined to have been under the influence of angel dust (PCP). Katie's murder was witnessed by numerous fairgoers, including her mother. As Joan cradled her daughter in her arms, the child's neck, head, and dress were covered with blood, her eyes were clear, and her face wore a look of surprise and release from the pain of her last living moments. A minute later she was dead.

"She was gazing at me and beyond me, and there was a warm feeling in me. Her head had fallen back. Then I raised her a bit, and I thought she was still breathing. I spoke her name a few times and told her I loved her. . . . Her chest began heaving and she started to vomit blood. It came out in such huge amounts, constantly—I didn't think she would have so much blood in her; I knew she was emptying out the blood in her body. I screamed for help, but there was nothing I could do to stop the vomiting.

When I had first gone to her, I saw some glimmer in her eyes, almost like some sort of recognition. But by the time I laid her on the ground, her eyes had a different look. Even when she was vomiting blood, they had changed to a more glassy look. When I first went to her side, she still looked alive—but not anymore.

There was no look of pain in her eyes, but instead it was a look of surprise. And then when things changed, she still had that expression on her face, but her eyes had glazed over a little bit. A woman came over—I guess she was a nurse. She started CPR. I didn't say anything, but I thought to myself, Why is she doing that? Katie is not in her body anymore. She's behind me, up there above me, and floating. Her life isn't inside her anymore, and she's not coming back. Her body is just a shell now. At that point, everything was different than it had been when I first went to her side—I had an awareness that my daughter had died. I felt she was no longer in her body, that she was somewhere else.

The ambulance came, and they lifted her out of the pool of blood and tried to force air into her lungs with an Ambu bag. Her eyes were still wide open and she still had that glassy look. The look on her face was a look of utter surprise, like 'What's happening?' It was a combination of being helpless, confused, and surprised, but definitely not a look of horror, and I remember being relieved that it wasn't, because I was looking for any sense of relief at that time. . . .

Do you know what it looked like? It looked like a release. After seeing him attacking her that way, it gave me a sense of peace to see that look of release. She must have released herself from this pain, because her face didn't show it. I thought, maybe she went into a state of shock. She looked surprised but not terrified—as terrifying as it was for me, it wasn't that way for her. . . .

Even though she was unconscious, I felt that somehow she knew I was there, that her mother was there when she was dying. I brought her into the world and I was there when she was leaving—in spite of the terror and horror of it, I was there."

Source: Nuland (1993), pp. 126–127.

generally expressed a rigid, moralistic, and repressive outlook on life. They seemed less able to "let go" and express inner feelings and thoughts than did those subjects reporting a great deal of fantasy. Those high on fantasy tended to be more tolerant of shortcomings in themselves and others and less dogmatic in their beliefs. Scores from projective tests revealed that subjects with the ability to exercise their imaginations in waking life reported more vivid fantasies during the hypnogogic state of sleep (Budzynski, 1976).

Our dreamlike experiences in the hypnogogic state of consciousness may not truly parallel the experience of the actual moment of dying. On the other hand, these findings may shed some light on near-death experiences (NDEs) in which individuals on the brink of permanent death are revived, often through some heroic medical procedure.

NEAR-DEATH EXPERIENCES

What does it feel like to die? What did Katie Mason experience in the final moments following her attack? What is it like to cross over from "being alive" to "being dead"? And how would a psychologist gather data to answer such a question?

Surprisingly, some fascinating information is available on the experience of dying. Recent developments in medicine have made it possible, in some instances, to bring people who are "clinically dead" back to life. Stopped hearts can sometimes be started again—and interviews have been conducted with these individuals by psychiatrist Raymond Moody (1975) and others, to gain an understanding of what the moment of death feels like.

Since Moody's breakthrough investigations, several researchers have described the NDEs of persons surviving a variety of near-death encounters, including falls of mountain climbers, automobile accidents, drownings, serious illnesses, including cardiac arrest, and miscellaneous other medical causes (Noyes and Kletti, 1977; Kastenbaum, 1991). Survivors often describe the experience of dying as an unpleasant one, at first, as they fight death. Upon "letting go," however, they are overtaken with a magical, hallucination-like state in which a sense of peace soon settles over them and they report visions, out-of-the body experiences, sharp and vivid images, and feelings of great understanding and joy (Moody, 1975, 1980, 1988).

Loss of control of the body and the mind is often experienced, as though the mind is taken to a special place while the body is left behind. Movement of the mind occurs through darkness or into a dark space and then travels through a tunnel or underpass

LIFE AFTER LIFE

"A man is dying and, as he reaches the point of greatest physical distress, he hears himself pronounced dead by his doctor. He begins to hear an uncomfortable noise, a loud ringing or buzzing, and at the same time feels himself moving very rapidly through a long, dark tunnel. After this he suddenly finds himself outside of his own physical body. . . . He glimpses the spirits of relatives and friends who have already died, and a loving, warm spirit, . . . a being of light, appears before him. . . . [H]e finds himself approaching some sort of barrier or border, apparently representing the limit between earthly life and the next life. Later he tries to tell others, but he has trouble doing so."

Source: Moody (1975), pp. 16–18.

Among individuals reporting the NDE in India, Australia and the United States, descriptions of tunnels, dark places and bright lights were remarkably similar. © *Marrone/1995*

filled with a bright light—a heavenly place filled with love and awe. Some people are allowed to enter the light, and some are not.

The mind then emerges into the bright light, where it is allowed to converse with people or a supreme being. Conversations do not occur in words but in thoughts and intuitions. In the midst of this light, escorts, in the form of angels or beings of light, accompany the mind in this phase of the near-death experience.

Often the escorts are predeceased family members or friends. The escorts are recognized by their personalities, not by their faces or bodily presentation (Blackmore, 1983; Dougherty, 1990). Lundahl (1992), in a review of NDE accounts, points out that the beings of light or angels have three major functions in the NDE: that of guide, that of messenger, and that of escort. Interestingly, he notes that while the being of light has been identified as an angel *or* a deceased family member, he knows of no published NDE account in which the being of light is identified as *both* family member *and* angel.

Recently, psychological researchers from various countries have attempted to determine both whether near-death experiences occur in other cultures and what community attitudes toward those phenomena are. Pasricha (1992), for example, found that of 2,207 persons interviewed in Channapatna, a region of southern India, twenty-six reported that they had died and were revived, and of these, sixteen reported having had a near-death experience. Blackmore (1993) examined the incidence, circumstances, and aftereffects of near-death experiences among 19 adults in India. Among the eight individuals (42%) who reported at least some elements of a classic NDE, the proportions of persons experiencing tunnels, dark places, and lights were remarkably similar to those reported in American and Australian studies, and these features seemed independent of the person's culture. Blackmore points out that these findings fit with what would be expected if these features are a product of brain physiology and are not dependent on culture.

Kellehear, Heaven, and Jia (1990) surveyed 197 Chinese undergraduates in the People's Republic of China concerning their attitudes on near-death experiences. In response to a hypothetical description of an NDE, participants chose from among a range of explanations and social reactions that they felt would most resemble their own. Fifty-eight percent believed that NDEs were probably hallucinations or dreams. Less than 9% believed that NDEs were evidence of life after death. Rural and younger participants were more likely to react positively to those reporting NDEs. Opinion polls of American health care professionals over the years have found that this group believes that NDEs are not "real" experiences (Oakes, 1981; Ome, 1986).

THE IMMORTALITY INSTINCT

"I know you want to keep on living. You do not want to die. And you want to pass from this life into another in such a way that you will not rise again as a dead man, but fully alive and transformed. This is what you desire. This is the deepest human feeling; mysteriously, the soul itself wishes and instinctively desires it."

—Augustine: Sermon 344.4

DIMENSIONS OF THE NEAR-DEATH EXPERIENCE

In numerous studies over the years, researchers have isolated some of the dimensions of the near-death experience. These dimensions include *hyperalertness, depersonalization, out-of-body experiences,* and experiences of the *transcendence* of time, space, and individual identity (Noyes & Kletti, 1976, 1977; Sabom and Kreutziger, 1977; Sabom, 1982; ; Oakes, 1981; Blackmore, 1983; Kastenbaum, 1991).

Hyperalertness dimension

Many subjects reported that their attention level was heightened but narrowed during the near-death experience so that thoughts and images became sharper and speeded up. Sensory experiences involving vision and hearing became highly intense, while the passage of time appeared altered and distorted. Subjects reported that, at other times, the experience appeared to reverse itself so that thoughts, images, and sensations became blurred or dull, and movements became robotic or mechanical.

Depersonalization dimension

Depersonalization is best described as a state of altered perception in which the individual feels he or she is unreal, disembodied, or lacking personal identity (Bates & Stanley, 1985; Marrone, 1990). The experience involves an altered perception of time, a feeling of unreality, altered attention, a sense of detachment, panoramic memory, and loss of control. The feeling of depersonalization was described by NDE survivors as involving a loss of ability to keep track of time, so that memories seemed to pass by at rapid speeds while actual time itself, in the overall experience, seemed to be slowed down significantly (Noyes and Kletti, 1977; Blackmore, 1983).

A panorama of memories, spanning the entire lifetime, allowed for a "fleeting review of significant past experiences momentarily restored with great intensity" (Noyes and Kletti, 1977:185). Scenes were distinct and vivid, and the emotions associated with each memory were fully experienced. Future events were also pictured, such as family and friends attending one's funeral or finding out about the death. Others experienced a great sense of calm when they realized their efforts to save themselves were futile. They then described being surrounded by an overwhelming feeling of warmth (Noyes and Kletti, 1977). Some individuals reported a distortion of the body—a change in shape and size—but a body experienced as apart or detached from self and the world. At these times, a wall appeared to exist between emotions and the self. Strange sounds were reported.

Out-of-body dimension

Cardiologist Michael B. Sabom (1982:33), among the earliest contributors to NDE research, and others have found that most subjects report near-death experiences as beautiful and rapturous journeys into an ethereal netherland, accompanied by a sense serenity and freedom. Like Moody (1975, 1980, 1988) and others, Sabom (1982) reports that the sense of being separate from one's own body (i.e., the autoscopic experience) is a strong component of the hundreds of cases he investigated.

The out-of-body experience is described as an awareness of what is happening to the body, but with an accompanying feeling of being separate from it. This feeling is described as floating above the body while viewing the efforts of others to revive it (Rodin, 1980). A calm, detached feeling prevails while events are observed in distinct detail. The mind is described as returning to the body, sometimes, but with a distinct sense of reluctance. Subjects reported that only when mind and body were reunited could the pain and distress of dying be fully experienced (Oakes, 1981). Individuals describe very clear vision, observing what is happening to their body as if watching a movie, and feelings of great height, distance, and detachment (Sabom & Kreutziger, 1977; Greyson, 1981; Grof & Halifax, 1977; Holck, 1978; J. Lee, 1974; Kastenbaum, 1981, 1991).

Among the many interesting cases documented by Sabom and colleagues (Sabom and Kreutziger, 1977; Sabom, 1982) are several that illustrate the individual's attempt to make contact with others while in the out-of-body state. A Vietnam veteran, for example, immediately experiences himself as hovering above his wounded body when a mine explosion leaves him close to death. He continues to watch his body and what is happening to it all the way to the surgical table in the field hospital:

Subject: I'm trying to stop them (the doctors). I really did try to grab a hold of them and stop them, because I really felt happy where I was. . . . I actually remember grabbing the doctor

Author: What happened?

Subject: Nothing. Absolutely nothing. It was almost like he wasn't there. I grabbed and he wasn't there or either I just went through him or whatever. (Sabom and Kreutziger, 1977:196).

Sabom reports that he was able to establish a positive correspondence between what the patient "saw" during the out-of-body experience and what did in fact take place during the life-and-death medical procedure. Having established a baseline for knowledge of medical procedures, Sabom concludes that, in each of the six cases cited, the individual recalled specific events and developments connected to specific medical procedures that they could not have obtained through guesswork or prior knowledge. In other words, there was some objective evidence that some individuals who reported a near-death experience did in fact gain information consistent with out-of-body status (Kastenbaum, 1991). Sabom concludes that some type of split between mind and body can occur during points of crisis, and that during this altered state of disembodied consciousness a person can make accurate observations of immediate reality, as well as enter into the mystical states of being often reported in near-death experiences.

Mystical dimension

Transcendence is an experience described by survivors as the mind leaving its earthly dimension and, for a time, entering another space, age, or place. Many persons have related that this entire experience was ineffable—difficult to describe with words.

Transcendental experiences were described as an encounter with a mystical being or invisible spirits, and as approaching a barrier or point of no return that if crossed would result in death (Greyson, 1985). The transcendence experience often included speaking with God or feeling that God or some higher force was present, or a feeling of being controlled by an external power. This force or being frequently appeared as an intensely bright white light, offering a glimpse of a realm of heavenly scenery and angelic escorts and guides (Moody, 1975). Other reported experiences included feelings of great understanding, harmony, revelation, unity and joy.

> **"I sat on the grass across from the grave and thought of my friend, trying to recall his features, and to fix them in my mind as they had been before he had been carried down that immense river which vanishes completely in the sea and which disperses everything beyond the recall of memory. And then I remembered his words: 'To die is to go into the Collective Unconscious, to lose oneself in order to be transformed into form, pure form.' "**
>
> Miguel Serrano. (1966). *C.G. Jung and Herman Hesse: A Record of Two Friendships*. Schocken Books, NY, p. 35.

THE WALL AND THE DOOR

The near-death experience must clearly pique our interest as a remarkable human experience. But were the survivors really dead? Do such reports provide evidence for survival after death or for the existence of heaven or paradise? Is death the joyful and ultimately fulfilling experience it seems to be from survivors' reports of near-death encounters? Or are such experiences simply psychological projections, wish-fulfilling fantasies or endorphin-induced hallucinations that serve to mask the terror of confronting our own demise? Is death the ultimate ending, a wall that forbids passage? Or is death merely a transitional state of being, a door to another, more heavenly realm of existence?

One explanation of near-death experiences postulates that they simply reflect the breakdown of the individual's personality as a result of the dysfunction and misfirings of a brain and nervous system in the act of dying. A second explanation postulates that near-death experiences are what they appear to be: experiences of life after death, a peek into the hereafter before being brought back to life. Each explanation offers a model or representation of how the world works: One version is rational, objective and scientific; the other version is metaphorical, subjective, and spiritual.

Herman Feiffel (1959) and Clyde Nabe (1982) offer a helpful metaphor of *death as a door* or *death as a wall* in their attempt to characterize these two basic philosophical perspectives regarding death. From the scientific or objective point of view, death is the breakdown of physical matter and personality structure and, as such, is the cessation of all existence for the person who dies. In short, death is a wall. Death is an ending, not an opening. In the second, spiritual perspective,

The metaphor of the wall and the door offers alternate explanations of death: the wall version is objective, rational and scientific while the door version is metaphorical, subjective and spiritual. © *Stock Illustration Source*

the possibility arises that what is real about us as persons may not correspond to our makeup as material beings, so that the dissolution of the body need not be viewed as necessarily resulting in the dissolution of the human person. In other words, death is a door, not a wall. Death is an opening to an afterlife, not an ending.

THE SPIRITUAL SIGNIFICANCE OF NDEs

"When you combine . . . reports of out-of-the-body experiences (OBEs), near-death experiences (NDEs), and phenomena from a variety of altered states of consciousness, I think we have an excellent case for believing that some nonmaterial part of our minds may survive death and that there may be intelligent, nonphysical beings in the universe, a matter of great intellectual and spiritual significance to us."

Source: Tart (1989), p. 85.

There are many variations on the wall and the door metaphor (DeSpelder Strickland, 1992). The secular, scientific position is that death is actually a final termination of existence. But for some people, it is experienced psychologically as a door to an afterlife. The Christian position is that death is initially a wall, a temporary ending that, at the time of the Resurrection, is transformed into a door to everlasting life. The Hindu concept of reincarnation suggests that death is always a door, a revolving door, to various and recurring states of life. Tibetan Buddhists believe that death involves entrance through a series of doors called *bardos* (Sogyal Rinpoche, 1992); Zen Buddhists and transpersonal psychologists (Tart, 1989) might respond that death is both a door and a wall—simply alternative ways of experiencing the same reality.

The Death-as-Door Thesis

From this perspective, the near-death experience is a peek into the hereafter, a visit with the Supreme Being in a heavenly realm inhabited by angels. Thanatologist Joanne Murley (1995:16), speaking from the death-as-door perspective, describes the NDE in this way:

> [D]eath may be understood as primarily a separation of spirit and matter, the intangible from the corporeal, consciousness from form. . . . When the body dies, the essence of the individual is energized in compassionate light and is liberated . . . The physical body no longer anchors the five senses; the body of light is activated and a vitality is restored which taps into a benevolent power . . . Spiritual understandings are nurtured; inner senses are increased.

Murley believes that the issues generated by NDE will undoubtedly continue "until scientific measurements can gauge, calibrate, and monitor consciousness beyond the grave."

Two recent papers published in the *Journal of Near-Death Studies* attempt to link near-death experiences with the release or mobilization of spiritual energies. Kason (1994), based on her exploration of both historical and research evidence, suggests that the awakening of latent spiritual energy is the "biopsychospiritual" basis of near-death experiences. This spiritual energy is known in various sacred traditions as *holy spirit, vital winds, chi, dumo,* and *fire* and in the Eastern yogic tradition as *kundalini.*

Kundalini is the mechanism, or power center, through which the cosmic and individual *prana* (i.e., breath) are intermingled and regulated. It is hypothesized that the awakening of kundalini, which involves a reversal of the activity of the reproductive system, may activate another chamber in the brain, which can lead to the experience of enlightenment or illumination. In a similar vein, Kieffer (1994) suggests that in the NDE, this same conscious, cosmic energy endeavors to make a last-ditch effort to save the brain by rallying all available organic resources into action. It is argued that the mechanism that powers and regulates this life-saving operation is kundalini. However, while Kieffer (1994) and Kason (1994) believe that the NDE can, in some cases, activate the kundalini, they point out that there is still little understanding of what is meant by the arousal of this power.

Tibetan thanatologist Sogyal Rinpoche (1992:289–290) sees a powerful correspondence between reports of the near-death experience and the description of the bardo in Tibetan Buddhist doctrine. The *bardos* refer to various doors the spirit must pass through after death. The out-of-body experience, for example, appears to reflect passage through the bardo of becoming. Rinpoche states,

> If we are very attached to our body, we may even try, in vain, to reenter or hover around it. In extreme cases the mental body can linger near its possessions or body for weeks or even years. And still it may not dawn on us we are dead. It is only when we see that we cast no shadow, make no reflection in the mirror, no footprints on the ground, that finally we realize. And the sheer shock of recognizing we have died can be enough to make us faint away.

The Death-as-Wall Thesis

From the death-as-wall perspective, Noyes (1979) compares the near-death experience to a strong nervous-system stress reaction whose function is to help us to adapt to dangerous circumstances. Hyperalertness, combined with the separation of some parts of the personality from the rest in depersonalization, is, according to Noyes, an adaptive mechanism that combines opposing reaction tendencies, "the one serving to intensify alertness and the other to dampen potentially disorganizing emotion" (Noyes, 1979:78). When this mechanism is working properly, a person is able to cope exceptionally well (coolly, calmly, objectively) in the midst of a crisis as though "in a dream" or "doing this mechanically" (Sarason & Sarason, 1989:138).

Noyes speculates that the destruction of the personality resulting from the breakdown of the brain and nervous system in the dying moment induces altered states of consciousness (e.g., sleep states, dream states, coma, states of rapture) in which experiences of a mystical type are known to appear (Noyes, 1979). These and other research findings generally support the hypothesis that the near-death experience is simply the result of psychophysiological phenomena connected to the dysfunction of the body at death. Robert Kastenbaum (1991), following a thorough review of major NDE research studies, summarizes some of the central arguments in supports of the "death as wall" hypothesis.

1. Not everyone experiences NDEs or "dies" a blissful, accepting death. Kastenbaum points to the majority of individuals who return from a close encounter with death but who do not report having had near death experiences. These survivors typically report no memories at all or only nebulous and ambiguous images. Other survivors, rather than reporting visits to some heavenly domain, report nightmarish experiences that neither increase their spirituality nor decrease their fear of death (Garfield, 1979). Kastenbaum (1991:442) maintains that ". . . since death is universal, how could the NDE be otherwise if it is truly a visit to the other side?" These and similar findings argue against the universality of the NDE, and Kastenbaum believes they weaken claims that the NDE is actually a visit to the hereafter.

> ## THE EXPERIENCE OF THE BARDO
>
> "In the bardo of becoming we relive all the experiences of our past life, reviewing minute details long lost and revisiting places, the masters say, 'where we did no more than spit on the ground'. Every seven days we go through the experience of death once again, with all its suffering. If our death was peaceful, that peaceful mind is repeated; if it was tormented, however, that torment is repeated too. And remember that this is with a consciousness seven times more intense than that of life, and that in the fleeting period of the bardo of becoming, all karma of previous lives is returning, in a fiercely concentrated and deranging way.
>
> Our restless, solitary wandering through the bardo world is as frantic as a nightmare, and just as in a dream, we believe we have a physical body and that we really exist. Yet all the experiences of this bardo arise only from our mind, created by our karma and habits returning."
>
> *Source:* Rinpoche (1992), pp. 290.

2. The primary NDE occurs sometimes in situations in which the individual is in no bodily peril of death, therefore it should not be considered as distinctively related to death (Stevenson, Cook & McClean-Rice, 1989–1990). For example, Stevenson, Cook, and Mclean-Rice (1989–1990) stated that of 107 patients reporting NDEs, 55% were rated as having had no life-threatening condition, although 82% of these patients believed that they had been dead or near death. Kastenbaum points out that some of these patients had decided for themselves that they had been "dead" or "clinically dead." Others (mis)interpreted what they had been told by medical staff. In reviewing the results of their research, Stevenson, Cook, and McClean-Rice (1989–1990: 52) speculate that ". . . having had the NDE itself may have led some people to believe retrospectively that their condition must have been worse than it otherwise seemed."

The out-of-body component of the NDE has also been reported frequently—and sometimes even created experimentally—apart from any death peril (Myers, 1975). For example, Gabbard and Twemlow (1984:16) found that people who had been in severe pain were more likely than others to experience a sense of distance from their bodies. They note that, "In hypnotic pain experiments, it is a common suggestion to dissociate the painful part from the body so that it is treated as not self." Furthermore, they report that individuals under anesthesia were more likely to report seeing brilliant lights and hearing peculiar sounds. According to Kastenbaum (1991:443) "The specific type of NDE that one experiences seems to be influenced by a number of circumstances, even though NDEs, as a class of phenomena, may occur to many kinds of people under many kinds of stress."

In other research, Gabbard and Twemlow (1986) compared NDEs to powerful, life-changing events as well as highly pathological disorders. Serdahely

Science will never prove or disprove life after death, according to psychiatrist Raymond Moody, M.D., whose book *Life After Life,* about NDEs, was a precursor of today's best-sellers. The book has sold about 12 million copies worldwide since its publication in 1975. "We can conclude that either the central nervous system causes the experience," he says, "or that the central nervous system state opens up some kind of window or portal into an afterlife. Science can't really make that determination." Moody remains unsure about what really happened in the 3,000 near-death cases he's investigated over the past 30 years. But he also confirms that studying death has changed his lifestyle. He avoids fats in his diet. He walks at least an hour a day, and while at work he regularly enters into a meditative state, between waking and sleeping, where he says he gets his best inspirations.

Source: Adapted from: Gurney Williams. (1994). Death and Royalties, *Longevity Magazine* (September 7).

(1992), for example, suggests the possibility that near-death experience (NDE) and multiple personality disorder are not disparate experiences, but variants of a single experience. Accounts of both experiences include references to out-of-body experiences and concomitant pain relief, a transcendental environment of light, a higher self or inner self helper, telepathic communication, time distortion, floating, references to "hell," psychic abilities and spheres of light and energy.

3. We hear reports of NDEs only from the survivors. Finally, Kastenbaum asks us to keep in mind that, in spite of the growing number of reports of NDEs, there is no evidence that what happens when a person actually dies

> . . . and stays dead has any relationship to the experiences reported by those who have recovered from a life-threatening episode. In fact, it is difficult to imagine how there could ever be such evidence; the very fact that a person recovered disqualifies their report of "permanent death." There is always an observing self that categorizes the observed self as inert or dead. This split consciousness may result in the opinion that "I was dead," but there was always another "I" lively and perceptive enough to make that judgment (1991:443).

THE NEAR-DEATH EVENT AS A MAJOR LIFE TRANSITION

Despite opposing and inadequate explanations as to how and why NDEs occur, the experience itself can have profound effects on the life of the individual. The person who views death as a wall, a final ending, may feel reassured that the suffering experienced during this life ends at death. However, someone else may find comfort in the belief that death is a door, that the personality survives physical death. Beliefs about what happens after death may be a source of solace to both the dying as well as the bereaved (Dougherty, 1990). For example, many of Sabom's subjects reported the near-death experience as a significant, if not a profound, life-changing event. The impact of the NDE for individuals included:

- A reduction in death anxiety
- The development of new attitudes regarding death
- A refocusing of life on the here and now as compared to a preoccupation with death
- An intuitive acceptance of both life and death
- A renewed will to live

- A sustained sense of self during long recovery periods after the NDE
- A change or enrichment in religious faith
- A new interest in the caring aspects of human relationships

Attitude changes following near-death events have been described by other researchers (Noyes, 1980; Greyson & Stevenson, 1980). The attitudes most often affected included a reduced fear of death, a sense of relative invulnerability, a feeling of special importance or destiny, a belief in having received the special favor from God or fate, and a strengthened belief in continued existence.

In an Australian study by sociologist Cherie Sutherland (1990), fifteen men and thirty-five women (ages 7–76) were interviewed about their NDEs years earlier to determine the impact these experiences had on their lives. It was found that, although before the NDE participants were no more religious or spiritually inclined than the general Australian population, following the NDE there was a significant shift toward spirituality. Over 75% said that they had a fear of death before the NDE, whereas none had a fear of death after the NDE. Data also show a change in attitudes toward suicide, with participants being opposed to suicide after the NDE. The most significant changes resulting from the NDE were reported to be spiritual growth, a loving attitude, knowledge of God, and inner peace.

Some individuals reported feeling that their NDE carried a message for others: "If people would accept death and [that] it's not a frightening experience, that it's going to happen, and they're going to have to experience it one day, then they would live their life a lot easier" (Sabom, 1982:133). Many individuals interpreted their near-death experience as a preview of their eventual death. The pleasant nature of the near-death experience appears to calm the fears of dying, allowing some to live the remainder of their lives with a greater sense of purpose and determination (Sabom and Kreutziger, 1977). Other research studies have shown that surviving a serious illness or a near-death encounter has led to a change in values, priorities, and feelings of love and caring toward others (Kastenbaum, 1991).

One in three people who come close to dying report a near-death experience, and many are left feeling happier and more content after the NDE experience. But a recent study by psychiatrist Bruce Greyson casts some doubt on this rosy picture (Grabmeier, 1995). Greyson compared 126 people who said they had an NDE with those whose brushes with death did not produce the NDE. He found that the positive effects of the NDE, such as renewed sense of altruism or personal wisdom, were often offset by problems caused by the experience. Problems involved the confusion created by the NDE, tension in old relationships caused by a shift in values and attitudes, and, for some, the sense that what may have seemed normal before the NDE "may not seem normal anymore" (Grabmeier, 1995:6)

A sense of "rebirth" or "reawakening" to the important aspects of life follows survival from a near-fatal event in some persons. The long-term impact, then, of an NDE on the future life goals of the individual is important to consider in the recovery process following serious illness or accidents (Dougherty, 1990). Robert Kastenbaum cautions, however, that one needs to be careful of a too-ready acceptance of the "fantastic voyage" implied by most life-after-death accounts. The "happily ever after" stance toward death may represent a form of denial when what is really needed by the dying is a demonstration of real concern and real caring in their present experience. He believes that the happily-ever-after theme threatens to draw attention away from the actual situations of the dying persons, their loved ones, and their caregivers over the days, weeks, and months preceding death. What happens up to the point of the fabulous transition from life to death, he says, recedes into the background, which could not be more unfortunate, because the background, after all, is where these people are actually living until death comes.

Entering the terminal phase of the dying process, we may fight against the experience of regression into self (Pattison, 1977). At this point, the goal of loved ones is to help us to turn away from the world of thoughts and concepts and accept surrender and release to the internal self. In this way, regression, withdrawal and death might occur more peacefully as we approach the wall, the door, or both.

Chapter Summary

In her popular and groundbreaking book *On Death and Dying,* Elizabeth Kubler-Ross presented her idea that the dying process could be viewed as a series of stages, which include: shock and denial, anger, bargaining, depression, and acceptance. With the introduction of her model, many thanatologists criticized the idea that dying proceeds in stages. These criticisms were based, for the most part, on a lack of empirical support in the research literature, the restrictive nature of the stage theory itself, and the way it was being used and misused by medical personnel and family members. E. Mansell Pattison offered a phase model of the dying process. The model proposes a three-phase process that includes an acute phase, a chronic living-dying phase, and a terminal phase. The model delineates a series of fears the dying person is likely to experience.

Charles Corr proposes a task-based coping model that offers a fuller range of challenges while supporting greater empowerment of the dying person in dealing with physical, psychological, social, and spiritual needs.

The actual moment of dying may resemble the drowsy state of slumber called the hypnogogic state of consciousness. Experiences in this state resemble those commonly reported to occur during near-death experiences. These include hyperalertness, depersonalization, out-of-body experiences (autoscopy), and the experience of transcendence of time, space, and individual identity. One explanation of near-death experiences postulates that they simply reflect the dysfunction and misfirings of a brain and nervous system in the act of dying. A second explanation postulates that near-death experiences are what they appear to be: experiences of life after death, a peek into the afterlife before being brought back to life. Despite opposing and inadequate explanations as to how and why NDEs occur, the experience itself can have profound effects on the life of the individual.

FURTHER READINGS

Corr, C. A., Nabe, C. M., & Corr, D. M. (1994). *Death and Dying, Life and Living.* Brooks/Cole, Pacific Grove, CA.

Kastenbaum, R. J. (1991). *Death, Society and Human Experience* (4th ed.). Macmillan, NY.

Kubler-Ross, Elisabeth. (1969). *On Death and Dying*. Macmillan, NY.

_____ . (1975). *Death: The Final Stage of Growth*. Prentice Hall, Englewood Cliffs, NJ.

Moody, R. A., Jr. (1988). *The Light Beyond*. Bantam, NY.

_____ . (1975). *Life After Life*. Mockingbird Books, Atlanta.

Larson, D. G. (1993). *The Helper's Journey: Working with People Facing Grief, Loss, and Life-Threatening Illness*. Research Press, Champaign, IL.

Pattison, E. M. (1977). *The Experience of Dying*. Prentice-Hall, Englewood Cliffs, NJ.

Rinpoche, Sogyal, (1992). *The Tibetan Book of Living and Dying*. HarperCollins, NY.

FOUR

The Work of Mourning

We tend to associate loss, grief and mourning with death, but they are actually inherent aspects of many life events. Psychological and sociological research has made clear that divorce, rape, physical and sexual abuse, as well as the loss of a job or sexual function or our youthful dreams all involve significant experiences of grieving and loss. In fact, loss and grieving are a part of all normal human maturation and development. The preschooler who leaves the security of home to enter kindergarten, the adolescent who graduates from high school and leaves for college, and the newly married couple who grow in size to a family with the birth of their first child, must, in the midst of their excitement and joy, also experience loss and grieving for what once was and is never again to be. Loss, grief and mourning are central phenomena in all aspects of human existence which we learn to accomodate in either a healthy or unhealthy way.

The loss and sorrow experienced with the death of someone deeply loved can distress us in ways that are particularly profound and powerful because death involves a finality and an emptiness that is immediate and highly disturbing. The death may remind us of our own finite nature and provoke feelings of *fear* that our own existence will some day come to a close. It may elicit feelings of *anger* directed at the departed for abandoning or betraying us (especially in suicide), feelings of *relief,* that the death has finally occurred, or feelings of self-disgust and *guilt* surrounding real or fantasized ways in which our love and concern could have been expressed to the deceased while they were still alive (Kalish & Reynolds, 1981; Harvey, 1996).

However hard we may try to avoid the disturbing feelings and emotions related to death and dying, we cannot escape the experience of loss in our lives. Each year, approximately 8 million people in the United States suffer the death of someone in the immediate family. Each year there are also about 800,000 new widows and widowers, and 400,000 infants, children, adolescents, and young adults die (CDC, 1995a; Sarason & Sarason, 1989:131). Whether the loss involves the death of a parent, a spouse, or a child, most of us will come through the experience without suffering permanent harm, but usually not without going through a powerful process that Sigmund Freud called the "work of mourning."

The Biological Roots of Grieving and Mourning

Like human beings, other animals grieve the death of their family and group members, as well as of their human companions. Ethologist Konrad Lorenz (1952) observed grieving in a greylag goose that had lost its life-long mate. The goose was anxious and restless, flying ever-greater distances in search of its mate, visiting places where the mate might have been found, incessantly signaling with a long-distance call. Bowlby (1961) has described grieving in domestic dogs as well as in jackdaws, geese, orangutans, and chimpanzees. Researchers have also described grieving and burial behavior in elephants (Douglas-Hamilton, 1975).

Each species initially attempted to recover a lost relationship or companion. The attempt was followed by a grieving process involving withdrawal, frequent hostility, rejection of a potential new companion, depression, loss of appetite, apathy, and restlessness (Bustad & Hines, 1984; deWaal, 1996).

There is both naturalistic and empirical evidence that the death of, or separation from, the mother can lead to grieving behavior in a variety of animals, including hamsters, elephants, and a number

GRIEVING AMONG THE ELEPHANTS

"Now I saw a scene of great natural drama. The cow, an adult, was lying on her side down the slope; one of her hind feet was wedged between a boulder and a thick tree and she was hanging from it. Her head was bent backwards at an acute angle and she was stone dead. Next to her stood three calves of different sizes. The eldest was moaning quietly but every so often gave vent to a passionate bawl. The second just stood dumbly motionless, its head resting against its mother's body. The smallest calf, less than a year old, made forlorn attempts to suck from her breasts. The eldest knelt down and pushed its head and small tusks against the corpse, in a hopeless attempt to move it."

Source: Douglas-Hamilton & Douglas-Hamilton (1975), p. 11.

GRIEVING IN AN "OFF-BRAND" TERRIER

"For eight years an unsightly black-and-white off-brand terrier, Eeyore, was Mr. Cardwell's constant companion. . . . Eeyore slept at Mr. Cardwell's feet, rode with him to work every day, and enjoyed many hunting and fishing outings with her master. . . .

"One morning Eeyore and Mr. Cardwell set out on a fishing expedition. Twelve miles from home an accident occurred. Neighbors were alarmed when Eeyore returned home, crawled under the house, and started whining. Mr. Cardwell had died at the wheel of his truck. Now nobody could coax Eeyore from her hiding place. Food and water remained untouched, and all rescue attempts by family and friends and volunteers from the humane society were fruitless. Eeyore would interrupt her moaning momentarily at the sound of Claire's familiar voice but she would not let her come near. She had retreated into a deep hole under the house where no one could reach her.

"The whining grew meeker as the last rescue attempts failed. After one and a half weeks of grieving, Eeyore died."

Source: U. Carson (1989), pp. 49–62.

of primates. For example, infant rhesus monkeys separated from their mothers first show increased activity and searching behavior, followed by behavioral depression, including a huddled posture, a typical "sad" facial expression, excessive whimpering, listlessness, withdrawal from social activities, alterations in heart rate and body temperature, and, in some cases, self-mutilation. Grieving behavior persists for many months. Most infants recover over a period of time, but some may die, with no apparent cause found on autopsy (Goodall, 1983; Crawley, Sutton, & Pickar, 1985).

Dolphins have been observed attempting to rescue dead or injured members of their own group from drowning by pushing them back above the waterline to breathe. In a rare species of Siberian dwarf hamster, in which lifelong male–female bonding is common, the death of one animal or separation of the pair induces a syndrome of increased body weight, reduced exploration, and reduced social interactions in the survivor (Crawley, Sutton, & Pickar, 1985). Reports from veterinarians and zoos indicate that animals separated from their owners often exhibit many self-destructive behaviors and their results, including violent attempts to escape, self-mutilation, severe malnutrition, and sudden death.

If deliberate burial of the dead is a sign of mourning for humans, we cannot ignore the burying behavior of elephants and other animals as rudimentary signs of ritualistic mourning. When encountering dead animals, elephants will often bury them with mud, earth, and leaves. Animals known to have been buried by elephants include rhinos, buffaloes, cows, calves, and even humans (Douglas-Hamilton & Douglas-Hamilton, 1975:24). Teleki (1973) has documented a case of a rudimentary mourning ritual in which a chimpanzee troop in Tanzania that witnessed the accidental death of a member of their group tore up vegetation, threw stones at the corpse, and then gathered around the body in a circle. They sat in silence while staring at the corpse or made wailing sounds, and then left the dead body alone. Comparative psychologist Eugene Marais (1969:139) described a mysterious and quasi-religious mourning ritual among South African baboons who huddle together with the setting of the sun, gaze at the western horizon, observe a period of silence, and "then from all sides would come the sound of mourning, a sound never uttered otherwise than on occasions of great sorrow—of death or parting."

Grief and the Mourning After

In old and young, human and nonhuman animals, the loss of a companion leads to a sequence of grieving behaviors that, although somewhat predictable, is neither unvarying nor smooth and, especially in the early phases of the grieving process, may oscillate violently from yearning, protest, and rage to withdrawal, depression, and silent despair. It is the overall process of grieving the loss of an attachment, "from protest through despair to some new equilibrium of feeling and behavior" (Bowlby, 1961:331), which is a similarity we share with many other animals. However, for human beings, grieving reactions are actually only the beginning of the much larger and longer process of mourning, a process that, although observed in rudimentary form in some other animals, may be unique to us as a species. Grief reactions, such as shock, protest, sadness, yearning, crying, and depression, help us to recognize the loss and prepare us for the work of mourning.

Sigmund Freud's (1957) definition of *mourning* describes it as the psychological work associated with the loss of a loved one through death. This definition encompasses not only the grief reactions to the loss of a loved one, but also the future resolution of the loss. From this perspective, in order for mourning to be resolved, the bereaved person must comprehend the "significance, seriousness, permanence, and irreversibility" of his or her loss (Krueger, 1983:590). In other words, in addition to feelings typical of grief, such as sadness, anger, and guilt, the individual must come to understand that the deceased person will never return and that life can be meaningful nonetheless.

"Blessed are those who mourn for they shall be comforted."

JESUS, Sermon on the Mount, Matthew 5:4

Anna Freud (1960), expanding upon her father's insights, maintained that, although the very young child is capable of grieving the loss of his or her parent, the child can mourn only when she or he has developed a mature concept of death, that is, a clear understanding of the finality, irreversibility, and permanence of the loss. The same might be said for the feelings of sadness, rage, and longing observed in primates and other mammals. These emotional expressions may qualify as grief reactions; but without an understanding of the finality and meaning of that loss, these reactions cannot accurately be termed mourning.

Mourning refers to the ways in which we come to live with loss, grief, and bereavement, to how we weave loss into the fabric of our lives (Webb, 1993). From this point of view, grief involves the process of experiencing the psychological, behavioral, social, and physical reactions to the perception of loss—but it doesn't take us far enough. According to Rando (1995:219, 220), grief is a complex set of passive responses to a stimulus (i.e., loss) that is "actually the beginning part of mourning. . . . The active processes of mourning are necessary to take the individual beyond the passive reactions of grief and represent the mourner's moving to reorient him- or herself in relation to the deceased, the self, and the external world."

Grief, according to Robert Wrenn (1994), manifests in four separate ways: (a) the expression of feelings such as sadness, anger and guilt, (b) body sensations such as hollowness in the stomach, lack of energy, and shortness of breath, (c) thought patterns and dreams involving preoccupation with, or sense of the presence of, the deceased, and (d) behaviors such as treasuring objects of the deceased, withdrawing from people, and having disturbances in appetite and eating. Beyond these typical grieving reactions, however, we also experience mourning reactions, both conscious and unconscious, that have to do with (a) undoing our ties to our loved one, (b) revising our assumptions about ourselves-in-the-world, (c) reintegrating new roles, skills, and behaviors into our lives, and (d) learning how to live fully and meaningfully in a world no longer occupied by the one we loved. Typical grief reactions to the death of a loved one may last a number of months or even longer. In contrast, mourning involves a search for meaning in our loss and profound changes in our assumptive world that can last for years and, for some of us, may last until we ourselves die.

Our grieving extends into the mourning after so that, although the cognitive, emotional, and behavioral reactions of grief may be over, mourning may not be over. The widow or widower may not be in acute grief a year after the death of a spouse, but he or she may not really consider dating or investing emotion in a new relationship until accommodation and integration of the loss is complete. In

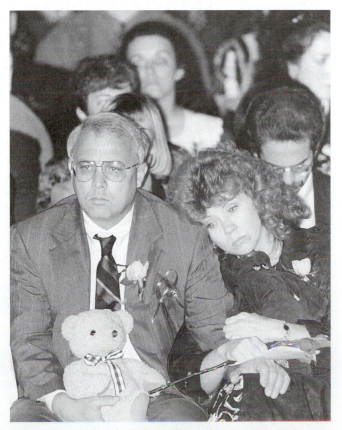

Relatives of a young victim of the bombing in Oklahoma City, Oklahoma held teddy bears given to them at a prayer service. In addition to grieving behaviors, such as treasuring objects associated with the deceased, loved ones experience mourning reactions which are both conscious and unconscious.

other instances, though the grieving process may appear to have been resolved, there may be temporary upsurges in grieving reactions during the mourning process—during anniversaries, upon hearing a certain song, or upon grieving a subsequent death. In this sense, "grief is a part of mourning, but mourning is not necessarily a part of grief" (Rando, 1995:220).

> Mourning encompasses much more than grief and . . . the distinction between grief and mourning is crucial to treatment and caregiving. Many caregivers assist the bereaved with the beginning process of acute grieving (expressing their reactions to the loss) but not with the important later mourning processes (reorienting in relation to the deceased, the self, and the external world). As a result, mourners are frequently left alone to reshape themselves and their world after the loss of a loved one, and they suffer additionally as a consequence (Rando, 1995:220).

The grieving process often involves painful and heart-wrenching expressions of loss. Mourning, on the other hand, through moving toward and working with our grief and sorrow, can bring us eventual comfort and a sense of personal reintegration and, for some, spiritual transformation. Shneidman (1980:179) states, "Mourning is one of the most profound human experiences that it is possible to have. . . . The deep capacity to weep for the loss of a loved one and to continue to treasure the memory of that loss is one of our noblest human traits."

The Process of Uncomplicated Mourning

There are many theories about the stages, phases, and tasks related to human grieving and the mourning after. Bowlby's (1980) theory, for example, describes four phases: (1) numbness and denial of the loss; (2) emotional yearning for the lost loved one and protesting the permanence of the loss; (3) cognitive disorganization and emotional despair, finding it difficult to function in the everyday world; and, finally, (4) reorganizing and reintegrating the sense-of-self so as to pull our lives back together.

Other theorists such as Zisook (1987) simplify the process by envisioning three stages: (1) shock, (2) emotional expression, and (3) recovery and resolution. Parkes and Weiss (1983) also propose a three-part process. The first phase involves the cognitive acceptance of the loss, the second concerns emotional acceptance of the loss, and the third pertains to change in the individual's model of self and outer world to match the new reality.

Harvey (1995, 1996) also proposes a three-phase process. Phase one begins with shock, outcry, and denial. In the second phase, the intrusion of thoughts, distractions, and a tendency to review the loss obsessively is followed by a period of emotional working through in which the mourner confides in others and continues cognitively to restructure an account of the loss. The third and final phase, according to Harvey, involves resolution and recovery, with enhanced feelings of controllability, increased willingness to feel the pain of loss, and the reintegration of a new self-concept.

Schneider (1984, 1989) offers an elaborate holistic model across five dimensions (the behavioral, physical, cognitive, emotional, and spiritual) involving

REACTIONS DURING UNCOMPLICATED GRIEVING

Physical
Nausea
Upset stomach
Tremors (lips, hands)
Feeling uncoordinated
Profuse sweating
Chills
Diarrhea
Vision problems
Fatigue
Bodily pains
Behavioral
Change in activity
Withdrawal
Suspiciousness
Changes in
    communication
Changes in interactions
Increased/decreased
    appetite
Increased smoking
Increased alcohol intake
Overvigilance
Excessive humor
Excessive silence
Unusual behavior
Cognitive
Denial
Confusion

Lowered attention span
Calculation difficulties
Memory problems
Poor concentration
Seeing an event
    repeatedly
Distressing dreams
Disruption in logical
    thinking
Blaming others
Emotional
Anticipatory anxiety
Fear
Uncertainty of feelings
Depression
Grief
Feeling hopeless
Feeling overwhelmed
Feeling lost
Feeling abandoned
Worrying
Wishing to hide
Wishing to die
Anger
Feeling numb
Identifying with the
    victim
Survivor guilt

Source: Adapted from University of California, Davis. *Critical Incident Debriefing Team Training Manual,* in R. M. Leash (1994).

discovery of what is lost with the death of a loved one and coping with that condition, discovering what still remains of our lives after the loss, and, finally, finding and exploring new ways of relating to life as a consequence of the loss.

Other theorists, rather than concentrating on the phases or stages of the mourning process, focus on the tasks to be completed during grieving and mourning. Worden (1991), for example, describes four tasks of mourning that must be completed if the process is to be brought to resolution: (1) acceptance of the reality of the loss, (2) experience of the pain of grief, (3) adjustment to the environment in which the deceased is missing, and (4) withdrawal of emotional energy and reinvestment in other relationships.

More recently, thanatologist Therese Rando (1995) elaborated upon three major tasks involved in the mourning process: (1) the undoing of the psychosocial ties that bind the mourner to the loved one with the eventual development of new ties, (2) addressing the necessary revision of his or her assumptive world through adopting new, and modifying old, roles, skills, and behaviors into a new identity and sense-of-self, and (3) learning how to live healthily in a new world that does not include the deceased by reinvesting in people, objects, hopes, beliefs, causes, ideals, goals, or pursuits.

The Mourning After

Increasingly, thanatologists have begun to question the idea that the mourning process has a definitive ending in recovery and renewal. Educator Richard A. Dershimer (1990), for example, criticizes the assumption of some stage and phase models that the process ends with "recovery." These models, according to Dershimer (1990:ix), attempt to categorize and "pathologize" the grieving

CARING INSIGHTS

The Stress of Loss

Our reaction to the death of someone we love, whatever the cause of death, is usually a highly stressful and personal reaction that involves characteristics of our personalities, our life experiences, our developmental level, and our unique temperaments. On the other hand, the degree to which dying and death impact our lives and arouse stress depends on important characteristics of the death itself, as well as the nature of our relationship with the deceased, the duration of our relationship with them, the trajectory of their death, and our own coping skills in dealing with critical stress-arousing factors associated with loss.

Trajectory and predictability of the loss

The trajectory of the death of a loved one, whether it is sudden and unexpected or drawn-out and anticipated will affect the intensity of our reaction to the death. Suddenness of onset impacts how prepared we are to cope with a particular death. An automobile accident, a drowning, or a random killing of a child or spouse is usually completely unexpected, the trajectory is swift, and our reactions are numbing and unpredictable. On the other hand, when an elderly parent has a chronic disease, this permits us to prepare gradually for their death and to anticipate coping in a world absent of someone truly loved and prized.

Nature and duration of the relationship

The loss of a loved one to whom we have a strong attachment of long duration and in whom we have invested great meaning is invariably more stress arousing than the loss of someone to whom our attachment is short and weak. The death of a child who has been invested with great meaning may be the most stressful of deaths for an adult, while the death of a parent may be the most stressful life experience for a child.

process as either "a mishap that must be put right or an illness needing to be cured—nothing more. Recovery uses the scientific approach based on the delineation of clearly stated goals, time frames, and treatment modalities, all intended to return the poorly functioning person to normality as soon as possible."

Therese Rando (1995:221) maintains that the concepts of "recovery" from, or "resolution" of, grief and mourning insinuate a once-and-for-all closure that typically is not achieved after the death of a dearly loved one because certain aspects of the loss remain with the mourner until his or her own death. She offers the notion of "accommodation" to the loss as an alternative concept that "captures more accurately the reality that a major loss can be integrated into the rest of life but that a truly final closure usually cannot be obtained and is not even desirable."

CARING INSIGHTS

Severity of the loss

The pain of loss varies in terms of the trauma confronting the individual. The death of one family member is surely less severe than the loss of an entire family or community. A parent driving a car in which a child is killed or run over, has a more severe trauma than a parent not involved in the accidental death of his or her child. A sudden death by accident, homicide, or suicide is more severe than an anticipated death, such as one caused by AIDS or another chronic illness.

Degree of loss of control

One of the most upsetting reactions to loss is the feeling that we are unable to exert any influence on the unfolding of events. This is often the case for survivors of natural disasters and war. Earthquake victims, for example, can do nothing to prevent or control the quake's initial impact, the aftershocks, and the destruction the quake has brought on self, loved ones, and community. Feelings of helplessness and hopelessness are common among survivors of natural disasters and community devastation.

Self-confidence and coping skills

Research studies continue to support the finding that lack of self-confidence often results in reduced personal effectiveness in dealing with loss, even though the person may really know how to handle the loss of a loved one or his or her own dying. For example, a recently widowed man may feel ill at ease in social situations that he was able to handle very well during his marriage. On the other hand, if self-confidence is intact but coping skills are not developed, reduced personal effectiveness is more likely. The young child's loss of a parent is likely to be more disruptive than an adolescent's or adult's loss of a parent, because coping skills and a sense-of-self are usually better developed as we mature. The capacity to reach out to and confide in others—individually or through support groups—serves as a potent coping skill in dealing with loss, grieving, and the mourning after.

From this perspective, the loss of someone deeply loved, like depression, abandonment, and the after-effects of childhood abuse, cannot be mastered or conquered. We can live with the loss of our beloved, and there can be healing and health and joy in life after we heal our deepest wounds. But there can never be full "recovery" in the sense of a return to an untroubled past or an unscarred sense-of-self. In this light, when someone to whom we are deeply attached dies, there is a sense of lingering presence, a sense of personal longing, and perhaps, a deeply felt lesson learned about life and death that continues to occupy our consciousness throughout our lives. Gerontologist Bruce J. Horacek (1996a, 1995:21), in challenging the assumptions that the mourning process is time limited, states that, in high-grief deaths, "the basic loss continues to exist like a phantom limb after amputation."

A Model of Mourning

The following model of uncomplicated mourning is meant to encompass many other stage, phase, and task theories of loss and mourning. Although different theorists may give the phases different names and focus on different aspects, the four phases presented here help to bring many of the different loss reactions together. Of course, people do not always follow predictable sequences or phases in their grieving and mourning, and for some the mourning process may never "resolve" and the mourner may never "recover." In fact, the forms of grief and mourning are so varied from person to person, across the life span, and from culture to culture that there is no uniform, predictable, and orderly sequence of stages or phases or tasks through which *all* mourners must pass. Many factors help to explain these differences (Dershimer, 1990), including personality variables, past loss events, developmental factors, anxiety about death, extent and quality of social supports, ethnic and cultural influences, death trajectory, gender, quality of the lost relationship, and spiritual/religious outlook.

The four phases of mourning presented here—**cognitive restructuring, emotional expression, psychological reintegration,** and **psychospiritual transformation**—are not discrete; the mourner may move back and forth among them, depending on numerous factors and issues in his or her life. In this light, it would be foolish to apply this or any other theory of mourning rigidly.

The Cognitive Restructuring Phase

Faced with news of the death of someone we love, we are challenged to overcome resistance to and denial of the event itself, as well as of its impact on our lives. Initial responses often involve statements like "That's impossible, he can't be dead," "You're mistaken," and "It can't be, I was just talking with her." Our initial reactions involve denial, numbness, shock, outcry, bewilderment, panic, despair and feelings of helplessness. We are overwhelmed with cognitive dissonance and resistance that manifest as disbelief and denial, and with reactions that may involve escapism, avoidance, and isolation.

Traumatic events challenge our cognitive world, and the cognitive schemas—those clusters of knowledge about objects or sequences of events that compose our cognitive world. In confronting the death of a loved one, our existing cognitive schemas must, in the short-term, *assimilate* the new experience. If the experience cannot be fit into the structure of existing schemas, the schemas must structurally change so as to *accommodate* the loss.

WEEPING AND OUTCRY

For several days following a death, our feelings may be blunted and we may be in a semidazed state of consciousness, interrupted by interludes of irritability, anger, and outcry. The outcry often involves bouts of uncontrollable weeping and sobbing, coupled with a yearning or longing for the loved one, and sometimes with restless moving about, wondering "why" the death occurred, thinking intensely about the lost loved one, and developing a "perceptual set" so that our attention is focused on environmental stimuli that remind us of the deceased. We may find ourselves literally searching for our loved one through our tears. Sleep may be difficult and dreams may be filled with dark emotions, fragmented images, and vivid memories of our loved one.

Based on their research, Labott and Martin (1988:206) suggest that weeping, sobbing, and uncontrolled crying—so common during the first few days of grieving—actually reflect the cognitive restructuring process. The shedding of tears, along with sobbing and moaning, signal the assimilation of new information into already-existing schemas, the giving up of old schemas, and the creation of new, more accurate ones that are then utilized to accommodate the new information about the loss. The onset of tears, according to Labott and Martin (1988), signals the shift from denial and increased arousal to decreased arousal, assimilation, and accommodation of the actuality of the event. Subjects in their research studies reported feeling better after they had cried, not during the period of weeping.

These cognitive and emotional reactions are to be expected even when the death trajectory involves a certain death at a known time. Whether sudden or anticipated, the reality may be very difficult to accept fully. According to thanatologist J. William Worden (1991:16), "Denying the facts of the loss can vary in degree from a slight distortion to a full-blown delusion." Our challenge in the initial phase of the mourning process is to cognitively restructure our thoughts and concepts about our world so as to assimilate and accommodate the news that a loved one no longer occupies that world. Confronted with the actuality of the death, we as mourners must gradually work through our disbelief, weeping and outcry as we respond to the reality of the death and absence of the loved one, and as we attempt to develop some cognitive account of the death itself.

COMPANION THROUGH THE DARKNESS

"*Journal:* The denial moves in. It must be a sick joke. He's really there, and as soon as I round this next corner, he'll be there, standing with that stupid grin on his face. As soon as I open the door, he'll be there. Answer the phone, it will be him. Look in that direction, and I know, I just know I'll catch a glimpse of him. I'm sure I do see him out of the corners of my vision, but he is never there when I focus, never there when I turn my head to catch him, The man sitting at the sushi bar with the aviator glasses, like the ones he used to wear, makes me jump up and then sit down quickly again, before someone sees me, looking for my husband. Not him. I speak to my friends and they all have this look on their faces like they are watching me lying on the pavement with my belly sliced open. The expression is one of mixed pity and disgust. They want to avert their eyes, but they can't. Propriety? Fascination? Did I say disgust?

Stephanie Ericsson. (1991). The Agony of Grief, *Utne Reader*, September/October, pp. 75–78.

Account Making

Beyond the challenge of acknowledging the reality of our loss, the cognitive restructuring process also involves coming to some understanding of why, when, where and how the death occurred, as well as the need to make some sense of the death. Nearly all grieving individuals will ask themselves, at some point after acknowledging their loss, why the death occurred: "Why now, when he was in the prime of his life?" "Why did she have to suffer so much?" "How did it happen?" "Was she in pain?" Deceptively simple questions such as these may pose a cognitive challenge to come to some understanding of the death and the loss. Although some grieving individuals will find no answers to the question "Why did my loved one die?", others will develop a cognitive strategy (or strategies) to supply an understanding for their loss. This is usually accomplished through *account making* (Harvey, 1995, 1996).

Accounts are our stories about the important events and aspects of our lives. They are our attempt cognitively to restructure a shaken or crumbled world by bringing understanding to the beginning, middle, and end of some event or sequence of events that has hit our lives. The process of accounting for the death of a loved one involves repeated reflecting, analyzing of information, remembering, sifting through images and memories, and allowing ourselves to be emotionally moved in the process (Harvey, 1995, 1996). The account may involve a single, powerful explanation, or it may consist of several reasons that, taken together, provide a stabilizing explanation for the event and offer the mourner a greater sense of control in dealing with the loss.

The account-making process also opens the mourner to confide in others as she or he communicates parts of the story of the death to close friends and family, which is instrumental to eventual peace of mind. Walter (1996) has found that account-making conversations between grieving loved ones often involve construction of a shared "biography" of the deceased. Harvey (1995, 1996) notes that account-making, by involving the mourner in social interactions with family and friends, can be a healing process in its own right, above and beyond the actual content of what is shared (Harvey, Orbuch & Weber, 1992).

Cognitive Restructuring Strategies

According to Beck, Rush, and their collaborators (1979:8), cognitive schemas constitute the person's "stream of consciousness" or phenomenal field and are defined in terms of the individual's self, world, past, and future. The trauma of the loss of one dearly loved provokes varying degrees of upheaval in all these cognitive structures and these "alterations in the content of the person's underlying structures affect his or her affective state and behavioral pattern" (Beck, Rush, et al., 1979:8). Schwartzberg and Halgin (1991), and other researchers (Janoff-Bulman, 1985, 1989a & b; Pollio, 1982), have noted some of the cognitive strategies adopted by grieving individuals in the account-making process, along with some of the changes in affective (i.e., emotional, feeling-based) states and behavior patterns. The cognitive restructuring strategies adopted by the individual in the account-making process involve attempts at finding understanding of, and meaning in, the death in terms of the mourner's *past, future, world* and *self* schemas.

Cognitive Restructuring Based on the Past   One cognitive restructuring strategy used in assimilating the news of the death of a loved one involves focusing on the past history of the decedent, especially their past habits, behaviors, lifestyle, or health-related practices. In the case of loss by suicide, for example, loved ones may seek answers by constructing a shared psychological history or biography of the deceased which provides a context in which the suicide may begin to make some sense (Walter, 1996). Psychologist Howard R. Pollio (1982:237) suggests

that ". . . remembering the past, seems not only to help us order and be ordered by our experiences, it also helps us note that the present 'time' was preceded by a preceding 'time,' which was preceded by an earlier one, and so on." In this way, we attempt to embrace the experience of loss through a sense of continuity over time.

According to Schwartzberg and Halgin (1991:242), in an effort to understand the cause of death, we may point out ". . . that the deceased person smoked too much, was overweight, drove too fast, was sexually promiscuous or did not exercise enough." One individual, grieving the death of a loved one, stated, "Yes I asked why, but he didn't take good care of himself. He was overweight. He had the odds against him. He smoked . . . I do wonder why, kind of. But still, it wasn't like he was in great shape and then he died" (Schwartzberg and Halgin, 1991:242). Another person, commenting on the insensitivity of others who employed the past-based strategy, stated, "When I told some people that my dad died of lung cancer, they immediately asked, 'Did he smoke?'—as though that would explain it all, make it all sensible and understandable. I wonder, if my father had died of a heart attack, would they have asked, 'Did he eat bacon and eggs every morning?' "

These strategies help us to maintain the belief in personal control of our self and our world by reinforcing the idea that the deceased person did not die arbitrarily, but rather as a result of his or her own past action or inaction. In other cases, we come to understand the death in terms of medical incompetence or misjudgements by physicians. Here, too, the strategy, based on past events, may help us maintain a belief that the person did not die randomly, but, instead, as a result of the past actions or inactions of others.

Cognitive Restructuring Based on the Future   Cognitive restructuring based on the future involves an attempt to assimilate and accommodate the death of a loved one in terms of how the loss has triggered, or might trigger, some future developmental changes in us. If the act of remembering allows us to restructure the past and find meaning in the event of loss, then, according to Pollio (1982:237), ". . . anticipating and planning . . . builds the future out of both the present and the past" and may allow us to glean some meaning from the loss.

Understanding the loss in terms of the future is especially likely when the relationship to the deceased person is one of dependency, such as losing a beloved parent, spouse or lifelong partner or friend. For example, a grieving adult, searching for meaning in the death of his elderly parent, says, "If there was any reason for my father's death, it was to open my eyes and force me to grow up" (Schwartzberg and Halgin, 1991:241). Other persons may use the death of a loved one to motivate them in their future pursuits, or to dedicate their future accomplishments as a tribute to the deceased. An adult woman, mourning the death of her mother, said, "The way I resolved my mother's death . . . is that I sort of made a deal with myself: I know that my mother's happiest time was when people said to her, 'You have a lovely family' or 'You have beautiful children,' so if I can go through life and show people what a good person I am because of my mother, she'll live on through me" (Schwartzberg and Halgin, 1991:243).

In the midst of the experience of loss, we may attempt to minimize cognitive disruption by comparing the death to more painful or upsetting scenarios that could have evolved in some imagined futuristic scenario. Finding ways in which a situation "could have been worse" is a common cognitive coping strategy in the aftermath of a death (Taylor, Wood and Lichtman, 1983). In other instances, the grieving person may focus on the pain and suffering their loved one would have had to endure if they had not died. In these cases, the survivor may find relief in the fact that the death has finally occurred. In these future-based cognitive strategies, the grieving person comes to understand the death in terms of its impact on their own future actions and beliefs, as well as on projected future experiences of the now deceased. In so doing, the mourner is better able to assimilate the cognitive impact of the trauma.

Cognitive Restructuring Based on the World   In other instances, grieving individuals assimilate the event of the death in terms of their understanding of how the world works, including objective scientific concepts or subjective religion-based teachings and insights. Science-based account making may center on the fact that the disease which killed the loved one ran in the person's family, for example. Such a grieving person may point out that, "Death is scientific . . ., you're biologically born, you live biologically, and you die because your brain ceases to function" (Schwartzberg & Halgin, 1991:342). This strategy may allow the grieving person to focus more on the inevitability of the death than on their emotional reaction to the loss. Once again, the individual is attempting to maintain a belief that the world is orderly and knowable, and that death is a predictable life event.

Schwartzberg and Halgin (1991:241) note that grieving individuals with strong beliefs based on religious teachings ". . . will often rely on their faith, not only for emotional solace, but also for a helpful explanation of why the death occurred." In summoning the existence of God, a higher power, the spirit of the ancestors, or another transcendent entity who ultimately controls fate, ". . . it remains possible for a grieving person to assimilate the traumatic event through belief that life continues to follow a meaningful path." One woman said of her mother's death, "I believe there's a force of good in the world, and when good, strong people die they become part of that, and that's where I feel she is."

Cognitive Restructurings Based on Self   As fundamental beliefs are brutally strained and the rules that previously guided our lives are nullified, our challenge is to revise and reintegrate our sense of self and the assumptions which constitute the self. The *self-schema* is the major cognitive schema ". . . containing every-thing a person assumes to be true about the world and self on the basis of previous experience. . . . It determines his or her needs, emotions, and behavior and gives rise to hopes, wishes, fantasies and dreams—all of which are signifi-cantly affected by the death of a loved one" (Rando, 1995:217).

Through a combination of cognitive restructuring strategies, we attempt to assimilate and accommodate the death of a loved one by struggling to find ways of explaining, understanding, conceptualizing, or minimizing the impact of the loss on our own sense of self (Schwartzberg and Halgin, 1991:242). Those of us who find an answer to the question of "Why?"—be it God's will, our mother's obesity, or the negligence of incompetent doctors—are striving to preserve the assumptions that had guided our lives before the loss by cognitively minimizing the traumatic impact of the event and the potential upheaval of our assumptive world.

COMPANION THROUGH THE DARKNESS *(continued)*

"Journal: The guilt emerges like a thick fog that permeates every airspace available, surrounds everything, tucks itself away in corners and hovers close to the ground, waiting to trip me. What did I withhold telling him out of principle? Out of laziness? Out of a stupid confidence that I had *time* to tell him? Did I tell him that day that I loved him? That week? Somehow, the only thing I can think was important was telling him I love him. I talk to the ground, to the air, to the pillow, I get on my knees on his snowy grave and weep the words into the snow, melting it, but finding only frozen ground beneath. I confess all to a dead body, waxen-faced in a coffin, that doesn't look a thing like him. I only want to crawl in next to him while I am simultaneously repulsed at the makeup morticians have smeared all over any part of him that might show.

That's grief."

Source: Stephanie Ericsson. (1991). The Agony of Grief, *Utne Reader,* September/October, pp. 75–78.

For some people, the cognitive restructuring process ends in a reconfirmation or strengthening of previously held beliefs and their own sense of self. In most cases, loved ones assimilate and comprehend the fact of the death in the days surrounding the funeral or memorial service. For others, however, the death of their loved one may be the catalyst for a dramatic cognitive upheaval in how they make sense of themselves and the world, and their cognitive restructuring may extend into weeks, months, or years. The closer the relationship, and the more unexpected, shocking, or sudden the death, the lengthier the process of cognitive restructuring is likely to be. The cognitive upheaval may involve profound changes that extend beyond the emotional expression phase of the mourning process, into the phase of psychological reintegration and, in some cases, to psychospiritual transformation.

THE EMOTIONAL EXPRESSION PHASE

Emotion is e-motion, movement out, seeking exit. As we emotionally confront our loss and experience the pain of separation from our loved one, very intense and varied emotional grief reactions unfold. Waves of tears wash over us with each reminder of the deceased, the belly tightens, and sleep is fitful as dreams in which the dead person is still alive haunt us. At times, the frustration and confusion associated with acknowledging and assimilating the reality of our loss may lead to protest reactions in the form of outbursts of intense anger, as when parents bitterly blame one another for the death of their child, or adult brothers and sisters accuse one another for having failed to do something that might have prolonged the life of their elderly parent.

Physical disturbances are common in the emotional expression phase: Weakness, sleep disturbances, loss of appetite, headaches, back pain, indigestion, shortness of breath, heart palpitations, and occasional dizziness and nausea may manifest (Stroebe & Stroebe, 1987). We may even begin to adopt the mannerisms and symptoms of the deceased. All of these grief reactions can be intensified and prolonged following premature and violent deaths.

Among the challenges we face during the emotional expression phase is feeling, identifying, accepting, and giving some form of expression to all of the emotional turmoil, cognitive confusion, and physical pain that may be experienced. As Worden (1991) has reminded us, not everyone experiences pain the

We sense a profound emptiness in our world during the emotional expression phase of the mourning process. Some of us may seek out the company of loved ones to cry, to share an account of the loss and to be held. Others may socially withdraw into depression and despair. © *Alan Oddie*

same way, or with the same intensity, but no one loses someone to whom they are deeply attached without experiencing some level of pain.

We sense a profound emptiness in our world during this phase of the mourning process (Carson & Butcher, 1992). Tense, restless anxiety may alternate with lethargy and fatigue. Weeping may be uncontrolled. Sadness may be mixed with anger that is targeted at doctors who failed, at friends and relatives thought to be unappreciative, even at the dead person for abandoning us. Even the motives of people who try to reach out to us are sometimes suspected, and we may alienate our family and friends with our emotional lability, irritability and quarrelsomeness. Most painful of all is our tendency to blame ourselves and to be overwhelmed with feelings of guilt and self-disgust for having treated the deceased badly or for having done too little to prevent the death or for not having taken the time to tell our parent, grandparent, spouse, child, or friend of our love and appreciation for them. "If only I had visited her on Mother's Day." "Why didn't I know how sick he really was?" "How could I have. . . ?" "Why didn't I. . . ?" "I should have known." The words repeat over and over as the feelings and emotions move to the foreground of our experience.

A sense of emotional disorganization and despair fills our lives, and we find it difficult to function in our normal, everyday environment. Interior emotional confusion is central to our experience now as we alternate between avoiding reminders of the deceased and cultivating memories of our loved one. In the midst of emotional devastation, some of us may desperately seek the companionship of others with a need to share our account of the loss experience, to cry and be held. Others may socially withdraw into darkness and depression.

COMPANION THROUGH THE DARKNESS *(continued)*

"*Journal:* And then there's the inertia. You know the walk has to be shoveled and instead of saying, 'In a minute . . .' you say, 'Maybe next week . . .' You know there's a million things to do, but you just have to sit for a while. Just for a while. And a while turns into months.

People say, 'How are you?' and they have that look in their faces again. And I look at them like they're crazy. I think, how do you think I am? I'm not strong enough for talk. The phone rings incessantly with the damned question, how are you, how are you, how are you, how are you? Finally, I say, 'Fine.' Just so they'll stop. And maybe they'll stop calling because they feel better now. Then one day, my strength is down, and I actually tell someone how I am and they can't handle it, they can't understand, and I never hear from them again.

A woman said to me, in a comforting tone of conspiracy, 'My mother had breast cancer and lost her right breast . . .' 'Oh,' I say, 'that's awful . . .' and wonder if that is supposed to be some sort of comparison. A tit, a husband—same thing? Strange how people want to join you in your intensity, your epiphany, by trying to relate—grabbing at straws of a so-called 'like' experience while simultaneously they are repulsed by the agony. They see you on the street, driving by and pretending they don't see you."

Stephanie Ericsson. (1991). The Agony of Grief, *Utne Reader,* September/October, pp. 75–78.

Secondary Losses and Psychic Scars

Two additional challenges to be encountered during the emotional expression phase of mourning involve identifying and grieving secondary losses associated with the deceased, and learning to cope with the psychological scar left in the wake of the death. It may take considerable time to meet these challenges directly, especially when the relationship with our loved one was of long duration and exceptional closeness (Rando, 1995).

A secondary loss is ". . . a physical or psychosocial loss that coincides with or develops as a consequence of an initial loss" (Rando, 1995:217). Secondary losses refer to the empty places we find in our own lives over time as we adjust to a world absent of the one we loved. The changes in our life and in our environment encompass the physical, emotional, intellectual, financial, social, and spiritual dimensions of life. The many roles fulfilled by our loved one are not wholly realized until months and years after the loss. Life changes may involve the mundane, such as placing one less setting at the dining-room table, rearranging the furniture, and simplifying our lifestyle due to financial changes. They may also include profound shifts involving the discovery of new avenues for physical, emotional, intellectual, and spiritual engagement. Remembering our loved one and grieving the loss of the relationship we once shared is sometimes deeply painful and may result in profound sadness, spontaneous crying, yearning, and bouts of depression. At the same time, we may obsessively question what we could have done differently so as to postpone the inevitable. These interior ruminations involving negative self-talk (Meichenbaum, 1985) may create a sense of failure within us, leaving us feeling helpless in a world that feels more threatening. Our challenge is to adjust emotionally to a world without the deceased while continuing to recollect and emotionally to re-experience our loved one and the relationship we shared (Raphael, 1983; Rando, 1995).

The misuse of alcohol and other drugs, both prescribed and not prescribed, is a danger that we must confront during the emotional phase of the mourning process. Experiencing the emotional pain of a loss is sometimes overwhelming and the temptation to "deaden" that pain with drugs may present an ongoing struggle because the death of someone we deeply love can create a painful psychic wound in us. Like a physical wound, the psychic wound will leave a scar, similar to a scar that remains after a physical injury. And like a healed scar, it may not in any way interfere with our overall functioning in our day-to-day life. Yet, on certain days and under particular circumstances, it may act up, it may ache, and require our attention. Rando (1995:218) states, "Not unlike the individual who has been victimized by being physically assaulted and robbed, the bereaved experience anxiety; anger; self-blame; guilt; an assault on their assumptive world; a sense of unfairness; a loss of control, predictability, safety, and security; feelings of helplessness and powerlessness; and posttraumatic stress reactions." The next phase of the mourning process, psychological reintegration, involves learning to live with the fact of a loved one's absence and moving forward in a new and somewhat strange world, despite the fact that the psychic scar caused by the loss of our loved one remains—perhaps forever.

THE PSYCHOLOGICAL REINTEGRATION PHASE

During the psychological reintegration phase of the mourning process, the mourner is challenged to integrate new coping responses, behaviors, cognitive strategies, and assumptions so as to deal better with a world without the deceased. As the mourner struggles to find some purpose in the life lost, he or she is confronted with the need to integrate new ways of being in the world.

A World Turned Upside Down

According to clinical psychologists Steven Schwartzberg and Richard Halgin (1991:241), as Americans, we typically see the world ". . . as benevolent, regard ourselves with favorable self esteem, and bring meaning to life-events by believing in an abstract sense of justice, a strong sense of personal control, and by minimizing the importance of chance in determining events in our lives." As unrealistic as these beliefs and assumptions may be, they provide a stable cognitive framework for making personal sense of the world, as long as they remain untested (Janoff-Bulman, 1989a & b).

After the crisis of the death of one dearly loved, however, these beliefs may shatter, may be turned upside down, and may no longer be useful to undergird our cognitive world and sense-of-self. For example, what happens to our beliefs in personal control of our world when we are forced to confront a loved one's painful illness and tears over which personal control is futile? Or how can you or I continue to believe that the world is just and fair, and that people get what they deserve, after experiencing the death of our child from SIDS, random gunfire, or an automobile accident? How?

Reflective Silence

Reflective Silence.

   It is not easy to find the words to express grief and, as caregiver, we can easily react to our own anxiety, letting it get in the way and thus prevent the words from being found.

Reflective Silence.
There is a special quality of reflective silence within a relationship, however, which can enable the griever to find his or her own words. As you listen and give attention, they will begin to trust you not to rush in with the useless platitudes or controlling questions, and will be able to risk sharing more of their feelings with you.

Reflective Silence.
This silence is not an empty silence but contains acceptance and understanding. This lets the bereaved know that you value them and what they have to say about their experience of loss. It also tells them, without words, that you know they must struggle to find their own words for their sorrow and their own sense of meaning for their existence.

Reflective Silence.

Source: Adapted from: S. Lendum and G. Syme. (1992). Gift of Tears: A Practical Approach to Loss and Bereavement Counseling. Tavistick/Routledge, New York, p. 83.

Beyond the process of recognizing, account making, and emotionally expressing our anguish and pain, there are deeper forms of cognitive restructuring involving accommodation to new assumptions about ourselves in the world without the one we love. These changes are long term, continuing past the grieving process into the larger mourning process. They include revising and restructuring our assumptions regarding our own existence in the world (Rando, 1995; Parkes, 1988), integrating memories and meanings associated with the deceased into new ways of being in the world (Horowitz, 1986), restoring our self-esteem and sense of self-mastery (Taylor, 1983), as well as encountering possible spiritual transformations in life (Dershimer, 1990; Doka & Morgan, 1993). Caregivers, in assisting the mourning individual in the psychological reintegration phase, must address these long-term changes in the mourner's world.

Psychological Reintegration and Coping Strategies

Coping strategies employed during the psychological reintegration phase can be divided into three classes (Carver 1989; Folkman & Lazarus, 1988; R. E. Smith, 1993): focusing on problems, focusing on emotions, and seeking social support.

Problem-Focused Coping   Problem-focused coping involves attempts by the mourner to confront and deal directly with the loss so as to lessen her or his distress. Problem-focused behaviors include planning, active problem solving, suppressing competing activities, exercising restraint, asserting oneself, and other activities directed at mastering the loss experience.

Emotion-Focused Coping   Emotion-focused coping is aimed less at dealing with the loss directly and more at managing our appraisal of the loss as well as our stress reactions and emotions connected to the loss. Some adaptive strategies involve minimizing the emotional impact of the death, controlling grief reactions through meditation or relaxation techniques, or positively reinterpreting or reframing the event of loss. Other emotion-focused coping strategies are maladaptive and are capable of precipitating profound complications in the mourning process. These include emotion-focused defense mechanisms such as denial, repression, escape/avoidance, and wishful thinking.

Seeking Social Support   A third class of reintegration strategies involves seeking social support, that is, turning to others for assistance, guidance, and emotional support. Thus, the widow or widower in mourning might choose to join a support group, while a bereaved teenager might choose to visit a school counselor for guidance and support.

Although mourners tend to use various combinations of these coping strategies, research indicates that men are more likely to adopt problem-focused strategies while women are more likely to seek social support (Ptacek, Smith, & Zanas, 1992). Women also appear to be more likely than men to report using emotion-focused coping strategies (Eccles, 1991).

Reintegration and Self-Efficacy

One particularly powerful factor in determining an individual's coping success during the psychological reintegration phase is the individual's perception of his or her own *self-efficacy* (Bandura, 1982). People tend to avoid activities and challenges they believe exceed their coping abilities and to undertake those they consider themselves capable of handling. Efficacy expectations influence the decision to attempt a new behavior or activity, the length of time committed to the attempt, and the effort that will be involved. Low efficacy expectations in the face of obstacles result in our experiencing serious doubts or giving up, while high efficacy expectations will result in greater efforts being extended to achieve desired results.

Some older widows, for example, are active in church or civic activities, social affairs, or travel. Others are largely isolated and uninvolved with life. Objective circumstances and resources may be similar for both sets of widows; however, the

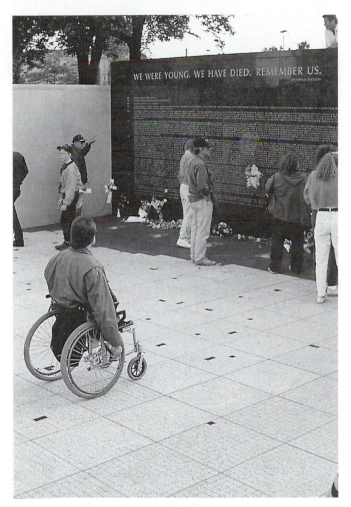

During the psychological reintegration phase of the mourning process, mourners may keep a lost person "alive" through symbolic representation and interaction. Memorials, such as the Vietnam Veterans Memorial in Washington, D.C., often facilitate this process. © *Steve Skjold/PhotoEdit*

former experience a high sense of self-efficacy while the latter do not. Many persons reach their later years with a high sense of self-efficacy, having learned throughout their life that they are capable individuals whose efforts will be rewarded. The circumstances of old age, the experience of multiple losses in later life, along with other changes over which they have no control may lead to a low sense of self-efficacy even among persons who felt otherwise when younger. In addition, the family and friends of older persons with an already low sense of self-efficacy may expect them to react to the losses of later life by giving up more easily and withdrawing. Changes in our assumptive world may be a source of distress or a source of increasing confidence, depending on their nature and our own perception of self-efficacy.

The Time to Heal

"It's been 10 months since my teenage son was killed in an accident. Word has gotten back to me that people are disappointed that I did not get to their graduation parties, or follow through on invitations to their cottages. The best gift you can give someone grieving is not to place expectations or standards upon them. It's a very confused world we are trying to function in during this time.

Life will never be the same. Yes, I have changed. Did you really want me to stay the same after looking death and mystery in the face? Priorities change. The soccer game that was important last year does not seem as important this year. It's not as easy to gear up for the activities that used to fill my time and interest.

It is a sad time, but it is also a very sacred and healing time. It takes time. It is a uniquely individual process, and only a few people seem to understand and respect that it's important that we be allowed to grieve, for that is the only way to heal. The tears have to be shed. The anger and frustration need to be experienced. Please don't be scared off by these stages. They are a normal and healthy process. There is incredible pressure from society, family and friends to 'get over this.' You don't get 'over' death and grieving, you go through it. Step by step, teardrop by teardrop. We don't want to be rescued from this healing work. You can't 'get our minds off it,' or 'know what is best for us.' . . . Just be there with us. . . . It will be friends who are supportive, accepting and non-judgmental. Friends will allow for this journey to be healing."

Source: Denise Anderson. (1995). I hear you. Please listen. *Thanatos,* 20(1), 11.

Inner Representations of the Deceased

During the psychological reintegration phase of the mourning process, the mourner is challenged to alter, relinquish, and modify old roles and behaviors, including a change from an actual relationship with the deceased to one based on symbolic representation and interaction. Mourners may keep a lost person "alive" internally by continuing to hear the voice of the deceased giving guidance, support, judgment, or criticism. Some mourners begin to identify strongly with the deceased person, or become aware of specific ways in which they feel similar to him or her. As a means of keeping a lost person psychologically alive, some people engage in very active behaviors, such as writing or talking to that person, that serve to maintain some type of relationship.

From the perspective that the death of a loved one is a traumatic event that disrupts a person's framework of basic assumptions, these strategies to keep the deceased person alive serve the important function of lessening the assault on the mourner's fundamental beliefs. By mitigating the finality of the loss but not denying the factual reality of the death, the mourner attempts to preserve the basic structure of his or her assumptions about self and the world so that the loss can be integrated into life. Although identification strategies may be problematic for some individuals, for others they are a source of comfort and solace (Schwartzberg & Halgin, 1991; Klass, 1995).

Beginnings and Endings

Based on years of study of grieving adults, Parkes (1972) describes the reintegration phase of the mourning process as beginning with feelings of emptiness, despair, and loss coupled with a desire to find oneself, and concluding with the establishment of a new identity and new patterns of behavior. Glick, Weiss, and Parkes (1974) found in their study of the mourning process that psychological reintegration was reported when individuals experienced the following:

- More control of their lives
- Fewer tears
- Fading of feelings of abandonment
- A personal sense of recovery and higher energy levels
- A growing interest in activities and in being with others
- Times of peace
- Less often seeking advice from others
- A new sense of respect for self and confidence in the ability to cope
- Less fear of being alone

TURNING POINT

"There he was! Walking toward me as if coming out of a mist. There he was—that lanky 17-year-old whose life I loved better than my own. He looked deeply into my eyes and with a grin on his face, the way he used to when he was 'buttering me up.' Not a word was spoken, but everything was said that needed to be said for my turning point to come.

It was time to resume life. I would not be bitter, but in loving memory I would be better. I would live again because I knew that my boy lived again. My own Christian faith was to be retrofitted. It offered meaning and purpose within the shadow of my loss. It asserted that though God does not intend my sufferings, He involves Himself in them. My pain and loss were not to be the end of life. Rather, it was to be a beginning—a beginning to a more compassionate life of quality and caring."

Source: Klass (1995), p. 256.

Many thanatologists (Glick, Weiss, & Parkes, 1974; Dershimer, 1990; Rando, 1995) point out that the reintegration phase of mourning involves the recognition that, although we do not love the deceased person any less, there are also other people to be loved. Having been immersed in countless endings surrounding the loss of our loved one, we now begin to sense some new beginnings, invest in new relationships, and experience a new dawning of life that slowly replaces the previous darkness.

Some mourners have difficulty with this task of investing energy in new love relationships, feeling that it somehow involves a dishonoring of the deceased's memory or because they fear investing emotional energy into another relationship that may also end in loss. The successful completion of the task of psychological reintegration is sometimes hindered when the bereaved holds onto past attachments and refuses to embrace new ones. This task may be the most difficult of all. Yet to leave it undone is be stuck in a condition of not loving (Rando, 1995).

THE PSYCHOSPIRITUAL TRANSFORMATION PHASE

In the mourning after the death of a loved one, when basic personal beliefs and assumptions are suddenly and dramatically questioned, the most fundamental existential and spiritual issues of a person's life may come into play. For some individuals, a close death may trigger a profound, growth-oriented transformation that fundamentally changes beliefs and attitudes about life, death, love, compassion, or God. The mourning process may lead to a spiritual awakening for people with no prior religious convictions, and strengthen the beliefs of those who already have a spiritual foundation. The question of whether or not human beings are religious and spiritual by nature has been argued for centuries. Observation suggests that, in one way or another, most of us find things that we regard as holy; commit ourselves to people or ideas that transcend immediacy; and try to find ways to link ourselves to life beyond this lifetime. People who are not aware of their psychospiritual yearnings are often surprised to learn how much they may have developed spiritually over the months or years of mourning the loss of one dearly loved.

Richard Dershimer, (1990) notes that the opportunity for such a transformative experience may occur particularly with an illness that allows time for the dying person and loved ones to deal gradually with the loss. By facing the reality of impending death with honesty and time to address the complex cognitions and emotions involved, the experience of watching a loved one die can potentially be transformative. The parent burying a child, the spouse sitting at the deathbed of a lifelong companion and friend are left to question the meaning and purpose of this life. This questioning process has been called a crisis in faith, or a turning point in life that could make everything different from then on.

REINTEGRATION

"I really don't feel there was much left of me. I really didn't know what I was or who I was or what kind of being I was. It seemed it always revolved about the two of us all the time. Your total self, how you cope—it seems like it always just revolves around two people. Even just thinking about something, I would say to myself, 'Well, I know that David would think the other way.' He was such a part of everything I did that it was a total aloneness. . . . I'm beginning to find myself now, and I'm beginning to feel good about this, because what I'm finding out is really neat."

Source: Shuchter (1986), p. 266.

Spirituality and Meaning

For an experience to qualify as spiritual, Klass (1995) sets forth two characteristics that are implied. First, the person encounters or merges with what was formerly understood as not self or other. Whether occurring in normal waking consciousness or in an altered state of consciousness (e.g., a dream, daydream, or fantasy), the experience involves a partial dissolution of ego boundaries "so the individual feels at one with another person, with the divine, or with the environment" (Klass, 1995:244). Second, the person becomes aware of a higher power, a higher intelligence, purpose, or order in the universe outside the person's control but to which the person may conform his or her life. At this point, according to Klass (1995:244), "the person feels his or her life is more authentic, more meaningful, . . . the person's thinking is 'set straight' or true, and his or her actions toward others are right and true." Such insights into leading a meaningful life have been codified in various religious traditions, as in the *doctrine* of Christianity, the *dharma* of Hinduism, the *tao* in Chinese religion, and, of course, the notions of "right living" and "right action" embedded in the Buddha's *Eightfold Path to Enlightenment*.

The belief in an afterlife—either as a continuation of previously held beliefs or as a new idea—may be the most common spiritual transformation observed in mourning individuals. Beliefs in an afterlife take different forms. Some people, particularly those with strong and traditional religious beliefs, tend to speak of a somewhat-concrete belief in the concept of heaven by thinking of it as a place where their departed loved one has gone. Some people use religion to find meaning in the loss and to gain solace in the comforting rituals that surround the death and period of mourning. McIntosh, Silver, and Wortman (1993), for example, in a study of 124 parents who had lost an infant to sudden infant death

In mourning the death of a loved one, the most fundamental existential and spiritual issues of a person's life may come into play. This questioning process has been called a crisis in faith, or a turning point in life that could make everything different from then on.
(© *Jean-Claude LeJeune/Stock, Boston*)

syndrome, found that religious and spiritual beliefs were positively related to cognitive processing, to finding meaning in the death, and to the parent's perception of social support, and were indirectly related to greater well-being and less distress among parents 18 months after their infants' deaths.

Ross and Pollio (1991) examined the meaning that death held for 26 adults, approximately half from church study groups and half graduate students in psychology. Participants completed a metaphor inventory and described the metaphors that most closely reflected their views of death. Metaphors focused on death either negatively (as a barrier to life's meanings), ambivalently (as an essentially negative condition made acceptable by a variety of mitigating factors), or positively (as a reinstatement or transformation of life's meanings). An analysis evaluating the influence of religiosity and spirituality on the meanings of death revealed that members of church groups viewed death significantly more frequently as a transformation of life's meanings than did nonchurch participants, who viewed death more frequently as a barrier to life's meanings.

Canadian thanatologist Frederick Boersma (1989) discusses the case of a woman who experienced the perinatal loss of four children due to birth complications, in which inner voice dialog occurred spontaneously through prayer and active imagination and reflected a spiritual experience of God/Christ that guided her through the mourning process.

Some may seek simplistic religious designs or precut spiritual models that fit any person and every situation (Dershimer, 1990). For others, a belief in the afterlife takes the form of a conception that the deceased person stays alive in the memories of people who are still living. Dershimer (1990) maintains that the specific ways in which people find meaning—such as a belief in heaven, reincarnation, or a spiritual order to the universe—may be less important than the process itself. In other words, the ability to reascribe meaning to a changed world through existential or spiritual transformation may be more significant than the specific content by which that need is filled. This perspective is compatible with an existential viewpoint that emphasizes the importance for individuals to ascribe meaning to their actions and their lives. Tillich (1952), for example, proposed that "existential anxiety" results when individuals acknowledge their own mortality or when they must come to terms with helplessness in the face of circumstances beyond their control. Frankl (1984) argued that the ability to find meaning in suffering, to find a spiritual or transcendent purpose, is vital for optimal

DO YOU BELIEVE:

In the healing power of personal prayer?
   YES 82%   NO 13%

Praying for someone can help cure their illness?
   YES 73%   NO 21%

God sometimes intervenes to cure people who have a serious illness?
   YES 77%   NO 18%

In the ability of faith healers to make people well through faith or personal touch?
   YES 28%   NO 63%

Doctors should join their patients in prayer if the patients request it?
   YES 64%   NO 27%

Source: From a poll of 1004 adult Americans taken for *Time*/CNN on June 12–13, 1996. Sampling error is + or −3.1%. "Not sures" omitted. In *Time* magazine, June 24, 1996, p. 62.

human functioning in the face of adversity (Dershimer, 1990; Schwartzberg & Halgin, 1991; Harvey, 1996).

Spiritual Meaning and Caregiving

Loss, grief, and mourning may cause some individuals to become bitter at life and to distance themselves from spirituality. The death of a loved one may lead to questioning or abandoning the faith that such persons had previously taken for granted. For mourners who cannot reconcile the "why" of their loss through traditional religious doctrine and ritual, other strategies may help give a sense of spiritual meaning or purpose to their suffering. For example, people may become involved in philanthropic, political, or caregiving work that specifically relates to the illness or manner of death experienced by their loved one. By so doing—by coping actively rather than passively—the mourner may discover meaning in the loss, as if to say, "This death was not in vain" (Schwartzberg & Halgin, 1991:244).

American philanthropist George Soros, for example, contributed more than $183 million to philanthropic projects in 1993, including the Project on Death in America. He says, "I chose the culture of dying as one of the areas I wanted to address . . . because of my experiences with the death of my parents, both of whom I was very devoted to and loved dearly." Koros was present at his father's death in 1963, "yet I let him die alone. The day after he died I went to my office. I didn't talk about his death. I certainly didn't participate in it. After reading Kubler-Ross, I learned that . . . I could have held his hand as he lay dying. . . . I just didn't know that it might have made a difference—for both of us." Years later, Soros, confronted with his dying mother, participated in her dying: "I reassured her. Her dying was really a positive experience for all of us." The attempt to bring meaning to these experiences of loss prompted Soros to found the Project on Death in America, with the goal of promoting "a better understanding of the experiences of dying and bereavement and by doing so help[ing] transform the culture surrounding death" (Soros, 1995:2).

SEARCHING FOR THE SACRED IN AMERICA: 1994

- Percent of Americans who say they feel the need to experience spiritual growth: 58

- Percent who have had a revelation from God in the last year: 20

- Percent who have seen or sensed angels: 13

- Percent who have had a religious or mystical experience: 33

- Percent who sense the sacred in church or at worship services: 50

- Percent who sense the sacred during meditation: 45

Source: Newsweek Poll of 756 adults conducted Nov. 3–4, 1994. Margin of error ±4%. *Newsweek,* November 28, 1994.

Psychospiritual Transformation and Faith

Spiritual/existential transformation involves *faith,* that is, the willful suspension of our order-seeking, controlling behavior. According to Dershimer (1990) we simply agree to accept that there is some greater order, purpose, structure, and meaning that is not self-evident in the seeming absurdity of events such as the premature death of our loved one. The exercise of faith and the acceptance of an order beyond our control does not mean we concede our free will or relinquish our desire to be in control. In a sense, we achieve our greatest control over our living when we choose to exercise faith. When confronted by a mourning parent whose child has died and who asks, "Why has God done this to me?" there is no satisfactory answer. When the mourner has worked through the mourning process, however, there may be an emergence of faith and a willingness to accept the pain and suffering, as well as to see his or her life as a part of some greater pattern that escapes the cause–effect logic of our scientific worldview (Klass, 1995).

> "My mother's death was more recent . . . She had this experience of walking up to the gates of heaven, and I was accompanying her. She was worried that she might drag me with her. So I reassured her that I was firmly ensconced on this earth and she should not worry. Her dying was really a very positive experience for all of us because of the way she handled herself and the way the family, not just me but particularly my children, could participate in it."
>
> GEORGE SOROS (1995), p. 2.

Psychospiritual Transformation and Joy

Having met the challenges of psychological reintegration and psychospiritual transformation, many mourners are able to identify positive, joyful, and triumphant aspects of their mourning experience. Kessler (1987), for example, discovered that many of her subjects regarded the mourning process as liberating: Over half mentioned feeling freed from previously limiting ties. Glick, Weiss, and Parkes (1974) found that many subjects in their study felt that they had become stronger and more confident people through the mourning process. Similar results are reported by Shuchter (1986), who found that, by the end of 2 years, the majority of widows and widowers studied were able to regard their grief and mourning as "growth-promoting." They perceived themselves to be more realistic, spiritual, patient, sensitive, autonomous, assertive, and open in their everyday lives. Their experiences enabled them to reflect on their personal values, put things in a new perspective, and appreciate more important things in life.

Complicated Mourning

The death of a loved one has been found to be the most powerful source of stress to most of us, and, in the presence of such stress, grieving and mourning can become complicated and unhealthy. Surely in the case of individuals already psychologically disturbed, the turbulence of loss and bereavement can precipitate and exacerbate already existing conditions. In *complicated mourning,* cognitive disorganization and emotional turbulence can persistently overwhelm the individual and may lead some persons to clinical depression and other maladaptive and unproductive behaviors that do not move toward resolution, reintegration, or transformation (Holmes & Rahe, 1967; Worden, 1991; Rando, 1995).

WHO IS GOD?

God • Abai • Adonai • Agaayun • Akua • Ala • Allah • Amaterasu • Amma • Amut • Arnam • Asdulaz • Asila • Banara • Bao • Bari • Bathala • Bhagawan • Bog • Boh • Bozymy • Brahma • Chaacs • Chiuta • Chukwu • Deews • Deus • Devel • Dieu • Dio • Dioz • Dok • Droue • Dumnezeu • Efozu • Foy • Gaddel • Gado • Gaia • Gatt • Gedepo • God • Godimli • Gospod • Gud • Gutip • Hananim • Hera • Hyel • Igziabiheir • Imana • Imbel • Indra • Ishwar • Isor • Isten • Jee • Jincouac • Jumala • Kalou • Kami • Khong • Khuda • Kot • Kunzi • Kwoth • Kyala • Leza • Lubah • Madaru • Manitou • Mawu • Maxam • Mulangu • Muneto • Naibata • Nan • Nawen • Ngai • Ngewo • Nialic • Nkulukumba • Nom • Norin • Nun • Nyambe • Nyasaye • Nzapa • Nzuaoco • Oghene • Olorun • Oqmasi • Ormazd • Owo • Owuso • Pai • Paz • Perendia • Prajow • Rabi • Ramwa • Rongo • Rua • Ruata • Rum • Shango • Shangti • Shashe • Shen • Shido • Shiva • Sibu • Sikwembu • Siyeh • Soko • Tanara • Tane • Tentei • Tev • Theos • Thixo • Torym • Tsuku • Tswashe • Tumpa • Ualare • Unguluve • Vishnu • Wain • Waqu • Were • Xwede • Yala • Yamba • Yataa • Yahwah • Yw • Zambe • Zikhle • Zin • God

Source: Who Is God? *Life,* December, 1990.

Thanatological researchers have, over the years, described various types of complicated mourning reactions, including chronic grief reactions, masked grief reactions, exaggerated grief reactions, and chronic depression (Lindemann, 1944; Worden, 1991; Aiken, 1994; Rando, 1995).

CHRONIC GRIEF REACTIONS

Chronic grief reactions involve reactions to the death of a loved one that are of long duration and do not lead to reintegration or resolution. The survivor yearns and sorrows for the lost loved one for years after the loss. Pincus (1976) isolated cases in which the delay or permanent repression of grief lasted 5, 10, 20 or even 40 years after the death. In such cases, extreme cognitive confusion and repression of emotions associated with the grieving process can precipitate both neurotic and psychotic disorders of various kinds. Persons experiencing chronic grief are often deeply depressed and apathetic, and suffer illogical fears, panic attacks, hallucinations, and other indications of a fragile and tenuous grasp of reality. One particular indication of chronic grief involves psychological mummification of the deceased (Aiken, 1994). In *mummification,* cognitive denial serves emotional repression so that everything connected to the deceased is kept in impeccable order—the deceased's clothes are laid out every day, the table is set for the deceased, and the bereaved individual continues the normal everyday routine of living just as though the deceased were still alive and present. Parkes and Weiss (1983) found that chronic grief is more likely to occur when a loved one dies without warning, when death ends a troubled relationship, or when the bereaved has intense feelings of dependency toward the deceased. Chronic grief is also seen in *anniversary reactions,* in which intense psychological reactions recur on the anniversary of the death.

MASKED GRIEF REACTIONS

Masked grief reactions involve the complete absence of grief reactions (Deutsch, 1937), along with the seepage of repressed emotions into substitute psychosomatic complaints, such as headaches, insomnia, and body pain. In most cases, these reactions go unrecognized by the person as connected to the death. In some cases, masked grief reactions may eventually be associated with stress-related life-threatening diseases, such as heart disease and cancer (Marrone, 1990). The *broken heart syndrome,* which refers to repeated findings that a widow or widower is more likely to die within the first 2 years following the death of a spouse, may be connected with masked grief reactions (W. Stroebe & Stroebe, 1987).

EXAGGERATED GRIEF REACTIONS

Exaggerated grief reactions are often associated with repressed grief reactions from previous losses that erupt in response to a current loss. These involve magnified and disabling reactions to loss that may manifest as phobias, panic reactions, psychosomatic symptoms, or extreme psychiatric disorders, such as paranoid delusions, hallucinations, and regression to a previous developmental level.

CLINICAL DEPRESSION

The difference between *clinical depression* (depression that would be classified as a chronic psychological disorder) and the profound sadness and acute depression experienced in the mourning process is a matter of degree. Clinical depression is classified as a *mood disorder* that includes such symptoms as sad mood, difficulty in sleeping or getting out of bed, loss of appetite, loss of energy, feelings of worthlessness, helplessness, and guilt, and thoughts and fantasies of suicide. In the extreme, those suffering from the most severe depression remain waxlike, motionless, and mute for hours, faces frozen in expressions of slumping grief.

Paying attention is an exhausting effort for the depressed. They cannot take in what they read and what other people say to them. Conversation is a chore, and sometimes they choose to sit alone and remain silent. They tend to speak slowly, after long pauses, using few words and a low, monotonous voice. At other times, they are agitated and cannot sit still. Some pace and wring their hands, sighing, moaning and complaining about how life is difficult. Confronted with a problem, no ideas for its solution occur. There is only the moment and its great heaviness. Depressed people sometimes neglect personal hygiene and appearance and tend toward hypochondriacal complaints of bodily aches and pains. Feeling utterly dejected and helpless, they are also without hope.

There is great variation in the symptoms and signs of depression across the life span. Depression in young children and preadolescents sometimes manifests as hyperactivity and aggressiveness. In adolescents and young adults, depression is often manifested as negativism, antisocial behavior, and a feeling of being misunderstood. In middle-age and older adults, depression is often characterized by distractibility, confusion, and memory loss.

An individual seldom shows all the aspects and symptoms of depression. The diagnosis is typically made only if significant signs are evident, such as a mood of profound sadness that is out of proportion to the person's life situation, compounded by a loss of interest and pleasure in previously enjoyable activities. Most recurrent depressions tend to lessen in intensity over time. But an average untreated episode may stretch on for 6–8 months or even longer (Davison & Neale, 1994).

Complicated grief reactions develop as a result of a number of factors. The *survivor's own history* of depressive illness, personality disorder or role in the family as "strong" or "weak," can influence complicated grief. The *relationship between the survivor and the deceased* may play a major role. If this relationship was of a dependent nature, or if it was based on ambivalent "love/hate" feelings, bereavement may be complicated. The *circumstances of the death* itself—whether the survivor was involved in the death, caused the death, or was involved in multiple losses—may affect the survivor's willingness to accept the death or degree of guilt experienced. In other cases, when a loss is socially negated or disenfranchised or when the *survivor is without any definable social network* to facilitate grieving, complications in the mourning process may require professional intervention.

Individual Differences and the Mourning After

In the process of grieving and mourning a profound loss, our challenge is to overcome the tendency toward cognitive denial, emotional repression, and behavioral passivity. Most people experience various combinations of these cognitive, emotional, and behavioral reactions, and occasionally experience deep depression, suicidal thoughts, and hallucinations. Intense emotional reactions, such as anxiety, fear, depression, guilt, and anger, are common and are powerful expressions of the mourning process for most people. And yet, some individuals do not go through the typical process of mourning. For instance, a person may choose to live out the role of a detached, unaffected family leader during the mourning after, remaining in denial and aloof from feelings and emotions while tending to the management of family affairs. In these cases, cognitive denial may be functioning as a temporary, but adaptive, coping mechanism.

STRUGGLING WITH THE MOURNING AFTER

"Every day, she says, is a struggle just to keep going. On her bad days, she cannot bring herself to get out of bed, and her husband comes home at night to find her still in her pajamas. . . . She cries a great deal; even her lighter moods are continually interrupted with thoughts of failure and worthlessness. Small chores, such as shopping or dressing, seem very difficult, and every minor obstacle seems like an impassable barrier."

Source: Seligman (1975), p. 1.

ADAPTIVE DENIAL

Clinical psychologists have typically thought of cognitive denial as maladaptive, particularly

IN MEMORY OF

"Scott David. It's been 12 yrs. since you left us, but I can still see your smiling face and hear your laugh. There is an empty place in my heart that nothing can fill. I miss you and love you so very much. The holidays will never be the same without you.

   Mom."

Source: Horacek (1996a), pp. 1/25.

because it distorts an accurate perception of reality. However, this need not always be the case. A distinction can be drawn between adaptive and maladaptive denial (Janoff-Bulman, 1989b). Denial is maladaptive when it leads people to engage in inappropriate or risky behaviors or, conversely, stops them from engaging in appropriate behaviors. For example, in the case of HIV (human immunodeficiency virus) transmission, maladaptive denial may lead a person to continue engaging in high-risk sexual or drug-taking activities because he or she feels that "it can't happen to me." *Adaptive denial,* on the other hand, enables people gradually to handle and integrate a significant assault to their fundamental belief system. When a person's basic beliefs about issues such as personal invulnerability, safety, or the benevolence or meaningfulness of the world have been severely strained, as they may be in the case of the death of a loved one, adaptive denial can allow the individual time to adapt to the demands of a new reality. For individuals coping with a significant death, old expectations about how the world functions are no longer valid. Reality is no longer what it was, and denial is sometimes the key mechanism by which the remnants of a coherent worldview can be maintained and a new one created (Janoff-Bulman, 1989b; Wortman & Silver, 1987, 1989).

EXTENDED MOURNING

In his classic paper "Mourning and Melancholia," Sigmund Freud (1957) said that the work of mourning is "complete" when the ego becomes free from and uninhibited by the lost loved object. It is important to note, however, that the mourning process may not have an end point and that the process may in no way signify clinical depression or any other psychological syndrome. Lorraine Siggins (1966) points out that in other writings, Freud recognized that a lost loved object is never totally relinquished, that mourning is never really completed, and that identification with the lost loved one is a healthy and necessary component of mourning. Gerontologist Bruce J. Horacek (1996a, 1995:21–24), following a thorough review of the evidence, concludes "that grief models over the past 25 years have not kept pace with the complicated reality of the mourning process. When a high-grief death occurs, there seems to be no clear, fixed end point. . . , [C]omplete emotional detachment or decathexis seems to be both impossible to achieve and undesirable. Unlike unresolved or chronic grief, this continuing grieving or loss does not significantly impair everyday functioning."

In a recent study of 1,269 obituary "In Memorium" tributes in a medium-sized American newspaper, Horacek (1996a) found that these printed tributes to deceased loved ones continued for from 5 to 50 years and that, in almost equal numbers, the person remembered was a mother, father, son, or daughter. Reviewing these many entries, Horacek found that the tributes reflected ongoing relationships with the deceased that were a mixture of both pleasant, happy memories and a bittersweet sense of continuing loss of the loved person. "There is nothing wrong or pathological about their grieving," Horacek (1996a:25) states. "What's wrong is that most of our traditional models of grieving are pathological." Horacek maintains that we need to rethink and reformulate our old, time-limited models of grieving and mourning and reeducate the grief counselors, psychologists, social workers, and other caregivers who continue to be guided by these models. "Most of these people need protection from many counselors, psychologists and psychiatrists who place unrealistic expectations on them," Horacek concludes. "We need to look at the old saying as it applies to each of us: 'Physician, heal thyself!' "

Horacek's review lends further support to an earlier report by the Committee for the Study of Health Consequences of the Stress of Bereavement of the Institute of Medicine (1984). In a review of research on death and dying, the committee concluded that a clear, fixed end point to grieving and mourning cannot be identified, that a person can adjust to a loss without totally withdrawing attachment, and that for many people the process of mourning continues for a lifetime without being pathological (Horacek, 1996a).

ABSENCE OF DEPRESSION

In other cases, an individual may not be in denial of a significant loss but simply not experience the distress of grieving and mourning. In fact, some psychologists and sociologists question Freud's assumption that depression and distress are key elements or ingredients in the mourning process, as well as the assumption that the absence of depression in the mourning process is a sign of underlying pathology. Camille Wortman and Roxane Silver, for example, take the position that depression, profound sadness or significant distress are not at all inevitable or a necessary component of the mourning process. They maintain that significant depression following a loss is not necessarily healthy "working through" of the loss. On the contrary, those adults with the greatest depression in the months following the death of a loved one are the ones who are still depressed several years later. They point out that such findings do not support the idea that depression is either temporary or a sign that the grief is being "worked through." Conversely, Wortman and Silver's analysis suggests that those who show little or no depression following the death are not more likely to have later difficulties. On the contrary, these adults seem to show the least long-term physical or emotional effects (Silver & Wortman, 1980; Wortman & Silver, 1987, 1989).

Based on the research evidence, Wortman and Silver suggest that rather than there being only one common pattern of resolution or accommodation in response to loss, there are at least three distinct patterns: (1) the "expected" pattern, which involves distress, anger, sadness, and depression followed by some kind of resolution or reintegration, (2) a pattern in which there is little or no distress or depression either immediately or in the longer term, and (3) a pattern of intense and prolonged distress and depression lasting many years. They point out that our cultural norm for grieving and mourning includes the expectations of heightened distress, "working through" the grief, and then getting on with your life. Any bereaved person who does not follow this pattern is likely to be perceived as deviant or unfeeling. In particular, the person who shows little despair or depression may be accused of "not dealing" with the grief, of being "in denial." Silver's and Wortman's research argues that the mourning process is unique to each individual and that those who are not expressing angry feelings or not crying and depressed may not necessarily be denying and repressing at all, but may be coping and healing in deeper and more subtle ways.

Grieving and Mourning: The Work Ahead

In the past few decades, our understanding of the work of coping with dying and death has grown exponentially. This knowledge has been drawn from empirical research, clinical insights, and personal anecdotes; from stage-based, phase-based, task-based, and developmental models; and from theorists in thanatology, psychology, psychiatry, sociology, nursing, gerontology, philosophy, biology, medicine, nursing, and theology. In light of this growing body of knowledge, future research, model building, and new ways of organizing our thinking about coping with dying should do a number of things (Corr, Nabe, & Corr, 1994). First and foremost, they should be *holistic,* in that they provide for understanding all of the dimensions in coping with death and dying: the physical, the psychological, the social, and the spiritual. Second, they should be *global,* in that they provide understanding and insight into the mourning process of all persons, of various ages, and across cultural, religious, gender, and class boundaries. Third, they should seek ways of *empowering* individuals who are coping with death and dying by emphasizing options and choices available to them (Corr, 1992). Fourth, they should focus on and emphasize the *participatory* or shared aspects of coping with death and dying, especially those that promote the gathering together of people in families, small communities, or networks that assist each other in the work of mourning. Fifth, they should be based on models of grieving and mourning that are *open-ended* and not arbitrarily time-limited. Finally, future research and models should be directed to providing broad-based *guidance* to physicians, nurses, other health care professionals, volunteers, and loved ones as to how best to facilitate both the endings and the beginnings that are so much a part of the mourning after.

Chapter Summary

There are many theories about the stages, phases, and tasks related to human grieving and mourning. The four-phase model presented in this chapter tends to bring many of the different loss reactions together. The cognitive restructuring phase involves the reorganization and restructuring of our thoughts and concepts so as to assimilate the news that a loved one no longer occupies that world. The phase of emotional expression involves the challenge of feeling, identifying, accepting, and giving some form of expression to all of the emotional turmoil, cognitive confusion, and physical pain that may be experienced. The psychological reintegration phase is concerned with integrating new coping responses, behaviors, cognitive strategies, and assumptions so as to deal better with a world without the deceased. And the psychospiritual transformation phase involves a profound, growth-oriented transformation that fundamentally changes beliefs and attitudes about life, death, love, compassion, or God.

Loss, grief, and mourning are, in every sense, central phenomena in human existence that we learn to accommodate in either a healthy or a problematic way. In complicated mourning, cognitive disorganization and emotional turbulence can persistently overwhelm the individual and may lead some persons to clinical depression and other maladaptive and unproductive behaviors that do not move toward resolution, reintegration, or transformation.

In the past few decades, our understanding of the work of coping with dying and death has grown exponentially. In light of this growing body of knowledge, future research and model building should seek to be holistic, global, empowering, participatory, and open-ended while providing broad-based guidance to loved ones and caregivers.

FURTHER READINGS

Dershimer, R. A. (1990). *Counseling the Bereaved*. Pergamon Press, New York.

Harvey, J. H. (1995). *Odyssey of the Heart: The Search for Closeness, Intimacy, and Love*. W.H. Freeman, New York.

Harvey, J. H. (1996). *Embracing Their Memory: Loss and the Social Psychology of Storytelling*. Allyn & Bacon, Needham Heights, MA.

Klass, D. (1988). *Parental Grief: Solace and Resolution*. Springer, New York.

Rando, T. A. (1993). *Treatment of Complicated Mourning*. Research Press, Champaign, IL.

Rando, T. A. (1986). *Loss and Anticipatory Grief*. Lexington Books, Lexington, MA.

Raphael, Beverly. (1983). *The Anatomy of Bereavement*. Harper Collins, San Francisco.

Stroebe, W., & Stroebe, M. S. (1987). *Bereavement and Health: The Psychological and Physical Consequences of Partner Loss*. Cambridge University Press, Cambridge.

Worden, J. W. (1991). *Grief Counseling and Grief Therapy: A Handbook for the Mental Health Practitioner*. Springer, New York.

PART TWO

Grieving and Mourning

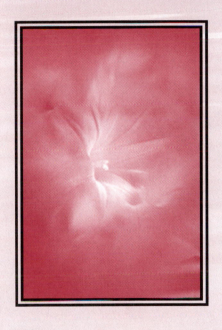

Death, Dying, and the Child

Loss, in its various forms, touches everyone, young and old alike. But the way we deal with loss is intimately tied to our understanding of life and death, as well as to our understanding of our own existence in the world. Infants and toddlers, for example, react both physically and emotionally to the loss of a significant other in their lives. Upon separation from a loved one, they experience varied, often intense, grief reactions, including yearning, crying, protest, anger, sadness, and depression. However, for a young child truly to mourn the death of a loved one, or for a terminally ill child to recognize that she or he is dying, the child must have formed a mature concept of death: that death is *universal* (i.e., all living things die); that death is *inevitable* (i.e., we might prolong life or postpone death, but eventually a living object will die); that death is *irreversible* (i.e., once dead, always dead—there is no returning to life); and that in death *the physical self will no longer exist* (Speece, & Brent, 1992; Speece, 1995).

Now I lay me down to sleep,
I pray the Lord my soul to keep;
And if I die before I wake,
I pray the Lord my soul to take.

Oxford Dictionary of Nursery Rhymes

During early childhood, as our physical development unfolds, personhood also emerges and expands. With personhood comes an understanding that we are part of a family, members of a larger community, and in relationship with one another, with the world, and with nature. In the midst of exploring life, we come to recognize that life also culminates in death. Arrival at such an understanding depends, ultimately, on the child's cognitive, emotional, and personal development of a sense-of-self—a sense of her or his own separate and unique existence.

The Cognitive Perspective

From the cognitive perspective, the child's conception and understanding of death depends on the child's progress through a series of developmental stages, with each stage involving qualitatively more complex forms of thinking than the preceding one. Swiss developmental psychologist Jean Piaget (1952), following decades of study, concluded that the child's cognitive development is like climbing a slippery hill, with slips and advances, fits and starts, with a gradual though uneven development of increasing sophistication. Even though some children advance more quickly than others, the sequence is universally the same: The first stage must precede the second, the second must precede the third, and so on. In this way, each stage holds both the fruits of the past and the seeds for the future.

Decades of study of children's cognitive grasp of death and dying reveals a process that begins to take shape in the first three years of life and reaches completion at 9 or 10 years of age for most children (Nagy, 1948; Speece, & Brent, 1992; Speece, 1995). Piaget described four stages of cognitive development: (1) sensorimotor, (2) preoperational, (3) concrete operational, and, (4) formal operational.

SENSORIMOTOR STAGE

Beginning at birth and lasting for about two years, we come to know the world by touching, grasping, smelling, sucking, chewing, pushing, poking, throwing, banging, shaking, and manipulating many of the objects we come across. Piaget called this the *sensorimotor stage* of development. As we develop, our explorations of the world change predictably. Beginning at 1 month old, we learn about the shape, texture, and substance of objects with the mouth (Gibson & Walker, 1984). At 5 months, we begin to acquire information with our hands or by coordinating the movement of the hands, eyes, and mouth (Rochat, 1989). This sensorimotor mode can be seen in the way young babies try to stuff crayons, toys, and limbs into the mouth—and in the way they pull, push, shake, squeeze, and bang everything they can get their little fingers on. For infants, an object exists in the world only for the moment and only as long as they are in direct sensory contact with it.

Peek-a-Boo!

According to Piaget, the crowning cognitive achievements of the sensorimotor stage involve language acquisition and the capacity for insight learning, that is,

DADDY WENT TO HEAVEN

"Chris was 2 and one-half when his dad died. I had explained that 'Daddy's body was dead. He didn't live anymore. Dead meant that Daddy was never coming back.' Apparently, some well-meaning family member also explained that Daddy had gone to heaven. When Chris asked where heaven was, this person pointed to the sky. Within days, Chris became anxious every time a plane flew overhead. He reached a point where he ran hysterically inside the house and finally refused to go outside to play."

Source: Oaks & Ezell (1993), pp. 117–118.

learning that occurs when a concept or the solution to a problem is suddenly grasped and followed by an immediate change in behavior. Central to our understanding of death and dying during the sensorimotor stage is the development of what Piaget termed *object permanence:* an awareness that objects continue to exist after they disappear from our view.

Piaget (1952) first noticed that whenever he covered a toy with his beret or a handkerchief, babies younger than 8 months did not protest, made no effort to retrieve the toy, and were unaware of its absence—even when the toy made noise. Given this lack of object permanence, it is no wonder that until babies approach their first birthday, they never seem to tire of playing *peek-a-boo,* a game in which each round is met with a fresh look of surprise. At this stage of infancy, "out of sight" quite literally means, "out of mind." Piaget believed that the phenomenon of object permanence was central to the child's development of a sense-of-self and of a clear understanding of the impermanence of his or her own life, as well as the lives of others.

Piaget's discovery of object permanence stimulated empirical research, as well as theoretical speculation that small children, although they react to separation with protest and despair, can mourn the loss of something or someone only at the point that they have realized that things (and people) are permanent in their perceptual lives. Object permanence is linked directly to social and emotional development. It is probably not a coincidence that just as babies become aware of objects that are out of view, they also begin to experience *separation anxiety,* a fear reaction to the absence of their primary caretaker. The baby who is not aware of her or his mother as separate from her- or himself will not seem emotionally distressed by her absence. However, the baby who has achieved object permanence is capable of missing mother or father and may well cry frantically the moment she or he slips out of sight (Hostler, 1978).

During the second year, developments in memory lend object permanence to people no longer in view. At 20 months old, babies who watch an adult hide a Big Bird doll in a desk drawer or behind a pillow are able to find the toy on the next day (DeLoache & Brown, 1983). The second year is also a time when babies become more verbal and more symbolic in their thinking. For the first time, words and images are used to symbolize objects. One object may now serve as a symbol for another, as when children pretend that their spoon is an airplane and their mouth a runway (P.L. Harris & Kavanaugh, 1993).

PREOPERATIONAL STAGE

According to Piaget, as preschoolers, between 2 and 6 years of age, we are in a *preoperational stage* of cognitive development during which we reason in an intuitive, prelogical, and magical manner. During this period, we have numerous fantasies, dreams, and nightmares, and are often preoccupied with subjects of magic, mystery, and death. Denyse Beaudet (1991), based on her studies of childhood cognition, suggests that the contents that appear in children's dreams and fantasies may extend to the very limits of the psyche itself. The universe that unfolds in the dreams of children includes shadow and light, night and day, and all the elements of nature, as well as phantasmagorical beings, humans, and characters from TV and literature. But at the center of this magical world, according to Beaudet, stands the "monster," defined as a threatening and deadly character that has an engrossing effect on the child's imagination. Beaudet found that more than a third of the dreams of 5- and 6-year-old children portray an encounter between child and monster in which the dreaming child either combats or kills the monster (coping), tames the monster (transformation), or is engulfed by the monster (symbolic death).

Hide-and-Seek

There are two important facets of this intuitive and magical stage of cognition, according to Piaget. The first is that we inhabit a world that is primarily *egocentric,* or self-centered. Still unable to adopt the perspective of another person, we tend to assume that other people can tell what we are thinking and feeling and that they know all the other people in our lives. Play *hide-and-seek* games with 3-year-olds, and they will often stand in full view and cover their eyes, assuming that if they cannot see you, then you cannot see them. Or eavesdrop on a conversation between 4-year-olds and you will hear each of them jabbering away and taking turns, oblivious to what the other is saying. These "collective monologues" offer further evidence of the egocentrism and magical thinking of preschoolers.

A second facet of this prelogical world concerns the concept of conservation, the idea that physical properties of an object stay the same despite superficial changes in appearance. Flatten a ball of clay and the preoperational child will think there is less clay. Then roll the clay into a long, thin snake, and the child will think there is more clay. Until roughly the age of 7, children can't seem to *center* on two object features at the same time (width and height, for example) or mentally *reverse* such operations as pouring, flattening, and spreading. Very simply put, "what you see is what you get" in this self-centered, magical stage of development. Piaget believed that both object constancy and conservation mark the beginning of a major advance in cognitive development, one that lasts until the age of 11 or 12.

After the Bombing, Oklahoma City, April 25, 1995

"Two very, very bad guys set a bomb," said Nathanael Block, 5, swinging his legs as he sat in the gym at Crestwood Monday. "If I could talk to them, I would say, You're not really good."

Peder Davis, a bouncy, tow-headed 5-year-old, shook his head.

"Yeah, but 'You're not really good' is what you say when a friend is being bad to you," Peder said. "That's not going to work."

"I would tell him: You shoot down this building? You put it back together," Peder said. "And I would say, You redo those people."

Source: Pam Belluck. (1995). Young Minds Are Left in Turmoil, *New York Times,* N.Y. Times News Service, downloaded @ AOL, 4/26/95.

Many of the dreams and nightmares of young children portray an encounter between the child and a monster (i.e. death) in which the dreaming child either fights and kills the monster, tames and befriends the monster, or is engulfed and destroyed by the monster. © *Michael Weisbrot/Stock Boston*

Children in the preoperational stage, unable to see fully from another's point of view or to take another perspective on the same subject, have difficulty distinguishing reality (what they know) from appearance (what they see). Egocentrism and failures at conservation may play a definitive role in the fears and anxieties experienced by dying children. Psychologist Hannelore Wass (1995:282), for example, suggests that their immature understanding of death may prevent young children from grasping the causal relationship between illness and painful surgical procedures. She states: "[C]hildren frequently replace separation anxiety with mutilation anxiety and . . . often act with anxiety, anger, and depression to the threats to their body integrity caused by medical treatments."

Cops and Robbers

As preschoolers' cognitive understanding of death unfolds, they tend to view death as any form of permanent separation, such as when a playmate moves to another part of town. The young child lives in a world of magic fairy tales where

OLD MOTHER HUBBARD

She went to the bakers

To buy him some bread;

But when she came back

The poor dog was dead.

She went to the undertaker's

To buy him a coffin;

But when she came back

The poor dog was laughing.

Oxford Dictionary of Nursery Rhymes

death is real but not yet fully permanent. Most children 3 to 6 years old, although they grieve loss and experience emotional pain, tend to lack an appreciation that death is a universal phenomenon and is a final and complete cessation of bodily functions. Instead, they are likely to view death as temporary and/or partial. For instance, when children play *cops and robbers,* or a video version of the game, one child will shoot a toy pistol or a toy laser gun at another child, who will fall down as if dead but then quickly return to life to play again. Young children who grieve the death and burial of their favorite pet will sometimes dig up the pet the next day to see if it has returned to life.

In her classic studies of children's comprehension of death, Nagy (1948) interviewed 378 Hungarian children from 3 to 10 years of age, ranging across a broad spectrum intellectually and from various religious backgrounds. She asked the younger children to draw pictures concerning death and those over 7 to write down everything they could think of about death. She found that the permanency of death is not clear in early childhood. Children age 3 to 5 believed death to be reversible and not final and tended to view separation and abandonment as equivalent to death. In fact, according to Nagy (1948:12), the child believes that the dead person continues to live, breathe, think and feel, but within the confines of the coffin. She writes, "In the cemetery one lives on. Movement is to a certain degree limited by the coffin, but for all that the dead are still capable of growth. They take nourishment, they breathe. They know what is happening on earth. They feel it, if someone thinks of them, and they may even feel sorry for them. Thus, the dead live in the grave."

Because of a strong sense of fantasy and the tendency to equate death with separation and abandonment, a child in this stage is likely to misinterpret and misunderstand death and sickness. The child may see sickness as a form of punishment for an actual or imagined action. The expression of grief by the parents may be viewed by the child as anger at or disappointment in them.

CONCRETE OPERATIONAL STAGE

At about the age of 7, we advance to what Piaget called the *concrete operational stage,* during which time we become capable of more complex physical activity and logical reasoning. At this age, we are beginning to empathize with others, are becoming more communicative and less egocentric. At the same time, a sense of moral judgement continues to develop. (Kohlberg, 1976).

While we are gaining in the ability to test reality (Hostler, 1978), magical thinking still persists. Nagy (1948), for example, found that children of ages 5 to 9 tended to personify death, representing death as a live person or some variation, such as an angel, a skeleton, a circus clown, or bogey man. Death in this age range is viewed as a taker, something violent that comes and gets you like a burglar or a kidnapper.

Little Dicky Dilver

Had a wife of silver;

He took a stick and broke her back

And sold her to the miller;

The miller wouldn't have her

So he threw her in the river.

Oxford Dictionary of Nursery Rhymes

Between the ages of 6 and 10, the evolution of the concept of death as a permanent cessation of life begins. However, the cognitive obstacles to abstract thought—the persistence of egocentrism and magical thinking—prevent its completion. In this stage, death is linked to forces in the outside world and becomes ". . . scary, frightening, disturbing, dangerous, unfeeling, unhearing, or silent. Death can be invisible as a ghost, or ugly like a monster, or it can be a skeleton. Death can be a person, a companion of the devil, a giver of illness, or even an angel" (Lonetto, 1980:7). There remains a fear that death is contagious, something that can be caught like a cold (Schaefer and Lyons, 1986). Nagy observed that children in this stage often feel that they can outmaneuver death—indicating that death's universality is not yet accepted by them.

According to Nagy (1948), a mature view of death as final, inescapable, and universal occurs in children after their ninth year. Support for Nagy's conclusions has been found in more recent research. Speece and Brent (1992), for example, investigated the age at which a mature understanding of death is achieved in children and the acquisition pattern for three components of a mature understanding of death, namely, universality, irreversibility, and nonfunctionality. Ninety-one children in kindergarten through grade 3 were interviewed. Based on their findings, Speece and Brent (1992) concluded that a mature understanding of death (i.e., comprehension of all three components) does not occur for most children until at least 10 years of age.

Cognition and Child Suicide

The lack of a mature understanding of death may play a role in the growing incidence of **child suicide.** There is evidence that suicide among 5- to 14-year-old Americans is a growing phenomenon. Suicide data for this age group

Solomon Grundy,

Born on a Monday,

Christened on Tuesday,

Married on Wednesday,

Took ill on Thursday,

Worse on Friday,

Died on Saturday,

Buried on Sunday,

This is the end

Of Solomon Grundy

Oxford Dictionary of Nursery Rhymes

were not reported until 1970 and, in that year, the official suicide rate for 5- to 14-year-olds was 0.3 per 100,000 population. In 1986, the last year for which official statistics for this age group were available, the reported suicide rate for children had increased almost threefold to 0.81 per 100,000 (Stillion, McDowell, & May, 1989; Stillion & McDowell, 1995). For youth age 10−14 years, suicide rates between 1980 and 1992 increased 86% for white boys, 233% for white girls, 300% for African American boys, and 100% for African American girls (NCHS, 1995a).

Numerous studies have found that the cognitive risk factor most closely associated with childhood suicide is an immature understanding of the finality of death (Joffe & Offord, 1983; Stillion & McDowell, 1995). Piaget and Inhelder (1969), for example, found that many children in the concrete operational stage of

MOTHER GOOSE NURSERY RHYMES: INCIDENTS OF VIOLENCE

INCIDENT	Number of Cases
Death by choking	2
Death by devouring	1
Cutting human being in half	1
Decapitation	1
Death by squeezing	1
Death by shriveling	1
Death by starvation	1
Death by boiling	1
Death by hanging	1
Death by drowning	1
Killing of pets and domestic animals	4
Body-snatching	1
Severing of limbs	7
Self-inflicted injury	2
Breaking of arms and legs	4
Devouring human flesh	1
Torture of human beings and animals	12
Whipping and lashing	8
Maiming of human beings and animals	15

Source: Geoffrey Handley-Taylor. In W.S. Baring-Gould, and C. Baring-Gould, (1967). *The Annotated Mother Goose*. World, New York, p. 176.

cognitive development (ages 5 to 12) do not comprehend the finality of death but, instead, tend to view death as a temporary and reversible state. Investigators have also found that many suicidal children are likely to view death as a transient and pleasant state (McIntire, Angle, & Struempler, 1972). It is not unusual for suicidal children who have lost loved ones to view death as a vehicle for a happy reunion. It seems that the lack of understanding of the finality of death plus the belief that death is a gateway to a happier situation are cognitions that increase the risk of suicide. Judith M. Stillion (1995:194), a leading figure in contemporary suicidology, believes that helping these children ". . . means leading them to a deeper understanding of the finality of death as well as finding ways for them to express their pain. Traditional play therapy and art therapy can be effective when combined with the skills of a good listener."

Another cognitive characteristic of young children that may be associated with child suicides, especially for children with learning disabilities, is an inability to see the multiple dimensions of a situation. Concrete operational thinking resembles in many ways the rigid thought patterns associated with suicide at later ages of development (Orbach, 1984; Pfeffer, 1986). Children simply are unable to envision multiple possibilities for the future and are, therefore, likely to experience excessive hopelessness when they are in a negative life situation. In addition to their cognitive limitations, children also lack the life experiences of adults. These years of experience teach us that problem situations that appear as hopeless or irresolvable often do turn out well in the long run. Learning-disabled children may be particularly disadvantaged in these areas (Stillion, 1995).

The ability to use methods of logic, such as deductive reasoning and systematic hypothesis testing, is the hallmark of Piaget's next stage, the formal operational stage of cognitive development.

On looking up, on looking
down
She saw a dead man on the
ground;
And from his nose unto his
chin,
The worms crawled out,
the worms crawled in.
Then she unto the parson
said,
Shall I be so when I am
dead?
O yes, O yes, the parson
said,
You will be so when you
are dead.

Oxford Dictionary of Nursery Rhymes

FORMAL OPERATIONAL STAGE

What distinguishes Piaget's fourth level of cognitive development is the ability to think *abstractly,* to reason on a logical, hypothetical level. In general, around 9 or 10 years of age, it is recognized that death is a process which takes place in us, the perceptible result of which is the dissolution of bodily life. Nagy (1948) found that children older than 9 years of age arrived at the realization that death comes to all, is irreversible, and is the final end to physical life. By then, according to Nagy, we know that death is inevitable.

During this stage, some children come to enjoy the heady contemplation of abstract concepts. Some preadolescents and many adolescents spend hours mulling over hypothetical possibilities related to abstractions such as life, death, God, love, and free will. Adolescents in this stage become more systematic in their problem-solving efforts and, unlike children in earlier developmental stages, are more likely to think things through, to envision possible courses of action, and to use logic to reason out the likely consequences of each possible solution before they act. Thought processes can be characterized as abstract, systematic, logical, and reflective (Weiten, 1994). However, unlike Piaget's first three stages, which generally appear on schedule in different cultures (Kagan, 1976), formal operational thought is not used by all adolescents and adults. In fact, most fall back on rules of thumb, known as "heuristics," in many problem-solving situations (Kassin, 1995). Piaget's point is that adolescents and adults are cognitively *capable* of formal operations and a mature understanding of death, whereas children are not.

The Psychodynamic Perspective

From the psychodynamic point of view, the child's understanding that "I" will die, that "I" am dying, or that another is dead or dying centers on the development of another facet of the sense-of-self: the differentiation of the "I" from the "not I" (Harding, 1973). Beginning with the work of Sigmund Freud, psychodynamic studies of the parent/child relationship reveal that the developing child, in concert with becoming more cognitively sophisticated and behaviorally independent of the parents, also undergoes a psychological progression from a relatively undifferentiated sense of self and other to a more differentiated, articulated representation of both the self and important others (Mahler, Pine, & Bergman, 1975; Bloom-Feshbach & Bloom-Feshbach, 1987).

SEPARATION AND INDIVIDUATION

According to Margaret Mahler's theory, the newborn's subjective world is initially self-absorbed. However, as the infant develops an attachment to the mother, a sense of merger with the parent takes place that creates a fluid, poorly defined self/other boundary. Over time, passing through several phases of increasing body awareness and interpersonal separation, the child gradually achieves a sense of psychological separateness. The final stage of this progression involves the establishment of an emotional foundation to the sense-of-self, around the age of 2 ½ to 3 years.

The organization of an emotional dimension to the sense-of-self, termed *libidinal object constancy,* is the psychological basis for a number of new developments, including the child's growing independence, his or her capacity for consolidation of a separate identity, and an emerging ability to relate to others in an interpersonally meaningful and mutual way. The setting of an emotional foundation, along with the achievement of object constancy, is thought to bring about a profound psychological reorganization that affects all of the child's future development. This stage is so fundamental that Mahler labels this period "the psychological birth of the infant" (Bloom-Feshbach & Bloom-Feshbach, 1987).

From a psychodynamic perspective, separation and individuation are two intertwined and interacting, but distinct, developmental lines: "Separation consists of the child's emergence from a symbiotic fusion with the mother . . . and individuation consists of those achievements marking the child's assumption of his own individual characteristics" (Mahler, Pine, & Bergman, 1975:4). In commonsense terms, the infant's initial overwhelming need for, and total dependence on, the parent for comfort and affection, in combination with limited cognitive capacities, leaves the infant feeling linked to the parent and vulnerable to parental separation. As the emotional dimension and object constancy develop, however, the child comes to represent internally the parent's giving of emotional security

---

CHILDREN'S INTERPRETATION OF DEATH

Infancy

- No concepts

Ages 3–5

- Temporary, capable of returning (grandma on trip)
- Not universal (old people only)
- Enfeebled life (live in casket)
- Fear of separation (who will take care of me?)

Ages 5–9

- Personification (bogey man)
- Catastrophic, powerful force (death picks you out)
- "It's not fair"—may be avoided by good behavior
- Not universal (I won't die)

Ages 9–12

- Permanent, personal, universal
- Will die some day
- Fascinated by the macabre (horror stories, blood, guts)

Early adolescence

- Fearful yet fascinated
- Adult understanding of death
- Strong, intense emotions
- Death is an enemy
- Represents loss of the newly discovered me
- Testing the limits of life (playing chicken)
- Religious and philosophical theories of life, death, and existence after death.

Source: Adapted from A. M. Sims, Survival (1990), pp. 34–35.

and becomes more separate as a psychological entity. The child is now able to meet new developmental challenges, as well as to tolerate more interpersonal separation (Fraiberg, 1971).

From this viewpoint, although the infant may not have formed a conceptual grasp of death and loss, the emotional effects of a parent or other caregiver on his or her life are real. By 6 months, for example, an infant perceives differences in caregivers and the degree to which physical and emotional needs are being met by them. A toddler may recognize that a pet is alive and a table is not, although "living" and "lifeless" are not yet cognitively distinguished at this early age. So, although a clear understanding of death may be wanting at this early stage of development, a clearer emotional and intuitive grasp of separation and loss appears to be active in early childhood.

SEPARATION AND THE DYING CHILD

Easson (1974) notes that the very young child lives emotionally as part of the parent–child relationship and, to a great extent, responds to and reflects the feelings of the parents. The fatally ill 2-year old, for example, will sense the pain and anguish of his or her parents. Often, these young children may exist in the here and now, at peace, until the grieving family members visit and exhibit sadness and anxiety (Rhodes & Vedder, 1983). While the 2-year-old child dying in a hospital has no known concept of his or her death, the child does have a real appreciation of the altered patterns of care received and of the separation from the usual caregivers. Many dying children react more to the daily treatment they receive at the hands of medical personnel, family, and friends than to the possibility of their actual death.

To help the young child die in peace requires that parents deal with their feelings so that they can support the adult–child bond. Since the ideas children have about death affect their emotional, cognitive, and social reactions, it is important to talk with children about death. For some adults, however, dealing with the dying child's feelings about death may be a difficult challenge. In a study involving interviews with 100 mothers, it was found that parents find it difficult to talk with young children about death (McNeil, 1983). They tend to feel inadequate about knowing what to say or how to say it. McNeil (1983) noted that the mothers had more difficulty dealing with questions on particular deaths involving actual situations than with general questions posed by their children out of natural curiosity.

LITTLE JENNIFER

"Observe the newborn infant or toddler exploring the world. The child's initial sense of unity with its surroundings is repeatedly ruptured in its interaction with those surroundings. Consider little Jennifer, as the infant's pleasure-seeking lips search for mother's nipple, the simple imperative takes form. . . '*mommy not I.*' In the collision between baby and coffee table, the statement is uttered once again. . . '*coffee table not I.*' And, too, as a toddler, drawn in fascination to the movement of sticky fingers, Jennifer touches each one accompanied by the statement '*my finger, my finger.*' And so on, by way of these experiences of lived-body, our *sense-of-self* or '*I-ness*' begins a seemingly endless process of delineation and affirmation."

Source: Marrone (1990), p. xii.

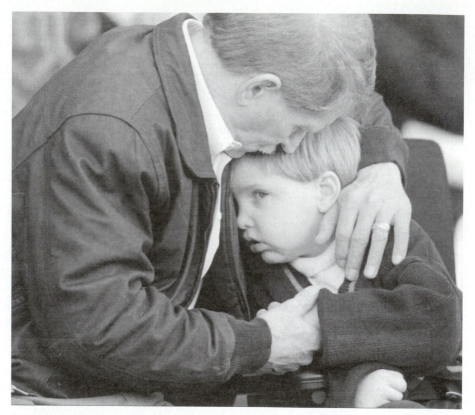

To help the young child die in peace requires that parents deal with their feelings and concerns so that they can support the adult–child bond. Many dying children react more to the treatment they receive at the hands of loved ones and medical personnel than to the possibility of their actual death.
AP/Wide World Photos

PSYCHODYNAMIC STAGES OF CHALLENGE AND CRISIS

While Freud believed that the significant stages of psychological development (i.e., oral, anal, phallic, latent, and genital) were completed early in life, other psychodynamic theorists extended Freud's basic developmental theory to other stages of life, including adolescence, adulthood, and old age. In fact, as a psychological theorist, Erik Erikson's major contribution lies in a field that has come to be called *life-span developmental psychology* (1963). The central idea of this approach is that we continue to change and differentiate throughout life as we meet new and different challenges and crises.

Erikson proposed eight psychosocial stages of development through which we progress in life, each of them characterized by a particular psychological challenge or crisis. The resolution of a stage conflict affects how we deal with each subsequent developmental stage, as well as our emotional, cognitive, and behavioral reactions to loss. If an earlier challenge is not adequately handled, the resolution of subsequent crises is hampered. Erikson's four stages of infancy and childhood involve the following conflicts and challenges.

CARING INSIGHTS

Children, Dying, and Death

- Communicating about death is easier when a child feels that she or he has permission to talk about the subject freely and believes we are honestly interested in his or her views and questions.

- Communication about death and dying depends on the child's level of cognitive development and his or her own personal experience. Very young children may be more concerned about separation from a loved one than about death itself.

- Young children can absorb only limited amounts of information in a single sitting. Answers need to be brief, simple, and repeated.

- A child often feels angry and guilty when losing a close family member. She or he needs assurance that she or he has been, and will continue to be, loved and cared for.

- Whether a young child should visit the dying or attend a funeral depends on age and ability to understand the situation, her or his relationship with the dying or dead person, and whether he or she wishes it. A child should be prepared in advance of visiting a dying loved one or attending the funeral. Children who choose not to visit or attend should never be coerced or made to feel guilty about the choice not to become involved.

- A child may need to grieve and mourn a deeply felt loss on and off until well into adolescence or young adulthood. Children may show little immediate grief but may express their sadness at unexpected times and in unique ways. Children need patience, understanding, and support to complete their "grief work."

Stage 1: Trust versus Mistrust

During the first year of life, babies are torn between trusting and not trusting their parents and the environment around them. If physiological, security, and belongingness needs are generally met, the infant comes to trust the environment and herself or himself in that environment. The sense-of-self, the capacity to negotiate separation and loss, as well as optimism about the future are essentially founded upon the child's faith in the predictability of the environment. On the other hand, frustrated by unmet needs, made anxious by multiple separations, separations of long duration, in a seemingly chaotic environment, infants and young children become suspi-

". . . healthy children will not fear life if their elders have integrity enough not to fear death."

Erikson (1963), p. 269.

cious, cognitively and emotionally defensive, anxious, and overly concerned with basic need fulfillment issues.

Stage 2: Autonomy versus Shame and Doubt

During our first three years of life, progressive physical development allows us greater autonomy and contact with our surroundings. We learn to deal with various forms of separation, to walk, to hold onto things, and to control our excretory functions. If we repeatedly fail in trying to master these skills, self-doubt and fear of loss may grow. Erikson noted that when parents and other adults belittle a child's efforts, the child may begin to feel shame and acquire a lasting sense of inferiority.

Stage 3: Initiative versus Guilt

Between the ages of 3 and 6, children become increasingly active, undertaking new projects, manipulating things in the environment, making plans, and conquering new challenges. Parental support and encouragement for these initiatives can lead to a sense of joy in exercising initiative and taking on new challenges. However, if the child is unable to acquire a sense of initiative and personal empowerment, strong feelings of self-negation, guilt, unworthiness, and resentment may persist.

Stage 4: Industry versus Inferiority

During the six or seven years preceding adolescence, children encounter a new set of expectations at home and at school. They must learn the skills needed to become fully functioning adults, including personal care, productive work, cooperative behavior, and independent social living. If children are stifled in their efforts to become a part of the adult world, they may conclude that they are inadequate, helpless, mediocre, or inferior, lose faith in their power to become industrious or overcome life's crises and challenges, and, in the extreme, become self-destructive and suicidal. For some children, according to Erikson (1963:163), rather than viewing the environment as trusted and predictable and caregivers as a source of nurturance and stimulation, "the environment is pictured not only as forbidding but also as destructive, while loved ones are in danger of departing or dying."

Erikson (1963) observed that a child "decides" early in life whether the universe is a warm and loving place to be or a place not to be trusted. The ability to deal with the threats and difficulties of later life is based on this primitive yet momentous subconscious conclusion. Failure to navigate these conflicts and challenges can, at a minimum, lower a child's feelings of self-esteem and, at worst, cause irreparable damage to the development of the sense-of-self. Erikson (1968) maintained that a major psychological factor that increases the risk of childhood suicide is a sense of **inferiority.** Children who feel inferior to others develop a poor sense-of-self and low self esteem. They frequently act out in ways that confirm their low opinion of themselves and increase the likelihood that they will receive negative feedback from significant others. In this way, they act so as to maintain or enhance their negative cognitions of self, past, and future, which may eventually lead to depression and suicide. In some cases, according to

Stillion (1995:193), "The sense of inferiority may become so extreme that the child views himself or herself as unworthy and expendable. When this happens, suicidal ideation may be the next step." Children who exhibit extreme feelings of inferiority ". . . should be encouraged to attempt activities in which they can succeed and be supported in these attempts. Competence is a powerful antidote to feelings of inferiority."

The Humanistic-Existential Perspective

Both the cognitive and the psychodynamic stage theories maintain that the concept of death and an understanding of the process of dying come into play only after the second or third year of life, and are not completed until 9 or 10 years of age. Although infants and young children do react emotionally to separation and loss, a concept of death as universal, irreversible, and permanent is not possible until the sense-of-self is more fully formed. But humanistic psychologists question whether psychological development progresses through a series of distinct, steplike stages as these theorists maintain. Is the development of a sense-of-self, as well as a clear understanding of death, like a step-by-step staircase, or is it smoother and more gradual, like a ramp? In any case, humanistic psychotherapists question whether stage theories of development are always the best way to understand a grieving child's experience in the moment.

From the humanistic-existential point of view, each human being is unique, and our understanding of the world, including our concepts of death and dying, are dependent on a unique array of personal experiences, many of which go beyond the child/parent bond and stages of cognitive development. Humanistic theories and research indicate that children's developmental stages, their individual experiences and characteristics, as well as their environmental, familial, and cultural experiences must be considered together before we can understand their grief. Some children can understand death to be final much earlier than is typically suggested by Piaget, Nagy, Erikson, and other developmental theorists (Stanbrook & Parker, 1987). Yalom (1980:16) has even hypothesized that children under 3 years of age "know about but deny death."

More recently, in their review of developmental theories concerning infants' and toddlers' reactions to death, Norris, Young, and Williams (1993) concluded that although the average toddler's cognitive skills may be limited, children age 3 years and younger have both emotional and cognitive responses to the death of someone they have known. Other researchers (Moller, 1996; Mcintyre, Angle, & Struempler 1972) also directly contradict the age-graded developmental models. They stress differences between persons of various age groups that are due to variations in social and cultural backgrounds and other experiences over the lifetime. To humanistic psychologists, the lack of consensus found here simply confirms that we cannot depend exclusively on age or developmental categories regarding children's understanding of death, but must also consider the uniquely personal experiences of the child.

EXPERIENCE AND THE DYING CHILD

One of the strongest critics of stage-based, age-based developmental theories is anthropologist Myra Bluebond-Langner (1977;1989). Her groundbreaking, in-

CARING INSIGHTS

The Dying Child

Parents, grandparents, and teachers often take a protective stance toward children when death enters their lives. We are reluctant to talk of death with children, believing they wouldn't understand, that they're not interested in such things, or that the trauma would be too devastating to one so innocent. Psychologists and sociologists have studied dying children's reactions for more than 50 years, and their findings and insights have shed new light on some very old myths and assumptions about dying children.

Based on these findings, many psychologists have concluded that, in caring for the dying child, caregivers should tell the child about the causes of the illness, should stress the importance of having medical treatment, and should explain the medical procedures that will be used (Wass, 1995). Children who are informed as to why their parents are exhibiting certain emotions are less likely to feel anxious, guilty, or unloved (Pattison, 1977; Rhodes & Vedder, 1983).

In caring for a fatally ill preschool child, parents, family members, and other caregivers should strive to alleviate the child's separation fears by being available, supporting, protective, and understanding. Dying children in this stage of cognitive development can deal very well with the pain of treatment, as long as they are certain that their caregivers will love and protect them. The dying child surrounded with love and caring will be more likely to die feeling certain that his or her loved ones will always care.

depth studies of dying children, 18 months to 14 years, have revealed the following:

- Terminally ill children as young as 3 years old come to know that they are dying, and that death is a final and irreversible process.
- Dying children integrate and synthesize information about death and dying based on their age, as well as their personal experiences, temporary concerns, life circumstances and self-concept.
- Very young dying children, although not yet able to express their understanding of death in words, exhibit certain behaviors which indicate that a child knows he or she is dying and what dying means. These include fear of wasting time, dislike of talking about the future, absorption with death and disease, increased fear with increased weakening, wanting to have things done right away, and setting up a distance from others by acts of anger or silence.

She notes that for dying children, time is not perceived as endless, as it is for most children. In fact, some young children reveal a cognitive change normally

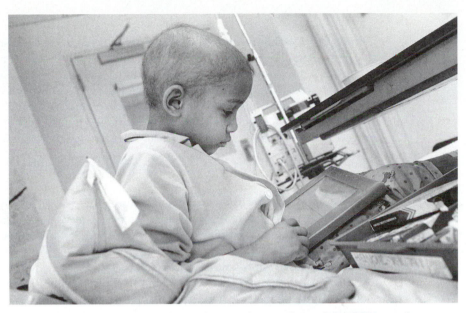

Although not yet able to express their understanding of death in words, very young dying children exhibit certain behaviors which indicate that a child knows he or she is dying and what dying means. Like dying adults, dying children are most fearful of being abandoned or rejected. ©*1992 Hazel Hankin/Stock, Boston*

seen in adulthood, that is, from viewing one's life in terms of time since birth to viewing it in terms of time until death (Santrock, 1985). These children will often push themselves to get things done. They may get angry when people take too long to answer questions or to bring things to them, or when others show emotional distress in their presence. In many cases, according to Bluebond-Langner (1977, 1989), dying children want to create and maintain the pretense that they are feeling well because they are fearful of being abandoned or rejected. In some cases, these fears may be stronger and of longer duration than fear of death itself.

Sociologist David Moller (1996:148) believes there are three important lessons to be learned from Bluebond-Langner's research. He writes,

> First, the experience of serious childhood illness is one of suffering, anxiety, and despair, all of which increasingly come to dominate the lives of parents and their dying children. . . Second, the experience of illness in the modern medical context is a salient factor affecting the child's perception of death and dying. . . A third important finding is that seriously sick children arrive at an understanding of their medical and human predicament within an environment of closed awareness and mutual pretense. . . The irony is that in seeking to protect children from the tragedy of terminal illness, the modern, medically based conspiracy of silence functions to exacerbate the anxieties and responsibilities of seriously ill and dying children. And, as we see from Bluebond-Langner's study, it is a conspiracy doomed in any event to fail.

FEELINGS OF DYING CHILDREN

Terminally ill children must face three powerful environmental stresses during their hospitalization: (1) separation from their parents and other family members (2) medical procedures that are new, painful and traumatic; and (3) deaths occurring around them during their hospital stay. According to Adams (1990), Webb (1993b), and Easson (1974), each child responds to these extraordinary stressors with a wide and unique array of emotions and feelings during the dying process. These affective states include fear, anxiety, anger, sadness, and loneliness.

Fear and Anxiety

Hospitalization and medical attempts to control the disease or physical damage mean that many dying children must suffer more invasive medical procedures, another surgery with possibly more disfigurement and/or intensive chemotherapy and radiation treatment with their sometimes intensely painful side effects. All of these measures are frightening and may raise the child's fear and anxiety level throughout the course of terminal care. According to social worker David Adams (1990:6), ". . . mutilation anxiety may prevail as they face invasive procedures, experience bodily changes, endure physical deterioration, and suffer increased pain. Children may also sense increased anxiety in their parents and caregivers and this, in turn, may heighten their own apprehensions. . . . Separation from mother and father, as well as from familiar surroundings, has a profound impact on these children."

Anger

Dying children ultimately must face the loss of self-control and independence that comes with the process of dying. They may bitterly resent the fact that they can no longer do what they want to do in the way they like. They may be angry because they are no longer physically able to do things they used to do. At a time when they should be asserting a newfound independence by exploring new horizons, they are restrained in a hospital bed or in their own bed at home. Dying children may resent being prevented from getting up and exploring as much as they resent having a terminal illness.

Adams (1990:7) notes that the anger of dying children

. . . may be directed at the disease, their parents, caregivers, themselves, or God. They might have had every reason to believe that they would get better with treatment. Now they may feel cheated—their trust in their parents and physicians is shaken as their disease progresses. They may be angry at the disease itself, for the control that it has assumed over their bodies and their lives. Physical limitations, increased pain, and isolation from family, friends, and activities tend to heighten their frustration.

As death approaches, and their bodies further weaken, children are faced with resolving the conflict between enjoying their increasing feelings of independence and mastery while growing increasingly dependent on parents and medical personnel to meet their basic physical, emotional and spiritual needs. According to Oaks and Ezell (1993), some dying children regress to an emotional level at

CARING INSIGHTS

On Dying Children

In her study of children with leukemia, Bluebond–Langner (1977) discerned a psychological process through which dying children progress during the course of their illness and treatment. This process includes the acquisition of information and changes in the child's perception of what is happening, along with certain events involving parents, hospital personnel, and treatment regimens.

Initially, the terminally ill child becomes aware that the illness is serious and perceives that he or she is seriously ill. This interval usually begins immediately after the parents learn of the diagnosis. Next, the child learns the names of various drugs and medical procedures and their side effects and perceives that he or she is seriously ill but will get better. This phase, according to Bluebond–Langner, usually begins after the child has been to the medical facility a number of times, has met other terminally ill children, and has been told of a remission. Over time, the child learns the purpose of various medical procedures and perceives that he or she is always ill but will get better. This period usually begins at the time of the first relapse and may continue through a series of remissions and relapses. Over more time, the child experiences the disease as a series of relapses and remissions and perceives that he or she will never get better. Finally, the child becomes aware that the disease is a series of relapses and remissions that will eventually cease at death and perceives that he or she is dying. This interval is often begun when the child learns of the death of a peer with the same disease.

which they are no longer independent. For others, as independence is lost, they become emotionally threatened and sometimes lash out at the possibility that their individuality, and their very existence, will cease to be. In their attempts to maintain the somewhat fragile sense-of-self, some dying children become ferociously independent to the point that they suspect and resist any offers of help from hospital personnel or family members.

Sadness

Terminally ill children often experience profound feelings of sadness as they grieve the loss of what they were and what they had before they became so ill (Adams, 1990; Papadatou and Papadatos, 1991). Dying children experience profound and multiple losses during the dying process. These losses include the following:

CARING INSIGHTS

Pain and Punishment

Dying children sometimes perceive hospitalization as a form of rejection by parents and family and, sometimes, blame themselves, thinking they deserve this rejection because they have been bad or unworthy. They frequently manifest this behavior through anger and disobedience. Parents, family members, and hospital personnel should help the child to understand that the hospitalization is not rejection and that the pain and suffering is connected with the disease state and is not, in any way, a punishment directed to the child personally.

- Declining contact with friends and classmates
- Reduced attendance at school and school functions
- Restrained participation in, or absence from family social activities
- Waning energy levels and ever decreasing mobility
- Alterations in body image and self-concept
- Feelings of discomfort or intense pain
- Feelings of helplessness and hopelessness

The dying child may withdraw in depression, rage in despair, experience bouts of spontaneous crying, and reveal other symptoms of depression, such as loss of appetite and sleep disturbances (Papadatou & Papadatos, 1991).

Loneliness and Isolation

Dying children face increasing physical and social isolation as a direct result of the disease and the need for frequent hospitalization. Some children face increasing psychological isolation as well when communication with loved ones and medical personnel involves evasion and pretense. When important information is restricted or overlooked by parents and caregivers, children may be left on their own to interpret what is happening (Easson, 1977).

Because dying children are often excluded from detailed knowledge of their disease and its ramifications, there may be little or no opportunity for parents and dying children to truly share their concerns and fears and provide comfort, security, and reassurance to each other (Adams, 1990; Papadatou & Papadatos, 1991; Harvey, 1995, 1996). Unfortunately, in contemporary society, children's feelings about loss and death sometimes become masked and repressed. According to French child psychiatrist Ginette Raimbault (1991:186), "To let children talk about death, about their fears and feelings, their hopes and despairs, their certainties and uncertainties, their love and hate, means we are allowing them to talk about life, *their* life, and we are providing them with the only possible help: the presence of another human being until the end."

From the humanistic perspective, children are as different in dying as they are in living. Parents and caregivers should not expect stereotyped behavior on the

Fleeting Smiles, Angry Outbursts

"The dying child will find that his parents, his relatives, and the people who treat him respond more readily to his few fleeting smiles rather than to his repeated angry outbursts. Somewhat to his dismay, the child who is dying will find that he cannot be too childish as he moves toward death. The youngster who has always been open and outgoing learns that, in death, he has to be more reticent and withdrawn."

Source: Easson (1977), p. 34.

part of the dying child. Some children are resilient and playful even when their life is ending. Other children are somber and withdrawn. Still others may find solace in their own spirituality. Sommer (1989), for one, suggests that spiritual needs are prominent in the lives of dying children and that caregivers addressing these needs and helping children meet them must aim toward two objectives: theological honesty (e.g., spirituality does not always provide answers) and speaking the language of children and entering into their world. According to Sommer (1989:89), "These children need to form relationships (to love and be loved), to be given a positive image of what lies beyond death, and to know they will be remembered."

Grieving Children

When someone very close to a child dies, the core of his or her existence is shaken. Trust in the consistency and predictability of support and comfort is disrupted and the effects on the child's psychosocial development can be profound and sometimes damaging.

For most young children, the first encounter with death involves the death of a parent, grandparent, sibling, pet, or other family member. In a study by Dickinson (1992) involving 440 college-age individuals, the most frequently cited first death experience involved relatives (57%), especially grandparents and parents.

THE DEATH OF A PARENT

The death of a parent is often the first death of a close relative that children experience and the one that is experienced most profoundly. The death creates an existential wound and leaves a role model vacuum in a child's life that may affect a child's adjustment and maturation. Psychologist Patricia Murphy (1986–87), for example, in a study of 184 male and female young Americans ages 18–24

CARING INSIGHTS

Hospice Care for Children

"Children's hospice care provides much-needed services by encouraging the ongoing involvement of family members and health care professionals with the dying child, and implementing practical knowledge and effective and appropriate palliative measures in children with life-threatening conditions. The hospice concept of care involves an interdisciplinary team working together to provide appropriate medical, psychosocial, and spiritual support. Application of the hospice concept can significantly enhance the lives of dying children, their families, and health care providers."

Source: Ann Armstrong-Dailey. (1991). Hospice Care for Children: Their Families and Health Care Providers. In *Children and Death*, Danai Papadatou and Costas Papadatos (eds.), Hemisphere, Washington, DC., p. 227.

found a relationship between self-esteem and loneliness reported by these young adults and their experience of parental death as young children. Analysis revealed that self-esteem was the single best predictor of loneliness and that experiencing the death of a parent during childhood significantly added to the prediction of variance in loneliness years later.

Research confirms that the death of a mother has a more immediate and profound effect on a child when she is the primary caregiver and organizer for daily living (Oaks & Ezell, 1993; Webb, 1993). The death of a grandparent may also profoundly affect children. In their study, Yates et al. (1989) examined the effects of life events on the severity of psychopathology in young patients as young as 9 years old, who were admitted to a private psychiatric hospital over a 10-year period. They found that the death of a grandparent in childhood, along with severe maternal bereavement, were related to childhood pathology more than any other life event.

Protest, Despair, and Detachment

Bowlby (1969) outlined three stages of bereavement in the young child dealing with the death of a parent: protest, despair, and detachment. The *protest* stage of the child's response involves anger and fear, the aim of which is reattachment to the lost parent. The second stage, *despair,* involves sadness, distantness, and unresponsiveness on the part of the bereaved child. The goal here is to come to terms with the separation and loss. The final stage is *detachment,* during which the child moves from depressed affect and lack of interest in other people to increasing activity, a return of attachment feelings, and openness to new relationships.

During this grieving process, children's reactions to the stress of loss might lead to various psychosomatic symptoms, including headaches, enuresis, and incontinence, as well as school phobia, depression, and poor school performance. Sood, Weller, and Weller (1992), in a comparative study of 38 bereaved children (ages 5–12 years), found increased complaints of headaches and gastrointestinal tract disturbances in this group 8 weeks after the loss, as compared to age-matched groups of depressed and normal children. Bereaved siblings may also regress in their behavior, have nightmares, and experience high levels of anxiety (Oaks & Ezell, 1993; Webb, 1993).

A child's emotional response to the death may not always be obvious to those who know the child because children can disguise their grief in various ways depending on their age and psychological development (Rando, 1984). In other cases, the child's grieving reactions begin long before the actual death occurs. Jane LeVieux (1993:81–82), director of The Caring Corner in Dallas, Texas, says,

> Children who have lost a parent as a result of a long-term illness are often the quiet observers of dying. The child knows that the parent is ill, in pain, and not the same individual he/she used to be. These children often experience intense reactions toward the infirmed parent. Their underlying fears of abandonment and guilt may begin long before the actual death occurs. They know something is wrong from whispered conversations, concerned looks, relatives showing up at different times, and significant changes in their daily routine.

Bereaved Children and the Family

Grieving children from stable families appear to suffer less psychosocial dysfunction than children from fragmented or dysfunctional families. Fristad et al. (1993), for example, studied a group of bereaved children (5–12 years old) from stable families and compared results to a group of depressed children from dysfunctional families and to a group of normal, nongrieving children. School behavior, interest in school, peer involvement, peer enjoyment, and self-esteem were similar for bereaved and normal children, and both these groups functioned significantly better than did the depressed children. The authors concluded that, as a group, the bereaved children from stable families did not experience significant psychosocial problems in their bereavement.

REACTIONS AND GRIEF STRATEGIES

Grieving children exhibit numerous emotional reactions and utilize several cognitive strategies in response to the loss of a loved one (Webb, 1993; LeVieux, 1993). Thanatologists Judy Oaks and Gene Ezell (1993) point out that, though often painful and disturbing, many of these reactions and strategies, including regression, hyperactivity, emotional outbursts, and overprotectiveness of the surviving parent, are both normal and integral to the healing process.

Regression to an earlier developmental stage is very common in grieving children. They may regress to thumb-sucking, bed-wetting, temper tantrums or other attention-seeking behaviors in their attempts to cope with the death of a loved one. In most cases, with time and nurturance, a child's regressive tendencies will subside and grow more subdued. On the other hand, children who are denied the opportunity to openly grieve a lost parent are likely to remain frozen at their psychological level or regress to an earlier developmental status. Shane and Shane (1990), for example, found that children who are denied the opportunity to grieve fully the death of a parent are sometimes incapable of giving up their emotional ties to the deceased parent throughout the life span. Full emergence of the sense-of-self is blocked, with the child remaining psychologically "frozen" in grief at the level attained, or regressing to an earlier level of cognitive and emotional development.

Hyperactivity and difficulty controlling emotions are also normal reactions in children. Children may be withdrawn and quiet or may act out negatively to get attention. Cheifetz, Stavrakakis, and Lester (1989), for instance, in a Canadian study of the emotional responses in sixteen children ages 4–17 years old found that the expression of depressive affect depends on maturation and that the young child may register grief only through anxiety, conduct disorders, and negativism. Angry outbursts, whining, and irritability occur frequently in both children and adolescents. *Difficulty concentrating* on tasks sometimes causes school grades to drop. Children who are old enough to understand death sometimes try to *protect the remaining parent* and are preoccupied with the remaining parent's potential death.

On the other hand, some children exhibit grief reactions and symptoms that point to a need for professional intervention by a clinical psychologist, a grief counselor, or school personnel (Oaks & Ezell, 1993; Webb, 1993). These include chronic health problems, which indicate that the child's stress is having negative physical effects, and difficulty in school, either with behavior or falling grades, that does not gradually improve over time. Any discussion that reflects suicidal fantasies or ideas warrants immediate professional counseling, as do other signals—including lethargy, withdrawal, loss of interest in activities that previously were enjoyable, and lack of appetite—especially symptoms that do not seem to lessen over time (Oaks & Ezell, 1993).

Constructing the Deceased Parent

In "Mourning and Melancholia," Sigmund Freud (1957) discussed the notion that one way of coping with the death of a loved one is to identify with that longed-for individual. The pain of the total and permanent separation is diminished by internalizing a part of the lost person. This phenomenon of *identification* with a deceased loved one through the representational process is central to normal development.

Silverman, Nickman, and Worden (1992:496), based on their study of 125 bereaved children ages 6–17, identified five stages in the child's attempt to maintain a representational identification with the dead parent: (1) locating the deceased parent (74% believed in "heaven"), (2) experiencing the deceased parent (81% believed their parents to be watching them), (3) reaching out to the deceased, (4) waking memories of the deceased parent, and (5) cherishing objects shared by the child and the dead parent. This attempt on the part of the bereaved child to establish a set of memories, feelings, and actions of the deceased parent is termed *constructing the deceased*. Grief, these authors suggest, should not be viewed as a psychological state that ends or from which one recovers; rather, it should be understood as a cognitive and emotional process that occurs in a social context of which the deceased is a part.

THE DEATH OF A SIBLING

As with the death of a parent, a child's reaction to the dying or death of a brother or sister can be profound and long-lasting (Webb, 1993). In the midst of this process of separation from a deceased sibling, children often show fear and panic, much of which is fear of the unknown (Who will play with me? Who will take care of me? Why did they leave me?). Powell (1991), for example, in a study of the impact of a SIDS-related death on siblings and of parental management of sibling grief in Irish families, found that the peak of family behavioral upset occurred during the first 3 months of bereavement in the majority (82%) of families. However, death-related problems in siblings, such as seeking parental affection or attention, separation anxiety, fear of being alone, and incessant curiosity about the death, remained unresolved for nearly 3 years after the loss. In spite of these ongoing problems, few families sought or were offered professional support in coping with their bereaved children.

Birenbaum and Robinson (1989–90) investigated the behavioral adjustment of sixty-one children (ages 4–16 years) during the terminal illness and first year following a sibling's death from cancer. Using the Child Behavior Checklist, data on behavior problems and competence were collected from children, parents, and teachers. Results indicate that the bereaved siblings demonstrated significantly higher levels of behavior problems and significantly lower social competence than normal children throughout the bereavement period. Judith Cook (1983a,b) found similar adjustment problems (e.g., school problems, fear of death) in a high proportion of sibling survivors of children who had died of cancer. Some siblings reported that they sometimes resented the special treatment given to the dying child. Overall, however, Cook found that siblings can tolerate and accept less parental attention and more anxiety if they know what is happening with the dying sibling.

For bereaved sibling children, the vagueness in the definition of the sibling bereavement role may also be a significant obstacle to their healing process. Following the death of a brother or sister, siblings find their status as brother or sister replaced by the status of "bereaved" brother or sister. Unfortunately, this role has no clear shape. Cook (1983a) maintains that difficulties result from the attempt of siblings to play this role that has been imposed on them. To play a role, it is first necessary to role-take, that is, to try on the role by looking at yourself from the point of view of others or by modeling your behavior on that of a role model. But people and circumstances conspire to make role-taking difficult for those siblings. Children are denied access to crucial information, either intentionally (as when parents send them to stay with relatives or lie to them about the gravity of the situation) or as a function of hospital rules and personnel that prevent them from visiting the dying sibling or from following the course of dying and reactions of others (e.g., their parents) to it. In many cases, "siblings are. . . excluded from anticipatory socialization to the bereaved role and forced to construct their own part in it" (Cook, 1983a:5–6).

Family members, too, typically shield surviving siblings from the events surrounding them. This approach to the trauma of death in a family is not helpful to children who are struggling to understand the circumstances. Rosenheim and Richer (1985) studied the anxiety level of two groups of children dealing with terminal illness and loss: One group was informed of the terminality; the other group was not. The age range in both groups was 6 to 16 years. The anxiety level of the informed group was found to be significantly lower than that of the uninformed group (Webb, 1993).

Bereaved children need explanations, comfort, and support, as do adults. Pretense and avoidance can be frightening to anyone in a stressful and painful setting, especially a child. Involving siblings in the family crisis, rather than isolating them, allows them to grieve and helps them learn coping strategies they can rely on in dealing with future losses. According to Oaks and Ezell (1993), siblings need to forgive themselves and to be absolved from their feelings of guilt about what they may have said, thought, or done to the dying sibling. To do so, they must be full participants in the mourning after.

THE DEATH OF A PET

Dogs are most often involved in children's first loss experiences (14%), followed by cats (5%), birds (2%), and fish, gerbils, hamsters, horses, rabbits, turtles, and snakes (Dickinson, 1992). This is not surprising, considering that about 63 million cats, 55 million dogs, 25 million birds, and millions of other assorted critters are kept as pets in the United States. It is estimated that at least 10 million of these companion animals die or are killed each year (Armstrong, 1994).

In Dickinson's study, 28% of the adults queried reported that their first experience with death involved the loss of an animal companion when they were, on average, 8 years old. Their emotional responses to the death of their animal companion were similar to those expressed by adults, with over one-third reporting that crying occurred immediately after the death. Details of the death, grieving, and body disposal were remembered in great detail 16 years later.

How we react to the death of an animal companion depends on a number of important factors, including our age at the time of the loss, our emotional and cognitive development, the length of time we knew the pet, the quality of the

---

LYING IN THE ROAD

Suddenly the feeling that this was all just a dream ended. Christopher was angry. It wasn't fair. Why did that dumb man have to hit Bodger?

"I ought to run *him* over with a truck."

"Oh, honey, Bodger ran right in front of him. The man didn't have time to stop."

They took Christopher home to bed where he relived the accident over and over in his mind. He tried to pretend that the truck had missed the dog, or that he hadn't called and Bodger had stayed on the other side. Or he pretended that they hadn't left the dirt road, where there were hardly any cars. Or that they had stayed home and waited.

But the bad dream always rolled on out of his control until the moment when Bodger was lying in the road.

Source: Carol Carrick. *The Accident* (1976). Seabury/Clarion, New York, p. 3.

bond between us, the circumstances surrounding the death, and the quality of family support available to us during the grieving process (Nieburg & Fischer, 1982).

Preschool children, for example, are less likely to become deeply attached to their pets and are less likely to view the pet's death as final and irrevocable. However, a long-held belief that very young children do not experience a meaningful response to the deaths occurring around them is falling away as research evidence grows. A study conducted by Mark Speece (1983), for instance, found that over half of the very young children he studied had some experience with death, and that, even as very young children, we respond to the death of our pet in observable ways. Some children in the Speece study, for example, repeatedly searched for their deceased cat, bird, or dog or tried to get the dead animals to move. At other times, children talked about the pet, or tried to bury it, dig it up, and bury it again.

Children at this early age display various emotions in response to death, including anger. One child in the Speece study became very angry when a pet bird, which had died, would not come back to life. That these children were trying to come to terms with the experience of death was indicated by their questions about the immobility of the deceased pet and what happens after death, and by their expressions of concern for the welfare of the living.

In general, preschool children appear to miss their deceased animals more as playmates than as sources that satisfy basic emotional needs over time. School-age children, on the other hand, tend to express profound grief over the death of a pet, but usually for a short time, and then tend to adapt quickly to the loss,

Experiencing the dying and death of an animal companion is often a powerful and profound loss experience through which young children learn that death is a part of the life process, that death is permanent and painful, and that the grieving process doesn't last forever. © *David Young-Wolff/PhotoEdit*

especially if a new animal is introduced following the period of grieving (Kamerman, 1988). It is usually older children and adolescents who have the most profound experiences with the loss of a pet. From early adolescence on, young people begin to develop an adult perception and understanding that death is final, permanent, inevitable, and irrevocable. Faced with the death of an animal companion, adolescents tend to grieve more intensely and for a longer period of time, in part because their relationship with their pet tends to be more intense and long-standing at this age (Levinson, 1972; Weisman, 1991).

Unfortunately, there are very few large-scale empirical studies on pet death and its relation to child and adolescent behavior and experience. In one Minnesota study, however, it was found that abused and disturbed youths suffered more pet death in childhood, had their pets for shorter times, and were most likely to have had their pets killed accidentally or purposely more than any other factor (Robin & ten-Bensel, 1985).

There has been a tendency to minimize a child's grief over the death of a pet, as though it were merely an "emotional dress rehearsal" and preparation for truly important losses yet to come. Recent research makes clear that the death of an animal companion is more than a "rehearsal" and, for children, adolescents, and adults, is often a powerful and profound loss experience.

In experiencing the loss of an animal companion in childhood, we learn many things: that death is a natural part of the life process, that death is permanent and painful, that the grieving process itself is tolerable and doesn't last forever, and that feelings of guilt, sadness, and anger following death are common and can be overcome (Levinson, 1972). Following a thorough review of pet loss and grieving, Kamerman (1988:116) notes:

> Because the opportunity for children and adolescents to witness death has diminished during this century due to increased life expectancy and the shift of the scene of death to institutions, the death of a pet frequently represents a child's or adolescent's first experience with death. The death of a pet fulfills the function that a higher infant mortality rate, a shorter life expectancy, and a more even distribution of death across age groups used to perform.

Chapter Summary

Infants and toddlers react both physically and emotionally to the loss of a significant other in their lives. Upon separation from a loved one, they experience varied, often intense, grief reactions, including denial, yearning, crying, protest, anger, sadness, and depression. However, for a young child truly to mourn the death of a loved one, or for a terminally ill child to recognize that she or he is dying, the child must have formed a mature concept of death: that death is universal, inevitable, and irreversible and that, in death, the physical self will no longer exist.

In this chapter we have reviewed the development of a mature concept of death from the cognitive, psychodynamic, and humanistic perspectives, with special focus on the interaction between the child's understanding of death and his or her needs when terminally ill, as well as the grieving strategies adopted by children in coping with the death of a parent, sibling, or animal companion.

FURTHER READINGS

Bloom-Feshbach, J., and Bloom-Feshbach, S. (1987). *The Psychology of Separation and Loss*. Jossey-Bass, San Francisco.

Feifel, H. (1977). *Meanings of Death,* McGraw-Hill, New York.

Morgan, M.A. (ed.) (1987). *Bereavement: Helping the Survivors*. King's College, London, Ontario, Canada.

Papadatou, D., and Papadatos, C. (eds.) (1991). *Children and Death*. Hemisphere, Washington, DC.

Piaget, J. (1952). *The Origins of Intelligence in Children*. International University Press, New York.

Piaget, J., and Inhelder, B. (1969). *The Psychology of the Child*. Basic Books, New York.

Webb, N.B. (ed.) (1993). *Helping Bereaved Children: A Handbook for Practitioners*. Guilford Press, New York.

Williamson, J. B., and Schneidman, E. S. (eds.) (1995). *Death, Current Perspectives*. Mayfield, Mountain View, CA.

Wolf, A. M. (1973). *Helping Your Children to Understand Death*. Child Study Press, New York.

Death, Suicide, and Young Americans

Adolescence is to adulthood what infancy is to childhood, the start of a new era, a "second birth." Beginning with a biological event (puberty) and culminating in a social event (independence from parents), adolescence corresponds roughly to the teen years, 13 to 20+. To many adults within our culture, the role of young people is to be perpetually happy, optimistic, and living life to its fullest. But, in fact, an ever-growing number of young Americans are very unhappy, angry, afraid, and self-destructive as they struggle to cope with the only period in the human life span in which the three leading causes of death are human-induced, and often intentional. Accidents, murders, and suicides, taken together, account for fully 77% of the deaths of young Americans today. No longer children, but not yet mature adults, many American adolescents face a dark and dangerous season in their lives (NCHS, 1995c).

"IT'S ONLY ROCK 'N' ROLL"

If I could stick a knife in my heart
Suicide right on the stage
Would it be enough for your teenage lust?
Would it help ease the pain?

Source: Mick Jagger and Keith Richards. (1987). It's only rock 'n' roll. In Jann S. Wenner (Ed.), *Twenty Years of Rolling Stone: What a Long, Strange Trip It's Been* (p. 319). Straight Arrow, New York.

Adolescence

The idea of adolescence as a transitional period between childhood and adulthood lasting 5 to 10 years did not gain widespread acceptance until the beginning of the twentieth century. In 1904, G. Stanley Hall, one of psychology's great pioneers, advanced a view of the adolescent years as filled with instability and inner turmoil, which he attributed to the adolescent's dramatic bodily changes brought on by puberty and the simultaneous psychological conflict associated with the issues of personal identity and sexual intimacy (Deveau, 1990).

Since Hall's theory of adolescence was first introduced, the ways we have viewed adolescence have spanned wide extremes. Robert Enright and colleagues (1987), in their sociological analysis of writings on adolescence published over the past 100 years, found that the shifts in our views of adolescence mirror changing social and economic conditions in the country. During World Wars I and II, for example, when America's young people were needed for factory work and military service, adolescents were described as competent, hard-working, and responsible, and the period of adolescence was thought to end at around 16 years of age. However, during economically depressed periods, such as the 1890s, 1930s, and more recent decades, when work was hard to find, young people were portrayed as incompetent, lazy, and immature (e.g., Generation X, Slackers) and the period of adolescence is perceived as extending past the teen years into the middle and late 20s. These trends suggest that, above and beyond the physiology of pubescence, the definition of adolescence is largely a social one and that ideas concerning this period of life can change greatly within a given culture over relatively short spans of time.

Psychological research suggests that, although it is assumed that adolescence is a period of great stress and unhappiness, many teenagers maneuver the tides of adolescence without any more turmoil than we are likely to encounter in other periods of life (Offer, Ostrov & Baker, 1981; Offer & Sabshin, 1984).) Moreover, and again contrary to a prevailing stereotype about adolescence, many adolescents report that they enjoy relatively good relations with their parents. They agree with them on basic values and on future plans, such as whether to attend college, and on many other matters. For most American teens, although frictions and collisions with parents and other authority figures flare up, the sense-of-self eventually takes root and the capacity for intimacy matures. For these young Americans, the value system of adult culture and the strengths and weaknesses of people, families, and institutions are put into more workable and useful perspectives, and the seas begin to calm (Bachman, 1987; Galambos, 1992). For some, however, the dark seas never calm.

FACTS OF TEENAGE LIFE AND DEATH

There have been many periods in the world's history when young people were at great risk with respect to physical and psychological harm. Warfare,

BURYING THE BROTHERS

Two corpses lie on separate tables at the Whitted and Williams funeral home in Oakland, California. Carefully picking over every detail from clothing to skin tone, Donnell Williams is getting ready for another burial. From his dark double-breasted suit to the bright sincerity in his eyes, Williams is the essence of the earnest undertaker. With one notable distinction: at 25, he may be the youngest mortician in the United States. He is a young African American man burying young African American men in an area of Oakland that the police call "the kill zone."

"So many young men, so many, I hate to see them come in," Williams said as he caught a spot near the eye of one corpse that was not tinted quite right and called an assistant over to touch it up. "I've had mothers come in and make 'pre-need' arrangements for their children—that's when they set up a funeral in advance because they know what's probably coming. Happens all the time. Last week I had a lady come in who had one son tragically shot, and she wanted to make arrangements for her other son," Williams said. "It was like she'd given up all hope. It was heartbreaking."

Summer and Christmas vacations are boom times for morticians in East Oakland, as in other troubled urban areas, but even in off months, there is never a shortage of customers. "I'd say I do about one girl for every 20 young men . . . the majority of our business is men between 16 and 25 years old. My age. Too many." Williams makes a point of hiring young men from the surrounding neighborhood, and if they tell him of some street thug they admire, Williams advice is simple. "I take them back, show them the bodies we have, and they can see the holes where they were shot or stabbed. And I tell them, 'You may be idolizing that person, but just look at this. Remember, we buried someone just last week who was like this person you idolize.'"

Source: Adapted from Kevin Fagan. (1994, May 11). "So many young men, so many." laments an Oakland mortician *San Francisco Chronicle,* p. A8.

revolutions, invasion, and conquest by foreign powers all take a great toll on the adolescent population, which often functions as soldiers or revolutionaries in such social convulsions. In 1994, the British relief agency Save the Children reported that children and adolescents are conscripted as soldiers in thirty-five countries, and in Mozambique alone an estimated 100,000 male children and adolescents were forced to serve in the rebel army during its 16-year civil war.

It is difficult to believe that young Americans today face a dangerous or more threatening world than those of preceding generations or of their counterparts in other places, such as Bosnia, Mozambique, and the Mideast. And yet, young Americans do seem to face a new and uniquely disturbing set of problems and circumstances that have been building for three decades or more. In fact, many social scientists have reached the conclusion that in the 1990s and into the next century, young Americans face a set of conditions and perils that have escalated to a point unlike those encountered by any recent generation (Takanishi, 1993; Weissbourd, 1996; Fox-Genovese, 1996).

Consider some simple facts of life and death for young Americans today.

• Young Americans are among the highest risk groups for contracting AIDS.
• More teenagers than ever suffer the effects of poverty.
• Teenagers' rates of drug use, eating disorders, and depression are rising. In 1990, 65% of adolescents reported using alcohol and other drugs by the ninth grade.

- Young Americans face collapsing public education, lower test scores, and astronomical college tuition costs.
- More than 12,000 young American are admitted to hospital emergency rooms each year with self-inflicted bodily injuries.
- Young Americans are fifteen to twenty times more likely to die from homicide than their counterparts in other industrialized nations.
- The U.S. rate of suicide for 5- to 14-year-olds has nearly tripled in recent decades. Between 1980 and 1992, the suicide rates for adolescents, ages 10–14, increased: 300% for African American males, 200% for white females, 100% for African American females, and 86% for white males.
- In 1992, firearm-related deaths accounted for 64.9% of suicides among people under 25. Among those ages 15–19, firearm-related suicides accounted for 81% of the increase in the overall suicide rate from 1980 to 1992.
- Suicide is the third-leading cause of death for young people between the ages of 15 and 24 in the United States (National Center for Health Statistics, 1995c) and the second-leading cause of death for young people in Canada and Australia.

Surveying these grim statistics, humanities professor Elizabeth Fox–Genovese (1996) suggests that we are leaving the "age of childhood," in which children were prized and made central to family and community life, and reverting back to a time, not so long ago, when children were viewed as miniature adults. She and other scholars (Weissbourd, 1996) believe that the dissolution of the

American teenagers face a set of conditions and perils that have been building for more than thirty years. During this period, suicide rates have risen three-fold making suicide the third leading cause of death for young people between 15 and 24 years of age. © *R. Marrone*

American nuclear family, geographic mobility, the pressures of consumerism, along with media abstractions of violence and egocentrism are creating a youthful world where teen pregnancy, drug and alcohol abuse, and adolescent suicide are seen as ways out for children who are slowly losing their childhood. She writes (Fox-Genovese, 1996:41):

> If the disquieting number of teen suicides seems to receive less attention than a few years ago, it still ranks as a national shame, and there is no reason to take lightly the evidence of drug and alcohol abuse by teenagers, and of pregnancies among teens, not to mention younger children. We are living in the midst of children who are anxious, pressured or disoriented, and they are too many to number. Wherever we turn, we confront social, cultural and economic patterns that seem to be cutting the remaining shreds of childhood out from under children's feet.

ADOLESCENCE, DEATH, AND DYING

Although commonly viewed as a single phase or stage of life, some social scientists believe adolescence consists of three distinct phases: young, middle, and late adolescence. From each of these phases, adolescents gradually piece together a *self-schema,* a cognitive framework for understanding themselves. Once formed, this schema remains fairly constant throughout the life span and serves as a central guide in many different contexts, including the encounter with death and dying. For young Americans, meeting the challenge of developing a self-identity, along with the capacity for intimacy with others, creates distinct concerns and issues in relation to dying and death that have a separate focus from those of younger children (Gordon, 1986).

Young Adolescence.   For the young adolescent (12–15 years), although there is an increasing awareness of the personal and family implications of death, death still seems very remote. The young adolescent recognizes that death will occur some day, but that day is placed in a far-off and vague future. Younger teenagers rarely form the idea that death will some day cut them off from a meaningful life.

"LIFE SUCKS SO MUCH"

"You know life sucks so much as it is now. A lot of teenagers don't know if it's going to get better or not, I guess. I guess this is their only way out. They feel they can't talk to people. We don't feel like we can talk to our parents or anybody. They say they understand, they don't."

These are the words of Alicia Marshall, 16, interviewed at a memorial service on a cliff overlooking the Pacific Ocean in San Pedro, California, where her two classmates, Amber Hernandez, 14, and Alicia Hayes, 15, had jumped to their deaths the day before. Witnesses said the two young women had tied their wrists together before they jumped to their deaths.

Source: Adapted from Principal says suicide intrigued teens who died. (1996, May 25). *San Francisco Chronicle,* p. A19.

Middle Adolescence.   In middle adolescence (15–17 years), our attitudes tend to reveal more interest in the quality of life than in how long we will live. Although, as middle adolescents we are beginning to impart more personal meaning to notions of death and dying, the prominent attitude is one of *death defiance*—high risk-taking and belief in our own invulnerability to harm and death. For some of us, middle adolescence is the peak of turmoil and rebellion, in which we are prone to intense emotional fluctuations and extreme reactions. We tend to exhibit a fight-or-flight response to stressful situations, try to bargain with adults, and think that we know it all. Parents become "worst enemies," peer approval becomes a top priority, and we are more likely to experiment or break rules as we try to establish our own beliefs and values (Deveau, 1990; Adams and Deveau, 1987). As middle adolescents, immersed in sexual exploration, dating, and love games, we tend to romanticize death, as seen in teenage films, literature, and rock 'n' roll music.

Late Adolescence.   In late adolescence (17 years plus), rationality and increasing maturity allow young people to face death and dying with less denial than their younger counterparts. During this period, we complete our physical and sexual maturation, begin to clarify our ethics and values, and continue to acquire adult social skills. We also begin to move into new social spheres and try to find peers—and perhaps a mate—with the same values. Goals, hopes, and aspirations are tested. Often, there is an excitement and enthusiasm for new situations and ideas (Pattison, 1977). Part of this capacity for projecting ourselves into the future, in concert with increased independent thinking, involves an increasing ability to imagine our own deaths. The idea that death will someday end that future can be emotionally devastating for some.

Accidents are the number-one cause of death for young Americans, especially for those in late adolescence. The accidental deaths are often the consequence of premature attempts to be involved with adult pursuits, such as driving and drinking, and there is often a family conflict in the background. Typically the death occurs in a motor vehicle accident of some kind. It is sudden and unexpected. It frequently occurs on a background of substantial family conflict. According to psychiatrist Beverley Raphael (1983, 1995), there has often been an argument beforehand about whether or not the adolescent should go. The whole outing may have been intended as an act of defiance of parental wishes or

ACCIDENTS AND HEARTBREAK

"Alan was 17 and had been working a year when he finally bought his motorbike. His mother, Mary, was apprehensive about its dangers. She had always been anxious and overprotective toward him. Her relationship with his father was fraught with provocations, alcohol, verbal and physical violence. She had asked Alan not to go out that night, but his father had abused her and Alan had said he'd be all right. The night went on and he failed to return. She worried and would not sleep, but she kept reasoning to herself that he would be with his mates.

"At 3:00 a.m., the police arrived to inform her that there had been an accident and they 'thought it was her son involved. Did she have a picture of him?' Her husband, Wal, finally woke. Identification proved that it was indeed Alan. He had run his bike into a car on the opposite side of the road. Blood alcohol levels were high. Mary wept profusely in the hours and days that followed, bemoaning her fate and the death of her son. Her doctor gave her heavy sedation, but to little avail. Wal took to drinking more, as he felt useless at home and heartbroken in his own way about Alan's death. He was deeply hurt and felt his wife gave him no support but was instead 'wallowing in self-pity.' Mary's grief continued unabated until she was referred for psychiatric assessment 2 years later following an overdose of barbiturates."

Source: Raphael (1983), p. 141.

simply for the thrill of risk taking. Police officers bring the message of the death to a shocked mother and father, who must then identify the dead body. Sometimes the mother is prevented from seeing the body, adding to the difficulty of accepting the reality and finality of her loss.

Late adolescents and young adults find it harder to deal with, and have more anxiety about, their own death than do younger individuals. Shneidman (1973, 1985), for example, discovered that most college students viewed death anxiously, as the end of existence, but were most disturbed by the idea that death meant there would no longer be any individual experiences. Death meant the end of the capacity of the person to reflect on life and living and to bring dreams and aspirations to fruition. Though college students see themselves as distant from death, when thoughts of death arise, they are often romanticized. Death is portrayed as a lover, as heroic, or as a mysterious, transformative experience. At this age, perhaps more than at any other, a person wants to continue to exist, for he or she is entering the creative and developing adult years.

When a young person learns that she or he is terminally ill and that death is imminent, there is the difficulty of coping with disappointment, frustration, and profound confusion. Feelings emerge of having been cheated out of a rightful portion of one's life. The feeling of frustration is often the most important emotion expressed by a dying young adult. A 17-year-old with AIDS who wanted to be an artist explodes in angry hatred at his disfigured and debilitated body; a 22-year-old graduate student becomes depressed because her creative ability was finally beginning to emerge just as her leukemia was worsening and death was imminent (Pattison, 1977; Rhodes & Vedder, 1983; Raphael, 1995).

There is considerable transition in thought and understanding of death during the adolescent years, and many factors have a direct bearing on the difficulties that young people have in coping with their own dying or the death of someone close to them. Gordon (1986) and Deveau (1990) have isolated a number of factors believed to influence the adolescent's conflicted and confusing reactions to death and dying, including the avoidance of death and dying in childhood; shyness, uncertainty, and lack of confidence in an emerging self-identity; the turmoil and panic of adolescence itself; and the media portrayal of death as violent and gruesome, especially in teenage-oriented films, comic books, TV shows, computer games, and rock 'n' roll music.

The Avoidance of Death in Childhood

As children, many of us were screened or sheltered from any real involvement in dying and death, and, consequently, we learned to engage in cognitive denial, emotional repression, and behavioral passivity in dealing with death and dying. Such topics were usually not discussed openly and systematically. As a result, many young Americans lack the preparation to cope with death (Gordon, 1986; Deveau, 1990). Interestingly, although parents, and society in general, attempt to shield young children from death, surveys suggest that an overwhelming majority of adolescents must deal with death during their youthful years, usually the death of a peer. In Schacter's (1991–92) survey of 13–19-year-old Americans, 87% indicated they had experienced the death of a peer, 13% had not (although most reported involvement and awareness of a relative's death), and 20% had had more than one experience with the death of a peer.

Shyness, Uncertainty, and Lack of Confidence

Certain behavioral characteristics surrounding shyness and feelings of insecurity sometimes inhibit young people from asking questions and expressing feelings and thoughts involving death and dying. Because adolescents sometimes tend to remain quiet, adults may assume they are uninterested and have no real concerns. In the midst of this social isolation, young people often turn to each other for support. Peers, however, may not be very supportive in sorting out difficult feelings connected with death and dying because they may not have had a similar personal experiences, or they may be too anxious to talk about what is happening (Gordon, 1986; S. J. Lee, 1990).

Adolescence = Turmoil and Disruption

Several contradictory assumptions underlie societal expectations of adolescents and young adults. Young people are expected to be more mature than children; therefore, they are expected to think rationally and understand what is happening. According to this line of thinking, adolescents should be able to handle any crisis and cope with whatever transpires. Because adolescents are capable of independent thought and action, it may be assumed that they are less dependent on adults for assistance and guidance in facing death and dying. In some cases, according to Adams and Deveau (1987), parents and adults may impose expectations and responsibilities that are beyond an adolescent's true capabilities. Parents and other adults often rationalize that, because issues related to death are seen as very personal, adolescents' privacy should be upheld. Consequently, they are often left on their own to manage difficult thoughts and feelings as they attempt to come to terms with their own dying or the death of a loved one (S. J. Lee, 1990; Raphael, 1995).

> **"Our youth love luxury; they have bad manners, contempt for authority, they show disrespect for elders and love chatter in place of exercise. Children are now tyrants, not the servants of their households. They no longer rise when elders enter the room. They contradict their parents, chatter before company, gobble up their food, and tyrannize their teachers."**
>
> –Plato, quoting Socrates in the fifth century, B.C.

Society is, and perhaps has always been, uncomfortable with adolescence, defining it as a time of turmoil and disruption, a time that adults wish would pass quickly so that young people could get on with their lives. This stereotyping of adolescents by adults as "going through a stage," "from another planet," "tyrants," "hormones with legs," and the like tends to create a pattern of interaction that separates adolescents from other adults. This so-called "generation gap" may hinder open and honest communication and discussion concerning dying, death, and the accompanying feelings and thoughts.

Death = Distance, Violence, and Destruction

From a societal perspective, we are still uncomfortable with illness, dying, and death. Death is held at a distance by our society. It is viewed as impersonal, and

A "TEENAGER" SPEAKS

"Perhaps the experiences of teenagers are more grievous than those of adults; personally I wouldn't know, since I have never been a 'grown-up.' All I know for certain is that I have encountered grief and I have already experienced it more than I care to in my lifetime. Volumes of books have been written and published on the subject of grief; even more on the subject of adult-related grief and child-related grief. But when it comes to teen-related grief, very few experts are willing to write up actual accounts, much less give advice. Personally, I believe that the hesitancy arises from the fact that teenagers cannot be categorized as easily as adults or children. After all, that was the reason the label 'teenager' came into existence. Teens cannot readily be placed in the category of either adult or child, because teens are in a transition which society has nicknamed 'that stage.' However frightening that may sound, teenagers are emphatically people, overwhelmingly subject to all human responses and behaviors. Unrecognized grief in young adults leads to physical, emotional, and mental turmoil and upheaval . . . and may lead to suicide attempts. . . . The task of seeking help should be the duty of caring and observant people who are part of that teenager's life. Society as a whole must start taking on the responsibility. Let's get responsible . . . let's save some young lives."

   -Susan J. Lee, Senior at River Dell Senior High
    School, Oradell, New Jersey

Source: S. J. Lee (1990), p. 49.

often is depicted by the media as violent and destructive (Kearl, 1995; Gordon 1986; Marrone, 1995). These portrayals may have a significant impact on young peoples' attitudes toward dying, death, and the mourning after. Wass, Raup, and Sisler (1989), for example, in a survey of 712 students (ages 12–18 years) from urban and rural schools found that the majority of adolescents reported high proportions of violent death on their favorite TV programs, and they reported ambivalence about allowing younger children to watch these programs. The fact that the majority of participants in this survey overestimated the annual incidence of homicide in the United States suggested to these researchers that an association exists between fear of death and dying in adolescents and the presentation of violent death by the electronic media.

Rock 'n' Roll 'n' Death

One way of gaining an understanding of the experience of young Americans and their relationship to death, dying, and suicide is, in the words of the Doobie Brothers (1976), to "listen to the music." Thomas Attig (1986:32) states, "Where traditional culture (family, school, church, political institutions) is perceived as silent, irrelevant, hypocritical, confusing, or corrupt, it is not uncommon for adolescents to turn to their music." The themes in American rock 'n' roll music, such as love, alienation, and death, allow young people to identify with personal concerns and fears, as well as with cultural heroes, values, ideals, hopes, and aspirations. From "bubblegum" pop love songs to "megadeath" heavy-metal rock 'n' roll music provides a connection between peers and an alternative frame of reference within which concerns can be acknowledged, if not addressed, in a shared language. Rock 'n' roll "provides many young Americans with mirrors of who they and society are, and intimations of what they and society might become" (Leming & Dickinson, 1994:127–128). In a real sense, rock 'n' roll amplifies the concerns of young people, sometimes through distorted speakers (Corr, Nabe and Corr, 1994).

Following the first-known sociological analysis of rock music by Thrush and Paulus (1970), Thomas Attig's (1986) psychological analysis focused on a number of death–related themes in popular music of the 1960s, '70s, and '80s, including: songs of alienation, drugs, old age, living in the shadow of death, and literal and symbolic immortality; songs about war, peace, nuclear devastation, hunger, the apocalypse, violence, guns, murder, mayhem, outlaws, death in the ghetto, and pornographic sex; and songs of loss, death, grief, mourning, and suicide. Sociologist Michael C. Kearl, in *Endings: A Sociology of Death and Dying* (1989), extended Attig's analysis into a study of the fate of rock performers and the theme of death in television and film. Charles A. Corr (1991) deepened the analysis of rock 'n' roll lyrics further with his attempt to portray rock lyrics more closely as a reflection of American adolescents' view of death and dying.

ROUND HERE, COUNTING CROWS, 1993

Maria says she's dying,
Through the door, I hear her crying
Why? I don't know

Then she looks up at the building
and says she's thinking of jumping.
She says she's tired of life;
she must be tired of something.

Round here we're carving out our names
Round here we all look the same
Round here we talk just like lions
But we sacrifice like lambs
Round here she's slipping through my hands

Source: From Counting Crows. (1993). Round here. On *August and Everything After.*

COFFIN SONGS AND CASKET TUNES

From American rock 'n' roll's very inception and popularization in the 1950s, the theme of death and dying has held a central place. The so-called "casket tunes," or "coffin songs," recorded in the 1950s and early '60s, included "Tragedy" by the Fleetwoods (1962), "Tell Laura I love Her" by Ray Peterson (1960), and "Leader of the Pack" by the Shangri-las (1964). Mark Dinning's "Teen Angel" (1960) tells the archetypal and tragic story of a fatal train wreck and the death of his "teen angel," who, rescued from the stalled car on the railroad track, runs back to the car and is killed while attempting to retrieve his high school ring, a symbol of their love. Standing by her grave, he sings, "I'll never kiss your lips again, they buried you today."

PROTEST SONGS

The 1960s, punctuated by cultural upheaval and protest of racial segregation and the Vietnam war, along with the assassinations of John F. Kennedy, Martin Luther King, Jr., and Robert Kennedy, gave birth to numerous antiviolence and antiwar protest songs, as well as songs about interracial love. Janis Ian's song about interracial dating, "Society's Child," reportedly was banned by many radio stations in the 1960s and may have provoked the murder of a Louisiana disc jockey brazen enough to have played the song on the local pop station during the height of the civil rights movement (Marrone, 1995). "I'm-Fixin'-to-Die Rag" by Country Joe and the Fish became an anthem for the Woodstock Nation of antiwar protesters, in the United States and Canada as well as in Western Europe.

TRIBUTES TO THE DEAD

Songs of tribute to slain presidents and political leaders, such as Dion's "Abraham, Martin and John" (1975), have continued into the 1990s, with James Taylor's tribute to Martin Luther King, Jr., entitled "Shed a Little Light" (1991). Don McLean's "American Pie" (1972), another tribute tune, views news of the plane-crash deaths of Buddy Holly, the Big Bopper, and other early rockers as a turning point in rock's loss of innocence.

The theme of drugs is prominent in the rock 'n' roll of the 1970s and early 1980s, while the drug-overdose deaths of rock stars such as Janis Joplin, Jimi Hendrix, and Jim Morrison created places of honor for them as rock icons. The drug/death theme is graphically captured in Paul Simon's "Save the Life of My Child" (1968), which depicts a scene in which a crowd is gathered beneath a young man perched on a ledge, threatening suicide, under the influence of drugs. Death also came prematurely to Buddy Holly (fatal crash, age 22), Elvis Presley (drug-related coronary, age 42), Keith Relf of the Yardbirds (electrocution by guitar, age 33), Jim Croce (plane crash, age 30), Ronnie Van Zant of Lynard Skynyrd (plane crash), Keith Moon of The Who (drug overdose), Brian Jones of the Rolling Stones (drug-related drowning), Sid Vicious of the Sex Pistols (suicide), Cass Elliot of the Mamas and Papas (age 30), Minnie Ripperton (cancer), Duane Allman (motorcycle crash), Karen Carpenter (anorexia nervosa), John Lennon (murder), Marvin Gaye (murder), Selena (murder, age 23) and Jonathan Melvoin (drug overdose, age 32) of Smashing Pumpkins. Kurt Cobain of Nirvana (drug-related suicide, age 27), joined this list of icons in 1994 (Marrone, 1995; Kearl, 1989).

GRIEF AND BEREAVEMENT

In the 1970s, themes of grief, bereavement, and personal loss were penned by James Taylor in "Fire and Rain" (1971), by David Gates (of Bread) in "Everything I Own" (1973), and by Jackson Browne in "For a Dancer" (1974). Taylor captures the typical denial preceding an imminent death, Gates mourns the death of his father, and Browne speaks to confusion in life and in the face of death: "I don't know what happens when people die, Can't seem to grasp it as hard as I try" (Attig, 1986:40). Melissa Manchester's "Don't Cry Out Loud" speaks to coming to terms with hurt, as do the love songs of Michael McDonald, formerly of the Doobie Brothers.

The themes of living in the shadow of nuclear devastation, social isolation, and ecological catastrophe are also prominent in the 1970s (Marrone, 1995). Marvin Gaye's album *What's Goin' On* and the single "Mercy, Mercy Me" are considered rock classics of ecological disaster, poverty, crime, and the isolation and alienation of the African American community from mainstream America. Chicago's intergalactic paean to nuclear and ecological devastation, "When All The Laughter Dies In Sorrow," speaks to a similar theme.

OLD AGE, SUICIDE, AND DEATH

A prominent aversion to aging is another major theme for the generation that coined the line "Don't trust anyone over 30" as well as for the generations that followed. In "My Generation" (1970), the lead singer of The Who repeatedly pleads to die before becoming old, with great repugnance towards old age itself. Blondie's "Die Young, Stay Pretty" (1971) paints a similar picture of old age as a repugnant state that is to be avoided at all cost, including death. Some songs, by contrast, express wonder about what it is like to be old and to see life from its ending. For example, in "When I'm Sixty-Four" (1967), the Beatles wonder about intimate connections with others in old age when they ask whether they will still be needed and cared for "when I'm sixty-four." In "Old Friends" (1968), Paul Simon sketches a touchingly lonely scene of two old friends sitting on a park bench, "winter companions waiting for the sunset" (Attig, 1986). The concept of life after death is treated in Joan Baez' rendition of the folk hymn "Will the Circle Be Unbroken?" (1969) in which the singer anticipates being reunited with her dead mother in a heavenly afterlife.

The theme of suicide is central to Elton John's "I Think I'm Gonna Kill Myself" (1972), the Little River Band's "Suicide Boulevard" (1981), and songs by Blue Oyster Cult, Paul Simon, and Queen (Attig, 1986). Rock musician Don McLean's "Vincent," a song from his 1972 album *American Pie,* explored van Gogh's pain as he may have contemplated his suicide. The romantic conceit of the song is that, although van Gogh's love for the subjects he painted is evident in his work, they would not love him as deeply in return (Attig, 1986).

A sampling of music popular in the 1980s and 1990s makes for interesting listening in regard to beliefs about the significance of life, death, suicide, unfinished business, and life after death. Examples include "In the Living Years" by Mike and the Mechanics, "The Rose" by Bette Midler, "I'll Be There" by the Escape Club, and "Round Here" by Counting Crows. "Tears in Heaven" by Eric Clapton is a hauntingly beautiful message to Clapton's 2-year-old son, who was accidentally killed in a fall from the window of a skyscraper. Eddy Vedder of Pearl Jam, as one of the leading male rockers of the 1990s, is a perfectly conflicted figure for his generation, as was Kurt Cobain of Nirvana. On Pearl Jam's first two albums, Vedder sang tales of isolation, estrangement, betrayal, bitterness, memories of child abuse, and suicidal fantasies, musing that he, "Cannot find the comfort in this world." A 1995 video by the rock/metal group Live, from their album *Throwing Copper,* offers a romantic visual variation on the funeral theme so present in contemporary rock videos. In this one, a series of images of a surreal and prayerful funeral service for a young woman is accompanied with wails of "I can feel it!" The 5-minute video culminates with the young woman's return to life and her birthing of a flailing baby, who joins the mother in a tender, fading kiss (Marrone, 1995).

HEAVY METAL AND SELF-DESTRUCTION

Some research studies support the speculation that a minority of young people, who are particularly troubled, experimenting with drugs, and from stress-filled family environments, are drawn particularly to heavy-metal, hard rock and songs with suicide, homicide, or satanic themes. Wass et al. (1988–89), for example, conducted a survey of hundreds of American young people concerning their rock music preferences and views on themes about homicide, satanism, and suicide to determine the number of adolescents who listen to this music and their attitudes about its effects on them as well as on other listeners. Results revealed that 9% of young adolescents in middle school, 17% of the rural, and 24% of the urban high school students were fans of this death-oriented rock. Three-fourths

Kiss of Death. **Since its very inception in the 1950s, the theme of death has held a central place in rock 'n' roll music. Young Americans who are particularly troubled, experimenting with drugs, and from stress-filled family environments are drawn particularly to heavy-metal, hard rock.** © *AP/Wide World Photos*

of these fans were male, and nearly all listeners were white. More of these fans claimed to know all the lyrics of their favorite songs than did the fans of other music; more fans of death-oriented rock said young children should be permitted to listen to rock music with destructive themes; and fewer of them believed that adolescents might commit murder or suicide after having listened to such songs.

In follow-up research, Wass, Miller, and Stevenson (1989) explored the rock music preferences of 894 ninth- through twelfth-graders in rural, urban, suburban public, and metropolitan parochial schools. Results revealed that 17.5% of participants were fans of rock music with lyrics that promote homicide, suicide, or satanic practices. As compared to nonfans, fans of suicide, homicide, and satanic rock were more likely to have parents who were never married or remarried and were more likely to be male European Americans enrolled in urban but not parochial schools.

In a 1993 Australian study of the possible relationships between adolescents' music preference and aspects of their psychological health and lifestyle, Martin, Clarke, and Pearce (1993) had 138 male and 109 female high school students complete self-report questionnaires on preferred music types and messages in the music. The Youth Self-Report and Profile provided information about suicide ideation, deliberate self-harm, depression, and delinquency. Brief risk-taking and drug-taking scales and questions about family environment were also administered. Results revealed a marked gender bias, with 74% of young females preferring pop music and 70.7% of young males preferring heavy rock/metal music. Significant associations appeared to exist between a preference for heavy rock/metal music and suicidal thoughts, acts of deliberate self-harm, depression, delinquency, drug taking, and family dysfunction. Feeling sadder after listening to the preferred music appeared to distinguish the most disturbed group of young people.

According to Wass, Miller, and Redditt (1991), themes in rock music might best be understood metaphorically, rather than literally, as symbols of deep concerns and emotions of young people. In this sense, rock music may serve a therapeutic purpose, providing the means for dealing with issues of emotional conflict, loss, and suicide and for managing the anxieties created by them.

In working with troubled youth, Macken, Fornatale, and Ayers (1980) and Marrone (1995) found that familiarity with the music on the part of counselors and significant adults allows for access to and comprehension of adolescent concerns and, in a real sense, is akin to learning and using a foreign language. They found that the very attempt to understand the music says much about the genuineness of the act of reaching out through a song.

Perspectives on Youth Suicide

Suicide is a behavior that is as old as humankind. And as far as we know, humans beings are the only species whose members kill themselves intentionally. Since the earliest-recorded suicides of Samson and Saul, around 1000 B.C., Western philosophers and poets have considered it, pondered its meaning, and written treatises about it. Shrouded in mystery and shocking in its implications, human beings have always struggled to understand this behavior that seems to violate the most basic of all human instincts: the instinct for survival itself (Stillion & McDowell, 1995).

ANGER, GUILT, SUICIDE, AND NIRVANA

"I love you, I love you."
-from Cobain's suicide note found April 8, 1994
"Asshole, asshole, asshole."
-chant of 5,000 Cobain fans, April 10, 1994, Seattle

A suicide note and a shotgun marked the spot in the guest house where Kurt Cobain's body was found sprawled on the floor on April 8, 1994. The lead singer and song writer in the immensely successful and popular grunge rock group, *Nirvana,* committed suicide three days earlier at age 27—the same age at which other rock icons had died, including Janis Joplin, Jim Morrison and Jimi Hendrix. Nirvana—with their stringy hair, plaid work shirts and torn jeans—appealed to a massive audience of young fans—and their major-label debut album, "Nevermind," sold almost 10 million copies.

Cobain didn't overdose on drugs like Morrison and Hendrix, but his personal pain and self-destructiveness were also bound up with drugs, as well as firearms. In early March, Cobain overdosed on painkillers and champagne while in Rome. On March 18, Cobain reportedly locked himself in a room of his spacious Seattle house with firearms and threatened suicide. On April 2, Cobain left a California drug rehabilitation facility, where he tried to overcome a long-standing heroin habit, purchased a shotgun and flew to Seattle. His body was discovered by an electrician a few days later. Later the same day, Cobain's wife, Courtney Love, and his two-year-old daughter, Frances Bean Cobain, arrived at their home via limo.

Rosy Nolan, a 15-year-old Cobain fan, interviewed outside a Berkeley, California, rock club on the eve of the announcement of Cobain's death, said, 'Wow, what a hero. It's more like, "What a stupid idiot." ' Another fan said, "He's a punk. He had a cush life. Are you gonna kill yourself and leave behind a 2-year-old daughter? Not!" In an obscenity-laced recorded farewell, his wife asked a crowd of 5,000 fans who had gathered in Seattle, to call the singer, "an asshole." Later, referring to Cobain's heroin addiction, his withdrawal symptoms, and her own feelings of guilt, Love said, "Tough love doesn't work. We should have let him have the thing (heroin) that made him feel better, the thing that made his stomach feel better.' Courtney Love reportedly attempted suicide a few days later with an overdose of heroin.

Source: Gina Arnold, (April 11, 1994) Wild Farewell for Kurt Cobain: Wife's angry words played for crowd, *San Francisco Chronicle,* p. D1 and "He Was a Geek and a God": The Story Behind the Tragic Death of Kurt Cobain, *Rolling Stone,* issue 682, May, 19, 1994, pp. 17–20.

Condemned by most of the world's great religions as a violation of God's law, suicide has sometimes been used as a form of execution. Perhaps the most famous such case is that of the philosopher Socrates, who was required to drink hemlock to end his life in 399 B.C. after being found guilty of corrupting the youth of Athens. In the twentieth century, the German general Erwin Rommel took poison rather than be executed for his role in a plot to oust Adolf Hitler from office.

In some societies, suicide has had a social dimension. In Japan, for example, the customs and rules of social class have demanded suicide under certain circumstances. Called *seppuku* (and popularly known as *hara-kiri,* which means "self-disembowelment"), it has long been viewed as an honorable method of taking your life. It was used by warriors after losing a battle, to avoid the dishonor of capture, and as a means of capital punishment to spare warriors the disgrace of execution.

In the Western world, since the eighteenth century, suicide has been thought of by some as a romantic type of death. The individual, in seemingly hopeless conflict with the world, decides to end his or her existence in what amounts to a final temper tantrum against a society that can no longer be tolerated. In so doing, the person symbolically obtains a final revenge on everything and everyone that has caused these feelings of depression and alienation. This notion led to the belief that some artistic individuals, such as writers, painters, and musicians, glamorize suicide, thinking that such a death will add to their reputations. In 1774, the German writer Johann Wolfgang von Goethe's novel *The Sorrows of Werther* reinforced this concept and was credited with creating a near-epidemic of romantic suicides in Europe. Since that time, among well-known artists who killed themselves are Vincent van Gogh, Virginia Woolf, Anne Sexton, Mark Rothko, Jerzy Kosinski, Ernest Hemingway, and Sylvia Plath.

In the effort to comprehend what appears to be a violation of the essence of the human condition, social scientists have attempted to place suicidal behaviors within various categories [for example, anomic, egoistic, altruistic, and fatalistic (Durkheim, 1951)] and types (for example, cluster suicides and copycat suicides). Researchers have also studied the biological, cognitive, affective, and behavioral states of suicidal people, as well as the environmental factors that predispose to suicidal behavior. As evidence has accumulated, it has become clear that suicidal behavior, especially adolescent suicide, is one of the most complex behaviors in the human repertoire and that we have only begun to unravel its mysteries (Weissbourd, 1996).

YOUNG AMERICANS AND THE SUICIDE CRISIS

During the first half of the twentieth century, the youth suicide rate in the United States was stable at one-half the national rate. Things began to change in the mid-1950s, when the number of suicides among the young began to rise markedly. In 1977, for the first time, the adolescent suicide rate surpassed that for the nation as a whole (G. B. Fulton & Metress, 1995). By 1984, the rate had tripled, and suicide became one of the leading causes of death for young Americans. In the early 1990s, the adolescent suicide rate stood at 12.9 per 100,000, almost triple the 1950 measure of 4.5 per 100,000 (National Center for Health Statistics, 1995c).

American statistics on youth suicide may be the proverbial tip of the iceberg, because it is generally accepted that many suicides go unreported or are misreported as accidents or death due to undetermined causes (particularly for young

---

Dear Mom, Dad, and everyone else,

I'm sorry for what I've done, but I love you all and I always will, for eternity. Please, please, please don't blame it on yourselves. It was all my fault and not yours or anyone else's. If I didn't do this now, I would have done it later anyway. We all die someday, I just died sooner.

Love,
John

Source: Alan L. Berman, (1986). Helping suicidal adolescents: Needs and responses, In Charles A. Corr and Joan McNeil (Eds.), *Adolescence and Death*, p. 151. Springer, NY.

Note: John was 17 years old at the time of his death.

CARING INSIGHTS

Warning Signs of Suicide

Often, suicidal people give warning signs, consciously or unconsciously, indicating that they need help, frequently in the hope that they will be rescued. These signs usually come in clusters, so several warning signs often will be apparent. The presence of one or more of these warning signs does not necessarily mean that the person is suicidal; the only way to know for sure is to ask them. In other cases, a suicidal person may not want to be rescued, and may avoid giving warning signs. Here are some of the typical warning signs.

- Withdrawing from friends and family
- Depression:
- Loss of interest in usual activities
- Showing signs of sadness, hopelessness, irritability
- Changes in appetite, weight, behavior, level of activity, or sleep pattern
- Loss of energy
- Making negative comments about self
- Recurring suicidal thoughts or fantasies
- Sudden change from extreme depression to being "at peace" (may indicate that a decision has been made to attempt suicide)
- Talking, writing or hinting about suicide
- Previous attempts
- Feelings of hopelessness and helplessness
- Giving away possessions

This list is not definitive: Some people may show no signs yet still feel suicidal; others may show many signs yet be coping OK. The only way to know for sure is to ask. If a person is highly perturbed, has formed a potentially lethal plan to kill him- or herself, and has the means to carry it out immediately available, then that person would be considered likely to attempt suicide.

Source: Adapted from Graham Stoney. (1995, Sept. 15). Copyright 1994 by Graham Stoney.

children). It has been estimated that the actual number of suicides may be two to three times greater than official statistics indicate (National Center for Health Statistics, 1995c). In certain subpopulations of American adolescents, the numbers appear to be much higher. In the case of gay adolescents, for example, a number of reports conclude that gay male youths are far more likely to commit suicide than their heterosexual peers, with these youths comprising as many as 30% of all completed suicides among young males in the United States (Garnets

& Kimmel, 1993; Ramafedi, Farrow & Deisher, 1993). Interestingly, as the suicide rate has soared for young people between 15 and 24 years of age, it has declined slightly for the middle-aged and the elderly, although suicide rates for elderly white males remain the highest in the country. The most recent national statistics reveal that an increasing percentage of elderly Americans killed themselves between 1990 and 1994 (National Center for Health Statistics, 1995b).

GUNS AND SUICIDE

Easy access to firearms is an environmental factor that significantly increases the risks of suicide, especially among junior high and high school students. Hudgens (1983) maintains that the rise in suicides during the past 30 years can be accounted for almost entirely by the dramatic rise in deaths caused by handguns. The National Task Force on Suicide in Canada (1987:41) echoed Hudgens' observations by calling for measures "to reduce the lethality and availability of instruments of suicide, including more stringent gun control." Hudgens points to the lower suicide rates in states with stringent gun control laws as further support for the association between access to handguns and youth suicide.

ATTEMPTED SUICIDE AMONG YOUNG AMERICANS

To a great degree, the suicide crisis among young Americans involves *attempted suicide* (i.e., parasuicide) as much as completed suicide. It is estimated that when U.S. statistics for all age groups are lumped together, suicide attempts outnumber actual suicidal deaths by a ratio of about 8 to 1 (Cross & Hirschfeld, 1986; National Center for Health Statistics, 1995a). However, this ratio of attempted to completed suicides is much higher for adolescents than for any other age group. Studies suggest that the ratio among adolescents may be 100 to 1 and possibly even higher (Sheras, 1983; National Center for Health Statistics, 1995c).

For certain subpopulations of young Americans, especially those targeted for victimization and ostracism, the rates for attempted suicide may be even higher. Using a national sample of female participants, the National Lesbian and Gay Health Foundation found 59% of lesbian Americans from 17 to 24 years of age had contemplated suicide, while as many as 35% actually attempted suicide (Hershberger & D'Augelli, 1995) A 1993 study of gay male youths found that 42% reported suicide attempts (D'Augelli & Hershberger, 1993). These rates for gay and lesbian young people are significantly higher than overall estimates of high school suicide attempt rates, which range from 8% to 13% (Garland & Zigler, 1993).

GUNS AND YOUNG AMERICANS

Question	% Yes
"Can you get a gun if you want one?"	59%
"Know someone wounded or killed by gunfire?"	39%
"Believe you're likely to die from guns?"	35%
"Carried a handgun in the last 30 days?"	15%
"Carried a handgun to school during last year?"	4%
"Shot a gun at somebody?"	9%
"Were you seriously threatened with a firearm?"	13%
"Were you shot?"	11%

Source: Harvard University School of Public Health Survey of Middle and High School Youth, Nationwide. (1993). p. 6.

SELF-MUTILATION AND DEPRESSION

Each year, 12,000 American youths are hospitalized for deliberate acts of self-mutilation (Fasko & Fasko, 1991). Data suggest that about 3% of adolescents mutilate their bodies, but the rates are substantially higher among young adolescents. In one study of adolescent body mutilation, Garrison et al. (1993) administered a questionnaire and conducted psychiatric interviews with 249 female and 195 male adolescents (ages 11–18 years) to determine the frequency and correlates of self-mutilation acts. Prevalence estimates were 2.46% in males and 2.79% in females, and significant relationships were found between self-mutilation and suicidal ideation, major depression, and undesirable life events. These authors concluded that the strong correlation between nonsuicidal self-destructive acts and both suicidal ideation and major depression suggests that a history of self-damaging acts should be taken into consideration when evaluating for possible depression and suicide risk.

In some cases, self-mutilation by individuals may be connected to an extremely abnormal grief reaction to the loss of a loved one. Thompson and Abraham (1986), for example, reviewed the cases of fifty-three male individuals who attempted self-circumcision after the death of their fathers. They suggest that sons at risk for genital self-mutilation after paternal death might have had an undue attachment to mother and an intensely ambivalent relationship with the deceased father, which then precipitated this extremely rare grief reaction.

SUBJECT: RE: SELF-DESTRUCTIVE BEHAVIORS

"From: Deb

I used to cut myself deliberately for a couple years. It's been 6 months now since I've done any self-injury. The last time I didn't cut, I burned myself with a hot glue gun. None of this behavior had anything to do with suicidal thoughts. It was a way for me to numb out painful feelings. I've been in therapy for a few years and I've been on medication. The drugs didn't help the urges but the therapy has helped me to find healthier ways to deal with painful feelings. Because I have a painful chronic physical illness it was easier for me to deal with the pain of cutting than the pain of feelings. Once you cut or deliberately self-injure it gets hard to stop. So if you're still at the thinking stage—don't do it. Get yourself some professional help with someone who knows how to treat this problem."

Source: Subject: Re: Self-Destructive Behaviors. (1995, April 28).

THE SOCIOCULTURAL PERSPECTIVE

One of the first scholars to study suicide scientifically was the French sociologist Emile Durkheim. In his comprehensive sociological theory, entitled *Suicide: A Study in Sociology* (1951), Durkheim viewed suicide not as the act of an isolated individual but as the act of an individual within a society. In his view, whether a person commits suicide is determined in large part by the person's adjustment to and investment in society, by the stability or instability of that society, and by the network of values and norms with which the society embraces the individual. Durkheim's sociological model described four major types of suicide: *anomic, egoistic, altruistic,* and *fatalistic.*

Anomic suicide.   Anomic suicide occurs when the equilibrium of a society is severely disturbed. In the United States, for example, the unforeseen crash of the stock market in 1929 resulted in a rash of suicides. In Austria, suicide rates took a sharp upturn immediately following World War II, possibly because of the stress created by the loss of the war and the occupation by enemy troops (Havighurst, 1969; Bootzin, Acocella, & Alloy, 1993). Sociologists Michael Leming and George Dickinson (1994:332) state that anomic suicides "result from the lack of regulation of the individual when the norms governing existence no longer control that individual." In essence, the individual feels let down and unsupported by the failure of social structures and institutions. The individual who commits suicide following the loss of a job would fit into the category of anomic suicide.

Egoistic suicide.   A very different type of self-annihilation, egoistic suicide, results from the individual's lack of integration into society. Egoistic suicides are often loners, intellectuals, celebrities, social isolates, or political radicals who have less conventional links to society and who have no supportive social network to see them through periods of stress and personal pain.

Altruistic Suicide.   At the opposite extreme to egoistic suicide is altruistic suicide. This occurs because individuals are totally immersed in the norms of their culture as well as in a value system that tells them that under certain circumstances it is either necessary or honorable to commit suicide. In the modern era, this cultural endorsement of suicide has been much more common in Eastern than in Western cultures. Typical examples include the Japanese practice of hara-kiri, the suicide missions of kamikaze pilots during World War II, and the self-immolation of a number of Buddhist monks protesting the war in Vietnam.

Fatalistic Suicide.   This fourth type of suicide occurs because the individual despairs at succeeding in a society that allows little opportunity for individual fulfillment and feels overcontrolled and oppressed by the society's stringent rules and regulations. Fatalistic suicides are more likely for individuals living under slavery, in prison, in a totalitarian state, or under extreme physical and economic conditions. The population model offered by sociologists G. B. Fulton and E. K. Metress (1995), for example, proposes that the youth suicide rate fluctuates according to the number of young persons and their proportion to the rest of the population. It is theorized that as their numbers increase, so does competition for available resources, such as jobs, academic honors, spots on athletic teams, and admission to college/university programs, as well as adult nurturance, concern, and guidance. Heightened competition may, in turn, lead to increased stress, depression, and risk of suicide. As the adolescent population has increased, young people in the United States have experienced a rise in many behaviors indicative of social stress, including drug abuse, alcohol abuse, eating disorders, crime, and delinquency (Weissbourd, 1996).

The youth suicide rate plateaued in the 1980s as the last of the baby boom generation moved into adulthood and the number of adolescents fell. On the basis of census data, the number of adolescents will continue to decline into the late 1990s and then increase again after the year 2000. If the population model is correct, the youth suicide rate should be expected to follow the same pattern.

Parental Role and Youth Suicide

For bereaved parents, the suicide of their child, whatever the underlying reasons, often brings social ostracism, shame, and guilt feelings. Miles and Demi (1991–92), for example, in a study of the frequency of guilt feelings experienced by bereaved parents, compared parents whose children had died by suicide, by accident, and by chronic disease. Guilt was reported by 92% of suicide-bereaved parents, 78% of accident-bereaved parents, and 71% of chronic-disease–bereaved parents. Particularly strong guilt feelings were reported by the parents of suicide victims, with 34% reporting guilt as the most distressing aspect of their grief.

Other research suggests that dealing with the reactions of persons outside the family can be a significant source of stress for the parents of a suicide victim because the parents tend to experience greater guilt, shame, and stigmatization and perceive the social environment as less supportive (Calhoun & Allen, 1991). A study of social impressions of parents whose children had committed suicide did find them to be less liked and more blamed for the child's death (Calhoun, Selby, & Faulstich, 1980). A study by R. G. Dunn and D. Morrish-Vidners (1987–88) found that mothers were particularly blamed and that parental blame generally focused on poor communication patterns, inadequate role models, and parents transmitting their own personal problems and inadequacies onto the child. In large numbers, parents blamed themselves, became deeply depressed, and responded to the death as an act of rejection, abandonment, and punishment (R. G. Dunn & Morrish-Vidners, 1987–88).

THE NEUROSCIENCE PERSPECTIVE

Adult patterns of sexual development begin at puberty and continue to unfold during adolescence. Hormonal changes are central to rapid growth in height, cognitive development, mood swings, bone and muscle density, breast development, and body and facial-hair patterns. During adolescence the vagina gradually lengthens and the uterus enlarges, and the penis and testes increase in size. Both male and female voices lower. Feelings of sexual desire, accompanied by fantasies, daydreams, and infatuations, explode as boys and girls experience erotic dreams accompanied by orgasm and ejaculation. These dramatic biochemical changes may also play a significant role in the etiology of adolescent suicide. Suicidologist Judith M. Stillion (1995:192) writes, "Puberty brings about many hormonal changes. Physically, young adolescents experience a growth spurt and other bodily changes that require them to readjust to their changing body on almost a daily basis. These hormonal changes spark some of the psychological and cognitive changes that make adolescence such an extremely painful period for many youngsters."

The Biochemistry of Depression

Depression in young people heightens suicide risk, especially for those between the ages of 15 and 19. But even at younger ages, young people can become so despondent, so completely without hope of things becoming better, that they attempt to end their lives. David Clark (1993), noting that about 3% of older adolescent girls and 1% of older adolescent boys attempt suicide each year,

CARING INSIGHTS

Suicidal Ideas, Triggers, and Signs

Suicidal ideation, triggering events, and warning signs form an interrelated triad that is present in many suicides. Suicidal ideas, threats, and attempts often precede a suicide. The most commonly cited warnings of potential suicide include (a) extreme changes in behavior, (b) a previous suicide attempt, (c) a suicidal threat or statement, and (d) signs of depression, hopelessness, and a sense of meaninglessness in life. Young children who have depression may have physical complaints, be agitated, or hear imaginary voices. Adolescents may have school difficulties, may withdraw from social activities, have negative or antisocial behavior, or may begin to use and abuse alcohol or other drugs. They may display increased emotionality, and their moods may be restless, grouchy, aggressive, or sulky. They may not pay attention to their personal appearance and may refuse to cooperate in family ventures. Many want to leave home because they are being physically or sexually abused or because they feel they are not understood and approved of. Or they may be emotionally sensitive and reactive to rejection in love relationships.

These actions and events in a young person's life often lead to progressive social isolation. When an individual is isolated from family and is without friends, that person inhabits an existential vacuum in which a pressing problem with great emotional impact may precipitate suicide. The precipitating problem—a poor grade in school, loss of a job, not being allowed to go somewhere or to buy something special, the breakup of a romance—may sometimes appear trivial to an objective observer. But the seemingly trivial problem may serve as the "last straw" of frustration and distress for that young person, resulting in an attempted or completed suicide.

concludes that suicide in the absence of a major mental disorder is almost as rare among adolescents as it is among adults. In adult populations, suicidal preoccupations and suicide attempts tend to be linked strongly to symptoms of a depression. Children and adolescents treated for a major psychiatric disorder, particularly major depression, are also at greater risk for death by suicide.

Although many suicides are committed by people who are not clinically depressed and although there are many clinically depressed people who do not attempt suicide, the link between the two is strong and long-standing (Bootzin, Acocella, & Alloy, 1993; Stillion & McDowell, 1995). In a study of 100 adolescents who had attempted suicide, Chabral and Moron (1988) found that

90% met the diagnostic criteria for depressive disorders. Suicide seems to run in families, and some researchers suspect that what is inherited is a biochemical susceptibility to depression (Egeland & Sussex, 1985).

Beginning with the revolution in psychoactive drugs in the 1950s and '60s, psychopharmacologists have shown that clinical depression is related to the level of certain neurotransmitters in the brain (Asberg & Traskman, 1981; Banki & Arato, 1983; Schildkraut, 1965). A deficiency of one particular neurotransmitter, serotonin, has been found in the brain of some people who have completed suicide and in the cerebrospinal fluid of suicide attempters (Asberg, Nordstrom, & Traskman–Bendz, 1986). Serotonin has been found to be instrumental in regulating emotion, feelings, and mood, leading some researchers to speculate that a deficiency of serotonin may be implicated in both depression and suicide attempts, especially impulsive suicide attempts. In support of this hypothesis, tests of the cerebrospinal fluid of suicide attempters, particularly those who had

Across the human life span and across national boundaries, males complete suicide at a rate that is 3 to 5 times higher than for females. Researchers suspect that higher levels of male aggression, rooted in hormonal and other biochemical factors, may explain this gender difference. Others disagree.
© *Miro Vintoniv/Stock, Boston*

chosen impulsive and violent methods, have found evidence of abnormally low serotonin activity (Edman et al., 1986; Roy, DeJong, & Linnoila, 1989). In addition, postmortem analyses of suicides have found subnormal amounts of serotonin and also impaired serotonin receptors in the brainstem and frontal cortex (Mann et al., 1986). Other lines of research into the biology of depression have implicated the neurotransmitters acetylcholine and norepinephrine (Asberg, Traskman, & Thoren, 1976; Banki & Arato, 1983; Bootzin, Acocella, & Alloy, 1993). This intriguing work has already led to the development of many antidepressant drugs for treating neurotransmitter deficiencies, although it has not, as yet, addressed the question of how the deficiencies arise in the first place.

Gender, Aggression, and Suicide

Data indicate that across the life span, including those 15–24 years of age, American males have a much higher risk of suicide than females (National Center for Health Statistics, 1995c). This significant difference between males and females carries through across the human life span and across national boundaries. In all developed countries, males complete suicide at higher rates than do females. The most recent suicide rates in thirteen developed countries reveal that males in all reporting countries are two to five times more likely to commit suicide than females. Male and female suicide rates in the United States across a 26-year period show that the sex differences remain more than three male deaths for every one female death by suicide (Stillion & McDowell, 1995).

Whenever a behavior shows clear and consistent sex differences, across both cultures and time, researchers begin to suspect that it may rest, at least in part, on genetically based biochemical influences. Because suicide is clearly an aggressive behavior, a possible explanation of the heightened adolescent male suicide rates may come from the research into the biochemical basis of aggression. According to Stillion and McDowell (1995), given that male aggression is greater than female aggression in humans as well as in many other species, and from the very earliest ages at which it can be measured, the most logical inference is that there is a genetic or prenatal basis for heightened male aggression. Males may simply inherit a tendency toward higher aggressive activity. Such a tendency, when directed at the self (i.e., "murder in"), may help to explain the consistent sex difference in adolescent suicide rates. Others disagree, however, pointing out that the high rate of attempted suicide among females argues against the biochemical theory and that the higher completion rate for suicide among males is more directly the result of their use of more deadly means, such as firearms (A. M. Allen, 1995).

Impulsivity, Depression, and Youth Suicide

During the childhood years (ages 5–14), there are two additional factors for suicide that may also be rooted in biochemistry. The first is a tendency toward *impulsivity,* a psychological pattern in which the individual's behavior is governed to an inordinate degree by stimuli that are immediately present in the environment while representations of events that are not immediately present remain weak. A child who has suffered from abuse or neglect over a long period of time will jump in front of a car without warning. Another child may run from the room in the midst of a parental argument, find the parent's gun, and shoot himself or herself almost in one movement (Stillion & McDowell, 1995). Although youth suicide almost always results from a host of problems, the act itself tends to be more impulsive in childhood than in other age periods, suggesting a blending of physiological, affective, and cognitive factors that may be unique to this phase of life (Joffe & Offord, 1983; Kosky, 1982).

IMPULSE SUICIDE

His parents were moving to Houston because the father had been transferred by his employer. He said he was not going with them. He was an honor student, involved in sports and extracurricular activities. He showed his friends the gun, but no one took him seriously enough to tell school personnel. He walked to the front of the classroom, put the gun in his mouth, and pulled the trigger.

Source: J. Oaks, and G. Ezell, (1993), p. 215.

Hyperactivity may also play a role in childhood suicide (Pfeffer, Plutchik, & Mizruchi, 1983). Hyperactive children are unable to sit for a long time or to consider all the repercussions of an action (Derryberry & Rothbart, 1984). They have a bias for action and seem to move almost anxiously from one situation to another. Hyperactivity by itself does not predispose a child to suicide. However, if the predisposition to depression is there, or if there are sufficient other behavioral, emotional, cognitive, or environmental factors present, hyperactive children may be more prone to self-destruction. Hyperactive children may have less protection against suicide than others, who can contemplate alternative solutions to problems more fully. More so than at any other period of life, triggering events may be minor occurrences. Because these children are at higher risk for suicide, a seemingly tiny incident may trigger an act of self-destruction (Stillion & McDowell, 1995).

Moods, Drugs, and Adolescent Death

Research suggests that, as adolescents, we are somewhat unpredictable and moody, prone to emotional turmoil and confusion of thought. In several studies on this issue, large numbers of teenagers wore beepers and were signaled at random times throughout an entire week. When signaled, they were to enter their thoughts and feelings in a diary. Results indicated that they did in fact show frequent and large swings in mood, from the heights of euphoria to the depths of the blues (Csikszentmihalyi & Larson, 1984). Moreover, these swings occurred very quickly, sometimes within only a few minutes. Older adults also show shifts in mood, but theirs tend to be less frequent, slower, and smaller in magnitude.

Many young people find it difficult to deal with the turmoil and volatility of these mood swings. Some turn to the use of alcohol, cocaine, heroin, methamphetamines, or various designer drugs, such as ecstacy, as a way to alter and modulate moods. For some, the use of drugs to modulate mood states can create more problems than it solves. Alcohol and other drugs can have damaging effects on the body and can cause additional emotional volatility, along with cognitive and perceptual distortions. Family and social problems resulting from the use of alcohol and drugs can create additional sources of conflict. Accidents, homicides, and suicides, the three leading causes of deaths among young Americans, are frequently associated with biochemical changes connected with the concurrent use of alcohol and other drugs.

THE COGNITIVE PERSPECTIVE

Do adolescents think and reason like adults? And could cognitive dysfunction in adolescence allow us some insight into adolescent depression and suicide? Jean Piaget believed that, in many respects, adolescents do reason as adults do. In the stage of formal operations, adolescents can assess the validity of verbal statements, reason deductively, and show many other logical capabilities. Yet Piaget contended that adolescents' thinking still falls short of that of adults in several important respects. For instance, adolescents tend to use their newfound cognitive skills to construct "totally" sweeping theories and generalizations about various aspects of life. These theories are sometimes overblown and naive because they are not founded on extensive experience with life. Similarly, teenagers tend to exhibit inclinations toward egocentrism, rigidly holding to their views, assuming that none other but their own point of view could possibly be correct.

The idea that adolescent thinking is inferior to, or at least different from, that of adults is echoed by other researchers and theorists. Elkind (1967), for example, suggests that adolescents often go seriously astray when they try to conceptualize the thoughts of other persons because they fail, at times, to differentiate others' thoughts from their own. This tendency toward egocentrism also leads them to assume that they are the focus of others' attention, a phenomenon Elkind termed *the imaginary audience*. Adolescents tend to see themselves as superstars, on center stage, with other people focusing attention on them. Consequently, they can become painfully shy, self-conscious, and anxious in everyday situations.

Some adolescents tend to believe that their feelings and thoughts are totally unique, that no one else on the planet could possibly grasp the significance of the "here and now" experiences of "what is." Elkind (1967) referred to this adolescent phenomenon as *the personal fable*. This is our personal and dramatic story of uniqueness, victimization, and heroism; we are special, in the vanguard, and our story is difficult for others, especially adults, truly to comprehend.

Other research suggests that, in some ways, the magnitude of difference between adolescent and adult ways of thinking is smaller than developmental theories and

THE "UNFORTUNATES"

"Many social commentators believe that drug- and alcohol-related problems are the sources of chaos in young adults' lives. This is not so. Drugs and alcohol are the direct result of grief, when no one is available and/or willing to help. People are so quick to point out that the use of drugs and alcohol is directly responsible for 'devil worship' and 'evil music' which 'messed-up' teenagers are longing for. The actual cause of chaos may have been the indifference of just such eager critics. When society gives up on these teenagers and labels them 'the unfortunates,' no more hope is held for their futures, which only weeks or months before seemed so bright and promising. Young adults who feel desolate often resort to the last and only choice they believe is left: the choice between continuing with their life or ending it."

–Susan J. Lee, Senior at River Dell Senior High School, Oradell, New Jersey

Source: S. J. Lee (1990), p. 50.

everyday experience might suggest. The most intriguing research pointing to this conclusion involves the question of whether adolescents and adults think about risk in different ways. That adolescents tend to play the edge—engaging in lots of high-risk behaviors, ranging from unprotected sex to reckless driving—is obvious. One widely accepted explanation for this is that young people suffer from what has been termed *adolescent invulnerability,* the belief that as adolescents we are somehow immune (or excluded) from the potential harm of high-risk behaviors (Baron & Brown, 1991). Surprisingly, this belief is not supported by all research findings. Studies by Fischoff (1992) and Quadrel (1990), for example, indicate that adolescents are no more likely to view themselves as impervious to negative outcomes from risky behavior than are their parents.

Why, then, are adolescents more likely to engage in high-risk behaviors? Several factors may play a role. Perhaps adolescents find the rewards associated with such actions, such as peer approval and feelings of triumph, so pleasurable that they are not deterred even by the threat of serious potential harm. Alternatively, many adolescents may belong to groups whose social norms (rules about what is and is not appropriate behavior) favor high-risk actions. In short, they engage in such actions because their friends both expect and encourage them to do so. Together, these and other factors may help explain the gap between adolescents' beliefs—their recognition that they are not invulnerable to harm—and their tendency to engage in actions that threaten their health or safety (R. A. Baron, 1995).

Cognitive Distortion and Suicide

From a cognitive perspective, what determines a person's response to a situation is not the situation itself but the person's interpretation of the situation. Cognitive researchers and therapists are fond of quoting the Greek philosopher Epictetus, who noted that people "are disturbed not by things but by the view they take of them" (Bootzin, Acocella, & Alloy, 1993:76). It has become increasingly clear that because humans use their intellectual powers to build their self-concepts, to construct their views of the world, and to weigh and judge their past life choices and future opportunities, cognitive risk factors play a significant role in suicidal behavior across the life span.

Psychologist Aaron Beck and his associates have accumulated a body of evidence that shows that the thoughts of depressed and suicidal individuals are characterized by four types of cognitive distortions: rigidity of thought, selective abstraction, overgeneralization, and inexact labeling (Beck, 1967; Beck, Kovacs, & Weissman, 1979; Beck, Rush, et al., 1979; Beck, Steer, et al., 1985). According to psychologists Judith M. Stillion and Eugene McDowell (1995), *rigidity of thought* is shown in the narrowing of the cognitive focus of suicidal individuals that results in their inability to consider more positive alternatives and to learn new coping techniques. *Selective abstraction* results when individuals center only on the bad or negative events and memories and overlook the positive ones. *Overgeneralization* refers to the tendency of depressed people to apply negative thoughts and appraisals to all current and future possibilities in their lives so that they eventually perceive little or no hope anywhere. Overgeneralization is indicated by the use of words like *always* ("I'm always in trouble"), *never* ("I'll never amount to anything"), *everyone,* and *every time*. Finally, *inexact labeling* occurs when individuals interpret a situation negatively, place a negative, all-encompassing label on themselves as a result of their negative interpretations (e.g., "loser," "nerd," "unlovable," "unattractive"), and from then on react to the label rather than to the realities of the situation. Instead of seeking new coping strategies for overcoming the negative situations in their lives, the label allows for a quick but mistaken explanation for all of life's problems. Evidence continues to accumulate that reveals that suicidal individuals become more rigid and dichotomous in their thinking, viewing life's joy and pain strictly in blacks and whites rather than shades of gray.

Once begun, all of these cognitive distortions are strengthened by the phenomenon that Meichenbaum (1977, 1985) called *negative self-talk,* the tendency for people to reinforce their misery by giving themselves continuous, self-absorbing messages relating to their inferiority, their hopelessness, and their helplessness. In time, they narrow their cognitive focus to suicide as the best and perhaps the only answer to their problems (Bootzin, Acocella, & Alloy, 1993; Stillion & McDowell, 1995).

Suicide Notes

Psychologist Judith Stillion (1995) offers examples of some of the types of cognitive distortion typically observed in suicidal individuals in the case of a 20-year-old male college student who tried to commit suicide by taking an overdose of pills mixed with alcohol. Jason left the suicide note reprinted in the next box.

According to Stillion, Jason's suicide note is a classic example of overgeneralization, as when he writes, "When a girl dumps me (which is *always* the case)," or when referring to his mother, "I think she *always* hated me." Jason goes on to pile negative upon negative as he comments on his mother's treatment of him, his boss's negative remarks, and the fact that even strangers call him names. Selective abstraction is evident in Jason's note as he selectively leaves out any reference to his mother's caring for him during his childhood, concentrating instead on the most recent events. Jason's letter also exemplifies the cognitive distortion of inexact labeling because he excludes any reference to his victories or achievements during his 20 years and because in the one sentence in which he recognizes his good grades, he immediately neutralizes the positive aspects of this accomplishment with the statement "I wouldn't have gotten a job anyway." In essence, Jason labels himself a loser by excluding any aspect of his life that would counter this claim. In fact, on his way from the emergency room to his hospital room after having his stomach pumped, Jason remarked angrily to a nurse, "Boy, am I a loser! I even mess up when I try to take myself out." Stillion (1995:190) writes, "He has forgotten that he has been a good student, that he has coped with life's hardships, and that he has achieved other victories, large or small, over the course of his 20 years. All those are gone, replaced with a label evoking utmost disgust and anger: 'Loser.' "

Stillion notes that Jason's tendencies toward egocentrism and self-absorption are also evident in the fact that Jason refers to himself either by name or as "I," "me," or "my" no less than 45 times in this short note. Stillion (1995:191) concludes that "the cognitive set of the suicidal individual is characterized by self-absorption, a form of renewed egocentrism so extreme that there is no room

JASON'S SUICIDE NOTE

"TO WHOM IT MAY CONCERN"
Jason Kelvin Joyner
(July 16, 1968–April 30, 1989)

Why?! Because my life has been nothing but misery and sorrow for 20-¾ Years! Going backwards: I thought Susan loved me, but I suppose not. 'I love you Jason' was only a lie. I base my happiness on relationships with girls—when I'm going steady, I'm happy. When a girl dumps me (which is always the case), I'm terribly depressed. In fact, over the last 3 years I've been in love at least four times seriously, but only to have my heart shattered—like so many icicles falling from a roof. But I've tried to go out with at least 30–40 girls in the last few years—none of them ever fell in love with me. My fate was: 'to love, but not be loved.'

My mother threw me out of the house in March. I guess she must really hate me; she doesn't even write me letters. I think she always hated me.

In high school, and even before that, nobody liked me. They all made fun of me and no girl would ever go to the proms with me.

I haven't anything to live for. Hope? Five years ago I wanted to end my life—I've been hoping for 5 years. Susan was just the straw that broke the camel's back. I simply cannot take it anymore! I only wanted someone to love; someone who would love me back as much as I loved her.

Yeah, I had pretty good grades, but the way my luck runs, I wouldn't have gotten a job anyway. I got fired over the summer 'cause the boss said, 'Jason you don't have any common sense.' Gee, that really made my day.

I walk down the streets of Madison and people call out of dorm windows: 'Hey, Asshole!' What did I do to them? I don't even know them! I've been pretty miserable lately (since 1979), so I think I will change the scenery. What's the big deal? I was gonna die in 40 or so years anyway. (Maybe sooner: when George decides to push the button in Washington, D.C.!)

Good bye Susan, Sean, Wendy, Joe, Mr. Montgomery, Dr. Johnson, Jack, and everyone else who made my life a little more bearable while it lasted.

Jason Kelvin Joyner
April 30, 1989

P.S. You might want to print this in the campus newspaper. It would make excellent reading."

Source: Stillion (1995), p. 189.

for humor or objectivity. Such narrowness of vision is the fertile soil in which suicide ideation flourishes."

Other analyses of suicide notes indicate that, for many people who kill themselves, death seems the only way out of a hopeless and insoluble situation. In a study comparing notes left by completed suicides with simulated notes written by a matched control group, Shneidman and Farberow (1970) found that the writers of the genuine notes expressed significantly more hopelessness and suffering than the control group. Interestingly, the genuine suicide notes also contained a greater number of instructions and lists of things to be done by family members and friends after the suicide was completed. In another study, Leenaars (1989) rated suicide notes from fatal suicides for various psychological factors and discovered differences by age. The suicide notes of young Americans more often reflected problems in interpersonal relationships, an inability to adjust to life's difficulties, and attachment to another person who did not meet the suicide's

What To Do

Suicidal people, like all of us, need love, understanding, and care. People usually don't ask directly, "Are you feeling so bad that you're thinking about suicide?" Locking themselves away increases the isolation they feel and the likelihood that they may attempt suicide. Asking if they are feeling suicidal has the effect of giving them permission to feel the way they do, which reduces their isolation; if they are feeling suicidal, they may see that someone else is beginning to understand how they feel. If someone you know tells you that they feel suicidal, above all listen to them. Then listen some more. Tell them, "I don't want you to die." Try to make yourself available to hear about how they feel, and try to form a "no-suicide contract": Ask them to promise you that they won't attempt suicide, and that if they feel they want to hurt themselves again, they won't do anything until they can contact either you or someone else that can support them. Take them seriously, and refer them to someone equipped to help them most effectively, such as a community health center, a counselor, a psychologist, a social worker, a youth worker, or clergy. If they appear acutely suicidal and won't talk, you may need to get them to a hospital emergency department. Don't try to "rescue" them or take their responsibilities on board yourself, or be a hero and try to handle the situation on your own. You can be the most help by referring them to someone equipped to offer them the help they need, while you continue to support them and remember that what happens is ultimately their responsibility. Get yourself some support too, as you try to get support for them; don't try to save the world on your own shoulders. If you don't know where to turn, chances are there are a number of 24-hour anonymous telephone counseling or suicide-prevention services in your area that you can call, listed in your local telephone directory. [Or see Chapter 12 of this book.]

Source: Adapted from a piece by Graham Stoney (1995, Sept. 15). Downloaded @ AOL. Copyright 1994 by Graham Stoney.

needs. The notes of middle-aged and elderly adults more often documented a wish to escape from pain and suffering and, less often, a wish to punish themselves or to make others suffer (Lester, 1994).

Hopelessness

Major cognitive theories of depression (Abramson, Metalsky, & Alloy, 1989; Beck, 1967) hold that hopelessness is the primary and most immediate cause of suicide, and there is strong evidence on their side. Of all the psychological predictors of attempted and completed suicides, hopelessness has been found to be the best predictor, even better than depression (Spirito et al., 1989).

People who are depressed suffer from low self-esteem and show varying levels of hopelessness and helplessness. Although many studies have shown that depression, hopelessness, and low self-esteem are positively interrelated, at least three studies have shown that hopelessness is the factor that could best predict the level of lethality of a suicide attempt (Wetzel, 1976; Goldney, 1981; Kazdin et al., 1983). Taken together, these studies indicate that young people who dislike themselves and are generally depressed may contemplate suicide, but the seriousness of such contemplation is greatly increased in people who also feel hopeless about the future.

One study, for example, compared a group of suicidal adolescents with a group of psychiatrically hospitalized but nonsuicidal adolescents. Though the two groups did not differ on the level of depression, the suicidal subjects were more likely to view negative events as stable characteristics of the environment: Nothing, in their view, was ever going to get better (Hart, Spirito, & Overholser, 1988). Not surprisingly, research has shown that suicidal adolescents are also poor problem solvers (McLeavey et al., 1987; Weissbourd, 1996).

Imitation Suicides and Cluster Suicides

Exposure to suicide—directly, as with the suicide of a friend or classmate, or indirectly, through a news report, video, or film—has also been considered a possible cognitive risk factor for youth suicide. D. A. Brent et al. (1993), for example, found that of 146 friends and acquaintances of twenty-six adolescent suicide victims, nearly one-third developed a depressive episode following the suicide. As compared to other groups who were either depressed before the suicide or who never became depressed, those who became depressed after exposure had a closer relationship with the suicide victims, showed more severe grief, and showed a greater exposure to suicide during their lives. These researchers concluded that depressive reactions occurring after exposure to suicide appear to be bona fide major depression, as a complication of bereavement.

Apparent outbreaks of suicide or suicide attempts by young people in a given community within a relatively short period of time are referred to as *serial, copycat,* or *cluster suicides.* These suicides, which appear to account for between 1% and 5% of all youth suicides in the United States, tend to mimic the suicide method of the target suicide (G. B. Fulton & Metress, 1995). In one case involving an apparent suicide pact that took place in New Jersey in 1987, four teenagers committed suicide by locking themselves inside a thirteen-car garage and sitting in a car with a running engine. Two were males, ages 18 and 19, and two were females, 16 and 17. The two young men died of a combination of carbon monoxide, cocaine, and alcohol poisoning, while the two young women died of a synergism of carbon monoxide and cocaine.

Within days of these deaths, the community—aware of previous incidents of cluster suicides—responded with various efforts to prevent other suicides. School officials provided counselors for students thought to be at high risk, such as those with a history of suicide attempts or close friends of the victims. A local suicide hotline was set up, as was a walk-in crisis intervention center. The garage where the deaths occurred was locked and placed under periodic police surveillance. In spite of these measures, 6 days later a 17-year-old male and a 20-year-old female attempted suicide in the same garage by the same method. A police officer found them unconscious after noticing that the garage door lock was broken. They survived and the garage door was removed (National Center for Health Statistics, 1995c).

Another case involved a series of suicides that followed a television documentary broadcast in Germany in 1987 (Klerman, 1987; G. B. Fulton & Metress, 1995). The video featured a graphic and explicit portrayal of a young man who died when he threw himself in front of a speeding train. Surrounded by controversy, the show was repeated a year later. Tracking reactions to the showing, the Mannheim Mental Health Institute reported a significant increase in suicide by railroad trauma in the weeks following each of the television showings (Klerman, 1987).

The degree to which exposure to another's suicide enhances the danger of imitating that act is being debated. In a study of two cluster suicides in Texas, research revealed that exposure did not increase the probability of suicide in those not already at risk. Those who did kill themselves were more likely to have made a previous attempt at suicide, to have lost a close friend or relative to violent death, or to have suffered a recent breakup with a girlfriend or boyfriend (G. B. Fulton & Mettress, 1995). In a more recent incident (Gleick, 1996:41), Alicia Hayes, 15, and Amber Hernandez, 14, of San Pedro, California, jumped to their deaths from a 150 foot cliff along the Pacific coast. Months earlier, Chris Mills, an eleventh grader at the same school had killed himself but crisis teams who went to the school talked mostly with students in his class. There was no opportunity to identify Alicia and Amber as particular copycat risks although both had a history of drug-taking and running away from home. Rosemary Rubin, a crisis consultant who worked with students after each of the crises, says, "People don't want to believe that children have problems where they could possibly think about ending their lives, yet that is what's going on. The crises are hitting right and left, and not only are the schools burned out, so are the crisis teams."

Cases of adolescent cluster suicides generate concern over the possible influence of exposure to suicide, the public health responsibilities of the media, and the development of appropriate community intervention strategies when youth suicides occur. The American Association of Suicidology (1995) has developed guidelines for the media, aimed at reducing the contagious effects of suicide reports. They recommend that the press avoid providing specific details of the method, romanticization of the suicide, descriptions of suicide as unexplainable, and simplistic reasons for the suicide. Further, they advise that news stories about suicide not be printed on the front page, the word suicide not be in the headline, and a picture of the person who committed suicide not be printed.

THE PSYCHODYNAMIC PERSPECTIVE

The ending of childhood begins at puberty and stretches through adolescence, as the responsibilities of adulthood become clearer. According to Erik Erikson (1963), we arrive at two major crises during adolescence: the conflict of identity versus role confusion, and the conflict of intimacy versus isolation.

The Identity Crisis: Who am I?

One of the most critical challenges of the adolescent period of life involves finding our own identity. This is Erikson's fifth developmental stage and one of the most important, because it introduces each of us to some form of *identity crisis*. This crisis, said to occur between the ages of 12 and 20, reflects the transition from childhood to adulthood, a period when we all create a sense of personal identity, both the kind of psychological beings we are and the kind of lives we plan to forge for ourselves. At this time of life, individuals ask themselves, "Who am I?" "What am I really like?" "What do I want to become?" Of course, these are questions we tend to ask ourselves at many points in life. But, according to Erikson (1963), during adolescence it is crucial that these questions be answered effectively. If they are not, individuals may drift along, uncertain of where they want to go or what they wish to accomplish. Failure to shape an identity leads to role confusion and a sense of isolation and alienation.

As adolescents, we adopt many different strategies to help resolve our personal identity crises. We try out many different roles—the rebel, the dutiful daughter or son, the athlete, the brain, the conformist, the vamp, the playboy—and we join different social or religious groups in search of answers to our many questions. In so doing, we consider many possible social selves and different kinds of persons we might potentially become. In Erikson's view, identity is achieved by integrating a number of roles into a coherent personal schema that provides a sense of inner continuity over time.

Relatively little of Erikson's theory has been verified by research. Nevertheless, some aspects of it have been studied. The concept of identity resolution has probably attracted the most attention. Waterman, Beubel and Waterman (1970) asked whether people who were successful in handling the crises of the first four stages were more likely to achieve a stable source of identity in the fifth stage. Their data suggest that this is indeed the case. While resolution of earlier crises may not be essential for ego identity, it does seem to be important.

Intimacy Versus Isolation: Can I Love and Be Loved?

A second challenge to be negotiated during adolescence involves the new interpersonal dimension of intimacy versus isolation. By intimacy, Erikson (1963) means the ability to express love, share with, and care for others without fear of losing ourselves in the act. Intimacy also involves a deepening sense of commitment, loyalty, and self-disclosure between friends. As we mature sexually, the capacity for, and interest in, romantic and sexual relationships also develops. Friendships, primarily with people of our own sex but also with members of the other sex, become increasingly important. Friendships confer many obvious benefits, including the opportunity to practice and improve a wide array of social skills (Berndt, 1992) and to develop further the capacity to share our thoughts, feelings, and dreams with another person.

The conflict for the young adult is whether to be vulnerable and open to the possibility of rejection, loss, and grieving in a relationship, or to live a sterile and shallow life protected from vulnerability but alone and lonely. To love someone else, Erikson argues, we must have resolved our earlier crises successfully and feel

C A R I N G   I N S I G H T S

Breaking Up is Hard to Do

The disruption of a love relationship between young people is a common precipitating factor for severe depression and suicide. A recent study of American college students (Robak & Weitzman (1995:278) revealed that grief reactions following a lost romantic relationship during early adulthood are very similar to grief responses following loss through death. Males and females showed no difference in how long it took to "get over" the loss of a relationship—about 7 months. Females exhibited less denial than did the males and reported greater feelings of loss of control and death anxiety. These severe grief reactions, although often recognized by friends, are just as often ignored and disenfranchised by family members, teachers, and other significant adults as "puppy love," histrionics, or melodramas. In the midst of searching for self-identity, sexual identity, and intimacy, the experience of loss, grieving, and mourning experienced by young people following the breakup of a relationship should be taken as seriously by adults as a loss by death.

secure in our identities. To form an intimate relationship, lovers must be trusting, autonomous, and capable of initiative, and must exhibit other hallmarks of maturity. Failure at intimacy brings painful loneliness and a sense of being incomplete. On the other hand, while deepening friendships confer benefits, the potential downside of such relationships should not be ignored. Many studies indicate that adolescents often experience intense conflict with friends and lovers that can leave serious psychological scars and, in some cases, precipitate suicide (Berndt, 1992).

Separation, Depression, and Suicide

Many psychoanalysts and family therapists point to adolescent/parent separation and the problems of "leaving home" as a key factor in the development of problems during adolescence, including drug abuse, psychosomatic illness, and suicide (Bloom-Feshbach & Bloom-Feshbach, 1987:236). Offer & Sabshin (1984), for instance, in their study of boys ages 14–17, found adolescent/parent separation to be central to adolescent rebelliousness. K. Sullivan and A. Sullivan (1980), in a study comparing teenagers in high school with teenagers after they have left home to go to college, found that boys, after leaving home, exhibited increased ability to express affection, more open communication, and more satisfaction with their parents. In another survey, of 142 college freshman before leaving home and again after being in college for 6 months, it was found that there was more aggression toward parents before leaving home than after, and that feelings of closeness were expressed more openly and more intensely when physical distance was greater (Kurash, 1979).

From another psychodynamic perspective, separation from parents in adolescence represents a major experience of loss and grieving and a major stepping stone to the development of self-identity and intimacy. Much of the confusion and depression felt by adolescents is caused by moving into an adult world in which relationships and responsibilities are significantly different from those known as a child. Psychoanalyst Michael Bloom (1987:264) notes that the successful navigation of this transition of parent/child separation depends on a number of important factors:

- The readiness of both parents and child to truly be independent
- The cognitive development of object constancy and other adaptive modes of thinking in the young person
- The past separation experiences of the parents and the adolescent
- Family systems and cultural impacts on the separation process itself

Bloom (1987:249–250) states that adolescent/parent separation "serves as a prototype for future separation experiences and is an important transition in the life course."

Thanatos

In psychoanalytic terms, suicide may seem something of a mystery, an obvious violation of the powerful life instinct by a destructive force that Freud termed *thanatos*. Yet Freud claimed that psychoanalysis had solved this puzzle with the discovery that people do not have the psychological capacity to violate the life instinct by killing themselves, unless in doing so they are also killing a love object with whom they themselves have identified. In other words, suicidal people are bent not so much on destroying themselves as on destroying another person, a significant other whose image they have incorporated into their own psyche (Bootzin, Acocella, & Alloy, 1993). Freud's psychoanalytic view of depression challenged the earlier biogenic models of mood disorders by explaining depression as rooted in an early trauma that is reactivated by a recent loss.

Similarly, psychodynamic theorists maintain that some children who are traumatized by an early devastating loss grow up believing that close interpersonal relationships cannot continue over time. Rejection by significant others early in life may cause young people to develop defenses against the pain they unconsciously come to expect as adults. If these defenses give way and such people confuse the overwhelming pain of the early loss with a current rejection or separation, they may commit suicide. They may even develop some internal clock by which they gauge how long they can expect such a relationship to endure before the inevitable separation. These are the people who tend to commit *anniversary suicide,* ending their lives on a date that has special personal meaning, like their birthday or their wedding anniversary (Bootzin, Acocella, & Alloy, 1993).

THE HUMANISTIC PERSPECTIVE

Carl Rogers (1959) supported the humanistic view that each person has the potential for healthy and creative psychological growth throughout the life span,

The psychodynamic perspective, unlike biochemical models of mood disorders, views depression as rooted in early and traumatic separation experiences of childhood. Young people may develop some internal clock by which they gauge how long they can expect a love relationship to last before the inevitable separation occurs. © *David Young-Wolff/PhotoEdit*

including adolescence. Roger's person-centered theory rejects Freud's historical determinism with its exclusive emphasis on the role of past experiences and memories. Instead, it emphasizes the development of self-esteem, the immediacy of our experiences, and the choices we make from moment to moment.

For both Abraham Maslow and Carl Rogers, the sense-of-self is like a seed planted within the individual. Given the right growing conditions—enough food, enough water, enough caring, enough self-esteem, and enough challenge—the self will fulfill its potential, flourish, and grow into a unique and creative person. From this humanistic perspective, all of what we are meant to be and are struggling to become is in there, the environment only serves to help or hinder development. If the environment interferes and fails to serve these needs, the self seed fails to develop completely or at all.

Incongruence, Faking it, and Existential Anxiety

Rogers divided the personality into the biological organism, the experiential field, and the self. By using our *organismic valuing process*—our feelings, emotions, and intuitions—we evaluate experience according to whether it helps or hinders our self-actualization. As long as our sense-of-self is congruent with our experience and the choices we make, we develop smoothly as fully functioning persons. At other times, in order to receive positive regard from the world, we

CARING INSIGHTS

Suicidal Ideation and Plans

Suicidal ideation, including the making of specific plans, is an essential phase in all but the most impulsive of suicides. There is a wide variation in the length of the time periods over which suicidal individuals consider suicide. They may range from a few minutes to many years. However, suicidal ideation moves from the general to the specific, from considering suicide as a possible coping behavior to accepting it as the best coping behavior, and accompanying that acceptance with detailed plans for carrying out the suicidal action. Once plans are formed, warning signs may be evidenced. The most common warning signs are verbal threats, self-injurious behaviors, and indications of closure, such as saying good-bye or giving away prized possessions to friends and relatives. These warning signs themselves may precipitate a triggering event. For example, saying good-bye to a friend may cause the friend to become suspicious and to call the authorities. The appearance of the authorities may trigger the suicide attempt. A negative life event may occur and become the triggering event, which may or may not be accompanied by warning signs. Triggering events, like warning signs, are not universally present in suicidal behavior. Triggering events, or "last-straw" phenomena, are not necessarily dramatic or particularly traumatic. They differ from regular negative life events in that they occur after the individual has already engaged in significant suicidal ideation and planning.

change our behavior in ways not consistent with the emotions and cognitions that underlie our sense-of-self (i.e., the organismic valuing process). This state of two-facedness, in which we project a false image of ourselves that is at odds with our true feelings and values as persons, is the stuff of depression, despair, and existential anxiety. Rogers termed this anxious and stressful circumstance the *state of incongruence.*

Incongruence results in part from differences between the self as *perceived* by others and the self as *experienced,* a situation that often results from negative appraisals from the world regarding our individual self-worth. Valuations of worth are messages like "We love you when you are good (or clean, or polite, or happy, or productive)." Since we are not always good, clean, polite, or happy, the message we get is that some of the time we won't be loved. So, in order to gain the love we need, we fake it—we take more showers, hide our sadness, cheat on tests, pad our resume, and lie to others, even though we know this behavior is at odds with our inner values, feelings, or intuitions. This interferes with the actualization process, especially when we have internalized these negative appraisals of self-worth and apply them to ourselves on an ongoing basis.

CARING INSIGHTS

Risk Factors for Youth Suicide

- Being male
- Being white
- Previous suicide attempt
- Depression and behavioral disorders
- Substance abuse
- Exposure to suicide
- Family history of suicide
- Turbulent home life
- Physical and/or sexual abuse
- Breakup of a love relationship
- Expendable child syndrome
- Presence of firearms in the home
- Nonsuicidal physically self-damaging acts

According to Rogers, both the organism and the self have related, but separate, self-actualizing tendencies. If the self is relatively congruent with the total experience of the individual, then the actualizing tendency is unified. But if not, the self and the individual may oppose each other. From the humanistic perspective, incongruence, faking it, and existential anxiety result in the emotional turmoil and cognitive confusion so common to adolescence. For some young Americans, they are an invitation to self-destructive behavior and suicide.

Love, Self-Esteem, and Suicide

From a humanistic point of view, either the environment in which the young person resides can support the development of the sense-of-self and feelings of self-esteem or that environment can hinder these developments and produce states of anxiety and meaninglessness. Consider one of the most powerful risk factors for youth suicide, the *expendable child syndrome.*

The expendable child experiences loss of love in the most extreme form. Parents of such children communicate very low regard for, hostility toward, and even hatred for them on a daily basis. In addition to emotional abuse, some of these children may experience physical and sexual abuse. These children believe they are unworthy and expendable, that their deaths will not matter to anyone (Sabbath, 1969). Vulnerable to low self-esteem, with less opportunity to develop good coping behaviors, these young American are at high risk for drug abuse, depression, and suicide.

Many studies have shown that suicidal children are more likely than others to be victims of child abuse and neglect (Orbach, 1984; Joffe & Offord, 1983; Pfeffer, 1981a, 1986; Green, 1978; Adams-Tucker, 1982). In addition, parental conflict, unclear role definitions, and inflexible structure often characterize the families of suicidal children and adolescents (Kosky, 1982; Orbach, Gross, &

SUICIDE AND PSYCHACHE

"As I near the end of my career in suicidology, I think I can now say what has been on my mind in as few as five words: *suicide is caused by psychache* (sīk-āk: two syllables). Psychache refers to the hurt, anguish, soreness, aching, psychological *pain* in the psyche, the mind. It is intrinsically psychological—the pain of excessively felt shame, or guilt, or humiliation, or loneliness, or fear, or angst, or dread of growing old or of dying badly, or whatever. When it occurs, its reality is introspectively undeniable. Suicide occurs when the psychache is deemed by that person to be unbearable. This means that suicide also has to do with different individual thresholds for enduring psychological pain.

"All our past efforts to relate or to correlate suicide with simplistic nonpsychological variables, such as sex, age, race, socioeconomic level, case history items (no matter how dire), psychiatric categories (including depression), etc., were (and are) doomed to miss the mark precisely because they ignore the one variable that centrally relates to suicide, namely, intolerable psychological pain; In a word, psychache."

Source: Edwin S. Shneidman. (1995). Suicide as psychache. In J. B. Williamson and E. S. Shneidman (Eds.), *Death: Current perspectives* (4th ed.). Mayfield, Mountain View, CA, p. 369.

Glaubman, 1981; Pfeffer, 1982). Several studies and clinical observations reveal that suicidal youth also have many negative experiences at school as well as at home. They tend to perform poorly at school, both academically and socially, and are often cast as "the weirdo," "the rebel," "the nerd," or "the bully" (Pfeffer, 1981a; Joffe & Offord, 1983; Connell, 1972).

Research by J. Jacobs (1971) suggests that the typical suicidal adolescent has a long history of stress and personal problems at home, extending from childhood. Unfortunately, for some teenagers, problems such as conflicts with parents, stepparents, or siblings, difficulties in school, and loneliness escalate during adolescence and young adulthood. As their efforts to cope with these problems fail, many teenagers rebel against parental and school authority, withdraw from social relations, turn to alcohol and drugs, and make dramatic and desperate gestures, such as running away from home, committing self-destructive acts on their own bodies, or attempting self-annihilation.

Suicide and Psychache

Research into the factors that precipitate suicide in young people is in its infancy. In terms of prevention, the most recent review suggests that whereas the treatment of depression and restricting access to handguns and other weapons are more useful tactics for suicide prevention in older adults, crisis counseling and educational programs are more useful in dealing with younger adults (Lester, 1994). And yet, from a humanistic point of view, we cannot be sure, because of the lack of research and theorizing on the *unique* features of suicide in different individuals and groups. According to suicidologist David Lester (1994:345−346), "All too often, the variables thought to be important in determining the appearance of suicidal behavior of those in one age group (such as depression or alcoholism) are demonstrated to be important for explaining the suicidal behavior for those in other age groups as well." In other words, in terms of insight into the act of suicide itself in one unique individual, no simple categorization or typology has proved to be very helpful.

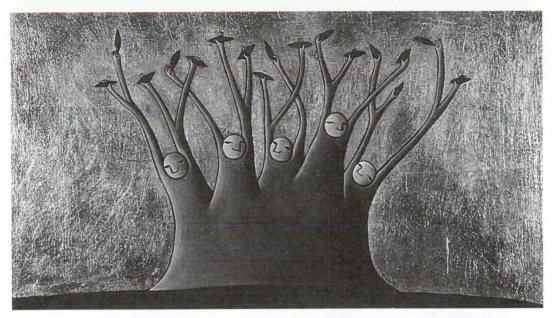

According to the humanistic point of view, the sense-of-self is like a seed planted within the individual. Given the right growing conditions, the self will fulfill its potential, flourish, and grow. An uncaring, unloving environment serves to hinder this development so that the self seed fails to develop completely—or at all. © *Stock Illustration Source*

In reviewing this field of study since its very inception, Edwin S. Shneidman (1985:29), the father of suicidology in the United States, concluded that "classifications [of suicide], taken singly or together, have either an arbitrary, esoteric, or ad hoc quality to them. They do not seem impressively definitive. I know for a fact the best known of them is of practically no use in the clinic, where the task is saving lives."

Chapter Summary

Beginning with a biological event (puberty) and culminating in a social event (independence from parents), adolescence corresponds roughly to the teen years, 13 to 20+. The development of self-identity, along with the development of a new capacity for intimacy with others, creates distinct concerns and capabilities in relation to dying and death that have a separate focus from those of younger children. The themes in American rock 'n' roll music, such as love, alienation, and death, may reflect some of these personal concerns and fears as well as cultural heroes, values, ideals, hopes, and aspirations, and offer some insight into their world.

When a young person learns that he or she is terminally ill and that death is imminent, there is the difficulty of coping with disappointment, frustration, and profound confusion. In the midst of preparations for entering the world of adulthood, feelings emerge of having been cheated out of a rightful portion of one's life. The feeling of frustration is often the most important feeling expressed by a dying young adult.

Suicide rates for young Americans have more than tripled in recent decades. In the effort to comprehend the event of suicide, social scientists have attempted to place suicidal behaviors within various categories and typologies. They have also studied the biochemical, cognitive, psychodynamic, and personal conditions of suicidal people, as well as the sociological factors that predispose to suicidal behavior. As evidence has accumulated from these various approaches, it has become increasingly clear that suicidal behavior, especially adolescent suicide, is one of the most complex behaviors in the human repertoire.

FURTHER READINGS

Alvarez, A. (1972). *The Savage God*. Weidenfeld & Nicolson, London.

Colt, G. H. (1991). *The Enigma of Suicide*. Summit Books, New York.

Durkheim, E. (1951). *Suicide* (J. A. Spaulding & G. Simpson, Trans.). Free Press, Glencoe, IL.

Fulton, R., Markusen, E., Owen, G., & Scheiber, Jane (eds.). (1984). *Death and Dying: Challenge and Change*. Addison-Wesley, Reading, MA.

Morgan, J. D. (ed.). (1990). *The Dying and the Bereaved Teenager*. Charles Press, Philadelphia, PA.

Pine, V. R., (eds.). (1990). *Unrecognized and Unsanctioned Grief*. Charles C. Thomas, Springfield, IL.

Plath, S. (1972). *The Bell Jar*. Bantam, New York.

Raphael, Beverly. (1983). *The Anatomy of Bereavement*. HarperCollins, San Francisco.

Schneidman, E. (1993). *Suicide as Psychache: A Clinical Approach to Self-Destructive Behavior*. Jason Aronson, Northvale, NJ.

Stillion, J. M., McDowell, E. E., & May, J. H. (1989). *Suicide Across the Life Span—Premature Exits*. Hemisphere, Washington, DC.

Weissbourd, R. (1996). *The Vulnerable Child: What Really Hurts America's Children and What We Can Do About It*. Addison-Wesley, New York.

SEVEN

Death, Adulthood, and a Parent's Tears

I n the span of years between 25 and 60, an increasing awareness of the physical signs of aging, coupled, perhaps, with the death of a parent, a child, a spouse, or a good friend, tends to break down the cognitive, emotional, and behavioral defenses we have erected against our fear of death. Key to this growing fear of death in adulthood is a cognitive shift in our time perspective, from viewing our life in terms of time already lived to viewing it in terms of the time we have left to live. For some, this shift in time perspective may trigger higher death anxiety and contribute to the onset of a period of confusion and despair in the adult years. For others, this period of life brings a sense of accomplishment, generativity, and personal fulfillment.

"We learn to trust the 'knowingness' that is our biological wisdom. . . . We learn to trust our 'gut' feelings and begin to follow our instincts instead of being ruled by the 'tyranny of the shoulds.' . . . As we draw within to know ourselves better, we become more receptive to intuitive messages."

Ng (1994), p. 33.

GENERATIVITY VERSUS STAGNATION

One of the major conflicts to be resolved by the maturing adult concerns *generativity versus stagnation.* According to Erik Erikson (1963), seeds planted in childhood and adolescence and rooted in young adulthood either generate and are brought to fruition during the adult years or are left to wither and die. Numerous studies suggest that those adults who have not been able to resolve the various tasks and dilemmas of childhood and adolescence face maturity and old age more anxiously, with what Erikson described as stagnation and despair. For these individuals, adult life becomes a drab, conformist routine, and they become increasingly dulled and resentful. Erikson (1980) noted especially that those persons who have not successfully established intimacy and love in their lives may find themselves at risk during the adult years, with a heightened likelihood of psychological isolation and depression. Suicide statistics consistently show higher rates of suicide among single people, of both sexes (National Center for Health Statistics, 1995a).

For others, adult life is full of the challenge to remain productive, creative, and engaged in all aspects of life. To Erikson, people who have successfully negotiated the six earlier developmental stages are grounded in a strong and dynamic experience of generativity and are likely to find meaning and joy in all the activities of life, including career, marriage, and family.

JUNG ON GETTING OLDER

Carl Jung (1933) characterized a person's values in youth as expanding in an outward direction. He believed that in the adult years, with increasing maturity, our values become more inward directed, more interior. As we come to act less from the desires of ego and more from the essence of self, our intuitive powers grow in strength, and we tend to take more complete control of our lives. Jung viewed adulthood as the most inspired period of the life span, in which change is evident in psychological growth, human potential is realized, spirituality is refined, and commitment to life and loved ones is expressed more fully than possible in earlier years. According to Jungian scholar Sharon Joy Ng (1994:33), as we mature, "[w]e learn to trust the 'knowingness' that is our biological wisdom. . . . We learn to trust our 'gut' feelings and begin to follow our instincts instead of being ruled by the 'tyranny of the shoulds.' . . . As we draw within to know ourselves better, we become more receptive to intuitive messages."

In *Modern Man in Search of a Soul* (1933), Jung observed that as we enter the second half of life, often after establishing a career and a family, many of us experience a profound transition or crisis. During this time, we begin to listen to our deeper urgings, to longings we had ignored in the first half of our lives. Concurrent with this sense of crisis and the shift in the sense of time, we launch a cognitive evaluation of our life choices and patterns (Santrock, 1985). This self-examination can lead to important psychological and social changes. People who were formerly driven by ambition may become interested in interpersonal relations, while those who were dependent on others may become independent and assertive for the first time in their lives (Ornstein & Carstensen, 1991).

Jungian theorists Janice Brewi and Anne Brennan (1992) suggest that midlife, which is often a time of increased personal awareness, is also filled with peril and turmoil, because everything held dear in life's first half may be questioned, criticized, or even rejected. And in the midst of questioning and surrendering our youthful dreams, we can become convinced that there is not enough time left to awaken, not enough time left to begin anew. Life, which in our youth seemed to stretch out into infinity, now emerges as finite and tenuous. The beginning signs of aging, the cognitive shift to "time 'til death," the increasing number of losses experienced during the adult years, and the stark contrast between our youthful dreams and our actual accomplishments all come together to create a *mid-life crisis*.

Central to resolving this crisis is the challenge of overcoming our fear of death, accepting its inevitability, and engaging the work of mourning the loss of our loved ones, as well as the dreams of our youth. Jung believed that when we cling to the past (for instance, when in middle age we try to maintain the appearance and prowess of youth), we are surrendering to our fear of death and, in a symbolic sense, are like children swallowed up by the monster in the center of our worst nightmare.

Adulthood and the Fear of Death

As researchers have attempted to plot changes in the fear of death over the life span, several possible age-related patterns have seemed plausible: Children, adolescents, and young adults, for example, are more fearful of death, since they have the most to lose—all those experiences not yet enjoyed and those relationships not yet explored. On the other hand, since the elderly are, on average, much closer to death, they might fear death more. As it happens, neither

Each year, American and European consumers spend billions of dollars for anti-wrinkle creams, hair coloring, diets, vitamin supplements and plastic surgery involving tummy tucks, face lifts, vein removal, nose jobs, and hair transplants in efforts to smooth over the signs of aging and approaching death. © *Tony Freeman/PhotoEdit*

of these two possible hypotheses is supported by research findings. Instead, the peak of fear and worry over death and dying occurs during the central years of adulthood, between the approximate ages of 35 and 60 years. Collectively, these findings are consistent with Jung's theory that one of the major tasks of the maturing adult is to come to terms with the inevitability of death (Riley & Foner, 1968; Bengston, Cuellar, & Ragan, 1976–77; Gesser, Wong, & Reker, 1987–88; Marzuk et al., 1988; G. B. Fulton & Metress, 1995). The greater fear of death during this period may be associated with experiences of loneliness, stagnation, and despair in adulthood, as well as with the experience of coping with the death of a parent, a spouse, a child, or a best friend.

MOURNING THE DEATH OF A PARENT

According to an old adage, when we lose a child we lose our future, but when we lose a parent we lose our past. In this sense, the death of a parent is a powerful symbolic life event that strips away any past illusions of immortality for the maturing adult and can be a powerful catalyst to further emotional and psychological growth. The death of a parent has been compared to a *developmental push,* forcing us to accept the fact of our own mortality so that we no longer think of ourselves as children but, rather, as mature and seasoned adults (Douglas, 1990–91; Osterweis, Solomon, & Green, 1984).

"When a parent dies, our whole world in a sense comes apart, and we have to question our lives in a way we haven't before. . . . People tend to isolate themselves a lot in grief, and a lot of times friends and other family members may not want to talk because they feel overwhelmed or frightened by it."

A. Kennedy (1991), p. 26.

Parental death during adulthood is the most common cause of bereavement in the United States. It has been referred to as one of the most important personal and symbolic life events for adults, because it involves the loss of the most unique and long-standing relationship we will ever have. The death of our parents during adulthood is especially shocking and disturbing to us, not only because of the specific loss to be mourned, but because the loss tends to put us face to face with the realization that we are now the orphans of time—the oldest generation in the family lineage and, thus, "next in line" for death (Douglas, 1990–91; G. B. Fulton & Metress, 1995).

Although the death of an elderly parent may end a long and full life or terminate a painful illness or disability, it may nevertheless provoke intense grieving in the surviving child. To lose someone we loved dearly who remained a central figure in our lives is painful, whatever his or her age. Interviews with adults mourning the loss of a parent point to the uniqueness of the bond between parent and child, its irreplaceability, the loss of enduring love, and the loss of a loved one who provided acceptance with allowance for mistakes and faults (Donnelly, 1987). Because our mother is most likely to have played the central role of nurturer in our lives, and because she is more likely to outlive our father, the death of our mother is often a more difficult loss for maturing adults. In most cases, the death of our mother leaves us without any parent.

On the other hand, although the death of a parent may have powerful personal and symbolic meaning, it may be experienced as a low-intensity grief

CARING INSIGHTS

Mourning a Parent's Death

1. Take time daily, even 10 minutes, to acknowledge that this death has occurred. Let your feelings surface—and be honest about them.
2. Network with those who can support what you're going through—a friend who has lost a parent, a hospice group, support group, or grief therapist.
3. Realize that death ends a life but not a relationship. Use imagination and dreams to access your deceased parent and express unfinished feelings, thoughts, and emotions.
4. Educate yourself about the grieving/mourning process—learn what to expect and how to facilitate the process.

Source: A. Kennedy (1991), p. 26.

event because it may require fewer life adjustments for the bereaved adult child. We are more absorbed in our own jobs, families, and activities as adult children. We may have relocated to another part of the country and see our parents only occasionally, perhaps on holidays or at annual family get-togethers. Ties with our parents tend to weaken as we forge strong ties with our spouse and children (R. Fulton, Markusen, Owen & Scheiber, 1984). In these cases, the loss of a spouse or a child is often much more emotionally crushing than the loss of an elderly parent.

There may also be personal and social pressure to deny the significance of the death of a parent, because, unlike the death of a young child or a spouse, the death of an older person is typically viewed as timely and appropriate. Intense or prolonged grief may not be expected or easily tolerated by others. Psychotherapist Alexandra Kennedy (1991:26) states, "When a parent dies, our whole world in a sense comes apart, and we have to question our lives in a way we haven't before. . . . People tend to isolate themselves a lot in grief, and a lot of times friends and other family members may not want to talk because they feel overwhelmed or frightened by it."

MOURNING THE DEATH OF A SPOUSE

One of the most potentially disrupting and studied forms of loss is the death of a spouse. Although the death of a long-term companion and mate is painful at any age, it appears to be particularly difficult during the early and middle adult years. In a study by Zisook, Shuchter, and Sledge (1993) comparing the grief responses of 350 widows and widowers (ages 26+ years) over the first year of bereavement, results strongly suggest that older widows and widowers perceive themselves as adjusting better to their loss and as suffering from less depression and fewer anxiety symptoms than their younger counterparts. Unlike the

CARING INSIGHTS

Getting Through the Night

"My husband and I had been married for 32 years when he died very unexpectedly of a heart attack. At first I was beside myself. I felt so devastated. The two of us spent so much of our time together that it seemed like we were seldom apart. And suddenly we were very apart.

One thing that I did for awhile that helped me was this: I wore his clothes. I know it may sound silly, but sometimes when I went on walks outdoors, I'd wear his favorite jacket. Somehow I felt a little of his protection. And at nighttime I would wear the tops to his pajamas. It was very comforting. I still have that jacket of his and I hardly ever wear it anymore. But I like remembering that it was his and that it gave me a sense of peace when I most needed it."

Source: Faye, of Fargo, North Dakota. downloaded @ AOL Grief Forum, (1995, September 16).

awkward social status of a young widow, widowhood in older women is considered more normal.

In an earlier study, Zisook and Shuchter (1986) examined the frequencies of bereavement-related feelings, experiences, and behaviors for seventy widows and widowers (ages 24–66 years) who were followed over a 4-year period. Results indicated that the majority of the younger bereaved spouses did not, even after 4 years, feel that they had made what they would call an excellent adjustment. Other researchers have also discovered that younger widows, because of their lack of preparation for widowhood, the need to care for younger children, and assorted practical problems, usually have more difficulty adjusting than older widows. Younger widows tend to receive less social support from family members and the wider community, making the transition from wife to widow more traumatic for younger women. The parents of a young widow are often her most important source of social support. For the young woman in mourning who does not have close relatives living nearby, widowhood can be especially demanding (Blau, 1961; Glick, Weiss, & Parkes, 1974; Lopata, 1973; G. B. Fulton & Metress, 1995).

The loss of a spouse, even when the death involves a long dying trajectory and the possibility of anticipatory grieving responses, may still be emotionally devastating for the surviving spouse. For instance, in a major study of spousal loss in those under 45 years of age, anticipatory grief did not remove the impact of death. Although the widowed often voiced relief that their spouse's suffering had ended, they felt desolated and pained when the death actually occurred. While sudden death brought the tendency for intense anguish, the anticipation of death did offer the potential to keep the grief responses within certain limits. Bereaved spouses reported the months following the funeral to be the most difficult period. As family and friends got on with their lives, the bereaved spouses were, in most cases, left to deal with the burden of loss on their own (Glick, Weiss, & Parkes, 1974; M. S. Stroebe, 1994; G. B. Fulton & Metress, 1995).

In reviewing numerous research studies on the health consequences of spousal death, a decline in health is consistently noted during the first year of mourning, followed by a return to levels similar to nonmourning persons after this time. However, for some widowed persons, mortality rates significantly exceed those for married persons of similar age and status. The finding that widows and widowers are more likely to die within a year or two following the death of a beloved spouse is termed the *broken heart phenomenon* (M. S. Stroebe, Stroebe, & Hansson, 1988; M. S. Stroebe, 1994).

MOURNING THE DEATH OF AN ANIMAL COMPANION

Loss of an animal companion is often described as a typical experience of childhood. It is that, but it can also be of parallel importance to adults, for whom a pet's death can trigger a grief almost as intense as that precipitated by the death of a human (Weisman, 1991). For the growing population of widows, widowers, and single adults who live alone, pets can be the only family member and an important source of companionship (Carmack, 1985; Cowles, 1985). For example, in a study conducted in the Netherlands, Endenberg, Hart, and Bouw (1994) reported that pet owners acquire them primarily for companionship, as well as to recreate pleasant childhood experiences. This was the case not only for persons who were living alone but also for those living in families.

Sadness and crying are reported almost universally in the literature on pet grief. In studies by Cowles (1985) and Weisman (1991), for example, all of the participants reported crying at the time of their pet's death, and most reported spontaneous crying, sometimes without an apparent stimulus, for several weeks following the death. The death also appeared to serve as a reminder of their own mortality in many of Cowles' subjects, with the accompanying anxiety and fear. Often, this fear was projected onto the pet as pet owners dwelled on thoughts of the fear the animal "must have felt" during the dying process. Many bereaved pet owners reported experiences of searching behavior, that is, unconscious attempts to locate their pet in particular places in the house; others noticed that they were careful where they walked so as to not step on the animal. One individual described waiting periodically for the pet to walk into the room. She said, "Sometimes you think you see a shadow and it's him. You have the feeling they're going to come in." All reported that these behaviors subsided between 2 days and a few weeks after the death (Cowles, 1985:6; Carmack, 1985; Weisman, 1991).

In the midst of mourning the death of a pet, we are likely to recall the characteristics of our companion that made him or her special. Grieving pet owners describe some of these qualities of specialness: "He was a special dog, he really was unusual. I've had dogs before, but this one was different," and "I can't really expect anyone to understand just how special our relationship was" (Carmack, 1985:151). Grieving adults miss what they perceive as unique qualities of the pet, as well as extraordinary qualities of their relationship with their deceased companion. Collars, tags, food dishes, blankets, and favorite toys were some of the items reported to have been kept as memorabilia (Cowles, 1985).

ALI: BOXER AND SAGE

Ali was our beautiful and muscular brindle Boxer. Clear-eyed and steady, he'd always struck the family as sort of sagelike. We'd joke sometimes about how he had probably functioned as chief guard dog at a Tibetan monastery in some previous life.

Ali was his own dog. He'd occasionally chase a ball or a stick, but only if he was in the mood to do so. Otherwise, he'd serenely watch the ball sail through the air and look back at me with an air of concern for my presumptuousness—or so it seemed. He was like that!

Ali immediately took to Ronya, a cocker spaniel puppy who, in contrast to Ali, always seemed to remain a puppy. The two of them would take off every morning, down the deer trail, Ronya barking at the leaves (and the deer and anything else that moved) while Ali trotted behind, quietly protective of his short, somewhat flabby friend. Our neighbors would spot the two of them sometimes 3 or 4 miles into the hills. We called it their "morning constitutional."

In his thirteenth year of age, Ali began to act strange—confused and disoriented, bumping into things, sleeping through the mornings. The veterinarian diagnosed a mild stroke. A month or so later, Ali wandered away from the property, putting the family into a weeklong frenzy of calls to the pound. We leafleted trees with his photo and called friends, until a neighbor found him and called us. He'd had another stroke, but this time it was major one. His eyes were glazed, his equilibrium was affected, he couldn't find his food and water. He looked weak and emaciated. The veterinarian said there was nothing to be done, except to consider euthanasia. We reluctantly agreed.

She gave us sleeping pills that we were to give to Ali before driving him back to the veterinary hospital. Back home again, the family gathered around Ali, who was lying on the living room carpet, on his favorite pillow, wrapped in his horse blanket. I placed the sleeping pills in the back of his throat, poured some water into his mouth, and held his jaws together until I could feel him swallow. In a matter of minutes his eyes, mostly glazed, began to close and his body grew limp. We held each other, and Ali, and we cried and sobbed on each other's shoulders, and comforted Ali with soft words and tender strokes. Ronya licked his snout. When he was deeply asleep, we drove back to the hospital. Ali was cradled in my arms when the veterinarian took him from me, a sad smile creasing her face.

A week later, still feeling his absence, we received a sympathy card from the veterinarian. She'd written, "Ali was serene to the very end. He was such a fine dog! I know you will all cherish your memories of him." Funny, isn't it, how such a loving gesture can turn tears of sadness into tears of joy.

R. M., personal recollection

The Death of a Child

For the vast majority of adults, the central testimonial to life and generativity during the adult years involves the birthing and raising of a child. To psychologist Terese Rando (1986c:8), "[a] baby signifies the potential for fulfilling dreams, starting over, rectifying past mistakes, and putting new insights into practice." As parents, the child brings powerful and profound forms of meaning to our lives. In stark contrast, the death of a child—whether sudden or anticipated, whether by accident, congenital birth defect, cancer, crib death, or homicide—creates a gaping and painful existential wound in the parents, a wound that may take many years to heal. And for some parents, that wound may never truly heal.

A CHILD'S SUDDEN DEATH

Deaths are not common in early childhood. In fact, mortality curves consistently decline following infancy to a minimum at about age 10 and then rise progressively throughout the remainder of the life span. Of the deaths that do occur, accidents are responsible for the highest number in small children and are among the leading causes of death in adolescence and young adulthood in the United States. In addition to accidents, other causes of sudden death in young children include sudden infant death syndrome (SIDS, or crib death), and murder.

Accidental Death

Sudden, accidental deaths in young children are complex and highly traumatic. Motor vehicle accidents, for example, are likely to involve other family members and tend to precipitate intense, long-lasting grief in the surviving family members. Symptoms of post-traumatic stress disorder are common if the parent was present at the death or was in any way involved. According to psychiatrist Beverley Raphael (1995:270), the shocking, unexpected nature of these deaths and their "killing" aspects all lead to great problems of adjustment and reintegration that will be heightened if the parent is in any way involved in the death of the child. "If the mother or father was driving the car in which the child was killed or, as sometimes happens, backed the car out

---

LIFE IN THE SHADOW

Mr. and Mrs. L were at home when they heard a loud crash. Mrs. L suddenly realized Melissa, her four-year-old, was not playing in the house where she had been a moment earlier. She ran, but said she felt almost paralyzed—she "knew it was her; she was hit." Vividly etched in her memory, replayed in slow motion are the details of the scene as she passed through her front door and out onto the street: the gathering crowd, the blood, the small still body.

This replayed constantly, in repetitive cognitions, with periods of repression over the two years following the death. There was all the helplessness, dread, and panic she felt at that moment—powerless rage at God and the driver. Her life had become disorganized and purposeless.

She had not mourned but had become fixed in that time and place, neither having her child nor relinquishing her.

Source: Adapted from Beverley Raphael (1995), pp. 261–275.

CARING INSIGHTS

When SIDS Strikes

"Counseling parents immediately after their child's death consists of providing them with the basic facts about SIDS and reassuring them that the death could neither be foreseen nor prevented. It's often helpful to give them written information on SIDS. . . . Convey autopsy findings to parents as soon as possible. Ideally, they should have the opportunity to discuss findings with the pathologist.

After the period of initial shock, parents may need extensive psychosocial support. Attempt to assuage their guilt by re-emphasizing what is known about SIDS, and provide calm support while allowing them to grieve and express their feelings. . . .

Make sure the parents know how to get in touch with a SIDS parents group or similar organization. . . . [S]ome parents may benefit from sharing their grief in group therapy with other affected parents; others, who may be more depressed or humiliated by it, may prefer individual talks with another SIDS parent, in person or by phone."

Source: De'Epiro (1984), pp. 303–322.

of the garage over the young child and fatally injured him, guilt and recrimination are overwhelming. Blame from the other parent and family members is also very great." Where the parents do not see the child's body, as is sometimes the case in floods and drownings, the death may seem even more surreal.

Often accidents are seen as preventable. Beatty (1989), for example, found that parents whose children died accidentally often felt they had failed to protect their children and suffered from feelings of guilt. Similarly, Nixon and Pearn (1977) found that parents of children who drowned reported greater recrimination, and Lord (1987) found significant frustration accompanying the grief that followed a drunk driving crash. Feelings of guilt were also found to predominate in the bereavement reactions of parents whose children died by suicide (Dunn & Morrish-Vidners, 1987–88).

Sudden death that occurs for medical reasons can eventually be understood. Sudden deaths from accidents, on the other hand, often appear as incomprehensible and senseless in the minds of loved ones. Extreme anger about the incident, survivor guilt, a hatred for the perpetrator, for example, and a desire to strike out and get revenge may dominate the parents' response. These feelings may be directed toward individuals, God, institutions, or the spouse. One bereaved and angry mother reported that when someone said to her, "I know how you feel," she wanted to say in return, "Give me your kid—I'll show you how it feels" (Gallagher, 1996:14).

Sudden Infant Death Syndrome

Sudden infant death syndrome (SIDS) is a particularly devastating loss for many parents. Each year about 6,000 infants in the United States are victims of this mysterious syndrome (National Center for Health Statistics, 1995a) that accounts for about 10% of deaths among American infants during the first year of life. SIDS is an unexpected, unexplainable death of an infant that often occurs at night. Parents are often left feeling devastated, angry, and filled with guilt.

In their attempts at account making, the majority of parents come to believe that the cause of their child's death was suffocation, a fact that medical science says may be the case. The second most common parental explanation of the death is that the child has choked on mucus or regurgitated food. Parents dwell on the last feeding, having doubts about what they did or failed to do. The third most common belief held by parents is that the cause of death was a previously unsuspected illness. Parents wish they had taken the baby to the doctor, particularly if he or she had a cold. Although medical researchers have some indication of a possible cause involving a brain dysfunction that causes faulty monitoring of carbon monoxide in the body with resulting suffocation, SIDS remains largely unexplained. The suddenness of the death, the age of the child, and the uncertainty about the cause of death all combine to make a SIDS death an extremely high-intensity grief experience.

The Murdered Child

Homicide-related bereavement occurs with startlingly high and annually increasing frequency in the United States (National Center for Health Statistics, 1995a; Kastenbaum, 1986). Only accidents claim more lives among young Americans. Parental grief responses to such deaths have been found to be complicated by overwhelming rage, fear, and a desire for retribution (Pouissant, 1984). In an investigation of siblings who had lost a brother or sister to accident or homicide, all surviving siblings reported symptoms of post-traumatic stress disorder, and 45% met the clinical criteria for the disorder. Thirty-five percent of the parents also met these criteria. Although symptom severity did not differ significantly among surviving siblings in the accident and murder groups, parents of murdered children reported more severe symptoms than parents of children who suffered accidental death (Applebaum & Burns, 1991).

CHILD MURDER AND ABUSE

Two thousand American infants and young children are murdered each year. One hundred forty thousand children and infants are seriously injured through physical abuse, while the number of children under 4 years of age who were murdered hit a 40-year high in 1994.

Profile: Most physical abuse fatalities are caused by angry, extremely stressed-out fathers, stepfathers, or boyfriends who unleash a torrent of rage on infants and children over such triggers as a baby's crying, feeding difficulties, or failed toilet training. Mothers are often responsible for deaths resulting from bathtub drownings, starvation, or neglect.

Source: Adapted from The U.S. Advisory Board on Child Abuse and Neglect. (1995). *A nation's shame: Fatal child abuse and neglect in the United States.* Washington, DC.

Murder attacks the basic sense of power over our life that society is supposed to provide and encourage (Klass, 1988). Moreover, the majority of murders are committed by relatives, friends, or acquaintances, which must certainly complicate grief (Danto, 1982). Thanatologist Dennis Klass (1988:116) has written that the "exaggerated narcissistic wound" created by homicidal death is kept open by criminal trials and the formal criminal justice system and is often reopened in appeals and second trials. From the parent's point of view, the legal system promises a satisfaction of revenge but rarely makes good on the promise. In addition, well-intentioned but misinformed family members and friends may attempt to minimize the death of the child in an effort to console the bereaved parent. They may say, "You're young, you can have another child," unaware that such a comment, though possibly true, is inappropriate. No other child will replace the one who has just died.

A CHILD'S ANTICIPATED DEATH

Most often, the child's death is sudden and unexpected, the result of an accident, murder, SIDS, or other medical emergency. Much less frequently, the death is caused by progressive, debilitating, or malignant conditions, with opportunities for *anticipatory grief*—the grief experienced prior to a death (Lindemann, 1944). When a child is dying or when a baby is born alive but with life-threatening disabilities due to prematurity, congenital defects, or similar causes, the ensuing period of anticipating and waiting for death can be a nightmare for parents, siblings, and grandparents. Frustration and a sense of futility may be overwhelming as surgery or other medical interventions are attempted and fail. Sometimes a baby born with one or more life-threatening conditions embarks on a life-or-death struggle that lasts for weeks or months. Sociologist David Moller (1996:157) writes, "[T]he chronicity and ambiguity of serious childhood illness create an atmosphere of living in a framework of impending loss, anticipating the possibility or probability of the death of the child, as well as having to deal with a variety of role-threatening losses and strains."

Phases of Anticipatory Grief

Based on their studies of parents of dying children, Futterman and Hoffman (1983:375) have constructed a model of the parental grieving process in anticipation of the death of their child. Parents pass through five phases of the anticipatory grieving process. The first phase involves *acknowledgment* and a progressive realization of the inevitability of the child's death. Once the reality of impending death has sunk in, the second phase, *grieving,* begins, with increasing emotional expressiveness that slowly diminishes over the course of the child's dying. The third phase, *reconciliation,* overlaps and facilitates grieving as the parents work through feelings of helplessness and hopelessness, as well as the assault to their sense of the "worth of life in general" and recast death into a more acceptable interpretation. For example, some parents may interpret the death as a religious or spiritual event or as the child's release from a life of suffering.

The timing of the fourth phase, *detachment from the parent–child bond,* is crucial to the parents' healing process, according to Futterman and Hoffman (1983:376). If detachment precedes death by too much, it is accompanied by guilt, sometimes

TWISTED GRIEF

According to medical examiners, police, and prosecutors, sudden infant death syndrome (SIDS) is a label that is too readily affixed to mysterious deaths of infants and young children. They estimate, in fact, that anywhere from 1% to as many as 20% of the nearly 6,000 U.S. babies who die of SIDS each year actually succumb to other causes, including murder. Generally the killer is the mother. Sometimes she slays for insurance or from frustration, but sometimes the murder results from a twisted bid for attention and sympathy.

Psychologists observed that the killers commonly suffer from a variant of Munchausen's syndrome, a bizarre mental condition that impels people to feign or induce illness in order to get care and attention from doctors and hospitals. In Munchausen's syndrome by proxy, people injure their children in their place. They may inject the youngsters with poisons or drugs, or mix blood in their urine. Parents have even been caught by surveillance cameras attempting to smother their offspring in their hospital beds (Toufexis, 1994).

Experts first described this syndrome in 1977. By 1992 some 200 cases had been uncovered, including a number of deaths previously attributed to natural causes or SIDS. One telltale sign is when more than one child in a family dies for unexplained reasons. A classic case is that of Marybeth Tinning of Schenectady, New York. All nine of her children died mysteriously between 1972 and 1985. Tinning was convicted of murdering the last one in 1986. Waneta Hoyt, also of upstate New York, is now awaiting trial for the suspected murders of her five children between 1965 and 1971. In the spring of 1994, Hoyt was interrogated by police 23 years after the death of her last baby. After 2 hours, she began to confess details of how she suffocated her children, one by one, with pillows, a towel, or her shoulder (S. Miller & Woodruff, 1994).

Most states now require an autopsy for all babies who die unexpectedly. On June 20, 1996, for the first time, the Centers for Disease Control and Prevention issued investigation guidelines to help coroners and police distinguish between crib death (SIDS) and homicide in infants who die suddenly. The standardized six-page form notes such things as the position of the infant's body, suspected injuries from child abuse and evidence of drug and alcohol use in the home (CDC, 1996).

reinforced by judgments of relatives and hospital staff of the parents' "lack of concern, callous behavior, and disinterest" toward the child. On the other hand, if dying precedes the detachment phase, parents experience greater difficulty in adjusting to the death. In the final phase, termed *memorialization,* begun before the actual death, parents distill certain characteristics of the child, usually positive, which are then solidified into their inner representation of the dead child.

Judith Cook (1983a, b) has identified a number of practical, emotional, and social issues that must be confronted by the parents during the course of their child's dying:

- Making child care arrangements for the ill child as well as for other children
- Experiencing feelings of helplessness and loss of confidence in parenting abilities
- Confronting financial difficulties
- Experiencing a sense of being avoided by others
- Suffering marital strains, feeling the need to protect their spouse from distressing feelings and upsetting events, feeling that their spouse may be

The pledge to love and caring that a mature parent feels for a helpless child is a form of sacred bond. The sacred or spiritual nature of the parent–child relationship makes it unique and makes the mourning after the death of a child such a long and agonizing process. © *Stock Illustration Source*

excessively preoccupied with the dying child, or seeing their spouse withdraw from the family unit

- fearing the inability to cope with the actual death of the child and having to cope with the inability of other family members to deal with the actual death
- Feeling that their family is being torn apart

Although anticipatory grieving may soften postbereavement mourning to some extent, the death of a child is still likely to create enormous difficulties for the entire family. For instance, after the child dies, other relationships that retreated to the periphery during the crisis must be restored or reconstituted (J. A. Cook, 1984). In addition to the work of anticipatory grieving, parents may be confronted with medical and ethical choices that could result in their child's death. Meanwhile the costs incurred in keeping the child alive and comfortable continue to mount. Following the death, the parents may express resentment toward the medical institution and its personnel, feeling as if they have survived the painful ordeal only to be billed for failed medical interventions (J. A. Cook, 1984; Raphael, 1995).

Anticipatory grieving is usually thought to ease the mourning process once the death occurs, with some thanatologists arguing that it isn't so much that grief has preceded the death but that the death is not unexpected—the parent has had time to strive for some understanding and to develop some coping skills (Kamerman, 1988; Rando, 1983, 1995). Well-being throughout life depends on

"Then there was the empty room at home, and it all came over me like a great tidal wave of grief. I was so sad, so empty, I thought I'd never feel whole again. I used to think about the funeral, and think about him. It was such a tiny casket. He was such a little person to die."

Raphael (1995), p. 269.

our ability to make sense of transitional experiences; in this case, the time before the death of a loved child would seem to be an opportunity for resolving old conflicts and ambivalent feelings, as well as for achieving a psychological closure to parenting (R. Cohen, 1988; Perkins & Harris, 1990). There is no uniform agreement on this, however. Empirical evidence (Shanfield, Benjamin, & Swain, 1988; R. Cohen, 1988) and clinical insights (Rando, 1986b; Raphael, 1983, 1995) suggest higher levels of psychiatric distress in parents whose children died suddenly. Other studies, however, argue that there is inconclusive evidence for a relationship between anticipatory grief and subsequent adjustment (Gallagher, Thompson, & Peterson 1981–82; Levav, 1982).

Childhood Leukemia

Deaths from malignant disease most often involve a process of gradual adaptation to the reality of the child's illness and fatal prognosis. Although childhood malignancy, especially leukemia, is viewed with repugnance, it is nevertheless accepted as a medical condition, not the result of personal action or inaction.

Acute lymphocytic leukemia is the principal type of leukemia that affects children. The disease is a form of cancer that often comes on quickly and severely. The abnormal cells resemble a type of white blood cell called lymphocyte. Other names for the disease are *acute lymphatic leukemia* and *acute lymphoblastic leukemia.* Intensive treatment with combinations of drugs active against the acute leukemias is an important recent advance in leukemia treatment research. With a combination of certain drugs, more than 90% of individuals with acute lymphocytic leukemia can be expected to achieve remission (American Cancer Society, 1996).

Deaths from leukemia create special problems. Though leukemia was once thought to be inevitably fatal, leukemia victims may now achieve prolonged remissions, which might suggest that the disease has been "cured." The parents and the child must resist hoping for the child's survival even as the day-to-day evidence is clear at times that the child is not dying. These lingering medical conditions may lead family members to an orientation of "living one day at a time," not investing in an ominous and indefinite future (Raphael, 1995).

FETAL, NEONATAL, AND POSTNEONATAL DEATH

Approximately 68,000 fetal and infant deaths occur each year in the United States (National Center for Health Statistics, 1995a). According to medical definition, *stillbirth* refers to fetal death that occurs between the twentieth week of gestation (pregnancy) and the time of birth, resulting in the delivery of a dead baby. *Neonatal deaths* are those that occur during the first 4 weeks following birth. *Postneonatal deaths* include those that occur after the first 4 weeks and up to 11 months following birth.

CARING INSIGHTS

"When Grief Descends"

"When grief descends, there is no redemption then in suffering, nothing saving or luminous about it, no higher meaning to its torment, not one thing bestowing of wisdom or grace. Every moment's pain, like a parody of first love, afflicts for hours, and every day flaunts its eternity. If we could choose our lot, who would not say: Woman, when you see suffering, run. But we cannot choose. . . .

When you meet such a woman, do not speak of inner sustenance, of benefit from sorrow or of healing. Nothing but restoration would suffice, and every day the anguish, rather than abating, multiplies. Do not say that time repairs, or talk of moving forward or of growing. Such consolations are absurd. Offer only this: I, too, have suffered and endured."

Source: Nessa Rapaport. (1994). *A woman's book of grieving.* William Morrow, New York, p. 6.

All reproductive or childbearing losses involve mourning, not only the actual ending of an unlived life, but also the symbolic death of the parents' dreams, hopes, and investment of meaning. Thanatologist Judith Savage (1989:19) writes, "Childbearing losses are mourned not only for what was, but also for what might have been." Generally, parental grief associated with fetal or neonatal death is related more to the nature of the actual and symbolic bond created between parents and offspring than to the length of the pregnancy or the age of the infant (Peppers & Knapp, 1980).

Pregnancy is a powerful life event for adults, the anticipated outcome of which is the birth of a vital, healthy infant, and the attachment of feelings and meanings placed on the child by the parents have been found to begin long before birth (DeVries, Dalla Lana, & Falck, 1994). Most parents begin to reshape their lifestyles, their roles, and their self-concepts during pregnancy in preparation for the birth. Parents may purchase furniture and toys for the child, choose a name for the baby, develop dreams, feel its movements, and, with newer medical imaging techniques, may actually see the fetus in the womb. In fact, from structured interviews with 105 women who had undergone ultrasound examinations of their fetuses and had subsequently lost their pregnancies, psychologist Rita Black (1992) found that 44% of these bereaved women reported that viewing the fetus with ultrasound made it more difficult to cope with the loss.

Stillbirth: A World Turned Upside Down

There are approximately 40,000 documented cases of stillbirth in the United States each year (National Center for Health Statistics, 1995c). The loss comes, tragically, when the fulfillment of pregnancy should be at hand, and falls on adult parents-to-be and adolescent parents-to-be, as well. The still birth may be quite unexpected, often sudden. Hopes built during the months of pregnancy are dashed. Instead of a crib, there is a grave; instead of receiving blankets, there are burial clothes; instead of a birth certificate, there is a death certificate. The world is turned upside down (Kirkley-Best & Kellner, 1982; Raphael, 1983, 1995).

The baby's death may occur with some forewarning. Either through congenital abnormality or intrauterine event, it may become obvious that the baby will not be viable or that it has already died. Some anticipatory grieving may commence when the death is discovered or when diagnosis is made of a nonviable deformity, such as anencephaly. However, on many occasions the mother senses something wrong—cessation of movements, unexpected sensations, something not quite right—that leads her to have the matter investigated. She may have kept this concern to herself or shared it with her husband. This may be the beginning of her working through her loss. The birthing process itself may be immensely painful for the parents, particularly if they must wait for the natural onset of labor to birth the dead baby.

In some instances, it may be that "a dull, sad quietness pervades the labor ward as the baby emerges, and its floppy body is hurriedly wrapped in a sheet and whisked away" (Raphael, 1983:126). One young woman said of her stillbirth, "After 7 days of induced labor, no one said a word, including me. The delivery room was dead quiet." In others, when the stillbirth is unexpected, there may be "frantic efforts at resuscitation as the silence becomes increasingly oppressive, raising everyone's anxiety, especially the mother's" (Raphael, 1983:126).

The cause of the death may be difficult to ascertain and even more difficult to explain to the distressed mother. The mother's comprehension of the death and her mourning for the baby she has lost are sometimes complicated further by the fact that she has been prevented from seeing and touching the baby. Although progress has been made over recent years, medical personnel and hospital systems are still sometimes reluctant to let her have any sight or contact at all with the dead baby, in the mistaken belief that this policy will aid in her recovery. But the majority of mothers are anxious to see their babies, to touch, hold, name them, and take part in the arrangements for the burial. They may find photos of the baby helpful. This is not always the case, however. One woman, approached by the hospital to okay a postmortem photograph of the baby wanted nothing to do with the baby, did not want to hold the baby, and certainly did not want a photograph of the child. "I regret that decision now," she says. "All I have now are her footprints and descriptions of Erica from my husband and my parents" The hospital changed its policy shortly thereafter and now takes photos of all stillbirths and makes them available to the parents if they should ever want them as evidence that the whole pregnancy produced something: a baby that was real and can be remembered.

Jane A. Nichols (1990:21), a grief counselor in a neonatal intensive care unit, states:

> My observation has been that most parents want to see, be with, and hold their baby. They believe it to be helpful to their own process and have reported in follow-up that it was a rich experience. If, however, a parent wishes to have only minimal contact with the baby, caregivers may feel confident in honoring that choice also. Parents should not be coerced in either direction; the option should simply be proffered in a neutral manner: 'Would you find it helpful?' "

Neonatal Death

Many aspects of the grieving and mourning processes following the death of a newborn baby are symptomatically comparable to those following stillbirth, except in neonatal death the parents have had some opportunity, even if limited, to get to know and to bond with the child. Raphael (1995:268) has observed that "although the bonding to the sick neonate may be inhibited by the threat to the child's life, its prematurity, or illness, in most instances, with modern obstetric practices, the attachment to the real baby has time to consolidate."

In all cases, sadness and depression are the predominant emotions, with cultural role and death-causation guilt often playing a significant role. There may be bouts of anger and rage, especially if the mother believes it should not have happened, either because she wanted the baby so much or because she perceives medical or personal care as failing. The father may also feel anger and sadness, but it is likely to be less intense than the mother's, unless he had particular hopes and fantasies invested in the pregnancy, the child, and the parenting role. Many men in these circumstances deflect awareness from their own feelings of loss and sorrow by taking on the roles of protector and nurturer of the grieving mother.

> ### Ambivalence, Anger and a Parent's Sorrow
>
> "I wished this horrible suspense of not knowing whether Michael would live or die would end. I became so desperately unhappy that I truly believed that I wanted him to die. I wished desperately that he would live, and I also wished that he would die. The two desires lived constantly in my mind side by side. I felt shattered. I was deeply angered. I wanted to hit people. . . . We left the hospital. We didn't know what to do with ourselves, not wanting to go home for the inevitable phone call. Finally we went home and the resident called to tell us that Michael had died 10 minutes after we left. We were shaking inside."
>
> *Source:* Bowie (1980), pp. 60–61.

The attitudes of the mother toward the pregnancy may fall anywhere on the spectrum from wanted to unwanted, and in some small proportion of cases the attitude may affect the chances of neonatal death. Bustan and Coker (1994), for example, evaluated whether a woman's negative attitude toward her pregnancy increases the risk of neonatal death. Data were collected from 8,823 women (ages 20–50 years) who attended health clinics for confirmation of pregnancy. Participants were interviewed about their medical history, behavioral risk factors, and attitude toward pregnancy and were followed throughout their pregnancy while receiving prenatal care. Results revealed that, among other factors, those women who reported during the first trimester that the pregnancy was unwanted were more than twice as likely to deliver infants who died within the first 28 days of life than were those who wanted and accepted their pregnancies.

The newborn's death may also have psychological effects on later parenting experiences and behaviors. Theut, Moss, and Zaslow (1992), in comparing twenty-five mothers who had experienced a previous neonatal death with a group of thirty nonloss mothers, found that mothers who had experienced a neonatal loss expressed more concerns about psychologically separating from their children than the comparison group and spent more time worrying about their children's physical well-being.

Spontaneous Abortion

It is estimated that about 20% of all pregnancies end in spontaneous abortion, with about three-quarters of these ending before 12 weeks (Dorland's, 1985). The woman who experiences spontaneous abortion may display significant grief immediately, or grief may be delayed until the time the baby's movements would have been felt or the date the baby would have been born or until some other trigger reminds her of the loss.

The swiftness and abruptness of the event itself may form obstacles to the parents' account making. They may find it difficult to make sense of events or their own reactions to those events. Grief may be complicated by the fact that in many instances there are no remains to be buried and no funeral to acknowledge the loss. One young mother was able to begin resolving her grief when she returned to the hospital, asked for and received the remains of her baby, took them home and buried them in her backyard. "She takes comfort in looking out the window and knowing her baby is there" (DeSpelder & Strickland, 1992:310).

"JUST A MISCARRIAGE"

"They said it was nothing . . . just a miscarriage. I was only a few weeks overdue. I had seen those pictures, and I know it was only tiny, but it was my baby, and it counted as a real baby.

I wanted to see it, but really all there was was blood. They said I couldn't see anything in that. When I got home I cried and cried and they couldn't understand. Jim tried to comfort me. He kept on saying it would be all right because we could have another baby right away. But that was another baby—it wasn't the same at all. It was this baby I was crying for and there'd never be another one just the same as it. Jim said we hadn't really been ready for it anyway, that it was just as well. That only made me feel worse, as though we'd got rid of it. Then I wanted it all the more, just to show it that we loved it and cared for it. Some days I would think of how it would have been—a little boy or a little girl.

Anyway, my tears went. I was a bit sad again now and then. Each month I used to think, now the baby would have been this big, now I would have been feeling the movements, now it would have been due. I felt a failure until I became pregnant again and then it faded. Really, I got over it all right when you look back. But it wasn't 'nothing.' For me I really did lose a baby, not just a miscarriage."

Source: Raphael (1995), p. 263.

Jackman, McGee, and Turner (1993) examined the experience of and preferences for management of fetal remains among twenty-seven women who suffered early miscarriages. Results showed that most women neither saw the miscarried fetus nor knew of burial details. Regardless of stated preferences for viewing and burial, all the subjects indicated that they wanted to be involved in making these decisions. These researchers concluded that specific recommendations for viewing and burial arrangements were not as important as the provision of choice for the parents involved.

Induced Abortion

In contrast to spontaneous abortion, which occurs naturally, *induced abortion* (sometimes called *artificial* or *therapeutic abortion*) is brought about intentionally, with the aim of ending a pregnancy by mechanical means or drugs. In these cases, even though the parents feel unable or unwilling to bring the baby to term, there is usually a lingering sense of loss and grief (Doane & Quigley, 1981; Peppers, 1987–88).

Statistics indicate that about three to four out of ten pregnancies end in abortion, resulting in a total of about 1.6 million induced abortions conducted annually in the United States. Although it might be assumed that women who elect to terminate a pregnancy voluntarily would experience little in the way of a grief reaction, this is not the case with all women. In fact, the results of a study conducted by Peppers (1987–88) indicate that there is a grief reaction to voluntary abortion that is, for the most part, similar to that experienced following involuntary fetal and infant loss. The grief reactions may begin when the decision is made to terminate the pregnancy or weeks later, and, according to Peppers (1987–88), the intensity of the grief appears to be associated with both the length of the pregnancy and the woman's perception of the pregnancy itself—that is, whether she perceived herself as "simply" pregnant or as a potential mother.

According to researchers (Peppers, 1987–88; Raphael, 1995), the woman's pattern of grief and mourning is symptomatically similar to that for spontaneous abortion, except that cognitive denial of the loss and emotional repression of grieving reactions are much more likely. The first appearance of sadness is often noted 6 weeks or so after the termination, when defenses are down or the loss of the baby is obvious because of the failure of anticipated body changes. Anger is more likely to be directed toward the self or toward those who are seen as having pressured the woman to have the termination. There are many loss rationales (Raphael, 1995:265).

> it was the only thing to do, I had no choice, I couldn't take care of a baby. So why should I feel like this? Thoughts about what the baby might have been like and fears about possible negative effects on future pregnancies may appear. Some grief and mourning may appear when the baby would have been born. The woman may find herself depressed and tearful some months later 'for no good reason,' she says—then she remembers that this is when the aborted baby would have been born."

In most cases, there is little social support offered by family and friends, and support groups rarely exist for woman and men dealing with the aftershocks of an induced abortion.

Of course, not every woman who undergoes pregnancy termination by induced abortion does so as a result of conflict about the pregnancy. Contraceptive practice may have failed, the abortion may have been needed to save the woman's life, or, as in the Peoples Republic of China, termination may be the method of that society for population control. In these cases, ambivalence toward the pregnancy may not be great, and the choice to terminate it may be clear and simple for the woman (Raphael, 1995). In these circumstances, grieving responses may be limited and resolved easily.

Phases of Parental Mourning

In *Centuries of Childhood* (1962), Phillip Aries notes that extremely high infant mortality rates in western Europe before the seventeenth century produced a situation in which children younger than the age of 5 were viewed, essentially, as

THE PERCEPTION OF LOSS FOR PARENTS IN MOURNING

On the Death of an Infant The infant is seen as the antithesis of death; the loss is viewed as dissynchronous and involving a loss of potential; parents perceive the loss as the result of incompetence, a failure to protect, or a violation of the natural order, and often experience guilt. Mourning is for loss of the parent role and part of their own identity with the child; social support may be minimal; loss of a fetus or newborn may be discounted by others.

On the Death of a Young Child or Adolescent The loss of the young child or adolescent is seen as the deprivation of a child on the verge of productivity, and as a loss of family system organization. Parents often experience a sense of futility and perceive the loss as a result of their incompetence or as failure to protect, with accompanying guilt and stigma. Social support may be avoided as parents withdraw from the social world.

On the Death of an Adult Child The loss of an adult child is seen as dissynchronous because old should die before young; the loss of this long-lasting relationship may stimulate survival guilt; loss of ability to procreate and carry on the family; loss of beneficiary; and loss of control and meaning. The loss may be exacerbated if there was reduced involvement with the adult child. Social support may be minimized by others in some instances.

Source: Adapted from DeVries, Dalla Lana, & Falck (1994), pp. 47–69.

nonpersons. The burial and mourning after the death of a young child was, in many instances, comparable to what would today be given to family pets (Kearl, 1989). Just a century ago, when communicable diseases were still common and infant mortality rates remained high, the death of a child continued to be an anticipated part of normal family life. In our more recent history, however, as infant mortality rates have plummeted and children have become highly prized and valued, the intensity of the emotional pain surrounding their deaths has dramatically increased.

Thanatologist Terese Rando (1983:xi) describes parental grieving as "severe, complicated, and long lasting with major and unparalleled symptom fluctuations over time." John H. Harvey (1996:44) describes a parent's grief as "the most inconsolable, incurable of any kind of grief." In fact, of the losses experienced in the adult years, the death of a young child now evokes the highest intensities of bereavement and the widest range of grief reactions among family members. For example, in a study by Littlefield and Rushton (1986) that investigated the range of grief intensity of bereaved parents, parent siblings, and grandparents in 263 Canadian families, it was found that grief reactions rippled throughout the family nexus so that:

- Mothers grieved more than fathers.
- Healthy children were grieved more than unhealthy children.
- Male children were grieved more than female children.
- Maternal grandmothers grieved more than either maternal grandfathers or paternal grandmothers, who in turn grieved more than paternal grandfathers.
- The mothers' siblings grieved more than the fathers' siblings.

Research findings consistently reveal that parental despair and depression following the death of a child are profound and long-lasting. Hazzard, Weston, and Gutterres (1992), for example, in a study of the grief reactions of forty-five parents whose children (sixteen boys and ten girls) had died 6 months to 4 years earlier, found that the parents of children who died suddenly experienced despair, anger, guilt, and depersonalization that appeared to remain fairly intense for at least 4 years after the child's death. Other longitudinal studies of parental grief reveal an intensification of grieving on anniversaries and birthdays and in the third year following death (Rando, 1983, 1995). In a study of bereaved parents at 2 and 7 years after the death of a child from cancer, Martinson, Davis, and McClowry (1991) found there was no difference between parental depression at 2 and 7 years. One mother in mourning said, "I went one night to the cemetery at 12 midnight, got out of bed and went up there and screamed . . . 'It's been six *years*.' But I guess in 50 years I'll still feel the same" (Gallagher, 1996:14).

The intensity and duration of parental grief have been attributed to a number of factors (DeVries, Dalla Lana, & Falck, 1994; R. H. Turner, 1970; Rando, 1986c, 1995; Moss, 1986–87; Raphael, 1983, 1995; Harvey, 1996; Finkbeiner, 1996):

- The untimeliness of the child's death
- The nature and quality of the lost relationship with the child
- The meanings and archetypal representations of the child for the parent
- The uniqueness of the parent–child relationship
- The loss of a parent's link between the past and the future
- The role the child played in the particular family
- The characteristics of the death itself
- The social support system available to the parents during the work of mourning

THE COGNITIVE RESTRUCTURING PHASE

We are all children, of course, in that the label "child" may be applied to anyone, from newborn infants to those in their 70s and beyond. Correspondingly, the death of a child is not an event restricted to any particular age range. Whatever the age, the scheme of nature is geared to the increasing vitality of the young and the declining strength of the old (Hocker, 1988). The old are "socialized to death," with the unspoken expectation that the child will be the survivor (Moss, Lesher, & Moss, 1986–87). As a result, the actuality of the death of the youngster is likely to be met with powerful forms of cognitive resistance.

The death of a parent is said to be part of the natural order of the universe, while the death of a child is always an *untimely* and unnatural interruption of the normal life course that often provokes intense parental denial, anger, and rage (Sanders, 1979–80; Harvey, 1996; Hocker, 1988; DeVries, Dalla Lana, & Falck, 1994; Perkins & Harris, 1990). Gallagher (1996:14) notes that "because children aren't supposed to die, the loss is not only painful but profoundly disorienting." To the parents, the death of their child is often associated with a view of the world as random or chaotic.

In addition to the general sense of untimeliness that most parents experience, the suddenness of the death, the age of the child, and the uncertainty about the cause of death may all combine to create powerful barriers to the parents' cognitive assimilation and accommodation of the actuality of the child's death. In the beginning phase of cognitive restructuring, disbelief is the initial reaction. According to one psychological researcher who has studied parental grieving, the bereaved parents' lives seem not to make sense to them during the initial phases of the mourning process. Many of the parents in the study "gave the appearance of individuals who have suffered a physical blow which left them with no strength or will to fight, hence totally vulnerable" (Sanders, 1979–80:317).

For the first few days, and possibly over several weeks, some parents will have a fear of going insane. They will have sensations such as whirling around, pressure in the head, heartache, and stomach pain. These somatic sensations are accompanied by a sad expression, profuse weeping, sighing, insomnia, and restlessness. This is followed by a period of account making and reality testing in which parents often speak of the dead child both in the present tense and the past tense (Bergman, Pomeroy, & Beckwith, 1969; Rhodes & Vedder, 1983; Harvey, 1995).

Shadow Grief

In the parents' initial attempts to understand and cope with the death, their thoughts are often filled with "if only." All the events leading up to the death, as though seared into consciousness, are gone over, revised, and revisioned—over and over—in the parents' attempts at account making. What could have been done differently, what actions or omissions contributed to the death? Answers are sought and sorted out in these attempts at understanding the loss and perhaps allocating blame for the death. The bereaved parent may become locked in the angry "if only" stage of separation from the dead child, with yearning for the child, restless searching, deep feelings of helplessness, but no real acceptance. There may be little overt grief, just fitful agitation and distress (DeVries, Dalla Lana, & Falck, 1994; Raphael, 1995).

In some cases, according to DeVries, Dalla Lana, and Falck (1994), loved ones become frozen in cognitive denial in their attempt to come to terms with the actuality of the child's death. Parents, as well as siblings, may become obsessed with the image and the presence of the lost child, keeping the child's room as it was at the time of death, clinging to toys and blankets, visiting the grave daily, and talking to the dead child. For some parents, the grief remains forever unresolved. The emotional agony caused by the child's death, rather than moving toward emotional expression, psychological integration, and psychospiritual transformation, creates *shadow grief*—an unresolved grief that becomes part of the parents' sense of self and, to some degree, that defines their very existence (DeVries, Dalla Lana, & Falck, 1994).

In interviews with mothers who had experienced the death of an infant years earlier, Peppers and Knapp (1980), for example, noted that some mothers had never progressed through their initial grief and, instead, lived with shadow grief. Frozen in denial, repression, and passivity, the death of the child may forever alter the parents' lives and their relationship to one another. In losing the child, the parents lose not only the relationship but a part of the self and a hope for the future. Even when deeply and fully mourned, the child is rarely forgotten and is almost always counted as one of the children.

THE EMOTIONAL EXPRESSION PHASE

Anger is a common response of the newly bereaved parent during the emotional expression phase of the mourning process. Physicians, nurses, and other health personnel are sometimes blamed for the death. For example, based on a study of the pediatrician's role in the grieving process of parents, Patterson (1989) suggests that pediatricians not attend the child's funeral, since other family members may need to deal with blaming the doctor, but that a meeting with the family about 4 weeks after the death can be therapeutic.

Anger may be directed toward the other parent, with the accusation "You never wanted this child anyway!" Anger may also be focused on the child, resulting in confusing emotions for parents (DeSpelder & Strickland, 1992:309). This range of emotional expression may be accompanied by auditory or kinesthetic hallucinations: A child cries in the night, waking parents from sleep, or the baby kicks inside the "haunted womb," yet there is no pregnancy, no live child. Such experiences only add to the intensity of the grieving process (Grimes, 1995).

"I was not just crying; I was crying at—crying at Trevor, at the doctors . . . at the God who had refused to dole out proper bone marrow, at the stepfather who posed as father around nurses and doctors. Cowboys don't cry, but if they do—if they must—they cry mad."

Source: Grimes (1995), p. 262.

The societal expectation that children should not die an untimely death often contributes to parents' feelings of *guilt* or self-disgust that they somehow failed and that society will condemn them (Rando, 1983; Raphael, 1983, 1995). Hospital personnel in neonatal and pediatric units know too well the pleas of grieving parents: "Better I should have died than my child"; "Why would God allow my child to die before me?" (Moss, Lesher, & Moss, 1986–87:209–218). Older parents of a young child may feel much more acutely the "out-of-turness" of their child's death (Rando, 1983). *Survival guilt,* a complex of feelings based on the belief that children should naturally outlive their parents, tends to intensify and extend the parental grief experience.

Miles and Demi (1983–84:308–309) found other forms of guilt to be a common feature of parental bereavement, particularly what they term *death-causation guilt* and *cultural role guilt.* Death-causation guilt is viewed as a consequence of the parents' belief that they caused the child's death, either directly or indirectly. Cultural role guilt stems from the belief that they didn't fulfill their obligations as parents.

Another source of parental guilt, discovered unexpectedly during the study by Miles and Demi (1983–84), is *grief guilt*—based on the parents' perceived failure to grieve correctly or to behave appropriately as a grieving parent. Cognitive denial, emotional repression, and behavioral passivity all play a role in creating grief guilt. Kamerman (1988:129) suggests that "the vagueness of the bereavement role, the barriers to effective role-taking, and the cultural encouragement of denial" also play a role in hampering the work of mourning by parents.

Brammer (1991) notes that a period of stabilized moods is sometimes experienced during the emotional expression phase, but this stabilization is usually short-lived as awareness of fears for the future and anger at the death of the child reemerge. Self-esteem usually falls, and feelings of sadness, dread, or depression take over once again. The length of these cycles of sadness and depression depends on the person's perception of the severity of the loss, the availability of coping resources, and cultural attitudes about the appropriate length of grieving. The task for loved ones and other caregivers during this period is to encourage the mourning parent to perceive of this time as a transitional life event, as a period of healing and change (Brammer, 1991).

Gender, Emotional Expression, and Grieving Style

Judith Cook (1983a, b) notes that parental grieving affects mothers and fathers in different ways, related to their respective gender roles. Mothers, because they are often emotionally closer to their children and have a greater role in caring for the child, tend to experience a greater intensity of sadness and depression than fathers. She found that mothers reported more depression and difficulty than fathers during the first year after the child's death. Moller (1996:160) notes:

> Fathers, in connection with their largely instrumental world view and the norm of American male inexpressiveness, emphasize their feelings of responsibility for managing the grief of the family unit. Fathers usually shoulder the emotional burden of grief in a solitary and private way. Mothers, on the other hand, suffer from repeated visualizations of the deceased child, see painful reminders of the child around the house, and experience an emptiness related to the child's absence from their daily routine. The more personal dimensions of the mother's grief— her deep loneliness and feeling of personal diminishment—make her grief typically more profound."

"I wanted to go to the cemetery and let my milk flow onto my daughter's grave."

DeSpelder & Strickland (1992), p. 309.

When the death involves a neonate or infant, *postpartum depression* may be intensified by the loss. Absent a baby, the mother may be confronted by physical reminders of the loss, such as the onset of lactation. One bereaved mother said, "I wanted to go to the cemetery and let my milk flow onto my daughter's grave" (DeSpelder & Strickland, 1992:309). At the same time, the father may feel personally and culturally constrained to "be brave" and "in control" so that he can give support to the mother who is recuperating physically as well as emotionally. In the process, the father's need to grieve often goes unmet, and his emotions may be repressed until long after the event.

Men are more likely to hide their distress, in keeping with male mores about not expressing certain emotions, such as crying, or appearing helpless. In fact, recent studies suggest that medical practitioners, distracted by men's displays of "strength," are much less likely to diagnose depression in a truly depressed man than in an equally depressed woman (Potts, Burnam, & Wells, 1991). Without a clear cultural prescription for proper mourning behavior, people fall back on more clearly defined role prescriptions.

Schwab (1992), who interviewed twenty bereaved couples (ages 27–60) between 1 month and 48 months after their child's death, found a number of problem areas that caused the marital relationship to suffer. These included the husbands' concern and frustration about the intensity and duration of their wives' emotional expression, wives' anger over their husbands' not sharing feelings connected to their grief, temporary breakdowns in communication, loss of sexual intimacy, and general irritability between spouses. Couples reported withdrawing from each other at various points in the grieving and mourning processes, either because of their own intense anguish or out of a desire to avoid increasing their spouse's emotional pain. Almost without exception, couples reported that the death of their child was the most emotionally devastating event they had ever experienced (Harvey, 1995, 1996).

Emotional Expression and Coping Strategies

One difference between men and women that might tend to promote differences in emotional expressiveness during the mourning process is that women are more likely to become involved when others are suffering, and may experience the feelings of other people more acutely and intensely than do men. The stresses associated with this empathic behavior may induce deeper sadness and depression in grieving woman (Turner & Avison, 1989). Other research suggests that women are not sadder or more depressed than men during the mourning process but simply are more willing to admit to being depressed and to seek relief. In one Canadian study of the coping strategies of twenty-seven couples who had experienced stillbirth, neonatal death, or sudden infant death syndrome, mothers and fathers were found to be similar in their use of various coping strategies. Among the exceptions, however, were the findings that mothers admitted to personal vulnerability and sought out and used social support to a significantly greater extent than did fathers (Feeley & Gottlieb, 1988–89).

> **"For years I was prepared for the loss of my sons (in war): and now comes that of my daughter. . . . Quite deep down I can trace the feeling of deep . . . hurt that is not to be healed."**
>
> –Sigmund Freud in a letter to a friend. (1957). In E. Jones, *The life and work of Sigmund Freud* (Vol. 3). Basic Books, New York, p. 20.

THE PSYCHOLOGICAL REINTEGRATION PHASE

Embedded within the reintegration phase of the parental mourning process are two distinct yet related realities that must be confronted: the *actual* relationship between the parent and child, and the *symbolic* nature of the parent–child bond. Parents in mourning, according to DeSpelder and Strickland (1992:308), "often speak of the lost companionship, lost dreams, and all the ways in which a particular child would have enriched their lives. Such talk is concerned with the actual loss. The symbolic loss relates to the meaning attached to the relationship, as when an individual, by parenting a child, becomes a nurturing, supportive guide." From this perspective, the death of a child creates three obstacles to psychological reintegration: (a) a crisis in the social environment brought on by the child's absence from the family itself, (b) the challenge of adopting new roles and a renewed sense-of-self, and (c) the parents' ongoing relationship with the inner representation of the child (DeSpelder & Strickland, 1992; Klass & Marwit, 1988–89; Marwit & Klass, 1995; Benedek, 1970).

Coping with the Actual Loss

Confronting the actual loss of the child involves tapping previously learned and newly learned coping skills and resources, such as family, friends, and a support network of other parents in mourning (e.g., Compassionate Friends, Survivors of Suicide, Emotions Anonymous). Overcoming behavioral passivity through the adoption of new roles, setting new goals, and initiating new ways of being in the world often facilitates the mourning process. Self-nurturing and frequent interaction with the family and support networks are important, but each person must ultimately discover his or her own method of getting through this painful period.

The challenge for the mourning parent is to let go of the deceased child to some degree while taking hold of new aspirations and relationships (Brammer, 1991). These attitudes and resources, combined with the passage of time, enable us to regain self-confidence and self-esteem. We begin to look to the future with some optimism and hope—and the tears lessen. This process often does not proceed in nicely calibrated steps, however, and we often recycle through previous phases of the mourning process. One father in mourning said, "You have to work at improving. If you don't, you're going to be down forever" (Gallagher, 1996:14).

THE METAPHOR OF AMPUTATION

"All grief contains the sense that a piece of the self has been cut out, but it appears that sense is exaggerated in parents after the death of a child. It also appears as if that sense does not diminish in character as the parent develops after the death of the child. One father . . . expressed it as, 'It is like I lost my right arm, but I am learning to live as a one-armed man.' A continuing sense of that amputation remains in the form of an empty historical track which is life-long in most bereaved parents. They report that they think thoughts like, 'He would have been 18 years old and graduating from high school this year.' An examination of renewed discomfort in bereaved parents often reveals that the trigger is a child of the age the deceased child would have been or developmental events in which the deceased child would have been participating at the time of the discomfort."

Source: Klass & Marwit (1988–89), p. 41.

Coping with the Symbolic Loss

The creation of an inner representation of the child is especially salient during the psychological reintegration phase of the mourning process, when the parent is remolding his or her assumptive world and learning new roles and ways of being in that world. The child may have many representations in the parents' psychic life because, as Raphael (1983:229) reminds us, a child is "a part of the self, and of the loved partner; a representation of generations past; the genes of the forebears; the hope of the future; a source of love, pleasure, even narcissistic delight; a tie or a burden; and sometimes a symbol of the worst parts of the self and others." As one bereaved father said, "Not only have I lost a son who might follow in my footsteps, but, without him, I have no feet" (Gallagher, 1996:14). As psychological reintegration progressed, it was important for him to acknowledge and mourn both the loss of his son and the loss of symbolic meaning and purpose in his life. One mother in mourning whose young son was murdered during a basketball game became a grief counselor. She says that she can no longer protect her own child from violence, "[b]ut maybe, some other child. Maybe that in turn will help me to not miss Erin so much" (Gallagher, 1996:14).

A parent's attachment to a child begins long before birth. But following the birth, as experiences are shared, the bond between parent and child takes on increasing complexity and depth. Over the years, as the child develops her or his own personality, the parent–child relationship, no matter how strong the feelings of affection and love, also involves feelings of anger, sadness, frustration, and disappointment. Ambivalent feelings toward the child create a challenge to coping with the symbolic loss of the child. Finnish researchers Achte et al. (1989–90:194), in a survey of the lullabies of twenty-six countries, found these ambivalent parental feelings expressed in lullaby themes from around the world.

These themes included death and funerals as well as threatening the child with violence if he or she does not go to sleep.

When the parent/child bond is broken by the death of the child, all of the issues in the creation and development of the biological and psychological bonds are put into play. Benedek (1959, 1975) notes that the experience of becoming a parent changes our assumptive world and activates memories of how we were parented and what it was like to be a baby. Such memories are associated with parental identification with the child: "[T]he child is a reproduction of the parent" (Klass, 1988:5).

The depth and intensity of the actual and symbolic loss of the child, along with the tension created by feelings of ambivalence toward the child, sometimes stimulate parents to continue their interaction with the deceased child through their inner representations of the child. Parents are likely to experience a sense of the dead child's presence in the world. Hallucinations involving sounds, sights, taste, or odors of the dead child may be experienced, along with vivid memories of the child (Klass, 1992–93). Touching, holding, cherishing, or gazing at familiar reminders of the child may become part of the parent's conscious and unconscious incorporation and memorialization of the characteristics and virtues of the dead child into the parents' own sense-of-self. Together, these feelings, behaviors, and cognitions play a major role in the parent's attempt at psychological reintegration.

Rock-a-bye baby,

in the treetop

When the wind blows,

the cradle will rock

When the bough breaks,

the cradle will fall

And down will come baby,

cradle and all

Reintegration Strategies of Parents in Mourning

Although studies show that psychological reintegration depends on social support in some cases, each parent is alone in his or her grief and mourning (Klass, 1988; Levav, Lubner, & Alder, 1988; Purisman & Maoz, 1977; Nichols, 1990). Parents may look to one another for support and understanding, but their differing patterns of mourning can cause misunderstandings in such a close relationship. The literature indicates speculatively, as well as empirically, that when each parent is suffering so intensely, it can be difficult to accept and acknowledge the pain of the spouse (Edelstein, 1984; Gilbert, 1989).

According to Helmrath and Steinitz (1978), the mother's acute stages of grief may last 6 months to a year, but the father's psychological reintegration may occur more rapidly. In fact, fathers report having fewer symptoms of grief, which, in general, do not last as long as the mother's grief following the death of their baby. In a study conducted at Children's Hospital Medical Center in Ohio, Nichols (1990) asked 180 parents when they had experienced "a sense of release" from the emotional pain of their baby's death. By the end of the first month, 2% of the mothers and 20% of the fathers said they felt release. By the end of 6 months, 18% of the mothers and 44% of the fathers felt released. Grief counselor Jane A. Nichols (1990:22–23) states, "Fathers, then, may join the ranks of family and friends who presume the mother 'should be over this by now,' and the mother becomes further isolated from human support. . . . It is easy for mothers to assume that this difference is the result of fathers having less love for the baby."

CARING INSIGHTS

Supporting Parents in Mourning

- Say you are sorry about what happened to (name) and about their pain.
- Allow them to express as much grief as they are feeling at the moment and are willing to share.
- Be available to listen, to run errands, to help with the other children, or to do whatever else seems needed at the time.
- Allow them to talk about their deceased child as often and as much as they want.
- Accept silence. Allow the mourners to lead the conversation.
- Talk about special memories and endearing qualities of the one who has died.
- Reassure them that they did everything they could, that their child received the best medical care, or of whatever else might be true and positive.
- Encourage the postponement of major decisions.
- Avoid pity. Simple understanding is enough. Acknowledge the loss, but don't dwell on it.
- If the mourners are unable to work through guilt or rage, suggest a consultation with a grief therapist or clergy or participation in a support group for parents in mourning.
- Thank them for sharing their personal pain.
- Send a personal note.

Believing this, women are often alarmed ("Does he love at all?"), resentful ("How dare he not love enough to grieve!"), or thrown into the despair of a second loss ("I can't love someone who does not love children. Who is this man I thought I knew? How could I have parented a child with such a person?") (Nichols, 1990).

Nichols (1990) suggests that a plausible reason as to why fathers experience emotional release sooner than mothers is that mothers remain hospitalized, protected, and relatively passive during the early days or weeks of bereavement, while fathers are called on to visit and console the mother, notify family members, make funeral arrangements, and so on. Performing these death–related tasks, though difficult, may be therapeutic and facilitate psychological reintegration in the fathers, whereas the passive role assigned the mother may inhibit the work of mourning.

This dissynchrony in the parents' grieving/mourning trajectory may cause difficulties between them, their families, and the social field during the psychological reintegration phase of mourning primarily because the parents may be preoccupied with their own distress (Clyman et al., 1980). Moller (1996:161) notes that not only are the parents using different coping strategies, but their differing reactions create distinct psychosocial patterns of need that make it difficult for them to find comfort in each other. In the absence of guiding norms for bereavement . . . men and women understandably rely on gender prescriptions that have influenced them all of their lives to provide some sense of stability and familiarity to the turbulance generated by the death of the child.

Finkbeiner (1996) observed that, although the parents share a common ordeal, the grieving and mourning reactions vary among the parents just as they do within an individual at different times. Some couples draw closer together, while others divorce. One parent becomes severely depressed and remains solitary, while the other befriends family members or joins a support group with other parents in mourning. In addition to the problems related to their relationship, parents must also face difficulties in explaining to the remaining children what has happened, in understanding their differing grief and mourning, and in responding to their questions and needs. In the case of neonatal death, there is the problem of what to do with the things they purchased and the gifts they received for the baby. This may only be resolved as they gradually mourn the loss and feel able to relinquish them.

 On the other hand, V. Thomas and Striegel (1995:308), in a phenomenological study of how twenty-six couples grieved and mourned the death of their baby, found that most couples had excellent coping strategies that derived from strengths within the couple relationship itself. Their results confirmed previous findings that the fathers' levels of depression and bereavement were significantly lower than the mothers' level. Their findings also suggested that mothers and fathers grieved differently, in that the mothers grieved for their babies while the fathers grieved for their wives. However, grieving and mourning differently did not mean that fathers were unable to provide the necessary empathy and support for the mothers. Thomas and Striegel (1995:308) concluded: "Although fathers' level of bereavement and depression were significantly lower than the mothers' level, the qualitative analysis suggested that fathers grieved for their wives by trying to 'hold it together.' " Nichols (1990:28), commenting on the caregiver's role in facilitating parental grief, states, "It was their child. It is their grief. They must do the grief work in their own way. As caregivers, we can only hope that we will not be the cause of additional suffering for them by insisting upon well-intentioned, but misguided, interventions."

Disenfranchised Grief and Parental Support

Disenfranchised grief, according to gerontologist Kenneth J. Doka (1996:204), "can be defined as the grief that persons experience when they incur a loss that is not or cannot be openly acknowledged, publicly mourned, or socially supported." For example, nontraditional relations, such as with exspouses, past lovers, former friends, foster parents, in-laws, roommates, colleagues, cohabitants, and homosexual partners, have both limited social acceptance and legal standing. As a consequence, mourners may not be given full permission to grieve the loss publicly. Neonatal deaths and abortions, although they can constitute high-grief losses, may also be treated by others as insignificant or even nonexistent. This disenfranchised grief results from a general belief that there is no loss to grieve, as if the infant did not count and no relationship had as yet been established (Doka, 1996).

Often, these parents feel themselves to be caught in a social system that fails to understand the enormity of their loss (Klass, 1988). What seems to be required is an appreciation of the severity of the loss and an accepting environment for the reintegration of self within a changed world (DeVries, Dalla Lana, & Falck, 1994). Such understanding, however, does not appear to be available to parents equally across the life cycle.

Even the health care profession has failed to comprehend fully the parents' needs (Pepper & Knapp, 1980; Rowe et al., 1978; Moller, 1996), and parent support groups have, in some instances, discounted bereaved parents of newborns as not knowing what real grief is (Nichols, 1986).

> **"It was their child. It is their grief. They must do the grief work in their own way. As caregivers, we can only hope that we will not be the cause of additional suffering for them by insisting upon well-intentioned, but misguided, interventions."**
>
> Nichols (1990), p. 28.

Within such an environment, these bereaved parents are expected to resume their lives as though nothing has happened. Parents often feel very unsupported by family and friends. Few can let them talk of the baby and their fears and sadness as they need to, to mourn their loss. Parents often feel they require ongoing assistance, but this may not be readily available to them. In Clyman and colleagues' (1980) study, 80% of the participants felt they needed continuing follow-up because of an inability to resume previous responsibilities.

Bereaved parents of young children, adolescents, and young adults are understood by society to have suffered a tragic loss. It has been shown that initially there is a great deal of support from friends and relatives, but expectations are that recovery will take place quickly and that the parents will not continue to mourn (J. A. Cook, 1983b). Many bereaved parents lose a part of their social world, since socializing often involves contacts made through their young children (de Vries, 1991; Sanders, 1989). Following a child's death, casual friends may avoid the parent because such acquaintances seem to be unsure about what to say (not mentioning the child's name for fear of causing pain) and because they do not want to be reminded that such a tragedy could also happen to them (Edelstein, 1984). Social invitations diminish, and social and emotional supports are withdrawn at a time when they are needed the most.

Although bereaved parents, especially the well educated, may make use of parent support groups, these types of interventions have not been found to be completely adequate at providing improvement in mental health or social functioning (Videka-Sherman & Lieberman, 1985). This failure may be due to the devastation of the loss. It has been argued that in order to be successful in assisting bereaved parents, support groups must do more than offer an opportunity for exploration of others' grief experiences. They must be able to motivate parents to overcome behavioral passivity, to reassert their ties with life, and to find meaning that can coexist with the experience of enduring grief (Nahmani, Neeman, and Nir, 1989; DeVries, Dalla Lana, & Falck, 1994). In this sense, support groups, grief counseling, and psychotherapy must help the parents to move beyond grief work into the deeper and longer-lasting work of mourning.

For other bereaved parents, their religious affiliations and convictions appear to provide social support. McIntosh, Silver, and Wortman (1993), in a study of 124 parents who had lost an infant to SIDS, found that two components of religion (religious participation and religious importance) were directly related to increased perception of social support and greater meaning found in the loss, and were indirectly related to greater well-being and less distress among parents 18 months after their infants' deaths. In these and other instances, the death of a child may bring the parents, the extended family, and friends closer together as they learn to share and cope with their pain and vulnerability and as they embrace each other in the light of a shared tragedy.

THE PSYCHOSPIRITUAL TRANSFORMATION PHASE

Many current models of grief and mourning do not account adequately for the unique characteristics of parental mourning and the complex grief reactions exhibited by parents after the death of child. Klass and Marwit (1988–89) underscore the uniqueness of the parent–child relationship as one that simply has no equal among human relationships.

Most bonds between individuals are contractual in nature in that people enter the bonds on the basis of an understood group of mutual obligations. The bond between spouses and between friends, for instance, is contractual and, as such, may be abandoned if the interactions between the participants are no longer reciprocal and mutually satisfying. However, the bond between parent and child—as with religious obligations or duty to God, to ancestors, or to an abstract principle—are *sacred bonds*. The pledge to love and caring that a mature parent feels for a helpless and dependent child is, obviously, not contingent on reciprocal behavior on the part of the child for the parent (Klass and Marwit, 1988–89). Psychoanalyst Therese Benedek (1970:68) maintains that "the sacred nature of the parent–child bond has deep roots which are grounded in the parents' investment in the helpless infant." In this sense, it is the sacred or spiritual nature of the parent–child relationship that makes it so unique and that makes the mourning after the death of a young child such a long and agonizing process.

The sacred nature of the parent–child bond is seen in certain psychospiritual changes observed in mourning parents. The parents' search for meaning in and understanding of their child's death often results in the formulation of religious/ spiritual *loss rationales,* or justifications of the child's death, that parent's utilize in an effort to manage their pain (Glaser & Strauss, 1964). In their study of the use of religion to give meaning to a child's death, J. A. Cook and Wimberley (1983:230), isolated three parental loss rationales that they term reunion, reverence, and retribution.

The most frequently used rationale was the notion that the child had gone to heaven, where parents and the dead child would eventually be reunited (*reunion*). Another frequent rationale was that the child's death served some religious purpose, for example, as an inspiration for parents to do good works (*reverence*). As J. A. Cook and Wimberley (1983:230) point out, this rationale is tied to the contemporary image of the child: "[A]s a social category assumed to include innocence and purity, it is especially appropriate that a child should serve as an example of religious faith to others." Finally, a child's death may be construed as

As parents search for understanding of their child's death, the most frequently used rationale is the belief that the lost child has gone to heaven, where the parents and the child will eventually be reunited. © *Jim Corwin/Stock Boston*

a punishment for the sins of the parents (*retribution*), though in one sense this explanation hardly seems comforting, in that "it validates the sense of guilt frequently experienced by survivors regardless of their actual role in an individual's death" (Cook and Wimberly, 1983:230).

In a more recent study of bereaved parents participating in a chapter of Compassionate Friends, a support group for parents in mourning, Dennis Klass (1995:261–262) found that virtually all the parents in the group rejected simple religious loss rationales for the death of their child, such as their child's death was

> **"[She] was a beautiful girl. She didn't deserve to die. I am a good mother. I cannot accept that God just lets things happen. I feel these changes in me. I see good things happening, like the way the kids at the school responded and the pages in the yearbook. There is a reason for this and good will come of it."**
>
> Klass (1995), pp. 261–262.

God's will. Instead, he found that in many cases profound forms of psychospiritual transformation were an integral part of the healing process for bereaved parents. He states: "[M]any of these parents-in-mourning find solace in connections with that which transcended the physical and biological world, and . . . with their perception of an underlying order in the world. These spiritual aspects of the resolution of the grief were central elements in the parents' rebuilding of their lives to be able to live in a changed world."

Many of these bereaved parents accepted that good may come from a bad thing. A bereaved mother, struggling with the question "Why did my daughter die?", said: "I just cannot accept that there is no reason for this. There has got to be some purpose. R was a beautiful girl. She didn't deserve to die. I am a good mother. I cannot accept that God just lets things happen. I feel these changes in me. I see good things happening, like the way the kids at the school responded and the pages in the yearbook. There is a reason for this and good will come of it" (Klass, 1995:261–262).

Klass (1995) discovered that some parents reinterpreted the death of the child in a way that allowed them to maintain their former assumptions about self and the world. This was often accomplished through a reinterpretation of former religious and spiritual beliefs and a reframing of the child's death so that it could be accommodated within their worldview in a new and compelling way. For other parents, the death of their child prompted a dramatic transformation of their sense-of self and their assumptions about the world. These included an objective adoption of new religious and spiritual beliefs and a search for new symbols and myths that brought meaning to their lives.

The parents in this study, according to Klass (1995:264), were forced by the death of their child to undertake a spiritual quest for individual meaning and solace, to restructure and reintegrate their sense-of-self and their assumptions about meaning in the world, and to "transcend the human limitations they find in the death of their child. They reveal what people in . . . 'the extreme situation' do and what all persons must do." These subjective transformations permitted ongoing interactions with the inner representations of the dead child and were central to creating a psychospiritual metamorphosis, a restructured worldview, as well as a renewed sense-of-self.

Chapter Summary

Jung viewed adulthood as the most inspired period of the life span, in which change is evident in psychological growth, human potential is realized, spirituality is refined, and commitment to life and loved ones is expressed more fully than possible in earlier years. To Erikson, adults who have successfully negotiated the six earlier developmental stages are grounded in a strong and dynamic experience of generativity and are likely to find meaning and joy in all the activities of life, including career, marriage, and family. The challenge is to overcome the greater fear of death during this period, a fear that may be associated with experiences of loneliness, stagnation, and despair in adulthood, as well as with the experience of coping with the death of a parent, a child, a spouse, or a best friend.

For the vast majority of adults, the central testimonial to life and generativity during the adult years involves the birthing and raising of a child. In stark contrast, the death of a child, whether sudden or anticipated, creates a gaping and painful existential wound in the parents, a wound that may take many years to heal and that, for some parents, may never truly heal. In fact, of the losses experienced in the adult years, the death of a young child now evokes the highest intensities of bereavement and the widest range of grief reactions among family members.

Having reviewed the parental mourning pocess, from cognitive restructuring and emotional expression through psychological reintegration and psychospiritual transformation, the power and intensity of grief associated with the death of a child appear to have no equals.

Although bereaved parents, especially the well educated, may make use of parent support groups in coping with the death of their child, these types of interventions have not been found to be completely adequate at providing improvement in mental health or social functioning. This failure may be due to the devastation of the loss, but it has been argued that support groups, grief counseling, and psychotherapy must help the parents to move beyond grief work into the deeper and longer-lasting work of mourning. They must be able to motivate parents to overcome behavioral passivity, to reassert their ties with life, and to find meaning that can coexist with the experience of the mourning after.

FURTHER READINGS:

Aries, Philippe. (1962). *Centuries of childhood: A social history of family life.* Vintage Books, New York.

DeSpelder, L. A., & Strickland, A. L. (1992). *The last dance: Encountering death and dying.* Mayfield, Mountain View, CA.

Finkbeiner, A. K. (1996). *After the death of a child: Living with loss through the years.* Free Press, New York.

Jung, C. G. (1933). *Modern man in search of a soul.* Harcourt, New York.

Kennedy, A. (1991). *Losing a parent: Passage to a new way of living.* HarperCollins, San Francisco.

Lindemann, E. (1944). Symptomology and management of acute grief. *American Journal of Psychiatry, 101,* 141−148.

Rando, T. A. (Ed.). (1986). *Parental loss of a child.* Research Press, Champaign, IL.

Raphael, Beverly. (1983). *The anatomy of bereavement.* HarperCollins, San Francisco.

Raphael, Beverley. (1995). The death of a child. In J. B. Williamson & E. S. Shneidman (Eds.), *Death, current perspectives* (pp. 261−275). Mayfield, Mountain View, CA.

EIGHT

Aging, Mourning, and the Search for Meaning

We are the only species, so far as we know, that is aware it will die. And in the normal course of events, this awareness moves to the foreground of our consciousness during the later years of life. In addition to the growing signs of aging, our journey through adulthood into old age involves an encounter with two aspects of life that are new to the second half of life: the increasing number of losses to death experienced during the later adult years, and the search for meaning in our living as we approach the day of our dying. Opposing the ideas of their mentor Sigmund Freud, Carl Jung and Erik Erikson came to understand human development as a lifelong process and to believe that the most powerful issues to be confronted in old age had little to do with sex, aggression, or memories buried in the personal unconscious. Jung, for instance, was interested in the ways in which aging adults search for meaning and

**"Do not go gentle into that good night,
Old age should burn and rave at close of day;
Rage, rage against the dying of the light."**

—Dylan Thomas, *Do Not Go Gentle into That Good Night*

personal fulfillment in life. He theorized that, following a series of turning points involving the loss of innocence in childhood and adolescence and the establishment of family and work in early and middle adulthood, the sense-of-self emerges fully and completely in later adulthood with the resolution of a new series of conflicts involving meaning, values, and spirituality.

Final Challenges

According to Erik Erikson (1963), our aspirations toward generativity and productivity are often satisfied in creating a family or excelling in our work in early and middle adulthood. In our later years, however, we may become more concerned with attempts to improve society. For example, a survey of 1,200 men and women by the American Board of Family Practice (a professional organization of physicians in family practice) found that the vast majority of aging adults viewed their later years as a time for acts of caring and the deepening of relationships (Goleman, 1990). Of those sampled, 84% agreed that the aging person becomes more compassionate to the needs of others and 89% saw this as a time to become closer to family and friends. Many believed that older people, by virtue of their position and experience, can help younger people get started, see their ideas take hold, and work toward positive change. On the other hand, Erikson emphasized that aging individuals can also stagnate and become excessively concerned with their own needs. Like Dickens' Scrooge in *A Christmas Carol,* the self-absorbed, egocentric person has little regard for others and focuses almost exclusively on personal needs and ambitions.

Many aging adults experience the loss of their dreams for the future. For some, it is a period when they realize that they have gone as far as they are going to go in their careers or that they will never achieve a perfect family or become famous in any way. Although most aging adults are able to become reconciled to the vanishing of their hopes for outstanding accomplishment, others experience great pain and become highly vulnerable to depression and suicide (Levinson et al., 1978; Viorst, 1986).

As aging adults, we can stagnate if we continue to believe that we will not achieve our earlier goals or, once having achieved them, if we find that they were really not all that worthwhile. Fortunately, stagnation is reversible (Erikson, 1963). Even Dickens' Scrooge could become caring and compassionate when he was shown his own miserable end (Seamon and Kenrick, 1994).

With the onset of old age, we are all confronted with the challenge of coming to terms with the approach of death. For those of us who stay healthy into old age, Erikson uncovered one last developmental journey to be completed. At this time, when our lifework has been completed, we can look backward and evaluate that life in something approaching its entirety. Erikson describes this last developmental task as involving a conflict between *integrity and despair.*

This last developmental stage represents an opportunity to attain full selfhood. By this challenge Erikson means an acceptance of one's life, a sense that it is complete and satisfactory. People who have gained full maturity by successfully completing earlier developmental tasks and challenges tend to possess the integrity to face death with a minimum of fear. People who view their past achievements with pride have a sense of integrity that Erikson refers to as *wisdom*

WHY DO WE AGE?

Why do our bodies age and some of our psychological capabilities decline over time? People have been trying to answer these questions for thousands of years. The hope is that if we could only discover what causes aging, perhaps we could find a way to halt it. But aging is not a disease and death is not a symptom to be halted or cured. The aging process is, instead, built into our cells, a part of our basic biological inheritance.

There are numerous theories of how we age, ranging from *wear-and-tear* theories (of the cell, of cell colloids, of nervous tissue, endocrine tissue, connective tissue, etc.) to *toxin* theories based on the accumulation of intestinal bacteria, metabolites, heavy water, cosmic rays, the actions of gravity, and so on. (Comfort, 1979; Austad, 1992). But although there are many theories as to how we age, there are really only two theories as to *why* we age. These are the *rate-of-living* theory and the *evolutionary* theory.

Rate-of-Living Theory First put forward by Max Rubner in 1908, the rate-of-living theory was based on Rubner's observation that large mammals, such as zebras or elephants, lived longer than small mammals, such as shrews and mice. Knowing that small animals have a more rapid metabolic rate per gram of body tissue and that animal cells are basically the same size regardless of the size of the animal, he concluded that each mammal species expends about the same amount of energy per gram of weight in its lifetime. Animals with the quicker metabolic rate spend their allotted energy more quickly and die young, while animals with slower rates live longer. A folk version of this idea claims that all mammals have about the same number of heartbeats per lifetime—the quicker the heartbeat, the sooner they die.

But there are many problems with the old version of the rate-of-living theory. For instance, for a given body size, birds have a higher body temperature and about twice the metabolic rate of mammals. The rate-of-living theory would predict that birds should be shorter lived than mammals of similar size. In fact, the reverse is true. Mice and rats, for instance, live three years or so, at the most, in the laboratory, and for a year maximum in the field. In contrast, the mouse-sized song sparrow has been reported to live eleven years in the field. Even among our domestic dogs, smaller breeds tend to live longer than larger breeds (Comfort, 1979).

The modern version of the rate-of-living theory proposes that the accumulation of defective molecules and toxic waste products in the cell lowers its efficiency. Multiplied over millions and millions of cells, the result is a general deterioration called aging. Leonard Hayflick (1985), the proponent of the programmed senescence theory of aging, believes that aging and death occur due to built-in clocks in our genetic structure. Hayflick showed that human cells have a limited ability to divide. Prior to this work, it was believed that, outside of the body, cells would continue to divide indefinitely. Hayflick's research showed that human cells divide only 50 times. This demonstration of the limited life span of the human cell contributed to a new version of the rate-of-living theory and changed our views of the aging process.

(Erikson, 1963). For example, if we believe that we have done our best, we can see our whole life as a meaningful experience This sense of integrity or wholeness will lead us to face our final days with peace and personal acceptance. But if we construe our past as a series of missed opportunities or directions, we can develop a feeling of despair. Those who despair see their past and future efforts as futile, and they dwell on what might have been. With the death of a spouse, a child, or close friends, along with the inevitable approach of death, this sense of gloom only darkens the remaining years (Seamon & Kenrick, 1994).

The Evolutionary Theory of Aging Evolution works by natural selection, a process that gives an advantage to the genes in organisms that survive long enough to reproduce many offspring. Because genes that make organisms reproduce more and survive better have an evolutionary advantage, they sweep through populations. Genetic mutations affecting the young will have enormous impact on that organisms' success in passing on its genes. Any new mutation that affects only old organisms would have hardly any effect. This is the central idea in the evolutionary theory of aging.

Consider the gene for Huntington's chorea, a disease which kills all of its carriers in middle age but has no negitive effects before middle age—in contrast to diseases like progeria, also thought to be carried by a single gene. Progeria produces horrific premature aging in children, with victims dying in their teens or early twenties. Only about 20 carriers of the gene for Progeria are known world wide, compared with tens of thousands of carriers for the gene for Huntington's chorea. The crucial difference between these diseases is the age at which the carriers die. Huntington's chorea acts after most of its carriers have reproduced, so that the gene can remain in, and spread through, human populations. Progeria prevents almost all carriers from reproducing (Rose, 1991).

As these examples show, natural selection stringently removes lethal genes expressed so early that individuals usually do not reproduce before death, but it does not influence those genes expressed late in adulthood. They are virtually immune to elimination by natural selection, which may be why certain diseases, like cancer, occur predominantly in old age.

Another variation on the evolutionary theory of aging holds that slowed aging is due to an evolutionary history of reduced vulnerability to predators and other "accidents." This theory, based on the waning power of natural selection as an animal ages, provides a general explanation both for aging and for why some species live so much longer than others. Exceptional longevity is found in some species of animal with special protection of some sort, for example, tree-dwelling, or spines and, of course, the well-protected turtle. According to evolutionary theory, their longevity is due not simply to current increased safety, but to an evolutionary history of safety which may have given the species time to evolve special physiological protective mechanisms against the ravages of old-age diseases.

The evolutionary theory agrees with the rate-of-living theory insofar as they both predict that aging will ultimately come about as a consequence of the gradual failure of physiological or cellular processes. The theories differ, however, in that the rate-of-living hypothesis assumes that the rate of failure is an inescapable consequence of the rate of biochemical processes, whereas the evolutionary theory assumes the rate of failure may be modified or even halted by natural selection under appropriate circumstances (Austad, 1992).

Suicide in Old Age

As we grow through adulthood and into old age, the risk of suicide also grows. Older adults have the highest suicide rate—more than 50% higher than that for young people or for the nation as a whole—and that rate is increasing. The elderly now account for one in five of the suicides committed in America.

The suicide rate for men grows gradually during the adult years before the major increase in old age. In contrast, middle age is the peak for suicides among women. Each year, more than 6,300 older, mostly male, adults take their own lives, which means nearly 18 older Americans kill themselves each day. After declining for nearly four decades, the suicide rate for Americans 65 and older

The most pressing unsolved problem of old age is that of overcoming loneliness, disempowerment, and social isolation. Persons who are both poor and old are among the most vulnerable of our population. Isolated in our ghettos and rural communities, they are the most prone to self-annihilation.
© *Documentary Photo Aids*

climbed almost 9% between 1980 and 1992 (CDC, 1996) and appears to have continued to rise in 1993 and 1994. During this period, men committed 81% of the suicides among the elderly, and guns were the most common method of suicide, chosen by 74% of men and 31% of women.

Suicidologists suggest that this increase results from people living longer with chronic illness, from the social isolation of the elderly, and from society's growing acceptance of suicide in recent years (CDC, 1996). Additional risk factors most often associated with elderly suicide include increasing interiority, chronic illness, an accumulation of multiple losses (including the death of a spouse, a child, and other significant persons), the loss of parental and work roles, widowhood, and the lessening of activity and resultant social isolation.

INTERIORITY

An important psychological risk factor for depression and suicide in old age is the increasing tendency toward *interiority*—the turning into ourselves in the search for personal meaning. Interiority can be healthy if it promotes positive self-knowledge, spirituality, and increased satisfaction with life. For some, however, the tendency toward interiority results in unhealthy self-absorption and increased social isolation. As responsibilities to the family decline, the amount of daily interaction with children and with the individuals they bring into our life also declines, resulting in the danger of social and psychological impoverishment and seclusion (R. C. Peck, 1968). Older individuals need to struggle against this natural tendency toward interiority and impoverishment to be productive and to find contentment during the final years of life. Those who fail to do so begin to slip toward the stagnation and despair poles of Erikson's continuum and increase their risk of despair, depression, and suicide (Erikson, 1980).

CHRONIC ILLNESS

There is reason to believe that suicidal risk in old age is greatly enhanced by biological factors. General organic and psychological declines, combined with chronic illness and chronic pain, undoubtedly contribute both to the depression that is endemic to old age and to the high suicide rates among the elderly (Dorpat, Anderson, & Ripley, 1968; M. Miller, 1978a,b). Studies have shown that 70% or more of elderly people who kill themselves visit a physician within 1 month of the suicide, and that as many as 10% consult a physician on the actual day of the suicide (Barraclough, 1971; Miller, 1978a,b; Rockwell & O'Brien, 1973). Some of these visits may be attributed to the fact that suicide among the elderly can be triggered by a diagnosis of terminal illness.

In the psychological sphere, elderly people experience increased passivity and loneliness. The passivity may be rooted in a lack of meaning in life because of a reduction in purposeful activity, often resulting from the experience of chronic pain. These feelings undoubtedly add to a growing sense of despair among a minority of older people. One study found that suicide notes among the elderly, more than among any other age group, often include references to loneliness, isolation, and pain (Darbonne, 1969).

CRYING: ONLINE

"Just like you and the others, I've also been prone to these spontaneous crying fits since my wife and mother died within nine days of each other around the end of 1994. It often starts when I remember something about my wife, but it has occurred while driving, bathing, doing anything and there seemed to be no trigger to them at all. They decreased in frequency for a spell, then started up again, showing me that grief really takes time, and the road out is one of many ups and downs. Yet after each episode, I somehow feel a bit better always, and the spells are less and less painful—but they've got a ways to go before they become painless. I will pray that you have the strength to continue your journey through grief and find happiness in life to lessen the pain."

Source: Grief Forum Message, Downloaded @ America On Line, March 2, 1995.

MULTIPLE LOSSES

Many elderly people must cope with a rapid succession of losses (such as job, status, spouse, peers, good health, social freedom) that does not allow sufficient time for resolution of the grief inherent in each loss. Although the experience of cumulative loss may happen at any time across the life cycle, it most commonly occurs during old age. When many losses are experienced within a relatively short period of time, the associated depression can become chronic. Indeed, depression has been found to be the most common of all illnesses among the elderly (Butler & Lewis, 1982). Retirement and the concomitant reduction in activity and financial loss appear to be special risk factors for elderly men (Breed & Huffine, 1979; Lyons, 1984; M. Miller, 1978).

ALCOHOLISM

Alcoholism also plays more of a role in the suicide of male adults between the ages of 35 and 64 than for any other age group (Roy & Linnoila, 1986). Alcohol abuse among aging men seems especially to enhance depression and to exacerbate negative life events, such as divorce, abuse, loss of employment, and illness (Dorpat & Ripley, 1960). Sociologists Debra Umberson and Meichu Chen (1994), for example, found that, compared with nonbereaved persons, bereaved adults experienced a significant increase in alcohol consumption, reports of psychological distress, and a decline in physical health status.

DEATH OF A SPOUSE

Widowhood, a major source of social isolation among the elderly, has been shown to increase the likelihood of suicide within this age group, especially among men (Benson & Brodie, 1975; Bock & Webber, 1972; Butler & Lewis, 1977; NCHS, 1995b). Although problems of adjusting to the death of a spouse are often worse for a woman than for a man, any man who has lost his wife by death or divorce is faced with loneliness and a need for companionship. A widow usually has more friends from whom she can seek sympathy and support than a widower. A widower, in contrast, may discover that he was much more dependent on his wife for social and emotional support than he realized. Compared to widows, widowers are typically not as close to other people and find it more difficult to make friends with other bereaved persons. Even when her husband is alive, a woman is more likely to have a confidante or close friend of the same sex. Married men may have friendships with other men, but such is less often the case. And those men who failed to develop close relationships with other men while their wives were alive typically become even more socially isolated as widowers (Breed & Huffine, 1979; Lyons, 1984; M. Miller, 1978a,b).

Isolation is dangerous for widows and widowers, as it is for most people. Grief following the loss of a lifelong spouse or companion is normal. When the individual is socially isolated, however, and absent of care and affection, the grieving process may become abnormal. The grieving widower may suffer various forms of anxiety and depression and, perhaps, die of a "broken heart" (Parkes, 1986).

Loss and Mourning in Old Age

The meaning of any loss, whether through death or through a loss of freedom or meaning, can only be evaluated by those who are most closely affected. Each loss will be difficult in its own way, but, as a general rule, research has shown that the most intense grief experiences in old age involve the death of an adult child and

CARING   INSIGHTS

The Grief Counselor's Tears

"It is important that the bereaved express their grief without fear of being judged or made to feel unusual. The bereaved can be very sensitive to the reactions of listeners, instantly becoming aware of embarrassment, shock, boredom—or the opposite—compassion and empathy. A few honestly shed tears or other expressions of feelings by the clinician affirm the client's own emotions better than words—sometimes with more comfort. But remember: clinicians must keep their emotional responses within reasonable bounds so that the focus is not shifted away from the client."

Source: Dershimer (1990), p. 83.

the death of a spouse. However, as is usually true, it is the meaning of the relationship terminated by death, be it the death of an adult child, a spouse, or an animal companion, that is central to the mourning after.

THE DEATH OF A PET

In addition to serving as sources of unconditional love in the lives of children, adolescents, young and middle adults, companion animals are objects of care and affection in the lives of many elderly persons. As a consequence of growing old in today's society, we may lose both the opportunity and the means of caring for others—and of giving of ourselves (Katcher, 1984, 1985). Stewart et al. (1985) reported that 86% of a sample of elderly pet owners indicated their major reason for owning a pet was for companionship. They also held strong beliefs that having a pet, especially an interactive companion, facilitated better health and that the death of an elderly owner's pet might result in ill health for the owner.

These beliefs have been supported by psychological studies over the years. In one investigation, it was found that talking to and stroking a pet promotes relaxation and lowers blood pressure in both the pet owner and the pet (Katcher, 1984). A study that investigated the impact of pet ownership on the health status of 108 recently widowed, urban woman (Akiyama, Holtzman, & Britz, 1987) found significant differences between pet owners and nonowners in regard to symptoms experienced and utilization of medications. Studies described at a National Institutes of Health workshop linked life with a pet with higher survival rates in patients with heart disease, increased self-confidence and independence in psychiatric patients, and improved ability of children to interact with others (National Institute for Health Statistics, 1995b).

Pets may also become part of an elderly person's pathology. Israeli psychologist Judith Stern (1985), for example, presents a case study of a 52-year-old female Holocaust survivor exhibiting excessive pet attachment and compulsive behavior related to animal care. Stern suggests that these manifestations were associated

SYMPTOMS EXPERIENCED BY WIDOWS (percentages)		
Symptoms	**Pet Owners**	**Nonowners**
Persistent fears	17.6%	31.6%
Feelings of panic	7.8	22.8
Increased drug intake	3.9	19.3
Constipation	0	12.3
Difficulty in swallowing	3.9	17.5
Cold sores	3.9	22.8
Headaches	3.9	22.8

Source: Akiyama, Holtzman, and Britz (1987), pp. 187–193.

with the delayed mourning process and served as a means of dealing with disturbances resulting from recurrent massive trauma situations this woman had experienced. Therapy employing dreamwork was used to decrease her inner turmoil and to give attachment to pets a vital quality that had been hidden because of her need for protection against repressed memories.

Companion animals also protect and aid socialization among the elderly and, in recent years, have become familiar mascots in many nursing homes, long-term care facilities, and hospitals. Occupational therapist Katherine Fick (1993) investigated the effect of the presence or absence of a dog on the frequency and types of social interactions among 36 male nursing home residents. A significant difference in verbal interactions among residents occurred with the dog present. Findings provide evidence of the value of animal-assisted therapy programs as an effective medium for increasing socialization among residents in long-term care facilities. Because an increase in social interactions can improve the social climate of an institution and because occupational therapists frequently incorporate group process into their treatment, the therapeutic use of animals is described as a valuable adjunct to reaching treatment goals.

In a variety of settings, pets can relieve loneliness, lower stress levels, increase social

DUKIE PASSED AWAY

Miss G, single, retired, in her seventies, acquired a 4-year-old beagle when a friend died. Miss G had promised to care for the animal in the event his mistress died. She wanted to go home to Scotland to spend her last years, but kept putting it off because she was apprehensive about the dog's ability to make the trip. When she went and took the dog, he was more than 11 years old. The dog died in quarantine one week before the end of the six-month period and one week past his twelfth birthday. Heartbroken, Miss G wrote to her veterinarian:

"I have the saddest news. Dear wee Dukie passed away on September 9th. I can't believe it. I'm sure you must know how I feel. I wish I had never come away. Dear Dukie, used to so much love and comfort! He was so upset when I left him at the kennel. I thought it better not to visit so I never saw him alive again. It's breaking my heart. Why, Dr. Harris, did it happen so near his time for freedom and eight days after his twelfth birthday? If he had only died in his own house with me beside him. I'll never forgive myself. . . . I just know my pet has gone and left me very lonely and sad."

Source: J. M. Harris, (1984) pp. 31–36.

interaction, contribute to a sense of purpose, and enhance self-esteem (Rynearson, 1978; Kay, 1984; Nieburg & Fischer, 1982). And the loss of this relationship, although often dismissed with insensitive remarks, can represent a major bereavement for an elderly person who may otherwise have only limited social contacts (Quackenbush, 1985; Kay, 1984). Similarly, grieving may occur when an older adult is no longer able to care for a pet, cannot pay for expensive veterinary care, must give up the pet when moving to new living quarters, or must have a sick, old animal euthanized, or "put to sleep." Older adults may also be concerned about what will happen to a prized pet if they should die (Kay, 1984, 1988).

Avery Weisman's work with bereaved pet owners (1991–1:243–244) revealed a strong reluctance on their part to tell others of their grief, but within the therapy group they spoke freely and with relief when they received acceptance and respect for their bereavement. According to Weisman, "Clients felt that their grief was both exceptionally strong and abnormally tenacious, and they wept accordingly, as if confessing something unmentionable. Most people apologized for crying." One client said, "I've actually mourned more than I did for my father." Veterinarians, cognizant of the power of the human/animal bond and sensitive to the grieving process, can provide support and referral. Psychologists, counselors, and loved ones can assist the bereaved in expressing their thoughts and feelings, as well as help the person resolve problems that arise as a consequence of bereavement (Stewart et al., 1985).

ADULT DEATH

"Helen and Ross, both age fifty, were grief stricken when their daughter Jenny, age twenty-five, died from malignant melanoma. The condition had been rapidly fatal over the six-month period following diagnosis. At that time they moved closer to where Jenny lived with her husband Stan and two young children, girls of five and three. Helen helped care for the children as Jenny's illness progressed, but, as she confessed to Ross, it was all she could do to attend to the children's needs, so great was her distress at her daughter's condition. She constantly thought of Jenny and prayed for her cure, although as the weeks progressed she could see this was impossible.

Following Jenny's death she and Ross moved in with Stan. There was often friction between them, yet they felt bound to 'do the best they could' for the children. Helen loved them but at another level resented the sacrifice she and Ross were now forced to make for them, and, as she kept telling herself, 'for Jenny.' She was recurrently depressed over the next two years until they moved back to their own home when Stan remarried. Helen felt that it was only then that she and Ross could really 'let go' their grief for their daughter. They had 'done their duty,' but now faced the terrible loss it meant for them."

Source: Beverley Raphael, (1995).

THE DEATH OF AN ADULT CHILD

The older parent who experiences the death of an adult child is likely to feel that his or her own death would have been far preferable to that of the son or daughter. Survivor guilt is often a key problem faced by these bereaved parents. They feel they should not have survived, yet are glad to be alive and guilty of that feeling (Raphael, 1995). The parents most often adjust to the actuality of their child's death, for there has usually been a degree of separation from the adult child already. Nevertheless, for some elderly parents, grief responses can be of high intensity. Moss, Lesher, and Moss (1986–87), for example, reported that 25% of elderly admissions to hospitals were precipitated by the death or severe illness of a child or child-in-law.

The deaths are difficult to adjust to because they are untimely and, like other deaths, they may be harder to accept if ambivalence and dependence levels were unduly high (Raphael, 1995). One study of parents who had lost sons in the 1969–70 war in Israel found that most resolved this loss reasonably well, and that good family relationships and death education beforehand facilitated this resolution (Purisman & Maoz, 1977). The parent may also be expected to take on parenting roles for the child's children, and, despite their own grief, many parents do this successfully.

Older bereaved parents may have fewer social contacts and may not have been active in the community (DeVries, 1991). Indeed, their favorite confidant and main source of social support may have been the child who died. It has been found that older parents whose adult children had died were less likely to turn to other relatives for help than those elderly individuals who had never had children (Cicirelli, 1983). Presumably, in the past the parents had relied on exchanges of help with their children. With these sources of support gone, these parents may feel especially isolated and in special need of help from loved ones, health professionals, and community service agencies.

Similar to parents who lose a newborn, parents of a married adult child who has died often receive little social recognition of their loss (Doka, 1996). It is not that the child is not recognized as worthy of grief, but that the child's spouse and

Despite their own grief, parents of a married adult child receive little social recognition of their loss because the child's spouse and children are the primary recipients of comfort and care. Bereaved parents of an adult child are often expected to take on parenting roles for the child's children. © *David Frasier Photolibrary*

children are the primary recipients of condolences and comfort (J. H. Arnold & Gemma, 1983).

ADULT CHILDREN AND AIDS

Losing a child to AIDS may precipitate a particularly difficult grieving process for parents, especially the parents of a gay son (Tross & Hirsch, 1988). Writer and photographer Susan Sontag (1989:24–25) points out that "the illness flushes out an identity that might have remained hidden from neighbors, jobmates, family, friends." Many of these parents, especially fathers, may have difficulty accepting a homosexual son (Kubler-Ross, 1987). This rupture in the relationship and the lack of acceptance often results in more distressing grief reactions for both the dying child and the bereaved parents. For example, in a comparative study of parents whose children died of AIDS versus cancer, the grief reactions of AIDS parents involved greater levels of depression, anxiety, guilt, somatization, obsessive-compulsion, and more intense overall distress (Normile, 1990).

Other parents may never be told of the diagnosis until the illness is in the very last stages. Sontag (1989:25) writes: "Like other diseases that arouse feelings of shame, AIDS is often a secret, but not from the patient. A cancer diagnosis was frequently concealed from patients by their families; an AIDS diagnosis is at least as often concealed from their families by patients."

THE DEATH OF A SPOUSE

Our marriage vows say till death do us part, but who among us is ever prepared for that final parting? Whether a spouse's death is anticipated or whether it comes unexpectedly, the event of death is always sudden. In the beat of a heart, a wife becomes a widow, a husband a widower. The transition is a very real, painful, and personal phenomenon. The trauma of trying to adjust to an indefinable role while beset with a multitude of urgent questions and decisions seems overwhelming.

Parkes (1992), in reviewing data on reaction to bereavement in the elderly, concludes that the elderly tend to suffer less extreme anguish on the death of a spouse than younger people, but there is a substantial minority of elderly widows and widowers in whom loss of a spouse can precipitate severe depression and even death. In fact, bereavement contributes to a substantial proportion of psychiatric problems in the elderly. Elderly people are more likely to perceive illusions of the dead spouse than younger people and are also more likely to disengage socially. Those whose grasp on reality is already tenuous may become disoriented, aggravating symptoms of organic brain syndromes.

Self-esteem appears to play a significant role in a widow's or widower's capacity to cope with the death of a spouse. R. J. Johnson, Lund, and Dimond (1986), for example, examined the stability of self-esteem as a coping resource during bereavement in adults ages 50–93 following the death of a spouse. Results revealed that initially effective copers (those higher in self-esteem) remained effective throughout the first year of their bereavement, while those lower in self-esteem continued to report high levels of psychological stress throughout the first year.

C A R I N G   I N S I G H T S

Mourning Exercises

The process of caring for a person in mourning is not as important as the emotional climate in which the caregiving takes place. According to psychotherapist Carl Rogers (1961, 1986) it is critical for us, as caregivers, to provide a warm, supportive, accepting climate, creating a safe environment in which the mourner can confront her or his feelings and thoughts without feeling threatened. The lack of threat reduces defensive tendencies, facilitates the exercise of freedom of expression and thus helps the mourner to open up. To create this atmosphere of emotional support and healing, we must meet three conditions.

1. *Genuineness.* We must be genuine with the mourner, communicating honestly and spontaneously. We should not be phony or defensive in any way.

2. *Unconditional positive regard.* We must also show complete, nonjudgmental acceptance of the mourner as a person, providing warmth and caring with no strings attached. At the same time we need not approve of everything that the mourner says or does. We can disapprove of a particular behavior while continuing to value the grieving individual as a human being.

3. *Empathy.* Finally, we must provide accurate empathy for the mourning person. We must suspend or bracket our own presuppositions about the world and perceive the world from the mourner's point of view, and we must be articulate enough to communicate our understanding to the mourner.

The degree to which a bereaved spouse tends to engage in *rumination* over the death of his or her deceased partner (i.e., the tendency to think about and relive memories, repeatedly) also has an effect on the grieving process, especially the depressive component. In one longitudinal study of 253 bereaved adults, women reported more rumination than men, and individuals with a ruminative style were more likely to have a pessimistic outlook at 1 month after the death. This negative view of future events was, in turn, associated with higher depression levels 6 months later (Nolen-Hoeksema, Parker, & Larson, 1994). In addition to issues involving psychological well-being, unfamiliarity with the family finances or lack of experience managing money while their husbands were alive can lead to chronic uncertainty and additional rumination about where and how to live and how to reconstruct their lifestyles (Blau, 1961; Lopata, 1973; O'Bryant & Morgan, 1989).

The death of a spouse affects all the family relationships of a widowed person. Older widows tend to grow closer to their own children, to daughters in particular. Although members of the extended family (brothers, sisters, aunts, uncles, etc.) are usually in close contact with the widowed person for a while after the death of the spouse, interactions with them become less frequent as time passes. This is particularly true if the children are grown (Aiken, 1994). Wolinsky and Johnson (1992), in a cross-sectional assessment of 2,354 widows (age 55+ years) and 4,113 widowers (age 70+ years) found that being widowed significantly increased the likelihood that an elderly person would be placed in a nursing home by family members.

There is evidence that a spouse's recovery from grief is quicker and more complete when the marriage was happy. Widows who were happily married, though admittedly lonely at times, typically become more competent and independent with time. A widow may miss the companionship of her husband, but she now has time to devote to interests and to develop abilities that have not been cultivated in the past. This is less likely to occur if a widow was extremely dependent on her husband and identified with him too closely. And strange as it may seem, widows who experienced the greatest of difficulty getting along with their husbands may find themselves least able to get along without them. Whatever the cause may be—feelings of guilt, years of unfinished business, or unresolved anger—adjustment is often quite difficult for widows whose marriages were unhappy (Connidis, 1989; Kalish, 1985b,c).

For many widowed persons, the religious and communal rituals of grieving, such as a wake, sitting shiva, or holding a memorial service, provide an important beginning to the mourning process by giving social and spiritual support to the expression of despair. Some people are encouraged to vocalize their feelings, to weep, to wail, and to grieve loudly and publicly at a funeral. Others are expected to remain detached, to "keep a stiff upper lip and wear a mask of composure." Letting the pain show may be especially difficult for men. Our social expectation of men is that they will be strong and silent. This gives them little room to express pain and may partially account for the fact that the death rate among widowers is three times greater than it is among widows. In fact, studies have shown that there is a connection between societal expectations of men to be less emotionally expressive and their vulnerability to depression, physical illness, and death after the loss of a mate (D. J. Levinson et al., 1978; Viorst, 1986).

The Broken Heart Phenomenon

Research on the effects of the grieving/mourning process on human functioning has brought new understanding and insight over recent decades. However, until recently, one phenomenon has tended to mystify researchers—the tendency of one elderly spouse, usually male, to die shortly after the death of the other. Although the death certificates in these cases may state various diseases as cause of death, such as cancer, heart disease, or "natural causes," the bereaved spouse appears to have died of a *broken heart*.

In a typical study, the effects of the death of a spouse were investigated in several thousand men and women in semirural Washington county, Maryland (Helsing, szelo, & Comstock, 1981). The widows and widowers were compared with still-married individuals who were similar in such factors as age, sex, race, education, and religious interests. The major finding was that, for widowers ages

55 to 64, the mortality rate was almost 61% higher than the rate for married men and 26% higher for widowers for all ages in a matched group. In contrast, the difference in mortality rates was only 3.8% between widows and married women in a matched group. In widowed men who remarried (at least half of them did), the death rate was 70% lower than for widowed men who did not remarry. In fact, death rates for widowers who remarried were even lower than the rates for men in the same age groups who were married throughout the period of the study. This tendency for bereaved spouses, especially widowers who remain unmarried, to die prematurely is termed the *broken heart phenomenon.* British psychologist Ann Bowling (1987) has verified this same phenomenon of increased mortality after bereavement in England, noting that the widowed have a greater risk of dying than married people of a similar age, with the excess risk being much greater for men (W. Stroebe & Stroebe, 1987).

Why do some of us react with what Freud called normal mourning in coping with the death of a lifelong spouse or companion, while others of us plunge into despair and chronic depression or succumb to our broken heart? There are a number of possible answers to this complex question that are associated with various perspectives on human functioning: the cognitive, psychodynamic, and humanistic-existential perspectives.

THE COGNITIVE PERSPECTIVE

Aaron Beck's cognitive-distortion model (Beck, 1967, 1976; Beck et al., 1979), one of the most original and influential of the cognitive approaches to the study of acute and chronic depression, offers a powerful perspective on the broken heart phenomenon. Beck argues that deep and chronic depression, as seen in broken-hearted spouses, results, primarily, from a disorder of thinking rather than of emotion or mood. He believes that the experience of deep depression can best be described in terms of a *cognitive triad of negative thoughts* about self, the past, and the future. A person who is depressed misinterprets facts in a negative way, focuses on the negative aspects of any situation, and, through selective perception, has pessimistic and hopeless expectations about the future.

According to Beck's theory, the person who progresses from extreme grief to clinical depression to premature death is the person who tends to attribute any misfortune to his or her personal defects. Any ambiguous situation is interpreted as evidence of the defect, even if there are more plausible explanations.

Absorption in these presumed defects of the self becomes so intense during the mourning process that it completely overwhelms any positive self-concepts the person may have developed prior to the death of the spouse.

The term *attribution* is used by social psychologists to refer to the causes a person assigns to things that happen. Beck's cognitive approach predicts that depressed individual's attributions will be personal; that is, depressed people will blame themselves when anything bad happens, rather than the environment or the inevitability of death. When something good happens, it is usually attributed to luck or seen as something that happened in spite of them.

Learned Helplessness

People who are dealing with the dying or death of a loved one sometimes feel helpless to control the situation they find themselves in. They think that no matter what they do, they will be unable to affect the way things turn out. Often, this is indeed the case. On the other hand, some people learn to be helpless as a result of certain situations they have encountered in the past, such as the death of a parent in childhood, or multiple stressors in their lives. Martin Seligman (1974, 1975) first popularized this concept, which is termed *learned helplessness.*

Like Beck's cognitive-distortion model, learned helplessness theory stresses the importance of the attribution people make in dealing with dying and death in determining whether they will become depressed in the particular situation (Abramson, Seligman, & Teasdale, 1978). There are three dimensions to these feelings of helplessness that have direct impact on the progression from extreme grief to clinical depression in the bereaved. The first has to do with whether the person sees the problem as *internal or external*. People facing loss may attribute the situation to their personal inability to control outcomes, or they may feel that anyone would have a hard time in the same situation. The second dimension has to do with the *global–specific* continuum. Someone may see a situation as proof that he or she is totally helpless or may see him- or herself as helpless only in the particular situation. The third dimension has to do with whether the situation is viewed as *stable (chronic) or unstable (acute)*. People may think their helplessness will go on for years or that it will last only a short time. The learned-helplessness hypothesis suggests that only certain kinds of attributions result in depression. Negative events, such as a death, may call up different sets of attributions from the same person, suggesting that attributions play a role only for that subgroup of depressed people suffering from a broken heart (Sarason & Sarason, 1989).

THE PSYCHODYNAMIC PERSPECTIVE

Freudian theories of depression emphasize unconscious feelings and reactions to new situations, all based on what has happened earlier in life. Focus here is placed on the history of our relationships with the people on whom we were most dependent as children, usually our mothers. John Bowlby, a British psychoanalyst, is one of the more prominent theorists to emphasize that separation of a child from an important figure during early childhood, whether because of death, abandonment, travel, or other reasons, creates repressed feelings that can impact our emotional relationships in adult life and precipitate depression and death by a broken heart (Bowlby, 1980).

From the psychodynamic perspective, the actual, feared, or simply fantasized loss of a parental figure in childhood, because it is anxiety-provoking, is repressed—pushed out of awareness—from where it still exerts its influence. Years later, with the death of our spouse, our emotional vulnerability may result in painful depression because the loss of a loved one has disturbed the emotions connected with the old, repressed memory of loss from childhood. As the depression unfolds, an observer often cannot tell, nor does the sufferer know, what loss is actually at the center of this extreme and protracted depression. In contrast with the conscious loss in the case of mourning, here there is a depressing loss of some unconscious object from the past. We tend to become absorbed with the idea and emotions connected with that previously loved person.

In normal mourning, we slowly withdraw our attachment to our deceased loved one, return to the self to heal, and are then free to seek new love attachments and connections. In clinical depression, according to S. Freud (1957), we are not free to seek fresh attachments, nor do we return to the self to heal. Instead, the part of the self we call conscience turns against the rest of the self, creating a drowning pool of thoughts of self-negation and guilt and a pattern of recalling past memories and projecting future scenarios that are themselves steeped in negativity, failure, and despair.

Researchers have provided data that suggest a correlation between the experience of depression in adults and early experiences of loss. Sociologist George Brown, for example, found that women who had lost their mothers before the age of 11 were at greater risk of depression than women who had not suffered the death of mother in childhood (G. W. Brown, Harris, & Copeland, 1977). Bowlby (1973) notes that maladaptive ways of thinking and behaving are more common among people who have few social supports, particularly within their families. However, even though lack of social support in our early years can be damaging, the possibility exists that new social relationships can have stress-buffering and therapeutic value. Psychotherapy, from this perspective, is a special social relationship directed at helping people face and overcome obstacles associated with extreme grief and depression.

DEATH AND LONELINESS

- Individuals who are socially isolated but healthy are twice as likely to die over a 10-year period as are healthy people who have close ties to other people.

- Living alone after a heart attack increases the risk of subsequent cardiac problems.

- Persons with heart disease have a significantly poorer chance of survival if they are single than if they are married; those with a close tie or confidant live longer than those without.

- Women with advanced breast cancer who take part in a support group live twice as long as those women who do not.

- People with malignant melanoma who participate in support groups live longer than those who do not.

Source: Foreman (1996).

Although not everyone thinks that early loss has been firmly established as a factor increasing the risk of later depression (Crook & Elliot, 1980), it remains an important part of the psychodynamic perspective on depression, mourning, and the broken heart phenomenon.

THE HUMANISTIC-EXISTENTIAL PERSPECTIVE

Whereas psychodynamic theorists emphasize the early loss of a loved object as a central cause of depression, humanistic-existential theorists focus on the loss of self-esteem in the here and now of the mourning after. The loss of the loved one is central during the work of mourning. But in depression, according to this perspective, the loss itself is not as important as the change in the individual's self-assessment as a result of the loss.

Many people base their self-concepts and sense of self-worth on the roles they play or on what they have: I'm the son of a famous father; I'm the parent of a beautiful, bright child; I'm the wife of an influential and wealthy man; and so on. Identifications of this kind offer external verification of people's worth in their own minds. In American culture, for example, a frequent cause of depression in men is loss of their job. The job represents the man's value in his own eyes. At least until the recent increase in the number of women employed outside the home, a frequent cause of female depression was loss of a mate. This represented not only the loss of a loved person, but also the loss of a major source of prestige and economic security, since a woman's status was traditionally based on her husband's role (Sarason & Sarason, 1989). From the humanistic-existential perspective, the broken heart phenomenon, clinical depression, and accompanying feelings of worthlessness and despair in reaction to the death of a loved one result from the collapse of the individual's sense of self.

DESPAIR AND THE SENSE OF SELF

"Despair is never ultimately over the external object but always over ourselves. A girl loses her sweetheart and she despairs. It is not over the sweetheart, but over herself-without-the-sweetheart. And so it is with all cases of loss. . . . The unbearable loss is not really in itself unbearable. What we cannot bear is being stripped of the external object. We stand denuded and see the intolerable abyss of ourselves."

Source: Kiekegaard (1843/1954) p. 160.

THE BODY/MIND CONNECTION

The key question of just how the death of a beloved spouse or companion, and the resultant depression and feelings of helplessness and despair, can contribute to the death of the surviving spouse could not be answered until the connection between body and mind could be found. Not too long ago, the broken heart phenomenon might simply have been labeled "psychosomatic" and left at that. For centuries, *psychosomatic* was the only word we had to describe the effect of mind on body in various physical diseases, and the term often served as a kind of conceptual trash bucket for physical diseases with no apparent physiological basis. "Psychosomatic" was another way of saying "It's not real, it's just in your head." (Marrone, 1990:85).

The breakthrough event that would establish the role of psychological factors in disease processes and mortality occurred in the 1950s in the laboratory of organic chemist Hans Selye. Selye wondered whether certain traumatic events, such as electric shocks, would cause any physical damage to the rats receiving them. Although, to all appearances the shocked rats suffered little in the way of harmful effects, Seleye's autopsies revealed significant tissue damage, including broken blood vessels, shrunken glands, and other physical effects. He termed the phenomenon *stress* (Selye, 1956).

Loss, Loneliness, and Immunosuppression

Central to present day understanding of the broken heart phenomenon are two key hypotheses which, when joined together, suggest a conceptual model of just how physical disease, psychological disorder, and death may result from the stress of dealing with the death of a lifelong spouse. Both hypotheses concern suppression of the immune system as a result of long-term stress.

Suppression of the immune system in short-term stress is a naturally-occuring event in many animals, including human beings. Short-term suppression of the immune response works to increase our chances of survival in highly stressful situations by protecting us from reacting to, say, the inflammation and swelling of a wound. Soldiers, for instance, often report not being unaware of a battle wound until they are well out of danger, at which point the inflammation and pain will be fully experienced. Under conditions of long-term stress, however, this same immunosuppression process can make us more susceptible to physical diseases, psychological disorders, and death. Prolonged stress has been shown to suppress physical growth, and the immune system, to diminish sex drive, to reduce the output of reproductive hormones, and to play an important role in cancer, coronary heart disease, asthma, gastrointestinal diseases, migraine headaches, and a host of other disorders (Marrone, 1990; Stroebe, 1994).

The first hypothesis, termed the *nuclear conflict hypothesis,* states that the presence of unconscious conflict involving the expression or repression of emotions—including anger, sadness, fear, and disgust (Bull, 1962)—acts as a central stressor. Because the emotional impulses are chronically repressed by the person, the corresponding behavioral expressions of anger, crying, trembling, etc., though physiologically activated, are not brought to expression. We are left suspended, as it were, in a state of muscular preparedness. This state of suspension, between the impulse to act and the impulse to repress action, is the chronic stressor which, like the injury to the soldier in battle, signals the release of opiate-like chemicals from the brain which suppress the immune system.

The second hypothesis, termed the *immunosuppression hypothesis,* states that stress in our life suppresses the immune system; when a nuclear emotional conflict remains unresolved, this suppression of the immune system becomes chronic, resulting in a breakdown of the body/mind complex in the form of various physical diseases and psychological disorders. The loneliness experienced by a surviving spouse, for instance, may be a chronic source of stress that suppresses the immune response. For example, in studies of immune system responsiveness in nonmedicated, psychiatric inpatients divided into high-loneliness and low-loneliness groups, results revealed that individuals in the high-loneliness group had significantly lower level of immunological compe- tence than the low-loneliness group (Marrone, 1990; Stroebe, 1994).

Margaret Stroebe (1994), drawing on these empirical studies as well as information from epidemiological research, found that what distinguishes be- reaved spouses who die from those who survive is a lack of contact with others during their bereavement. Those broken-hearted spouses who died tended to isolate themselves and immerse themselves in helplessness and despair. They tended not to remarry, had no one to talk to or care for, lived by themselves, and became progressively more isolated and alone. The general picture is one of loneliness, lack of support, and little integration with other people.

The absence of their loved one may also affect the nutritional status of widowed persons. Rosenbloom and Whittington (1993), for example, in a study of recently widowed persons (age 60+ years) and married persons of similar age, found that widowhood changed the social meaning that eating held for them, producing negative effects on eating behaviors and nutrient intake. Stroebe (1994) suggests that the direct effects of grief (e.g., depression and helplessness) and the secondary consequences associated with the stress of bereavement (e.g., loneliness, and decreased nutrient intake) underlie the bereavement–mortality relationship seen in the broken heart phenomenon.

While further research will be needed to find out why wives are less affected by the loss of a spouse than husbands, Stoddard and Henry (1985) propose that the greater impact of bereavement on men is due in part to the fact that men are more likely to have only one strong emotional relationship in their lives, and when this bond is severed their health is more severely compromised. They suggest that American social norms about affectional bonds between men and others require men to become independent from parents and siblings and to maintain a social distance between themselves and others. Since men commonly rely on women—namely, wives—to supply their social networks for them, a bereaved husband is more often psychologically isolated than a bereaved wife, and is more physiologically vulnerable to disease and death. They further suggest that elderly people, especially men, must learn to empower themselves, overcome behavioral passivity, develop social relationships that enrich their lives, and develop coping strategies to insulate themselves from life events that are both profound and highly stressful.

> **"Age is strictly a case of mind over matter. If you don't mind, it doesn't matter."**
>
> —Jack Benny

Aging, Empowerment, and Meaning

Aging, like death, is inevitable, universal, and irreversible. The fact that our population is aging is no longer shocking. However, as a society, the phenomenon is still "new," not fully understood, and easy to "put on the shelf." For aging Americans, however, questions of how to cope with aging, how to remain empowered as persons as we age, and how to conduct the search for meaning and purpose in our remaining years, has not been put on the shelf. In fact, persons who are older today are survivors, having lived through more medical breakthroughs, technological changes, economic disruptions, and social transformations than occurred throughout the remainder of recorded history. As elders, we are pioneers, creating new definitions of wellness, learning to empower ourselves, searching for new motifs of meaning to give significance and purpose to our remaining years, and creating lifestyles for ourselves and for the years ahead that previous generations did not experience and, probably, never even imagined.

In 1900, the average life expectancy was 47 years. People could expect to grow up, marry, raise children, and enter the postparental era. Their life then

AGING: THE UPSIDE

- The frequency of female orgasms increases in each decade of life, up through the eighties.

- Male erections may not be as fast or as firm as they once were, but their staying power increases.

- It's easier to quit smoking as you get older.

- Your perspiration will be less odiferous.

- During middle age, people who want to live longer should weigh 6 to 14 pounds over what the ideal height/weight tables recommend.

- As the years go by, many people gain a much broader perspective on their lives—leaving behind many stressors, such as being a slave to the clock or calendar or trying to climb the corporate ladder.

- You'll probably outgrow those pounding, painful headaches.

- Because they have fewer small blood vessels near the skin, older people heal with much less redness and scarring from wounds.

- After age 60 our bodies react less strenuously to things that trigger hay fever symptoms, hives, and food allergies.

- We get more hours for productivity because older people sleep about 1 hour less per day.

- People ages 45 to 64 spend fewer days away from their jobs fighting an illness than do people ages 15 to 44.

- If you haven't already developed lupus, rheumatoid arthritis, schizophrenia, chronic depression, you're less likely to do so.

- Violent acts, one of the greatest threats to health and well-being, tend to decrease with age; people do tend to mellow with age.

- Our sense of humor improves because we tend to stop "editing" ourselves.

- People get happier as they get older and begin reaping the rewards of whatever decisions were made in the past.

- Older people tend to nourish relationships with loved ones and appreciate how hard these relationships are to build.

Source: Peggy Noonan. (1994). 50 Things That Get Better as You Get Older, *Longevity* (September) pp. 41–56. Downloaded @ AOL, 4/21/95.

was, essentially, complete. Today, men and women 85 and older—about 3 million strong—are the most rapidly growing age group in America (NIHS, 1995b). Many demographers predict that 20 million to 40 million people will be 85 or older in the year 2040, and 500,000 to 4 million will be centenarians in 2050. In fact, U.S. Census Bureau estimates predict that about 1 out of every 100 youngsters born between 1979 and 1981 will reach 100 years of age (NIH, 1995). This phenomenon of the aging of the U.S. population is sometimes termed the *graying of America.* From a global perspective, the aging of the human population will be one of the world's most important social issues of the next half-century. The United Nations anticipates that by the year 2025 there will be 822 million people in the world age 65 and over, a number that exceeds the present combined populations of Europe and North America (NIHS, 1995b).

Researchers have found that the oldest of old Americans—those who had passed their 100th birthday—were experts in survival. They were independent, stubborn, optimistic and curious nonconformists who felt empowered as persons. Comedian George Burns died in 1996 at 100 years of age. © *AP/Wide World Photos*

AGING, BEAUTY, AND THE BODY

For much of our lives, most of us are unaware of the aging process because the changes occur gradually and there is plenty of time to develop cognitive strategies for coping with them. But evidence of the aging process eventually becomes undeniable. As we move into our 40s, 50s, and 60s, the obvious physical signs of aging—wrinkles, middle-age flab, failing vision, and the loss and graying of hair—bring the realization that the twilight of life is approaching. Psychological reactions to this realization are as diverse as the different physical patterns of aging. Some view old age as a time of crisis and become anxious and depressed. They see themselves as "over the hill" and feel their days are numbered. But others view old age as a time for gaining new purpose in life, self-understanding, and personal fulfillment (R. E. Smith, 1993).

The physical signs of aging affect our outward appearance and the functioning of every organ. There are dramatic changes in the shape of our bodies as we age, and changes in our reproductive organs and sexual responsiveness. Difficulties in falling asleep and staying asleep become more common, and our reaction times to stimuli are slower. Vision, hearing, and the sense of smell become less acute. Bones become fragile and more easily broken. Muscles lose power; joints stiffen or wear out. Circulation slows, blood pressure rises, and because the lungs hold

CARING INSIGHTS

Memory, Use it or Lose it

K. Warner Schaie (1989), in a longitudinal study of 1,620 adults between 22 and 91 years of age, found that the speed of information processing slows in old age. This slowing of information processing is especially detrimental to short-term memory, which is the stage of memory that involves conscious, purposeful manipulation of information (Sdorow, 1995). Short-term memory enables us to perform functions such as mental arithmetic. On the other hand, although older adults do more poorly than adolescents and young adults on cognitive tests of memory recall, an important factor that may explain this difference is that older persons have been out of school for many years. This was demonstrated in Schaie's Seattle Longitudinal Study when researchers compared the recall ability of college students, their peers not attending college, and older people not attending college. The average age of the younger groups was 22, the average age of the older group was 69. The results showed that the recall ability of the college group was better than that of the other two groups. But there was no difference in the performance of the groups of older persons and younger persons who were not attending college. This suggests that it might be the failure to use their memory, rather than simply brain deterioration accompanying aging, that accounts for the inferior performance of the elderly on tests of recall. The old adage of "Use it or lose it" is summarized in the words of researcher K. Warner Schaie, who said, "Those who wish to maintain a high level of intellectual functioning in old age must maintain flexible behaviors and attitudes, remain involved in a broad spectrum of intellectually stimulating activities, and practice their problem-solving abilities" (Sdorow, 1995:147).

less oxygen, we tend to slow down (Cavanaugh, 1990). Internally, there is the progressive loss of cells in the brain, kidneys, and other vital organs.

Approaching old age, many adults respond to signs of physical aging by focusing more attention on their bodies (R. L. Gould, 1972). Bernice Neugarten (1968) found an increase in "body monitoring" among aging men and women. Confronted with an aging body, many aging adults become concerned with its upkeep. They may spend an increasing amount of time before a mirror, begin an exercise program to tone up their muscles, or resort to hair color, wigs, creams, or other cosmetic products.

Adults who value themselves for their beauty, strength, or other physical traits tend to experience negative psychological reactions as soon as their bodies begin to show wear and tear. In contrast, people who place importance on nonphysical attributes, such as intelligence or interpersonal skills, usually continue to function well and feel young for many years after their hair turns gray and their muscles weaken (Troll, 1985). Robert Peck (1968) analyzed the specific developmental tasks of old age and concluded that one of the most important is acceptance of our inevitable physical decline, accompanied by a shift from valuing physical powers to valuing wisdom and relationships. D. J. Levinson and co-workers (1978) also found that as they entered the later years of life, many of their subjects redefined the self, placing less emphasis on physical appearance and performance and more emphasis on knowledge and experience. In this way, they focused on the remaining productive activities where their functioning was less affected by the physical aging process (R. E. Smith, 1993).

Aging adults not only think more about their bodies but also become more concerned about their health. A national survey of 25,000 aging Americans revealed that 42% of the respondents thought about their health more than about almost anything else, including love, work, or money. Rubinstein (1982) found three predominant health-oriented response patterns among aging Americans. *Health vigilants* pursued health with a vengeance and believed that diet, vitamins, and exercise could conquer virtually any health threat. *True believers* thought illness could best be resisted through positive thinking, faith, prayer, optimism, and friendship. *Fatalists* believed that their health was determined by fate and luck or by genetic endowment and that they could do little to influence it. Not surprisingly, psychological assessments revealed that the fatalists were the most unhappy of the three groups. In contrast, the health vigilants, who took maximum responsibility for their own health, were physically and psychologically the healthiest of the three groups studied.

SELF-ESTEEM AND EMPOWERMENT IN OLD AGE

Many persons cope with changes in their lives as they grow older with little disruption of functioning. At the same time, it is fairly well documented that mental health concerns, along with physical health concerns, increase with advancing age. Older persons in America experience many stresses, crises, and losses, in addition to the need to cope with a devalued social status. They are less likely to seek mental health care than other segments of the population, and, as a consequence, minor issues may escalate to major concerns before intervention is sought.

In addition to social isolation, elderly persons in America are often faced with the challenge of overcoming psychological despair in old age. In general, attitudes toward older persons are negative, and older persons frequently internalize these negative societal perceptions. These attitudes, combined with frequent losses, contribute to lowered self-esteem among older persons, along with an increasingly external locus of control, behavioral passivity, and a lack of feelings of self-efficacy (Bandura, 1982). The circumstances and multiple losses of later life, over which we have no control, may lead to a low sense of self-efficacy even among persons who felt otherwise when younger. In addition, older persons with an already low sense of self-efficacy may be expected to react to the losses of later life by giving up more easily and withdrawing.

Kuypers and Bengtson (1973) proposed the social breakdown syndrome (SBS) as an explanation of negative adjustment in old age. The SBS explains the process of interaction between social inputs and self-concept that results in a self-perpetuating cycle of negative psychological functioning for many elderly persons (J. E. Myers, 1990). The first stage of this model describes an existing precondition of susceptibility to psychological breakdown, possibly as a result of identity problems, declining health, or loss of status. In the second stage, other persons, such as family members or health professionals, label the older person as incompetent or deficient in some aspect of behavior. This negative labeling by others leads to the third stage, induction into the sick role. At this point, the elderly person is treated as though she or he is ill, senile, helpless, or, in some other way, lacking in the ability to fully think, feel, or behave. As the older person begins to identify more strongly with the sick role (stage four), self-efficacy becomes impaired and the older person also begins to perceive him- or herself as inadequate and incapable of independent action. The effects of labeling and ageism make older persons particularly susceptible to this social breakdown syndrome.

Empowerment, the process of helping people feel a sense of control over their lives, can be an effective strategy for countering the social breakdown syndrome and for enhancing a sense of self-efficacy and self-esteem among older persons. Empowering strategies include changing ageist stereotypes and beliefs, developing valued roles for elders in the home, hospital, or community, and improving access to social services for older persons. The encouragement of self-efficacy through empowerment is a vital strategy, not only for interrupting and reversing the breakdown cycle, but, it appears to increase longevity. For example, in psychological assessments conducted at the University of Georgia's Gerontology Center and sponsored by the National Institutes of Health, researchers found that the oldest of the old Americans—those who had passed their 100th birthday—were experts in survival and empowerment who tended to be independent, stubborn, and curious nonconformists who scored low in depression and emotional stability and high in optimism and empowerment measures. Psychologist Leonard Poon (1995), director of the center, states, "They tend to be independent, they tend to dominate,. . . they want their way. They also tend to be suspicious. They won't just take one's word on something. They tend to question what you have to tell them. It fits into what a survivor would be."

By helping older persons experience a sense of control and power in the management of their lives and by promoting older persons as valued, capable, and self-determined, a sense of empowerment can be fostered. This may require significant modifications in the environment as well as in individual perceptions. For example, one way to empower persons is to provide a means of involvement that promotes a sense of ownership and control. Service on community advisory boards and hospital and nursing home resident panels are examples of strategies for involving older persons in decision making on their own behalf. In general, elderly individuals placed in the role of passive recipient, such as

"The remarkable fact is that most older people learn how to contain their oldness, and they are not depressed. Failure to credit the resilience and resourcefulness that successful aging requires (and that most people find within them) is a more significant public-health problem than late-life depression."

Jacobson (1995), p. 17.

occurs in hospitals and in convalescent and nursing homes, tend to become and remain disempowered. For the medical model to incorporate empowerment, a paradigm shift from an illness model to a holistic/wellness model may be required.

EMPOWERMENT THROUGH WELLNESS

Wellness is an active process of living in which persons strive to achieve a sense of balance and integration among their mind, their body, and their emotions (Leafgren & Elsenrath, 1986). Wellness focuses on self-responsibility, on the need to be assertive in creating the life we want rather than passive in just reacting to circumstances. Through an emphasis on freedom of choice, wellness strategies increase the responsibility of individuals for self-care. Wellness is essentially an empowering philosophy that has a goal of helping individuals identify areas of their lives over which they have control, and assisting them to make choices that enhance their physical, psychological, and spiritual well-being. Individual behavior is notoriously hard to change. It may be that the best way to ensure change is through creating a positive, nurturing environment in which caregivers communicate a sincere belief in the capability of individuals to assume responsibility for their own total well-being. Such an environment, according to Myers (J. E. 1990), is inherently empowering.

A philosophy of wellness across the life span is one way to respond to the challenge of living longer and to create a world where empowerment is the norm for all persons, regardless of their life circumstances or their age. Central to a sense of integrity and empowerment in old age is the search for meaning and purpose, a search that may involve both subtle and dramatic changes in our views of living and dying.

Coming to Terms with Death: Motifs of Meaning

In *Fear and Trembling and the Sickness unto Death,* existential philospher Soren Kierkegaard (1843) argues that the price we pay for not coming to terms with our own death is despair. A person in despair, according to Kierkegaard, is a person who lives his or her life as though life were no different from death. In not coming to terms with death, the person in despair also avoids the insights that life is precious, that existence is delicate, that a life filled with vibrancy, choices, and risks is the truest antidote to loneliness and despair, and that the dignity with which you live your life is the dignity with which you die.

In Henrik Ibsen's *Peer Gynt,* as Peer is pondering his life of despair and anticipating his death, he offers some of the most powerful lines of the play:

How unspeakably poor a soul can be
When it enters the mist and returns to nothing!
O beautiful earth, don't be angry with me
That I trod your sweet grass to no avail.

O Beautiful sun, you have squandered
Your golden light upon an empty hut.
There was no one within to warm and comfort.
The owner, I know now, was never at home.

Nearly 140 years after Kierkegaard's death, existential psychologist Rollo May died in Tiburon, California. In *My Quest for Beauty* (1985:70), May recaptured Kierkegaard's insight in these words: "Only when we confront death, in some form or other, only when we realize that life is fragile, do we create beauty. It is parallel to the fact that only when we confront death do we authentically love."

As we enter the final season of life, a number of different death meanings are typically synthesized into our personal value system (Kalish, 1985a,b). These *motifs of meaning* are part of our search for personal strategies for coming to terms with death.

DEATH AS AN ORGANIZER OF TIME

Death, of course, defines the end point of our lives. More central to our search for meaning, however, is the shift in the way we mark our own lifetime and organize our lives, from "time since birth" to "time 'til death" (Neugarten, 1968, 1977).

Research reveals that this change in time perspective, from looking back on life to looking ahead to life, does nor occur for every adult. Not all adults think of their lives in terms of time 'til death. In one study of aging adults, for example, Keith (1981–82) found that only about half her sample seemed to think about or to define precisely "time remaining." But such a recognition of time remaining may be a useful (perhaps even a necessary) aspect of coming to terms with our own death.

In Keith's study, those adults who did talk about their lives in terms of "time remaining" had more favorable attitudes toward life, spent less time regretting past mistakes or lost opportunities, and experienced less fear of death. Other research has confirmed this pattern: Older adults who continue to be preoccupied with the past, who avoid thinking about the future and the time remaining in their lives, are more likely to be fearful or anxious about death than are those who face the future (and their own deaths) more fully (Pollak, 1979–80).

> "It's not much longer I'm going to be able to do things I've loved so much—skiing, horseback riding, all the physical things. I've just enjoyed having my body be able to pretty much do anything I wanted it to. But that time is being diminished. . . .
>
> "[The best part of being 56 is] the wisdom, the perspective you gain that allows you to be more compassionate, more forgiving about some of your hostilities and anger."
>
> *Source:* Robert Redford, *Chicago Tribune,* May 15, 1994, p. 4.

DEATH AS A FEAR TO BE CONQUERED

As we mature and season through the adult years, not only may "time 'til death" mark a new time line for our lives, but our fears regarding death itself tend to manifest. Fears of death may include fear of the pain or suffering or indignity that may be involved in the process of dying; fear that we will not be able to cope well with the pain of separation from loved ones; fear of whatever punishment may come after death; and a vague and fundamental fear of loss of the self.

Pervasive as they are, these fears are extremely difficult to conquer, in part because we defend ourselves against them in devious ways, most typically with emotional repression, cognitive denial, or behavioral passivity. If you ask adults directly whether they are afraid of death, a majority will say no. If you approach the subject more indirectly, such as by asking about a person's feelings about the deaths of others or about expectations of or fear of pain, you will find somewhat higher levels of fear in aging adults.

When researchers attempt to tap unconscious fears, virtually everyone shows signs of such fear. For example, Feiffel and Branscomb (1973) gave several hundred subjects lists of words, printed in various colors. The subject's task was to read off the color of the word, not the word itself. Half the words in the series were death related, half were neutral. If it takes subjects longer to read the colors of death words than of neutral words, this implies some resistance to these words and may reflect unconscious anxiety or fear about death. Feiffel and Branscomb found that 71% of their subjects said no when asked directly, "Are you afraid of your own death?" But it nonetheless took these subjects significantly longer to read off the colors of death-related words than of neutral words.

In the later years, many adults grope toward new ways of thinking about death, eventually accepting it in a different way, so that the fear recedes in old age. This does not mean that older adults are unconcerned with death. On the contrary, they are more likely to talk about it and think about it than are younger adults (Kalish, 1985a,b). But while death is highly salient to the elderly, it is apparently not as frightening as it is in midlife (Bee, 1992). Part of the strategy for overcoming death anxiety in our later years may be connected with making preparations for dying and death. For example, in her national survey, Matilda White Riley (Riley & Foner, 1968) found that 80% of adults of all ages "believe" that a person should make plans for death, such as preparing wills and living wills and making funeral arrangements. But the older we are, the more likely we are to have actually made such preparations. Riley found that those over 60 years of age are more than twice as likely as those under 40 to have made out a will or to have made funeral or cemetery arrangements. More recent research has shown that the act of preparing for death in very concrete ways does indeed lower death anxiety (Riley & Foner, 1968; Bee, 1992).

Age is not the only factor that plays a part in our coming to terms with the fear of death. The degree of spirituality or religious feeling in our lives seems to make some difference. After reviewing the few studies addressing this link, Kalish (1985a,b) concludes that, in general, adults who describe themselves as deeply religious or who go to church regularly are less afraid of death than are those who describe themselves as less religious or who participate less regularly in religious activities. In some instances, however, researchers have found a curvilinear relationship, with both those who are deeply religious and those who are deeply irreligious being less fearful than those who may be uncertain about or uncommitted to any spiritual tradition.

More interesting, perhaps, is the link between fear of death and a sense of personal worth or competence. Several facets of this area have been studied over the years. Adults who feel they have achieved the goals they set out to achieve or who think of themselves as not too discrepant from the person they wanted to be are less fearful of death than are those who are disappointed in themselves (Niemeyer & Chapman, 1980–81). Adults who feel that their life has some purpose or meaning also appear to be less fearful of death (Durlak, 1972), as do those who feel a sense of personal competence (Pollak, 1979–80; Harvey, 1996).

Such findings suggest at least the possibility that those aging adults who have successfully completed the major tasks of adult life, who have adequately met the demands of the roles they occupied, and who developed inwardly, and spiritually, are able to come to terms with death with less fear and greater balance.

"Death is an evil;
the gods have so judged;
had it been good,
they would die."

—Sappho

DEATH AS PUNISHMENT AND LOSS

Many religions have long traditions that emphasize that death is a punishment, and many adults believe that a "good" person will be rewarded with longer life. Anthropologists, who have obtained a great deal of information on the various myths and legends focusing on the origin of death from around the world, point out that in most of these myths humans are believed to have been created initially without death. As with Adam and Eve in the Garden of Eden, death came into the world as punishment for messengers of the gods or humans who had disobeyed divine law, overpopulated, or had become jealous, angry, or selfish

A great aunt rocks and comforts her little grand niece. For some elders, the counterpoint to life's finality is an appreciation of the patterns and rituals of daily life and the loved ones who bring joy and meaning to these fleeting moments. © *Documentary Photo Aids*

(Corcos & Krupka, 1985). The difficulty many adults have in surrendering their ideas and ideals of youthfulness and expectation of a long life and in accepting and prizing their maturity and time remaining may be tied to the meaning we invest in the equation: *death = punishment.*

Perhaps, more pervasively, death is seen by most of us as a *loss* of some kind—loss of the ability to complete projects or to carry out our plans, loss of our body, loss of experiencing, of taste or smell or touch, loss of relationships with people, and so on. The specific losses that we associate with death appear to change as we move through the adult years.

Young adults are more concerned about loss of opportunity to experience things and about the loss of family relationships. Older adults may be more concerned with the loss of time to complete some inner work. In a study by Kalish and Reynolds (1976), adults of various ages were asked what they would do with their time if they had only 6 months to live. Younger adults were more likely to plan to spend time either experiencing things or relationships, while older adults were much more likely to spend time reading, contemplating, or praying—suggesting that we develop a greater concern with our spiritual life as we age. Of course, some of these losses may occur during a person's lifetime. A loss of hearing in old age will cut out the Bach chorales and the doo-wop harmonies, widowhood may deprive us of our mate, companion, and caresses, and the aging process itself will lower our energy levels, physical stamina, and memory recall. Coming to terms with death involves recognizing and accepting that death guarantees all losses.

DEATH AS COUNTERPOINT

The dignity with which you live your life, is the dignity with which you die.

The various motifs of meaning associated with coming to terms with death and dying tend to configure around the negative in many ways, around fear, loss, and punishment. And yet the cognitive time-shift to "time 'til death" can also inspire an appreciation and prizing of each remaining moment of life. In a real sense, the finality and irrevocability of death can serve as a counterpoint to another, perhaps more dramatic cognitive shift involving a slowing of the sense-of-time, along with a localization of conscious awareness to the now, the here, and the dear.

"After my heart attack my attitude toward life changed. The word I use for it now is the post-mortem life. I could just as easily have died, so my living constitutes a kind of extra, a bonus. One very important aspect of this post-mortem life is that everything gets doubly precious, gets piercingly important. You get stabbed by things, by flowers and by babies and by beautiful things—just the very act of living, of walking and breathing and eating and having friends and chatting. Everything seems to look more beautiful rather than less, and one gets the much-intensified sense of miracles."

Source: Abraham Maslow, 1970, as quoted in Rollo May (1985), p. 69.

Psychologist Norman Paul (1986) also notes the paradoxical nature of the experience of loss and the process of coming to terms with death, which is often obscured by negativity. By paradoxical he means an expanded appreciation of its nature, which can include a consideration of the survivor's own joy at being alive.

As we grow older, we experience increasing numbers of deaths and funerals and, as a consequence, we are subject to increasing experiences of loss, grief, and sorrow. Our parents may die, or a child, surely friends and co-workers. We leave another funeral or memorial service feeling the sun against the face; and later, struck by the laughter and touch of those we love, the moments come to life, for the moment. Here and now, the counterpoint to death's finality is an appreciation of the patterns and subtext of our daily routines and rituals and the loved ones who bring joy and meaning to these fleeting moments. Suddenly, the irreversibility of death suggests the counterpoint of reversibility and change in our lives. If death has the capacity to deform us, then life still has the capacity to transform us. If death can inspire fear and loathing, then life can inspire triumph and joy.

Chapter Summary

Awareness that we will die moves to the foreground of our consciousness during the later years of life. In addition to the growing signs of aging, we encounter an increasing number of losses, and many of us launch a search for meaning and purpose in our living and dying. As our lifework moves toward completion, we face our last developmental task of resolving the conflict between **integrity and despair.**

As we grow through adulthood and into old age, the risk of suicide also grows. Older adults have the highest suicide rate—more than 50% higher than that for young people or for the nation as a whole—and that rate is increasing. Risk factors most often associated with elderly suicide include increasing interiority, chronic illness, an accumulation of multiple losses (including the death of a spouse, a child, and other significant persons), the loss of parental and work roles, widowhood, and the lessening of activity and resultant social isolation.

Statistics indicate that in a typical year, approximately 14 million Americans, or 7.05% of the population 15 years and older, experiences the death of a spouse. The tendency for one elderly spouse, usually male, to die shortly after the death of the other is termed the broken heart phenomenon. The questions of why some of us react with what Freud called normal mourning while others of us plunge into despair and chronic depression or succumb to a broken heart was reviewed from a number of points of view, including the cognitive, the psychodynamic, and the humanistic-existential.

As elders, we are pioneers in creating new definitions of wellness, learning to empower ourselves by creating new lifestyles for ourselves. Central to our work in old age is the search for meaning and the search for personal strategies for coming to terms with death.

FURTHER READINGS

Barrow, G. (1996) *Aging, the Individual, and Society,* 6th ed., West. Publishing, St. Paul, Mn.

Beck, A. T., Rush, A. J., Shaw, B., & Emery, G. (1979). *Cognitive Therapy of Depression.* Guildford Publishing Company, New York City, NY.

Erikson, E. H. (1980). *Identity and the Life Cycle.* Norton, New York.

Binstock, R. H., & Shanas E. (eds.) (1985). *Handbook of Aging and the Social Sciences,* 2nd ed. Van Nostrand, New York.

Kalish, Richard A. (ed.) (1985). *The Final Transition.* Baywood, Farmingdale, NY.

Parkes, C. M. (1986). *Bereavement: Studies of Grief in Adult Life.* International Universities Press, Madison, CO.

Parkes, C. M., & Weiss, R. S. (1983). *Recovery from Bereavement.* Basic Books, New York.

Silverstone, B., & Hyman, H. K. (1992). *Growing Older Together: A Couple's Guide to Understanding and Coping with the Challenges of Later Life.* Pantheon, New York.

Stroebe, W., & Stroebe, M. S. (1987). *Bereavement and Health: The Psychological and Physical Consequences of Partner Loss.* Cambridge University Press, Cambridge, England.

PART THREE

Caring and Preparing

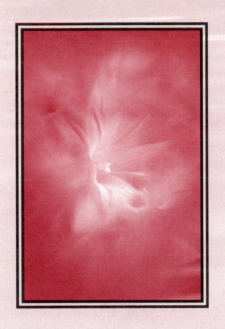

Caring for the Dying

Disasters often reveal the positive and compassionate side of human nature in ways that can truly inspire. Consider the bombing of the Federal Office Building in Oklahoma City, Oklahoma, on April 19, 1995. In one shattering instant, 168 men, women, and children were killed by the bomb blast, while hundreds of others were left injured and maimed. It was the second multifatality terrorist attack in the United States, but, unlike the bombing of the World Trade Center in New York a year earlier, the massive toll of dead and injured in Oklahoma City, including very young children, cut at America's heart. The specter of toddlers crushed by building debris and bomb fragments and the sight of parents and spouses limp with grief and sorrow shocked the nation and the world.

A horrifying tragedy like this can sour us on humanity. We might conclude that "people are insane" or that "our society is in a state of decay and falling apart." But "people" or "society" did not set the bomb that killed and maimed so many. In fact, two or three individuals are the alleged perpetrators. When we examine the actual incident, we see that during the few minutes following the blast, scores of caring people pulled others to safety while risking their own lives. And in the days and weeks that followed, volunteers from all over the United States, Canada, Europe, Japan, and other nations searched the rubble, inch by inch, for survivors, while others provided support for the victims, their families, as well as exhausted volunteers.

Within hours, teams of volunteers from around the nation intervened, including psychologists, social workers, and grief counselors. Many had experience from earlier disasters, including the Sioux City, Iowa, crash of United Airlines Flight 232 and the campus mourning program organized for students and professors affected by the loss of thirty-three college students in a plane explosion over Scotland. One-on-one counseling sessions with the dying and their loved ones were initiated, while makeshift support groups gathered in church basements and nearby government buildings. People from around the world sent clothing, funds for housing, scholarships for young survivors, and words of sympathy and outrage. Others hung teddy bears, flowers, and words of encouragement and sorrow on the cyclone fencing surrounding the bomb site. Tens of thousands of acts of caring and helping unfolded within days of the disaster as loved ones and strangers responded to a single, desperate act of mindless terror.

Altruism and Caregiving

Selfishness, violence, and a cold insensitivity to the suffering of others have always been a part of the human landscape. Their existence, although reflecting the brutal and violent aspects of our nature, may not be enough to indict all of human nature. In fact, if we take a closer look at the Oklahoma bombing and its aftermath, a more hopeful image emerges. From this point of view, we are biologically programmed to be cooperative, supportive, and altruistic, neurologically wired to be our brother's and sister's keeper, and intrinsically motivated to attain a sense of belongingness and meaning in our lives by reaching out to others in need. Along with the dark side of our nature, there is a hero or heroine within each of us whose caring and compassion forms an invaluable part of the human fabric of existence.

This brighter alternative to the neo-Darwinian view of humans as brutal competitors in a dog-eat-dog world maintains that if we create the right environment, then empathy, compassion, and caring behavior will unfold naturally and that both the caregiver and the care-recipient will grow and thrive from their participation in it (Larson, 1993). The weight of the evidence suggests that, although a harsh and unloving childhood can inhibit the full expression of these tender, human qualities, compassion and caregiving are part of our biological inheritance (Maslow, 1954, 1973; Gray, 1991; Kohn, 1990).

THE DEVELOPMENT OF ALTRUISM AND CAREGIVING

The human capacity for empathy and caregiving begins expressing itself early in life. Zahn-Waxler and Radke-Yarrow (1982:126), for example, found that many children are able to engage in discernible caregiving behavior by the age of 1½ to 2 years. Very young children attempt to comfort a distressed person in simple ways—by patting, hugging, or presenting an object—along with more sophisticated and complex attempts to help. These latter include expressing verbal

This Pulitzer Prize winning photograph captures the last dying moments of a toddler fatally wounded by the bomb blast in Oklahoma City, Oklahoma. Touched by the suffering of others, individuals from around the world searched the rubble, honored the dead, and comforted the living. © *Charles H. Porter/Sygma*

sympathy, offering suggestions about how to solve problems, trying to cheer others up, and sometimes trying alternative helping responses when a given technique is not effective. The authors state that these behaviors in young children "appear to be intended to reduce suffering in others and to reflect concern for the victim in distress. Many of the acts would undoubtedly be judged as altruistic if an older child or adult were performing the very same behaviors."

Our capacity for compassion and empathy continues to develop through adolescence and the early adult years. The newborn baby cries reactively in the presence of another in distress, but as adults we can take the role of the distressed other and imagine how it would feel to be in those same circumstances. As children, we begin to develop our role-taking ability around the age of 2 or 3. By late childhood and adolescence, we can empathize beyond our immediate situation and become empathically aroused by someone else's general life circumstances or prospects for the future. Hoffman (1982) and Kohn (1990) observe that with increasing cognitive proficiency, we become capable of a more generalized empathic response. As we approach adolescence, we begin to empathize with the suffering of an entire group or class of people (e.g., the terminally ill, people with AIDS, bereaved parents, bombing victims).

"Two animals trading favors each derive an overall advantage. An animal who does not return favors . . . ceases to receive them."

Masson. J.M. 1995, p. 171

Laboratory experiments and naturalistic observations of other animals, including dogs, squirrels, foxes, rats, elephants, dolphins, and various primates, reveal that animals of the same species fight, bicker, threaten, and sometimes even kill one another in their competition for resources. On the other hand, animal research also shows that animals have an almost universal tendency toward cooperation and altruism and tend to become aroused in the presence of a distressed member of their species (de Waal, 1996). Many of these animals will act in ways that reduce the other's distress (Gray, 1991; Hallett, 1967; Larson, 1993). In some studies, it has been demonstrated that those animals who had been in pain themselves were most likely to engage in cooperative, altruistic behavior toward others in similar situations (Masserman, Wachking, & Terris, 1964; Church, 1959; Gray, 1991). For example, when chimpanzees fight and inflict wounds on one another, they will often return to the other injured animal, inspect and even clean an injury she or he inflicted (de Waal, 1996).

Dutch primatologist Frans de Waal (1996) has observed numerous examples of helping behavior among monkeys. In one example, he witnessed Azalea, a monkey born with a chromosomal condition similar to Down's Syndrome in humans, whose elder sisters carried her around and protected her against other monkeys. de Waal also observed that whenever keepers tried to move the monkeys from an indoor to an outdoor section of their enclosure, adult males would hold the door open until Wolf, an old, near-blind female, could go through. According to Gray (1991:112), "This sort of helping occurs all the time in the animal world. It occurs when a mated pair of foxes work together to raise their mutual young, or a pack of wolves work together to kill an antelope, or a troop of macaque monkeys work together to repel a troop invading their territory. Most of the advantages of social living lie in cooperation."

Among human beings, helping responses of 85% to 100% are common in laboratory experiments as well as outside the laboratory (Kohn, 1990). National surveys, such as the Gallup poll (1986), consistently reveal that about 50% of the American population reports performing some kind of volunteer work during the past year, with 80 million American adults engaging in volunteer work in any given year (Larson, 1993). For example, although denial and avoidance still characterize much of society's response to the AIDS crisis, there has also been a tremendous caring response from community-based grassroots organizations of volunteers who provide supportive care for people with AIDS (Omoto & Snyder, 1990). Canadian John Saynor (1988), in a discussion of the stigmatization of AIDS patients associated with homophobia, points to the unselfish giving and support demonstrated by both the homosexual and heterosexual communities throughout Canada toward persons afflicted with AIDS.

Vast amounts of natural helping also occur in American self-help groups where participants voluntarily assist one another in coping with shared problems, such as various 12-step programs (e.g., Alcoholics Anonymous, Narcotics Anonymous, Emotions Anonymous), Compassionate Friends, Survivors of Suicide, and many others (Doka & Tatelbaum, 1996). About 15 million Americans have at one time or another participated in self-help groups, and more than 10 million each year will participate in these groups by the turn of the century (M. K.

Jacobs & Goodman, 1989). Add the hundreds of thousands of adults caring for their frail or terminally ill loved ones, along with the informal support occurring among friends and relatives on a daily basis, and the estimate of voluntary caregiving occurring in America rises to a staggering figure.

Theoretical explanations for these events come from vantage points in biology, psychology, and sociology. Evolutionary psychologist Harvey Hornstein (1976), for example, contends that we must travel back in time to the savannahs of Africa, where, about 3.5 million years ago, our 60-pound ancestors were struggling to survive. Their survival hinged on whether or not they could develop the capacity for coordinated and cooperative activities. Physically, they were no match for the other predators; only their superior intelligence could save them. Fortunately, at about that time, Hornstein notes, their brains underwent a pivotal growth spurt that empowered them to think and feel their way into the minds of their fellow hominids, making cooperation and other forms of prosocial, caregiving behavior possible. Without this ability to empathize (i.e., to feel emotionally and sympathetically aroused in the presence of another's distress), we as a species would, in all likelihood, not have survived, falling prey to physically superior species.

Evolutionary theorists describe a model of reciprocal altruism, a kind of psychobiological Golden Rule guided by the following wisdom: If I help you now, you'll help me in the future, and this increases both our chances of survival. The reward for helping is the increased likelihood of receiving help in the future. Much of the behavior that fits this pattern goes on throughout the animal kingdom, especially among primates, which are the best at remembering previous helpers and nonhelpers (Larson, 1993; Gray, 1991; de Waal, 1996).

Sociologists and social psychologists assume that compassion and altruism are enduring qualities acquired through various forms of social learning. They view caregiving as conditioned early in life through a process in which people see the reactions of others to caring acts and learn that responding with empathy and compassion is both rewarded and rewarding. Finally, biologically oriented researchers look at altruism as genetically transmitted and point out that it would make sense that caregiving is inborn in a species like ours, whose young are so entirely defenseless at birth and for the first few years of life (Gray, 1991).

CAREGIVERS' FEARS

We are capable of caring for one another in countless ways. This is certainly the bright side of our nature. However, in a society like ours, which tends to deny thought and repress feelings associated with death, caring for another person who is in the throes of death can reveal a vulnerable, more fearful side to our nature. Whether tied to a dying loved one by bonds of affection and time or, as a medical professional, joined to the dying by bonds of professionalism and service, we are likely to encounter the dying with a mixture of compassion, anxiety, and fear.

Thanatologist Lewis Aiken (1994:309) notes that because we have little or no experience with death and dying, "the average person does not know how to relate to the terminally ill person at anything other than a superficial level. After reassuring a dying person and trying to cheer him or her up, the conversation usually turns to more pleasant, but psychologically less meaningful topics." Medical professionals are also inclined to avoid discussing death with patients

CAREGIVING@WELL.COM

The WELL (Whole Earth Lectronic Link), a computer-based bulletin board, is a virtual community of more than 10,000 persons centered in Sausalito, California, but inhabited by computer "posters" (message writers) from Tokyo, Paris, Costa Rica, London, and other points near and far. Members include children, teenagers, working people, professionals, artists, writers, and musicians. Communicating through e-mail and various forums, WELL members have celebrated weddings, argued, fallen in love, and grieved.

For example, in the summer of 1994, KJ announced that she was suffering from an advanced stage of cancer and didn't expect to live more than two months. Dozens of people who had never seen her, except for her online words, took turns at her bedside via computer. As she weakened and could no longer work her laptop, a friend tapped out her messages to other WELL members. KJ finally died, but not alone.

Philcat's son, who was diagnosed with leukemia a few years earlier, stimulated an online support group of virtual friends, including psychologists and nurses, who continue to support the family as they deal with the ups and downs of chemotherapy.

Singer David Crosby of the rock group Crosby, Stills and Nash found out that the computer world of virtual community can be a kind and compassionate place. The 53-year-old musician had been a frequent poster on the WELL until September 1995, when a Crosby, Stills & Nash concert tour had to be canceled because of his deteriorating health. When word of his condition leaked out, Crosby confirmed the news online. "Yes, I'm sick," he wrote. Diabetes and an undiagnosed case of

hepatitis, aggravated by years of drug abuse, had destroyed his liver. "The prognosis," he wrote, "is that I will die from liver failure within a few months without a transplant." His condition worsened over the next few weeks, and on November 2 he was rushed to the hospital. On the WELL, a new "topic" was created to provide a place for people to send the "beams" of good luck that WELL members traditionally send to those in need. A few days later, Crosby was back online to report that he had mastered the hospital's phone system and was able to send messages from his bed. "I'll keep trying to check in," he promised, "until they unzip me."

In the fall of 1995, when Crosby entered the UCLA Medical Center in Los Angeles to undergo a liver transplant, he took a laptop computer with him. For the next 2 months he posted messages from his hospital bed to his friends on the WELL. Readers of the WELL got a candid and often touching firsthand account of his ordeal. But Crosby got something valuable in return: nearly 1,000 messages of support and encouragement that he says helped him survive the experience. "I'd be there at 3 or 4 in the morning, unable to sleep and in a lot of pain, and all of a sudden, there would be all these other sparks out there in the darkness," he says. "It really put wind in my sails."

Just five days after the operation, Crosby was back at the computer, sending his first post-op message: "Don't feel sick any more. Thank you all so much." Crosby says the Apple PowerBook 540C computer that fellow musician Graham Nash lent him for his hospital stay gave him more comfort than all the pills and drugs he had to take.

Source: Adapted from *Time* magazine, downloaded @ America On Line, February 19, 1995; and Howard Rheingold, Tomorrow, *San Francisco Chronicle,* February 19, 1995.

whenever they can, and to avoid terminally ill patients, especially when death is near. Waldman (1990), for example, found that many health care providers, including physicians, nurses, social workers, and occupational therapists, believed that the expression of grief connected to the death of a patient was an unprofessional reaction that aroused feelings of inadequacy and incompetence in them.

Most of us can accept death in the abstract, in the news, on the screen, or in a novel, as a *concept* about the inevitability, universality, and irreversibility of the ending of physical life. However, being confronted with the affective (emotional) demands of caring for the dying on an ongoing basis puts us eye to eye with powerful and sometimes numbing forms of fear. Based on extensive experience in working with caregivers and the terminally ill, psychologist Dale Larson (1993) has isolated a number of these fears, including fear of our own death, fear of hurting, fear of being hurt, and fear of being engulfed in another's emotional world.

Fear of Our Own Death

Daily encounters with life-threatening illness and the dying process can often rouse a caregiver's own fear of mortality. Doctors, nurses, social workers, grief counselors, family members, and friends can do the work of caring for the dying for lengthy stretches of time without *consciously* experiencing this fear, through various forms of cognitive denial and emotional blocking. But then, suddenly, in the case of a loved one, we anticipate a future without that person, or a memory penetrates our consciousness, or we empathize with the pain and torment, and we are overtaken by fear. In the case of a patient, medical personnel often hide behind the mask of professionalism for long stretches of time. "Then, suddenly," according to Larson (1993:43), "we have a patient with our birthday, or who looks like our child or our sister, or has our mother's name and instantly we have an 'ego chill' experience in which we lose our sense of 'this is not me' who is dying." In that moment, our sense of vulnerability takes over as the repressed feelings of fear connected with our own death are experienced. How we react to and cope with this fear determines whether our empathy turns to personal anguish so that we unconsciously detach ourselves emotionally from our patient or loved one, or whether we continue to provide care in a compassionate and mindful way.

When our death fear is activated, we might find ourselves exiting the situation entirely. In one study, Amenta (1984) discovered that hospice volunteers with lower scores on a measure of death anxiety continued working in the program for longer periods than did volunteers with higher scores, suggesting that the group with high death anxiety had greater difficulty keeping their emotional equilibrium on an ongoing basis. In another study (Brockopp, King, & Hamilton, 1991), it was found that palliative care nurses who worked with dying patients on a frequent and continuing basis had more positive attitudes toward death and less death anxiety than nurses who did not work regularly with the dying. This research suggests that various strategies for coping with our fear of death are the result of important learning experiences connected with working with the dying over time.

As caregivers, our challenge, in each moment, is to recognize the source of our distress and to reclaim our balance by shifting back into the perspective of caregiver. The challenge may be ongoing because, as Larson (1993) makes clear, the fear of our own mortality is something we constantly face in the role of caregiver.

Fear of Hurting

Another personal challenge to caregivers involves the fear of hurting the person we are helping. Administering chemotherapy to a high school athlete, doing a spinal tap on a 7-year-old leukemia victim, giving another injection to an elderly patient already in pain, delivering the news of a death to a family, or making many other such routine interventions can be quite painful to all involved. Helping frequently hurts, and, according to Larson, this hurt is often combined with time pressure, the urge to be perfect, and the frequent necessity for caregivers to make decisions based on vague or incomplete information. As a result, many caregivers work with a "terror of error" that can stress them, grind them down, and make it more difficult to be emotionally involved with the people they care for (Larson, 1993:43; Petzold, 1982). Mistakes inevitably do occur, and the emotional consequences for the caregiver can be powerful, persistent, and, sometimes, emotionally devastating.

A NURSE REMEMBERS

"Early in my nursing career, another nurse and myself were caring for the patients on a pediatric unit. An infant was receiving blood and I could not monitor it because we got an admission with croup and the second nurse sent me to assist. The baby received too much normal saline after the transfusion and went into congestive heart failure, and his existing heart condition was compromised and he died. If I would have been more knowledgeable and insistent about having a doctor come in for a late deceleration, that baby would be about 4 years old today."

Source: Larson (1993), p. 23.

Fear of Being Hurt

The fear of being hurt is also a frequent concern for caregivers. This can take many forms: fear of direct physical aggression (e.g., being kicked, spat on, hit); fear of being the target for the rage of others, such as patients, family, and friends; and fear of feeling hurt and sorrow when our patient or loved one finally dies. The urge to protect ourselves from hurt often results in our distancing ourselves from the dying person or objectifying the person. Caregiver fear and grief is a regular part of the daily routine, and it builds up over time if not confronted and worked through. Larson (1993) and E. Kennedy and Charles (1990) suggest that feelings repressed and unacknowledged over long periods of time can generate ongoing stress and activate grief and fear from other parts of the caregiver's life. The tears and fears held back years ago are often activated in the presence of other losses, often without our awareness of their source.

Fear of Being Engulfed

The fear of being engulfed is best captured by the thought that "if I let myself become involved, I'll be sucked into the bottomless pit of . . . emotional neediness" (Larson, 1993:45) When activated, this fear can hinder a caregiver from feeling empathy and compassion for the care-recipient, thereby creating an experience of deep personal distress. A patient whose cries of pain once aroused our sympathy now appears overly needy and manipulative, and we feel used and defensive. In other cases, we become so immersed in the grief and distress of the dying that we find it difficult to shake these sad and depressing feelings. So we go home sad and depressed and feel guilty about stealing time from our own family members and friends (Rawnsley, 1990; E. Kennedy & Charles, 1990).

DEATH AND THE CAREGIVERS

"Anyone who works with the dying and remains genuine while dealing with them does not treat them as mere objects, strangers, or mannequins but learns to admit feelings, fears, pain, powerlessness and anger. Otherwise, these workers become removed and hard, in an unhealthy, routine manner. They then lose some of their humanity and must shield themselves from any arousing emotions."

Source: Petzold (1982), p. 254.

Taken together, these fears often lead to additional stress in the caregivers' lives that may manifest in numerous ways: blaming ourselves and feeling immersed in helplessness and hopelessness; avoiding emotionally charged topics of conversations with patients or loved ones; becoming emotionally wrought for no apparent reason; becoming careless in our communication—interrupting more, questioning more, trying to take back some control of our lives by telling people what to do, how to act, think or feel; or not paying attention to the impact we are having on others (Larson, 1993; Petzold, 1982). The sensitive caregiver must risk perceiving the experience of dying from the dying person's perspective, or function mechanistically. Rawnsley (1989, 1990:147) points out that, in the process of divesting caregiving activities of personal meaning, both the caregiver and the care-recipient are dehumanized and diminished.

Dehumanization and depersonalization are often the case for individuals who die in hospitals and nursing homes in America. Although medical professionals, as well as the population at large, are becoming more and more aware of the needs of the dying and their survivors, the educational process is a slow one, and the fears connected with death and dying are very powerful. Fortunately, there are alternatives to dying in a medical institution, including dying at home in the care of a loved one or as part of one of the more than 2,000 hospice programs operating in the United States today.

Dying in a Hospital

From a psychological or social point of view, American hospitals may not be the best places to die. Busy physicians and nurses, preoccupied with administrative duties and technical tasks, often have little time to try to understand and deal with the psychological and social needs of dying patients. "The hospital staff can be seen moving swiftly and efficiently in and out of intensive-care rooms or terminal wards, checking their watches, administering medicines, and connecting, disconnecting, and tuning machines. If they do stop to talk with patients, it is usually only for brief moments before they move on to more pressing duties" (Aiken 1994:299). According to Benoliel (1974:219), a vocal critic of medical and nursing school training, the behaviors of some doctors and nurses dealing with dying patients all too often reflect, "a lack of appropriate and consistent norms for professional behavior."

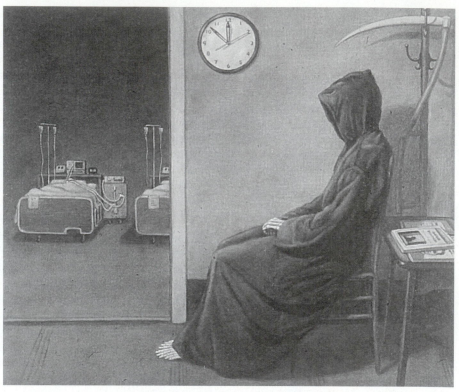

As medicine and the hospital culture have evolved during the twentieth century, they have become the instruments by which death is culturally banished, psychologically denied, and institutionally hidden. The result has been a hospital culture whose needs often supercede those of its patients.
© *Stock Illustration Source*

In 1995, fuel was added to the argument of critics of the medical profession with publication of the results of a $28 million, longitudinal study of the treatment of persons dying in American hospitals. The 4-year investigation, which followed dying patients, their families, and the physicians and hospital staff who cared for them in five American hospitals, was published by the *Journal of the American Medical Association* (Knauss & Lynn, 1995). Of the 9,000 dying persons who participated in the study, results revealed the following.

• Half the dying patients who were able to communicate reported that they were suffering moderate or severe pain during the last weeks of their lives that was not relieved by the medication administered.

• Nearly 40% of dying patients spent at least 10 days in a coma, attached to a mechanical ventilator or in an intensive care unit, where they were isolated from their families most of the time.

• Of those dying patients who had completed living wills and other directives stating that, if comatose or unconscious, they did not want to be artificially resuscitated, nearly half were artificially resuscitated against their wishes by physicians who did not know about their directives because of an all-but-complete lack of communication.

- Nearly one-third of the dying patients and their families spent all or most of their life savings for unsought, unrequested, and vain efforts to postpone inevitable death.
- Nurse advocates who were assigned to encourage doctors to communicate with their terminally ill patients and families, to determine their wishes about terminal care, and to avoid futile and unwanted high-tech efforts when near death had virtually no effect on outcomes. The 5,000 patients assigned nurse-advocates spent the same amount of time in intensive care and suffered almost as much unrelieved pain, and almost as many were kept alive artificially, against their wishes.

The report, which provided a searing indictment of the way Americans die in the nation's hospitals, revealed a hospital culture whose needs superceded those of its patients, and it prompted calls for widespread changes in how physicians, nurses, and other hospital personnel treat people in their final days of life.

LIFE, DEATH, AND MEDICINE

Beginning with its triumphs over infectious diseases nearly a century ago, medicine has become the institution within which American society wages its "war" against death. According to sociologist Michael Kearl (1989:442),

> "as the medical establishment has grown in power and prestige, . . . its practitioners have come to professionally monopolize its healing rituals, the costs of its services have skyrocketed, making the quality of health care dependent on the ability to pay. Further, medicine has become the instrument by which death is culturally banished, institutionally hidden, and psychologically denied. For the dying individual, the medicalization of death has resulted in deindividualization and loss of control."

THE PHYSICIAN

As the medical institution has evolved during the twentieth century, physicians have come to occupy the status of high priests in American society. After all, it is the medical doctor to whom we entrust our lives, to whom we turn to salve our pain and to birth our babies. The physician is also responsible for being on the front line in the "battle" against death, for diagnosis, care, and notification of death.

Involved as it is with issues of life and death, the occupation of medical doctor is among the most prestigious in American society. The high-priest status of the medical doctor is also reflected in a mean annual income of $150,000, double the income of other professionals such as dentists and lawyers, and triple and quadruple the average income of America's K–12 teachers (American Medical Association, 1995). And yet, according to Kearl (1989:423), "it is also one of the most self-destructive of all professions. Physicians commit suicide at three times the rate of the population at large. As many physicians take their own life each year as graduate from Harvard Medical School." In addition, the cultural high-priest status of physicians, their professional authority, as well as their income, are undergoing dramatic change in this era of managed care.

BiZarro   by Dan Piraro

Today, in addition to their increasingly tarnished image as high priests, doctors are pressured more and more to serve as society's double agents. Medical ethicist Marcia Angell (1993:1) states, "[D]octors are no longer simply agents for their patients. They are now agents for society's needs as well. They are, in short, double agents, expected to decide whether the benefits of treatment to their patients are worth the costs to society." What precisely are doctors supposed to do as double agents? In a nutshell, doctors are supposed to tailor their care of patients to save money for third parties, including Medicare, hospitals, health maintenance organizations (HMOs), and other managed care entities. Their changing status is affecting physicians' attitudes toward their own profession, as well as their finances.

The American Medical Association, in a 1995 national survey of physicians, reported a drop of annual earnings for physicians from $156,000 to $150,000 in 1994, the first drop in earnings reported in the past 14 years. In a 1995 survey of young physicians conducted by the California Medical Association, nearly one-third said they would not choose to become a physician if making that decision today, while 79% reported that their patient-care decisions were sometimes or frequently influenced by financial issues. Less than 10% reported that they were satisfied or very satisfied with managed care organizations, while about two-thirds said they were dissatisfied with the amount of time they could spend with patients (CMA, 1995).

DEATH AVOIDANCE

Studies have found that many physicians are highly death avoidant (Glaser & Strauss, 1965; Kubler-Ross, 1969; Backer, Hannon, & Russell, 1982). In reviewing these studies, Kearl (1989) offers a number of reasons for this tendency on the part of physicians actually to avoid dying patients under their care. One factor is the basic personality structure of many physicians, who have been found to have, on the average, an inordinately high fear of death, often stemming from childhoods that were struck by a death or serious illness in the family (Toufexis & Castronoro, 1983; Schulz & Aderman, 1980). A second reason for physicians' death avoidance is medical training itself, during which medical students tend to be taught that death is evidence of personal and/or professional failure (Rabin & Rabin, 1970). In many cases, the lack of medical education on issues of death and dying, along with various medical school rituals, may have a desensitizing and dehumanizing effect on medical students' attitudes toward death and dying (Backer, Hannon, & Russell, 1982; Kearl, 1989). Another reason for this death avoidance hinges on the fact that the dominant medical model has been historically cocooned in the Cartesian-Newtonian scientific view of the world (Marrone, 1990). As a consequence, the average physician tends to have a narrow idea of the factors necessary for quality of life, and a limited understanding of the more elusive psychosocial factors that play a role in death and dying as well as in life and living (Kearl, 1989).

Italian thanatologist Franco Toscani (1990) argues that the physicians' avoidance of death and resistance to palliative care and comforting of the dying patient, as opposed to "curing" the dying patient, is rooted in scientific elitism. He says it encompasses several psychological factors, including a denial of death through banalization and routinization, the perception of death as a threat to the self-image as a physician, and a medical "machismo" image that harmonizes uneasily with the "maternal" image of comfort care.

Israeli psychiatrist Meira Weiss (1993) explains some of the routine behavior of physicians in the hospital setting as directed at marking the territorial boundaries of his or her high-priest(ess) status and threats to that status. This behavior also functions to permit physicians control over entering and departing from the more culturally marginal regions of human experience, such as those dealing with death, waste, or sex, experiences that people try to avoid, deny, or mask in everyday life. In this sense, according to M. Weiss (1993:236), the high-priest status of physicians creates a controlled space in which "everyday reality is masked and turned into play, creating a boundary between the medical reality and the social world." As a result, medical professionals, especially during this era of managed care, HMOs, and cost/benefit analyses, often forget that human beings are more than simple biological organisms struggling to survive or money machines generating new revenue streams. They sometimes forget that the dying, in addition to their biological needs, also have social, psychological, spiritual, and comfort needs that must be addressed.

Death = Failure = Evasion

Physicians and nurses undergo extensive training in the science of saving lives, and their inability to save a life tends to symbolize powerlessness as well as a failure to control. As a consequence of their frustration, some medical personnel tend to exhibit anger and resentment toward dying patients by treating them differently from other patients. "Good patients," according to Aiken (1994:299), "are those who make the staff look good, they do what they are expected to and do not cause a lot of trouble. 'Bad' patients, on the other hand, are those who cause trouble by not getting well or by dying at the wrong time."

Avoiding a dying patient as much as possible is one particularly well-used method of coping. In fact, research by Gordon and Klass (1979) has shown that staff contact with a patient declines abruptly when the illness is diagnosed as "terminal." Medical personnel report that when they've exhausted all forms of medical intervention, it is difficult to walk into the patient's room each day because there is an unspoken but pervasive idea that the death of a patient represents a failure on the part of attending physician, nurses, and other medical professionals (Kearl, 1989:425; Barrow & Smith, 1983:364). According to Aiken (1994:299), "The hospital staff may become abrupt and tense with dying patients and confess that they don't want them to die on their shift." Sociologist D. Sudnow (1967), in a classic investigation of the organizational aspects of dying in an institution, studied a hospital staff in which it was common practice for aides or orderlies to prop up or ignore patients who died on their shift, leaving it for orderlies on the next shift to take responsibility for wrapping and moving the body to the hospital morgue.

Kastenbaum and Aisenberg (1976) found that the typical response of medical staff members confronted with talk of dying by the patient often involves *evasion* through distraction and professional role-playing. Of course, not all medical staff members employ the same approach in responding to a patient's desire to discuss death and dying. Other strategies noted by these researchers include: (1) reassurance ("You're doing so well"), (2) denial ("Oh, you'll live to be a hundred"), (3) changing the subject ("Let's talk about something more cheerful"), (4) fatalism ("Well, we all have to die sometime"), and (5) authentic discussion and communication ("What happened to make you feel this way?").

GRAND DECEPTION

"What tormented Ivan Ilych most was the deception, the lie, which for some reason they all accepted, that he was not dying but was simply ill and that he only need keep quiet and undergo a treatment and then something very good would result. He, however, knew that do what they would nothing would come of it, only still more agonizing suffering and death. This deception tortured him—their not wishing to admit what they all knew and what he knew, but wanting to lie to him concerning his terrible condition, and wishing and forcing him to participate in that lie. Those lies, lies enacted over him on the eve of his death and destined to degrade this awful, solemn act to the level of their visitings, their curtains, their sturgeon for dinner—were a terrible agony for Ivan Ilych. And strangely enough, many times when they were going through their antics over him he had been within a hair-breadth of calling out to them: 'Stop lying! You know and I know that I am dying. Then at least stop lying about it!' But he had never had the spirit to do it. The awful, terrible act of his dying was, he could see, reduced by those about him to the level of a casual, unpleasant, and almost indecorous incident (as if someone entered a drawing-room diffusing an unpleasant odor) and this was done by that very decorum which he had served all his life long. He saw that no one felt for him, because no one even wished to grasp his position."

Source: Tolstoy (1960, pp. 137–138).

SOCIAL DEATH AND DEPERSONALIZATION: "THE COMA IN 502"

Sociologists have long recognized *social death,* in which the person is alive but is treated as if dead by medical personnel, family, and friends (Doka, 1996). Sociologist Jeanne Guillemin (1996:101), for example, notes the plight of intensive care unit (ICU) patients who have to live attached to machines, be "worked on" by teams of strangers, lie among other patients near death or already dead, be surrounded by and totally dependent on wires and machines, while often alone and in pain. She states, "For years, medical staff have known about '**I.C.U. psychosis,**' the severe and not uncommon disorientation of patients reacting to the windowless, mechanical environment. For years, the only remedy has been to set a clock where the patient could see it." In all these cases, according to Doka (1996:205), where the dying person is in ICU., comatose, or isolated in a nursing or convalescent home, loved ones experience a form of disenfranchised grief in which "spouses and others may experience a profound sense of loss, but that loss cannot be publicly acknowledged for the person is still biologically alive."

Death is not the ultimate tragedy of life, according to Norman Cousins (1979). The ultimate tragedy is **depersonalization**—dying in a strange and sterile environment, isolated from spiritual nourishment, unable to reach out to a loving hand, separated from the persons and experiences that make life worth living, and disconnected from hope. Cut off from their own feelings of empathy and caring, some medical personnel depersonalize patients by robbing them "of their personhood—depersonalizing them into transparent stereotypes and objects of manipulation" (Marrone, 1990:12). Depersonalization, which is reflected in the tendency to refer to patients by a specific disease and room number rather than by a personal name, is most marked when the patient is most helpless.

The depersonalization of the hospital patient is seen most clearly in patients who are comatose. Physicians may not talk to comatose patients believing that they do not hear or respond, that speaking to them will not affect their clinical

C A R I N G   I N S I G H T S

Relating to Comatose Persons

La Puma and colleagues (1988) suggest that when caring for comatose persons, physicians, nurses, staff members, and loved ones should identify themselves to the persons, greet and recognize the persons by name, tell them the reason for their visit, explain any new developments, describe any procedures that are planned for the day, and say words that might be comforting, because they may hear, they might recover, and, most importantly, they are fellow human beings in need of care and affection.

outcomes, and that time spent chatting with a comatose patient is a waste of time. According to La Puma et al. (1988:20–21), "[N]ot talking to comatose patients may promulgate the notion that these patients are dead or nearly dead, and promote the inappropriate withholding or withdrawing of therapy. . . . Comatose patients may, however, hear, may have normal brain-stem auditory evoked responses and normal physiological responses to auditory stimuli. . . . [N]ot talking should not become a self-fulfilling prophesy."

DEATH NOTIFICATION: THE CONSPIRACY OF SILENCE

The physician's tendency toward death avoidance often becomes clear when a patient has been diagnosed with a terminal illness. Numerous studies have shown that many physicians resist informing these patients of their terminality, insisting that the terminally ill do not want to know about the critical nature of their situation because such knowledge would shatter all their hope and, thereby, accelerate their death. Sociologist Michael Kearl (1989:427) cites a University of Texas study of 3,000 physicians in which 47% said they try to avoid telling a patient directly that he or she is dying, and another 27% admitted that "they avoid a dying person altogether."

Many medical personnel rationalize these conspiracies of silence on professional grounds, arguing that a patient should not be told he or she has only 6 weeks, 6 months, or any finite amount of time to live, because (1) such information may cause the patient to give up or attempt suicide, (2) the physician may not really know how long a person has to live (e.g., there is always the possibility of remission), and (3) there is always the possibility that a cure will be found (McCormick 1980; Shneidman, 1973). Unfortunately, this silence, which is supposedly for the good of the patient, often leaves him or her to face death psychologically alone, a petrified, dehumanized body coupled to a collection of sterilized tubes and stainless steel devices. (Aiken, 1994)

To the dying patient, according to Aiken (1994), it may appear as though loved ones, physicians, and nurses are collaborating in a conspiracy of silence, a conspiracy that the patient may also comprehend and accede to. Glaser and Strauss (1965) elaborated on four different renditions of the game of silence: *closed awareness,* in which the medical staff knows that certain of their patients are dying but these patients are simply not informed and remain unaware of their impending death; *suspicious awareness,* a variation of the closed awareness scenario in which the patient suspects that he or she is dying and is left wondering why this crucial information is not forthcoming; and *mutual pretense awareness,* a further modification of the closed awareness game in which family, medical staff, and the terminally ill patient are all aware that death is imminent but all pretend it is not. Glaser and Strauss (1965) note how often children are forced to play this complex game of mutual pretense, hypocrisy, deception, and false hope. Finally, with increasing frequency, medical personnel are coming to realize that the overwhelming majority of terminally ill patients, including children, do wish to be told the truth and feel betrayed if it is withheld (Blackhall et al., 1995). As a result, increasing numbers of medical professionals engage in an *open awareness* scenario so that they, along with loved ones and the terminally ill patient, acknowledge the likelihood of death and are open with one another in honestly discussing that likelihood, with all its ramifications (Blackhall et al., 1995; Ferrigno, 1996).

Research suggests that, for physicians, conspiracy of silence strategies are taught in their medical school training. Williams (1992), for example, conducted research in the gross anatomy laboratory of a medical school to explore the communication restrictions among faculty and students during human cadaver dissection. The cognitive and affective responses of participants were explored over a 14-week period. Focus was on the history and maintenance of the faculty's tacit prohibition against discussion of their own and their students' attitudes about illness, dying, and death. According to Williams, a twofold strain was observed: one involving the difficulty medical professors encountered in handling their own discomfort with this yearly ritual, and the other involved the anxiety experienced by medical students, for whom this was a first experience. The parallel tension remained unrecognized throughout the course and was, in fact, heightened by a "conspiracy of silence" between professors and students and between students and their peers. Williams points to the need of medical school faculty to become comfortable with their own concerns about death and dying if they are to encourage their students to acknowledge and express similar concerns.

This gap, between what a majority of dying patients desire from the physician and the physician's perception of the patient's needs, is not confined to the West. Kai et al. (1993), for example, assessed patient–physician communication about terminal care in Japan by examining the accuracy of physicians' estimation of their patients' preferences regarding information about diagnosis and prognosis, the place of death, and the therapeutic strategy at terminal stage (life prolongation versus pain control). A questionnaire was administered to 201 inpatients (age 40+ years) in one urban and two rural hospitals. Forty physicians in charge of these patients estimated their attitudes. Results revealed that although 80% of the patients

THE GAME

"Consider, for example, the story of Mrs. Phillips, a 73-year-old widow diagnosed with terminal stomach cancer. After exploratory surgery two weeks earlier, her family was informed of the prognosis, but she was not. Mrs. Phillips started noticing a change in her family members' behavior and began receiving many unexpected visits, such as from her grandchildren, who usually only visited during the summers. She had only seen her physician once since her surgery, and nothing had been discussed at that time. She became very suspicious and angry. According to a son, all of the family members refused to talk about 'it' and did not want her informed. Finally, after three days of this, the son convinced his siblings that their mother should be told the truth, and they requested that her physician be the one to confront her.

But Mrs. Phillips knew, as do most terminally ill patients, and did not have any great difficulty accepting her fate. What she did feel was anger, anger toward both the physician and *her* family for withholding her information. 'I'm entitled to any information about myself. It's only my body that has deteriorated, not my mind.' She then felt a growing distance between herself and family members and experienced loneliness. She wanted so much to discuss her fate, but the family would only 'talk about mundane things' or about themselves. Mrs. Phillips was not a winner in the ritual of exit game of death."

Source: Kearl (1989), p. 427.

preferred candid information on diagnosis and prognosis, regardless of the nature of their disease, physicians were correct in estimation in only one-half of the cases. One-sixth of the physicians' guesses were in the opposite direction, and about one-third failed to make any estimation at all. Seventy percent of the patients wished to die at home, while physicians estimated this correctly only 50% of the time. Japanese physicians also underestimated the fact that two-thirds of the patients preferred pain control over life prolongation.

DEATH NOTIFICATION OF THE PATIENT

Notifying a person that he or she is dying is never an easy task. Following some degree of shock and denial, the first question put to the physician is usually, "So how long do I have left to live?" In his review of patient death notification techniques, psychotraumatologist R. Moroni Leash (1994) has noted a number of suggestions made by physicians as to how to go about this delicate task. Australian physician R. C. Charlton (1992:615−621) notes that the patient's question "How long do I have to live?" is really an impossible question because "the time left can rarely be quantified (and estimates will invariably be wrong), so the doctor should concentrate on the good quality of life that exists at present." Charlton suggests that the discussion of prognosis in terms of finite time "is appropriate only when the prognosis is appropriately measured in a few days to a few weeks," because exact estimates for longer periods cannot be made with any certainty. As an alternative, it is suggested that longer periods of prognostic time be given in terms of median survival rates—for example, "You have a 50/50 chance of living another 5 years." This notification technique allows the patient to adapt his or her personal philosophy to the situation, such as "I'll beat the odds" or "I may not be here in a few years, so I'll make the best of my life now" (Langlands, 1991:1428; Leash, 1994).

Leash (1994) also notes that familiarity with various patient-engaging responses may be enormously helpful at this time. For example, he cites responses such as "Statistically, it looks bad . . . (but) some people, against all the odds, do amazingly well" and "The situation is serious, but far from hopeless—you have a chance of doing well." He also advocates forms of "indirect reassurance," such as "What will you do for your holiday next year if you are fit enough?" (Leash, 1994:195; Brewin, 1991). In some cases, the medical professional might consider turning the question back to the patient, saying, "How long do you want to live?" Leash observed that the answers to such queries were often surprising and candid, such as "until after Christmas" or "until after my son John's graduation in June," and were additionally helpful in allowing the physician to encourage the patient or to inform the patient sensitively that her or his hopes for life probably were not realistic or helpful (Leash, 1994:195; Fletcher, 1992). Hogshead (1978) recommends that, when telling a patient that his or her condition is terminal, physicians should do the following.

On March 21, 1984, Colleen, a 20-year-old model, shot herself with a .22-caliber rifle. By midnight her mother had been notified of the shooting, which was to prove fatal, and frantically called the hospital to ask about her condition. "Her condition," she was told, "is the bullet went in one side of her head and came out the other side. What do you want me to tell you?"

Source: People Weekly Magazine, March 14, 1988, p. 86.

- Keep the information simple.
- Try to understand what the diagnosis means to the patient.
- Don't reveal all the information at once, but don't say anything that is not true.
- Wait for the patient's questions, and answer them honestly.
- Don't argue with the patient who attempts to deny information.
- Ask the patient to repeat or paraphrase what has been said.
- Don't destroy all hope in the patient.

DEATH NOTIFICATION OF LOVED ONES

Based on his extensive study of death notification techniques among health care providers and death notification requirements among bereaved families, Leash (1994) has developed the *Sequential Notification Technique.* The value of this technique, according to Leash, is that it does not involve a prolonged dialogue with the family, but does provide sufficient structure to prepare the family for the ultimate statement of death. He states (1994:51−52):

> After gathering the necessary information and bringing the family to a suitable location, the notifier should then:
>
> - Ask the family members what they already know about the situation.
> - Bridging from what they know, give a *brief* description of additional events that led up to the patient's arrival at the hospital.
> - Give information regarding resuscitative efforts made on behalf of the patient at the hospital.
> - Conclude with the victim's response to treatment, the statement of death, and a brief explanation of the cause of death.

Some medical schools have already integrated these and other notification techniques into the curriculum. Tolle et al. (1989), for example, report on an educational program that models humanistic attitudes and encourages empathic behavior in internal medicine residents, using role-playing sessions focusing on physicians' interactions with family members after a patient's death. The program is judged successful by participants because training sessions are held during orientation, have direct clinical relevance to their work as physicians, and are realistic simulations of family death-notification issues that are likely to arise in a variety of hospital situations.

MEDICAL EDUCATION, DENIAL, AND REPRESSION

By learning how to repress feelings and how to deny attitudes and apprehensions about death and dying, many medical students learn the defensive maneuver of objectifying themselves and observing death from an impersonal and purely biomedical point of view. Ley and Corless (1988) suggest that scientific thought has sliced understanding of the person into parts and that the emotional, cognitive, social, and spiritual concerns of the person have not been considered the proper role of the community of physicians or a part of medical school education. Thorson and Powell (1991), for example, examined changes in attitudes toward older persons and in attitudes toward personal death anxiety in

Death Notification

Based on his extensive experience as a psychotraumatologist, R. Moroni Leash (1994:53) offers the following example of a family death notification, which follows Sequential Notification Technique guidelines:

"Hello, Mrs. Jones. My name is Moroni Leash. I am a social worker here at the hospital. What could you tell me about what happened to Mr. Jones today?"

"Well, Fred and I were at home when he started having pain in his arm. It bothered him more and more, even after he took his medicine. He went to the bedroom to lie down and rest, and when I checked on him 15 or 20 minutes later, I noticed he wasn't breathing and I couldn't wake him up. I called for an ambulance right then. Please tell me how he's doing!"

"Mrs. Jones, Fred came in under CPR, and we continued that for some time, about 30–40 or more minutes. There are certain medicines and procedures that can sometimes restart a heart that has stopped beating. We did everything we could, but it became obvious that we wouldn't be able to revive him."

"Is he . . . dead, then?"

"Yes, Mrs. Jones, he died a couple of minutes ago."

three entering classes of medical students. As graduating seniors, these students again completed scales measuring attitudes toward older persons, death anxiety, and dying. Significant attitudinal changes did not occur among the physicians-in-training.

This objectified, disembodied approach to medical intervention helps the physician to maintain professional distance from the patient so as not to become emotionally involved—but at great cost to the patient and, in the long run, to the physician as well (Redding, 1980; Kearl, 1989). In addition, this education in denial, repression, and depersonalization continues to produce a hospital culture that often dehumanizes patients in their final days of life, is insensitive to their pain, isolates them without regard for their psychological, social, and spiritual needs, in many cases, disregards their dying wishes regarding terminal care, and treats them as revenue streams, at least until the stream of money runs dry. This hospital culture is headed by high-priest physicians who, often, have little or no training in how to communicate with their dying patients and their families about what death involves and what their rights are. In some cases, they appear to be more committed to maintaining their own opulent lifestyles and artificial authority than in changing the hospital culture to one that is humanized and committed to recognizing the dignity of the dying person.

THE NURSE AS NURTURER

Nursing students do not appear to undergo the same degree of desensitization to death in their training as do medical students. Sandor Brent et al. (1991), for example, in an investigation of attitudes toward dying patients among 424 undergraduate and graduate nursing students, found that death aversiveness significantly decreased, attractiveness significantly increased, and overall attitude became more positive as the number, extent, and specificity of death-related experiences increased during nursing school training. Unlike the medical student's education, the nurses' educational experiences made a significant contribution toward reducing their aversion and increasing their attraction toward the care of dying patients.

Other researchers have questioned whether resistance to dealing with dying patients is based on the attitudes that medical professionals bring to their careers. Sandor Brent et al. (1992), for instance, compared beginning medical and nursing students with no professional death-related experience in order to discover the attitudes they bring to their careers prior to their professional socialization. On five of the six attitude measures, female nursing students expressed a more positive attitude than male medical students and, contrary to conventional wisdom, the attitudes of female medical students were no more positive than those of males. Among physicians-in-training, hours of death-and-dying course-work and life experience did exert a significant influence on attitudes toward talking to dying patients about death, but did not change any of the other attitude measures over time.

Although some physicians continue to deny or rationalize their own attitudes toward death, terminal illness, and telling dying patients of their terminal prognosis, recent research suggests that these attitudes are changing. Dickinson and Tournier (1994) surveyed 1,664 physicians soon after graduation from medical school in 1976 to determine their attitudes toward death and terminally ill patients and their families. A follow-up survey of respondents was made 10 years later to ascertain if changes had occurred in their attitudes. Results revealed that physicians in 1986 were more open in telling dying patients their prognosis than in 1976. Ley and Corliss (1988) argue that the hospice movement and the aging U.S. population may be factors that are bringing aspects of personhood back into consideration by health care professionals. Heller (1996) points out that the AIDS epidemic, in forcing young physicians and medical students to treat patients closer to their own age, may be playing a role in breaking down old stereotypes, in stimulating empathy, and in making young physicians more sensitive to the psychological, social, and spiritual needs of dying patients. In light of these changes, it is interesting to note that it was not until 1972 that the specific area of death-education courses for medical students was first addressed (Liston, 1975). Before this course, instituted by David Barton at Vanderbilt University, medical students were completely on their own in dealing with dying patients.

PROFESSIONAL BURNOUT

Part of the resistance by medical professionals to dealing authentically with death and dying may well be the result of the absence of legitimate venues and rituals

"[We] may cry for rest, peace and dignity, but we will get infusions, transfusions, a heart machine, or tracheotomy if necessary. We may want one single person to stop for one single minute so we can ask a single question—but we will get a dozen people around the clock, all busily preoccupied with heart rate, pulse, electrocardiogram or pulmonary functions . . . Is the reason for this increasingly mechanical, depersonalized approach our own defensiveness? Is this our way to cope with and repress the anxieties that a terminally ill or critically ill patient evokes in us? Is this our way . . . to displace all our knowledge onto machines, since they are less close to us than the suffering face of another human being which would remind us of . . . our own mortality?"

Source: Kubler-Ross, E. (1969:8–9).

for handling their feelings of loss and grieving. The absence of such opportunities may also play a role in professional burnout.

In a paper on minimizing professional **burnout** in caregivers, Nursing Professor Marilyn Rawnsley (1990:144) argues that the relationship between a physician, nurse, or other professional caregiver and a terminally ill person is a unique one in that the caregiver's grief is both unrecognized and expected to be so. She states:

In view of the context and content of the encounters . . . and the way in which the relationship predictably ends, the caregiver is postulated to be a hidden survivor. Lacking the legitimacy of kinship, masked by professional precepts, and constricted from confronting personal loss through any socially sanctioned ritual, the survivor is unrecognized and thus is deprived of valid grief.

"A TRANQUILIZER, A SHOT . . . ANYTHING!"

"A young black woman came to visit her brother in the hospital, only to find that he had died unexpectedly an hour before her visit. She cried out her grief unrestrainedly, sobbing violently and calling her brother's name over and over. The medical resident grabbed the passing consultation psychiatrist and said, 'Please give her some tranquilizers, a shot, anything. She is completely out of control!' The psychiatrist refused but took the young woman into a quiet room and stayed with her. Within a half hour her acute grief abated and she was able to collect herself, begin the painful task of calling her family, and start the arduous process of preparing for an unexpected funeral.

"Health care providers are often at a loss as to how to deal with expressions of grief. . . . [T]he outright expression of grief frightens us and leaves us feeling helpless. Many a medical student or young resident, left with the difficult task of informing family members of a recent death, ask, 'What are we to do if they fall apart and cry?'

"The expectation that we keep tight control over emotions and repress our grief takes its toll on many of us."

Source: Seeland (1990), pp. 53–54.

The professional caregiver—whether physician, nurse, psychologist, social worker, or grief counselor—is challenged to overcome a very basic conflict between (a) growing close to the dying patient and having to deal with disenfranchised and unrecognized grief later and (b) remaining aloof and removed from the dying patient in the here and now and, thus, becoming a reluctant helper confronted with a different set of problems likely to culminate after the patient's death.

The key to change involves legitimizing grief and providing the opportunity for professional staff to talk about their experiences. Waldman (1990:156) states, "This grief must be legitimized, sanctioned and finally . . . addressed in a manner facilitating verbalization and conver-

sation. Grief is an active, not a passive process. Freud rightfully labeled it 'work.' Our first labor, then, must be to untie the ribbons on the mask which hides this very real issue."

GENUINE CARING

Although there is a tendency for some medical personnel to become detached specialists and professional spectators who protect themselves from disturbing thoughts and emotions, many other doctors and nurses genuinely care for their dying patients. These medical professionals have learned to cope with death and dying and to accept death as a natural event rather than as a sign of their failure to keep the patient alive at all cost (Ferrigno, 1996). Patterson (1989), for example, discusses the unique characteristics of pediatricians in terms of how they help in ministering to the needs of the dying child and his or her family. Pediatricians have been found to have more need to assist and attend to their patients, to be protective of mothers, and to be more desirous of love and affection from others.

In another study, Gerber (1990) collected verbal reports from twenty male cardiac or cancer surgeons concerning two of their patients whose surgery had not been successful and who were likely to die within the next year. Many surgeons in this study, in genuinely facing the death of another human being, reported experiences of transformation in their own self-understanding, including a sense of self-forgiveness and acceptance, a strengthened feeling of human connectedness, an enhanced sense of meaning about what they were doing, and a feeling of openness and hope for the future. Research findings also suggest that physicians' attitudes toward death and terminally ill patients change positively as they age. Durand et al. (1990), for example, in a survey of 441 family physicians, found that physicians age 50+ years had a significantly more positive attitude toward death than did physicians ages 25–34, as did those who had a strong religious or spiritual orientation, or those who had received death-education instruction during their medical school training.

Medical and nursing schools in the 1990s are likely to offer their students some version of a course in death and dying, and continuing education requirements in many states now involve short courses in dealing with death and dying. Merman, Gunn, and Dickinson (1991), in a report on a 1991 survey of 111 U.S. medical schools and offerings related to death-and-dying education, found that twelve (11%) provided no formal teaching in death and dying at all. Of the ninety-nine schools that did, thirty provided one or two lectures in the first two years, fifty-one of the schools taught death and dying as a shorter module of a larger required course, and eighteen schools taught it as a separate course. Lecture was the predominant teaching method, and patient participation was usually restricted to a class presentation.

Critical of some of these training seminars and modules, Gunn and Dickinson (1991) describe a death-and-dying seminar developed at Yale University that enables students to learn the personal impact of serious illness, coping techniques used in daily living, characteristics of the caring physician, and skills needed to provide compassionate care. These and similar training programs are designed to assist medical personnel in establishing greater rapport with terminally ill persons and their families and thus to help them view death less fearfully and with greater dignity for the dying patient. One important component of some of these

training programs, termed the ***psychological autopsy,*** involves an in-depth postmortem analysis by medical and nursing personnel of the psychosocial aspects of the patient's death and how they may have contributed to or eased the dying process (Kastenbaum, 1991; Aiken, 1994). Data are gathered from interviews, documents, and other materials to determine the mode of death, personnel and patient mood states during the course of the dying trajectory, and psychosocial stressors present during caregiving (Young, 1992).

The promotion of humanistic education in schools of medicine and nursing is encouraging and may introduce purpose into a sphere that has been described as "a highly sophisticated and profoundly primitive halfway medical technology" (Rawnsley, 1990:146). But, as Rawnsley points out, the physician and nurse do not have to bear the entire burden of emotional care for the terminally ill patient. Other nonmedical professionals, such as psychologists, trauma counselors, social workers, grief counselors, and pastoral counselors, have a role to play in caregiving to the terminally ill. Krant (1974:91) suggests that the presence of other professionals trained to deal with the issues of meaning, communion, and support for the dying patient might allow the physician and nurse to direct all of her or his energies into the "life-oriented, cure-structured primary role."

Although specific education aimed at training new health care professionals to deal with death and dying may be both a viable and a desirable option, it is clearly not current practice in medical and nursing education programs or in most hospitals. At the present time, according to Rawnsley (1990:146), "interested individuals from the fields of social work, ministry, nursing, psychology, physical and rehabilitation therapy, and others comprise an amorphous subculture within the health care provider system. In general, these caregivers, invisible behind disciplinary barriers, practice in relative isolation from their colleagues and each other."

Dying at Home

Home care is essentially a 24-hour-a-day endeavor whose main ingredient is the presence of a willing-and-able family member or friend to attend to the various tasks that constitute proper care for the terminally ill and dying. In spite of the more formal services offered by nursing homes and convalescent hospitals, informal caregivers continue to provide 80% of long-term care to older adults in the United States (U.S. Select Committee on Aging, 1994).

To many families, home care is recognized as a critical factor in preventing or delaying nursing home placement of their loved one (Pilisuk & Parks, 1988). The home setting provides an alternative to the sometimes-dehumanizing experience of hospitals and convalescent homes, offering greater opportunities for maintaining old relationships and connectedness to neighborhood and community. It can, however, become a heavy burden and create great stress in both the caregiver and care-recipient.

HOME CAREGIVING IN AMERICA

Although anyone can become a caregiver, home caregivers tend to be women who on average are 57 years old. Adult children caring for a frail or terminally ill

parent tend to be between 40 and 59 years old. Most are married women with families of their own, but an estimated 44% of caregiving daughters and 55% of caregiving sons are employed outside the home (Blieszner & Alley, 1990). These statistics suggest that many adult children caring for their parents have family and work obligations that may conflict with caregiving responsibilities.

Caregiving spouses tend to be in their late 60s and 70s. When compared to the general population, older caregivers are less likely to be employed and more likely to be poor or near poor and in fair to poor health. The majority of caregivers have been providing care for 1 to 4 years, 80% of family caregivers provide unpaid assistance 7 days a week, and primary caregivers report spending between 4 and 6 hours a day in caregiving duties (Stone, Cafferata, & Sangl, 1987; Pilisik & Parks, 1988; Barrow, 1996).

In the past 20 years, the older population in America has grown twice as quickly as all other age groups. The 85-and-older age group is expected to be seven times its present size by the year 2050 (National Center for Health Statistics, 1995a). This population trend, which could result in a large number of chronically ill and terminally ill elderly people in need of caregiving services is accompanied by several other trends that suggest that home caregiving may become more difficult to provide in the years to come.

The most commonly cited of these trends are an increase in life expectancy, a decrease in the birth rate, and an increase in the participation of women in the labor force (Montgomery & Borgatta, 1989; Pratt & Kethley, 1988; Wisendale & Allison, 1988). The increased life expectancy may result in caregivers themselves being older adults. Individuals in their 60s or 70s may find themselves being the primary caregivers for terminally ill parents or other relatives in their 80s or 90s. The increase in childlessness and the trend toward having fewer children will result in there being fewer adult children to care for a greater number of older adults in the future. The trend toward more women being employed leaves these traditional caregivers little time to care for an elderly relative. The increased divorce rate, along with increased geographic mobility and dispersion of families, will also make it difficult for families to provide the care needed by the elderly and the dying in the future (Barrow, 1996).

BURDEN AND STRESS: HOW HOME CAREGIVERS COPE

Social isolation has been cited as the most stressful infringement on the caregivers of moderately and severely impaired persons (U.S. Select Committee on Aging, 1994; Blieszner & Alley, 1990; Montgomery, Gonyea, & Hooyman, 1985). Role conflict resulting from the competing demands of the care-recipient, other family obligations, and employment responsibilities have also been reported as among the major complaints of caregivers. Seventy-seven percent of employed women who also provide care reported experiencing a conflict between work and caregiving demands, and 35% believed that being a caregiver adversely affected their work role (U.S. Select Committee on Aging, 1994).

In addition to competing roles, many caregivers must adjust to a change in their relationship with the care-recipient (Blieszner & Alley, 1990). Barusch's (1988) study of elderly spouse caregivers found that the most prevalent problem involved ongoing grieving over the loss of the spouse they once knew.

CARING INSIGHTS

Caregiving at Home

- Maintain close ties with relatives and friends.
- Discuss your care-recipient's wishes regarding health care, terminal medical care alternatives, and disposition of his or her personal assets.
- Find sources of help such as chore services, housekeeping, home-delivered meals, senior recreation, day care, respite care, and transportation assistance.
- With the care-recipient's consent, become familiar with his or her financial records, bank accounts, will, safe deposit boxes, insurance, debts, and sources of income before he or she becomes incapacitated. Talk and plan together now about how these affairs should be handled.
- Anticipate potential incapacitation by planning as a family who will take responsibility such as power-of-attorney, living will, and in-home caregiving if an aging relative becomes incapacitated.
- Closely examine your family's ability to provide long-term, in-home care for a frail and increasingly dependent relative. Consider the family's physical limits.
- Plan how your own needs will be met when your responsibility for the dependent older relative increases.
- Explore alternative sources of care, including nursing homes and other relatives' homes, in case your situation changes.
- Don't offer personal home care unless you thoroughly understand and can meet the responsibilities and costs involved.
- Don't assume that poor interpersonal relationships between you, or other members of the household, and the care-recipient will disappear.
- Don't hamper the care-recipient's independence or intrude unnecessarily on his or her privacy.
- Don't label your efforts a failure if home care is not possible and you must seek an alternative.
- Call the American Association of Retired Persons for more information: 800-424-3410.

Seventy-six percent reported worrying about their own health and what would happen if they became ill. Many expressed some form of generalized anxiety about the future, and 67% reported feeling depressed.

Caregiving at home is a time-consuming responsibility that inflicts various limitations on the caregiver's personal life. Distinctions are often made between the caregiver's objective burden and subjective stress, with **objective burden** referring to the management and performance of physical tasks involving the

This ninety year old woman sits alone in her bedroom, looking out a window, wondering what the future holds for her. Her family lives far away and seldom visits her. She doesn't feel well most of the time, doesn't want to be burden, but is afraid of dying alone. © *Documentary Photo Aids/Mark Jury*

care-recipient, and ***subjective stress*** referring to the psychological strain on the caregiver (Montgomery, Gonyea, & Hooyman, 1985; Pilisuk & Parks, 1988). Both burden and stress must be examined in assessing the appropriateness of the home care relationship.

The emotional stress and physical burdens of caregiving often lead to deterioration in the relationship as well as in the caregiver's own health. Several studies have shown that the degree of caregiver stress increases as the care-recipient's level of functional impairment becomes more severe (Blieszner & Alley, 1990; U.S. Select Committee on Aging, 1994). Many caregivers experience problems with the physical burdens of caregiving, such as difficulty in lifting or moving their loved one and difficulty in performing personal care tasks.

The most common coping response of the caregiving spouses studied by Barusch (1988) was to seek help when they had problems, especially in the areas of care management and health problems. The second most common response was simply not to cope with growing problems by minimizing their importance or denying that they were problems in the first place. Spouses reported not coping with sexual problems, guilt feelings, feeling their spouse was overly dependent, arguments with their spouse, excessive demands made by others, worries about future financial problems, managing money, and worries about their own health. One study found that 12% of caregivers drank alcohol to cope with the psychological strains of caregiving (Barusch, 1988). Deterioration in the relationship between the caregiver and the care-recipient can sometimes result in various forms of physical and psychological abuse, especially in the case of the frail or terminally ill elderly patient.

ELDER ABUSE: DEFINITIONS AND SIGNS

Passive neglect: Unintentional failure to fulfill a caretaking obligation; infliction of distress without conscious or willful intent.

Psychological abuse: Infliction of mental anguish by demeaning name-calling, insulting, ignoring, humiliating, frightening, threatening, isolating.

Material/financial abuse: Illegally or unethically exploiting by using funds, property, or other assets of an older person for personal gain.

Active neglect: Intentional failure to fulfill caregiving obligations; infliction of physical or emotional stress or injury; abandonment; denial of food, medication, personal hygiene.

Physical abuse: Infliction of physical pain or injury; physical coercion; confinement; slapping, bruising, sexually molesting, cutting, lacerating, burning, restraining, pushing, shoving.

SIGNS: Increasing depression, anxiety, withdrawal/timidity, hostility, unresponsiveness, confusion, physical injury, new poverty, longing for death, vague health complaints, anxiousness to please, proclivity to shop for physicians

Interventions designed to help caregivers cope with caregiver burden and stress have focused on individual coping strategies, respite services (e.g., adult day care), support groups, and other group interventions. Results from studies evaluating the effectiveness of different interventions have been mixed. Caregivers themselves report having the most success when they could somehow change a stressful situation and reported highest levels of satisfaction when they could change it alone (Barusch, 1988).

Respite Care

Compared with caregivers receiving no respite care, caregivers of Alzheimer's patients who had formal adult day care were able to keep their relatives out of institutions for a longer time (Lawton, Brody, & Saperstein, 1989;). Participants reported high levels of satisfaction with these respite services, yet respite neither alleviated caregiver burden nor promoted caregiver mental health significantly. A program that provided adult day care services to older adults with dementia did report a reduction of caregiver burden (Eddowes, 1988). A study by Larkin and Hopcraft (1993) examined the role of an in-hospital respite program on the stress level of twenty-three family caregivers of patients with Alzheimer's disease. Data on family stress levels obtained before, during, and following respite suggest that stress was alleviated to some degree by the respite program.

Group Interventions

Caregivers who have little time to meet their family, work, and caregiving responsibilities often feel they have no time left for support groups or other interventions. Many do not seek outside help until they have reached a crisis point. One study of family caregivers of dementia patients showed that, at posttreatment, caregivers who participated in support groups showed no greater change in caregiver depression, life satisfaction, coping, or social activity than did caregivers on a waiting list who received no group intervention (Haley, 1989). In another study, individuals caring for impaired elderly who received a combination of services, including seminars, support groups, family consultation services, and respite care, reported benefiting from the experience. One interesting finding from this study was the reluctance of participants to utilize services. In spite of free access and encouragement to use the services offered, almost one-third of caregivers did not do so (Montgomery and Borgatta, 1989). In some cases, private corporations have come to recognize their stake in caring for the elderly and dying, although only 3% of American companies have policies to assist employees who are caring for frail or terminally ill loved ones (Barrow, 1996). Some companies, such as Stride Rite Corporation, IBM, and The Travelers Insurance Company, have had elder care programs in place for many years.

The literature has illustrated that a variety of coping skills is often needed by caregivers in order to deal with a variety of problems. Barusch (1988) recommends that training programs teach techniques for personal control in order to help caregivers cope without outside help, but also provide information about community resources and discuss caregiver feelings about seeking and accepting help in an effort to prepare the caregivers for a time when they may be unable to cope alone. For many home caregivers, especially those who have made a realistic assessment of their responsibilities and who take advantage of community and family support opportunities, home caregiving can be a meaningful and workable experience, in spite of the burden and stress it imposes on them. Gerontologist Georgia Barrow (1996:314) notes that "the very fact of a death occurring at home can ward off psychological damage to the family. . . . Keeping a dying family member at home can both make it easier for relatives to accept the death and prevent the patient from being alone in the dying process." Internet resources and books are available to those considering caring for a dying family member at home. Some of these resources are presented in Chapter 12.

The Hospice Alternative

The word *hospice,* which means "host" or "guest" in Latin, was introduced during the Middle Ages to refer to a place where weary pilgrims were sheltered and cared for on their way to the Holy Land. Today, *hospice* refers to a comprehensive philosophy of compassionate care for the terminally ill. The centerpiece of this philosophy is that dying patients should be enabled and empowered to carry on an alert, pain-free life and manage other symptoms so their final days are spent with dignity and quality at home or in a homelike setting.

The Hospice movement has evolved in response to the recognized need to manage care better for patients and families in the end stages of illness when cure and rehabilitation are not possible. Unlike the dominant medical model, which focuses almost exclusively on the patient, the diagnosis, and the treatment

AFFIRMING LIFE

"The purpose of hospice is to provide support and care for people in the final phase of a terminal disease so that they can live as fully and comfortably as possible. Hospice affirms life and regards dying as a normal process. Hospice neither hastens nor postpones death. Hospice believes that through personalized services and a caring community patients and families can attain the necessary preparation for a death that is satisfactory to them."

Source: National Hospice Organization (1996)

regimen, hospice care is multifocused and includes coping with the psychosocial, spiritual, and economic issues as well as the medical problems related to the terminal illness. The goal for the patient, according to Carroll and Graner (1994), is to achieve and maintain comfort physically, emotionally, and spiritually. For the family, the hospice program attempts to nurture a sense of fulfillment and accomplishment so that loved ones may eventually be able to feel that they did all that they could, not in the realm of high-tech, life-prolonging medical intervention, but in the delivery of compassionate and comforting care (Lattanzi-Licht & Connor, 1995).

The modern hospice program took shape in the mid-1960s, when the efforts of two exceptional physicians, Elizabeth Kubler-Ross and Dame Cicely Saunders, intersected to bring the physical, psychological, social, and spiritual needs of the dying to the attention of professionals and laypeople. While Kubler-Ross was working at the University of Chicago Hospital, British physician Cicely Saunders founded St. Christopher's Hospice in London in 1967. Trained as a nurse, social worker, and physician, some have called Saunders "a whole Hospice team wrapped up in one person" (Gentile & Fello, 1990:1).

Saunders' approach to working with the dying began with a philosophy of comfort care. Here are the major elements of that care, as enunciated by Saunders (1980):

1. Control of the patient's pain and discomfort
2. Communicating effectively through discussions of death and dying between patients, family members, and medical staff
3. An interdisciplinary team approach
4. Facilitating death with dignity and a sense of self-worth rather than a depersonalized death with feelings of isolation and despair

As implied by this list, hospice care is centered on meeting not only the physical needs but also the social, emotional, and spiritual needs of terminally ill patients. The focus of this kind of treatment, according to Gentile and Fello (1990), is on coping with pain and depression, which are common companions of fatal illness, without making extraordinary efforts to prolong life. Hospice differs from other types of terminal health care in that the treatment is comfort-centered rather than cure-centered. The person rather than the disease is the focus of treatment, and care and quality of life is the all-consuming goal. This commitment to quality of life extends beyond the dying person to include the entire family as the unit of care.

Although active euthanasia (i.e., mercy killing) has frequently been proposed as a means of avoiding a painful death, Saunders has been a highly vocal opponent of efforts to legalize euthanasia. Aiken (1994:304) points out that to Saunders and other hospice advocates,

CARING INSIGHTS

Entering a Hospice Program

Only patients who are dying from cancer, AIDS, or other terminal illnesses are accepted for hospice treatment. Other criteria for admission include a prognosis of death in weeks or months, not years, and an agreement on the part of the referring physician to continue his or her association with the patient and cooperate in the treatment. The patient must live within a reasonable distance of the hospice, and a primary caregiver (spouse, relative, trusted friend) must agree to take continuing responsibility for the care of the patient. These criteria vary somewhat with the particular setting, but they have been adopted by most hospices. Once a patient has been accepted for hospice care, a treatment program centered on the features just described, but also designed to meet the patient's individual needs, is put into action.

the pain experienced by dying people—not only physical but also psychological and spiritual pain—does not require a speeding up of death but can be controlled in a specially designed environment. Thus, the goal of hospice treatment is similar to that expressed in Saunders' original (1980) conception of the term—an easy or painless death, but not one that is hastened by an external agent."

HOSPICE IN AMERICA

As the work of Saunders and Kubler-Ross became known in the United States, groups of Americans came together in Marin County, California, and New Haven, Connecticut, to establish the first American hospice programs. Whether by design or as the result of funding problems, America's hospice programs, though philosophically similar in conception to the British hospital-based model, began to deliver care to the dying primarily in their own homes. As the hospice movement spread across the United States, programs took on various shapes and sizes (Lattanzi-Licht & Connor, 1995).

Today, the National Hospice Organization reports more than 2,400 hospice programs in operation or in the planning stages in the United States, each being a unique combination of program designs. One model of a hospice is that of a house where people go for visits and counseling. A second model is hospice care in a separate ward or palliative care unit of a hospital, where patients are cared for by a roving interdisciplinary hospice team. A third model, which has become the predominant American model, is home care service with the goal of allowing patients to remain in their home environment as long as desired and possible.

Other models include combinations of the home care, hospital care, and drop-in counseling models. In all programs, standards of care are developed in seven areas: (1) the patient and family as the unit of care, (2) interdisciplinary

HOSPICE CARE: VALUE AND EFFECTIVENESS

In 1995, the National Hospice Organization (NHO) released the results of its study of hospice care in the United States. The report, entitled *An Analysis of the Cost Savings of the Medicare Hospice Benefit,* outlined some surprising findings:

- In 1994 hospices tended to more than 340,000 deaths in this country, up 24% from 1993.

- One out of every three cancer and AIDS deaths occurs under the auspices of hospice care. Seventy-eight percent of hospice patients have cancer as their primary diagnosis.

- There are currently more than 2,476 operational or planned hospice sites in the United States. Since 1990 this figure has grown by an annual average of 10%.

- Three out of four hospices nationwide are Medicare certified.

- In the final month of life, Medicare spent about $4,667 for cancer patients who opted for hospice care, as opposed to $8,723 for cancer patients receiving traditional institutional care.

- A 1992 Gallup Poll revealed that nine out of ten Americans surveyed would opt for the services hospice provides if faced with a terminal illness.

Source: NHO/ (703)243-5900: NHO Bookstore/ (800)243-5900

team services, (3) continuity of care, (4) home care services, (5) pain and symptom control, (6) bereavement, and (7) quality assurance. Saunders' model—prescribing an interdisciplinary team, communicating effectively, treating symptoms of terminal disease, including the patient and family—has become the fastest-growing caregiving alternative for the terminally ill in the United States today (Gentile & Fello, 1990; Lattanzi-Licht & Connor, 1995).

As hospice continues to expand and programs multiply, advocates for hospice have begun to express concern over the quality and quantity of services offered. Lattanzi-Licht and Connor (1995:160), for example, believe that the services provided by hospice will have to be of consistent high quality if hospice programs are to continue to grow, a goal, they believe, that has not been generally attained. They state:

Hospice programs still vary considerably in the quantity and quality of services they deliver. . . . Hospice programs must be careful not to become so rigid that they are unable to accommodate creative solutions to the needs of the dying people they were originally intended to serve. If hospice programs serve only those who are easy to care for or who meet strict admission criteria, the spirit of caring that has made the movement special will be lost and hospice will be just another cog in the great health care machine.

PAIN MANAGEMENT FOR THE TERMINALLY ILL

Among the many valuable contributions of the hospice movement to the health care system has been the development of sophisticated pain management techniques. The majority of terminally ill patients suffer moderate to severe pain problems in their final weeks or months of life, and pain is often what patients and families fear most. The hospice view of pain goes beyond the physical, however, to a view of pain as psychological, social, and spiritual as well. The interdisciplinary hospice team, combining the skills of various specialists and caregivers, seeks to address pain in all its manifestations.

Drugs and Pain Management

Hospice researchers Marian Gentile and Maryanne Fello (1990) point to some of the most important pain management concepts and insights to come from decades of hospice pain management research.

- Chronic pain management requires regularly scheduled delivery of appropriate analgesia in advance of the return of pain.
- Patients do not exhibit signs of drug addiction (e.g., drug-seeking behavior, ever-escalating dosages) when placed on an appropriate pain management program.
- Various routes of administration (i.e., sublingual, rectal, oral) can be equally effective as the intravenous (IV) route when used in equianalgesic ratios.
- Morphine and its derivatives are by far the most useful drugs in the management of intractable pain. Drugs often used for pain management include morphine, levorphanol, hydromorphone, oxymorphone, methadone, meperidine, fentanyl, codeine, oxycodone, propoxyphene, and hydrocodone.
- Knowledge and administration of combinations of drugs, such as narcotics with nonsteroidal antiinflammatory drugs, can be very effective for alleviating bone pain.
- Careful assessment of pain and all its components is essential to developing an effective intervention.

Hospice pays a great deal of attention to pain control. Efforts are made, however, not to sedate patients (or allow patients to sedate themselves) so much that communication is hindered. Oversedation, according to Aiken (1994:306),

> would interfere with the important goal of bringing patients and family members together. By providing a warm, homey atmosphere in which pain is controlled, patients can remain alert, active, and productive until they die. Meanwhile, death can be discussed openly, without unnecessary fear and without the feeling that it is the end of everything. In this way, dying becomes more meaningful and acceptable to the patient.

Massage in Pain Management

Medical massage is not exactly new. Hippocrates saw "rubbing" as an essential tool for physicians and nurses, and massage is still common in European medicine. Renewed interest in massage by American medical professionals does, however, reflect the growing conviction that certain low-tech, patient–centered treatments can help restore the "human" dimension to medicine while yielding real clinical benefits to patients (Marrone, 1990:40).

Nurses report that patients receiving various forms of massage take fewer narcotics, hypnotics, and sedatives for pain and sleeplessness, and it helps them cope with hospital stress. Appropriate touch that creates a relaxation response results in decreased heart rate, blood pressure, and skin temperature, and it creates conditions for patients to facilitate their own healing (J. Cohen, 1995; Curtis, 1994). McCaffery and Wolff (1992), reporting in a special issue of *Hospice Journal,* present guidelines for patients and caregivers regarding the use of massage and other methods of stimulating the skin to relieve pain or produce comfort in dying patients. Methods include superficial massage, superficial heat and cold, menthol application to skin, transcutaneous electrical nerve stimulation (TENS), positioning, and movement. Massage therapists are increasingly a part of the hospice team.

Whereas massage programs are geared to enhancing patients' comfort, in other medical settings massage therapists use massage for specific medical purposes. Zhang and Wang (1994), reporting on the use of acupressure in the treatment of lumbar back pain, found that applying finger pressure to traditional Chinese acupuncture points on the body was effective in relieving pain in nearly 40% of the cases, and moderately to mildly effective in more than 95% of the cases studied. Another study involved treating sixty-three chronic pain patients with a twice-weekly regimen of massage and shiatsu acupressure for 4 weeks. Eighty-six percent of the patients reported decreased pain and increased mobility by the fifth session. With regular massages, it was found that the patients needed less medication, cognitive function improved, and brittle skin became more elastic.

Clearly, there seems to be more to massage than a good rubdown. And after a long period of neglect, American medicine is finally beginning to reinstate massage as a pain control technique and the aid to good health that Hippocrates recommended. Begun by five Atlanta nurses in 1987, the National Association for Nurse Massage Therapists (NANMT) had grown to over 500 members by the end of 1995. The association successfully applied to the National Federation for Specialty Nursing Organizations to make massage a recognized specialty, and at least a dozen of its members have introduced "touch therapy" programs to hospitals (Cohen, 1995). Massage therapists now work in oncology, organ-transplant, hospice, and intensive care units, and get requests from many other departments for their services.

THE HOSPICE PATIENT

In 1992, according to Lattanzi-Licht and Connor (1995), 53% of hospice patients in the United States were men, of whom 68% were 65 years of age or older. Of the population of women, 72% were over 65. Eighty-five percent of care-recipients were caucasian, 9% were African American, 3% were Hispanic American, 1% were American Indian, and 2% were members of another racial or ethnic group. Fifty-five percent of patients lived with a spouse, 20% lived with a child, 10% lived with a significant other, and 5% lived with a parent. Ten percent of hospice patient had no primary caregiver in the home.

U.S. Hospice Patient Population: 1985–1994

Year	Number
1985	158,000
1987	177,000
1989	186,000
1990	210,000
1992	246,000
1994	340,000

Source: Lattanzi-Licht & Connor (1995), p. 147, N.H.O., 1995.

THE INTERDISCIPLINARY TEAM

The thrust of hospice requires the development of a specialized, holistically directed interdisciplinary team that works together to look for solutions to a patient's medical, psychosocial, and spiritual problems. With such a broad approach and such a wide scope of issues, one individual or discipline cannot adequately meet all needs. Hospice care requires an extraordinary interdisciplinary group effort involving a diversity of talent, cultural and ethnic background, lifestyle, and educational background, plus a blend of talents and skills (Gentile & Fello, 1990).

The Nurse Coordinator

In an age of nursing shortages, many nurses with a holistic and compassionate view of terminal care are drawn to the hospice program. According to hospice nurses Marian Gentile and Maryanne Fello (1990:98) of the Forbes Hospice in Pittsburgh, Pennsylvania, nurses are drawn to hospice work for a number of reasons.

> The first is the satisfaction of the work itself. To assist the patient and family during the dying process carries many rewards. Becoming involved after a family has been told 'there is nothing more to be done' can restore the family's faith that it will not be abandoned even though curative medical treatment has been exhausted. Helping a family know what to expect, putting effective symptom management skills into practice, and supporting with effective counseling skills makes a hero of many nurses in the eyes of grateful families.
>
> The second draw is the role of the nurse within the hospice team itself. Medical intervention takes a back seat to nursing intervention in terminal care. This fact thrusts the nurse into a primary role for both direct care and the coordination of the care provided by other members of the team. . . . [N]urses (and others) who are drawn to hospice tend to be religious, realistic revolutionaries and they find in a hospice program a setting that is just short of an ideal medium for fundamental, holistic, independent nursing practice.

This description of the hospice nurse by Gentile and Fello is supported, in part, in a study by Brockopp, King, and Hamilton (1991). In a comparative investigation of attitudes toward death and dying among palliative care nurses, psychiatric nurses, and orthopedic nurses, these researchers found that palliative care nurses had more compassionate and more positive attitudes about death and the dying, and had less fear concerning the death of self and others.

Because the majority of hospice patients need some assistance with symptom management and other problems related to their physical care, the nurse may find herself or himself in the central role of coordinating the medical care of most patients. It is the hospice nurse who has day-to-day contact with the patient and families, who visits regularly, who conducts psychosocial assessments, and who calls frequently to give added reassurance and guidance (McCracken & Gerdsen, 1991). In addition to her or his other duties, the hospice nurse is both liaison to the family and facilitator for the family as members attempt to deal with the dying and death of their loved one. Ann McCracken and Leigh Gerdsen (1991), of Hospice of Cincinnati, describe the psychosocial assessment methods used by the hospice nurse in working with the family's emotional needs and daily problems. The nurse facilitates patient–family communication throughout the dying process, prepares the family for the actual death, and assists the family at the time of death as well as through part of the mourning after. The formalized bereavement program includes literature, memorial services, and education/support groups, and follow-up care is provided to family members for up to one year after the patient's death.

The Home Health Aide

The home health aide is one of the most valuable members of the hospice team. Working closely with the hospice nurse, the aide's role is to help provide personal care and light housekeeping duties in the home and to give the primary caregiver a break from the daily rigors of caring for the dying. The aide also plays an important informal role. Because the aide tends to spend the most time with the dying person and family members, relationships tend to become intimate. There is less professional distance in these relationships, and the challenge often arises for aides to maintain these intimate relationships while remaining objective enough not to become immersed in family problems and entanglements (Gentile & Fello, 1990; Carroll & Graner, 1994).

The Grief Counselor

The team member most concerned with family dynamics and interactions is the hospice grief counselor. The counselor's specialized training as a clinical psychologist, clinical social worker, or marriage, family, and child counselor is brought into practice in the usual ways of seeking out community resources, such as finding help with financial, legal, and insurance issues, while also employing special therapeutic and communication skills to help the families work through their issues. With hospice patients and their families, these problems take on exaggerated importance because the crisis of dealing with a dying family member affects lives so intensely and in so many different ways.

"We are not always able to cure, we are always able to care."

Most important, the grief counselor is faced with the challenge of facilitating the family to consider various options and alternatives while, at the same time, permitting family members and the dying person to make the actual decisions day to day. This is sometimes a forbidding challenge, because many families have great difficulty focusing on decision-making tasks in the midst of the emotional crisis, and may pressure the grief counselor to rescue them. Sorting through these issues can facilitate peace of mind for the patient and caregivers but also permits insight into the more critical areas of the family system. In describing the work of the hospice grief counselor, Gentile and Fello (1990:99) point out that the task of helping family members to deal with the crisis of terminal illness and all its ramifications "requires much emotional fortitude and keen perceptive talents on the part of the counselor."

Volunteers

Volunteers are of enormous benefit to the hospice program and to individual patients and families, by providing caregiving, family support, housework, grocery shopping, and even babysitting. Hospice volunteers are carefully selected and trained, with each hospice program gearing its selection-and-training program to its own needs. Training usually involves at least 20 to 40 hours of lectures, group discussion, outside reading, and instruction in physical care, including hands-on nursing care. Then the volunteers begin assisting the hospice staff, all the while becoming deeply involved and committed to the care of the terminally ill patient and his or her family. S. Schneider and Kastenbaum (1993)

As children and adolescents, we learn to empathize and become aroused by someone else's pain and suffering. For many hospice volunteers, these empathic skills result in acts of caring and kindness, along with a belief in maintaining human dignity in the terminal phases of the dying process.
© *Elizabeth Crews*

found that hospice volunteers tend to have strong religious beliefs and values and often rely on personal prayer as a way of coping with the burdens and stresses of working with the dying and their families.

The most common area of hospice volunteering is the home care setting. Volunteers in the home act in the capacity of a friend, one who knows how to care for a sick person. Most commonly, the volunteer provides respite for the caregivers by affording them an opportunity to get out of the home during the volunteer's visit (d'Artois, 1995). In describing the hospice volunteer, Gentile and Fello (1990:3) state, "Their perspective is one of kindness and caring, along with a belief in maintaining human dignity in the dying process. They give much of themselves and reap only the gratification that comes from helping people in their darkest hour." In addition, volunteers perform many duties for the hospice main office, including clerical work and fund raising, and may also serve on hospice boards in helping to define policy and to write funding proposals.

Specialized Therapists

Based on their individual training, physical therapists, speech therapists, and massage therapists contribute to the work of the interdisciplinary team in various ways. For example, the physical therapist may teach family members techniques for proper positioning of the patient, as well as various body transfer techniques. The physical therapist will also train the patient in various exercises meant to maintain mobility and strength for as long as possible. The massage therapist may work with the patient in stress reduction and pain abatement, while occupational and speech therapists concentrate on maintaining communication skills and a semblance of the patient's former life. Some hospice programs also include music and art therapists as part of the interdisciplinary team.

Music therapist Marie West (1994) notes that music therapy can help the dying person to cry, laugh, feel angry, and express a fuller range of emotions and may support the dying individual in his or her spiritual quest and search for meaning. Music has also been found to increase relaxation by lessening muscle tension and anxiety and in regulating respiratory rate, cardiovascular rate, blood pressure, breathing rate, and pain levels (Eschelman & McKay, 1988). Music therapy appears to have a special role to play in work with the dying child, where it can help to distract the child from feared medical interventions and the sterile hospital environment, thus creating a calming and tranquilizing effect in a child who is feeling anxious and confused. The patient's own ethnic heritage and personal musical preferences, such as classical, rock, jazz, country/western, or new age and ethnic music, play a central role in the choice of music employed by the music therapist.

The Nutritionist

The nutritionist's main task is to counsel both the family and the dying person on the special needs of the dying patient (Gentile & Fello, 1990; Carroll & Graner, 1994). Nutritional deficiencies in the terminally ill usually result from nausea (possibly accompanied by vomiting), mouth soreness (which may be caused by treatment or vitamin deficiencies), or anorexia. It is quite common for terminally ill persons, especially cancer patients, simply to have no appetite or to find food unappealing. Cancer patients often report that many foods taste different from what they recall prior to becoming seriously ill.

In a real sense, the nutritional content of the food is far less important during the terminal stage of life than simply being able to eat and enjoy the experience of eating. Although no amount of nutrition will stop the progress of the disease, attempting to maintain protein stores can help skin integrity, and the patient may not weaken quite so quickly. More critical is the issue of hydration. The nutritionist attempts to help families look at these nutritional problems from their own perspective. For them, the emphasis is on getting their loved one to take in as much food and liquid while knowing that the patient's food and fluid intake will continue to decline during the process of dying (Gentile & Fello, 1990; Carroll & Graner, 1994).

The Hospice Physician

The hospice physician's major task as medical director is to act as liaison between the hospice program, with its holistic, palliative model, and traditional

BLUE AND DYING

"Patients must be able to confide in someone without any fears. We may not have answers, but we are well trained to listen. If a patient says, 'My favorite color is blue,' we accept that. A family member might say, 'But your favorite color is pink!'"

"If a patient wants to speak about his/her death, a volunteer will not change the subject. Family members tend to avoid discussion of this topic."

Source: Quoted in d'Artois (1995), p. 12.

medicine, with its allopathic, cure-dominated model. "The hospice medical director," according to Gentile and Fello (1990:100), "must display compassion and patience to the other team members while often acting as a stabilizing force within the group framework. The medical director plays a variety of parts." As a trained physician, the hospice physician must possess expertise in the clinical aspects of symptom management in order to develop an effective palliative care program based on the patient's prior medical history. In addition, the hospice physician may actually manage the medical care of some hospice patients or act as a consultant to the care in other cases. Acting as a teacher, the medical director works with the rest of the hospice staff and interdisciplinary team to understand the various disease processes and their clinical implications. N. M. Murphy (1992) discusses the value of a hospice physician, who in the spirit of love, compassion, and forgiveness, can catalyze and guide a meeting of family members. Coping with death or serious illnesses with the aid of such a physician can result in an experience of profound learning and change for all involved.

Clergy

Spiritual care is an integral part of the hospice program, and hospice clergy have two important roles to play in caring for the terminally ill: one role as spiritual guide to the dying patient, and another role in teaching family members and health care professionals about death and dying (Charlton, 1992). All team members must attend to the physical, social, psychological, and spiritual needs of the patient and family members as death becomes imminent and questions and fears arise. Gentile and Fello (1990) believe that many of the patients to which hospice chaplains minister have become estranged from formal religion beliefs and practices and hope to reconnect themselves with their spiritual roots. A chaplain with a caring and compassionate nature may, with sensitivity and discretion, help the dying person to explore spiritual issues and engage the search for meaning and dignity during the process of dying.

As Abraham Maslow (1954) suggested in his theory of human motivation, basic physical, social, and psychological needs must be satisfied to a significant degree before the highest needs for spiritual nurturance and support can be adequately addressed. In this sense, the chaplain's involvement in the interdisciplinary team is to ensure that other needs are met so that spiritual and existential concerns can take their rightful place in the final moments of life. The chaplain's work, unlike that of some other members of the hospice team, continues into the mourning after, when spiritual care may be the most important element in family support.

There is no single pathway or procedure that works for everyone. According to Carroll and Graner (1994:54), the unique purpose of hospice care is to aid patients and families, in their individual ways, to manage the wide range of concerns and issues related to terminal care. As they state, "We are not always able to cure, we are always able to care."

Allopathic and Holistic Models of Healing

Western medical concepts and techniques have their centuries-old roots in a mechanomorphic point of view—seeing human beings as machines and medicine as committed to fighting diseases of the machine with curative agents and procedures. The allopathic model, as the exclusive medical model for centuries, has served us in profound and powerful ways in curing, as well as managing, numerous human diseases and disorders. However, as physicians' power over life and death has increased, their personal interactions with the dying has deteriorated. As the mechanical aspects of the model have become preeminent, the human elements have taken a secondary, if not peripheral, role in the healing process.

With the evolution of such different specialties as pulmonology, cardiology, endocrinology, radiology, and oncology, individual care has become impersonal and piecemeal. Patients find themselves at the mercy of specialists whose examinations are not explained in everyday language. No longer is the individual viewed or treated as a whole person (Kearl, 1989). Despite the changes in our knowledge of and attitudes toward holistic healing, the allopathic point of view remains the predominant one in most Western hospitals and medical com-

THE PILGRIM PROJECT

The Pilgrim Project, launched by grief counselor Brendan Cavanaugh in 1978, provides a volunteer support and training program to terminal cancer and AIDS patients and their loved ones in Montreal, Canada. The training courses focus on five major areas: medical, social, psychological, philosophical, and spiritual, and include would-be volunteers, people who want to become better caregivers in their families, and patients who seek insight into their disease and ways of coping with it. On the medical level, participants learn about terminal diseases, how the body responds to changes they induce, and how to behave defensively in their interactions with the medical community. On the social level, participants are familiarized with community resources as well as with practical advice on coping strategies, from finding someone to cut the grass to locating an agency that might fund a new prosthesis for a terminally ill patient. On the psychological level, volunteers are paired with terminally ill patients and assist them in dealing with emotional issues as well as family dynamics. Cavanaugh notes that as the disease progresses and the patient experiences loss of energy, reduced mobility, and increased dependence, "people become philosophical. They start to think about the meaning and value of their lives and they need someone who will listen. . . . When death is staring people in the face, they often have renewed interest in their religious background. If they have lost contact with their church, they may need help to get in touch with a priest, minister or rabbi." At present, the Montreal project has more than 170 volunteers and 90 patients and has begun to spread to other communities in which similar volunteer services to the terminally and chronically ill are nonexistent.

Source: d'Artois (1995), pp. 12–13.

plexes. A product of the scientific worldview, this allopathic model has been described along a number of dimensions (Langford, 1984; Marrone, 1990):

- It focuses on vulnerability and death as failure to cure.
- It views disease states as problems, as "something wrong" or as alien enemies to be destroyed (e.g., war on cancer, battle against AIDS).
- It concentrates on symptoms.
- It is invasive and intrusive.
- It deals exclusively with linear, cause–effect strategies.
- It uses language that alienates and mystifies.
- It takes a professional stance that the healer knows more about the healing process than does the patient.
- Practitioners take a strong, specialist approach.
- It seeks a normative, empirical basis for understanding disease states while disregarding the unique makeup and circumstances of the individual patient.

"We are witnessing an explosion of new healing and caring possibilities as these once–separate models, allopathic and holistic, intertwine and merge into one."

Shapiro, Larsen, and Jacokes (1991) maintain that understanding unexpected patient outcomes often requires a shift in the physician's analytic paradigm. They suggest that shifting to a psychosocial perspective (1) can highlight previously ignored dimensions of patient and family that affect care, (2) can reveal parallels of emotional response (e.g., anger, guilt) between patient/family and physician, and (3) can help address the physician's emotional distress and burnout.

A number of researchers and theorists from medicine, psychology, sociology, and gerontology (Langford, 1984; Cousins, 1983; Chopra, 1990; Marrone, 1990; Barrow, 1996) maintain that a complementary holistic model is emerging in the healing professions that views the patient as person and the role of caregiver as caring for the whole person, including his or her medical, psychological, social, and spiritual needs. Langford (1984) and Marrone (1990) have described this holistic model along a number of interesting dimensions:

- It makes a distinction between "curing a disease" and "healing the person."
- It looks at the entire person and seeks to create a context or environment where the healing process can unfold.
- It recognizes and facilitates the patient's responsibility (i.e., ability to respond) in the healing process.
- It is holistic in nature and is reflected not so much in new technologies and strategies as in shifting attitudes and values.
- It recognizes diseases as an opportunity to learn and grow, and symptoms as embodying messages that, when listened to, can be healing and enriching.
- Its use of language attempts to demystify the healing process.
- It focuses on life and accepts surprise, movement, and flux as part of the healing process.
- It is an open system that places great value on compassion, loving care, and the uniqueness of the person.

We are witnessing an explosion of new healing and caring possibilities as these once-separate models, allopathic and holistic, intertwine and merge into one

(Marrone, 1990). This is evidenced by recent breakthroughs in psychoneuroim-munology, body/mind psychotherapies, and health psychology, by new death-and-dying course offerings in medical and nursing schools, and by the establishment of more than 2,000 hospice programs in the United States in the last 25 years. Joining the two models together is creating a unified paradigm that removes all the old constraints and begins to suggest even newer and more powerful insights into the processes of healing, caring, communicating, conscious living, and conscious dying.

Chapter Summary

Faced with the challenge of caring for the dying person on an ongoing basis puts us eye to eye with powerful and sometimes numbing forms of fear, including the fear of our own death, fear of hurting, fear of being hurt, and fear of being engulfed in another's emotional world. Denial and repression of these fears may help to explain the dehumanizing treatment of dying persons in American hospitals.

Despite the availability of lifesaving equipment and medical expertise, a typical hospital or nursing home is not, from a psychological or social perspective, the best place to die. Research has pointed to a number of factors associated with the dehumanized treatment of patients in America's hospitals. One factor concerns physicians who have been found to have, on the average, an inordinately high fear of death. A second is the idea, implicit throughout medical training, that death is evidence of failure. The lack of medical education in the areas of dying and death is a third reason. Fourth, because the dominant model of the medical institution views the human being as a machine, the average physician tends to have a limited view of the factors necessary for quality of life and a limited understanding of the more subtle psychosocial factors that play a role in death and dying.

One alternative to dying in a hospital involves home care, which is essentially a 24-hour-a-day job whose main ingredient is the presence of a willing-and-able family member or friend to attend to the various tasks that constitute appropriate care for the terminally ill and dying. The home setting provides an alternative to the sometimes-dehumanizing experience of hospitals and convalescent hospitals, offering greater opportunities for sustaining relationships and connectedness to neighborhood and community. It can, however, become a heavy burden and create great stress in both the caregiver and the care-recipient. The literature has illustrated that a variety of coping skills are often needed by caregivers in order to deal with a variety of problems.

The hospice alternative has evolved in response to the identified need to manage care better for patients and families in the end stages of illness, when cure and rehabilitation are not possible. Standards of care were developed in seven areas: (1) the patient and family as the unit of care, (2) interdisciplinary team services, (3) continuity of care, (4) home care services, (5) pain and symptom control, (6) bereavement, and (7) quality assurance. At the present time, there are 2,400 hospice programs planned or in operation in the United States, and the number is growing.

A number of researchers and theorists from medicine, psychology, and sociology maintain that the success of the hospice movement is a reflection of the fact that a complementary holistic model is emerging in the healing professions that views the patient as person and the role of caregiver as caring for the whole person, including his or her medical, psychological, social, and spiritual needs.

FURTHER READINGS:

Aiken, L. (1994) *Dying, Death, and Bereavement* (3rd ed) Allyn & Bacon, Needham Heights, MA.

Chopra, D. (1990). *Quantum Healing: Exploring the Frontiers of Mind/Body Medicine.* Bantam Books, New York.

Cousins, N. (1979). *Anatomy of an Illness.* Bantam Books, New York.

Cousins, N. (1983). *The Healing Heart.* Norton, New York.

Gentile, M., & Fello, M. (1990). Hospice Care for the 1990s, *Journal of Home Health Care Practice 3(1):*1−15.

Kearl, Michael C. (1989). *Endings: The Sociology of Death and Dying.* Oxford University Press, New York.

Kennedy, E., & Charles, S. C. (1990). *On Becoming a Counselor: A Basic Guide for Nonprofessional Counselors.* Continuum, New York, p. 26.

Larson, D. G. (1993). *The Helper's Journey: Working with People Facing Grief, Loss, and Life-Threatening Illness.* Research Press, Champaign, IL.

Leash, R. M. (1994). *Death Notification: A Practical Guide to the Process.* Upper Access, Hinesburg, VT.

Masson, J.M. (1995) *When Elephants Weep: The Emotional Lives of Animals,* Dell, N.Y.

McGurn, Sheelagh. (1992). *Under One Roof: Caring for an Aging Parent.* Hazelden, New York.

Sudnow, D. (1967). *Passing On: The Social Organization of Dying.* Prentice Hall, Englewood Cliffs, NJ.

U.S. Select Committee on Aging. (1994). *Home Care and Community-Based Services: Overcoming Barriers to Access,* #103-16 (March 30). gopher://ftp.senate.gov:7 . . .mmittee_publications (May 6, 1996).

Wrenn, R. L., Levinson, D., and Papadatou, D. (1996). *Guidelines for the Health Care Provider: End-of-Life Decisions.* University of Arizona Health Services Center, Office of Contining Education, Tuczon, AZ 85724. Telephone: 520-626-7832.

Preparing for Death and Dying: Anxieties, Issues, and Tasks

Whether we believe that death is a part of life, the end of life, or the start of a new life, we cannot escape the fact that we will die. In Ecclesiastes 3:19–20, the Bible says, "As one dies, so dies the other. They all have the same breath, the man has no advantage over the beasts . . . all are from dust, and all turn to dust again." Although we may come to accept the inevitability of our own death, actually preparing for our death and dying—that is, considering the issues and engaging the tasks concerned with our demise—may be very far from our minds much of the time. At other times, however, questions about our own preparations for death may become a central concern, as we mourn the death of a parent, spouse, friend, or animal companion or face our own imminent death.

Tasks and issues concerned with preparing for dying range from the simple—such as whether we choose to be buried or cremated— to the profoundly complex right-to-die decisions—such as whether to sustain our lives, through heroic medical procedures if we are

NOT THINKING ABOUT DEATH

"There are two ways of not thinking about death: the way of our technological civilization, which denies death and refuses to talk about it; and the way of traditional civilization, which is not a denial but a recognition of the impossibility of thinking about it directly or for very long because death is too close and too much a part of daily life."

Philipe Aries. (1981). *The Hour of Our Death*. Knopf, New York, p. 22.

comatose or in intractable pain, or *not* to sustain our lives, through indirect or active euthanasia, suicide, or assisted suicide.

Whether you have thought about or have already answered any of the following questions reveals the degree to which you have begun preparations for your own death and dying.

- Do you know how you want your body disposed of (burial, cremation, donated to a medical school)?
- What kind of last rites do you desire (funeral, memorial services, a party)?
- Have you decided on how much your funeral or memorial service should cost?
- Have you decided on a casket design, tombstone design, obituary, cemetery plot or where you'd like your ashes scattered?
- Is there a particular song or symphonic piece you'd like played at your funeral or memorial service?
- Do you have a will, a living will, or some other advance directive concerning health care?
- Do you have life insurance? Burial insurance?
- Are you willing to have an autopsy done on your body?
- Are you willing to donate the organs of your body for use by others after you die?
- Do you want to be maintained in a vegetative state, on life-sustaining machines, if there is little or no hope of your recovery? If so, for how long? If not, when should the equipment be removed, and by whom?
- Would you consider taking your own life to end chronic, excruciating pain?
- Would you like a physician to assist you in killing yourself if your physical pain became unbearable? Would you consider taking your life with the assistance of a friend or family member? What if your depression and psychological pain became unbearable?
- Would you trust another person to make these final decisions for you if you become unable to make them for yourself? If so, who is this trusted person?

To answer these and related questions, we must be willing and able to imagine our own death and dying and to examine it from various points of view. In the sections that follow, we consider the anxiety experienced in imagining and examining our own death, along with the ethical issues and practical tasks to be considered in preparing for dying and death. As we consider these many issues and tasks, we will face the following challenges:

- Focusing upon and embracing the inevitability of our own death
- Pondering questions concerned with dying with dignity
- Overcoming the anxieties associated with the questioning process itself
- Reflecting upon the impact of our death on the loved ones who touch us and are, in turn, touched by our existence

Anxieties

Should we avoid thinking about or preparing for death? After all, isn't it just a morbid exercise in anxiety and depression? Or should we prepare for our own dying and death and confront the fears and anxieties this exercise is sure to arouse? Avoid or confront? This dilemma of how to deal with the anxieties aroused in imagining our own death and dying have been pondered throughout human history.

DEATH: AVOIDANCE OR CONFRONTATION?

Zeno, who founded the philosophy of Stoicism in the Third century, B.C. chose one horn of the *avoid-or-confront dilemma* in his attempts to achieve total and complete indifference to the anxiety and fear connected with death. Zeno taught his many disciples that they could best deal with death by using their strength of character or will power to drive the problem of death from their minds. Death, to Zeno, was the enemy to be chased from human consciousness. Years later, Zeno discovered that this "out of mind" solution to the problem of death anxiety only worked if death was also "out of sight." So what were we to do when death reared its ugly head in spite of our attempts to deny the problem or avoid preparation? Zeno's second line of defense involved an appeal to God, fate, and divine providence to cope with the unwelcome anxiety and fear (Choron, 1963; Kenyon, 1990–91).

Seneca (4 B.C.—65 A.D.), a later Stoic philosopher, chose the other horn of this dilemma in dealing with death and dying. Seneca's solution was clear. To overcome our death anxieties and fears, we must run at death headlong, face it unflinchingly, prepare for it, and think about it all the time. When we were truly familiar with the face of death, Seneca reasoned, when we had immersed ourselves in all the aspects and nuances of death, the fears and anxieties would melt away and we would truly be free of its grip on the soul (Kenyon, 1990–91).

The French philosopher and essayist Michel de Montaigne (1533–1592) came to a similar point of view centuries later (1991:95):

> We come and we go and we trot and we dance, . . . and never a word about death. All well and good. Yet when death does come—to them, their wives, their children, their friends—catching them unawares and unprepared, then what storms of passion overwhelm them, what cries, what fury, what despair! . . . To begin depriving death of its greatest advantage over us, let us adopt a way clean contrary to that common one; let us deprive death of its strangeness, let us frequent it, let us get used to it; let us have nothing more often in mind than death. . . . We do not know where death awaits us: so let us wait for it everywhere. To practice death is to practice freedom. [One] who has learned how to die has unlearned how to be a slave.

But it wasn't too long before both Seneca and Montaigne realized that this "medicine" of thinking about and preparing for death all the time was worse than the "disease" it was meant to cure. Constantly thinking about death, rather than leading to an easing of death anxiety, caused just the opposite to occur. "Tis certain," Montaigne wrote, "that for the most part, the preparation for death has administered more torment than the thing itself" (Dali, 1947:389). Not to think about death at all, or to be prepared for death all the time, are extreme poles of a continuum, and each strategy for solving the problem of death anxiety fails miserably, sooner or later.

THE FLOATING PERSPECTIVE

In recent decades, a psychological perspective has emerged that allows us to remove ourselves from the horns of this prickly dilemma by adopting a *floating perspective* on the question of how death and anxiety might touch our lives. According to Canadian thanatologist Gary M. Kenyon (1990–91:68), the floating perspective is based on the psychological insight that recognizes "that our relationship with the question of our own mortality is not frozen at some point on a continuum." From this point of view, loss, grief, and mourning continue to touch our lives throughout the life span, from childhood to old age, and our personal acknowledgment of death, as well as our willingness and ability to prepare for death, is part of a process that changes over time. This insight, Kenyon (1990–91:68) points out, is central to the floating perspective, the essence of which is that "there is no lasting position on death that might be called the right one." Instead, our awareness and concern with death are permitted to float along the avoidance/confrontation continuum throughout life because, in the final analysis, death can be neither completely confronted nor completely denied.

> **"If one of us dies before the other, I think I'll move to Paris"**
>
> Sigmund Freud

DEATH, ANXIETY, AND THE UNKNOWABLE

Both avoidance of death and confrontation with death presuppose that a state of death anxiety must be overcome, in the one case by putting death out of our mind, in the other case by always being prepared for death. Some people believe that preparing for death, or even reflecting on your own death, will create only morbid depression, anxiety, and panic. But here, too, we have the same set of polar opposites: avoid or be anxious/confront or be anxious. These solutions are too simple because they assume that we must be in perpetual upheaval and continuously anxious about something that we cannot, in the end, really know.

We can never really get at death or truly comprehend the finality of our lives because, as another Stoic philosopher, Epicurus, stated it, "As long as we exist, death is not with us, but when it comes, we do not exist" (Kenyon, 1990–91:68). If we can never truly know death *from the inside,* perhaps it is inappropriate to be so anxiety-ridden about it in the first place (Kenyon, 1990–91:70). Maybe anxiety is the result of trying too hard to know something that cannot be known (Cole, 1987). Sigmund Freud strongly believed that the human ego cannot truly and fully imagine its own death or final dissolution. In fact, it is rumored that in one of his lighter moments, Freud turned to his wife and uttered, "If one of us dies before the other, I think I'll move to Paris" (Larson, 1993:42).

From the floating perspective, if some attitude or point of view towards death and dying is considered helpful to us (in the sense that it is adopted during a

"Once, in the Orient, I talked of suicide with a sage whose clear and gentle eyes seemed forever gazing at a never-ending sunset. "Dying is no solution," he affirmed. "And living?" I asked. "Nor living either," he conceded. "But who tells you there is a solution?"

Wiesel (1966), p. 15FF.

particular point in life) or something that seems to make sense to us in the here and now, then it is consistent with the floating perspective. On the other hand, any view of death that is considered the ultimate remedy for death anxiety or an exclusive answer to the "problem of death anxiety" is highly questionable. Kenyon (1990–91:68) writes that "any rigid position on the problem, any position taken as a solution to the problem, rather than as a guide or a temporary explanation, is unacceptable." In this light, the floating perspective is best described as an attempt to continue examining our view of death as an ongoing project throughout our lives. In this way, our understanding of and preparations for death may change as our lives change.

DEATH ANXIETY, CREATIVITY, AND INTEGRITY

It is safe to say that, for most of us, there is always some anxiety connected with the fundamental issue of our own mortality. And in some cases, anxiety and fear can overwhelm and freeze us in denial. However, this is only one part of the total picture. It is one thing to claim that there is anxiety connected with death, and quite another to suggest that to be anxious is the only way we can honestly deal with death. In this light, the most significant point about death anxiety is that it needn't be an end point but, instead, can be viewed simply as a part of the process of searching for life's meanings.

Martin Heidegger, in *Being and Time* (1927), declares that death and the threat of nonexistence are, indeed, threatening. But the realization of our future death is also a precondition for a fuller and deeper understanding of our life. As such, meditating on personal death, while likely to make us anxious, is also a precondition for freeing ourselves from death anxiety and fear (Tomer, 1994). In *Being and Nothingness* (1943), Jean Paul Sartre speaks of thoughts of death as reducing us to our very essence. Psychologist Adrien Tomer (1994:4) points out that Heidegger, Sartre, and other philosophers, such as Frankl (1963), make the meditation on personal death "a precondition for achieving meaning and freedom of fear in everyday life." In this light, the anxiety associated with death can be seen as something positive—as a wellspring of creativity and self-actualization, as well as a source of personal integrity and strength.

Realizing that death is the ultimate destiny for each of us is no easy thing. And yet, research studies suggest that planning for our death and the mourning after can ease some of our anxiety about death and, in this way, improve the quality of our lives. For example, research by Henderson (1990) on the effects of preparing for death found that individuals who received support on specific planning—and, thus, control over their dying—showed a decrease in their anxiety about death as compared to others who did not prepare for death. The experimental group received intervention in the form of counseling and filling out a questionnaire regarding specific treatments (e.g., cardiopulmonary resuscitation, feeding tubes), advance directives (e.g., living wills), proxy decision making (e.g., durable power of attorney), body disposal, funeral arrangements, and other questions related to preparations for dying. Scores on the Death Anxiety Scale decreased for this group, while the control group's score remained statistically unchanged. Results revealed that coming face-to-face with the details of dying strengthened and empowered these individuals and lessened their reported anxiety.

FACING DEATH GENTLY

For many of us, preparing for dying involves the central challenge of overcoming the anxiety associated with the issues of death and dying. But overcoming death anxiety in a scientific culture requires more personal strength, more self-awareness, and more willingness to assume personal responsibility for our death and dying than was ever required by our ancestors. To prepare for our own death today requires that we go beyond the simple questions of willing our personal belongings and disposal of our bodies, to profound questions involving the definition of our own personhood, to our own imaginings of pain, and to the deepest moral and ethical questions of life and death.

> **"The chief problem about death, incidentally, is the fear there may be no afterlife. . . . Also, there is the fear that there is an afterlife but no one will know where it's being held."**
>
> Woody Allen

Throughout our lives, we face similar situations that challenge us. Implicitly or explicitly, we either choose to deal with the situation confronting us or default on it and walk away. In the first case, we encounter the situation and give ourselves the chance to resolve and come to terms with it. The resolution may not be complete, or even satisfactory, but, as Muller (1987) notes, if the situation is met honestly, our dealing with it becomes a part of us, and we become more ourselves for doing so. In the second case, we default, and the chance to grow is passed up. If major challenges are met by default often enough, the self does not become itself (what it might become) and it does not flourish or thrive.

The floating attitude of openness and receptivity to death is, in a real sense, a challenge different from avoidance or confrontation with death and dying, because our intention is to face death gently and mindfully—and to prepare consciously for death as the process unfolds. According to Kenyon (1990–91), the floating perspective advocates working with the issue of preparing for death as a personal, ongoing project. Authentically embracing such a project allows for changing our attitudes toward and meanings of death, as well as for transforming feelings of anxiety and fear into feelings of triumph and joy. According to philosopher Karl Jaspers (1970:76), by giving ourselves permission to feel, think, and imagine our deaths freely and realistically as well as to float from one point of view to another, "we are not contradicting ourselves if death makes us despair and, at the same time, makes us conscious of our innermost being, if we fail to understand, and feel trustful at the same time."

Issues

Death-related issues have occupied a central place in America's public debate for more than three decades. Some argue that medical technology is being used to "maintain" the dying and, perhaps, even the dead; or that the dying are being maintained so that their organs can be "harvested" for use by others as organ donations in heroic transplant operations. Arguments have been raised and concerns have been voiced that medical technology has effectively blurred life-and-death questions, such as what actually constitutes death. Should we define the death of a person in terms of medical data, such as heart rate, respiration rate, and brain activity? Or does the death of a person mean the end of that person's consciousness of self? and others? and the world? These are some of the right-to-die questions we must answer for ourselves as we prepare to die with dignity and grace.

In the span of a few decades, technology had transduced the chilling fear that a living person would be treated as a corpse to the chilling fear that a corpse would be treated as a living person.

THE RIGHT TO LIVE / THE RIGHT TO DIE

Right-to-die issues are very complex and very new to us, especially when we consider that for much of our history, up to the early twentieth century, our ancestors were concerned, not with the "right to die," but with the "right to live." Throughout history, the mystery surrounding death, coupled with a general distrust of physicians, manifested itself as a fear of being "buried alive" after being pronounced erroneously "dead" (G. B. Fulton & Metress, 1995). Mant (1976), for example, who studied cases of premature burial, beginning in the sixteenth century, states: "One reads of persons hearing sounds from a fresh grave, disbelief and then many hours' delay before the formalities are completed for exhumation. When the coffin is eventually opened we are told of the twisted shrouds, the doubled-up body, often with fresh injuries which have been bleeding, and all the signs of suffocation."

In order to prevent premature burial, various safeguards were proposed, such as testing the body for signs of life by applying hot irons or boiling water; embalming; decapitation; cremation; allowing the body to begin putrefying before burial; and elaborate devices, escape mechanisms, and speaking tubes built into coffins and grave sites. J. D. Arnold, Zimmerman, and Martin (1968) describe one coffin-escape device that worked in this way: an above-ground, hermetically sealed box containing a flag and a bell is attached to a 3-inch-diameter tube that enters an opening in the coffin, below ground. A glass ball, sitting on the chest of the deceased and inside the tube, is spring-loaded to the box, above ground. Any movement of the chest—say, by breathing—moves the ball, which releases a spring, which instantly opens the box, admitting light and air into the coffin while, at the same time, a flag raises and a bell begins ringing. The tube also acts as a speaking tube that amplifies the voice of the prisoner in the coffin below, who can then call for help. Interestingly, as elaborate as they were, these devices were never documented to have resulted in the rescue of a single victim of premature burial. With improving technology, such as the invention of the stethoscope, along with increasing trust of physicians, the use of these devices died out (so to speak).

Somewhere near the middle of the twentieth century, public fears of being pronounced dead too soon were replaced with concern about not being pronounced dead soon enough. G. B. Fulton and Metress (1995:7) state:

Irreversible cessation of cardiopulmonary function, the traditional standard used to declare death, had gradually given way to machines that could restart a stopped heart (defibrilators) and even regulate its beating if necessary (pacemakers). Respiratory function could be maintained indefinitely through the use of mechanical pumps called ventilators. The problem had become one of knowing when the person, whose vital functions were being maintained by this technology, had passed the point where, except for the technology, he or she would have been pronounced dead.

In the span of a few decades, technology had transduced the chilling fear that a living person would be treated as a corpse to the chilling fear that a corpse would be treated as a living person.

Physicians—once suspected and distrusted—are today frequently accused of "playing God," not only because they all too often assume an aura of omnipotence, but because so many of their devices and inventions for prolonging life seem to border on the miraculous and astonishing. Scientists can restructure the genetic code and create new life forms. Humans have been cloned. Hearts are routinely transplanted. There may be no limit, except perhaps by government regulation, to the future technologies medical science can use to control the forces of life and death in the modern world. Ironically, because of medical "advances," we now find it difficult to define what actually constitutes life and death.

R.I.P. SOFTWARE

"It's one of the stickiest questions in modern medicine: How do doctors decide when to stop treatment for a patient they believe is not going to recover? At London's Guy's Hospital, they turn to a computer program. The software—named the Riyadh Intensive Care Program after the city where it was developed, but chillingly dubbed R.I.P. for short—takes into account the patient's medical history, current condition and treatment administered. Its prediction may simply be "Outcome Uncertain"—but if it's death, either treatment is terminated or the patient is moved to a hospice.

"Although R.I.P. is right '95 times out of 100,' says David J. Bihari, F.R.C.P., director of intensive care at Guy's, it's not infallible. But physicians can be wrong too, he says, often being swayed by their desire to fix everything. And prolonging the life of a hopelessly ill patient he sees as the equivalent of torturing them to death. Bihari points out that in England one in four patients with recoverable illness is denied access to the intensive care unit because there are no beds. He sees programs like R.I.P. as an 'ethically correct' means of helping doctors decide how limited beds are apportioned.

Source: P. Noonan. (Dec. 1994). Death by Computer, *Longevity,* downloaded @ AOL 01/25/96.

Ethical Knots

Physicians have traditionally believed they must prolong life as long as possible without question. This idea, central to the Hippocratic oath taken by all graduating physicians, has become part of the right-to-die debate. The collision between classical medical ethics and contemporary right-to-die issues actually involves not a single practice, but at least three practices intimately connected with death, namely, ***aid in dying*** (ceasing the patient's artificial life support in cases of terminal illness), ***assisted suicide*** (providing a terminally ill person with the means to end his or her life after the person has requested such help), and ***mercy killing*** (actively causing a terminally ill person's death, most commonly by injection

THE HIPPOCRATIC OATH

"You do solemnly swear, each man by whatever he holds most sacred

That you will be loyal to the Profession of Medicine and just and generous to its members

That you will lead your lives and practice your art in uprightness and honor

That into whatever house you shall enter, it shall be for the good of the sick to the utmost of your power, your holding yourselves far aloof from wrong, from corruption, from the tempting of others to vice

That you will exercise your art solely for the cure of your patients, and will give no drug, perform no operation, for a criminal purpose, even if solicited, far less suggest it

That whatsoever you shall see or hear of the lives of men which is not fitting to be spoken, you will keep inviolably secret

These things you do swear. Let each man bow the head in sign of acquiescence.

And now, if you will be true to this, your oath, may prosperity and good repute be ever yours; the opposite, if you shall prove yourselves forsworn."

American Medical Association

of lethal drugs, pain medications, or asphyxiation). Other controversial issues facing the medical establishment involve abortion, embryo experimentation, genetic engineering, consent to treatment, resource allocation, organ transplantation, living wills, defining death, defining moral personhood, and defining the "persistent vegetative state." As American medical technology has spread around the world, these issues have become part of the public debate in countries of both the West and the East.

One of the most famous cases involving a collision between medical ethics and a person's right to die involved Karen Ann Quinlan, a young woman in a permanent vegetative state. In the 1970s, Karen Ann's parents initiated a court battle in the state of New Jersey for the right to disconnect the life-support machines to which she was attached. The hospital repeatedly refused these requests on ethical grounds. The New Jersey Supreme Court asserted that it had little doubt that if Karen could have regained consciousness for a single moment and surveyed her own situation, she would have chosen to have the respirator disconnected. The court ruled in favor of permitting her father to have this done (Battin, 1994). Disconnected from life-support devices, Karen nonetheless lived on in a vegetative state for nearly a decade before she died in 1985 (Hill & Shirley, 1992).

Since the right-to-die opinion was handed down by the court in the case of Karen Ann Quinlan, most states have passed statutes establishing procedures for abandoning life-sustaining treatment of the dying. In 1986, for example, Florida courts ruled that the removal of artificial feeding tubes from persons with no prospect of regaining cognitive brain function was permissible (Barrow, 1996). In 1987, a paralyzed man who starved to death after his wife removed his feeding tube did so under the New Jersey Supreme Court's landmark right-to-die decision. Idaho legally permits the terminally ill or their families actively to hasten death, and doctors who cooperate are fully protected under the law. Nevertheless, the judges asked to settle these cases have little to guide them in dealing with a variety of ethical knots and practical issues, including (Keilitz et al., 1989):

- Determining a terminally ill patient's "competence" or "capacity" to express his or her wishes
- Determining what is and is not considered life-sustaining medical treatment
- Determining the legal significance of a living will and other advance directives laying out the patient's final wishes and directives regarding life-sustaining procedures

Although numerous legal, medical, and bioethics projects, such as the project established by the National Center for State Courts, have taken steps toward formulating guidelines for these issues, they continue to be hotly debated. Families in many states are still fighting similar court battles today (Hill & Shirley, 1992).

Natural-Death Legislation

Most states have natural-death laws in place that, in general, affirm the patient's right to refuse treatment while still fully conscious. Some states have drawn an established line of authority for decision making to end the life of a person incapable of making the decision for him- or herself that begins with the dying person's spouse. Many states now recognize previously prepared documents, such as living wills and Durable Power of Attorney for Health Care directives, stating that an individual in his or her right mind has requested death with dignity and that life shall not be extended beyond the point of meaningful existence. However, as gerontologist Georgia Barrow (1996:316) states, "given society's deeply ingrained abhorrence of suicide, assisted suicide, and the legally sanctioned taking of human life under any circumstances, the right to die can still be extremely difficult to obtain." For example, Barrow points to the 1990 *Cruzan v. Missouri* case, in which the U.S. Supreme Court ruled, in a 5-to-4 decision, that the parents of a comatose woman did not have the right to insist that hospital workers stop feeding her. The justices ruled that, although a conscious patient has the right to refuse all medical treatment, a family member cannot speak for an unconscious or comatose child. Another part of their ruling made clear that this right-to-die issue was to be decided on a state-by-state basis.

Based on this ruling, the State of Missouri eventually allowed the parents of 33-year-old Nancy Beth Cruzan to have her feeding tube removed, and Nancy Beth eventually died. Interestingly, Cruzan would have been allowed to die in the State of Missouri without a court battle had she provided a living will or Health Care directive spelling out to her parents her own wishes regarding heroic medical procedures (Hill & Shirley, 1992). Since the Supreme Court's 1990 ruling, all states have adopted some form of natural-death legislation recognizing the wishes of the dying person as spelled out in some form of advance directive (Horacek, 1996b). On the other hand, as Barrow (1996:3170) points out,

> States with natural-death legislation do not all agree . . . as to the binding quality of a signed document requesting death-with-dignity, and court cases in several state courts are now testing the legality of documents such as the Durable Power of Attorney for Health Care, the living will and other advance directives. In other states, although documents requesting natural death are not legally binding, those who sign them hope they will be "morally" binding.

EUTHANASIA: DIRECT AND INDIRECT

Euthanasia, in Greek, means "the good death," and usually involves the active intervention of a medical doctor, at the dying patient's request, to bring that patient's life to an end. In spite of recent Circuit Court rulings in California and New York that have challenged the illegality of euthanasia, euthanasia remains illegal almost everywhere (Russell, 1996). In the United States, it is considered assisted suicide; in the United Kingdom, it is considered attempted murder; and even in the Netherlands, where the practice is winked at, the statutory penalty for assisting another's death is 12 years in prison (*Economist,* 1991:21).

Although polls reveal that a majority of American adults of all ages support the right to die by refusing treatment, when it comes to hastening death actively, older people are less supportive than younger and middle-aged people. For example, Huber, Cox, and Edelen (1992) found that of 200 adults (ages 21–93 years) interviewed regarding right-to-die issues, 90% favored some kind of personal control over death circumstances. Those more likely to want some control over their death circumstances included individuals with more education, higher incomes, or in health-related professions, and women. Older persons were, in general, less likely to want the same degree of control. We can wonder if the older person takes the topic more personally and worries that someone would hasten his or her death without consent.

Seale & Addington-Hall (1994) report on results from two surveys in England focusing on 3,696 persons in twenty medical institutions throughout the country who actually requested euthanasia and chose to die

"Pain, pain, pain . . . Sometimes it's so hard to describe the pain. It's a pain like—well, the way I feel when pain gets over me . . . It's like . . . EATING AWAY AT MY BONES."

Moller (1990), p. 76.

BY TOM MEYER/THE CHRONICLE

early. Data were gathered through structured interviews with relatives and others who knew people in the samples to determine the degree to which requests for euthanasia were determined by the experience of pain, other distressing symptoms, social dependency, and demographic factors, such as religious belief and social class. Results revealed that pain was the primary factor leading to requests for euthanasia, especially in death from cancer. Social class, place of residence of the deceased, and strength and type of religious faith were largely insignificant in influencing opinions about an earlier death.

Two terms are important to any discussion of the right to die: (1) *indirect euthanasia,* the process of allowing persons to die without using "extraordinary means" to save their lives, and (2) *direct euthanasia,* performing a deliberate act to end a person's life (Horacek, 1996b). Barrow (1996) notes a number of ways, both direct and indirect, that physicians and other medical personnel could hasten the end for patients who wish to die:

- Kill the terminally ill patient by injection or other means.
- Decide not to begin—or simply stop—an intravenous drip or respirator.
- Wait until the weakened body is infected with pneumonia and then avoid using antibiotics.
- If the person is in pain or unable to sleep, administer fatally high doses of a narcotic or barbiturate and thereby hasten death.

However, the American Medical Association policy statement on voluntary, direct euthanasia reads:

The intentional termination of the life of one human being by another—mercy killing—is contrary to that for which the medical profession stands and is contrary to the policy of the American Medical Association. The cessation of the employment of extraordinary means to prolong the life of the body when there is irrefutable evidence that biological death is imminent is the decision of the patient and/or his immediate family. The advice and judgment of the physician should be freely available to the patient and/or his immediate family.

Philosopher James Rachels (1993:253) points out that the debate for and against the legalization of euthanasia often appeals to a well-known distinction between indirect and direct euthanasia: Indirect is considered moral, direct is considered immoral. This is the position adopted, for example, by the American Medical Association. Rachels maintains that the distinction between killing and letting die, on which the direct/indirect distinction is founded, is morally irrelevant. He states: "If one simply withholds treatment, it may take the patient longer to die, and so he may suffer more than he would if more direct action were taken and a lethal injection given. . . . [B]eing 'allowed to die' can be relatively slow and painful, whereas being given a lethal injection is relatively quick and painless."

"We do not see best when our eyes are filled with tears."

Thomas Sullivan (1993)

Philosopher and bioethicist Margaret Pabst Battin (1994:101) offers arguments in support of both direct and indirect euthanasia on grounds of "mercy, autonomy and justice." Legal scholar Glanville Williams (1993) also disagrees with the AMA position and, instead, lends support for voluntary, direct euthanasia on a number of major grounds:

- It is cruel to refuse a terminally ill patient who is in agony the right to die.
- It is cruel to allow the agony of family and friends in seeing their loved one in a desperate situation.
- The principle of personal liberty and freedom overrides any utilitarian or social considerations against permitting direct euthanasia.

Philosopher Thomas Sullivan (1993:264), in support of the AMA position, defends the distinction between indirect and direct euthanasia by emphasizing the difference between intending and foreseeing. He argues that traditional law forbids intentional termination of life, whether by killing or by letting die, but not the withholding of extraordinary medical means of prolonging life. He states:

I fully realize that there are times when those who have the noble duty to tend to the sick and the dying are deeply moved by the sufferings of their patients, especially of the very young and the very old, and desperately wish they could do more than comfort and companion them. Then, perhaps, it seems that universal moral principles are mere abstractions having little to do with the agony of the dying. But of course we do not see best when our eyes are filled with tears.

While the debate rages on, both on moral and ethical grounds, the legal consequences of these and other alternatives vary from state to state and country to country, as do physicians' attitudes and actions. For example, some physicians use code words on patient charts for "hopeless case," such as " Code-90 DNR" (do not resuscitate) or "CMO" (comfort measures only). Both indicate that extraordinary life-saving measures should not be applied (Barrow, 1996). All in all, these life-and-death issues present complex, ethical knots, but some of the

EUTHANASIA: PRO AND CON

"I have always argued for more and better hospices, more and better pain management. I want as little euthanasia as possible. But . . . there will always be some cases, perhaps 10% of [terminal] cases, where the doctor at a certain point just runs out of things to do. It's purely a quality-of-life decision. The doctor is doing his best. . . . [But] if the patient's body has deteriorated so much that life isn't worthwhile to them, then they want euthanasia. They want assisted suicide. They want to die. . . . And that's not a hospice or a medical decision. It's a highly individual civil liberty."

Derek Humphry
Executive Director of the
Euthanasia Research and
Guidance Organization
and cofounder of the
Hemlock Society

"The nation is at a point where the aid-in-dying issue can go either way. [But] people do not favor this. If voters gain greater understanding of what 'death with dignity' and other such terms really mean, we're not going to be looking at a bleak future where euthanasia is the American way of death and people are expected to request their lethal injection at an appropriate time. I think people will look back and say, 'Oh my goodness, do you realize what we almost did?' "

Rita L. Marker
Executive Director of the
International Anti-Euthanasia
Task Force

Worsnop (1995), p. 15.

right-to-die concerns can be stated as specific questions.

1. What is the difference between killing a person, and allowing a person to die, between stopping treatment and not beginning it?
2. What is a person? Does simply being "alive" confer personhood, or are there other criteria for personhood, such as consciousness of self and purposeful activity?
3. Are there reasonable and unreasonable medical treatments? What is the difference? And who should decide the difference—the physician, the patient, the family?
4. At what point should the decision not to prolong life be made? Who should make the decision?
5. Does the individual ever have the right to take his or her own life? If so, under what conditions?
6. Should other people ever be permitted to assist someone in taking his or her own life? If so, should that be a physician, more than one physician, a family member, a friend, a committee, a court?
7. Should a person be allowed to commit suicide only if they're terminally ill? What about people in intractable and chronic physical pain? What about people in intractable and chronic psychological pain?

The answers to these right-to-die questions vary on moral, legal, and ethical grounds. On personal grounds, however, the search for answers to some of these questions may be central to our preparations for dying with dignity.

SUICIDE, PAIN, AND THE RIGHT TO DIE

Does a terminally ill patient with little quality of life and in chronic and excruciating pain have the right to take his or her own life? Are we truly masters of our fate? Doesn't our constitutional right to "life, liberty and the pursuit of

A DESIRE FOR SUDDEN DEATH

"The startling medical advances of this century have created unparalleled opportunities for ill and suffering people, but these same forces have combined to make the experience of dying a terrifying, fearful, lonely vigil for many. Devoid of traditional myths, rituals, and family support, many patients now die in sterile institutional settings, often appearing as mere appendages to life-supporting machines. This shift from the moral to the technical order manifests itself in doctor's fascination with gadgets, the emphasis upon parts of the body, and a concomitant blurring of distinctions concerning death, personhood and individual rights. The patient is reduced to a secondary role in his or her own death, thus engendering a widespread desire for a sudden death."

Leslie M. Thompson. (1984). Cultural and institutional restrictions on dying styles in a technological society. *Death Studies, 8,* p. 223.

happiness" extend to our choosing how, when, where, and under what circumstances we die? These are complicated questions with profound moral and ethical implications.

Several groups, such as EXIT, founded in England, and The Hemlock Society, its affiliate in the United States, advocate control over your own dying, which includes committing suicide, if necessary, to escape terrible pain or great bodily deterioration. Derek Humphrey, founder and president of the Hemlock Society, has advocated the right to commit suicide for decades. His best-selling book, *Final Exit* (1992), outlines humane methods of committing suicide. AIDS caregivers also tend to advocate the right to commit suicide, and several have assisted AIDS patients in ending their lives (Barrow, 1996).

Physician-Assisted Suicide

The right to commit suicide with the help of a physician has occupied a central place in the public debate over the right to die for more than a decade. The question has long stirred heated debate among religious leaders, jurists, and medical ethicists (Moller, 1996). Soon, Oregon residents may have the right to decide for themselves, a right that residents in no other state currently have. Oregon will become the first state where doctors can legally prescribe lethal drugs for terminally ill patients who request help in taking their own lives. (Similar initiatives have been defeated in Washington and California).

Oregon's new law, known as the Death With Dignity Act, basically provides terminally ill adults with the right to obtain a prescription from a physician for medications that can be used to end their lives "in a humane and dignified manner." The law imposes three main conditions on doctor-assisted suicide.

1. Two doctors must determine that the patient has a life expectancy of a half a year (six months) or less.
2. The patient must request a doctor's assistance in suicide three times, the last time in writing, with the statement dated and signed by the patient in the presence of two witnesses.
3. The physician must wait at least 15 days after the initial request—and at least 2 days after the final written request—before writing the prescription for the lethal drugs.

NURSES, EUTHANASIA and ASSISTED SUICIDE

Eight hundred fifty-two critical care nurses were surveyed in the United States in 1996. Results revealed the following:

- 17% reported that they had received requests from patients or family members to perform euthanasia or assist in suicide.

- 16% percent reported that they had engaged in such practices.

- 4% reported that they had hastened a patient's death by only pretending to provide life-sustaining treatment ordered by a physician. Some nurses reported engaging in these practices without the request or advance knowledge of physicians or others.

- The method of euthanasia most commonly described was the administration of a high dose of an opiate to a terminally ill patient.

D. A. Asch. (1996, May 23). The role of critical care nurses in euthanasia and assisted suicide. *New England Journal of Medicine, 21*(334). Available: http://www.nejm.org/publi. . .O334/0021/1374/1.htm.

Under the new law, physicians who follow the guidelines cannot be prosecuted or disciplined by professional organizations, such as examining boards and medical societies. Physicians also have the right to refuse a patient's request for the lethal medications. Doctors may be present, but are not required to be, at the time the lethal dose is taken. The law is intended to distinguish between the prescription of lethal medications at the request of a mentally competent, terminally ill adult and euthanasia or physician-assisted suicide. The law states: "Nothing in this Act shall be construed to authorize a physician or any other person to end a patient's life by lethal injection, mercy killing, or active euthanasia." Prescribing the lethal medication to a dying patient "shall not, for any purpose, constitute suicide, assisted suicide, mercy killing or homicide." Additionally, "No medication to end a patient's life in a humane and dignified manner shall be prescribed until the person performing the counseling determines that the patient is not suffering from a psychiatric or psychological disorder, or depression causing impaired judgment."

By the new law, at least one of the two witnesses to the patient's written request for the lethal prescription must be a person who is not a relative of the patient, does not stand to benefit from the estate of the patient, and is not an employee of the hospital or nursing home where the patient is being treated. Still pending, however, are court challenges to Oregon's law legalizing assisted suicide.

In the interim, more than thirty states have made assisted suicide a criminal offense. Physician Jack Kevorkian, who has helped more than forty people to end their lives since 1990, had sought to overturn a 1994 Michigan Supreme Court ruling that there is no constitutional right to physician-assisted suicide and that those who help can be prosecuted. At the same time, Pope John Paul II has issued an encyclical strongly condemning any form of assisted suicide under any circumstance (Barrow, 1996; Moller, 1996).

In 1996, two federal appeals courts, in San Francisco and New York, struck down laws making it a crime for a physician to assist in a suicide (Russell, 1996). The ruling by the U.S. Court of Appeals in San Francisco maintained that physician-assisted suicide is part of the liberty protections of the 14th Amend-

Dr. Jack Kevorkian meets the press in homemade cardboard stocks before his arraignment on assisted suicide charges in Michigan, where the state supreme court has ruled that assisted suicide can be prosecuted. The retired pathologist advocates doctors helping the terminally ill who wish to end their own lives.
© *AP/Wide World Photos*

ment's guarantee of due process as regards the right to privacy. The U.S. Court of Appeals in New York argued that people have the same right to hasten death by taking drugs prescribed by a physician as they do by refusing artificial life supports. Supporters of assisted suicide and right-to-die advocates hailed the two rulings as great strides toward establishing a right-to-die with dignity in America. The U.S. Supreme Court will rule on a number of right-to-die cases in the near future.

Physical Pain and the Right To Die

Many jurors and ethicists maintain that new rulings and initiatives are unlikely to quiet the national debate on physician-assisted suicide. Other experts argue that interest in assisted suicide would decline dramatically if terminally ill persons had more access to hospice care and effective pain management (Worsnop, 1995). Cherny, Coyle, and Foley (1994), drawing a distinction between the right of dying patients to relief from suffering and their right to die, argue that increased efforts directed toward the relief of excruciating pain, severe anxiety, profound existential distress, and intense family fatigue will diminish the impression of patients that elective death is the only answer.

These critics of assisted suicide argue that support for the practice is driven primarily by the fear of dying alone and in intractable pain. Support would plunge, opponents say, if home-based hospice care of the terminally ill became more widely available and if medical and nursing schools did a better job of

"The pain is evil. It's destructive, bad and even demonic. The cancer makes me nervous, anxious, obsessive. The pain and suffering is so bad that it must be evil. . . . Really, there is no meaning to the pain. Pain like this has to come from the devil. At certain times I feel the pain is punishing me. But for what? That I just can't see."

Moller (1990), p. 76.

humane but also cost-effective, since they reduce the amount of time spent in hospitals.

Part of the instruction needed is a change in values so that physicians can be comfortable prescribing "large" doses of narcotics without fear that they are addicting their patients to pain-control drugs. These fearful attitudes are still present in many physicians and nurses and are impediments to effective pain control (Heller, 1996). In a real sense, the burden for changing medical and nursing school training procedures, including requiring death-and-dying course work and instruction in pain control and comfort care for the dying, rests with the organizations that accredit medical and nursing schools. Once these accreditation panels and committees begin to require these changes in training before school accreditation is granted, change will be much more likely.

Psychological Pain and the Slippery Slope

In Australia, an aging population, life-extending technology, and changing community attitudes all played a part in the passage of landmark right-to-die legislation in 1995. After 6 months of debate and a final 16 hours of impassioned parliamentary oratory, Australia's Northern Territory became the first jurisdiction in the world to allow doctors to take the lives of terminally ill patients who wish to die (Moller, 1996).

Under the 1995 Australian Northern Territory Rights of the Terminally Ill Law, an adult patient can request death, probably by lethal injection or pill, to put an end to suffering. The patient must be diagnosed as terminally ill by two doctors, one of whom must have psychiatric qualifications. After a "cooling off" period of 7 days, the patient can sign a certificate of request. After 48 hours the wish for death can be met. Both advocates and critics of assisted suicide point to the question of **the slippery slope.** This begins with the question of where to draw the line on who is to be assisted and who is not to be assisted in taking their life and, once decided, becomes the problem of slipping from that line into more questionable practices.

Consider this case from the Netherlands: Hilly Bosscher endured 25 years of repeated beatings by an alcoholic husband before the marriage ended in divorce. One of her two sons committed suicide at 20 years of age; the other died of lung cancer at the same age. When the 50-year-old former social worker from the Dutch town of Ruinen went to see psychiatrist Boudewijn Chabot, she had but one desire: She wanted to die and she wanted the doctor to help her.

Over the next 4 months, Chabot tried to ease Bosscher's depression and change her mind about suicide, but she did not respond to counseling and refused all medication. Having already made an attempt to kill herself by overdosing on drugs, she thought about other methods. Chabot consulted with seven colleagues, all of whom concurred that Bosscher's prognosis was dismal. Finally, Chabot agreed to help her. On September 28, 1991, he handed Bosscher twenty

"If you're worried about the slippery slope, this case is as far down as you can get."

George Annas, Boston University

sleeping pills and a toxic liquid mixture. Along with this deadly cocktail, she swallowed some antinausea medicine. Then she lay down on her bed while a friend, Chabot, and another doctor sat by her side. She kissed a portrait of her sons and, while Bach played on a tape recorder, she peacefully drifted into death.

The Netherlands boasts one of the worlds' most liberal policies on mercy killing, but the Bosscher case caused a major uproar. Never before had a physician reported helping a depressed but otherwise healthy patient commit suicide. Of the estimated 2300 cases of euthanasia and 400 cases of assisted suicide in the Netherlands each year, virtually all involve patients suffering from a terminal illness or unbearable physical pain. The Bosscher case set out to draw a new line in the sand. Officials charged Chabot with violating the strict guidelines that permit doctors to help patients end their lives. But in a landmark decision, the Netherlands' highest court ruled that, although Chabot neglected to have another physician examine Bosscher personally, the psychiatrist would not be punished. The court ruling recognized the right of patients experiencing severe psychic pain to choose to die with dignity. In essence, the court ruled that intolerable psychological suffering is no different from intolerable physical suffering.

In the United States, where debate flares around Jack Kevorkian and assisted suicide for the terminally ill, the Dutch decision troubles ethicists deeply. Critics are worried that the Netherlands has pointed the way to "assisted suicide on demand." "If you're worried about the slippery slope, this case is as far down as you can get," warns George Annas, health law professor at Boston University. "Terminal illness at least gives you some line to draw," writes Arthur Caplan (1994), director of the University of Pennsylvania's Center for Bioethics. (Toufexis, 1994:61). Nevertheless, critics and advocates alike recognize that right-to-die issues are far tougher to decide when they shift from abstract principles to the reality of desperate persons in physical or psychological pain searching for a way out of their private hell.

In summing up the state of the euthanasia/mercy-killing controversy, thanatologists Gere Fulton and Eileen Metress (1995:219) remind us that the American legal system has demonstrated both ambiguity and tolerance in dealing with indirect euthanasia as well as mercy killing. There have been celebrated cases where those who have broken the law have received surprising leniency and, in some cases, no punishment at all. They write:

> Indirect euthanasia—allowing death to occur by withholding or discontinuing treatment that no longer benefits the patient—has become widely accepted. So, too, has indirect euthanasia such as produced by escalating use of pain-control drugs, realizing that this will likely shorten the patient's life. The intent is to provide relief from pain; the death of the patient is a foreseeable but indirect effect of the treatment. It is only those direct acts intended to end the life of the patient, so-called mercy killing, that seem to be so controversial. . . . Physicians, at least until Dr. Jack Kevorkian, have been quite unlikely to be successfully prosecuted for assisting in the death of their patients."

The debate and the court cases will, most likely, continue to bring these issues to the foreground in the ongoing public dialog, cautioning us, at each turn, to

Ethicists are immersed in debate over numerous issues connected with the impact of medical technology on our definitions of life, death, and personhood—and the East/West dialog has brought the debate to truly global proportions.

proceed with great wisdom and care. Philosopher and ethicist Margaret Pabst Battin (1994:9) writes that: "the situation is growing increasingly volatile. Indeed, I think the right-to-life issues, including . . . the withholding and withdrawing of treatment, assisted suicide, and active euthanasia, will become the major social issue of the next decade—that is, the focus of the most volatile public controversy—replacing abortion in that role." But, regardless of how we proceed as a society, it is clear that the right-to-die remains an issue we must come to grips with personally, now, for ourselves, if we are to prepare for our own death with dignity.

LIFE/DEATH, EAST/WEST

Right-to-die issues are not confined to the West. Unquestionably, as advanced medical technology is introduced into a country's health care system, the ethical knots of right-to-die issues and other legal and moral conundrums are soon to follow. In many Asian cultures, for example, the doctrine, or *dharma,* of Buddhism is identified as the authority par excellence on matters pertaining to the ethics and morality of life-and-death issues, and is closely linked to the rites and ceremonies associated with the transition from this life to the next. The themes of impermanence, decay, and death are omnipresent in Buddhist literature, and Buddhist ethics appear to have played a prominent role in the evolution of traditional Indian, Chinese, and Japanese medicine (Zysk, 1991). It is likely that as Buddhism spread through Asia it interacted with indigenous medical traditions, promoting the cross-fertilization of ethical ideas and practices.

In a monograph on the subject of death in Asia, Becker (1990) asserts that the Buddhist tradition, especially in Japan, is very tolerant of suicide and euthanasia. Evidence of this is the Buddha's tolerance of suicide by monks and the many Japanese stories and legends praising suicide by monks and Samurai as well as ordinary citizens. Becker suggests that Buddhism values self-determination and praises those who decide when and how they will die when they do so in order to have a dignified, conscious death. But the pervasive influence of Buddhist ethics in Asian approaches to healing has not produced consensus on these issues of life and death.

Brain Death and Personhood

Over the last 20 years, the West has slowly accepted that a "person" is dead if the whole brain is dead, even if the rest of the body continues to function. But the term "death by brain criteria" is somewhat ambiguous, since it refers to at least three different types of brain malfunction (Kastenbaum, 1991, Iserson, 1994): ***whole-brain death,*** in which the whole brain, including the brainstem, has ceased functioning; ***cerebral death,*** in which the brain itself has ceased functioning but the lowest centers of the brainstem and cerebellum still function; and ***neocortical death,*** in which there is a lack of function in the "thinking" part of the brain, the neo- (new) cortex. In this regard, Becker (1990) points out that a key point in

"If the medical and legal professions continue to prefer the whole-brain position, then there may also continue to be a felt obligation to maintain life in those who no longer show the ability to have conscious experiences or social interaction. And should advocacy develop for the intermediate concept of cerebral death, then implications for life support would again be altered. A consensus on what death is—or when deadness has been established—is necessary if society is to cope in an intelligent and coherent way with the many new problems that continue to arise in clinical medicine."

Kastenbaum (1991), p. 34.

Buddhist ethics is not whether there is still bodily warmth or neural activity in the brain, but whether the person is permanently unconscious, unaware of self, and lacking in purposive action and mindfulness.

Most Christian and Jewish scholars accept the concept of death by whole-brain criteria, based on the doctrine that the soul departs the body at the moment of death. "Yet," according to Iserson (1994:16) "religions such as Taoism, Confucianism, Zen-Buddhism, and Shintoism which stress integration of mind and body have difficulty accepting death by brain criteria." To many Eastern (as well as some Western) ethicists, it is troubling to declare the permanently unconscious as "dead," because they consider this an example of inappropriate mind–body dualism.

On the other hand, some ethicists believe that only a "neocortical" definition of death recognizes the centrality of consciousness and personhood. This definition recognizes the importance of meeting death mindfully, a central and powerful tenet of Buddhism that rests on the idea that the last moments of our life can be particularly influential in determining both the quality of our dying and the quality of our next rebirth (Gervais, 1986). Neocortical death is not recognized in the United States, Britain, or Canada. While some bioethicists argue in favor of this criteria of death, others argue for the cerebral death criteria (Kastenbaum, 1991). The most widely accepted and only legal definition of brain death in the United States at this time is "death by whole-brain criteria,"

Based on the "whole-brain criteria", it would appear that Buddhist ethics would wholeheartedly endorse a "whole-brain death" definition of death, since neocortical function is absent in whole-brain death. And yet, according to Hughes (1995) and Becker (1990), there has been strong resistance to the adoption of any brain-death standard in Japan, both from the public and within the medical profession. Much of this resistance is due, in no small measure, to the association between brain death and organ harvesting. The brain-death criterion allows organs to be harvested with minimum delay, thereby enhancing the prospects for a successful transplant. Japanese tradition, however, requires the performance of rituals over a lengthy period of time before an individual is considered to be truly dead. In addition, there is also reluctance on the part of Asians to plundering of bodily organs of future ancestors and their spirits.

Some commentators suggest that there is growing acceptance of brain-death criteria among some Japanese professionals as universities develop criteria and as pressure from potential organ recipients grows. A more positive attitude towards organ transplantation is revealed in research by Tsomo (1993). The author, who surveyed Asian teachers from many different traditions about their attitudes toward organ donation, discovered that an overwhelming majority were positive toward organ transplantation, believing that the corpse is merely an empty vessel.

Asian teachers believed, for the most part, that to give of yourself in the form of organ donation is a great thing, an act of profound compassion Also, it should be noted that countries such as the Philippines have raised objections to Japanese patients' going abroad for transplants rather than building an organ-retrieval system of their own (Hughes, 1995).

Personhood and the Right-To-Die

For our purposes, it seems useful to identify a related issue associated with the right-to-die that has become central to an East/West dialog on the question of biomedical ethics. This is the issue of the meaning of **personhood** as it applies to the definition of death (Becker, 1990).

Personhood is a central problem for both Buddhist ethics and Western medical ethics, and, consequently, a very promising area for a dialog between the two. For bioethicists, struggles over abortion, animal rights, and brain death have brought personhood to the forefront of the debate (Becker, 1990; Hughes, 1995) Opponents of euthanasia and advocates for the disabled and animals assert that merely being alive should bestow "personhood" and a "right to life." Other bioethicists believe that human beings and animals take on ethical significance to the extent that they are "persons." Some, such as Tooley (1984), would set a standard of personhood that excludes almost all animals, newborns, and the severely retarded or demented from the definition of "person." Interestingly, some Western bioethicists have argued for standards of "personhood" in which they begin to sound remarkably Buddhistic (Becker, 1990; Hughes, 1995). These standards of personhood include:

- Neurological integrity
- Sentience (the power of perception by the senses)
- Awareness of the difference between self and other
- The ability to be conscious of yourself over time
- The ability to engage in purposive actions

These same bioethicists have become increasingly troubled by questions about the autonomy, continuity, and authenticity of personhood and the sense of self (Hughes, 1995). For example:

- Do antidepressants or powerful pain medications create an inauthentic self, or is the self more authentic when it is free of physical or psychological pain?
- Are we respecting a patient's autonomy by respecting the treatment preferences they expressed when they were healthy, or those they express in the throes of illness?
- Is it ever possible for a patient to give truly free and informed consent to treatment?

As is evident, the question of what constitutes personhood weighs heavily on virtually all the other ethical, moral, and legal questions connected with the right to die (Becker, 1990). Ethicists from around the world continue to be immersed in debate over numerous issues connected with the impact of medical technology on our definitions of life, death, and personhood. The East/West dialog has deepened the questions being asked about death with dignity and brought the debate to truly global proportions.

Tasks

There are important tasks we can complete now that will serve us well in preparing for our death and dying. One such task involves educating ourselves about our rights and powers as patients in America's hospitals and nursing homes. Other tasks involve both decision making and the preparation of documents involving a formal will, a living will, a Durable Power of Attorney for Health Care, organ donation, and funeral arrangements.

INFORMED CONSENT

Informed consent means that patients share in their health care decision making by becoming informed and by basing their choice, acceptance, or rejection of medical treatment on the information available to them. The Patient Self-Determination Act, which took effect December 1, 1991, requires hospitals and other medical institutions to tell patients that they have the right to refuse treatment or artificial life-support procedures. Hospitals must also ask patients whether they have living wills or other documents that spell out their wishes in the event they become incapacitated. Nursing homes that receive Medicare or Medicaid funding must also inform patients of these rights.

THE LIVING WILL

There are things you can do today to let others know how you would like decisions handled in the event that you become unable to make them for yourself. The living will makes it easier for a loved one to know how to make difficult health care decisions on your behalf and can help avoid family conflict. Living wills are very personal and conform only to your desires and preferences (Hill & Shirley, 1992). They state only the preferences of the individual making the will and do not "name" anyone to speak on your behalf (unlike a Durable Power of Attorney for Health Care). Laws regarding the validity of living wills vary from state to state, although most states now recognize

ETHICS: EAST/WEST

Jennifer Tsai and Kang Cheng Chiu, both 20-year-old engineering students at the University of California, Berkeley, walked along Baker Beach holding hands, enjoying a break from summer school. Suddenly, a rogue wave swept over them, washing them out to sea. Tsai's body was recovered that night, while Chiu's body remained missing. Both were members of the Chinese Buddhist Society.

In the days after Tsai's death, her family tried to maintain a constant vigil at the county morgue, playing music and performing rituals, based on their belief that Buddhists who die an accidental death, especially by drowning, need many prayers and a great deal of care from loved ones so that their spirits can rest in peace. The parents protested a planned autopsy on Tsai's body by the San Francisco medical examiner, saying this unnecessary invasion would deeply disturb her spirit. Citing First Amendment rights, a San Francisco Superior Court judge ruled that a coroner's autopsy was unnecessary because a number of witnesses saw what happened to Tsai at Baker Beach. Tsai's parents and other weeping relatives claimed her body the same day and prepared for her funeral and cremation. The San Francisco City Attorney said he knew of just one other successful challenge to an autopsy, it involved an Orthodox Jewish family.

Source: H. K. Lee. (1995, June 15). Buddhist family wins autopsy dispute. *San Francisco Chronicle*, p. A23.

CARING INSIGHTS

The Freedom to Choose

Patients do not always realize that they have the right to accept or reject any treatment or prescription that their physician may offer them. According to Georgia Barrow (1996), those suffering a serious or life-threatening illness for which several treatment plans are possible or optional should gather as much information as possible and then select what they believe to be the best plan. In terms of cancer treatment, for example, surgery, radiation, chemotherapy, and special diets are all available as treatment options. Patients should become aware of the risks involved with each option and then base their consent to treatment on three principles:

1. They are competent to give consent.
2. Consent is being given freely (e.g., not coerced by economic situation or relatives).
3. Consent is being given with a full understanding of the situation.

an individual's right to refuse medical treatment and to request the care that he or she prefers.

A living will provides written instructions concerning health care in the event of terminal illness and, in addition to offering clarity to loved ones regarding our final desires, also saves on medical bills. Medical researchers (Hanson & Rodgman, 1996) report that Medicare patients who do not leave verbal or written instructions about the kind of treatment they wanted spent more than three times in hospital charges ($95,305) for their final hospital stay than patients who left a living will or other advance directive ($30,478). Among the general population of hospital patients, these researchers found that patients who are black, poorly educated, underinsured, or cognitively impaired are least likely to prepare a living will and that, although decedents with living wills forego specific treatments, they remain intensive users of routine medical services. Choice in Dying, the nation's largest distributor of living wills, sent out 400,000 forms in 1995. But no one knows how many living wills have actually been signed or executed.

Despite the legal requirements and public enthusiasm for written advance directives, such as living wills, few patients actually complete them. But two studies have shown that simple educational interventions increase the number of directives completed. Luptak and Boult (1994), for example, studied the effectiveness of an interdisciplinary intervention designed to help ambulatory frail elders to record advance directives (e.g., living wills, durable power of attorney). In collaboration with physicians and a trained lay volunteer, a social worker provided information and counseling to thirty-four elderly persons (ages 65–86 years), to their families, and to their proxies in a series of visits to a

CARING INSIGHTS

Say What You Mean

To give a living will added force, describe as full a range as possible of physical and mental conditions and the sorts of care you would not accept in each case. Hill and Shirley (1992:51) warn: "Vague advance requests for 'no treatment at all' are not likely to be taken seriously by even the most sympathetic caregiver."

Don't simply say, "Heroic medical procedure are not acceptable," or that "life-prolonging procedures" should end when you have a "terminal illness for which there is no reasonable expectation of recovery." Instead, be as specific as possible. For instance, you might say, "Should I ever have a terminal illness, with irreversible brain damage that makes me unable to recognize people or to swallow, I would (or would not) want these measures taken: cardiopulmonary resuscitation to start my heart beating, use of respirator if I can't breathe, feeding by a tube into the stomach, treatment with antibiotics, if pneumonia or other infections develop." If you feel that a hospice program would provide the best care during your last months of life, specify so.

After completing a valid living will (one that complies with the specific rules of your state), give copies of the living will to all individuals who are likely to be involved in your medical care. Include on the form the location of the original document. Keep it with other important papers. If you have a safe deposit box, do not put it in the box if you are the only one who has access to the box.

geriatric evaluation and management clinic. Nearly three-quarters of the sample (71%) chose to record some form of advance directive. And of these, 96% named a proxy and 83% recorded specific treatment preferences.

Courts have generally supported the rights of patients and their surrogates to refuse life-sustaining treatment, including nutrition and hydration. On the other hand, there are times when a family member of an incompetent patient insists that everything possible be done for the patient (including resuscitation after cardiac arrest) and the physicians are uniformly opposed to resuscitation as a violation of the standards of medical practice. In cases involving such a conflict, physicians are routinely advised to stand their ground and refuse to resuscitate patients when there appears to be no medical justification. The official position of the Society of Critical Care Medicine, the American Thoracic Society, and the American Medical Association is that no physician should be obligated to provide useless or futile treatment, even when asked to do so by patients or surrogates. Defining which therapies are futile is a current topic of debate for ethicists.

Example of a Living Will

The following document is only a guide. It should not replace necessary consultation with a qualified legal professional regarding your state's regulations regarding a living will's length of effectiveness, requirements for witnesses, or other factors.

Living Will of (**fill in your name**)

To my physician, attorney, family, friends, and any medical facility or health care professional whose care I may come under or happen to be under and all others who may be responsible for decision making with respect to my health or well-being:

On this (**fill in ordinal number, e.g., first, second**) day of (**fill in month**), (**fill in year**), I, (**fill in first name, middle name, and last name**), born (**fill in birth date**), being of sound mind, willfully and voluntarily direct that my dying and death shall not be artificially prolonged under the circumstances set forth in this declaration:

If, at any time:

1. I should be in a coma or a persistent vegetative state and, in the opinion of two physicians who have personally examined me, one of whom shall be my attending physician, have no known hope of regaining awareness and higher mental functions no matter what is done, or

2. I should have an incurable injury, disease, or illness certified to be a terminal condition by two physicians who have personally examined me, one of whom shall be my attending physician, and the physicians have determined that my death will occur as a result of such incurable injury, disease, or illness, whether or not life-sustaining procedures are utilized, and where the application of such procedures would serve only to prolong artificially a hopeless illness or the dying process, I direct that life-sustaining or -prolonging treatments or procedures (including the artificial administration of food and water, whether intravenously, be gastric tube, or by any other similar means) shall not be used and I do not desire any such treatment to be provided and/or continued.

3. I would like to live out my last days at home rather than in a hospital, long-term care facility, nursing home, or other health care facility if it does not jeopardize the chance of my recovery to a meaningful life and does not put undue hardship on my family or significant other.

4. I direct that I be permitted to die naturally, with only the administration of medication and/or the performance of any medical procedure deemed necessary to provide me with comfort and/or to alleviate pain. In the absence of my ability to give directions regarding the use of such life-sustaining procedures, it is my intention that this document and my wishes with respect to dying shall be honored by my family and physicians as a definitive expression of my legal right to refuse medical or surgical treatment and to accept the consequences from such refusal.

As a consequence of the foregoing instructions, I hereby direct my Personal Representative, my Trustee, the beneficiaries under my Will, and my heirs that none of them may or shall maintain or cause to be maintained any legal or administrative action that has as its foundation or as one of its claims or causes of action the failure of a physician, nurse, hospital, clinic, or any other natural or legal person or entity whatsoever to prolong my life while, because of an incurable injury, disease, or illness certified to be a terminal condition, under the procedures described above.

This statement is made after careful consideration and is in accordance with my strong convictions and beliefs. I want the wishes and directions here expressed carried out to the full extend permitted by law. Those concerned with my health and well-being are asked to take whatever action is needed (including legal) to realize my preferences, wishes, and instructions. Insofar as they are not legally enforceable, let those to whom this is addressed regard themselves as morally bound by these provisions.

I am an adult of sound mind and otherwise legally competent to make this Declaration, and I understand its full import.

Signed by:
(**fill in your full name and address**)

Signature of the above:
Date: (**fill in date**)

Under penalty of perjury, we state that this Declaration was signed by (**name of individual signing**) in the presence of the undersigned, who, at the Declarant's request, in the Declarant's presence, and in the presence of each other, have hereunto signed our names as witnesses this (**fill in ordinal number, e.g., first, second**) day in the month of (**fill in month**), in the year of (**fill in year**).

Each of us individually states that: The Declarant is personally known to me, and I believe the Declarant to be of sound mind. I did not sign the Declarant's signature to this Living Will Declaration.

Based upon information and belief, I am not related to the Declarant by blood or marriage, a creditor of the Declarant, entitled to any portion of the estate of the Declarant under any existing testamentary instrument of the Declarant, entitled to any financial benefit be reason of the death of the Declarant, financially or otherwise responsible for the Declarant's medical care, or an employee of any such person or institution.

Name: (**fill in name**)
Address: (**fill in address**)

Name: (**fill in name**)
Address: (**fill in address**)

CARING INSIGHTS

Legal Advice

As health care technology increases in both sophistication and cost, the legal and ethical issues surrounding death and dying will continue to increase in complexity. As technology continues to advance, the regulatory, legal, and ethical issues will remain fluid and will change as new situations arise. Given the fluidity of the situation, and the sometimes-vast differences in regulations and statutes from state to state and nation to nation, most experts in the field advise consumers to seek out an attorney who specializes in the field to help them with the tasks of completing their wills, living wills, advance directives, and instructions regarding organ donation. Consult a lawyer before setting up a power of attorney, durable power of attorney, living will, joint account, trust, or guardianship. Be sure to ask for the cost of a legal consultation *before* visiting any lawyer.

Copies of this Living Will have been distributed to:

Name: (**fill in name**)
Address: (**fill in address**)

Name: (**fill in name**)
Address: (**fill in address**)

The original Living Will is located in (**fill in**) at (**fill in address**).

DURABLE POWER OF ATTORNEY FOR HEALTH CARE

A standard power of attorney can be set up to give one person power to handle personal or financial matters for another. Because the standard power of attorney loses its effectiveness if the principal becomes legally incompetent, a *durable* power of attorney may be better. A durable power of attorney becomes operative only after a person becomes incapacitated.

A Durable Power of Attorney for Health Care permits you (the Declarant) to express in writing (while you're still capable of making decisions about your health and well-being) your desire to appoint another person (the attorney-in-fact) to make medical and health care decisions in the event that you become unable to participate in decision making about your medical care and treatment. The attorney-in-fact, who is a person of your own choosing, is empowered to make health care and medical decisions, based on your preferences and desires as well as any instructions you have given them. As with your living will, copies of the Durable Power of Attorney for Health Care should be given to all people who are likely to be involved in decision making regarding health and medical services (Hill & Shirley, 1992).

Laws regarding the validity of Durable Power of Attorney for Health Care vary from state to state. While not all states require that a Durable Power of Attorney for Health Care be used in conjunction with a living will, many experts recommend that a Durable Power of Attorney for Health Care be named when completing a living will. Be sure to check with a qualified legal professional in your state regarding specific language and rules.

FORMAL AND HOLOGRAPHIC WILLS

As a general principle, each of us is free to leave her or his property to anyone by executing a valid will, a formal legal document that is probated through the court system. According to law professor Sheryl Scheible Wolf (1995), every state has statutory formalities for executing wills, which must be strictly complied with in most states. Although the statutes governing wills vary considerably among states, many states recognize wills that were validly executed in another state. The strict, formal requirements are imposed to ensure that the writer of the will, the testator, realizes the importance of the act and to protect against fraud.

In general, any adult of "sound mind" may dispose of property by will. A will is invalid if the testator lacked mental capacity or if another person unduly influenced the testator to the extent that the will does not represent the testator's true intentions. A formal will must be attested to and signed by at least two witnesses, often according to a prescribed ceremony (Wolf, 1995).

Although all states recognize and prefer formal wills, approximately half the states also permit handwritten, unwitnessed wills, known as *holographic wills*. There are many commercially available books and computer software programs for wills and other such documents. Some of these, such as those published by Nolo Press, allow documents to be customized for state of residence (Heller, 1996). However, as Sheryl Wolf (1995) points out, even where holographic wills are recognized, they should be used with caution.

REMEMBER FLUFFY

In 1994, the New York City Bar Association issued a pamphlet with detailed postmortem pet guidelines for individuals planning on providing for their pets in their wills. Tips included the following.

- Since wills can take months to settle, make provisions on an outside document.

- Find several people who agree to care for the pet just in case one or more back out at the last minute.

- Set aside money in a trust fund for food and veterinary care, but not too much, because relatives can become very upset when a pet outinherits them.

FUNERAL ARRANGEMENTS

The relative freedom afforded us with respect to willing our property to others does not extend to the disposition of our bodies after death. The body is not considered property in any conventional sense and, therefore, does not become part of the decedent's estate (Scarmon, 1991–92). The right to control our bodies ends at death, and any remaining rights regarding disposal and funeral rites passes on to the living. Fortunately, during life we can specify funeral and burial directions, to simplify the responsibilities of our survivors. According to Wolf (1995), considerations span the continuum from the most general (e.g., body disposal) to the most detailed (clothing and jewelry to be worn) and should include:

- Whether the body should be buried, cremated, or be offered to medical research
- Whether funeral home visitation, a memorial service, or religious ceremony is desired
- The type of casket to be used, and whether it should be open or closed
- The nature of the obituary, and whether to make a request for gifts to some specific charity in lieu of flowers

It is important to talk with our loved ones about these issues, because unless our close relatives agree with our predeath plans and wishes, there is little certainty that they will be implemented. According to Wolf (1995), traditional law has never recognized the right to decide the disposition of our own body. In addition, once death has occurred, immediate arrangements must be made for disposal of the deceased's body. Wolf (1995:1976) writes:

> Family members and close friends may be emotionally unprepared to make the many necessary decisions for funeral arrangements at this time without some written guidance. . . . [I]t is advisable to give a copy of funeral and burial instructions to someone who is likely to be available when death occurs and to discuss the arrangements with family members to obtain their concurrence in advance. A will typically is not read until after disposal of the body, so a separate writing containing funeral plans is preferable."

Although the courts have asserted that the individual's expressed intentions should be respected to the extent that is proper and reasonable, they have often balanced those intentions against any conflicting wishes of the survivors (Iserson, 1994). Similarly, a decedent's instructions for a nonrelative to decide on funeral and burial arrangements may be overridden by the surviving family members. A durable power of attorney can cover funeral and burial arrangements and could well forestall relatives with other wishes (Heller, 1996). Cremation has become a less expensive and more accepted option in recent years, prompting some states, such as Texas, to enact statutes allowing individuals to make binding decisions regarding cremation (Wolf, 1995). The *Preparing for Dying Worksheet* presented in chapter 12 will aid decision-making about body disposal and funeral arrangements.

ORGAN DONATIONS

Although there are numerous restrictions on our freedom to dispose of the whole body, we have considerable freedom in donating specific organs. Such donations, especially for transplantation, can alleviate a family's sense of loss and add meaning to the death of a loved one. Gifts of anatomical parts at death provide the primary source of transplant organs. Many types of organs, such as corneas, glands, and skin, can be stored in organ banks until needed (Crown,

THE COST OF FUNERAL SERVICES

Nondeclinable professional service charges	$668.33	*Average Retail Selling Price for Caskets*	
Embalming	226.23	Minimum alternative container	163.19
Other body preparation (cosmetology, casketing, hair)	90.71	Cloth-covered wood	490.87
		20-gauge steel, nonsealer, crepe interior	816.90
Use of viewing facilities	189.04	18-gauge steel, velvet interior	1754.41
Use of facility for ceremony	185.76	Copper, sealer, velvet interior	3255.40
Other use of facility	193.93	Select hardwood, crepe interior	1919.89
Transfer of remains to funeral home	87.74	Other	1848.89
Hearse (local)	117.49		
Limousine (local)	94.65	*Average Retail Selling Price for Burial Vaults*	
Other auto	66.99	Two-piece concrete box	421.59
Acknowledgment cards	19.32	12-gauge nongalvanized steel vault	827.73
Forwarding remains to another funeral home	794.58	10-gauge galvanized steel vault	1207.17
Retrieving remains from another funeral home	738.22	Asphalt-coated concrete steel vault	595.88
Direct cremation (family provides container)	824.03	Concrete vault with nonmetallic liner	720.14
Immediate burial (family provides container)	835.99	Other	786.36
Direct cremation (funeral home provides container)	886.10	**AVERAGE ADULT FUNERAL GROSS SALE**	$4104.16
Immediate burial (funeral home provides container)	835.99		

Adapted from the National Funeral Directors Association's 1991 Survey of Funeral Operations, based on the general price lists required by the Federal Trade Commission.

1982; Iserson, 1994). Other vital organs, such as hearts, livers, and kidneys, must be transplanted after brain death but before "circulatory" death, to avoid tissue damage or deterioration that might be harmful or fatal to the recipient. Predeath authorization for organ donation can lessen delay and be crucial to a successful organ transplant.

During life, vital organs may not be donated because of criminal prohibitions against suicide and homicide (Weissman, 1977). The federal National Organ Transplantation Act in 1984 banned the sale of human organs by living persons and established $50,000 fines and imprisonment for violations (Iserson, 1994; Wolf, 1995). By 1987, all states had enacted some version of the Uniform Anatomical Gift Act, which permits an individual to direct organ donation without the consent of surviving relatives. The act allows a competent adult to donate specific organs, prosthetic devices, or the entire body to any hospital, physician, medical or dental school, or storage facility to be used for education, research, therapy, or transplant. No obligation to contribute organs has ever existed. Absent evidence of the deceased's opposing wishes, the closest relatives traditionally have been authorized to make organ donations (Iserson, 1994).

Americans appear to have conflicting feelings and attitudes toward organ donation. In one Gallup poll of American attitudes toward organ donation, 73% said they were very likely to donate organs of their loved ones, whereas only 27% said they would want their own organs taken (Iserson, 1994). Robbins (1990), in a study of the personality factors related to organ donor card signing in ninety-four undergraduate and graduate students (ages 19–56 years), found that nondonors scored higher on the Death Anxiety Scale, the Collett-Lester Fear of Death Scale, and a scale of physical anxiety. Donors scored higher on a Likert scale reflecting acceptance of dying and on measures of self-efficacy.

Swedish researcher Margareta Sanner (1994) studied the deeper motives, attitudes, and reactions of people (ages 18–75 years) toward organ donation, transplantation, autopsy, dissection, and other procedures having to do with body disposal following death, along with their religious beliefs and beliefs about death. She discovered that reactions, beliefs, and motives concerning these procedures with the dead body could be summarized and understood according to six motive complexes: illusion of lingering life; protection of the value of the individual; distrust, anxiety, and alienation; respecting the limits set by nature or God; altruism; and rationality.

GETTING OUR AFFAIRS IN ORDER

One thing everyone, young or old, can do to plan for the future is to get his or her financial and personal records in order. Caring for a terminally ill person or preparing for your own old age or death can be managed more successfully by making decisions and arrangements *before* a crisis develops. Because caregivers often have little knowledge of the loved one's vital information and records, the task is much simpler if papers are already in order. The following checklist, although it may not cover everyone's unique situations, can help you get started organizing your own financial and personal records or the records of a loved one.

Personal Records

A personal records file should include the following.

1. Full legal name
2. Maiden or other names ever used by the individual
3. Social Security number
4. Legal residence
5. Date and place of birth
6. Names and addresses of spouse and children (or location of death certificate, if any are deceased)
7. Names of parents, including maiden or other names ever used by the individuals
8. Location of will or trust
9. Location of birth certificate

10. Location of certificates of marriage, divorce, and citizenship
11. List of employers and locations and dates of employment
12. Education and military records
13. Religious affiliation, name of church or synagogue, and names of clergy
14. Memberships in organizations and awards received
15. Names and addresses of close friends, relatives, doctors, and lawyers or financial advisors
16. Requests, preferences, or prearrangements for burial

Financial Records

A financial records file is a place to list information about insurance policies, bank accounts, deeds, investments, and other valuables. Here is a suggested outline.

1. Sources of income and assets (pension funds, interest income, etc.)
2. Social Security and Medicare information
3. Investment income (stocks, bonds, property)
4. Insurance information (life, health, and property), with policy numbers
5. Bank accounts (checking, savings, credit union, IRAs, CDs)
6. Location of safe deposit boxes
7. Copy of most recent income tax return
8. Liabilities: what is owed to whom and when payments are due
9. Mortgages and debts: how and when paid
10. Credit card and charge account names and numbers
11. Property taxes
12. Location of all personal items, such as jewelry and family treasures

A trusted family member or friend should know the location of this personal records file and of all important papers and documents.

How will we die, and where, and when? These are truly unanswerable questions. So how can we truly prepare to die? We cannot see into our futures in specific ways. And yet, according to philosopher Margaret Pabst Battin (1994:3), "we can still know a great deal about how we are likely to die—it is a new picture, different from what it would have been forty or fifty years ago. Furthermore, while we often think of dying as something that will eventually happen to us, we fail to see that our own deaths are a component of our lives about which we can make major, morally significant choices." To ponder our own deaths, to conjure up imaginings of pain and loneliness in our final days, is no easy thing—and yet we must do these things if we are to truly honor our own fleeting existence as well as those we leave behind in the mourning after.

Chapter Summary

Tasks and issues concerned with preparing for dying range from the simple tasks, such as body disposal choices, organ donation decisions, living and formal will preparation, and funeral arrangements to the profoundly complex right-to-die decisions—such as whether to sustain our lives, through heroic medical procedures if we are comatose or in intractable pain, or **not** to sustain our lives, through indirect or active euthanasia, suicide, or assisted suicide. The challenges in considering these issues and tasks are to focus on and embrace the inevitability of death, to begin pondering questions concerned with dying with dignity, and to consider the impact of our death on the loved ones who touched us and who were, in turn, touched by our existence.

The floating perspective is based on the psychological insight that recognizes that our capacity actually to encounter the anxiety connected with death and dying and to prepare for our own death is part of a process that changes over time. The floating perspective is best described as an attempt to continue examining our views of death as an ongoing project. In this way, our understanding of and preparations for death may change as our lives change.

FURTHER READINGS

Battin, M. P. (1994). *The Least Worst Death: Essays in Bioethics on the End of Life*. Oxford University Press, New York.

Hill, T. P., and Shirley, D. (1992). *A Good Death: Taking More Control at the End of Your Life*. Addison-Wesley, Reading, MA.

Moller, D. W. (1996). *Confronting Death: Values, Institutions and Morality*. Oxford University Press, New York.

Niemeyer, R. A. (1994). *Death Anxiety Handbook: Research, Instrumentation and Application*. Taylor & Francis, Washington, DC.

Pojman, L. P. (1992). *Life and Death: Grappling with the Moral Dilemmas of Our Time*. Jones and Bartlett, Boston.

Pojman, L. P. (ed.). (1993). *Life and Death: A Reader in Moral Problems*. Jones and Bartlett, Boston.

Quill, T. E. (1993). *Death and Dignity: Making Choices and Taking Charge*. Norton, New York.

Wolf, S. S. (1995). Legal perspectives on planning for death. In H. Wass and R. A. Niemeyer (eds.). *Dying: Facing the Facts*. Taylor & Francis, Washington, DC, pp. 163–184.

Zysk, K. G. (1991). *Asceticism and Healing in Ancient India: Medicine in the Buddhist Monastery*. Oxford University Press, Oxford.

ELEVEN

Honoring the Dead, Comforting the Living

I f we imagine ourselves gazing at this planet from a bird's-eye (or a satellite's-eye) view, at the nearly 6 billion human inhabitants, each immersed in a different cultural tradition, spiritual outlook, and world view, we might begin to appreciate the amazing array of meanings and interpretations we place on the events of life and death. Life, for some, is objective and material. Death is simply the end of existence, a wall, and the idea of an afterlife has an illusory, mystical quality. For others, life itself is illusory and mystical, and the realm between death and an afterlife is a door, an objective transition between states of being.

To some, the event of death is a sacred and magnificent release from the pain and suffering of this gross earthly existence. To others, death is a terrifying and unfortunate waste of life. But whether we view death as life's black hole, or as the pearly gateway to an unimaginable paradise, the fact is that death is a constant, universal, and inevitable ending, not only for the individual who has died, but for all who were touched by that person's existence. Whatever our religious background, ethnic heritage, spiritual outlook, or personal experience, the ritual disposal of the body of our dead and the gathering of loved ones for the mourning after are two of the few cultural universals known about the human inhabitants of this little blue planet.

Endings

"Disposing of the dead" is a harsh-sounding phrase, but it refers to an activity that all societies must perform. As with all human rituals, body disposal rituals are formal, stylized, and repetitive and are performed in special places, at set times. According to Leming and Dickinson (1994), these rituals function primarily to reinforce group ties, to lessen psychological tensions in the participants, and to stabilize the pattern of community life disrupted by the crisis of death. Sociologist David Wendell Moller (1996:79) writes:

> [F]unerals . . . are ceremonial emblems of humanity's attempt, on both an individual and a collective basis, to respond to the turmoil generated by the deaths of individuals. They . . . provide legally and culturally sanctioned ways of disposing of dead human bodies while reinforcing systems of support for grieving survivors. Less obviously, funerals are an embodiment and a reflection of social life in a given time, place, and culture.

The ritual preparation and disposal of the dead also reflect an attempt by family and community members to honor the dead and to prepare the deceased for the afterlife. Throughout recorded time, people in many cultures have believed that if the physical body of the deceased is not properly cared for, the soul of that person would not find its final resting place in the afterlife. As a consequence, the soul or ghost of the person would resort to haunting and taunting the living in strange and evil ways. The fetal posture of the skeletal remains of many ancient people, for instance, is believed due to tying the arms and knees to the chest to keep the soul from walking about and annoying the living (Jonas, 1976). Ancient funeral rituals and burial customs attest both to the belief in an afterlife and to an almost-instinctual refusal on our part to accept death as the complete and final end of our existence. The belief that human beings survive death in some form occurs in nearly all religions and societies.

SACRED ACTS

"The reverence and rituals surrounding the disposal of the body reflect religious traditions going back thousands of years, as well as up-to-the-minute fads. All of the elements of the burial— the preparation of the body, the garments or shroud, the prayers, the method of disposal, the place and time of burial—become sacred acts by which a particular community of believers bids at least a temporary farewell to one of its own."

Source: Whalen (1990), p. 33.

THE ELEMENTS OF BODY DISPOSAL

Throughout human history, no matter how complex the preparation of the dead body and how elaborate the mourning ritual, ultimately, the dead body has been released to the basic planetary elements of earth, fire, water, and air for final disposal: buried in the earth, turned to ashes by fire, set adrift on the sea, or left above ground, in the open air, to be devoured by the wind, animal predators, family, or foe.

Earth

Ground burial of a corpse in a covered or enclosed pit, a cave, or some other earthen structure in which it eventually decomposes is probably the most common method of disposal of the dead (Middleton, 1991; Aiken, 1994). It is also the most ancient method, dating back to the Paleolithic era. Communal burial places, called *cemeteries* or *mausoleums,* mark some of the oldest locations of human settlement and are regarded by many as blessed and hallowed ground. The method of ground burial in which the corpse is placed in an opening in the ground and covered with earth was probably prompted by the belief "that a body planted in the soil will rise again like a flower rises from a seed" (Aiken, 1994:134; R. Fulton, 1992). Burial in the ground is the most common form of body disposal in the Western world today.

GRAVE DANCING

During the Middle Ages, various rites, such as the "dance of the dead" were performed to prevent the deceased from returning to interfere with the living by speeding the soul to its place in the afterlife. Between the fourth century and the sixteenth century, the ritualistic dance of the dead turned many cemeteries into "dance floors." Ivan Illich describes the dance of the dead as follows:

> From the fourth century onwards, the Church had struggled against the pagan tradition of crowds dancing in cemeteries: naked, frenzied, and brandishing swords. Nevertheless, the frequency of ecclesiastical prohibitions testifies that they were of little avail, and for thousands of years Christian churches and cemeteries remained dance floors. Death was an occasion for the renewal of life. To dance with the dead over their tombs was an occasion for affirming the joy of being alive and a source of many erotic songs and poems. By the late fourteenth century, the sense of these dances seems to have changed: from an encounter between the living and those who were already dead, it was transformed into a meditative, introspective experience. In 1424 the first "Dance of the Dead" was painted on a cemetery wall in Paris: . . . king, peasant, pope, scribe and maiden each dance with the corpse. Each partner is a mirror image of the other in dress and feature. In the shape of his body Everyman carries his own death with him and dances with it through his life."

Source: Ivan Illich. In R. Fulton (1984), p. 112.

Burial Practices Generally, the body is buried within several days of the death, but for some groups the burial must be completed before sundown on the day of the death or within 24 hours. The amount of time between death and burial is usually related to the time needed to prepare the body, to make necessary funeral arrangements, and, above all, to gather together family members, friends, and neighbors for the last rites.

Traditionally, graves have been dug rather deep, usually 6 feet or so, to prevent seepage, odors, and exhumation of the dead by animals or other grave robbers. Today, with sealed, steel caskets that are often placed in steel or concrete vaults, it is not necessary to dig the grave as deep. Typically, graves are dug 4.5 feet deep with 18 inches of earth above the casket or vault (Leming & Dickinson, 1994).

Behold, I show you a mystery; We shall not all sleep, but we shall all be changed. . . . in a moment, in the twinkling of an eye, at the last trump: for the trumpet shall sound, and the dead shall be raised incorruptible, and we shall be changed.

I Corinthians 15:51–52 AV

In Western cultures, the pit is dug wide enough for the body to lie horizontally, although certain cultures have buried the body in a sitting position or even upright. Some Australian aborigine tribespeople, for example, bury their dead in a vertical position with a space above the head. Dead Japanese may be seated in tublike coffins and buried. The Ik of Uganda place the dying person in the fetal position, since death for them represents a "celestial rebirth." Buddhists who choose burial are buried on their backs with the head facing north, which is believed to have been the Buddha's dying position.

In other horizontal burials, the face was often turned toward the west, perhaps emphasizing the setting (i.e., death) of the sun. However, in ancient Egypt, from 2500 B.C. onward, the body was placed with the head to the north and the face to the east. This easterly orientation of the face was presumably chosen to indicate rebirth in the hereafter as reflected in the rising sun (Lessa, 1976; Aiken, 1994). The placement of the head was of secondary importance in early Christian burials, in which the feet face the east so that the last trumpet, which was to be played by angels from that direction, could be heard best and responded to more quickly (Aiken, 1994). In all instances, the positioning of the corpse was meant to facilitate the journey to the afterlife. Based on his extensive study of burial customs, J. Mack Welford (1992:8) writes: "The soul journeyed to a far land, either a shadowy and gloomy

Traditionally, graves were dug about 6 feet deep to prevent disturbance of the body or problems caused by decomposition. Today, the lid of a sealed casket usually lies just 18 inches below the surface. © *Robert Marrone*

PRETTY EAGLE FLIES HOME

"The remains of Pretty Eagle, a great war chief of the Crow tribe, were flown home to rest among his people. Pretty Eagle, who lived from 1846 to 1903, was a member of the Piegan Clan and Fox warrior society. His body and the bodies of sixty-one other tribal members were removed from burial sites along the Bighorn River of Montana in the early 1900s and sold to museums, according to Crow Cultural Director John Pretty On Top.

The American Museum of Natural History in New York City released the remains after a 7-year campaign by the chief's great grandson Hugh White Clay. 'It's a great day, not only for me but for my boy and for the whole tribe,' White Clay said."

Source: San Francisco Chronicle, June 3, 1994, p. A3.

land beneath the earth (the tomb, the Sheol of the Old Testament Jewish tradition, etc.) or, more cheerfully, a happy land beyond the seas (Isle of the Blessed, Avalon, Valhalla, etc.) or in the sky (heaven)."

The presence of various kinds of valuables and other possessions in prehistoric graves, such as food, ornaments, chariots, weapons, flowers, and implements, also suggests the belief in an afterlife, as do the presence of the bodies of murdered servants and wives. The tomb complex of Emperor Qin Shihuang, who ruled China from 221 to 210 B.C. contained more than 6,000 life-size terra cotta soldiers, horses, and chariots, all painstakingly produced to be buried with the emperor in the belief that they would drive away intruders (Baker, 1994).

Embalming   Embalming is the art of preserving bodies after death generally by the use of natural or human-made chemical substances. Much evidence demonstrates that embalming is religious in origin, conceived as a means of preparing the dead for their journey into the afterlife. It is believed to have originated among the Egyptians, probably before 4000 B.C., and was used by them for more than thirty centuries (Mayer, 1990).

Life after death was of preeminent importance to the Egyptians, who believed that spiritual survival depended absolutely on the body's physical survival. Consequently, they devoted a great deal of time and effort to the art of preserving dead bodies (Welford, 1992). Egyptian embalming methods consisted of removing the brain and viscera and filling the bodily cavities with a mixture of herbs and other substances. The embalmers then immersed the body in carbonate of soda, injected the arteries and veins with turpentine and other balsams, filled the cavities of the torso with bituminous and aromatic substances and salt, and wound around the body cloths saturated with herbs, balsams, carbonate soda, and aromatic ingredients.

The success of the Egyptian arts of mummification and embalming are confirmed with each new archeological find of ancient burial sites. In many instances, the soles of the feet of mummies, when unwrapped after as many as 3,000 years, are often still soft and elastic. Historians estimate that by 700 A.D., when the practice faded out among them, the Egyptians had embalmed millions of bodies, several million of which are probably still preserved in undiscovered tombs and burial grounds (Bram, 1979).

From the Egyptians, the practice of embalming spread to other ancient peoples, including the Assyrians, the Jews, and the Persians. The Assyrians used honey in embalming, the Persians preferred wax, and the Jews used spices and aloes (Bram, 1979). Other ancient societies also practiced embalming, among them prehistoric Indian tribes of Peru and Ecuador and the aborigines of the Canary Islands. In Tibet, bodies are still often embalmed according to ancient formulas and techniques (Comptons, 1995; Mayer, 1990).

From the ancient peoples, embalming spread to Europe, where it became a widespread practice. Descriptions of methods used in Europe for almost 1,200 years have been preserved in the writings of physicians. These methods included evisceration, immersion of the body in alcohol, insertion of preservative herbs into incisions previously made in the fleshy parts of the body, and wrapping the cadaver in tarred or waxed sheets. Vanderlyn Pine (1984:274) describes embalming in the Middle Ages this way:

> During the Middle Ages, the Christian version of embalming included removing some organs, washing the body with water, alcohol, and pleasant smelling oils, chemically drying and preserving the flesh, wrapping the body in layers of cloth sealed with tar or oak soap, and mummifying in a way similar to the Egyptians. These tasks were performed by specialists who acted solely as embalmers.

Leonardo da Vinci (1452–1519), the great Italian artist, developed a system of intravenous injections for preservation of the dead body to enable him to draw anatomical plates. His methods inspired early embalmers, whose practices influenced modern embalming procedures (Welford, 1992). During the nineteenth century, French and Italian scientists perfected techniques of embalming by injection of preservative chemical solutions into the blood vessels, which allowed the preservatives to reach more distant parts of the cadaver.

Embalming in America   In the United States, embalming grew in popularity after the Civil War as a practice that made it possible to ship dead bodies back home from distant battlefields for burial. The most celebrated example of this occurred in the case of Abraham Lincoln, whose body was shipped by rail from Washington, D.C., where he was assassinated, to Springfield, Illinois, for burial. All of this took place during a warm part of the year, when decomposition of the body was likely to occur rapidly. The problem was that the funeral train made many stops along the way to accommodate the needs of grief-stricken Americans. If normal biological processes of decomposition had not been delayed through embalming, they would have transformed Mr. Lincoln's body into an object of social repugnance long before the train reached its destination. Embalming was not practiced routinely, however, until the late nineteenth or early twentieth century. When it finally became legal in the United States, some embalmers carted embalmed corpses from town to town, displaying their wares in barbershops, county fairs, and town hall meetings (Welford, 1992).

Embalming in the modern era means the removal of blood and other bodily fluids from a corpse and their replacement with artificial preservatives that help to retard decomposition and to color and soften the skin. Removal of the blood involves severing the main artery in the neck and allowing the blood to escape by gravity or, more likely, by electric pumps that permit blood to be removed from very small capillaries at the extremities of the body. In modern embalming procedures, the blood is replaced by a solution of formaldehyde in water, called formalin. Cavity fluid is removed and replaced with a preservative of formalin

"For Sale: Beautiful pine-finish coffin, slightly used."

Classified ad, *Petaluma Weekly News,* Petaluma, California, January 9, 1995.

mixed with alcohols, emulsifiers, and other substances (Iserson, 1994). Embalming fluids may or may not contain skin tints and lanolin, which work to restore the cosmetic appearance of the corpse (Mayer, 1990).

Modern embalming practices serve a number of functions. First, embalming prevents the spread of disease by disinfecting the corpse. Second, embalming can serve to slow decay in the bodily tissues of the corpse. Third, embalming permits extended viewing of the body during a wake or a funeral with an open casket. In this capacity, embalming has psychological significance because it may help mourners to evade thoughts of the decay of the body of the person who has died and may play a role in death denial, or at least in permitting mourners to deflect their attention from the full implications of death. For persons who prefer to donate their bodies for teaching or research purposes, careful preservation of the body is especially important and embalming techniques in such cases are much more stringent than those used in typical funerary embalming (Iserson, 1994; Aiken, 1994).

Triple-depth Burials   The luxury of a single, permanent burial site has come under increasing criticism in recent years as the human population continues to soar. Given that there is a finite amount of burial space on earth, the argument is made that, in time, the world would become one vast graveyard (Aiken, 1994; Iserson, 1994). One thousand individual graves take up an acre of land, and 1,000 acres are set aside for each million inhabitants. New York City estimates that 4,000 acres now used for cemeteries could provide housing for 200,000 families. In many urban areas, cemeteries are relocating to suburbs and exurbs to make room for new highways, airports, and shopping malls. As long ago as 1920, the county of San Francisco, in California, began moving its burial grounds out of town to nearby Colma, now sometimes called Cemetery City. Due to lack of space, double-depth and triple-depth burials are used in some densely populated nations, such as China. In the United States, Babyland of California permits three infants to be buried in one adult space.

> **I mean that's what death is, really, it's the last big move of your life. The hearse is like a van, the pallbearers are your close friends, the only ones you could really ask to help you with a big move like that. And the casket is that great, perfect box you've been looking for your whole life. The only problem is once you find it, you're in it."**
>
> Jerry Seinfeld, on moving and boxes, *Seinfeld*.

Air

Some cultures do not bury their dead, but simply leave the corpse to rot on the ground, in a tree, or on a specially constructed scaffold. Such open-air disposal is practiced by certain Australian aborigines, North America Indian tribes, the Nandi tribe of Kenya, and many Polynesian societies (Aiken, 1994; Welford, 1992).

Consider the Parsee people of India, who neither bury nor cremate their dead, believing that to do so would poison the earth and the water. These followers of the ancient religion of Zoroastrianism shoulder their dead to a site outside of Bombay, where they have constructed the Seven Towers of Silence. It is here that they perform their unique funeral rites. These elaborate scaffolds, called *dakhmas,* have no roofs, to allow flocks of vultures easy access to the body. When a

Some cultures do not bury their dead. Plains Indians used tree burial or a scaffold, as shown here, so that the body could return to all of the elements.
© *Documentary Photo Aids*

Parsee dies, the procession is led by six bearers dressed in pure white, who places the corpse on top of the Tower of Silence so the hungry birds can pick the bones clean. A few days later, the bearers return and cast the remaining bones into a pit.

Cannibalism   In prehistoric times, instead of being picked clean by vultures or other animals, the corpse was consumed by other humans, a practice called *mortuary cannibalism*. Archaeological evidence of mortuary cannibalism has been found in the remains of Peking man of some half million years ago and also of Neanderthal man of roughly 100,000 years ago (Aiken, 1994). The word *cannibal* comes from the Arawakan language name for the Carib Indians of the West Indies. The Caribs were well known for their practice of cannibalism, as were certain Australian aborigine tribes and the Luiseno Indians of southern California in more recent times. Cannibalism existed, until recently, in parts of West and Central Africa, Sumatra, Melanesia, and Polynesia; among various Indian tribes of North and South America; and among the aborigines of Australia and New Zealand. It is still believed to be practiced in remote areas of the island of New Guinea (Lessa, 1976; Iserson, 1994).

The reasons for cannibalism are varied. Sometimes there was simply limited food. Some groups liked the taste of human flesh. But mostly the reasons had to do with revenge or punishment for crimes, ceremony, ritual, or magic. Some victorious tribes ate their dead enemies. In some rituals the body was eaten by relatives, a practice called *endocannibalism*.

Water

Water burials were common among certain Pacific Island peoples and among early northeastern European cultures, who apparently did not share the Zoroastrian concern that dead bodies would contaminate the water (Aiken, 1994). In

May I Show You Our Wine List?

"Gustatory cannibals actually relish human flesh. . . . The notoriety of these cases attests to their rarity. . . . In 1981, a Japanese student, Issed Sagawa, ate his girlfriend. . . . Not to be outdone, in 1992, Jeffrey Dahmer, a Milwaukee chocolate-factory worker, admitted to killing, dismembering, boiling and eating seventeen young men over a 13-year period. He said he ate one man's biceps after seasoning it with salt, pepper, and A-1 sauce. But his killings look minimal next to those of Fritz Haarmann, the 'Hanover Vampire,' who in 1924 was convicted of biting twenty-seven men to death and producing sausage from their flesh, which he ate and sold. An accomplice picked up the victims in gay bars or at dances, and experts believe more than fifty victims succumbed to the sausage pot. Haarmann was executed, but his accomplice served only 12 years in prison.

The most notorious gustatory (and power-motivated) cannibal on the big screen was Hannibal Lecter, the victim-devouring psychiatrist featured in *The Silence of the Lambs.* His last on-screen words were, 'I'm going to have an old friend for dinner.' "

Source: Iserson (1994), p. 376–377.

the South Pacific, it was customary to place the body in a canoe and to launch it on the water. To these seafaring folk, water burial seemed a natural way to dispose of a corpse, and their custom was simply to dispose of the body at sea or, in other instances, to place the body in water until the flesh was gone and then gather the bones for burial. A special type of interment occurring in northern and western Europe during the pre-Christian era was ship burial. Ship burial was based on the belief that the deceased must make a sea journey to the land of the dead (Comptons, 1995).

Water burial was a custom in many ancient cultures, in which the bodies of heroes were often cast adrift in boats as part of elaborate funeral ceremonies. The funerals of pharaohs in ancient Egypt, for example, involved either a water burial or an earth burial, depending on the political will of the people. The funeral included a procession of the deceased pharaoh, first to the Nile River and then across the river in a boat. A gathering of people on the west bank of the Nile voted by voice and gesture on whether the dead pharaoh had been a good king or a bad king. The outcome of the vote determined if the body was ceremoniously buried in an elaborate tomb or unceremoniously dumped into the river (Iserson, 1994).

Burial at sea is still practiced today whenever a person dies aboard ship and the body cannot be preserved until land is reached. A mortician in San Rafael, California, who offers ocean-going burials from a 44-foot motorboat, says, "You don't have to buy a piece of land or a tombstone, there's no mowing of the grass, no planting of flowers. The sea is always alive, it's a beautiful place to be" (Rhodes & Vedder, 1983:91–92). Cremation remains, too, are often scattered at sea. In fact, Americans Hans Barth, an engineer, and David Humble, an entrepreneur, have patented the "Velella," a plastic, football-size container described as the world's first seaworthy urn. The container has a keel and a wind-catching groove that promises to sail a loved one's cremains into the sunset for up to 2 years. The urn then biodegrades, releasing the ashes to the sea (*Newsweek,* 1995).

Fire

Cremation is the practice of burning a human corpse, reducing it to ashes on a funeral pyre or in a specially constructed furnace. The ashes, gathered and blessed, are generally kept in an urn, buried, or scattered to the wind and the sea.

Fiery Farewell

Human ashes have been tossed overboard and out of planes. Brian Kelly took it a step further, arranging to have his ashes loaded into a fireworks shell that exploded Friday night in a red-and-green starburst with a silver tail.

Kelly, a Michigan fireworks handler who died last month of complications from intestinal surgery, went out with a bang during the grand finale at a convention of fireworks technicians about 40 miles northwest of Pittsburgh. The fireworks were created by his boss at Independence Professional Fireworks in Osseo, Mich., after Kelly told his sister: "I just want to be a big firecracker."

Source: Adapted from Fiery farewell. (1994, August 15). *San Francisco Chronicle*, p. A5.

In traditional cremation ceremonies, such as the Hindu, the body is covered with clarified butter, swathed in white cloth, and placed on a bed of logs and tree branches, and the next of kin lights the funeral pyre as the mourners look on.

More modern cremations are conducted by funeral directors and mortuary workers employing high-temperature gas and electric furnaces called *cremation chambers*. To begin the cremation process, the human remains are placed in the cremation chamber.

Crematories typically only require that the body be enclosed in a container, (of wood or cardboard) in which it can be handled easily and safely. Within minutes, open flames raise the temperature to 1600–2400°F for a period of 2–3 hours. The time varies with each human's remains. Since most of the human body is water, the water evaporates. At the high temperatures reached during cremation, the rest of the soft tissues are consumed by combustion. When the cremation is performed in a chamber that utilizes a secondary afterburner, the partially cremated remains are moved into this secondary chamber for completion of the process. In chambers without an afterburner, the partially cremated remains may be repositioned to facilitate complete burning. To reposition the human remains or to remove the cremated remains from the cremation chamber, a broad hoelike instrument is used.

After the cremation process is complete, the *cremains,* or cremation remains, are removed from the chamber and placed in a metal or clay tray for cooling. When the cremains have cooled, they are collected and ground up or pulverized into a coarse powder. The processed powder is placed into an urn or some other type of attractive container, according to the wishes of the family. Most cremated remains weigh between 4 and 8 pounds, depending on the weight and bone structure of the corpse (Aiken, 1994; Iserson, 1994).

Metal objects, such as jewelry and dental gold, may break down into small pieces during the cremation process. These small pieces, along with larger pieces of metal (e.g., hinges, screws, and prostheses), are removed from the cremains using a magnet or some other means, then disposed of according to local laws and crematory policy. The family chooses the final disposition of the ashes. Pending this decision, the funeral professional will hold the remains for a limited, specified time. The family may select inurnment in a permanent location, such as a *mausoleum* or a *columbarium niche,* cemetery plot (many cemeteries allow urns to be buried in the same plot as a previously interred casket or other urn), or other special location of the family's choosing. Alternatively, the remains may be scattered on a holy river (in the manner of the Hindus), at sea, in a cemetery *scattering garden,* or in some other location, so long as it is in accordance with local laws. Relict Memorials, a Mill Valley, California, company, combines the

CREMATION TERMINOLOGY

Cremation The irreversible process of reducing human remains to ashes and bone fragments through extreme heat and evaporation.

Cremated remains (cremains) The ashes and bone fragments remaining after the cremation process.

Crematory/crematorium The facility that houses the cremation chamber.

Cremation chamber The mechanical device used to perform the actual cremation process.

Cremation container The container required to transport the human remains to the crematory. It could be the casket used at the funeral or a special rigid, leak-proof, combustible box designed for cremation. The cremation container will be destroyed during the cremation process.

Final disposition The final resting place for the cremains.

Human remains The body of the deceased.

Inurnment (1) placing the cremated remains in an urn or other container in preparation for final disposition; (2) placing the urn/container in its final resting place.

Pulverization process The reduction of the cremated remains to an unidentifiable consistency to facilitate inurnment and/or to make the cremated remains acceptable for scattering. Depending on the pulverization device used, very small bone fragments may or may not remain after processing.

Cremation process Depending on local laws there may be a waiting period of up to 48 hours from the time of death before the human remains may be cremated. Before cremation, mechanical devices such as pacemakers must be removed because they may explode during the cremation process, causing extensive damage both to the integrity of the human remains and to the cremation chamber.

cremains with granitelike materials to form tombstones, grave markers, or even bronze plaques for a mantelpiece. Relict memorials are priced at $300 and up.

Only since 1961 has legislation in California, Indiana, Washington, and other states permitted the scattering of private ashes. This California law was rescinded in 1984 following a scandal involving an unscrupulous pilot who mixed cremains and scattered them randomly over the land. Present California law outlaws the scattering of cremains over any land and, although it is still often done, it cannot be offered as a commercial service (Heller, 1996).

Cremation has grown in popularity during recent years, especially in predominantly Protestant countries. For example, from 1975 to 1991, the ratio of cremations to deaths rose from 7% to 18.5% in the United States, and from 12.4% to 34.25% in Canada (Aiken, 1994). Interestingly, Jacobs and Wilkes (1988), in their analysis of 32,019 death certificates for major causes of death in New York City between 1982 and 1986 found that individuals who died of acquired immune-deficiency syndrome (AIDS) were cremated more frequently regardless of race or location of death.

CARING INSIGHT

Creating Meaningful Funeral Ceremonies

"The one who conducts the funeral . . . must have a capacity for empathy, understanding of the situation of mourners and knowing something of what they are feeling. He (or she) must be ready to accept the mourners as they are, not trying to press upon them attitudes or patterns of behavior that are not genuinely their own. . . . Since no two situations are identical, there must be sufficient flexibility in the funeral to make it relevant and meaningful in each situation."

Source: A.D. Wolfelt. (1995). Creating meaningful funeral ceremonies. *Thanatos, 20*(1), 7.

According to Aiken (1994:137), the practice of cremation "has several advantages over other methods of disposal, including economy, space conservation, public health considerations, and emotional comfort to people who are horrified by the thought of slow body decay." In some instances, however, there are legal complications and religious opposition. Murder is more easily concealed by cremation than by burial, so the causes and circumstances of death must be carefully determined before a corpse is cremated. Cremation may be an alternative to embalming, viewing, and a funeral, or it may follow those activities as a step between them and final disposition.

THE FUNERAL BUSINESS

Societal issues change, and with these changes come demands for new approaches to the problems associated with a rapidly changing world. The lessening sense of permanence in modern society, the pressing problems of the nuclear family, geographic mobility, the high-tech revolution in medicine, and various other changes in our world require new thinking about the meaning of life and death. Over the past few centuries, with the gradual removal of more and more areas of life from the realm of spiritual influence and religious control, we have become a more secular society.

America's death system is one of the areas becoming increasingly secularized. Over the years, the funeral industry has taken on more and more roles in America's burial rituals, funeral arrangements, body disposition procedures, last rites, and aftercare services. Mortician John Reynolds (1996:13) maintains that the expansion of the funeral industry, most recently into the area of aftercare for grieving loved ones, "marks a paradigm shift of historic magnitude as we observe the continued evolution of the funeral home as a community resource for the bereaved. Indeed," he continues, "one of the most dramatic sociological aspects of this transformation may be that the public has sanctioned the funeral home as a legitimate provider of human services."

The funeral industry in the United States began to emerge during the nineteenth century as carpenters and cabinet makers found the sale of coffins to be profitable. Gradually, these craftspeople began to offer other services along with the sale of coffins and, in a matter of decades, undertaking as a profession mushroomed. Today, there are over 20,000 funeral homes and approximately 50,000 licensed funeral directors in the United States who generate revenues in excess of $6 billion annually (Service Industries Annual Receipts, 1990:785).

Jessica Mitford (1963), in *The American Way of Death,* found many unethical practices within the funeral industry. She asserted that many of these shady practices occur because the average person has little knowledge of the costs of funerals and that when a person negotiates with a funeral home, it is during a period of stress and confusion, a time when they are more likely to be influenced and persuaded by funeral directors and salespeople. Thirteen years after publication of her book, a two-year investigation of the ethical character of the funeral

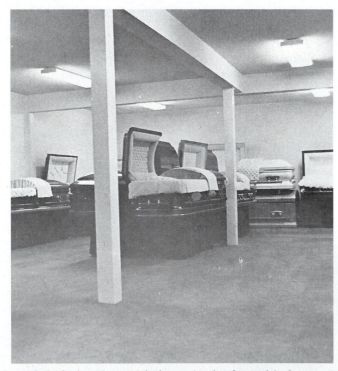

The FTC has identified widespread abuses in the funeral industry. During the distress and confusion, a bereaved person is much more easily influenced by funeral directors and salespeople. © *AP/Wide World Photos*

LANGUAGE USED IN THE FUNERAL PROFESSION

In the Slumber Room

- casket, *not* coffin
- case, patient, or Mrs. Smith, *not* corpse
- cemetery or memorial park, *not* graveyard
- cremains, *not* ashes
- deceased or departed, *not* dead person
- baby or infant, *not* stillborn
- funeral director, *not* undertaker
- internment, *not* burial
- memory picture, *not* last look
- monument, *not* tombstone
- preparation room, *not* embalming room
- professional car, *not* hearse
- slumber room, *not* laying-out room
- service, *not* funeral
- slumber robe, *not* shroud
- space, *not* grave
- vital statistic form, *not* death certificate

In the Back Room

- *coffins:* tin cans, containers, stovepipes
- *restoration:* pickling, curing the ham

Source: William Bailey. (1983). *Euphemisms and other double-talk.* Doubleday, New York, p. 127.

The FTC contended that there were widespread abuses in the funeral industry that primarily involved persons being overcharged or unfairly charged for services never delivered or charged for services never requested.

Research by sociologist Robert Fulton (1965) revealed that more people believe that the funeral industry takes advantage of a grieving individual than the facts of specific cases actually indicate. He believes that the funeral director is often made a scapegoat on whom grieving family members displace their frustration and anger, and that much of the public concern over the ethical character of the funeral industry is due to the practices of the large, bureaucratic funeral home chains located in major urban areas. He maintains that the small funeral home offers a personal and caring touch along with technical knowledge, a combination that does not produce resentment from the public (Rhodes & Vedder, 1983).

Given their roles and the criticism of the profession over the years, some researchers have investigated the attitudes and job satisfaction of funeral directors. In a Canadian study of 149 funeral directors' job satisfaction and commitment, Schell and Zinger (1985) found that funeral directors appeared to have low levels of career preference for this occupation, perceived low productivity of other members, and reported moderate job satisfaction and job commitment. The major reason given for remaining in the funeral-directing profession was their perceived personal growth and returns relative to their personal and financial investments.

Numerous researchers, based on studies of funeral practices and perceived insensitivity of funeral directors to the bereaved, have called for increased training and education. For example, in one study of the attitudes and practices of funeral directors toward newborn deaths and parental mourning practices, Benfield and Nichols (1984) discovered that the funeral directors' sensitivity to the needs of grieving parents extended only so far: The more intimate the contact requested by the parents, the less likely were they to offer such contacts. For example, 81%

said they would offer parents the option to see their dead baby, 64% to touch the baby, 27% to hold the baby, and 11% to dress the baby. The authors suggest that improved doctor–funeral director cooperation and expanded funeral director education and training may enhance the ability of funeral directors to help families achieve a healthy outcome during the grieving process, especially when a newborn infant dies.

Reynolds (1995:3) points out that, although funeral directors have provided aftercare to many grieving families, they have not received "broad enough inclusion into the family of helping professionals." Part of the problem, according to Reynolds, may rest with the training of funeral directors in the United States: "I know of no school that is offering peer support groups to its students to help them deal with their feelings about dealing with death on a daily basis. . . . If the profession itself doesn't recognize the emotional needs of its students, how can the public be expected to?"

Burial and Cremation Practices in America

An extensive study by Dawson, Santos, and Bardick (1990), of the University of Notre Dame, attempted to investigate American attitudes toward funeral practices and to isolate the reasons why some Americans choose to bury their loved ones while others choose cremation. Respondents were next of kin of deceased persons who had died 10–30 months prior to the survey in six metropolitan areas and whose kin were either buried or cremated. The 703 respondents were primarily white (93.6%), Protestant (61.0%), or Catholic (21.8%), and disproportionately female (70.6%).

In addition to issues related to body disposal, family members were questioned about which factors influenced their choice of burial or cremation. Choices included preference of the deceased, religious tradition, persuasion by funeral home personnel, and cost of disposal. Respondents were also questioned about viewing the body, social gatherings, flowers, donations, and other features of the funeral or memorial service. Overwhelmingly, respondents were influenced by the preference of the deceased in choosing burial or cremation and, interestingly, were least influenced by funeral directors and mortuary

CEMETERY INVESTIGATION

On September 13, 1995, investigators from the California State Cemetery Board began exhuming bodies and examining cemetery books and maps at a number of Los Angeles cemeteries based on numerous consumer complaints and two class-action suits that were recently filed. Complaints included the following:

- Bodies may have been buried in one cemetery site and then moved to another, less expensive site after the funeral so the original site could be resold.

- Bodies were plucked from caskets minutes after last rites and stacked in mass graves so the burial plots could be resold.

- Family members were, in some cases, not allowed to witness the casket containing their loved one being lowered into the ground.

- Sixty discarded gravestones were improperly discarded.

- Human remains were discovered in the cemetery's cremation chamber.

Source: Adapted from California State Cemetery Board, Sacramento, CA (1995).

> **"White people deal with death in a funny sort of way. . . . [T]hey don't cry over their dearly departed. . . . [W]hat they usually do is to say something like, oh, she was a nice old soul (sniff, sniff) and they go on about their business. But black folks say Ahhhhh, and they just holler . . . say things and carry on, just scream and get it all out."**
>
> Richard Pryor in Perry (1993), p. 59.

personnel. The dying wishes of loved ones generally seemed to eclipse other considerations, at least in this sample.

Other results revealed that age or sex of the deceased apparently played no role in whether cremation or burial was chosen by respondents. However, respondents who chose cremation over burial were significantly less religious than the burial sample, were more likely to be Protestant (63.4%) than Catholic (18.1%), had higher educational levels, higher employment levels, and higher family incomes, and were more likely to be married, single, divorced, or separated and less likely to be widowed.

For the cremation sample, the most common form of final disposition of cremains was the burial of ashes (40.4%), then scattering of ashes to the wind (28.7%), and then ashes going to the family (21.5%). The use of columbarium niches was less common and very few reported not claiming the ashes (3.8%).

Flowers were more often present at burials than at cremations, and religious donation requests were more likely during burial ceremonies. But medical and organ donation requests were more likely before cremations. The use of monuments or markers at the site of disposition was significantly more frequent for burials, although markers were also used in the majority of cremations.

Visiting and viewing the body was much more prevalent for burials (75%) than for cremations (22%), as was having the traditional social gathering after disposal of the body. As expected, embalming was more prevalent with burials (64%), but was also reported for 14% of the cremations. Only about one-third of the total sample of respondents reported having had services or ceremonies in a church, while a somewhat larger proportion used a funeral home. Dawson, Santos, and Burdick (1990:135), in reviewing the results of their research concluded "that the funeral industry is becoming as involved as the clergy in carrying out final arrangements, . . . that the funeral home is taking the place of the church for an increasing number of final arrangement activities," and that " . . . variation in the occurrence of final arrangements support the position that there is no one form of traditional American funeral."

In another study of the body disposal preferences of American college students (Cottrell et al., 1984), students were asked their preference between a traditional funeral (embalming, viewing, graveside service) and nontraditional services (cremation, body donation, simple burial). The results of this study indicated that the majority of college students, unlike the American populace at large, would prefer a nontraditional method of body disposal. Further analysis showed a significant difference in that those who preferred a traditional method did so because of reasons related to religion, family considerations, or social acceptability while those choosing nontraditional disposal methods did so out of economic, simplicity, or altruistic concerns. Catholics were more likely to state a preference for traditional methods of body disposal, while students of the Jewish and Protestant faiths were more likely to state a preference for nontraditional methods. Interestingly, it was found that exposure to a college-level death-education course had no significant effect on choice of body disposal methods.

Ashes to Ashes, Dust to Dust

The importance of funeral preparations, various death rituals and ceremonies, and the method of disposition of the body in helping survivors accept the reality of death has long been recognized. Over recent decades, however, as American funeral directors and their assistants have continued to take over many of the death-related tasks that must be carried out when a death occurs, attention has been focused on the increasing passivity of survivors and on the effects that funeral rituals, or the lack of them, may be having on individual survivors (Doka, 1984; Raether, 1985; Dawson, Santos, & Burdick, 1990).

As funeral directors and their assistants take over the tasks of preparing for the burial, the survivors become increasingly passive, and the emphasis shifts from the deceased to the ceremony. © *AP/Wide World Photos*

There is concern that a lack of active participation by survivors in the final arrangements of the deceased, the decrease of involvement in the funeral as a shared, social event, the deritualization of the death experience, and an increased secularization of funeral rituals may all have negative effects on survivors and on American society as a whole. The role that an increase in the use of cremation plays in the changing American funeral, and the status of the crematorium as a sacred place, is also unclear (Davies, 1996).

Cassem (1976), for instance, warns that the emergence of efficient, low-cost final arrangements, often involving immediate disposal of the body by cremation, might result in a harmful, death-denying culture. French thanatologist Jaques Ascher (1989) points out that body-centered funeral rites, involving viewing the dead body, are important to the human psyche. Supporting his contention with examples from the mass murders of the Armenians by the Turks and of the European Jews by the Nazis, Ascher maintains that the perpetrators of these crimes used absence of the body and denial of death as a way to sever the connection between victims and survivors. But a number of researchers have questioned the assumption that the traditional American funeral involving viewing of the dead body focuses attention on the death and thereby facilitates emotional expressions of grief and sympathy by the survivors (R. Fulton, 1976; Glick, Weiss, & Parkes, 1974). Based on contradictory research findings, Moller (1996:91), for example, hypothesizes "that the traditional funeral ceremony, with viewing of the deceased, is helpful for people who suffered from extreme disorientation as a result of their closeness to the dead person. People less close, who experienced less disorientation, may find viewing the body unhelpful and unpleasant."

R. Fulton (1976) points to a shift in the function of the funeral, no matter what form of body disposition is employed, from emphasis on the deceased person to an appreciation of the funeral as a rite of separation and integration for survivors. Lewis Aiken (1994) suggests that this shift may have already taken place. He concludes that the funeral has changed from mainly a rite for honoring the dead to an event where concern is increasingly focused on the needs and feelings of the survivors.

Thanatologist Paul Irion (1990–91), after examining changes in funeral services in mainstream-faith communities, concludes that changes in our under-standing of death and grief in the past decade have produced corresponding changes in funerals. He notes that a growing intentional awareness of the psychological and sociological insights into the grieving and mourning processes are making the funeral ritual a more effective resource for coping with death and bereavement. James Wentzy (1995), for example, found that members of New York City's gay community, finding traditional rituals deficient, have created death-affirming innovations. When another member of the People with AIDS Coalition dies, members of the family gather with gay community members to honor the deceased while white helium balloons are released from New York's St. Peter's Episcopal Church. In some instances, the ashes of one partner are mixed with the ashes of a predeceased lover in honor of their long-term commitment to one another. Ashes are then scattered in a place meaningful for the couple. The rainbow flag, symbol of gay pride, is often draped over coffins. The question of whether traditional funeral rites are simply disappearing or whether they are slowly being replaced with more contemporary and more meaningful practices will probably be debated for years to come.

Gatherings

Originally the funeral was primarily for the benefit of the dead, to acknowledge and honor their virtues and contributions to family and community and to prepare them for the passage to the afterlife. Sociological theorist Emile Durkheim (1965) argued that the ceremony and ritual of a funeral, in addition to being a last rite of passage for the deceased, also serves to establish a condition of social well-being for the survivors and the community left behind. To offset and buffer the crisis of loss through death, the gathering group will invoke the ceremony and ritual of the funeral or memorial service. Durkheim theorized that during the funeral ritual, the group uses its influence on its members to make sure their feelings come into agreement with the situation of loss by showing that they have been affected by the loss. Durkheim (1965:447–448) wrote:

> "To allow them to remain indifferent to the blow which has fallen upon it [the group] and diminish it would be equivalent to proclaiming that it does not hold the place in their hearts which is due it; it would be denying itself. A family which allows one of its members to die without being wept for shows by that very fact that it lacks moral unity and cohesion; it abdicates, it renounces its existence."

"And yes, Norman *was* beheaded, cleaned and plucked. ... But we all know Norman's wacky sense of humor, and we can take comfort knowing he would've gotten a kick out of this."

VIRTUAL MEMORIAL GARDEN

Friends and families are now saying their goodbyes to the dead on the Internet's Virtual Memory Garden (VMG), a growing collection of cyberepitaphs and remembrances posted on bereavement bulletin boards for anyone with a computer and a modem. The parents of an autistic 12-year-old who died in February wrote, "Our youngest. Even though he was autistic, he was a joy of life and meant the world to everyone who knew him. Rest easy, son, in the light." The VMG also includes a Pet's Corner to remember favorite animal companions.

British teacher Lindsay Marshall describes his pages on the World Wide Web of the Internet as a place for common people to pay homage to the dead in their own words. "I intend the VMG not to be place of death, but a place where people can celebrate their family, friends and pets. To tell the rest of the world about them and why they were special. . . . At the moment you see simple text much as you would in your local newspaper, but in the future . . . you will see cyberpyramids and datashrines appearing. Certainly there will be electronic crypts as pages devoted to whole families are assembled." Marshall says he is committed to the idea of keeping his obituary pages free to all who want to share their memories. The pages can be found via the World Wide Web at: http://catless.ncl.ac.uk/Obituary/memorial.html

Source: Adapted from Heather Irwin. (1995, July 25). The dead live on—on the Internet. *Newhouse News Service.*

These ceremonies and rituals function to help individuals to form certain thoughts, to recall certain memories, and to express certain emotions and feelings, together with family and friends, in an effort to soften the impact of the loss.

From this sociological perspective, the death of a community member disrupts the society's smoothly running functions. Funeral rituals and memorial services are equilibrium-producing systems in that they strengthen the individual's recommitment to the community and, in this sense, are a key to a stable society (Dawson, Santos, & Burdick, 1990). According to Leming and Dickinson (1994:367), "[A]ll societies seem to have some social mechanism for managing death-related emotions and reconstructing family interaction patterns modified by death. These customs are passed down from generation to generation and are an integral part of a society's way of coping with a major event like death."

For some, specific religious practices, such as daily meditations, prayers, sacraments, visits by the clergy, and community worship, give meaning to dying and death. These rituals allow survivors to express both positive and negative emotions connected with the grieving process, and, in a real sense, spiritual practices and funeral rituals help people cope with a reality that otherwise may be too painful to bear (Oaks & Ezell, 1993). Thanatologist Lonnie Yoder (1986), for example, analyzed the function of the funeral meal in different cultural and religious settings and concluded that the demise of the funerary meal has resulted in psychological and social impoverishment. She argues that both the immediate bereaved and the larger social community benefit from the gathering for the funeral meal because the meal functions as a group experience that focuses on the needs of the living, and it is a shared experience in a familiar, structured setting that enables the living to do significant grief work.

Most recently, Bosley and Cook (1993) examined the experience of funeral rituals for thirty-two adults (ages 27–79 years) who had lost either a parent or a spouse, with the goal of isolating specific elements of the funeral ritual that had therapeutic value or promoted healing in the participants. Based on interviews

CARING INSIGHTS

The Funeral/Memorial Service

- Decide on the place and time of the funeral or memorial service.
- Make a list of immediate family, close friends, and colleagues. Notify each one of the death. Telephone, telegraph, fax, or e-mail to distant persons who knew the deceased and inform them of the death.
- Write an obituary, include the time and place of services; deliver, telephone, or fax the information to appropriate newspapers.
- Notify insurance companies, employers, membership organizations, lawyer, and executors of will and estates. Get several copies of the death certificate.
- Arrange for members of the family to take turns greeting visitors, answering phone, and preparing food. Send thank you cards to these participants sometime after the services.
- Coordinate food for the day of the services, as well as the days following.
- Select pall bearers, and notify each. Plan for the disposition of the flowers after the ceremony.
- Check carefully all life and casualty insurance and death benefits. Monitor incoming mail for debts and installment payments due. Consult with creditors as regards delayed payments.
- If the deceased was living alone, inform utility companies, landlord, and post office where to forward mail. Make sure the decedent's home is secure.
- Consult an accountant as to some future date regarding payment of federal, state, and local income and property taxes.

Source: Adapted from Ernest Morgan. (1995). *Dealing creatively with death.* Barclay House, Bayside, NY, p. 233.

about their behaviors, feelings, and attributions of meaning, these researchers isolated five prevalent therapeutic themes. The funeral functioned as a tool of acceptance of memories of the deceased, allowed for the expression of strong emotions, affirmed faith, allowed for social support, and allowed for reconnecting with the family's heritage. Welford (1992:9) states: "The funeral has not only been used as a commemoration of an individual life, it has also been used as a religious statement and as a means of allowing the social group to establish its presence and support."

The funeral appears to have a similar therapeutic function for children. In one study, conducted at Massachusetts General Hospital in Boston, Silverman and

Worden (1992) interviewed 120 children (mean age 11.6 years), all of whom had experienced the death of one of their parents, about their view of the funeral ritual. Ninety-five percent of them attended the funeral. Interestingly, although they could recall little about the funeral shortly after the death, 2 years later they reported that it was important to them that they had attended because being present helped them to acknowledge the death, provided an occasion for honoring their deceased parent, and made it possible for them to receive support and comfort from family, friends, and other community members.

The social norms that define a society's burial and funeral rites are not laws of nature, no matter how steeped in tradition they may be. And the endurance of norms is not proof of any reason or logic that validates them as correct, "true," "right," or even "neccessary" (Morris, 1993:645). Instead, these rituals and rites of gathering together to honor the dead and to lend emotional support to the survivors speak to layers of our being that are deeper, more visceral, and more meaningful than any reason or logic could ever capture.

PAYING FINAL RESPECTS

Whether it be Buddhist, Christian, Hindu, Muslim, or Unitarian, the scope of the funeral ritual often extends far beyond the basic funeral or memorial service itself. First, there may be the ritual of dying itself, the actual separation of self from society. This may include the traditional deathbed scene, complete with life reviews and final words, or the contemporary practice of segregating the dying from the living in separate rooms, convalescent homes, and hospitals.

Following the ritual of separation comes a number of rites of transition for both the deceased and the bereaved. There is the first pronouncement of death

A sunrise ceremony showing part of the quilt bearing the names of thousands who have died of AIDS was held in Washington, D.C., on the mall of the capitol. © *AP/Wide World Photos*

to the immediate family, typically limited to the physician, shaman, or other type of healer. From the immediate family, the news spreads outward, like ripples on a lake, from friends to more distant relatives to employers and so on (Kearl, 1989). If someone is not immediately informed of the death, there may be feelings of being slighted, if not deeply hurt. Various bureaucracies must also be informed: government agencies, employers, schools, insurance companies, and other institutions that provide benefits to which the deceased is no longer entitled.

Finally, the community is informed of the loss of one of its members. In small communities, the information is often conveyed person to person, through a note on the local post office or grocery store bulletin board or by the tolling of church bells. In larger communities, such news appears in the obituary section of the local newspaper. And so, informed of the death, loved ones, friends, clergy, and acquaintances gather around the deceased and complete the final rite of passage.

Hindu Rites

When a death takes place in Hindu society, family and friends gather to offer solace to the survivors and to prepare the body for viewing: laying it out with the hands across the chest, closing the eyelids, anointing the body with oil, and placing flower garlands around it. This is done by persons of the same gender as the deceased, and the process will be presided over in the home of the deceased by the dead person's successor and heir.

Because Hindus believe that cremation is an act of sacrifice, whereby one's body is offered to God through the funeral pyre, cremation is the preferred method of body disposal. In preparation for cremation, family members will construct a funeral stand, consisting of a mat of woven coconut leaves stretched between two poles and supported by pieces of bamboo. The uncasketed body of the deceased will be carried on the platform from the deceased's home to the place of cremation by close relatives. This funeral procession will be led by the chief mourner, usually the eldest son, and will include musicians, drum players, and other mourners (Habenstein & Lamers, 1974; Whalen, 1990).

When the procession reaches the place of cremation, usually a platform (*ghat*) located on the banks of a sacred river, the body will be removed from the bier and immersed in the holy waters

---

PURPOSES OF FUNERARY CUSTOMS

Social customs associated with burial and mourning of the dead serve a variety of purposes:

- Disposing of the physical body
- Reallocating property
- Honoring and paying tribute to the deceased
- Facilitating the expression of grief and providing support to the bereaved
- Experiencing a rite of passage for both the deceased and the bereaved from one status to another
- Assisting the deceased in afterlife activities
- Reassignment of roles vacated by the deceased
- Providing an opportunity to reestablish contact with friends and relatives
- Reaffirming group solidarity
- Rearranging the surviving social group that may have been disrupted by the death

Adapted from Aiken, 1994, p. 133.

of the river. The body will then be smeared with *ghi* (clarified butter) and placed on the funeral pyre for burning. Usually the deceased's son (chief mourner) recites the prayers and the invocation of ancestors. At this point, the chief mourner, who has brought burning coals from the house, will light the pyre while a priest recites an invocation. Although outlawed by the British in 1829, the practice of *suttee,* the act of the Hindu widow throwing herself on her husband's funeral pyre in willing cremation, still occasionally occurs. After the body has been consumed, mourners will ritually wash themselves in the river in a rite of purification. Three days later, relatives will return to gather the ashes and bones, which are placed in an urn or vase and given to the chief mourner. It is then the responsibility of the chief mourner to cast these remains into the sacred river.

Between 10 and 31 days after the cremation, a *Shraddha* (elaborate feast) is prepared for all mourners and priests who have taken part in the funeral ritual. During the feast, gifts are given to the *Guru* (religious teacher), the *Purohita* (officiating priest), and other *Brahmins* (religious functionaries). At the close of the Shraddha, which may last hours or days, depending on social status, the mourning period officially comes to an end, though later Shraddhas may be given as memorial services. Next to Hindu wedding ceremonies, funerals are the most important religious ceremonies.

Points on a Wheel   The single physical lifetime of Christian doctrine contrasts with the multiple lifetimes of Eastern religions. In many religions, Hinduism and Buddhism in particular, life and death are likened to points on a constantly moving wheel. Each person has a succession of lives, being reborn or reincarnated after death into a life form determined by the person's character and actions during the previous lifetime (*karma*). In the *Bhagavad-Gita,* Krishna tells Arjuna, "For death is a certainty for him who has been born, and birth is a certainty for him who has died. Therefore, for what is unavoidable thou shouldst not grieve."

According to the doctrine of reincarnation, souls (*jivas*) pass through *samsara,* a succession of human and animal forms. Each successive life form is determined by a person's thoughts and actions and the lessons he or she learned in the previous life. Hinduism teaches that only when the soul is purified and the individual finds identity and unity with the cosmos (**nirvana,** enlightenment; Brahman, Atman, the Universal Power) can the continuous cycle of life, death, and rebirth be broken (Bouquet, 1991). Then and only then will all ignorance and craving disappear and the individual flame go out as the spirit merges with cosmos. Indian psychologists Roma Pal and Greesh Sharma (1985) maintain that because Hindus view aging, life, and death as parts of an inevitable continuum, death does not have the traumatic connotations for Hindus as it has for Westerners, and the Hindu belief in reincarnation has a tremendous mental health value.

Buddhist Rites

As a Buddhist lies dying, a religious teacher will often gather with family and neighbors to pray or recite mantras at the bedside, to bring solace and to create an environment that might have a wholesome effect on the transition to the next rebirth. Buddhists believe that, following the moment of death, the essence of

"**Underlying man's personality and animating it is a reservoir of being that never dies, is never exhausted, and is without limit in awareness and bliss. This infinite center of life, this hidden self, or** *Atman,* **is no less than** *Brahman,* **the Godhead.**"

Huston Smith. (1958). *The religions of man*. New American Library, New York, p. 34.

the person remains in an intermediate state, between death and rebirth, for no more that 49 days. Based on their extensive observations of Buddhist funeral practices, Leming and Premchit (1993:233) conclude that to Buddhists, "[t]he funeral is primarily a social event that affirms community values and group cohesiveness."

When a Thai Buddhist dies, for instance, family members, friends, and monks assist in the funeral preparation. The body is cleansed, dressed, and placed within a casket that is kept either in the deceased's home or at the *wat* (temple) for a period of three days (Leming & Premchit, 1993). During this 3-day period, monks will visit with the grieving loved ones every evening to chant the Buddhist scriptures (*Abhidhamma*). Family and friends who attend these evening gatherings often bring ornate and colorful floral arrangements as gifts.

On the fourth day the body will be taken to the charnel ground (cremation site), which is usually a distance from the wat. During these ceremonies, monks will chant important Buddhist scriptures called *sutras*. At the conclusion of the final service, there will be a final tribute of flowers and three lighted candles presented to the deceased. The casket will then be removed and placed on a carriage in preparation for the procession to the cremation site (Leming & Premchit, 1993).

During the procession, a long white cotton cord is attached to the casket and eight monks (the number is flexible), together with lay devotees, will carry the cord. In the urban areas, the carriage will be motorized, while in traditional funerals and/or funerals in rural areas the carriage will be pulled by walking members of the procession. Upon arriving at the site of the cremation, the casket is carried around the crematorium three times, which symbolizes traveling in the cycle of birth/death/rebirth. The casket is then placed in front of the crematorium while relatives pose for pictures, after which they will walk around the casket three times.

The stage is now set for the actual cremation. Just prior to the lighting of the fire, the biography of the deceased is read while a sandalwood flower with one incense stick and two small candles (i.e., *dok mai chan*) is distributed to all in attendance. The mourners are all invited to come forward and deposit the dok mai chan before the casket. By so doing, mourners are deemed participating in the actual cremation. The head mourner then lights the fire and the casket and body are consumed. The next morning the ashes and pieces of bone are gathered, placed in a receptacle, and enshrined in the monastery (Leming & Dickinson, 1994). Typically, there is dancing and musical performances associated with the funeral so that sorrow and loneliness may be lessened.

Muslim Rites

If a Muslim is near death, it is expected that he or she will be attended by relatives and close friends around the clock. Just prior to death, the dying person will recite the following Islamic confession of faith: "There is no god but God,

The parents and relatives of a 15-year-old Moslem combatant with the Bosnian army grieve over his body during the funeral. © *Corinna Dufka, Corbis-Bettmann*

and Muhammad is his messenger." The dying person is also encouraged to request forgiveness from anyone he or she may have offended or insulted, because, according to the tradition of Islam, "God will not forgive violation of human rights unless those wronged have forgiven" (Rahman, 1987:128).

While Hindus and Buddhists prescribe cremation, the world's 900 million Muslims forbid cremation. According to the Qu'ran, Muhammed taught that only Allah will use fire to punish the wicked. Islamic tradition also forbids embalming, and, consequently, it is expected that burial should take place as soon as possible after the death, preferably before the next sunset. According to Rahman (1987), burial is occasionally delayed one or two days to allow out-of-town family members and friends an opportunity to attend the funeral.

In preparation for burial, the family will call into their home or the hospital a person of the same gender as the deceased who knows the prescribed ritual for washing and preparing the body. The eyes and mouth of the deceased will be closed, the arms straightened alongside the body, and the body washed and wrapped in a white seamless cloth (shroud) similar to that worn for the pilgrimage to Mecca (Eichelman, 1987). When the body has been fully prepared according to the prescribed ritual, it will be placed in a simple wooden coffin. Occasionally, Muslims will be covered only by the white shroud when they are buried. At a Muslim funeral, mourners will often approach the corpse and whisper instructions as to how the deceased should answer Munkar and Nakir, the black-faced, blue-eyed angels who, it is believed, will visit the grave and

. . . every living plant utters the name of God.

interrogate the deceased regarding his or her beliefs and deeds in life (Abdul Latif Al Hoa, 1987).

When it is time for the funeral, the body will be transported from the home or the hospital to the mosque. Muslims consider burying the dead a good deed, so when worshipers leave the mosque and see the coffin in the courtyard, they will participate in the procession to the cemetery even though they were not acquainted with the deceased. At the mosque, the body will be placed on a stone bier (*musalla*) in the outer courtyard.

The body is now transported from the mosque to the cemetery on the shoulders of the male mourners in the procession. According to Habenstein and Lamers (1974:163):

> It is customary for every man in good health to carry the coffin on his shoulders for seven steps at least, and for passers-by to accompany the procession at least seven steps. When a new bearer pushes under the coffin, another steps out so that eight or ten people are always under the load. These customs insure that the remains will have an escort, even though the dead person may have no relatives. At a prearranged spot, hearse and funeral cars await the procession. Where distances to the cemetery are short, the body will be borne to the grave totally on foot.

At the cemetery the body is placed into the grave, with the head facing Mecca, and mourners place handfuls of dirt on top of it. The sexton then fills the remainder of the grave using a shovel. At the gravesite, rather than placing cut flowers, Muslim mourners plant living flowers in the ground because they believe that every living plant utters the name of God. Prayers are recited during this process, and the service concludes with the preaching of a sermon. Some Muslim grave sites are extraordinary. The Mogul emperor Shah Jahan built the world famous Taj Mahal as a mausoleum for his wife and himself. The Taj Mahal, which is one of the finest examples of Islamic architecture, was finished in 1654. It took 20,000 workers 22 years to complete the project.

After returning from the cemetery, all of the participants will sit for a meal that is served at the home of the deceased. Occasionally, some food from this meal is placed over the grave for the first 3 days after the death. Mourning continues for another 3 days while family members receive social support and consolation from friends and members of the community. Though Islamic women are allowed to express emotion openly during the mourning process, men are encouraged to retain their composure as a sign that they are able to accept the will of Allah. A widow is required by the Qur'an to go into seclusion for 4 months and 10 days before she is allowed to remarry (Eichelman, 1987; Whalen, 1990).

Baha'i Rites

The Baha'i faith, which originated in Persia in the nineteenth century as an outgrowth of the Shi'ite branch of Islam, also forbids cremation and embalming and requires that the body not be transferred more than an hour's journey from the place of death. Several million Baha'is live in Iran, India, the Middle East, and Africa, and an estimated 100,000 Baha'is live in the United States. Because Bahaism has no ordained clergy, the funeral may be conducted by any member of the family or the local assembly. All present at the funeral must stand during the recitation of the Prayer of the Dead composed by Baha'u'llah (Whalen, 1990).

Judaic Rites

Orthodox Judaism, according to Habenstein and Lamers (1974), prescribes some of the most detailed funeral rites of any religious group. As death approaches, family and friends must attend the dying person at all times. When death finally arrives, a son or the nearest relative closes the eyes and mouth of the deceased and binds the lower jaw before *rigor mortis* (stiffening of the body) sets in. Relatives place the body on the floor and cover it with a sheet, placing a lighted candle near the head, unless the death occurs on the Sabbath, when no lighting of candles is permitted. All the mirrors in the house are covered, to deemphasize the beauty and ornamentation of the flesh at a time when another body has begun to decay. This and similar practices are attempts to avoid personal vanity during tragedy and to reduce the usual superficial concern with appearance. The chief mourner, usually a spouse or eldest son, is expected to take responsibility for the funeral arrangements and, during the service, is expected and encouraged to express her or his grief openly.

Judaism, in its traditional form, forbids embalming and cremation. After a ritual washing, the body is covered with a white shroud and may be placed in a wooden coffin. At the funeral, mourners symbolize their grief by tearing a portion of an outer garment or wearing a torn black ribbon. Orthodox Jews discourage flowers and ostentation at the funeral, and mourners do not leave the graveside until the grave has been completely filled (Habenstein & Lamers, 1974; Whalen, 1990).

The Jewish funeral service includes a reading of prayers and psalms, a eulogy, and the recitation of the Kaddish, the prayer for the dead. Orthodox Jews observe a primary mourning period of 7 days during which mourners do no work, are visited frequently, are brought their food, and are encouraged to talk of the deceased. Reform Jews reduce this period to 3 days. There follows a period of 30 days of gradual readjustment and then, near the end of a year, a gravestone is erected and the official period of mourning is completed. During a second yearlong mourning period, the Kaddish prayer is recited at every service in the synagogue.

In Judaism, the faith of some 18 million people, the Old Testament of the Bible only hints at belief in an afterlife, but later Jewish thought embraced beliefs in heaven, hell, resurrection, and final judgment. In general, Orthodox Jews accept the concept of a resurrection of the soul and the body, while Conservative and Reform Jews prefer to speak only of the immortality of the soul (Whalen, 1990).

Catholic Rites

For Roman Catholics, the Mass is the principle celebration of the Christian funeral. The Catholic ritual employs candles, incense, and holy water, and in many parishes the priest encourages the family members to participate in the ritual as speakers and singers. The celebration of the Mass is followed by the committal service at the grave site, where the priest blesses the grave and leads

Heightening the Holiness: The Work of Jewish Burial Societies

"It has always been a Jewish duty to bury our dead properly. Jewish law requires that we show proper respect for a corpse, protect it from desecration, and ritually cleanse and dress the body for burial. A *chevra kaddisha* (burial society) is a loosely structured group of Jewish men and women who see to it that the bodies of Jews are prepared for burial according to these rules.

Some time ago, a friend asked me if I would like to become a member of the chevra kaddisha being formed in Atlanta, and I immediately answered yes. I did not think many people would respond to this call; I also thought my background as a surgeon's assistant would eliminate the squeamishness that others might feel.

At the first meeting—to everyone's surprise—there was a tremendous turnout. Rabbi David Epstein outlined the requirements and pointed out that two different groups would be needed: *shmira,* watching the body for protection against desecration; and *tahara,* the ritual purification of the body. Not surprisingly, more people volunteered for shmira—a far easier task—but we had enough people for both groups.

Soon after that meeting, we were called to perform this *mitzvah* for the first time. There were nine women that evening: all of us novices. On the way to the funeral home, we had disguised our fears about what would transpire with lively chatter. Once we entered the room where the body lay, however, we were silent. There was death lying on the table—that mysterious, deepest fear of the unknown that reduces us all to a common humanity. The trepidation all of us felt upon entering the room where the body lay, and the complete physicality of the preparations for tahara, served as a remarkable contrast to the spirituality of the occasion and the emotions of everyone present.

We formed a silent circle around the covered body, and our preconceived feelings of dread overcame us. Many of us were shaking, some turned white. Still, there was an unmistakable peace here, in this room.

Following the training given by Rabbi Epstein and using a book he had prepared, we ritually washed our hands three times and recited the prayer of Rachamim, requesting kindness for the body. Carefully, we began washing the body on the right side first through a sheet wetted down by a hose. We uncovered only the part of the body we were washing and cleansed it lovingly. We cleaned and filed the nails, removed visible dirt, bandages, and other foreign matter. The body must be cleansed of anything that might come between the purifying water and the body itself.

There is a strict order to this cleaning. We started at the head: the eyes, ears, nose, mouth, and continued down the right side, then the left. When we saw the woman's face, much of our tension lightened. This elderly woman looked so peaceful, so relaxed. She seemed to have found an inner quiet that oddly calmed us.

Now she was ready for tahara, the actual purification by water. We cranked the table on which the body was strapped so that it was perpendicular to the floor. Then we poured three large pails of water over the body in immediate succession, taking care that the flow was continuous.

Afterward, we lowered the table to its horizontal position and dried the body with a sheet. With a peculiar maternalism, we clothed the body in pure white garments, each specially tied. On this table, all wear the same clothing and all are equal: male and female, rich and poor.

The meticulous care with which we performed these acts, and the time we spent with this woman, heightened our feelings of holiness. A funeral home deals with bodies; we were dealing with a person, and we felt the power of this mitzvah as we worked. We were calmed, humbled, hallowed.

Source: Betsy Kaplan. *Lilith* (#22) (Box 3000, Dept LIL, Denville, NJ 07834), p. 7.

the mourners in the Our Father and other prayers for the repose of the soul and the comfort of the survivors. Prior to the liturgical changes of the Second Vatican Council in the 1960s, the typical funeral included recitation of the Rosary at the wake, black vestments for the priest, black candles, and prayers recited in Latin. The *Dies Irae,* a thirteenth century funeral dirge, was a standard musical piece played at Catholic funerals.

Nowadays, those attending a Catholic wake may still say the rosary, but often there is a scripture service instead (Whalen, 1990). During the Mass, the central rite of the Catholic funeral ritual, the priest's vestments are likely to be white or violet rather than black, prayers are likely to be said in English and often emphasize the hopes of resurrection rather than the terrors of the final judgments. Altar girls have joined altar boys as assistants. Catholics are usually buried in Catholic cemeteries or in separate sections of other cemeteries.

According to Whalen (1990), the Catholic Church raises no objections to embalming, flowers, or an open casket at the wake. At one time Catholics who wished to have a church funeral could not request cremation, but this injunction has been lifted unless, according to canon law, it has been chosen for reasons that are contrary to Christian teaching. The church used to deny an ecclesiastical burial to suicides, those killed in duels, Freemasons, and the ladies' auxiliary of Masonic lodges. Today, the church refuses burial only to "notorious apostates, heretics, and schismatics" and to "sinners whose funeral in church would scandalize the faithful" (Whalen, 1990:33). Catholics who join Masonic lodges no longer incur excommunication, although they still may not receive Communion. The church has also softened its position denying funeral rites to suicides based on the understanding that anyone finding life so unbearable as to end it voluntarily probably was acting with a greatly diminished free will.

Christianity carries over Judaism's respect for the body and firmly acknowledges resurrection, judgment, and eternal reward or punishment. Although the Catholic Church declares that there is a heaven and a hell, it has never declared that anyone, even Judas, has actually been condemned to eternal punishment. Men and women of heroic virtues, known as saints, are believed to be in heaven. Unlike Protestant churches, Catholicism also teaches the existence of a temporary site of purification known as purgatory, for those destined for heaven but not yet free from sin and selfishness.

Protestant Rites

Most people in the United States identify themselves as Protestants, and their funerals follow a similar form. Family and friends gather at the funeral home to console one another and pay their final respects. The next day, a minister conducts the funeral service at the church or mortuary. Typically, the service includes hymns, prayers, a eulogy, and readings from the Bible. In nearly 85% of the cases today, the body is buried after a short graveside ceremony. Otherwise, the body is cremated or donated to a medical school (Whalen, 1990; R. Fulton, 1992).

Many Christian funeral customs date back several thousand years to earlier practices and beliefs. The custom of walking in a funeral procession, for instance, was introduced in Britain at the time of the Roman invasion of 43 A.D., as was wearing black clothing and raising a mound over the grave (R. Fulton, 1992; Hambly, 1974).

Mormon Rites

Joseph Smith, founder of the Church of Jesus Christ of Latter-day Saints, taught his followers that one of their greatest responsibilities as Mormons is to care for their dead and to offer vicarious baptism to the dead so they could be admitted into heaven. Mormons believe in the separation of the body and the spirits at death. The spirits of the just would be resurrected at the millennium in connection with the Judgment Day (Oaks & Ezell, 1993).

The funeral rite in the Church of Jesus Christ of Latter-day Saints resembles the standard Protestant funeral in some ways, except that the Mormon Church forbids cremation. Another significant difference is in the attire worn by the deceased. Devout Mormons receive the garments of the holy priesthood during ceremonies when they are adolescents. According to Whalen (1990), these sacred undergarments are to be worn day and night throughout a Mormon's life. When a Mormon dies, his or her body is then attired in these garments in the casket. These sacred garments, which resemble long johns but with short sleeves and cut off at the knees, are embroidered with symbols on the right and left breasts, the navel, and the right knee, which remind the wearer of the oaths taken in the secret temple rites.

Mormon burial outer clothing is specified. For men, this includes white pants, white shirt, tie, belt, slippers, and an apron. Mormons put a white temple cap on the head of the corpse just before the casket is closed for the last time. If the deceased is a woman, a high priest places a temple veil over her face with the last casket closing. Mormons believe the veil will remain there until her husband calls her from the grave to resurrection (Habenstein & Lamers, 1974; Whalen, 1990).

Christian Scientist Rites

Some religious groups, such as Christian Scientists, have less formalized and elaborate funeral services. Because their founder, Mary Baker Eddy, denied the reality of death, Christian Scientists have no set funeral rite. The family of a deceased Christian Scientist often invites a Christian Science reader to present a brief memorial service at the funeral home (Whalen, 1990).

Unitarian-Universalist Rites

Unitarian-Universalists enroll many members who would identify themselves primarily as agnostics, humanists, positivists, or New Age spiritualists who hold to a temporal or secular interpretation of death's meanings. Unitarian-Universalism is based on the conviction that each of us evolves religious beliefs from our own personal life experience (Irish, 1993). The use of religious symbols is minimized, and there are no admonitions regarding body disposition through burial or cremation. Sociologist Donald P. Irish (1993:156) writes,

> There are no prescribed actions that are standard before or after a death. . . . Specific patterns tend to arise within given meetings or congregations in response to the needs of the individual and family members and to the sensitivity and resources of that community. . . . Minimally, the sole involvement of a funeral director might be to transport the body to a crematorium. The remainder of the services would be arranged and carried out by the religious community itself.

"One of the reasons people write books, especially death and dying books, is to promote their own symbolic immortality. As long as their books can be read, their influence will outlive their biological body."

Leming & Dickinson (1994), p. 185.

In a typical funeral or memorial service, the minister, loved ones, and community members celebrate the virtues, creativity, and good works of the deceased and say little about any afterlife.

Elements of Secular Rites

Temporal and secular interpretations of death provide a merging of death meanings that emphasize the empirical and natural world view of death. According to Glenn M. Vernon (1970:33), "[W]hen death is given a temporal interpretation and is seen as the loss of consciousness, self-control, and identity, the individual may conclude that he or she can avoid social isolation in eternity by identifying him- or herself with specific values." This involvement with values, while not pertaining to religious values or a belief in the supernatural, may nevertheless provide a spiritual or infinite frame of reference that transcends the finite individual. From this secular perspective, a person may die, but his or her concerns and accomplishments will continue to exist after death in a form of symbolic immortality.

Symbolic immortality refers to the belief that the meaning of the person can continue after he or she has died (Lifton & Olson, 1974). According to Leming and Dickinson (1994:185),

> If we define religion as a system of beliefs and practices related to high-intensity value meanings, then it is possible for individuals with secular orientations to be "religious" in their outlook without affirming an afterlife. . . . For the religious, symbolic immortality is often related to the concept of soul, which either returns to its preexistent state, goes to an afterlife, is reincarnated in another body, or is united with the Cosmos. For the person whose primary orientation is temporal or secular, symbolic immortality is achieved by being remembered by others, creating something that remains useful or interesting to others, or by being part of a cause or social movement that continues after the individual's death.

Individuals whose interpretations of death meanings are primarily temporal and secular share many of the following beliefs and attitudes (Vernon, 1970; Irish, 1993):

- They tend to reject or deemphasize a belief in the afterlife.
- They tend to believe that death is the end of the individual.
- They tend to focus on the needs and concerns of the survivors.
- They tend to be present-oriented for themselves but present- and future-oriented for those who will continue after them.
- Any belief in immortality is related to the activities and accomplishments of the individual during his or her lifetime, including biological offspring, social relationships, and work and community projects the individual has created.

According to Leming and Dickinson (1994), there is a strong temptation to view the person with a temporal or secular orientation as being very different

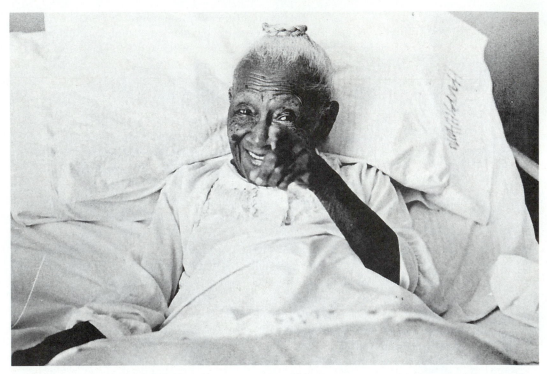

In the moment of death of a loved one we may wish to turn away, yet we are drawn back to find ourselves face to face with death, knowing in our deepest wisdom that death has a thousand doors to let out life. © *Documentary Photo Aids*

from the person who finds comfort in a traditional religious interpretation of death. For the individual with religious commitments, a sense of security and comfort are to be found by being in relationship with the supernatural. For the person with a secular or temporal orientation, these same benefits are found in becoming involved with other people, projects, causes, and personal spiritual values. In fact, both individuals will strive to bring order and meaning to their dying and death by placing death in the context of a "higher" order.

Endings: The Morning After

Death creates endings and separations, but it also creates gatherings of loved ones who, in facing death, may create new openings and devotion to life, living and caring. In coming together to bury or cremate one of our own, and to comfort one another, we may begin to savor and celebrate each breath of life, because familiarity with the face of death and dying tends to bring life and living into a position of ultimate importance for each of us. Philosopher Alan Watts (1987:260) writes, "if you can really open your eyes just for a moment, you will see that . . . in getting up in the morning, in dressing, in going to work, in sitting in a train, in washing your hands, in greeting a friend in the street, . . . everyday life and experience is the supreme religious experience."

"We must all die; we are like water spilt on the ground, which cannot be gathered up again. . ."

II Samuel 14:14, RSV

Death has a way of awakening us to our own humanity and spirituality. George Santayana (1944:3) writes that "in the turbid stream of nature there are clear stretches and traceable currents, and it is interesting to follow the beginnings and developments of a run here and a whirlpool there." Ultimately, however, "we watch the silent glassy volume of water slip faster and faster towards the edge of some precipice." Perhaps, in that moment, we realize that death is life's only certainty. In the Bible, Samuel says, "We must all die; we are like water spilt on the ground, which cannot be gathered up again" (II Samuel 14:14 RSV).

Death touches each of us. Whatever our religious, spiritual, or philosophical orientation may be, we have each experienced death, dying and loss, be it the death of a parent, a spouse, or a best friend, or the loss of our own dreams, hopes, and ideals. Each of us has gathered at the death scene or paused at the sight of the dead and dying on the highways, at the altar, in the funeral home, or beside the deathbed of one we truly love. And in that moment, we wish only to turn away. And yet, we are drawn back again. Fascinated and fearful, we open our eyes to find ourselves face to face with death, with the fact of our own mortality, with our own impermanence, with the transient existence of those we love, and with the mourning after. And in that moment we experience, not numbing fear or anxiety, but humility, dignity, and a certain groundedness in the flesh-and-blood biology of who we truly are, not who we think we are.

And we know now, perhaps for the first time, that we have physically, psychologically, and spiritually embraced death and have gracefully entered into the light. We can turn away from death in the next moment, deny death, repress our deepest emotions, and disempower ourselves in death's shadow. And yet we know, in our deepest wisdom, that death has a thousand doors to let out life, and, though there is no escape from the darkness of death and dying, there is always the dawn, the light, and the morning after.

FURTHER READINGS

Fulton, R. (1992). Funeral customs. In *World book encyclopedia* Vol. 7, World Book, Chicago.

Irish, D. P., Lundquist, K. F., and Nelsen, V. J. (Eds.). (1993). *Ethnic variations in dying, death, and grief.* Taylor & Francis, Washington, DC.

Iserson, K. V. (1994). *Death to dust: What happens to dead bodies?* Galen Press, Tucson, AZ.

Leming, M. R., and Dickinson, G. E. (1994). *Understanding dying, death and bereavement* (3rd ed.). Harcourt Brace, New York.

Mayer, R. A. (1990). *Embalming: History, theory and practice.* Appleton & Lange, Norwalk, CT.

Mitford, Jessica. (1963). *The American way of death.* Fawcett Publications, Greenwich, CT.

Watts, A. (1972). *The book: On the taboo against knowing who you are.* Vintage Books, New York.

Weisman, A. D. (1993). *The vulnerable self: Confronting the ultimate questions.* Insight Books, New York.

TWELVE

Resources

Educational and Advocacy Organizations

AIDS Resource Foundation for Children
182 Roseville Avenue, Newark, NJ 07107
Foundation that operates homes for children with HIV, AIDS, or AIDS-related complex.

Alban Institute
4550 Montgomery Ave., Suite 433 North, Bethesda, MD 20814-3341; telephone: 301-718-4407
This nondenominational research, consulting, and educational organization provides congregations with support and services and continuing-education programs.

Alliance for Aging Research
2021 K St. NW, Suite 305, Washington, DC 20006; telephone: 202-293-2856
Promotes research on aging and offers information booklets.

Alzheimer's Association
For services and publications for Alzheimer's patients and their families, many of which are useful for any elderly person, telephone: 800-272-3900. (Also see World Wide Web Site, p. 403.)

Alzheimer's Family Care
For Alzheimer's patients taking the drug Cognex (and their families), Parke-Davis, the manufacturer, has set up a 24-hour information line: 800-600-1600.

American Association of Retired Persons
601 E St. NW, Washington, DC 20049; telephone: 202-434-2277
Offers publications on such issues as housing, finances, health, and safety.

American Association of Suicidology
2459 South Ash Street, Denver, CO 80222; telephone 303-692-0985
Organization of professionals from various disciplines that promotes studies of suicide prevention and of life-threatening behaviors.

American Bar Association Commission on Legal Problems of the Elderly
1800 M St. NW, Washington, DC 20036; telephone: 202-331-2297

American Cancer Society
1599 Clifton Road NE, Atlanta, GA 30329; telephone: 800-227-2345
Association supporting education and research programs focusing on cancer prevention, recognition, diagnosis, and care.

American Diabetes Association
Telephone: 800-232-3472

American Foundation for AIDS Research
Second Floor, East Satellite, 5900 Wilshire Boulevard, Los Angeles, CA 90036
Fund-raising organization for conducting AIDS research.

American Geriatrics Society
770 Lexington Ave., Suite 300, New York, NY 10021
Medical specialty group dedicated to improving the health and well-being of older adults. For free publications, telephone: 212-308-1414.

American Heart Association
Telephone: 800-242-8721

American Hospital Association
840 North Lake Shore Drive, Chicago, IL 60611
Organization promoting efficient hospital administration through education of hospital administrators and personnel.

American Institute of Life-Threatening Illness and Loss
630 West 168th Street, New York, NY 10032
Association promoting improved care for critically and terminally ill persons and assistance for their families.

American Jewish Committee
165 East 56th St., New York, NY 10022; 212-751-4000
The committee is devoted to protecting civil and religious rights for all people. It compiles research on church–state issues, Israel and the Middle East, and Jews in the United States and the former Soviet Union.

American Medical Association
515 North State Street, Chicago, IL 60610

American Sudden Infant Death Syndrome Institute
275 Carpenter Drive NE, Suite 100, Atlanta, GA 30328
Organizations working to identify the cause of and find a cure for sudden infant death syndrome.

Arthritis Foundation Information Line
Telephone: 800-283-7800

Association for Death Education and Counseling
638 Prospect Avenue, Hartford, CT 06105-4298; telephone: 203-586-7503.
Association of individuals and institutions interested in responsible, effective education and counseling of the dying and bereaved.

Association of Nurses in AIDS Care
704 Stony Hill Road, Suite 106, Yardley, PA 19067
Association providing leadership and educational services for its members and working to develop national standards for AIDS care.

Association of SIDS Program Professionals
Massachusetts Center for SIDS, Boston City Hospital, 818 Harrison Avenue, Boston, MA 02118
Association that organizes activities for professional development, produces practice standards, and connects practitioners who work with families who lost a child to sudden infant death syndrome.

Bereaved Parents
P.O. Box 3147, Scottsdale, AZ 85271
Association of parents grieving the deaths of children from autoerotic asphyxiation that provides counseling to families and supports research. (See also World Web Site, p. 403.)

Better Vision Institute
1800 North Kent Street, Suite 904, Rosslyn, VA 22209; telephone: 703-243-1528
Candlelighters Childhood Cancer Foundation
7910 Woodmont Avenue, Suite 460, Bethesda, Maryland 20814, 1-800-366-2223.
This is an international organization of parents whose children have cancer or have died from this disease. A Candlelighters publication states the group's focus this way: "Candlelighters' parents share the shock of diagnosis, the questions about treatment, the anxiety of waiting, the despair of loss, the hope of remission, the joy of cure."
Center for Loss in Multiple Births
c/o Jean Kollantai, PO Box 1064, Palmer, AK 99645
Provides peer support for parents bereaved over the death of one or more multiple-birth children during pregnancy, labor, or childhood.
Center For Loss And Life Transition
3735 Broken Bow Road, Fort Collins, Colorado 80526, 1-970-226-6050.
The Center For Loss And Life Transition specializes in providing quality workshop presentations to a variety of sponsors throughout the country. A wide range of topics within the areas of death, grief, loss and life transition are available to choose from. Custom programs are often specially designed to meet the needs of the many sponsors.
Center for the Rights of the Terminally Ill
P.O. Box 54246, Hurst, TX 76054-2064
Advocates against euthanasia, assisted suicide, and abortion.
Centers for Disease Control
National AIDS Clearinghouse, P.O. Box 6003, Rockville, MD 20849-6003
Collects, analyzes, and disseminates information on HIV/AIDS.
Children of Aging Parents
1609 Woodbourne Road, Levittown, PA 19057; telephone: 215-945-6900
Children's Hospice International
901 North Washington Street, Suite 700, Alexandria, VA 22314
Organization promoting the inclusion of hospice care in pediatric facilities.
Choice in Dying
200 Varick Street, New York, NY 10014; 212-366-5540.
Educates the public on the legal and psychological implications of terminal-care decision making.
Compassion in Dying
PO Box 75495, Seattle, WA 98125; telephone: 206-624-2775
Organization providing education about the legal, ethical, and psychological implications of decisions concerned with terminal care.
The Compassionate Friends
P.O. Box 3696, Oak Brook, Illinois 60522-3696, 1-708-990-0010.
This is a support group for bereaved parents who "need not walk alone. We are Compassionate people who care and share and listen to each other." Group discussions range from helping the grieving accept death to handling family holidays after the death of a child. A wide range of literature and other information is available.
Concerned Relations of Nursing Home Patients
PO Box 18820, Cleveland Heights, OH 44128
Association promoting nursing home care that offers dignity and comfort regardless of ability to pay.

Eldercare America
1141 Loxford Terrace, Silver Spring, MD 20901
To find out about elder care workshops or to order video tapes, telephone:
301-593-1621.

Family Caregiver Alliance
425 Bush St., Suite 500, San Francisco, CA 94108
For a free newsletter and list of fact sheets for families and caregivers of
brain-impaired adults, telephone: 415-434-3388.

Foundation for Hospice and Homecare
519 C Street NE, Washington, DC 20002
Focuses on improving the quality of life of the dying, the disabled, and the
elderly, particularly as related to health care.

Hartford Seminary for Social and Religious Research
77 Sherman St., Hartford, CT 06105; telephone: 203-232-4451. Founded in 1981,
the center studies emerging issues in faith and religious practice.

Helping Other Parents in Normal Grieving
Sparrow Hospital, 1215 East Michigan Avenue, PO Box 30480, Lansing, MI 48909
Self-help group for newly bereaved parents.

Hemlock Society
PO Box 11830, Eugene, OR 97440-4030; telephone: 503-342-5748.
Organization that advocates voluntary euthanasia and assisted suicide for persons
with advanced terminal diseases. The society strives to foster a climate of public
opinion tolerant of people's right to terminate their lives at a time and in a
manner of their own choosing.

Hospice Association of America
519 C Street NE, Washington, DC 20002; telephone: 202-546-4759
Promotes the concepts of hospice, provides forums for nurses, offers hospice
start-up programs, and consults on hospice-related matters, such as Medicare
payments.

Hospice Education Institute
5 Essex Square, Suite 3-B, PO Box 713, Essex, CT 06426
Offers education on hospice, death and dying, and bereavement.

Hospice Nurses Association
PO Box 8166, Van Nuys, CA 91409-8166
Association of registered nurses who provide hospice care.

International Organization for Near-Death Studies
PO Box 502, East Windsor Hill, CT 06028; telephone: 203-528-5144
Supports the scientific study of phenomena associated with near-death
experiences.

International Anti-Euthanasia Task Force
University of Steubenville Human Life Center, P.O. Box 760, Steubenville, Ohio
43952; telephone: 614-282-3810. Opposes voluntary euthanasia, assisted suicide,
and so-called death-with-dignity laws. It publishes a bimonthly newsletter.

International Workgroup on Death, Dying, and Bereavement
c/o John Morgan, King's College, 266 Epworth Avenue, London, Ontario,
Canada N6A 2M3. Association of professionals concerned with care for the
terminally ill and bereaved and with issues of research and education in health
care.

Legal Counsel for the Elderly
American Association of Retired Persons, PO Box 96474, Washington, DC 90090

Leukemia Society of America
600 East 3rd Avenue, New York, NY 10016
Organization that raises funds to fight leukemia by means of research, health care, and education.

Make-a-Wish Foundation of America
2600 North Central Avenue, Suite 936, Phoenix, AZ 85004
Grants the wishes of terminally ill children up to 18 years of age.

Make Today Count
PO Box 6063, Kansas City, KS 66106-0063
Self-help organization for individuals with life-threatening illnesses and for their families.

Medic Alert Foundation.
To order bracelets and necklaces that alert doctors to medications, allergies, and other conditions and provide contacts, telephone: 800-633-4294.

Medicare Hotline
Telephone 800-638-6833

Mothers of AIDS Patients
1811 Field Drive NE, Albuquerque, NM 87112-2833
Association providing support for families of AIDS patients during the illness and after death.

National Academy of Elder Law Attorneys
To order the free booklet "Questions and Answers When Looking for an Elder Law Attorney," send a legal-sized SASE to 1604 North Country Club Road, Tucson, AZ 85716. Telephone: 602-881-4005.

National AIDS Hotline
Telephone: 800-342-2437

National Association for Home Care
519 C St. NE, Stanton Park, Washington, DC 20002
For the free brochure "How to Choose a Home Care Agency," telephone: 202-547-7424.

National Association for Medical Equipment Services
For free brochures on buying medical equipment, send SASE to Dept. MC, 625 Slaters Lane, Suite 200, Alexandria, VA 22314-1176.

National Association of People with AIDS
1413 K St. NW, Washington, DC 20005.
Association promoting local groups of persons diagnosed with AIDS, AIDS-related complex, or HIV to develop greater community awareness and to promote greater participation of local organizations in AIDS-related health care and social services.

National Association of Professional Geriatric Care Managers
1604 North Country Club Road, Tucson, AZ 85716
For referrals and information on hiring a caregiver for your needs, telephone: 602-881-8008.

National Center for Elder Abuse
810 First Street, Suite 500, Washington, DC 20002
For information on abuse of elders, contact this resource center at 202-682-2470.

National Center for Nutrition and Dietetics Consumer Nutrition Hot Line
For answers to nutrition questions and referrals to a registered dietician in your area, telephone: 800-366-1655.

National Citizens' Coalition for Nursing Home Reform
1224 M St. NW, Suite 301, Washington, DC 20005. Organization devoted to reforming long-term care in nursing homes and related systems.

National Council of Churches of Christ in the USA
475 Riverside Drive, New York, NY 10015; 212-870-2227. Representing thirty-two Protestant, Anglican, and Eastern Orthodox denominations, the council was formed in 1950 to promote "oneness in Jesus Christ" through research, publishing, education, refugee assistance, and disaster relief.

National Council of Guilds for Infant Survival
PO Box 3586, Davenport, IA 52808
Group providing consolation to parents who lost a child to sudden infant death syndrome (SIDS), supplying information about SIDS, and raising funds for medical research.

National Council of Senior Citizens
1331 F St. NW, Washington, DC 20004, telephone: 202-347-8800
An advocacy organization that defends Medicare and Social Security benefits.

National Council on Patient Information and Education
666 11th St. NW, Suite 810, Washington, DC 20001
For pamphlets on prescription medications and the elderly, telephone: 202-347-6711.

National Council on the Aging
409 Third St. SW, Second Floor, Washington, DC 20024
Includes the National Institute of Senior Centers, the National Institute on Adult Day Care, and the National Institute on Financial Issues and Services for Elders. For a list of resources and brochures on family home care, telephone: 202-479-1200.

National Eldercare Institute
University of South Florida, Suncoast Gerontology Center, 12901 Bruce B. Downs Boulevard, MDC Box 50, Tampa, FL 33613; For referrals on programs throughout Florida and nationwide information on long-term care, telephone: 813-974-4355 or (in Florida only) 800-633-4563.

National Eye Care Project
Telephone: 800-222-EYES
For referrals to ophthalmologists who provide free eye exams and treatments for qualifying older people.

National Family Caregivers Association
9621 East Bexhill Drive, Kensington, MD 20895-3104
To receive information on membership, a newsletter and a support network, telephone: 301-942-6430.

National Federation of Interfaith Vounteer Caregivers
368 Broadway, Suite 103, Kingston, NY 12401; telephone: 914-331-1358
Provides care, shopping, transportation, friendly visits, and more for home-bound elders.

National Health Information Center
PO Box 1133, Washington, DC 20013-1133
For referrals to agencies or groups that can best answer your health questions.

National Hospice Organization
1901 North Moore Street, Suite 901, Arlington, Virginia 22209, 1-703-243-5900
Hospice is a non-profit, community-based organization of volunteers, lay persons and professionals who provide a specialized health care program for the terminally ill. The aim of Hospice is to provide a supporting environment where the terminally ill can live their lives fully and meaningfully, and be able to die in a hospice support facility or at home with the companionship of family and friends. While many people are aware of its focus on the needs of the dying, Hospice also offers support to the family before, during and following the death of the terminally ill person.

National Institute for Jewish Hospice
8723 Alden Drive, Suite 652, Los Angeles, CA 90048
Association for individuals, businesses, and organizations interested in helping
terminally ill Jewish persons and their families.

National Institute of Mental Health Office of Scientific Information
For free brochures on depression and other mental disorders, telephone:
800-421-4211.

National Institute on Aging
For information, referrals and resources on all aspects of aging from this federal
agency, call 800-222-2225.

National Osteoporosis Foundation
Telephone: 800-223-9994

National Parkinson's Foundation
Telephone: 800-327-4545

National Right to Life Committee
419 7th St. NW, Suite 500, Washington, DC 20004
Organization opposing abortion and euthanasia.

National Self-Help Clearinghouse
25 West 43rd Street, Room 620, New York, NY 10036
Organization that maintains up-to-date information on self-help groups.

National Shut-in Society.
1925 North Lynn Street, Suite 400, Rosslyn, VA 22209; telephone: 703-516-6770
Writes letters and makes phone calls to the home-bound.

National SIDS Resource Center
8201 Greensboro Drive, Suite 600, McLean, VA 22102
Organization that develops materials on sudden infant death syndrome (SIDS),
apnea (temporary cessation of breathing), methods to monitor apnea, and grief
over SIDS death.

National Sudden Infant Death Syndrome
1314 Bedford Avenue, Suite 210, Baltimore, Maryland 21208, 1-800-221-SIDS.
The foundation and its many community chapters provide information, literature
and support to parents who have lost children to SIDS (crib death) or
SIDS-related symptoms. The national organization also provides films, training
support materials and a parent-to-parent contact referral service.

Older Woman's League
666 11th St. NW, Suite 700, Washington, DC 20001
For information on women's health issues, send SASE or
telephone: 800-825-3695.

Parents Without Partners
401 North Michigan Avenue, Chicago, Illinois 60611-4267, 1-800-637-7974.
This is a non-sectarian organization with over 700 chapters, all concerned with
the welfare of single parents and their children. With their motto, "Sharing by
Caring," Parents Without Partners assures them that they are not alone.

Pregnancy and Infant Loss Center
1421 West Wayzata Boulevard, Wayzata, MN 55391
Organization working to increase public understanding about perinatal death and
to establish support groups for persons grieving such deaths.

Pregnancy and Infant Loss Support
St. Joseph's Health Center, 300 1st Capitol Drive, St. Charles, MO 63301
Self-help group of parents who have suffered a perinatal loss.

Project Inform

1965 Market Street, Suite 220, San Francisco, CA 94103

Information clearinghouse on experimental drug treatments for persons with HIV or AIDS.

The Samaritans

500 Commonwealth Avenue, Boston, Massachusetts 02215, 1-617-247-5220 (Hot Line), 1-617-536-2450 (Business Line).

This is a special group of volunteers who are interested in the welfare of both individuals considering suicide themselves or persons who have lost a friend or relative to suicide. The Samaritans also operate a 24-hour telephone service. Specially trained volunteers listen to the caller's concerns and attempt to be as helpful and supportive as possible.

SEASONS: Suicide Bereavement

c/o Tina Larson, P.O. Box 187, Park City, UT 84060

Self-help group of persons grieving a suicide.

Self-Help for Hard-of-Hearing People

7910 Woodmont Avenue, Suite 1200, Bethesda, MD 20814; telephone: 301-657-2248 or (for the hearing impaired) 301-657-2249

Senate Special Committee on Aging

SD-G31, U.S. Senate, Washington, DC 20510-6400

For information and a free publications list, telephone: 202-224-5364.

Shepherd's Center of America

6700 Troost Avenue, Suite 616, Kansas City, MO 64131; telephone: 816-523-1080

Provides home services, including companion aides, shoppers, and handypersons.

SIDS Alliance

10500 Little Patuxent Parkway, Suite 420, Columbia MD 21044

Clearinghouse that provides medical and other scientific information about SIDS, offers bereavement support, and promotes SIDS research.

Society for Compassionate Friends

PO Box 3696, Oak Brook, IL 60522-3696; telephone: 708-990-0010

Self-help organization for bereaved parents.

Stroke Connection of the American Heart Association

Telephone: 800-553-6321.

The Simon Foundation for Continence

Telephone: 800-237-4666

The THEOS Foundation

322 Boulevard of the Allies, Suite 155, Pittsburgh, Pennsylvania 15222, 1-412-471-7779.

THEOS (They Help Each Other Spiritually) offers mutual self-help assistance to young and middle-aged widowed persons. A variety of written materials, brochures and a monthly magazine are available.

UNITE

c/o Jeanes Hospital, 7600 Central Avenue, Philadelphia, PA 19111-2499

Self-help support group for persons bereaved after miscarriage or infant death.

United Network for Organ Sharing (UNOS)

PO Box 13770, Richmond, VA 23225; telephone 1-800-243-6667

Well Spouse Foundation

PO Box 801, New York, NY 10023

To find out about support groups for partners of the chronically ill, as well as letter-writing round-robbins; telephone: 212-724-7209.

The Widowed Persons Service
601 "E" Street NW, Washington, DC 20048, 1-202-434-2260.
This organization was jointly formed by the National Retired Teachers
Association, the American Association of Retired Teachers and Action for
Independent Maturity. It offers support for those living through bereavement in
the form of individual and group-oriented outreach programs, telephone referral
services, public education programs for family adjustment, and financial and legal
counseling services.

Youth Suicide National Center
445 Virginia Avenue, San Mateo, CA 94402
Educational organization that develops and distributes materials about youth
suicide and youth suicide prevention programs.

Youth Suicide Prevention
65 Essex Road, Chestnut Hill, MA 02167
Volunteer association of parents, professionals, and civil service workers concerned
with preventing youth suicide.

Journals

Death Studies
c/o Taylor and Francis
1101 Vermont Ave. N.W., Suite 200
Washington, DC 20005

The Euthansia Review
c/o The Hemlock Society
P.O. Box 66218
Los Angeles, CA 90066

The Hospice Journal: Physical, Psychosocial, and Pastoral Care of the Dying
c/o Haworth Press
12 West 32nd Street
New York, NY 10001

Illness, Crises and Loss Journal
c/o Charles Press
P.O. Box 15715
Philadelphia, PA 19103

Journal of Personal and Interpersonal Loss
c/o Taylor and Francis
1900 Frost Road, Suite 101
Bristol, PA 19007-1598
e-mail: sample-pil@tandfpa.com

Journal of Psychosocial Oncology
c/o Haworth Press
12 West 32nd Street
New York, NY 10001

Mortality
c/o Carfax Publishing Co.
P.O. Box 25,
Abingdon, Oxfordshire
OX14 3UE, United Kingdom

Omega—The Journal of Death and Dying
c/o Baywood Publishing Company
26 Austin Avenue
Amityville, NY 11701
Rainbow Connection
477 Hannah Branch Rd., Burnsville, NC 28714
National organization that provides extensive mail order resources on bereavement,
grief and loss, as well as limited trainings. For their 2 free 20 page catalogs write
to the address above or call 704-675-9670."
Suicide and Life-Threatening Behavior
c/o Guilford Press
72 Spring Street
New York, NY 10012
Thanatos
P.O. Box 6009
Tallahassee, FL 32314

World Wide Web Sites

American Cancer Society
http://charlotte.npixi.net/acs
The American Cancer Society online.
Alzheimer Disease Web Site
http://med.www.by.edu/Alzheimer/home.html
Serves as reference for physicians, researchers and caregivers interested in
Alzheimer's disease and other related dementias.
Avon's Breast Cancer Awareness Crusade
http://www.com/Avon/avon.html
Provides information about breast cancer and breast health. Includes a list of more
than 250 breast cancer support groups across the United States.
Batesville Casket Company
http://www.batesville.com
Allows web cruisers to view the casket showroom and lists of funeral products and
services, including a wide array of urns. Includes the Grief Resource Center
which lists a handful of support and social service agencies and advice on dealing
with grief.
Bereaved Parents' Resources
gopher://gopher.rivendell.org/11/resources/parents
Central listing of information and support groups for parents in mourning.
Bereavement Resources Directory
http://asa.ugl.lib.umich.edu/chdocs/support/bereave.html
Central listing of bereavement resources available on the Internet.
Cardiovascular Institute of the South
http://www.cardio.com/
Center for the advanced diagnosis and treatment of heart and circulatory disease.
Reports covering prevention, diagnosis, and treatment of circulatory problems.
Center for AIDS Prevention Studies
http://www.caps.ucsf.edu/capsweb
Up-to-date reports of epidemiological and behavioral studies of prevention of and
intervention for HIV disease.

The CHATBACK Trust

http://www.tens.co.uk/chatback/

Serves as a place where children who have disabilities can have their own dialog via e-mail.

Children and Grief Resources

http://www.psych.med.umich.edu/web/aacap/factsFam/grief.htm

Children Now:

http://www.dnai.com:80/~ children

Nonprofit children's advocacy group. Provides information related to education, health, welfare, and safety of American children.

ChronicIllnet

http://www.calypte.com

Focuses on chronic illnesses, including groundbreaking research articles, a nationwide calendar of events, news, and articles

Compassionate Friends

http://pages.prodigy.com/ca/lycq97tcf.html

Information on resources and support groups for parents in mourning.

Cremation

http://www.twoscan.com/2s...erals/cremation.html

Offers information on cremation and connections to on-line resources, including The Internet Cremation Society, Internet Cremation Society FAO and the Laurel Memorial Cremation Society.

Cyberkid's Club:

http://mack.rt66.com/kidsclub/home.htm

Offers site where children can meet and write each other, read, shop, and play games.

Cyber-Psych

http://www.charm.net/~pandora/psych.html

Offers psychological information and relevant links for mental health information and resources.

DeathNET

http://www.rights.org/~deathnet/open.html

Serves as an international archive specializing in all aspects of death and dying including DeathTALK, ERGO! Information Center, Garden of Remembrance, Human Rights Campaigns, The Living Will Center, Media Monitor, Student Research Center and more.

Eldercare Web

http://www.ice.net/~kstevens/ELDERWEB.HTM

Provides information on aging including health care, living arrangements, statistics and demographics, provider locator and more.

Estate and Funeral Planning

http://www.twoscan.com/2s...b/memoriam/text.html

Offers information and resources for estate and funeral planning, death notices and obituaries, eulogies and elegies, prayers for the departed and dealing with bereavement. Estate planning links to information on safe deposit boxes, nursing home planning, pre-planned funerals, death benefits, life insurance and books of interest.

Funeral Arrangement for Loved Ones

http://www.twoscan.com/2s.../funerals/main2.html.

Offers information on funeral arrangements, legal rights and cremation as well as a directory of funeral directors.

Heart Mind Body Institute
http://www.power.net/hbm/hbm1.html
Explains new nonsurgical approaches in the prevention and reversal of coronary heart disease.

Health Fair On-Line
http://www.medaccess.com
The Locator section lists more than 600,000 physicians and 6,000 hospitals with descriptions and maps to help you find them, as well as accreditation information and lists of services offered by each hospital. A series of health-care pamphlets can be downloaded for off-line reference.

Hospice in Canada
gopher://152.160.1.32/11/resources/hospice/canada
Listing of hospice programs thoughout Canada, with relevant information.

Hospice in the United States
gopher:/152.160.1.32/00/resources/hospice/usa/hous.txt
Listing of hospice programs thoughout the United States, with relevant information.

The Interactive Patient
http://medicus.marshall.edu/medicus.htm
Presents a program that allows physicians and other health professionals to simulate an actual patient encounter; intended as a teaching tool for patient/professional communication.

Internet Resources for Caregivers
gopher://152.160.1.32/00/resources/caregivers/careint.txt
Central listing for information regarding issues in personal and professional caregiving.

Internet Resources on Aging and Loss
gopher://gopher.rivendell.org/11/resources/aging
Central listing of information for elderly persons coping with death and dying.

Internet Suicide/Homicide Resources
gopher://152.160.1/resources/suicide/suus.txt
Central listing of resources (e.g., articles, support groups, chat networks) related to dealing with suicide and homicide.

Living Wills
http://www.twoscan.com/2s...iam/wills/main2.html
Offers information on living wills, legal assistance and directories and associations concerned with living wills and other advance directives.

MedWeb
http://www.emory.edu/whscl/medweb.html
Serves as a link to many biomedical Internet resources.

Missing-Link Page for Missing Children
http://www.cris.com/~altoren/
Focuses on raising awareness about missing children. Includes a gallery of missing children and news and information on how you can help or receive help.

National Alliance for the Mentally Ill Home Page
http://www.cais.com/vikings/nami/index.html
Focuses on improving the lives of people who have severe mental and emotional disorders, and their families.

National Parent Information Network:
http://ericps.ed.uiuc.edu/npin/npinhome.html
Provides information about parenting.

OncoLink

http://www.oncolink.upenn.edu/

Serves as a resource directory, pointing you to sources of information and communication on cancer.

Parkinson's Web

http://neuro-chief-e.mgh.harvard.edu;/parkinsonsweb/Main/PDmain.html

Serves as a resource directory, pointing you to sources of information on Parkinson's disease.

Prayers for the Departed

http://www.twoscan.com/2s...m/prayers/main2.html

Allows you to post prayers for the dead and includes suggested prayers for the departed and to assuage your own grief. A treasury of Latin prayers is also presented.

Psychiatry and Psychology

http://www.leland.stanford.edu/~corelli;

Offers links to mental health information and resources. Includes personal reading list in areas of psychiatry, psychotherapy, and Jungian psychology.

Roxane Pain Institute

http:///www.Roxane.com

Offers cancer and AIDS pain management services, including articles, newsletters, and lists of upcoming pain management seminars.

Safer Sex Page

http://www.cmpharm.ucsf.edu/~troyer/safesex.html

Provides safer-sex information; allows access to Web Chat, an interactive forum for persons with questions about safer sex, HIV transmission, condoms, etc.

SafetyNet Domestic Violence Resources

http://www.interport.net/~asherman/dv.html

Contains domestic violence resources and statistics and domestic violence handbook with a warning list and safety plan.

Sociology of Death

http://www.Trinity.Edu/~mkearl/death.html

A key web site for accessing important information on the sociology of death, including: general resources; death across cultures and time; symbolic immortality and longevity; death and social institutions, political economies, medicine, and religion; moral debates; and personal impacts of death.

Sudden Infant Death Syndrome Information

http://q.continuum.net/~sidsnet/

Provides information about SIDS.

Suicide save.org

http://www.save.org

http://www.psych.med.umich.edu/web/aacap/factsFam/suicide.htm

Seeks to educate about suicide and to speak for suicide survivors.

Thanatology Forum

http://www.rights.org/~deathnet/thana.html

Serves to facilitate productive communication among health professionals and others regarding all aspects of thanatology, including clinical case histories, research findings, epidemiology, reviews of the literature, the history of thanatology, forensic issues and book reviews.

United States Public Health Services

http://phs.os.dhhs.gov/phs/

Provides information from the U.S. government about agencies, programs, health information, news and public affairs, and other health-related sites.

Violence Prevention
gopher://gopher.edu.gov.on.ca:70/11/english/shcools/violence.prev
Provides information on school violence, statistics, and prevention.
Virtual Memorial Gardens:
http://catless.ncl.ac.uk/Obituary/memorial.html
http:www.dgsys.com/~tgolden/1grief.html
Web sites dedicated to postings honoring deceased persons and pets.

Self-Help and Inspirational Books

For Hospice Books, brochures, and video resources, call the National Hospice Organization store at 800-646-6460.

For information about the following books or for a catalog of books in the following categories, contact Rainbow Connection for a copy of the Compassion Books Catalog. Compassion Books is the official mail-order book service of the **Association for Death Education and Counseling.** They can be reached by phone at 704-675-9670 or by fax at 704-675-9687, or write to: Rainbow Connection, 477 Hannah Branch Road, Burnsville, NC 28714.

BOOKS FOR CHILDREN*

General Books for Grieving Children

150 Facts About Grieving Children
Linn, Erin
Important information to help caring adults recognize characteristics of children going through grief of any type.

Aarvy Aardvark Finds Hope (Book)
O'Toole, Donna
Illustrated read-aloud story of the pain and sadness of loss and the hope of grief recovery. 6 years to adult. See also videos.

Aarvy Aardvark Finds Hope, (Audiotape)
O'Toole, Donna
The story of loving and losing, friendship and hope read by the author, with musical background. See book and teaching guide.

Aarvy Aardvark Finds Hope (Teaching Guide)
O'Toole, Donna
Guide to use with book/tape to teach the grief process. Includes discussion questions, creative-expression projects.

After the Funeral
Winsch, Jane Loretta
With simple words and multicultural illustrations, goes to the heart of children's fears and comforts them.

Feelings: Inside You and Outloud Too
Polland, Barbara
Helps adults help children identify, label, and understand their feelings and learn how to tell their feelings to someone else.

---

*The following is listed from the 1996-1997 catalog of Compassion Books, a division of Rainbow Connection, owned and directed by Donna O'Toole. Availability of the books is subject to change. For availability and order information, please contact Rainbow Connection at 704-675-9670 for a complete copy of the Compassion Books catalog, or write to 477 Hannah Branch Rd., Burnsville, NC 28714.

Fall of Freddie the Leaf
Buscaglia, Leo
A metaphorical story of life and death and the changing seasons of life. With color photographs. For all ages.

The Hurt
Doleski, Teddi
When Justin doesn't express his feelings a hurt grows inside him, but when he learns to express his feelings the hurt shrinks and goes away.

I Know I Made It Happen
Blackburn, Lynn Bennett
A validating book to help children overcome the fear and guilt that they might have caused the death or serious illness of a friend or loved one.

I'm Mad
Crary, Elizabeth
Recognizes a child's anger as a real and legitimate feeling and offers options for how anger can be worked through.

Love You Forever
Munsch, Robert
Shows how love can survive death and is passed down for generations to come.

You Hold Me and I'll Hold You
Carsen, Jo
Demonstrates the power and comfort of touch and nurturing during times of loss and fear. For all ages.

Cemetery Quilt
Ross, Kent and Alice
Young Josie learns about a special quilt that commemorates the life and death of the members of her family. The story speaks quietly to the universal fear of loss and separation as well as to the affirmation that life is valued and remembered and has continuity.

Death of a Sister or Brother

Am I Still a Sister?
Sims, Alicia M.
Written by an 11-year-old girl as she grieves and searches to find her identity while remembering her baby brother. Ages 8 to 12.

Children Facing Grief
Romond, Janis Loomis
A collection of poignant and inspirational letters from bereaved brothers and sisters, ages 6–15, to help others who are experiencing grief.

The Empty Place
Temes, Roberta
Story of a young boy whose sister suddenly dies. The boy receives comfort and help from a babysitter whose brother had died.

Molly's Rosebush
Cohn, Janice
Illustrated storybook that will validate the feelings children experience over a miscarriage.

No New Baby
Gryte, Marilyn
A story for children whose mother miscarries. Deals with the child's guilt and sadness and the need to be included and to have answers. Ages 3–7.

Stacey Had a Little Sister
Friedman, Judith
Stacey has mixed feelings about her new baby sister, but when the baby dies of SIDS, Stacey is sad and misses her. With parent's guide.

Thumpy's Story
Dodge, Nancy
A wise and tender story of a family of rabbits that shows people of all ages how they can help one another after a beloved child dies.

When I Die Will I Get Better?
Breebaart, Joeri and Piet
Written by a 5-year-old boy—who is assisted by his father—about the creative way he healed after the sudden death of his young brother.

Where's Jess?
Johnson, Joy & Marv
Book to validate and answer the questions and concerns of very little people who have a brother or sister who dies.

Death of a Pet

Goodbye, Mitch
Ruth Wallace-Brodeur
Shows what a child experiences when the cat he loves becomes sick and dies. Useful to teach about illness and death.

It Must Hurt a Lot
Sanford, Doris
After a boy's dog is killed, he learns many things he wants to share: to express his feelings and to help friends who are hurting. Ages 4–10.

The Tenth Good Thing About Barney
Viorst, Judith
Illustrated, provocative book for children about the death and burial of a pet cat, feelings of grief, what happens after death.

Sunflower Mountain
Foster-Morgan, Kathleen
A young boy, whose Grandpa has recently died, finds a friend in Mister Pete and his beloved dog, Governor, then learns how death is a part of life.

Death of a Parent

Dad! Why'd You Leave Me?
Frost, Dorothy
Ten-year-old Ronnie feels anger, sorrow, confusion over the sudden death of his father, but experiences support of family, friends, God.

Everett Anderson's Goodbye
Clifton, Lucille, and Grifalconi, Ann
Young African-American boy struggles through conflicting emotions as he tries to come to grips with the death of his father.
Ages 5–12.

Geranium Morning
Powell, E. Sandy
After Timothy's father is killed in a car accident, he meets Franny—a girl whose mother is dying. Their friendship and sharing brings hope to both.

How It Feels When a Parent Dies
Krementz, Jill
Collection of photo-essays with thoughts and feelings of eighteen children, ages 7–16, whose parents have died.

Onion Tears
Kidd, Diana
Nam-Huong, a refugee, is haunted by the loss of her parents and homeland. She is helped by a foster mother and a teacher. Inspiring.

A Quilt for Elizabeth
Tiffault, Elizabeth
After her father's death, Elizabeth and her grandmother make a quilt from his clothes, share their stories and their tears. A comforting, realistic story.

The Rag Coat
Lauren Mills
Evocative story that will charm readers with its message of the guidance and love a young girl can feel from her father, even after his death.

Saying Goodbye to Daddy
Vigna, Judith
Clare's mother and grandfather help her cope with the sudden death of her daddy in a car accident. Very sensitive. Ages 5–8.

Secret Places, The
Campbell, James
Shows the many tough changes Ryan experiences after his father's sudden death. A believable, uplifting story.

Death of a Grandparent

Annie and the Old One
Miles, Miska
As she prepares to die, an aging Navajo grandmother teaches her granddaughter about the cycles of life and death. Ages 6–12.

Grandad Bill's Song
Yolen, Jane
A lyrical and poetic book that shows how different members of a family respond to the death of a loved one.

Gran Gran's Best Trick
L. Dwight Holden
Deals sensitively with the illness and death of a grandparent who has cancer. The child is allowed to be a part of life, death, and family.

My Grandson Lew
du Bois, William Pene
Illustrates that grief reaches across the years, that those who love us, whom we love, are not soon forgotten. Ages 4–8.

Nana Upstairs and Nana Downstairs
dePaola, Tomie
Picture book that recognizes that even after a family member dies the love connections continue in heart and home.

Pablo Remembers
Ancoma, George
A colorful and instructive story about the Mexican fiesta of the day of the dead and how Pablo is able to commemorate those he loves.

Death of a Friend

Bridge to Terabithia
Paterson, Katherine
Newbery Award Winner. The story of a friendship between a boy and girl, an ensuing tragedy, and resurrection of hope. Ages 8–12.

The Class in Room 44
Blackburn, Lynn
Helps children understand and label their feelings related to the death of a classmate, to validate their ideas for commemoration.

I Had a Friend Named Peter
Cohn, J.
Describes the experiences of young Betsy after she learns of her friend's sudden death, how parents can help. Ages 5–10.

The Saddest Time
Simon, Norma, and Rogers, Jacqueline
Three compassionate stories of death—an uncle, a school friend hit by a car, and a grandparent. Ages 5–12.

Death and Loss Education

Badger's Parting Gifts
Varley, Susan
A story of the death of old Badger. As the animals talk about Badger they remember the gift of the skills and kindnesses he taught them.

Death is Natural
Pringle, Laurence
Illustrated book to help children understand death's place in the life cycle, especially as explained by nature.

God Is Always with Me
Caswell, Helen
A picture book that responds to a child's questions about why things change. A reassuring and sensitive reminder that love is forever.

The Great Change
White Deer of Autumn
Moving Native American story: Grandmother uses nature to explain death—the great change—to a grieving granddaughter.

Lifetimes: The beautiful way to explain death to children
Mellonie and Ingpen
Describes the cycles of life, beginning and endings in plants, animals and people. With illustrations. Ages 3–10.

Tell Me Papa
Johnson, Joy and Marv
A grandfather gives a detailed explanation of what happens when someone dies and the meaning of the funeral. Ages 4–8.

Water Bugs and Dragonflies
Stickney, Doris
Helpful booklet to be used to explain the mystery (spiritual dimensions) of death to young children. Ages 4–8.

WORKBOOKS AND ACTIVITY BOOKS—CHILDREN AND TEENS

A Book For Kids Like You
Burrel, Rachel and Coe, Barb
A 64-page workbook of letters, quotes, and drawings by the kids at Fernside, a center for grieving children. Lots of fill-in space.

A Child Remembers
Traisman, Enid
A write in memory book for bereaved children age 8–12. Pages for remembering, a good-bye letter, a story about us, pages for clippings, much more.

Create a Book
Sturdy blank book of heavy paper that helps children create their own story of loss and love. The cover can also be designed by the child.

Forever in My Heart
Levine, Jennifer
A creative, interactive storybook and workbook that helps children learn ways they can help themselves as well as a parent who is dying.

Fire in My Heart—Ice in My Veins
Samuel-Traisman, Enid
A fill-in scrapbook/journal to help teenagers experiencing a loss express feelings, sort out their thoughts, gather memories.

Goodbye Forever
Jim & Joan Boulden
Children ages 5–8 learn what "dead" means, what happens when people die, how to trust their feelings, saying good-bye, and remembering with love.

In the Hospital (Book and Audiotape)
Alsop, Peter and Harley, Bill
Songs and stories dealing with being sick, being different, being scared, and having fun anyway. For all ages.

A Keepsake Book of Special Memories
Van-Si, L., and Powers, L.
Guides children in preparing a book of photos, pictures, and writings to remember/commemorate someone who has died.

Let's Talk
Jim and Joan Boulden
Children ages 5–12 are given helpful information about divorce. Children gain understanding as they color, draw, and write their way through the book.

The Last Goodbye I
Jim and Joan Boulden
Serves as a way youth can gain information about grief and also process their feelings after a death has occurred. Ages 8–12.

The Last Goodbye II
Boulden, Jim and Joan
Informs about the grief process through interactive exercises and activities to be completed by the reader. Ages 13 and up.

My Stupid Illness
Tartakoff, Katy
Colorful interactive workbook gives children dealing with serious illness a way to express their experiences and document their lives.

The Penny Whistle Sick-in-Bed Book
Brokaw, B, and Gilbar, A.
Sick youngsters, and those who care for them, will love this treasure of games, crafts, puzzles, and even recipes to lighten up the blah days.

Remembering Special Days
Levine, Jennifer
A workbook to support grieving children focusing on the importance of remembering. Offers creative suggestions for special holidays/events.

Saying Goodbye
Boulden, Jim
Award-winning booklet that has color-in cartoons, drawings, and activities to help children understand the finality of death, the continuity of love.

Someone Special Is Very Sick
Jim & Joan Boulden
A workbook–coloring book about coping with feelings and concerns related to the serious illness of a loved one. For 5- to 7-year-olds.

So Much to Think About
Rogers, Fred
Activity book for children dealing with the death of a loved one that is just like Mr. Roger's Neighborhood, safe and warm and comforting.

*When a Grandparent Dies
Liss-Levinson, Nechama
A child's remembering workbook for Shiva on through a year of Jewish grieving rituals and holidays. For ages 7–12.

When a Parent Marries Again
Heegaard, Marge
Children are validated for both the losses and gains, blessings and strains inherent in the remarriage of a parent and merging of families.

When Mom and Dad Separate
Heegaard, Marge
Interactive workbook that teaches children about marriage and why divorce happens. Art projects and creative problem solving are stressed.

When My Daddy Died
Hammond, Janice
Coloring book/workbook to assist children in dealing with the many emotions and concerns when a father dies. Preface for adults.

When My Mommy Died
Hammond, Janice
Coloring book/workbook to use with the very young following the death of a mother. Contains a preface for adults.

When Someone Has a Very Serious Illness
Heegaard, Marge
Workbook to assist children in gaining information about an illness affecting them, or a loved one, and to express feelings.

When Someone Is Very Sick
Jim & Joan Boulden
Examines serious illness as it occurs at all ages. The objective is to legitimize feelings and encourage discussion. Ages 8–12.

When Something Terrible Happens
Heegaard, Marge
Interactive workbook designed to help children who have experienced traumatic loss. Explains grief through art activities.

When Someone Very Special Dies (Workbook)
Heegaard, Marge
A workbook that can be illustrated by children as they are guided through feelings and questions related to grief. Ages 5–12.

TEENAGERS FACING LOSS AND GRIEF

Adolescence and Death
McNeil & Corr
Researchers and practitioners discuss how adolescents face death and dying. Addresses bereavement issues of the teen years.

After a Suicide: Young People Speak Up
Kuklin, Susan
Young people tell how they have helped themselves, and been helped, after someone they loved killed themselves. Photos throughout.

The "C" Word: Teenager's and Their Families Living with Cancer
Dorfman, Elena
Candid and inspiring personal stories and photographs of five teenagers—and their families—as they deal with cancer.

Coping When a Parent Has Cancer
Strauss, Linda
Teens are given straight information about the disease process of cancer, common personal and family grief reactions, what to expect.

Coping with Grief
Buckingham, Robert, and Huggard, Sandra
Speaks to youth, helping them identify, cope with, and find help in dealing with the many losses of adolescence.

The Creative Journal for Teens
Capacchione, Lucia
Offers teens easy techniques for journal writing that enable the expression of feelings and self understanding.

Death Is Hard to Live With
Bode, Janet
For teens. The author uses cartoons, pop art, and interviews with teens to keep the information pertinent and dynamic.

The Dying and Bereaved Teenager
Morgan, John, ed.
Information on the needs and reactions of dying and grieving youth and the interventions needed by family, school, counselors.

Education of Little Tree (Book)
Carter, Forrest
Stories of wisdom, healing, growth, and adventure as told through the eyes of a 5-year-old orphan raised by his Cherokee grandparents.

The Education of Little Tree (Audiotape, 2 Cassettes)
Carter, Forrest
The ABBY award-winning story described above is read by actor Peter Coyote. An inspiring gift for any teen struggling to find hope and love.

Facing Change: A Book About Loss and Change For Teens
O'Toole, Donna
Speaks directly to teens. The author provides an abundance of information and coping choices to assist teens in understanding,

processing, and growing through their losses. Chapters include *How to Use Creative Coping, 75 Ways to Help Yourself,* and *Getting The Support You Need.* This is more than a book about loss and change. It is also a book about possibilities.

Fire in My Heart—Ice in My Veins
Samuel-Traisman, Enid
Fill-in scrapbook/journal to help teenagers experiencing a loss express feelings, sort out their thoughts, gather memories.

Grieving (The Need to Know Library)
Spies, Karen
Large print and photos add to the direct and solid information about experiences young people may have after a loved one dies.

Help for the Hard Times: Getting Through Loss
Hipp, Earl
Teens will like the cartoons/drawings scattered throughout this text. Helps teens understand grief over many kinds of loss.

How It Feels When a Parent Dies
Krementz, Jill
Collection of photo-essays with thoughts and feelings of eighteen children, ages 7–16, after the death of a parent.

The Last Goodbye II
Boulden, Jim and Joan
Informs about the grief process through interactive exercises and activities to be completed by the reader. Ages 13 and up.

Learning to Say Goodbye
LeShan, Edna
Wise and caring classic written directly to youth to help them overcome the problems they face when losing a parent. Ages 8–14.

My Brother Has AIDS
Davis, Deborah
Thirteen-year old Lacy's older brother has AIDS. How she deals with her shame, pain, and resentment provides hope and inspiration.

The Power to Prevent Suicide: Teens Helping Teens
Nelson, R., and Galas, J.
A guide of specific activities and actions teenagers can do to be peer helpers and be actively involved in saving the lives of their peers.

Preventing Youth Suicide
McEvoy, Marcia, and Alan
A comprehensive handbook for all phases of school-based programs. Contains step-by-step help for prevention as well as responder teams.

Straight Talk About Death for Teenagers
Grollman, Earl
"Straight-from-the-heart" information about what a teenager can expect from the grieving process, how to handle it.

Teenage Grief
Cunningham, Linda
A comprehensive training manual for initiating and facilitating grief support groups for teens who have experienced a death.

Teenagers Face to Face with Bereavement
Gravelle, K. And Haskins, C.
Seventeen young adults discuss the death of parents, siblings and friends in this sensitive and caring book. The book is candid and hopeful.

Teen Grief: 5 Teens Telling Their Story (audio tape)
Tape created by five teens with losses ranging from hospice to homicide. They describe their experiences, their growth.

Teens with AIDS Speak Out
Kittredge, Mary
Teens with AIDS tell what AIDS is, how it spreads, and what teens have to say about an illness that might someday end their lives.

When a Friend Dies: A Book for Teens About Grieving and Healing
Gootman, Marilyn
Especially during the teen years the death of a friend is a significant event. This book guides and validates teens with gentle wisdom and advice.

When a Parent Dies
Bratman, Fred
Speaks directly to young teens to guide them through the loss experiences related to a parental death. Photos throughout.

YOUNG PEOPLE FACING LIFE-THREATENING ILLNESS

Afraid to Ask: A Book For Families to Share About Cancer
Fine, Judylaine
Information and opportunities to talk about what to expect when someone in a family develops cancer; treatment, effects, emotions.

An Alphabet About Kids with Cancer
Berglund, Rita
Manages to inspire and celebrate life while informing kids about feelings and treatment related to childhood cancer.

Another Look at the Rainbow
Center for Attitudinal Healing
Thirty-four children (6–21) candidly share their stories, their feelings, and what they have learned about life with a terminally ill brother or sister.

Be a Friend: Children Who Live with AIDS Speak
Wiener, Best, and Pizzo, et al.
Through writings and drawings children living with HIV infection and AIDS candidly share their feelings, hopes, and fears.

The "C" Word: Teenager's and Their Families Living with Cancer
Dorfman, Elena
Candid and inspiring personal stories and photographs of five teenagers—and their families—as they deal with cancer.

Coping When a Parent Has AIDS
Hermie-Draimin, Barbara
A caring, to-the-point book to prepare readers for the changes and problems they will face during and after a parent's illness.

Coping When a Parent Has Cancer
Strauss, Linda
Young people are given straight information about the disease process, personal and family grief reactions, and what to expect.

Forever in My Heart
Levine, Jennifer
Informative, interactive story workbook that helps children learn ways they can help themselves as well as stay close when a parent is dying.

How to Help Children Through a Parent's Serious Illness
McCue, Kathleen
Carefully guides caregivers on how they can help children gain resilience, regardless of the parent's medical outcome.

In the Hospital (Book and Audiotape)
Alsop, Peter and Harley, Bill
Songs and stories dealing with being sick, being different, being scared, and finding strength and hope. For all ages.

I'll See You in My Dreams
Jukes, Mavis
About how young children can use their imaginations to comfort themselves and to say good-bye to someone who is dying.

Little Tree
Mills, Joyce
A tree that grows deep when it cannot grow tall provides a healing metaphor for children with serious medical problems.

Losing Uncle Tim
Jordan, MaryKate
Daniel's favorite uncle has AIDS. It isn't easy but Daniel visits his Uncle Tim right to his death and is rewarded with tender memories.

My Journey of Hope
Kovar, Sarah Jean
Book of courage written by 11-year old Sarah. She writes to tell other children what to expect if they are dealing with cancer.

*My Mom Is Dying: A Child's Diary
Westberg McNamara, Jill
Kristine learns her mother is dying and writes letters to God for help. Gradually she finds solace and learns her feelings are all OK. Helpful notes for parents are included in the back of the book.

My Brother Has AIDS
Davis, Deborah
When 13-year-old Lacy's older brother returns home with AIDS her life turns upside down. She deals well with resentment and pain.

My Stupid Illness
Tartakoff, Katy
Interactive workbook gives children dealing with serious illness a way to express their experiences and document their lives.

Nightmares in the Mist (Book, Activity Book and Guide)
Farrington, L., McGuire, L., and Dillon, I.
Provides a wealth of creative help for children experiencing fear of any kind, but especially related to a parent's illness. The kit includes an illustrated 36-page storybook, a 24-page child's activity workbook, and a 48-page adult guide.

No Longer Afraid
Sanford, Doris
With the help of parents and medical personnel, young Jamie learns how she can stay involved with life and friends while being treated for cancer.

On the Wings of a Butterfly
Maple, Marilyn
A dying child—and her parents—find comfort in her friendship with a caterpillar who is preparing to change into a Monarch butterfly.

Sammy's Mommy Has Cancer
Kohlenberg, Sherry
Shows how the whole family has ups and downs when someone is sick and how they can help each other cope.

*Someone Special Is Very Sick
Jim and Joan Boulden
Workbook-coloring book about coping with feelings and concerns related to the serious illness of a loved one. For 5- to 7-year-olds.

You Can Call Me Willy
Verniero, Joan
Story of Willy, an 8-year-old living with AIDS, is sensitively written, honest, humane, and full of care and hope.

What About Me?
Peterkin, Allan
A young child coping with her brother's serious illness seeks and receives assurance after she asks, "What about me?"

When Mommy Is Sick
Dherkin-Langer, Ferne
A young child faces the confines, concerns, and feelings related to her mother's illness. Provides information and support.

When Someone Is Very Sick
Jim & Joan Boulden
Examines serious illness as it occurs at all ages. The objective is to legitimize feelings and encourage discussion. Ages 8–12.

PROFESSIONALS AND PARENTS—HELPING CHILDREN AND ADOLESCENTS

Annie Stories
Brett, Doris
A clinical psychologist shares how storytelling can help children deal with loss and fear. Nine retellable "Annie Stories.

Bereaved Children and Teens
Grollman, Earl, ed.
Experienced grief counselors contribute to this resource. Includes information on religious differences, how parents and schools can help, needs of grieving teens, and the influences of culture.

Bereavement Support Group for Children (Leader)
Haasl and Marnocha
Five-session grief support group program is outlined with objectives and details for how to facilitate specific activities. See workbook below.

Bereavement Support Group (Participant Workbook)
Hassl & Marnocha
(See above) Fill-in activities and information for a five-session child's bereavement support group program. Winner of the NHO Award.

Children Who Grieve
Beckman, Roberta
Manual for providing grief support groups for children. Seven sessions are provided. Contains many useful group activities.

Death and the Classroom (A Teacher's Guide)
Cassini and Rogers
Practical suggestions on how teachers and schools can effectively plan and provide help for dying and grieving young people.

Drawing Out Feelings
Heegaard, Marge
Guide on how to use art therapy and Marge Heegard's five workbooks for children, including *When Someone Very Special Dies.*

Fernside Idea Book
Burrell, R., Coe, B., and Hamm, G.
Guidebook for group facilitators working at the Fernside Center for Grieving Children, packed with information and group activities.

Forever in My Heart
Levine, Jennifer
Informative, interactive storybook that helps children identify feelings and learn how to help themselves when a parent is sick or dying.

Growing Through Grief (A K–12 Curriculum)
O'Toole, Donna
Award-winning curriculum to help young people through all kinds of loss. Includes developmental charts, role play scripts, complete sessions outlines and activities, over 100 reproducible handouts.

Grieving Child, The (A Parent's Guide)
Fitzgerald, Helen
Guide from a practicing counselor written for parents helping their children cope with the death of a loved one.

Healing Childhood Grief (A School-Based Expressive Art Program)
Black, Anne, and Simpson-Adams, Penny
Certified art therapists share their educational art program for bereaved children. The approach uses movement, sound, art, guided imagery, writing, and ritual to help children, ages 6 to 12, access their unique healing energy. Eight creative arts group sessions, complete with learning objectives and activity guidelines, are provided.

Helping Children Grieve
Huntley, Theresa
Explains how children at various ages understand and react to the death of a loved one. Brief, readable, and informative.

Helping Bereaved Children (A Handbook for Practitioners)
Boyd, Nancy
A child and family therapist brings to life a variety of counseling interventions to help children who have suffered a loss. Contains reproducible assessment tools and current research findings.

Helping Children Cope with Grief
Wolfelt, Alan
Practical and helpful interventions and guidelines outlining emotional, physical, and behavioral expressions of children's grief.

Helping Children Cope with Separation and Loss
Jewett Jarratt, Claudia
Skilled advice, specific techniques, and innovative ideas for helping children deal with losses of all kinds.

*Healing the Bereaved Child
Wolfelt, Alan
Extensive guide book (over 300 pages) in which grief therapist Wolfelt discusses, in depth, just how adults can companion children through grief, to help nurture them and to help them grow into the future.

Homemade Books to Help Kids Cope
Ziegler, Robert, MD
How-to book of techniques and instructions to make personalized storybooks to help children deal with loss and trauma.

Interventions with Bereaved Children
Smith, Susan, and Pennells, Margaret
Offers guidelines and how-to's for working in a variety of settings using drama therapy, play therapy, group, individual and family work.

Life and Loss: A Guide to Help Grieving Children
Goldman, Linda
User-friendly guide that provides essential tools and resources that will help children who are grieving all kinds of loss.

Children Mourning, Mourning Children
Doka, Ken, ed.
Readers will learn how children respond to loss and life-threatening illness. Clearly stated and easy reading. A video accompanies this book.

Part of Me Died, Too: Stories of Creative Survival
Fry, Virginia Lynn
Gives rituals and expressive art activities to help youth express emotions and commemorate loved ones.

Teenage Grief
Cunningham, Linda
Comprehensive, well-researched training manual for initiating and facilitating grief support groups for teens who have experienced a death. Contains information and activities for working with grieving teens.

Helping Children Cope with the Loss of a Loved One
Kroen, William
A primer for anyone dealing with a bereaved child. Offers insights and information from the respected *Good Grief Program*.

Talking About Death: A Dialogue Between Parent and Child
Grollman, Earl A.
Illustrated, simple, and straightforward discussion of death to be read to children. Includes a valuable parents' guide. Ages 3–8.

Thank You for Coming to Say Goodbye
Roberts, J., and Johnson, J.
Provides compassionate information on how to involve children in funerals—what to do before, during, and after the service.

TRAUMATIC LOSS—SUDDEN AND VIOLENT DEATH

Books for Children and Adolescents

About Traumatic Experiences
Berry, Joy
Illustrated explanation of trauma as it relates to a variety of losses. An excellent general book on the topic.

Children Are Survivors Too: A Guide Book for Young Homicide Survivors
Aub, Kathleen
Essential information for all working with bereaved children of trauma and violence. Besides twelve provocative and inspiring stories written by youth ages 6–18, the guide provides chapters on victimization, traumatic grief reactions, and child development theory.

Ellen Foster
Gibbons, Kaye
Young Ellen Foster is victimized by neglect and abuse. When her mother dies, she feels totally alone. Story of quiet courage, humor, and sweet inspiration. Ages 13 through adult.

I Wish I Was in a Lonely Meadow
Dougy Center
Children from the Dougy Center in Portland, Oregon, tell their stories and experiences following the death of a parent through suicide.

Just One Tear
Mahon, J. L.
A 13-year-old boy's father is murdered. This is the diary he keeps that shows his feelings and how he learns to endure and heal.

Listen for the Fig Tree
Bell Mathis, Sharon
How an African-American teenage girl is able to survive and grow—against great odds—after her father is murdered.

We Don't Like Remembering Them As a Field of Grass
Dougy Center
Written by children who have had a loved one murdered. They share their stories, their art, what helps them, their wishes for others.

When Something Terrible Happens
Heegaard, Marge
Interactive workbook designed to help children who have experienced traumatic loss. Explains grief through art activities.

Why Did It Happen?: Helping Children Cope in a Violent World
Cohn, Janice
Storybook for children that shows how a young boy is helped to come to terms with a violent act in the neighborhood. Includes adult's guide.

Books for Adults

Children and Trauma: A Parent's Guide for Helping
Monahon, Cynthia
Teaches adults about the effects of trauma on children, and offers a blueprint for restoring a child's sense of safety and balance.

Compassion Fatigue
Figley, Charles
Eleven chapters addressing how those who work with traumatized persons are themselves put at risk. Specific preventative suggestions are given, as well as tools for assessment and intervention.

The Forgiving Place: Choosing Peace After Violent Trauma
Gayton, Richard
Readers are invited to revisit their encounters with violence—and are shown specific exercises to help them work through the pain. The author, a clinical psychologist, himself experienced the murder of his wife.

The Many Faces of Bereavement: The Nature and Treatment of Natural, Traumatic, and Stigmatized Grief
Sprang, G., and McNeil, John
Scholarly, yet very readable text. Provides a hard-to-find blend of theory, process, and practice related to different types of grief. Especially pertinent are the chapters on sudden, stigmatized, and traumatic deaths.

No Time for Goodbyes (3rd ed.)
Harris Lord, Janice
About coping with the sorrow, anger, and injustice of homicide and violent death. Includes chapters on many related topics.

Post-Trauma Stress
Parkinson, Frank
A comprehensive guide for processing the stress caused by violence and natural disasters. Designed for ease in reading.

Surviving: When Someone You Love Was Murdered
Redmond, Lula
Important information for anyone working with survivors of homicidal death. Includes clinical intervention, how-to's on conducting groups.

Triumph over Tragedy
Petrocelle, B., & Frederick, C.
How the author fought through the darkness of his grief—to reengage in life—after his wife was killed by a drunk driver.

Trauma Victim
Hyer, Lee and Associates
An extensive text (758 pages) containing in-depth information for understanding and helping those who have experienced PTSD and trauma.

What Will We Do?: Preparing Schools to Cope with Crisis
Stevenson, Robert
Highlights programs that have been effective in dealing with violent and traumatic deaths. Specific guidelines and protocols are given.

When Disaster Strikes
McEvoy, Alan
Helpful guidelines for working with shock and grief—and returning a school to normal activities—when a community disaster strikes.

When Father Kills Mother: Children and Trauma
Hendricks, Black, and Kaplan
A thorough discussion of the grief and stress disorders of children when a parent has been murdered. Concise interventions are given.

Who Lives Happily Ever After?: For Families Whose Child Has Died Violently
Turnbull, Sharon
Addresses feelings, anguish, rage, blame, physical grief, your other children, your partner, spiritual needs, judicial system, the media.

Undaunted Spirits: Portraits of Recovery from Trauma
Buares, Mary
Sixteen interviews with highly successful people who have grown through tragedy.

AIDS AND HIV POSITIVE

AIDS and the Hospice Community
Amenta & Tehan
Up-to-date discussion of policies, treatment, and care practices of hospice programs in providing quality services to persons with AIDS.

AIDS Care at Home
Greif, J., and Golden, B.
Thorough, practical guide details just how to provide safe, comfortable care in home settings. Extensive information on related topics.

AIDS, Sharing the Pain: A Guide for Caregivers
Kirkpatrick, Paul
Guide to understanding and providing care that is compassionate. Christian perspective but embraces all faiths.

Children, Families, and HIV/AIDS
Boyd-Franklin, N., Steiner, G., and Boland, M.
Landmark work presents a family-focused, culturally sensitive approach to the psycho-social and therapeutic issues involved in care.

Families Living with Drugs and HIV
Barth, Pietrzak, and Ramier
Offers current information and intervention for what can be done to help millions of families affected by drug use and HIV.

Guide to Living with HIV Infection
Barlett and Finkbeiner
Current medical facts, practical advice, and emotional support for those with HIV, ARC, and AIDS from John Hopkins AIDS Clinic.

The HIV Drug Book
Project Inform
Only reference available that lists and describes all the drugs used by people with HIV, their effects and interactions. Extensive master index.

*Nutrition and HIV: A New Model for Treatment
Romeyn, Mary
Essential reading for thousands of people struggling to stay well with HIV and AIDS. Thoroughly researched, readable, and compelling.

Support Groups: The Human Face of the HIV/AIDS Epidemic
Barouh, Gail, Ph.D.
Indispensable guide about how to conduct AIDS-related support groups is based on extensive practice. Informative and wise.

Surviving with AIDS: A Comprehensive Program of Nutritional Co-Therapy
Callaway, C., M.D., and Whitney, C.
Cookbook and daily reference guide to help PWAs utilize a clinically tested nutritional program to supplement medical treatment.

Teens with AIDS Speak Out
Kittredge, Mary
Teens with AIDS tell what AIDS is, how it spreads, and what teens with it have to say about a disease that threatens their life.

What Everyone Can Do to Fight AIDS
Garwood, A., and Melnick, B.
An up-to-date, complete, and accurate guide to AIDS. An invaluable resource in educating persons of all ages. Easy to read.

SUICIDE—PREVENTION AND INTERVENTION

After a Suicide: Young People Speak Up
Kuklin, Susan
Young people tell their agonizing stories in the hope of helping others and diminishing the stigma associated with those whose loved ones have killed themselves. Photos throughout.

After Suicide
Hewitt, John H.
Guide for dealing with the aftermath of death by suicide of a loved one.

Cruelest Death: The Adolescent Suicide
Lester, David
Thorough discussion of teenage suicide, prevention programs, assessment tools, studies, what professionals and parents can do.

Mourning, After Suicide
Bloom, Lois A.
Beginning resource that addresses the anger, questions, and grief work of those surviving the suicide of a loved one.

The Power to Prevent Suicide
Nelson, R., and Galas, J.
A guide of specific activities and actions teenagers can do to be peer helpers and be actively involved in saving the lives of their peers.

Preventing Youth Suicide
McEvoy, M., and McEvoy, A.
Comprehensive handbook for all phases of school-based programs, with step-by-step help for prevention as well as for responder teams.

The Suicide of My Son: A Story of Childhood Depression
Carlson, Trudy
Through the story of one victim's life, the author illustrates how caring adults can recog- nize the symptoms that threaten a child's life.

Suicide Intervention in the Schools
Poland, Scott
Step-by-step guide for setting up and maintaining a suicide intervention and response team program in schools.

She Never Said Good-bye: One Man's Journey Through Loss
Dykstra, Robert
Searingly honest and inspirational sharing of one man's struggle to find faith and hope again after his wife killed herself.

Suicide Prevention: A Curriculum for Teens and Young Adults
Smith, Judie
Curriculum with five sessions includes attitudes about suicide, warning signs, needed skills for prevention/intervention, and resources.

Suicide Survivors' Handbook: A Guide for the Bereaved and Those Who Wish to Help Them
Carlson, Trudy
Handbook loaded with practical information. For newly bereaved persons as well as all who intend to help them.

Words I Never Thought to Speak
Alexander, Victoria
Stories of many who have lost someone through suicidal death, have grieved their losses and gained resiliency.

WHEN A CHILD DIES

Bereaved Parent
Schiff, Harriet Sarnoff
Practical step-by-step suggestions to help parents cope with the many cycles of their grief. Written by a bereaved parent.

For Bereaved Grand Parents
Gerner, Margaret
The author, who lost a young son and granddaughter, talks about grief—helping your child and yourself. Suggestions for listening skills.

The Fall of a Sparrow
Koppleman, Kent
How a father searched for and found meaning after the death of his son. Recommended for all fathers.

Goodbye My Child
Wheeler and Pike
Practical comforting booklet for parents anticipating or experiencing the death of a child, decisions to be made, dynamics of parental loss.

Healing a Father's Grief
Schatz, William
Short booklet that addresses specific problems that a father might face in dealing with the death of a child.

Help for Bereaved Parents
Tengbom, Mildred
Supportive booklet for parents going through the trauma and sorrows of the death of a child.

Meditations for Bereaved Parents
Osgood, Judy, ed.
Thirty-five bereaved parents share their anguish, anger, and healing insights in order to help others.

Our Children Live Forever in Our Hearts
Children's Mercy Hospital
Memory-and-comfort book with pages that invite the insertion of photos, mementos, and personal remembrances.

*Only Spring: On Mourning the Death of My Son
Livingston, Gordon
The author, a psychiatrist and writer, shares his journey through hope, torment, loss, and even joy in this candid account of how he and his family deal with the illness and death of their son.

Parental Loss of a Child
Rando, Therese A., ed.
Comprehensive analysis of all types of
parental bereavement, with clinical
interventions and therapeutic support
procedures.

Recovering from the Loss of a Child
Donnelly, Katherine Fair
Compassionate, reassuring accounts from
parents who have survived their grief after the
death of a child.

*The Worst Loss: How Families Heal from the
Death of a Child*
Rosof, Barbara
Comprehensive and readable. Wise
counseling, research findings, and kind
wisdom.

CHILDBEARING AND INFANT LOSS

Bittersweet . . . hellogoodbye
Sister Jane Marie Lamb
Extensive resource manual to assist in
planning farewell rituals when a baby dies.
Over 200 pages of commemoration ideas.

*Empty Arms: Coping After Miscarriage,
Stillbirth and Infant Death*
Ilse, Sherokee
Hope-filled guide for families experiencing
miscarriage, pregnancy termination, stillbirth,
or SIDS. For caregivers and the bereaved.

Empty Cradle, Broken Heart
Davis, Deborah L.
Comprehensive and sensitive book showing a
wide range of experiences following the death
of a baby and offering ways to cope.

Facing Death, Finding Love
Church, Dawson
How the author used creative expression and
ritual to transform the death of his child into
spiritual growth.

Healing Together: For Couples Whose Baby Dies
Lister, Marcie and Lovell, Sandra
Useful booklet encouraging couples to share
their grief while respectfully acknowledging
their different styles of expression.

Little Footprints
Ferguson, Dorothy
Memory booklet for parents with brief
messages that validates the loss of an infant
and that has room for personal writings,
clippings, photos.

Miscarriage: A Shattered Dream
Ilse & Burns
Comprehensive medical information, emotional support, and helpful suggestions on
dealing with life and grief after a miscarriage.

Molly's Rosebush
Cohn, Janice
Illustrated story book that validates the
feelings children experience over a miscarriage.

No New Baby
Gryte, Marilyn
Story to help children who have experienced
a loss through miscarriage of a hoped-for
sibling. For ages 3–8.

Parents' Grief
Parrott, Carol
Booklet of information and helpful
suggestions to help parents help themselves
and their other children after a baby dies.

The SIDS Survival Guide
Horchler, J., and Morris, R.
Gives critical information about surviving a
SIDS death in an organized, easy-to-assimilate
format.

Silent Sorrow: Pregnancy Loss
Kohn and Moffitt
Thorough presentation of the concerns
related to pregnancy losses of all kinds.
Includes suggestions for meaningful
remembrance rituals.

Stacey Had a Little Sister
Friedman, Judith
Stacey has mixed feelings about her new baby
sister, but when the baby dies of SIDS, Stacey
is sad and misses her. With parent's guide.

When Hello Means Goodbye
Schwiebert and Kirk
Poetic, helpful, and practical guide for parents
whose child dies before birth, at birth, or
shortly after birth.

FOR BEREAVED ADULTS

After Goodbye
Menten, Ted
Collection of stories about love and loss written down by a master storyteller.

Being a Widow
Caine, Lynn
Self-help book full of practical advice and words of wisdom from the author of the bestseller *Widow*.

Beyond Sorrow: Christian Reflections on Death and Grief
Montgomery, Herb and Mary
Brief comforting words and helpful suggestions along with quotes and photographs.

Courage to Grieve
Tatelbaum, Judy
Clearly written on all aspects of grief and grief resolution, including a practical self-help section.

Does Anyone Else Hurt This Bad and Live?
Eneroth, Carlene Vester
Practical tips, humor, and understanding are given to those who are hurting. Briefly written in a hopeful tone to enlighten and encourage.

Don't Take My Grief Away
Manning, Doug
Consoling guide for those who have lost a loved one, based on the premise that grief is not an enemy, but a friend.

The Fall of a Sparrow
Koppleman, Kent
A father's journey through loss teaches some unique ways of processing grief through commemorative action.

Finding My Way: Healing and Transformation Through Loss and Grief
Schneider, John
Explains how grief is a wholistic process and how pain can be transformed into growth.

Footsteps: Through the Valley
Sims, Darcie
Through brief quotes and with a loving invitation, the author walks with the newly bereaved person through the valley one step at a time.

*Going Solo
Menden, Ted
Heralds the strengths of women in the face of loss. Here are their personal stories of pain, determination, humor, and promise.

Goodbye My Friend: Grieving the Death of a Pet
Montgomery, Mary and Herb
Thirty-two-page booklet that validates the importance of pets, the grief experienced at their loss, and the value of memorializing. All ages.

Getting Through the Night
Price, Eugenia
Comforting words for finding your way after the loss of a loved one. Christian perspective.

Good Grief
Westberg, Granger
Small handbook to understand the stages of all types of griefs and losses.

A Grief Observed
Lewis, C. S.
Journal of a famous author, written after the death of his wife, freely confesses his doubts, rage, and rediscovered faith.

Grief Therapy
Katafiasz, Karen
Booklet that gives wise counsel and encouragement. Illustrations throughout.

Helping the Bereaved Celebrate the Holidays
Miller, James
Sourcebook for helping communities and faith groups plan instructional and remembrance events for bereaved people.

Healing and Growing Through Grief (rev. ed.)
O'Toole, Donna
Colorful, large-type booklet. Gives information on the grief process, helpful resources, encouragement.

Healing Grief
Medic
Useful and compassionate 24-page booklet that provides basic information about loss and grief in many different situations.

Healing Power of Humor
Klein, Allen
Techniques for getting through loss, with a special emphasis on the value of humor in times of terminal illness and grief.

Holiday Help
Gibson, Sherry
Offers many practical and creative ways newly bereaved people can cope with loss during Thanksgiving and Christmas holidays.

How to Go on Living When Someone You Love Dies
Rando, Therese A.
Experienced clinician writes for the layperson about the dynamics of grief in specific situations and techniques for grief resolution.

How to Survive the Loss of a Love
Colgrove, Bloomfield, and McWilliams
Ninety-four main suggestions for surviving, healing, and growing. See also the "Surviving" workbook.

How to Survive the Loss of a Parent
Akner, Lois
Shows why the loss of a parent is different from other losses and how it is possible to work through the grief in constructive ways.

I'm Grieving As Fast As I Can
Feinberg, Linda
Guides young widowed persons through the special needs and challenges unique to their age group.

I Know Just How You Feel
Linn, Erin
Positive suggestions on how to talk with bereaved persons without using cliches or hurtful language.

If There's Anything I Can Do
Eneroth, Carlene Vester
Quick-reference guide with dozens of practical suggestions for helping others cope with grief. Easy reading.

Life After Loss (rev. ed.)
Deits, Bob
Wise, reassuring, practical, and readable guide to adults dealing with losses of all kinds.

Living When a Loved One Has Died
Grollman, Earl A.
Easy-to-read book of simple, straightforward thoughts to help the bereaved confront loss and then go on with living.

Living With An Empty Chair
Temes, Roberta
This best selling classic explains that although there is now an empty chair that feelings and relationships remain in meaning and in memory

Meditations for the Widowed
Osgood, Judy, ed.
33 widowed men and women share openly their pain and despair, and their discoveries that help them build new lives.

Men and Grief
Sraudacher, Carol
A helpful guide for professionals and men about how culture and gender issues affect men's grief. Suggested counseling interventions are given.

*Motherless Daughters
Edelman, Hope
Motherless Daughters gives essential information for millions of women whose mothers have died. Written in a captivating and readable format.

*Mourning and Mitzvah: A Guided Journey For Walking The Mourner's Path Through Grief to Healing
Brener, Anne
This marvelous book is an exploration in depth of the place where psychology and religious ritual intersect. Offers many useful activities.

*The Mourning Handbook
Fitzgerald, Helen
This highly readable book is immensely comprehensive. It is filled with compassionate, wise, helpful advice on all aspects of death and dying.

*A Pilgrimage Through Grief: Healing The Soul's Hurt After Loss
Miller, Jim
Drawing from an age-old tradition—the act of pilgrimage—the reader is invited to

journey, at their own pace, through grief to recover hope.

Picking Up The Pieces: Healing Ourselves After Personal Loss
Hensen, Barbara
We highly recommend this inspiring book. Especially helpful for those having multiple losses including death, injury, illness and mobility.

Recovering From the Loss of a Parent
Fair-Donnelly, Katherine, new edition
The author explores the many emotions that arise after a parent dies, and tells inspiring stories of how people overcame their anguish.

She Never Said Good-Bye: One Man's Journey Through Loss
Dykstra, Robert
A searingly honest and inspirational sharing of one man's struggle to find faith and hope again after his wife killed herself.

Surviving, Healing and Growing: The Workbook
Colgrove, Bloomfield, McWilliams
The accompanying workbook to "How To Survive The Loss of a Love." With ninety-four activities to help yourself through losses of all kinds.

Surviving Grief: And Learning To Live Again
Sanders, Catherine
This information based on life and research shows bereaved people how to actively pursue their own healing. Highly recommended.

A Time To Grieve: Meditations For Healing
Staudacher, Carol
Each page of this book is a gem. The brief meditations offer comfort, hope and healing insights. A beautiful gift book to share with a friend.

Understanding Grief: Helping Yourself Heal
Wolfelt, Alan
The author provides information and activities to guide and support people who are grieving the death of a loved one

What Helped Me When My Loved One Died
Grollman, Earl A.
Collection of personal stories from people who have lost loved ones. Covers a wide range of relationships and ages.

When Bad Things Happen to Good People
Kushner, Harold J.
A rabbi wrestles with the problems of human suffering.

What Will Help Me? How Can I Help?
Miller, Jim
Two books in one. Book 1 has 12 gentle suggestions to help the griever. Reverse the book for ways to help someone else.

What to Do When a Loved One Dies
Shaw, Eva
Full of usable information on all aspects of death, dying, and grief.

When Will I Stop Hurting?
Kolf, June Cerza
Helpful advice and encouragement for those dealing with a recent death. Christian perspective.

Why Are the Casseroles Always Tuna?
Sims, Darcie D.
Loving look at the lighter side of grief that affirms the normalcy of grief again and again through laughter as well as tears. Also available in audio.

Winter Grief, Summer Grace: Returning to Life After a Loved One Dies
Miller, Jim
Compassionately explores the feelings of grief and offers inspiring passages of comfort and hope. Beautiful nature photography.

When Someone Dies
Greenlee, Sharon
Picture book explaining the hurt, fear, and confusion felt by adults and children after the death of a loved one.

Why Her—Why Now: A Man's Journey Through love and grief
Elmer, Lon
True account of life's darkest moments and a book of healing in which the author shares his truest, clearest, most honest feelings. Hopeful.

Windows: Healing and Helping Through Loss
Hannaford, M. J., and Popkin, M.
Educational workbook provides an interactive format to learn how to help yourself and others recognize, understand, and heal from loss.

Woman's Book of Grieving
Rapoport, Nessa
Lyrical reflections take us into the heart of healing. Inspiration through honest, courageous writings.

RESOURCES FOR PROFESSIONALS

Adolescence and Death
McNeil and Corr
Explores how adolescents encounter death and dying and addresses special bereavement issues of the teen years.

Am I Allowed To Cry?: A Study of Bereavement Amongst People Who Have Learning Difficulties
Oswin, Maureen
The author of this book has done years of research related to the grief of mentally challenged persons. Here are her guidelines for helping.

Bereavement and Support: Healing in a Group Environment
Hughes, Marylou
How to develop and facilitate vital, effective support groups. Included are eight structured sessions, evaluation tools, information on working with special populations, and much more.

Beyond the Innocence of Childhood, Vols. I, II, and III
These three books make up a definitive resource for how children and adolescents—and their families—can be helped as they face death, serious illness, and/or bereavement. Over 40 chapters by well-known practitioners, educators, and clinicians.

Volume I: Factors Influencing Children's and Adolescents' Perceptions and Attitudes Toward Death
Adams, David, and Deveau, Ellie, eds.
Highlights answering children's questions, children and death, gender differences, teachable moments, perceptual and cognitive development related to death, violent death in popular culture and media, AIDS, cultural differences in managing serious illness, and death rituals and funeral ceremonies.

Volume II: Helping Children and Adolescents Cope with Life-Threatening Illness and Dying
Adams, David, and Deveau, Ellie, eds.
Chapters cover: the use of art, storytelling, music therapy, therapeutic play, humor and laughter, pets and empowerment, camps as therapeutic adjuncts, palliative care, lessons from dying adolescents, imagery for pain control, story resources, and much more.

Volume III: Helping Children and Adolescents Cope with Death and Bereavement
Adams, David, and Deveau, Ellie, eds.
Highlights anticipatory grief: religion, spirituality, and the bereaved adolescent; long-term effect of sibling death; impact of parental death; legacy of AIDS; aftermath of suicide; domestic violence; death in the school, and support groups for children and adolescents.

Compassion Fatigue
Figley, Charles
Eleven chapters addressing how those who work with traumatized persons are themselves put at risk. Specific preventative suggestions are given as well as tools for assessment and intervention.

Creating Meaningful Funeral Ceremonies
Wolfelt, Alan
For those wanting to help persons plan meaningful funeral rituals that are founded on knowledge of the grief process.

Death and Grief: A Guide for Clergy
Wolfelt, Alan
Compact yet comprehensive text for clergy to enhance their ability to assist others at times of death and grief.

Death and Spirituality
Doka, Kenneth, and Morgan, John
Current information, approaches, interventions, and resources to assist the use of faith in times of crisis.

Death: The Trip of a Lifetime
Palmer, Greg
Explores the different ways people live with—and ritualize—death in many countries and cultures. See video of same name.

Dying—Facing the Facts (3rd ed.)
Wass, H., and Neimeyer, R.
Essential resource for all those interested in death studies. The chapters cover such diverse areas as psychology, nursing, medicine, AIDS, family studies, philosophy, religion, education, and the humanities.

Disenfranchised Grief
Doka, Kenneth, ed.
Comprehensive discussion related to losses that are not openly acknowledged, socially sanctioned, or mourned in public.

Drawings from a Dying Child: Insights into Death
Bertoia, Judi
Poignant example of how expressive therapies can help children cope with their illness and with their preparation for death.

Ethnic Variations in Dying, Death and Grief
Irish, Donald, et al., eds.
Beliefs about death, burial, and mourning practices of various ethnic/religious groups. Illustrative episodes.

Encountering Death: Structured Activities for Death Awareness
Welch, Smart, and Zawistoski
Thought-provoking activities that can be used within groups or classes related to death and dying. Reproducible pages.

Finding My Way: Healing and Transformation Through Loss and Grief
Schneider, John
Wholistic and developmental approach to grief that demonstrates how losses of all kinds may either fragment the self or be transformed into personal growth.

Grief a Family Process: A Developmental Approach
Shapiro, Ester
Expands on grief reactions as a developmental process that occurs across time—for families as well as individuals. The approach is holistic and expansive.

Grief Counseling, Grief Therapy (2nd ed.)
Worden, J. William
Covers tasks of grief, normal and complicated grief reactions, and grief counseling and self-care strategies.

Grief, Dying and Death
Rando, Therese A.
Comprehensive college text that offers theoretical background and clinical interventions for caregivers.

Grief Ministry: Helping Others Mourn
Williams, D., and Sturzl, J.
Two experienced grief ministers provide detailed information on the skills and practices needed to facilitate grief and burial rituals.

Grief Ministry: Facilitator's Guide
Williams, D., and Sturzi, J.
This companion guide to the book above includes ten complete sessions—to train church members in community grief ministry.

Growing Through Grief
O'Toole, Donna
Award-winning K-12 curriculum to help young people through all kinds of loss. The eight individual sessions are divided into three grade-level groupings, grades K–3, 4–8, 9–12. Over 100 reproducible handouts.

Healing The Bereaved Child: Grief Gardening, Growth Through Grief and Other Touchstones for Caregivers
Wolfelt, Alan
Guidelines and specifics on how adults can companion children so they can grieve and grow.

Helping Bereaved Children
Boyd, Nancy
Up-to-date discussion of the latest research, counseling , and interventions for helping grieving children.

The Helper's Journey: Working with People Facing Grief, Loss, and Life-Threatening Illness
Larson, Dale
Inspiring view of helpers. Identifies skills and practices for effective caregiving and stress management.

How Different Religions View Death
Johnson and McGee
Belief systems of various faith groups—their death practices, beliefs, and impact.

Helping the Bereaved: Therapeutic Interventions for all Ages
Skinner-Cook, A., and Dworkin, D.
Offers insights, interventions, and assessment guidelines for helping children, adolescents, and adults in a variety of settings.

How to Design and Facilitate Grief Support Groups
Logan, Kim
For those wishing to form and facilitate support groups. Six sequential sessions are outlined.

How to Take Care of You
Vineyard, Sue
Helpful guide to self-care.

Imagery for Getting Well: Clinical Applications
Davis Brigham, Deidre
Extensive, in-depth volume that teaches professionals just how they can design and use imagery to help with specific needs and illnesses.

Into the Light
Olson, Sharon
Combines prose and female nude photography to illustrate, in the feminine voice, the transformative nature of grief.

The Many Faces of Bereavement: The Nature and Treatment of Natural, Traumatic, and Stigmatized Grief
Sprang, G., and McNeil, John
Scholarly yet readable text provides a hard-to-find blend of theory, process, and practice related to different types of grief. Especially pertinent are the chapters on sudden, stigmatized, and traumatic deaths.

*Peer Programs: Leader Manual
Tindall, Judith
In-depth facilitator's book that shows how to plan, implement, and facilitate peer helpers program. To be used with the two books below.

Peer Power: Participant Book
Tindall, Judith
Develops adult peer counseling skills: attending, empathy, summarizing, questioning, genuineness, attentiveness, confrontation.

Peer Power: Participant Book #2
Tindall, Judith
Provides adult peer counselors with applications for the skills in Book #1 and special training in coping with loss, suicide, drugs, etc.

Parental Loss of a Child
Rando, Therese A., ed.
Comprehensive analysis of all types of parental bereavement, with clinical interventions and therapeutic support procedures.

Play Therapy with Children in Crisis
Nancy Boyd, ed.
Play therapy resource with crisis intervention techniques using art, dolls, puppets, games, and storytelling.

Psychology of Death, The (2nd ed.)
Kastenbaum, Robert
Critical review of recent findings, trends, and concepts about death and death attitudes. Every aspect of death is systematically covered.

Secret World of Drawings: Healing Through Art
Furth, Gregg
Art techniques to be used in counseling dying and bereaved people of all ages.

Statements on Death, Dying and Bereavement
Corr, C., Morgan, J. and Wass, H.
Ten documents, assumptions, and principles to guide worldwide work in death, dying, and bereavement.

Storymaking in Bereavement
Gersie, Alida
The use of stories/storytelling in bereavement counseling and groups is explained. Many story examples are given.

A Time to Mourn, a Time to Comfort
Wolfson, Ron
On the death practices and complete mourning rituals of the Jewish tradition.

Surviving: When Someone You Love Was Murdered
Redmond, Lula
Important Information for anyone working with survivors of homicidal death. Includes clinical intervention, how-to's on conducting groups.

Trauma Victim
Hyer, Lee and Associates
In-depth information for understanding and helping those who have experienced PTSD and trauma.

What Will We Do?: Preparing Schools to Cope with Crisis
Stevenson, Robert
Highlights programs that have been effective in dealing with violent and traumatic deaths. Specific guidelines and protocols are given.

Treatment of Complicated Mourning
Rando, Therese
Examines the unique issues placing mourners at high risk for complicated mourning. Includes descriptive intervention strategies, assessment tools, and traumatic stress reactions.

When Father Kills Mother: Guiding Children Through Trauma and Grief
Hendricks, Black, and Kaplan
Thorough discussion of the grief and stress disorders of children when a parent has been murdered. Concise interventions are given.

CREATIVE LIVING— CONSCIOUS DYING AND HOSPICE

101 Tips for Volunteer Recruitment
McCurley, S and Vineyard, S.
Hundreds of effective tips to help recruit volunteers for every possible job. See also the book *Volunteer Power* below.

101 Ways to Raise Resources
McCurley, Steve, and Vineyard, Sue
Nearly 1,000 tips to help you get money, goods, volunteers, and support. Gives many how-to lists for planning, conducting events.

Being Human in the Face of Death
Roth and LeVier, eds.
Teaches caregivers who work with dying people to unlock one of the most valuable resources they have—their own humanness.

Caregivers Handbook
Boulden, Jim
Concise and practical how-to reference for volunteers and family members caring for a dying relative or friend.

Comforting the Confused
Hoffman, S., and Platt, C.
Practical guidelines for communicating with persons with all levels of dementia disability. Specific protocols given.

Creating Meaningful Funeral Ceremonies
Wolfelt, Alan
For those wanting to help persons plan meaningful funeral rituals that are founded on knowledge of the grief process.

Crossing the Bridge: Creating Ceremonies for Grieving and Healing from Life's Losses
Metrick, Sydney Barbara
Essential guidance in creating and using rituals and commemorative ceremonies to transform grief into positive change.

Dealing Creatively with Death
Morgan, Ernest
Practical information on death practices, simple burial, memorial services, and more.

Dying at Home: A Family Guide for Caregiving
Sandar, Andrea
Helpful, thorough, practical, encouraging guide for every person caring for a loved one at home.

Ethnic Variations in Dying, Death and Grief
Lundquist & Nelson, eds.
Beliefs about death, burial, and mourning practices of a variety of ethnic and religious groups.

Encountering Death: Structured Activities for Death Awareness
Welch, Smart, and Zawistoski
Directed activities to be used in groups to help individuals recognize and alter their beliefs, fears and attitudes about death.

Final Gifts
Callanan, M., and Kelley, P.
By hospice nurses documenting the symbolic communication of persons nearing death, how to help and hear.

Gentle Closings
Menten, Ted
Short stories that give reassurance and courage to people who have a loved one who is dying.

Gone from My Sight
Karnes, Barbara
A pamphlet to help caregivers recognize
the signs of approaching death—from
1–3 months prior to death, up to the final
hours.

*Give Sorrow Words: Working with a Dying
Child*
Judd, Dorothy
Will help readers understand the personal
tensions of working with a child who is
dying. Includes information on children's
attitudes and awareness of death and
common emotional responses.

Help for Families of the Terminally Ill
Tengbom, Mildred
Assists families who cope with their own
problems as they work to help a terminally ill
member.

The Healing Path: A Soul Approach to Illness
Barasch, Marcian
Looks into the spiritual dimensions of illness,
and provides insight and suggestions to lessen
suffering.

How to Live Between Office Visits
Siegel, Bernie
How to look into our hearts, listen to
ourselves, draw on our strengths, and
confront our difficulties—for the health
of it.

The Healing Journey
Simonton, C., and Henson, R.
The holistic program of the Simonton Cancer
Center. Clear, useful information for anyone
living with cancer.

*Hospice Movement: A Way of Caring for the
Dying*
Stoddard, Sandol
Outlines the development of the hospice
movement, its principles and practice.

*The Helper's Journey: Working with People
Facing Grief, Loss, and Life-Threatening
Illness*
Larson, Dale
Inspiring view of helpers. Identifies skills and
practices for effective caregiving and stress
management.

How We Die: Reflections on Life's Final Chapter
Nuland, Sherwin
Detailed information about what happens
and what behaviors and symptoms to expect
as a person's body is dying.

How Different Religions View Death
Johnson and McGee
Belief systems of various faith groups—their
death practices and beliefs.

Hospice Care for Children
Dailey, A., and Goltzer, S.
Authoritative resource for all those
caring for children with life-threatening
illness. Provides pain and symptom control
protocols.

I Don't Know What to Say
Buckman, Robert
Authoritative and empathic guide that
demystifies the dying process and offers
practical advice for families of the
terminally ill.

Life to Death: Harmonizing the Transition
Boerstler, R., and Kornfeld, H.
The authors teach their comeditation
process, a holistic process that helps to
bring the mind and body of the patient
into alignment and to quell the fear and
anxiety that can arise as one approaches
death.

Living with Life-Threatening Illness
Doka, Kenneth
Positive guidebook to help the seriously ill
person and his/her family. Outlines good
coping, tasks and issues to be faced.

*Our Greatest Gift: A Meditation on Dying and
Caring*
Nouwen, Henri
Reflecting on his faith and on the life and
teachings of Christ, Nouwen gently reveals
the gifts that the living and dying can give to
one another.

Midwives to the Dying
Schneider, M., and Bernard, J.
Hospice nurses have written this detailed
guide for those helping others on life's natural
journey to death.

No Time for Nonsense
Jevne and Levitan
Creative, life-enhancing ideas that can decrease tension when dealing with life-threatening illness.

Noninvasive Approaches to Pain Management in the Terminally Ill
Turk, D., and Feldman, C.
Precise and practically guided interventions. Supplements medical care to help people cope more effectively with pain.

A Time to Live, a Time to Die: Important Concerns When Death Draws Near
Ash, Beatrice
A minister and hospice caregiver shares six concerns dying people often face, and gives suggestions on how they can be faced and resolved.

A Time to Live: Living with a Life-Threatening Illness
Karnes, Barbara
Booklet of insights and ideas to enhance the quality of life for anyone facing a life-threatening illness and a limited prognosis.

A Loving Voice
Banks, C., and Rizzo, J.
Fifty-two brief and read-aloud short stories for older adults—especially those confined by illness.

Mortal Acts
Feinstein, David, and Mayo, Peg
The authors provide eighteen empowering rituals and exercises for confronting and transforming the fear of loss into an ability to embrace life.

Pain and Possibilities
Rico, Gabrielo
Teaches how to find and tell your story and how to use writing to express and reformulate the pain of loss and grief.

Panda Bear's Journey: A Heroic Tale of Heart and Home
Alden, Rio
Celebrates courage, self-determination, and the spiritual journey.

The Picture of Health
Capacchione, Lucia
Resource is about healing with art will guide you through many easy, insightful activities that draw out and reduce stress.

Refuge
Williams, Terry Tempest
Transforms loss into promise, pain into grace. A story of a family living with cancer, a story of nature, a story of a heroic journey!

Rituals of Healing: Using Imagery for Health and Wellness
Achterberg, J., and Dossey, B.
Two seasoned practitioners give many specific exercises and visualization scripts to help us help our body restore and maintain health.

Rituals for Our Times
ImberBlack, E., and Roberts, J.
Two seasoned mental health practitioners show how to plan meaningful rituals and how to use them to mark transitions and assist healing.

Tibetan Book of Living and Dying
Rinpoche, Sogyal
Guide to the ancient Tibetan tradition provides an inspiring introduction to meditation practices and a compassionate way to care for the dying.

The Tao of Healing
Trevino, Haven
For healers and for all who seek health.

The Tao of Dying
Smith, Doug
Photos, wisdom, and insight about how one can care for people without trying to change or cure them.

Therapeutic Touch: Learning to Accept Your Power to Heal
Kreiger, Dolores
Practical advice and precise skill-building exercises to teach the value and practice of touch.

When You're the Caregiver
Miller, James
Two books in one. Gives guidance to those caring for a loved one. By turning the book around it guides the person who is ill.

Where Is Heaven?
Menten, Ted
Stories of seventeen dying children shows the way young children find meaning and spiritual insight as they face death.

MUSIC AND THE SPOKEN WORD AND . . . LOSSES OTHER THAN DEATH

Aarvy Aardvark Finds Hope: A Story for People of all Ages
O'Toole, Donna
Story about loving and losing, friendship and hope. Read by the author, with a musical background.

Listen: 8 songs (cassette)
Monks of Western Priory
Soothing songs, including *Listen, The Dawn Has Come* and *All I Ask Is That Now and Forever You Remember Me As Loving You.*

Listen with your Heart: 12 songs (cassette)
Edwards, Deanna
Deanna Edwards sings her classics *Walk in the World For Me, Follow in the Way of Your Heart, Listen With Your Heart,* plus 9 others.

Losing a Parent (cassette)
Kennedy, Alexandra
A grief therapist combines stories and interactive exercises that comfort and empower persons facing the serious illness and/or death of a parent.

Music Brings my Heart Back Home (cassette)
Edwards, Deanna
Deanna Edwards sings *Teach Me To Die, You're Going Home, Take My Hand, Peacebird, Remember Me,* and others.

Pachelbel Canon in D, with Ocean Waves
Khalsa and Sills, Gary

Radiant Coat, The (cassette)
Pinkola Estes, Clarissa
Dr. Estes tells and explains the stories she has used to help sick and dying adults face their fears about dying.

The Red Shoes (cassette)
Pinkola Estes, Clarissa
Tells how to nurture the spiritual aspect of self, especially during periods of illness, transition, and emotional challenge.

Rise Up: Songs of Healing and Liberation
The Monks of the Weston Priory
Healing and grace are woven together in these songs: *For I am That Song, So Loved By God,* and *When Someone We Love.*

Songs of Healing (cassette)
Gass, Robbie, and On Wings of Song
Songs of healing. Includes *Go in Beauty, May We Dwell In The Heart, Wherever You Go, Life Is Eternal, Listen Listen, Listen,* and, *Who Knows Where The Time Goes.*

Teenage Grief
5 Teens
Audiotape of five teens talking about losses ranging from hospice to homicide. For individual or group use.

Wherever You Go (cassette)
The Weston Priory
Comforting songs of love and presence include *Wherever You Go I Will Go,* a tribute to the love that transcends time and the death of a loved one.

Wrap Myself in a Rainbow (cassette)
Alexander, Paul
Gently guides the listener into the rainbow, where each color becomes a soft quilt of comfort. Side II brings songs of rainbows and hope.

A Family That Fights
Bernstein, S.
Picture-storybook that validates children caught in the web of family violence. It is an important resource for schools, churches, and hospitals.

Banana Beer
Carrick, Carol
Charlie, the orangutan, never knows what to expect from his alcoholic father. Charlie deals with feelings and learns what he can do.

Dinosaurs Divorce
Krasny Brown, L., and Brown, M.
Reassuring picture book helps children dealing with the confusion and anxieties apt to arrive when parents are divorcing.

Fire Diary
Rosenblatt, Lily
After 9-year-old April loses everything in a house fire, she puts her thoughts and feelings down in her diary. A counselor helps her heal.

How It Feels When Parents Divorce
Krementz, Jill
Nineteen youngsters, ages 7–16, share their deepest feelings about their parents' divorce. Photos throughout.

I Can't Talk About It
Sanford, Doris
When the girl in this story is sexually abused she is engulfed in shame and fear. How she comes to find help is a comforting story.

No More Secrets for Me
Wachter, Oralee
Four separate stories on the theme of sexual abuse, how young people can get help, and how they can defend themselves.

When a Family is in Trouble
Heegaard, Marge
Compassionate workbook that can be used with children to help them understand and cope with the problems related to addiction in families.

Something Must Be Wrong with Me
Sanford, Doris
Illustrated story of how a young, sexually abused boy gets help and learns he is not responsible for what happened.

When Andy's Father Went to Prison
Hickman, Martha
When Andy's father is sent to prison, the family moves to be near him. With a friend's help, Andy realizes his loss and learns to face his fear and shame.

When Mom and Dad Separate
Heegaard, Marge
An interactive workbook that teaches children basic concepts about marriage and divorce. Art projects and creative problem solving are stressed.

When a Parent Marries Again
Heegaard, Marge
Children are validated for the losses and gains, blessings and strains inherent in the remarriage of a parent and the merging of families.

VIDEO RESOURCES

Aarvy Aardvark Finds Hope
When Aarvy Aardvark's family is taken far away he is so sad and upset that he can't eat or sleep. He wishes he could die. Gradually Aarvy regains his will to live. But it is only after a tender ritual of remembrance is performed that Aarvy regains his vitality to play. Shows grief as a natural healing process. It also demonstrates just how others can help when a friend is grieving. Training guide included.

After the Violence
In their own words, we hear the stories of bereaved individuals, mothers, a father, and a sister. They explain how their loved ones died as murder victims of our increasingly violent society. They openly talk about their many feelings, including revenge, anger, and intense pain and sorrow. Recommended for mature teens and adults.

AIDS and Kids: The Whitney Project
A true story about HIV/AIDS and much more. When members of a sixth-grade class in Pecos, New Mexico, learn about a girl their age in Illinois who has AIDS, they want to help. The students become pen pals with young Whitney. Eventually they meet Whitney and have a *Whitney Williams Day*. Informs youth on ways they cannot become infected with HIV. Includes discussion guide.

Being Present: Opening the Door to Intuition
Helps caregivers of the seriously ill increase sensitivity to the intuitive as well as the practical aspects of caregiving. Examples of "being present" are shown in hospital and in home settings.

By the Waters of Babylon: A Spiritual Pilgrimage for Those Who Feel Dislocated
Adds a nondenominational, spiritual dimension to the experience of grief and to the feelings of dislocation and disorientation that grief often renders. Viewers are invited to use the feelings of being lost and homeless to find a holy place of peace and of communion with a greater meaning. Includes a leader presentation guide.

Castles in the Sand
Documentary of Josh Littman, a young TV newscaster with cancer. Josh, his wife, and children experience the rollercoaster swings of hope and despair, remission and final decline. The viewer becomes aware of the need both to face and to avoid death, the disorientation and invasion of treatment and illness, and of how family and medical personnel provide hope and support.

Children Mourning, Mourning Children
Cokie Roberts hosts this educational video that features noted grief experts sharing insights into how children understand death and how children express grief. Accompanying book is available.

A Child's View of Grief
Filmed with Alan Wolfelt at the Center for Life Transition. Portrays children and adolescents (and their parents) who are grieving the deaths of a parent, a brother, or a sister. Children and their parents tell how they cope, what helps them, and the kind of help they appreciate.

Common Threads: Stories from the Quilt
Academy Award–winning documentary tells the stories of five adults and one child (and their families) who lived and died with AIDS; the meaning that is felt as their lives are commemorated in the AIDS quilt. Narrated by Dustin Hoffman, original music by Bobby McFerrin.

Coping with Loss
The Challenger space shuttle tragedy is the starting point to show the reactions of schoolchildren to sudden, unexpected death. Educators and therapists provide information on how children and grieving adults can be helped. Support groups for adults are seen in progress. Profiles the family of a person who is dying, and discusses the importance of grieving and emotional support.

Death: The Trip of a Lifetime
A poignant and strange journey that spans more than twelve countries to discover how people's beliefs, customs, and rituals affect the way they live their lives. Divided into four 1-hour programs:

(1) ***The Chasm*** looks at how death is portrayed in the media, the arts, and the rituals of many lands.
(2) ***The Good Death***—how people across the world take great measures to control the moment of death and work to create "a good death."
(3) ***Letting Go***—Funeral and grief rituals through the eyes of many cultures and faiths.
(4) ***Going for Glory***—how different cultures manifest belief in an afterlife and how these beliefs affect our lives in this world.

Divorce and Other Monsters
Shows the affects of divorce on young children. Young Sandy is feeling angry, guilty, and dejected about her parent's divorce. In sharing her feelings with her parents, a teacher, and a friend, Sandy learns that by expressing her feelings and her fears, she begins to find ways to deal with them. For adults and children.

The Fall of Freddie the Leaf
Like Leo Buscaglia's much-loved book of the same name, *Freddie* illustrates how the changing seasons represent the inevitable cycles of life. Children and adults will enjoy watching this program together. An excellent resource for stimulating talk about life and the mysteries of death. For all ages.

The Grit and Grace of Caregiving
Seven guiding principles are revealed and explained to help family members or professionals care for themselves as they are caring for others. Caregivers are validated and informed. The conclusion is a stirring affirmation of the life-giving possibilities caregiving can offer.

How Do I Go On?
A video for those courageous people who are struggling to redesign their lives after a crisis. Viewers are led through a five-step process that encourages the honest facing of feelings, the deliberate exploration of options, and the careful reassembling of future plans.

It's in Every One of Us
Works beautifully in rituals or ceremonies as a reminder that our connections to others are deep, and enduring. The song, "It's In Every

One of Us"—a song of peace and love—is sung as images of people of all ages and all races are portrayed. A moving, uplifting sensory experience of hope and connection.

Keeping the Balance: When a Sibling Is Seriously Ill

Explores the feelings and reactions of siblings coping with the serious illness of their brothers and sisters. Young people share their experiences of being "the normal child." They explore the frequent conflict between their feelings of love and concern and their resentment over the attention denied to them because of the sibling's illness. With their parents, they offer advice on how families can help sick kids, and their siblings, to cope with chronic illness. For adults and children. (Winner of the National Film Festival award.)

Invincible Summer: Returning to Life After Someone You Love Has Died

A meditative blend of words, original music, and stunning nature photography that gently leads the viewer through the seasons of the year. Teaches the naturalness of the grief process. Winner of the 1990 John Muir Medical Film Award.

Let's Get a Move On

The feelings of loss children may experience when moving are dealt with. Although the subject is difficult this video is able to lighten up feelings without denying the courage it takes to make changes. Advice to help children cope with change is given through song, dance, and narration.

Living With Grief—Personally and Professionally

Five seasoned death educators/counselors (Ken Doka, William Worden, Theresa Rando, Sandra Bertman, and Ellen Zimmer) team up with narrator Cokie Roberts to talk about living with grief and the role of caregivers with dying and bereaved persons. Divided into four sections: (1) What Is Grief—Who Experiences It? (2) Dealing with the Grief of Dying Patients and Their Families, (3) The Caregiver's Grief—How to Deal with It, and (4) Somewhere to Turn—Support Groups and Other Ways to Help.

Listen to Your Sadness

Shows how unrecognized and unrealized losses of the past can affect current losses and a generalized experience of depression and despair. The viewer is invited to look at healing past and present losses through a four-part process of healing.

Loneliest Journey: A Docudrama

Men and women whose spouses have died describe their experiences following the first year after the death. They discuss adjusting to a new life while trying to keep the meaning and value of the past intact.

My Grandson Lew: Memories Don't Die

A mother and young son demonstrate how sharing feelings and memories helps heal their grief. Remarkable in its simple and moving message—that children grieve and retain images and memories of those they love, even from a very early age; that acknowledging and validating these memories helps.

Managing the Transitions of Your Life

Five-part video offers guidance and hope for facing any loss or change. Sections include (1) Only One Thing Never Changes: Change, (2) In the Beginning is an Ending, (3) In Between Emptiness, (4) The End Is a New Beginning, and (5) Change Won't Change But We Can. Includes a journaling and facilitators guide.

No One Ever Told Us

The TeenAge Grief training group, known across the United States as TAG, has extensive experience working with bereaved teens. In this video TAG group leaders and teens themselves tell us how they have dealt with all kinds of death—murder, suicide, sudden death, illness of parents, friends, and grandparents. The video normalizes grief and is a nice introduction to a discussion on how youth can grow through grief.

The Pitch of Grief

A powerful look at the emotional process of grieving through intimate interviews with four bereaved men and women, both young and old. Helpful not only for the bereaved person, but for family, friends, and health care workers and for all who will someday face the loss of a loved one. Widely used as a training film by Hospice programs. Winner of the Film of the Year Award by the National Hospice Organization.

A Ray of Hope: Managing Holidays and Special Days

Viewers learn how to be true to their needs and how to take care of themselves during a holiday season or any day they honor as a special day of remembrance. Paul Alexander, grief counselor, hosts the program. He is joined by men and women who share what they did—and what they didn't do—to get through those special days that can be so difficult to face after a loved one dies.

Round Trip

Five people talk about how their lives have changed and how they no longer fear death after having had a near-death experience. Their clear, candid testimonies are spoken with conviction and gratitude.

Rainbow's Remedy

Using lighthearted props and spoofs, Rainbow the Clown takes the viewer through the pain of loss, into the loneliness and despair of mourning and then shares her search for hope, balance, and healing. The viewer also meets Eloise Cole, a bereavement specialist and bereaved parent, and the creator of Rainbow. For individual and group use.

Surviving When Someone You Love Was Murdered

Grief therapist Lu Redmond shows how to use groups to work with persons who have had a loved murdered. A series of enacted group therapy scenes that illustrate the unique issues, as well as the intense suffering and anger, that homicide survivors often experience. Redmond outlines special concerns of survivors and offers clinical observations throughout.

Teen Grief: Climbing Back

A video for teens, a teaching video for adults to learn how to help teenagers, and a discussion guide.

Video 1: Teen Grief: A powerful and intimate look at the process of grief as experienced by thirteen young people ages 13 to 20. Captures the emotional ups and downs common to many teens after the death of a close friend or family member—whether by sudden death, long-term illness, or suicide. Segments of a grief support group show how the youth use the sharing of feelings, stories, and remembrance ceremonies to help them realize and heal their losses.

Video 2: Companion teaching tape to the video above teaches adults to recognize and understand the unique elements of teen grief. Grief counselor Marsha Lattanzi-Licht offers information about the developmental needs of grieving teens and provides advice on how adults can give effective support.

To Touch a Grieving Heart

Answers questions that grieving people most want to know: How long should people grieve? What do I say to someone who has lost a loved one through violence or suicide? Should I help someone forget about the one who dies, or should I help them remember? Educational sections are articulately presented by grief counselor and educator Kathleen Braza, who also shares some "healing rituals" and "memory work" that can help a person process his or her grief.

This Healing Path

Addresses concerns important to surviving siblings. An invaluable resource to siblings, their parents, and all who wish to walk with them before and after the death of their brother or sister. The young people share their pain, sadness, anger, fears, and dreams as well as many questions they have about their future.

A Teen's View of Grief: An educational Videotape for Caregivers

Training video to help bereavement caregivers better help grieving adolescents between the ages of 12 and 19. Includes material from an actual bereaved-teen support group.

The Tenth Good Thing About Barney

For children to open up many issues related to death and dying. When Barney the cat dies, the young boy who loved him is broken-hearted. To help console her son, the boy's mother and father help him plan a backyard funeral and suggest he think of ten good things to say about Barney. As the boy is finally able to think of the tenth good thing he is comforted.

Whitewater: The Positive Power of Grief
Uses a metaphor of the rough waters of a fast-moving river to describe critical periods of grief. Viewers are encouraged to flow with the river, to learn navigation skills to ensure their safe journey, eventually into calm waters, where the physical presence of a loved one is transformed into memory. Age, ethnic and racial diversity.

We Will Remember
A 10-minute meditation that uses natural photography, soothing music, and gentle words to give permission and encouragement in using the memories of the past for healing in the present.

What About Me?: Kids and Grief
Highlights eleven boys and girls, ages 4–14, while they discuss grief experiences due to the death or chronic illness of a sibling, parent, or grandparent. Coming from a variety of ethnic and cultural backgrounds, these

children want to give others hope they will recover. For children ages 5 and up and for all adults who wish truly to develop insights into the world of the grieving child.

When Kids Say Goodbye
Nationally known entertainer/educator Peter Alsop and Canadian funeral director Paul Janisse team up to answer kids questions about death and to give support for their fears and concerns. The action happens when Peter and three young friends visit Paul's funeral home. Together Paul and Peter speak gently and openly with the kids and sing songs and act out what grief looks and feels like.

Windows: Healing and Helping Through Loss
Integrated video-based educational training program designed to educate individuals, groups, and communities in helping themselves and others during periods of loss and grief. Includes a 2-part video, Leader's Guide, Promotional Guide, Promotional Posters and Booklets and a Participant Workbook. In two parts: (1) Recognizing and reconciling all kinds of loss situations, (2) Skills to help individuals help those who are grieving.

Preparing for Dying Worksheet

The following worksheet presents many of the practical tasks we have discussed in Chapter 10 but in a simple question and answer format. Take the time to answer each question either on your own or with your closest loved one and leave a copy to be read in the event of your death.

PREPARING FOR DYING WORKSHEET

Full Name: _____

Maiden/Other Name: _____

Usual Address: _____

Birth Date: _____ Birth Place: _____

Social Security Number: _____

Spouse's Full Name: _____

1. How you should dispose of my body:
[   ] Interred (buried), not embalmed.
[   ] Interred (buried), embalmed.
[   ] Cremated, not embalmed.
[   ] Cremated, after embalming.
[   ] Do above after organ/tissue donation.
[   ] Donate entire body (precludes organ donation).

2. I wish to donate:
[   ] My entire body for research, study, or transplant.
[   ] Any organs or tissues that can be used for transplantation or study.
[   ] The following specific organs or tissues:
[   ] Corneas (eyes)
[   ] Heart/lungs
[   ] Liver
[   ] Pancreas
[   ] Skin
[   ] Bone
[   ] Other _____
[   ] I have already made arrangements for this with: _____

3. I [   ] do [   ] do not have funeral or burial insurance. The policy is with
(company) _____
and the policy number is _____

4. I prefer _____ funeral home or funeral director.
They [   ] have, or [   ] have not been previously contracted.

5. I prefer my hair and makeup be prepared by the following individuals:
[   ] hair _____
[   ] makeup _____
[   ] funeral home _____
[   ] no preference

6. I want to be dressed in _____
[   ] shroud only
[   ] shroud over clothing
[   ] no preference

7. I would like to be buried with (jewelry, favorite possessions, etc): _____

8. I prefer a
[   ] funeral (with the body present)
    [   ] open casket
    [   ] closed casket

[   ] memorial (without the body present)
[   ] no formal service

9. I prefer a [   ] publicly announced or [   ] family-only funeral or memorial service.

10. I prefer services to be:
[   ] In a church/mosque/synagogue
[   ] at the funeral home/crematory
[   ] at the graveside only
[   ] at home or
[   ] somewhere else (specify) _____

11. I want a [   ] religious, [   ] fraternal order, [   ] military/veterans, or [   ] secular ceremony *(These are not necessarily mutually exclusive)*

12. I want the service run by a (enter name if known)[   ] minister: _____
[   ] priest: _____
[   ] rabbi: _____
[   ] other: _____

13. I have a preference for [   ] music [   ] readings [   ] prayers [   ] other: _

14. I [   ] do or [   ] do not want "calling hours" [   ] with or [   ] without an open casket.

15. I want to be interred (buried) at _____ cemetery.

16. I own a [   ] plot or a [   ] mausoleum. The deed for the plot is kept at: _____
It is in the name of _____

17. I [   ] do or [   ] do not want to be buried with anyone else.
If with someone, whom? _____

18. I want a specific type of
[   ] casket: _____
[   ] vault: _____
[   ] grave marker: _____

19. I want this written on my marker: _____
_____

20. I want this symbol/decoration on my marker: _____

21. I [   ] do or [   ] do not want a veteran's marker.

22. I was in the _____ (branch of military) from _____ to _____
(dates). I was discharged at _____ (place) on _____ (date).

23. My discharge papers are located at: _____

24. If cremated, I want this done with my ashes:
[   ] inurned [   ] buried [   ] kept at home [   ] scattered [   ] other: _____

25. I want a specific type of
[   ] urn: _____
[   ] columbarium: _____

26. I want my ashes scattered
[   ] at sea
[   ] at another site: _____

27. The following people should be notified of my death.
Name: _____
Address: _____
Phone: _____

28. I prefer to have or not to have the following people at my funeral, if possible.
Name: _____
Address: _____
Phone: _____
[   ] Come to funeral; [   ] Not come to funeral

29. Other family and friends are listed in my address book, rolodex, computer listing, which is located at _____
The computer listing is accessed by typing _____

30. I want mourners to send [   ] flowers [   ] donations. To whom? _____

31. I want something special in my obituary:_____
_____

Send copies of the obituary to the following periodicals:
_____
_____

32. I have a cost limit on any of the services mentioned above: _____
_____

33. My lawyer is _____ Phone: _____

34. My life insurance company/agent is _____ Phone: _____

35. My will is located at: _____

36. The executor of my estate is: _____

Adapted from Iserson (1994).

References

REFERENCES

Abdul Latif Al Hoa (1987). *Islam*. Bookwright Press, New York.

Abraham, K. (1953). Contributions to the theory of the anal character. In K. Abraham (Ed.), *Selected papers on psychoanalysis* (pp. 441–451). Basic Books, New York.

Abramson, L. Y., Metalsky, G. I., & Alloy, L. B. (1989). Hopelessness depression: A theory-based subtype of depression. *Psychological Review, 96,* 358–372.

Abramson, L. Y., Seligman, M. E. P., & Teasdale, J. D. (1978). Learned helplessness in humans: Critique and reformulation. *Journal of Abnormal Psychology, 87,* 49–74.

Achte, K., Fagerstrom, R., Pentikainen, J., & Faberow, N. L. (1989–90). Themes of death and violence in lullabies of different countries. *Omega, 20*(3), 193–204.

Adam, K. S., Bouckoms, A., & Streiner, D. L. (1982). Parental loss and family stability in attempted suicide. *Archives of General Psychiatry, 39,* 1081–1085.

Adams, D. W. (1990). When a Child Dies of Cancer: Care of the Child and the Family. In J. D. Morgan (Ed.), *The dying and the bereaved teenager,* (pp. 3–21). Charles Press, Philadelphia.

Adams, D. W., & Deveau, E. J. (1986). Helping dying adolescents: Needs and responses. In Corr, C. A., & McNeil, J. N. (Eds.), *Adolescence and death* (pp. 79–96). Springer, New York.

Adams, D. W., & Deveau, E. J. (1987). How the cause of a child's death may affect a sibling's grief. In M. A. Morgan (Ed.), *Bereavement: Helping the survivors* (pp. 79–96). King's College, London, Ontario, Canada.

Adams-Tucker, C. (1982). Proximate effects of sexual abuse in childhood. A report on 28 children. *American Journal of Psychiatry, 139,* 1252–1256.

Adler, A. (1943). Neuropsychiatric complications in victims of Boston's Cocoanut Grove disaster. *JAMA, 123,* 1098–1101.

Adler, N., & Matthews, K. (1994). Health psychology: Why do some people get sick and some stay well? *Annual review of Psychology, 45,* 229–259.

Aiken, L. R. (1994). *Death, dying and bereavement* (3rd. ed.). Allyn and Bacon, Boston.

Akiyama, H., Holtzman, J., & Britz, W. (1987). Pet ownership and health status during bereavement. *Omega, 17(2),* 187–193.

Aldous, J. (1978). *Family careers: Developmental change in families.* Wiley, New York.

Aldridge, D. (1993). Is there evidence for spiritual healing? *Advances, 9*(4), 4–21.

Allen, K. M., Blascovich, J., Tomaka, J., & Kelsey, R. M. (1991). Presence of human friends and pet dogs as moderators of autonomic responses to stress in women. *Journal of Personality and Social Psychology, 61,* 582–589.

Alzheimer's Association, (1996), *Alzheimer's disease: Fact sheet* [On-line]. Available: http://www.alz.org/dinfo/factsheet/ADFS.html)

Amenta, M. M. (1984). Death anxiety, purpose in life and duration of service in hospice volunteers. *Psychological Reports, 54,* 979–984.

Amenta, M. M., & Bohnet, N. L. (1986). *Nursing care of the terminally ill.* Little, Brown, Boston.

American Association of Suicidology. (1995). *Adolescent Suicide.* Denver, CO.

American Cancer Society. (1996). *Leading sites of new cancer cases and deaths estimates (1995)* [On-line]. Available http://www.cancer.ord/cffll.html

American Heart Association. (1996). *Cardiovascular disease statistics: 1992* [On-line]. Available http://www.amhrt.org/heartg/ac9.htm

American Medical Association. (1995). *Current levels of physician compensation* [On-line]. Available http://www.practice-net.composit.html

Angell, M. (1993). The doctor as double agent. *Kennedy Institute of Ethics Journal, 3,*(3), 1–3.

Applebaum, D. R., & Burns, G. L. (1991). Unexpected childhood death: Posttraumatic stress disorder in surviving siblings and parents. *Journal of Clinical Child Psychology, 20*(2), 114–120.

Aries, P. (1962). *Centuries of childhood: A social history of family life.* Vintage Books, New York.

Aries, P. (1974). *Western attitudes toward death: From the Middle Ages to the present.* Johns Hopkins University Press, Baltimore.

Aries, P. (1975, June). A moment that has lost its meaning. *Prism,* 27–29.

Arkow, P. (1977, June). Pet therapy: A study of the use of companion animals in selected therapies. *American Humane,* 1–42.

Armstrong, R. (1994, March 28). The world is going to the dogs. *Newsweek,* 8.

Arnold, J. D., Zimmerman, T. F., & Martin, D. L. (1968). Public attitudes and the diagnosis of death. *Journal of the American Medical Association, 206*(9), 1949–1954.

Arnold, J. H., & Gemma, P. (1983). *A child dies: A portrait of family grief.* Aspen, Rockville, MD.

Aronson, E. (1992). *The Social Animal* (6th ed.). Freeman, New York.

Asberg, M., Nordstrom P., & Traskman-Bendz, L. (1986, December). Cerebrospinal fluid studies in suicide. *Annals of the New York Academy of Sciences, 487,* 243–255.

Asberg, M., & Traskman, L. (1981). Studies of CSF 5-HIAA in depression and suicidal behavior. *Experiments in Medical Biology, 133,* 739–752.

Asberg, M., Traskman, L., & Thoren, P. (1976). 5-HIAA in the cerebrospinal fluid. A biochemical suicide predictor. *Archives of General Psychiatry, 33,* 1193–1197.

Ascher, J. (1989). Ashes or burial. *Psychologie Medicale, 21*(4), 415–416.

Ashcroft, L. (1987). Defusing "empowering": The what and the why. *Language Arts, 64*(2), 142–156.

Aspinwall, L. G., & Taylor, S. E. (1992). Modeling cognitive adaptation: A longitudinal investigation of the impact of individual differences and coping on college adjustment and performance. *Journal of Personality and Social Psychology, 63,* 989–1003.

Attig, T. (1986). Death themes in adolescent music. In C. A. Corr & J. N. McNeil (Eds.), *Adolescence and death* (pp. 32–56). Springer, New York.

Azevedo, E. M. (1996). *Personal communication.*

Bachman, J. G. (1987, February). An eye on the future. *Psychology Today,* 6–7.

Backer, B. A., Hannon, N., & Russell, N. A. (1982). *Death and dying: Individuals and institutions,* Wiley, New York.

Bailey, K. G. (1987). *Human paleopsychology.* L. Erlbaum, Hillsdale, NJ.

Baker, K. (1994, August 3). Buried but not dead. *San Francisco Chronicle,* p. E1.

Bandura, A. (1982). Self-efficacy: Mechanism in human agency. *American Psychologist, 37*(2), 122–147.

Banki, C. M., & Arato, M. (1983). Amine metabolites, neuroendocrine findings, and personality dimension as correlates of suicidal behavior. *Psychiatry Research, 10,* 253–261.

Barber, T. X. (Ed.). (1976). *Advances in altered states of consciousness and human potentialities* (Vol. 1, pp. 103–111). Psychological Dimensions, New York.

Baron, J., & Brown, R. (Eds.). (1991). *Teaching decision-making to adolescents.* Erlbaum, Hillsdale, NJ.

Baron, R. A. (1995). *Psychology,* Allyn & Bacon, Boston.

Baron, R. A., & Byrne, D. (1991). *Social psychology: Understanding human interaction* (6th ed.). Allyn and Bacon, Boston.

Baron, R. S., Cutrona, C. E., Hicklin, D., Russell, D. W., and Lubaroff, D. M. (1990). Social support and immune function among spouses of cancer patients. *Journal of Personality and Social Psychology, 59,* 344–352.

Barraclough, B. M. (1971). Suicide in the elderly. In D. W. Kay & A. Walk (Eds.), *Recent developments in psychogeriatrics* (pp. 89–97). Kent, England, Headly Brothers.

Barrow, G. M. (1996). *Aging, the individual, and society* (5th ed.). West, St. Paul, MN.

Barrow, G. M., & Smith, P. A. (1983). *Aging, the individual, and society* (2nd ed.). West, St. Paul, MN.

Barusch, A. S. (1988). Problems and coping strategies of elderly spouse caregivers. *The Gerontologist, 28*(5), 677–685.

Bass, David M. (1985). The hospice ideology and success of hospice care. *Research on Aging, 7,* 1.

Bates, B. C., & Stanley, A. (1985). The epidemiology and differential diagnosis of near-death experience. *American Journal of Orthopsychiatry, 55,* 542–549.

Battin, M. P. (1994). *The least worst death: Essays in bioethics on the end of life.* Oxford University Press, New York.

Beatty, J. R. (1989). Parental bereavement: A Comparison of Grief Experiences. *Dissertation Abstracts International, 50*(5B), 2145.

Beaudet, D. (1991). Encountering the monster in children's dreams: Combat, taming, and engulfment. *Quadrant, 24*(1), 65–73.

Beck, A. T. (1967). *Depression: Clinical, experimental, and theoretical aspects.* Hoeber, New York.

Beck, A. T. (1976). *Cognitive therapy and the emotional disorders.* International Universities Press, New York.

Beck, A. T., Kovacs, M., & Weissman, A. (1979). Assessment of suicide ideation: The scale for suicide ideators. *Journal of Consulting and Clinical Psychology, 47,* 343–352.

Beck, A. T., Rush, A. J., Shaw, B., & Emery, G. (1979). *Cognitive therapy of depression.* Guilford, New York.

Beck, A. T., Steer, R. A., Kovacs, M., & Garrison, B. (1985). Hopelessness and eventual suicide. *American Journal of Psychiatry, 142,* 559–563.

Becker, C. B. (1990). Buddhist views of suicide and euthanasia. *Philosophy East and West, 40,* 543–56.

Bee, H. L. (1992). *The journey of adulthood.* Macmillan, New York.

Benedek, T. (1959). Parenthood as a developmental phase. *American Psychoanalytic Association Journal, 12,* 389–417.

Benedek, T. (1970). *Parenthood, its psychology and psychopathology.* Little, Brown, Boston.

Benedek, T. (1975). Discussion of parenthood as a developmental phase. *Journal of the American Psychoanalytic Association, 23,* 154–165.

Benfield, D. G., Leib, S., & Vollman, J. (1978). Grief responses of parents to neonatal death and parent participation in deciding care. *Pediatrics, 62*(2), 171–177.

Benfield, D. G., & Nichols, J. A. (1984). Attitudes and practice of funeral directors toward newborn death. *Death Education, 8*(2–3), 155–167.

Bengston, V. L., Cuellar, J. B., & Ragan, P. K. (1977). Stratum contrasts and similarities in attitudes toward death. *Journal of Gerontology, 32,* 76–88.

Benoliel, J. Q. (1974). Anticipatory grief in physicians and nurses. In B. Schoenberg (Ed.). *Anticipatory grief* (pp. 381–383). McGraw-Hill, New York.

Benson, R. A., & Brodie, D. C. (1975). Suicide by overdose of medicines among the aged. *Journal of the American Geriatrics Society, 23,* 304–308.

Bergman, A. B., Pomeroy, M. A., and Beckwith J. B. (1969). The psychiatric toll of the sudden infant death syndrome. *GP, 40,* 99–105.

Berman, A. L., & Carroll, T. A. (1984). Adolescent suicide: A critical review. *Death Education, 8,* 53−64.

Berndt, T. J. (1992). Friendship and friend's influence in adolescence. *Current Directions in Psychological Science, 1,* 156−159.

Bilatout, B. T. (1993). Hmong death customs: Traditional and acculturated. In D. P. Irish, K. F. Lundquist, and V. J. Nelsen (Eds.), *Ethnic variations in dying, death, and grief* (pp. 79−100). Taylor and Francis, Washington, DC.

Birenbaum, L. K., & Robinson, M. A. (1989−90). The response of children to the dying and death of a sibling. *Omega, 20*(3), 213−228.

Black, R. B. (1992). Seeing the baby: The impact of ultrasound technology. *Journal of Genetic Counseling, 1*(1), 45−54.

Blackhall, L. J., Murphy, S. T., Frank, G., Michel, V., & Azen, S. (1995). Ethnicity and attitudes toward patient autonomy. *JAMA, 274,* 820−825.

Blackmore, S. J. (1983). *Beyond the body.* Granada, London.

Blackmore, S. J. (1993). Near-death experiences in India: They have tunnels too. *Journal of Near-Death Studies, 11*(4), 205−217.

Blau, Z. S. (1961). Structural constraints on friendship in old age. *American Sociological Review, 26,* 429−439.

Blieszner, R., & Alley, J. M. (1990). Family caregiving for the elderly: An overview of resources. *Family Relations, 39*(1), 97−102.

Bloom, M. (1987). Leaving home: A family transition. In J. Bloom-Feshbach & S. Bloom-Feshbach (Eds.), *The psychology of separation and loss* (pp. 1−55). Jossey-Bass, San Francisco.

Bloom-Feshbach, J., & Bloom-Feshbach, S. (1987). *The psychology of separation and loss.* Jossey-Bass, San Francisco.

Blue, G. F. (1986). The value of pets in children's lives, *Childhood Education, 63*(2), 84−90.

Bluebond-Langner, M. (1977). Meanings of death to children. In Herman Feifel (Ed.), *New meanings of death.* McGraw-Hill, New York.

Bluebond-Langner, M. (1995). Worlds of dying children and their well siblings, In J. B. Williamson & E. S. Schneidman (Eds.), *Death: Current perspectives.* Mayfield, Mountain View, CA.

Blumenthal, S. J. & Kupfer, D. J. (1986). Generalizable treatment strategies for suicidal behavior. In J. J. Mann & M. Stanley (Eds.), *Psychobiology of suicidal behavior* (pp. 327−340). New York Academy of Sciences, New York.

Bock, E. W. & Webber, I. L. (February, 1972). Suicide among the elderly: Isolating widowhood and mitigating alternatives. *Journal of Marriage and the Family, 34,* 24−31.

Boersma, F. J. (1989). Listening to voices within through prayer and active imagination: Implications for analytical hypnotherapy. *Medical Hypnoanalysis Journal, 4*(4), 168−173.

Bootzin, R. R., Acocella, J. R., & Alloy, L. B. (1993). *Abnormal psychology: Current perspectives.* McGraw-Hill, New York.

Bordewich, F. M. (1988, February). Mortal fears: Courses in death education get mixed reviews. *Atlantic Monthly, 261,* 30–34.

Borgatta, E. F., & Borgatta, M. L. (1992). Death and dying. In *Encyclopedia of sociology* (Vol. 1, pp. 413–418). Macmillan, N.Y.

Bosley, G. M., & Cook, A. S. (1993). Therapeutic aspects of funeral ritual: A thematic analysis. *Journal of Family Psychotherapy, 4*(4), 69–83.

Boss, M. (1976). Flight from death—mere survival: And flight into death—suicide. In B. B. Wolman & H. H. Krauss (Eds.), *Between survival and suicide* (pp. 19–44). Gardner Press, New York.

Bouquet, A. C. (1991). Transmigration of the soul. In *Encyclopedia americana* (Vol. 27), Grolier, Danbury, CT.

Bowie, W. K. (1977). Story of a first-born. *Omega, 8*(1), 1–17.

Bowie, W. K. (1980) Story of a first-born, In *Caring Relationships: The Dying and the Bereaved.* R. Kalish (Ed.), Baywood Publishing Company, Farmingdale, NY, pp. 45–61.

Bowlby, J. (1961). Processes of mourning. *International Journal of Psychoanalysis, 42,* 317–340.

Bowlby, J. (1969). *Attachment and loss: Vol. 1. Attachment.* Basic Books, New York.

Bowlby, J. (1973). *Separation: Anxiety and anger.* Basic Books, New York.

Bowlby, J. (1980). *Attachment and loss: Vol. 3. Loss, sadness, and depression.* Basic Books, New York.

Bowling, A. (1987). Mortality after bereavement: A review of the literature on survival periods and factors affecting survival. *Social Science and Medicine, 24*(2), 117–124.

Bram, L. (Ed.). (1979). *New encyclopedia* (pp. 489–490). Funk & Wagnalls, New York.

Brammer, L. (1991). *How to cope with life transitions: The challenge of personal change.* Hemisphere, New York.

Breed, W., & Huffine, C. (1979). Sex differences in suicide among older Americans: A role and developmental approach. In O. J. Kaplan (Ed.), *Psychopathology of aging* (pp. 239–309). Academic Press, New York.

Brent, D. A., Perper, J. A., Moritz, G., & Allman, C., (1993). Bereavement or depression? The impact of the loss of a friend to suicide. *Journal of the American Academy of Child and Adolescent Psychiatry, 32*(6), 1189–1197.

Brent, S. B., Speece, M. W., Gates, M. F., & Mood, D. (1991). The contribution of death-related experiences to health care providers' attitudes toward dying patients: I. Graduate and undergraduate nursing students. *Omega, 23*(4), 249–278.

Brent, S. B., Speece, M. W., Gates, M. F., & Kaul, M. (1992). The contribution of death-related experiences to health care providers' attitudes toward dying patients: II. Medical and nursing students with no professional experience. *Omega, 26*(3), 181–205.

Breslau, N., & Davis, G. C. (1987). Posttraumatic stress disorder: The etiological specificity of wartime stressors. *American Journal of Psychiatry, 144,* 578–583.

Brewi, J., and Brennan, A. (1992). Midlife and the spirituality of the child. *Quadrant, 25*(1), 59–71.

Brewin, T. B. (1991). Three ways of giving bad news. *The Lancet, 337,* 1207–1209.

Brim, O. G. (1976). Theories of the male mid-life crisis. *The Counseling Psychologist, 6,* 2–9.

Brockopp, D. Y., King, D. B., & Hamilton, J. E. (1991). The dying patient: A comparative study of nurse caregiver characteristics. *Death Studies, 15,* 245–258.

Brody, E. M. (1981). "Women in the middle" and family help to older people. *The Gerontologist, 21,* 471–480.

Brokenleg, M., & Middleton, D. (1993). Native Americans: Adapting, yet retaining. In D. P. Irish, K. F. Lundquist, & V. J. Nelsen (Eds.), *Ethnic variations in dying, death, and grief* (p. 107). Taylor and Francis, Washington, DC.

Brown, F. H. (1989). The impact of death and serious illness on the family life cycle. In E. Carter & M. McGoldrick (Eds.), *The changing family life cycle: A framework for family therapy* (2nd ed.) (pp. 457–482). Allen & Bacon, Boston.

Brown, G. W., & Harris, T. (1978). *Social origins of depression.* Tavistock, London.

Brown, G. W., Harris, T., & Copeland, J. R. (1977). Depression and loss. *British Journal of Psychiatry, 130,* 1–18.

Brown, J. A. (1990). Social work practice with the terminally ill in the Black community. In J. K. Parry (Ed.), *Social work practice with the terminally ill: A transcultural perspective* (pp. 67–82). Charles C. Thomas, Springfield, IL.

Budzynski, T. S. (1976). Some applications of biofeedback-produced twilight states. In T. X. Barber (Ed.), *Advances in altered states of consciousness and human potentialities* (Vol. 1, pp. 103–111). Psychological Dimensions, New York.

Bull, N. (1962). *The body and its mind.* Las Americas, New York.

Bureau of National Affairs. (1988). *82 key statistics on work and family issues. The national report on work and family.* (Special report #9). (ED 305 502).

Bustad, L. K., & Hines, L. (1984). Relief and prevention of grief. In *Pet loss and human bereavement* (pp. 70–81). Iowa State University Press, Ames.

Bustan, M. N., & Coker, A. L. (1994). Maternal attitude toward pregnancy and the risk of neonatal death. *American Journal of Public Health, 84*(3), 411–414.

Butler, R. N., & Lewis, M. I. (1977). *Aging and mental health: Positive psychological approaches.* Mosby, St. Louis.

Butler, R. N., & Lewis, M. I. (1982). *Aging and mental health: Positive psychological and biomedical approaches* (3rd ed.). Mosby, St. Louis.

Byron, L. (1980). Epitaph to a dog. *The best-loved poems of the American people* (p. 610). H. Felleman (ed.) Garden City, N.Y.

Calhoun, L., & Allen, B. (1991). Social reactions to the survivor of a suicide in the family: A review of the literature. *Omega, 23*(2), 95–107.

Calhoun, L., Selby, J., & Faulstich, M. (1980). Reactions to the parents of the child suicide: A study of social impression. *Journal of Consulting and Clinical Psychology, 48*(4), 535–536.

Cameron, P., Playfair, W. L., & Wellum, S. (1994). The longevity of homosexuals: Before and after the AIDS epidemic. *Omega, 29*(3), 249–272.

Carlson, N. (1977). *Physiology of behavior.* Allyn and Bacon, Boston.

Carmack, B. J. (1985). The effects on family members and functioning after the death of a pet. In *Pets and the Family* (pp. 27-39). Haworth Press, New York.

Carr, B. A., & Lee, E. S. (1978). Navajo tribal mortality: A life table analysis of the leading causes of death. *Social Biology, 25,* 263–274.

Carrese, J. A., & Rhodes, L. A. (1995, September 13). Western bioethics on the Navajo reservation. Benefit or harm? *JAMA, 274,* 826–829.

Carroll, J. T., & Graner, M. E. (1994). Hospice is managed care. *Journal of Home Health Care Practice, 6*(2), 49–54.

Carson, R. C., & Butcher, J. N. (1992). *Abnormal psychology and modern life.* HarperCollins, San Francisco.

Carson, U. (1989). Do animals grieve? *Death Studies, 13,* 49–62.

Carver, C. S. (1989). How should multifaceted constructs be tested? Issues illustrated by self-monitoring, attributional style, and hardiness. *Journal of Personality and Social Psychology, 56,* 577–585.

Cassem, N. H. (1976). The first three steps beyond the grave. In V. R. Pine, A. H. Kutscher, D. Peretz, R. C. Slater, R. De Bellis, R. J. Volk, & D. J. Cherico (Eds.), *Acute grief and the funeral* (pp. 16–29). Charles C. Thomas, Springfield, IL.

Castles, M. R., & Murray, R. B. (1979). *Dying in an institution: Nurse/patient perspectives.* Appleton-Century-Crofts, New York.

Cavanaugh, J. C. (1990). *Adult development and aging.* Wadsworth, Belmont, CA.

CDC. (1996). *AIDS surveillance statistics: National and international* [On-line]. Available: http: //www.lib.berkeley.edu/PUBL/guide10.html

Chabral, H., & Moron, P. C. (1988). Depressive disorders in 100 adolescents who attempted suicide. *American Journal of Psychiatry, 145,* 379.

Charlton, R. C. (1992). Spiritual need of the dying and bereaved: Views from the United Kingdom and New Zealand. *Journal of Palliative Care, 8*(4), 38–40.

Cheifetz, P. N., Stavrakakis, G., Lester, E. P. (1989). Studies of the affective state in bereaved children. *Canadian Journal of Psychiatry, 34*(7), 688–692.

Cherny, N. I., Coyle, N., & Foley, K. M. (1994). The treatment of suffering when patients request elective death. *Journal of Palliative Care, 10*(2), 71–79.

Chopra, D. (1990). *Quantum healing: Exploring the frontiers of mind/body medicine.* Bantam Books, New York.

Choron, J. (1963). *Death and Western thought.* Collier Books, New York.

Church, R. M. (1959). Emotional reaction of rats to the pain of others. *Journal of Comparative and Physiological Psychology, 52,* 132–134.

Cicirelli, V. G. (1983). Adult children and the elderly parents. In T. H. Brubaker (Ed.), *Family relationships in later life* (pp. 31–46). Sage, Beverly Hills, CA.

Clark, D. C. (1993, May). Suicidal behavior in childhood and adolescence: Recent studies and clinical implications. *Psychiatric Annals, 23*(5), 271–283.

Clark, J. M. (1950). *The dance of death in the Middle Ages and the Renaissance.* University of Glasgow Press, Glasgow, Scotland.

Clyman, R., Green, C., Rowe, J., Mikkelsen, C., & Ataide, L. (1980). Issues concerning parents after the death of their newborn. *Critical Care Medicine, 8*(4), 215–218.

Cohen, J. (1995, May 13). The healing touch. *Longevity* [On-line]. Downloaded from America Online.

Cohen, R. (1988). The death of an adult child, acute grief and a closure to parenting. In O. S. Margolis, O. S. Margulis, A. H. Kutscher, E. R. Marcus, H. C. Raether, V. R. Pine, I. B. Seéland, and D. J. Cherico (Eds.), *Grief and the loss of an adult child* (pp. 31–36). Praeger, New York.

Cohen, S. (1988). Psychosocial models of the role of social support in the etiology of physical disease. *Health Psychology, 7,* 269–297.

Cohen, S., & Syme, S. L. (Eds.). (1985). *Social support and health.* Academic Press, New York.

Coleman, L. (1987). *Suicide clusters.* Faber & Faber, Boston.

Comfort, A. (1979). *The biology of senescence* (pp. 57–91). Churchill-Livingstone, London.

Compton's *Encyclopedia.* (1995, January 2). [Online]. Downloaded from America Online.

Connell, H. M. (1972). Attempted suicide in school children. *Medical Journal of Australia, 1,* 686–690.

Connidis, I. A. (1989). *Family ties and aging.* Butterwoths, Toronto.

Cook, J. A. (1983a). *The bereavement of siblings following childhood deaths.* Paper presented at the meeting of the American Sociological Association, Detroit.

Cook, J. A. (1983b). A death in the family: Parental bereavement in the first year. *Suicide and Life-Threatening Behavior, 13*(1), 42–61.

Cook, J. A. 1984. Influence of gender on the problems of parents of fatally ill children. *Journal of Psychosocial Oncology, 2,* 71–91.

Cook, J. A., & Wimberly. D. A. (1983). If I should die before I wake: Religious commitment and adjustment to the death of a child. *Journal for the Scientific Study of Religion, 22,* 222–238.

Cook, S. (1973). *Children and dying.* Health Sciences, New York.

Copenhaver, B. P. (1978). Death: IV. Western religious thought: 4. Death in the Western world. In W. T. Reich (Ed.), *Encyclopedia of bioethics* (Vol. 1, pp. 253–255). Free Press, New York.

Coppersmith, E. (1980). The family floor plan: A tool of training, assessment, and intervention in family therapy. *Journal of Marital and Family Therapy, 6,* 141–145.

Corcos, A., & Krupka, L. (1985). How death came to mankind: Myths and legends. In R. Kalish (Ed.), *The Final Transition* (pp. 165–178). Baywood, Farmingdale, New York.

Corr, C. A. (1991). Understanding adolescents and death. In D. Papadatou & C. Papadatos (Eds.), *Children and death* (pp. 33–51). Hemisphere, Washington, DC.

Corr, C. A. (1992). A task-based approach to coping with dying. *Omega, 24,* 81–94.

Corr, C. A. (1993). Coping with dying: Lessons we should learn and not learn from the work of Elisabeth Kubler-Ross. *Death Studies, 17,* 69–83.

Corr, C. A., & McNeil, J. N. (1986). *Adolescence and death.* Springer, New York.

Corr, C. A., Nabe, C. M., & Corr, D. M. (1994) *Death and dying, life and living.* Brooks/Cole, Pacific Grove, CA.

Cottington, E. M., & House, J. S. (1987). Occupational stress and health: A multivariate relationship. In A. Baum & J. E. Singer (Eds.), *Handbook of Psychology and Health* (Vol. 5, pp. 41–62). Erlbaum Assoc., Hillsdale, NJ.

Cottrell, R. R., Eddy, J. M., Alles, W. F., & St. Pierre, R. W. (1984). An analysis of college students' attitudes and beliefs concerning body disposal. *Death Education, 8,* 113–122.

Cousins, N. (1979). *Anatomy of an illness.* Bantam Books, New York.

Cousins, N. (1983). *The healing heart.* Norton, New York.

Cowles, K. V. (1980). Loss of a pet: Significance to the owner, implications for the nurse. *Nursing Forum, 19,* 372–377.

Cowles, K. V. (1985). The death of a pet: Human responses to the breaking of the bond. In *Pets and the family* (pp. 135–141). Haworth Press, New York.

Crawley, J. N., Sutton, M., & Pickar, D. (1985). Animal models of self-destructive behavior and suicide. *Psychiatric Clinics of North America (NIMH), 8(2),* 299–310.

Cremerius, J. (1989) Freud's Sterben—Die Identitat von Denken, Leben und Sterben [Freud's death: The consistent pattern of his thought, life, and death]. *Jahrbuch der Psychoanalyse, 24,* 97–108.

Crook, T., & Elliot, J. (1980). Parental death during childhood and adult depression: A critical review of the literature. *Psychological Bulletin, 87,* 252–259.

Cross, C. K., & Hirschfeld, R. M. A. (1986). Epidemiology of disorders in adulthood: Suicide. In G. L. Klerman, M. M. Weissman, P. S. Applebaum, & H. L. Roth (Eds.), *Psychiatry: Vol. 5. Social, Epidemiologic and Legal Psychiatry* (pp. 161–176). Basic Books, New York.

Crown, J. L. (1982). Anatomical gift form. *Probate and Property, 11,* 9–12.

Csikszentmihalyi, M., & Larson, R. (1984). *Being adolescent: Conflict and growth in the teenage years.* Basic Books, New York.

Cuellar, J. A., & Ragan, P. K. (1977). Stratum contrasts and similarities in attitudes toward death. *Journal of Gerontology, 32,* 76–88.

Cummins, V. A. (1978, September). *Death education in four-year colleges and universities in the U.S.* Paper presented at the First National Conference on the Forum for Death Education and Counseling.

Curran, D. K. (1987). *Adolescent suicidal behavior.* Hemisphere, Washington, DC.

Curtis, M. (1994). The use of massage in restoring cardiac rhythm. *Nursing Times, 90*(38), 36–7.

Cusack, O., & Smith, E. (1984). *Pets and the elderly: The therapeutic bond.* Haworth, New York.

Cutter, M. A. G. (1991). Euthanasia: Reassessing the boundaries. *Journal of NIH Research, 3*(5), 59–61.

Dali, S. (Ed.). (1947). *Essays of Michel de Montaigne.* Doubleday, Garden City, NY.

Danto, B. L. (1982). A psychiatric view of those who kill. In B. L. Danto, J. Bruhns, & A. H. Kutscher (Eds.). *The human side of homicide* (pp. 3–20). Columbia University press, New York.

Darbonne, A. R. (1969). Suicide and age: A suicide note analysis. *Journal of Consulting and Clinical Psychology, 33,* 46–50.

d'Artois, B. K. (1995). The Pilgrim Project: Companions on the journey. *Thanatos, 20*(1), 12–13.

D'Augelli, A. R., & Hershberger, S. L. (1993). Lesbian, gay, and bisexual youth in community settings: Personal challenges and mental health problems. *American Journal of Community Psychology, 21,* 421–448.

Davidson, G. W. (1977). Death of the wished-for child: A case study. *Death Education, 1,* 265–275.

Davidson, G. W. (1979). Hospice care for the dying. In H Wass (Ed.), *Dying: Facing the facts* (pp. 158–181). McGraw-Hill/Hemisphere, New York.

Davies, D. J. (1996). The sacred crematorium. *Mortality, 1*(1), 83–93.

Davison, G. C. & Neale, J. M. (1994). *Abnormal Psychology* (6th ed.). John Wiley & Sons, New York.

Dawson, G. D., Santos, J. E., & Burdick, D. C. (1990). Differences in final arrangements between burial and cremation as the method of body disposition. *Omega, 21*(2), 129–146.

Deaton, R. L., & Berkan, W. A. (1995). *Planning and managing death issues in the schools—A handbook.* Greenwood Press, Westport, CT.

Deaton, R. L., & Morgan, D. (1992). *Managing death issues in the schools.* Monograph No. 1, Montana Office of Public Instruction, Helena, MT.

De'Epiro, P. (1984) When sudden infant death strikes, *Patient Care,* March 15, 1984.

DeHart, D. D., & Mahoney, J. M. (1994). The serial murderer's motivations: An interdisciplinary review. *Omega, 29*(1), 29–45.

DeLoache, J. S., & Brown, A. L. (1983). Very young children's memory for the location of objects in a large-scale environment. *Child Development, 54,* 888–897.

deMause, L. (1974). The evolution of childhood. *History of childhood quarterly, 1*(4), 504–575.

Derryberry, D., & Rothbart, M. K. (1984). Emotion, attention, and temperament. In C. E. Izard, J. Kagan, & R. B. Zajonc (Eds.), *Emotions, cognition and behavior* (pp. 132–167). Cambridge University Press, Cambridge.

Dershimer, R. A. (1990). *Counseling the bereaved.* Pergamon Press, New York.

DeSpelder, L. A., & Strickland, A. L. (1992). *The last dance: Encountering death and dying* (3rd ed.). Mayfield, Mountain View, CA.

Deutsch, H. (1937). Absence of grief. *Psychoanalytic Quarterly, 6,* 12–22.

Deveau, E. J. (1990). The impact on adolescents when a sibling is dying. In J. D. Morgan (Ed.), *The dying and the bereaved teenager* (pp. 63–77). Charles Press, Philadelphia.

DeVries, B. (1991). Friendship and kinship patterns over the life course: A family stage perspective. In L. Stone (Ed.), *Caring communities: Proceedings of the symposium on social supports* (pp. 97–107). Minister of Industry, Science and Technology, Ottawa, Canada.

DeVries, B., Dalla Lana, R., & Falck, V. T. (1994). Parental bereavement over the life course: A theoretical intersection and empirical review. *Omega, 29*(1), 47–69.

de Waal, F. (1996). *Good natured: The origins of right and wrong in humans and other animals.* Harvard University Press, Cambridge.

Dickinson, G. E. (1986, April 18–20). *Effects of death education on college students' death anxiety.* Paper presented at the Forum for Death Education and Counseling, Atlanta.

Dickinson, G. E. (1992). First childhood death experiences. *Omega, 25*(3), 169–182.

Dickinson, G. E., and Tournier, R. E. (1994). A decade beyond medical school: A longitudinal study of physicians' attitudes toward death and terminally ill patients. *Social Science and Medicine, 38*(10), 1397–1400.

Doane, B. K., & Quigley, B. Q. (1981). Psychiatric aspects of therapeutic abortion. *Canadian Medical Association Journal, 125,* 427–432.

Doka, K. J. (1984). Expectation of death, participation in funeral arrangements, and grief adjustment. *Omega, 15*(2), 119–129.

Doka, K. J. (1986, April 18–20). *Disenfranchised grief.* Paper presented at the Annual Forum of the Association for Death Education and Counseling, Atlanta.

Doka, K. J. (1996). Disenfranchised grief. In G. E. Dickinson, M. R. Leming, & A. C. Mermann (Eds.), *Dying, death, and bereavement* (3rd ed.) (pp. 203–206). Dushkin Publishing Group/Brown and Benchmark Publishers, Guilford, Ct.

Doka, K. J., & Morgan, J. D. (Eds.). (1993). *Death and spirituality.* Baywood, Amityville, NY.

Doka, K. J., & Tatelbaum, S. (1996). *Clashing paradigms.* Paper presented at the Annual Forum of the Association for Death Education and Counseling, Hartford, CT.

Dombeck, M., & Karl, J. (1987). Spiritual issues in mental health. *Journal of Religion and Health, 26*(3), 183–197.

Donnelly, K. (1987). *Recovering from the loss of a parent.* Dodd, Mead, New York.

Dorland's Illustrated Medical Dictionary (26th ed). (1985). Saunders, Philadelphia.

Dorpat, T. L., Anderson, W. F., & Ripley, H. S. (1968). The relationship of physical illness to suicide. In H. L. P. Resnik (Ed.), *Suicide: Diagnosis and management* (pp. 208–219). Little, Brown, Boston.

Dorpat, T. L., & Ripley, H. S. (1960). A study of suicide in the Seattle area. *Comprehensive Psychiatry, 1,* 349–359.

Dougherty, C. M. (1990). The near-death experience as a major life transition. *Holistic Nursing Practice, 4*(3), 84–90.

Douglas, J. (1990–91). Patterns of change following parent death in midlife adults. *Omega, 22,* 123–137.

Douglas-Hamilton, L., & Douglas-Hamilton, O. (1975). *Among the elephants.* Viking, New York.

Dugan, D. O. (1987). Death and dying: Emotional, spiritual, and ethical support for patients and families. *Journal of Psychosocial Nursing and Mental Health Services, 25*(7), 21–29.

Duhl, F. S., Kantor, D., & Duhl, B. S. (1973). Learning space and action in family therapy: A primer of sculpting. In D. Bloch (Ed.), *Techniques of family psychotherapy: A primer* (pp. 26–43). Grune & Stratton, New York.

Duke, M., & Nowicki, S., Jr. (1979). *Abnormal psychology: Perspectives on being different.* Brooks/Cole: Pacific Grove, CA.

Dunn, A., Hudrson, B., Katz, J., & Wilkinson, T. (1990, September 26). Small heroics. *Los Angeles Times,* p. A1.

Dunn, R. G., & Morrish-Vidners, D. (1987–88). The psychological and social experience of suicide survivors. *Omega, 18*(3), 175–215.

Durand, R. P., Dickinson, G. E., Sumner, E. D., & Lancaster, C. J. (1990). Family physicians' attitudes toward death and the terminally-ill patient. *Family Practice Research Journal, 9*(2), 123–129.

Durkheim, E. (1951). *Suicide* (J. A. Spaulding & G. Simpson, Trans.). Free Press, Glencoe, IL. (Original work published 1897)

Durkheim, E. (1965). *The elementary forms of the religious life.* Free Press, New York.

Durlak, J. A. (1972). Relationship between attitudes toward life and death among elderly women. *Developmental Psychology, 8,* 146.

Eagle, M. N., & Wolitzky, D. L. (1992). Psychoanalytic theories of psychotherapy. In D. K. Freedheim (Ed.), *History of psychotherapy: A century of change* (pp. 341–363). American Psychological Association, Washington, DC.

Easson, W. M. (1974). Management of the dying child. *Journal of Clinical Child Psychology, 3*(2), 25–27.

Easson, W. M. (1977). The Dying Child: Management of the child or adolescent who is dying. Charles C. Thomas, Springfield, IL.

Eccles, J. (1991). Gender-role socialization. In R. M. Baron, W. G. Grazino, & C. Stangor (Eds.), *Social psychology* (pp. 109–158). Holt, Rinehart & Winston, Ft. Worth, TX.

Economist. (1991, July 20). What is the "good death"? *The Economist, 21–22,* 24.

Eddowes, J. R. (1988). Caregivers of demented elders: The impact of adult day care service on reducing perceived degree of burden. (ERIC Document Reproduction Service No. ED 305 536).

Edelstein, L. (1984). *Maternal bereavement: Coping with the unexpected death of a child.* Praeger, New York.

Edman, G., Asberg, M., Levander, S., & Schalling, D. (1986). Skin conductance, habituation and cerebrospinal fluid 5-hydroxyindoleacetic acid in suicidal patients. *Archives of General Psychiatry, 43,* 586–592.

Egeland, J. A., & Sussex, J. N. (1985). Suicide and family loading for affective disorders. *Journal of the American Medical Association, 254,* 915–916.

Egendorf, A. (1986). *Healing from the war.* Houghton-Mifflin, Boston.

Egger, S. A. (1984). A working definition of serial murder and reduction of linkage blindness. *Journal of Police Science and Administration, 12,* 348–357.

Eichelman, D. (1987). Rites of passage: Muslim rites. In M. Eliade (Ed.), *The Encyclopedia of Religion* (12th ed.). Macmillan, New York.

Eisenberg, L. (1980). Adolescent suicide: On taking arms against a sea of troubles. *Pediatrics, 66,* 315–321.

Eisenbruch, M. (1984). Cross-cultural aspects of bereavement, II: Ethnic and cultural variations in the development of bereavement practices. *Culture, Medicine and Psychiatry, 8,* 315–347.

Eliot, T. S. (1971). *The complete poems and plays: 1909–1950.* Harcourt, Brace and World, New York.

Elkind, D. (1967). Egocentrism in adolescence. *Child Development, 38,* 1025–1034.

Elliot, G. (1972). *The twentieth century book of the dead.* Random House, New York.

Endenburg, N., Hart, H., & Bouw, J. (1994). Motives for acquiring companion animals. *Journal of Economic Psychology, 15*(1), 191–206.

Enright, R. D., Levy, V. M., Harris, D., & Lapsley, D. K. (1987). *Journal of Youth and Adolescence, 16,* 541–559.

Erikson, E. H. (1963). *Childhood and society.* Norton, New York.

Erikson, E. H. (1968). *Identity: Youth and crisis.* Norton, New York.

Erikson, E. H. (1980). *Identity and the life cycle.* Norton, New York.

Eshelman, D. M., & McKay, M. (1988). *The relaxation and stress reduction workbook.* New Harbinger Publications, Oakland, CA.

Estes, C. P. (1994, April 19). Coming to terms with death. *USA Today, p. 18.*

Eysenck, H. J. (1980, December). Health's character. *Psychology Today,* 28–32.

Faberow, N. L., & Litman, R. E. (1970). *A comprehensive suicide prevention program: Suicide Prevention Center of Los Angeles, 1958–1969.* DHEW, Los Angeles.

Farrell, J. J. *Inventing the American way of death, 1830–1920.* (1980). Temple University press, Philadelphia.

Fasco, S., & Fasco, D. (1991). Suicidal behavior in children. *Psychology: A Journal of Human Behavior, 27,* 11–16.

Federal Bureau of Investigation. (1996). *Uniform crime reporting program: Crime index: 1994* [On-line]. Available: http://www.fbi.gov/ucrpress.htm)

Feeley, N., & Gottlieb, L. N. (1988–89). Parents' coping and communication following their infant's death. *Omega, 19*(1), 51.

Feiffel, H. (1990, April). Psychology and death. *American Psychologist, 45,*(4), 537–543.

Feiffel, H. (Ed.). (1959). *The meaning of death.* McGraw-Hill, New York.

Feiffel, H., & Branscomb, A. B. (1973). Who's afraid of death? *Journal of Abnormal Psychology, 81,* 282–288.

Ferrigno, J. (1996). *Personal communication.*

Fertziger, A. P. (1991). Artificial organs, organ transplantation, and dealing with death. *Loss, grief and care, 5*(1–2), 69–75.

Fick, K. M. (1993). The influence of an animal on social interactions of nursing home residents in a group setting. *American Journal of Occupational Therapy, 47*(6), 529–534.

Finkbeiner, A. K. (1996) *After the death of a child: Living with loss through the years,* The Free Press, NY.

Fischhoff, B. (1992). Risk taking: A developmental perspective. In J. F. Yates (Ed.), *Risk taking* (pp. 133–162). Wiley, New York.

Fletcher, W. S. (1992). Doctor, am I terminal? *The American Journal of Surgery, 163,* 460–462.

Fogle, B., Abrahamson, D. (1990). Pet loss: A survey of the attitudes and feelings of practicing veterinarians. *Anthrozoos, 3*(3), 143–150.

Folkman, S., & Lazarus, R. S. (1988). Coping as a mediator of emotion. *Journal of Personality and Social Psychology, 54,* 466–475.

Food and Drug Administration. (1996). *Alzheimer Disease Report (1996) [On-line]. Available: http://www.erols.com/jjjams/00000079.htm)*

Foreman, J. (1996, April 29). How loneliness may be bad for your health. *San Francisco Chronicle,* p. A4.

Foulkes, D. (1966). *The psychology of sleep.* Scribners, New York.

Foulkes, D., & Vogel, G. (1965). Mental activity at sleep onset. *Journal of Abnormal Psychology, 70,* 231–243.

Fox-Genovese, E. (1996, June 3). It takes a family. *The New Republic,* 41–44.

Fraiberg, S. (1971). Separation crisis in two blind children. *Psychoanalytic Study of the Child, 24,* 355–371.

Frankl, V. (1984). *Man's search for meaning* (3rd ed.). Simon & Shuster, New York.

Freedman, J. L., & Fraser, S. C. (1966). Compliance without pressure: The foot-in-the-door technique. *Journal of Personality and Social Psychology, 4* (16), 195–202.

Freidman, P., & Linn, L. (1957). Some psychiatric notes on the Andrea Doria disaster. *American Journal of Psychiatry, 114,* 426–432.

Freud, A. (1960), Discussion of Dr. John Bowlby's paper. *Psychoanalytic Study of the Child, 15,* 53–62.

Freud, S. (1930). Civilization and its discontents. In J. Strachey (Ed.), *The standard edition of the complete psychological works of Sigmund Freud* (Vol. 21). Hogarth, London.

Freud, S. (1957). Mourning and melancholia. In J. Strachey, (Ed.), *The standard edition of the complete psychological works of Sigmund Freud* (Vol. 22). Hogarth, London. (Originally published 1917).

Friedman, M., & Rosenman, R. H. (1974). *Type A behavior and your heart.* Knopf, New York.

Fristad, M. A., Jedel, R., Weller, R. A., Weller, E. B. (1993). Psychosocial functioning in children after the death of a parent. *American Journal of Psychiatry, 150*(3), 511–513.

Frye, J. S., & Stockton, R. A. (1982). Discriminant analysis of post-traumatic stress disorder among a group of Vietnam veterans. *American Journal of Psychiatry, 139,* 52–56.

Fryer, J. (1987). AIDS and suicide. In J. D. Morgan (Ed.), *Suicide: Helping those at risk* (pp. 193–200). King's College Press, London, Ontario, Canada.

Fulton, G. B., & Metress, E. K. (1995). *Perspectives on death and dying.* Jones and Bartlett, Boston.

Fulton, R. (1965). The sacred and the secular: Attitudes of the American public toward death, funerals and funeral directors. In R. L. Fulton (Ed.), *Death and identity* (pp. 89–105). Wiley, New York.

Fulton, R. (1970). Death, grief and social recuperation. *Omega, 1,* 25.

Fulton, R. (1976). The traditional funeral and contemporary society. In V. R. Pine, A. H. Kutscher, D. Peretz, R. C. Slater, R. De Bellis, R. J. Volk, & D. J. Cherico (Eds.), *Acute grief and the funeral* (pp. 201–224). Charles C. Thomas, Springfield, IL.

Fulton, R. (1992). Funeral Customs. In *World book encyclopedia* (Vol. 7, pp. 171–172). World Book, Chicago.

Fulton, R. (Ed.). (1976). *Death and identity.* Wiley, New York.

Fulton, R., Gottesman, D. J. & Owen, G. M. (1983). Loss, social change and the prospect of mourning. *Death Education, 6,* 137–153.

Fulton, R., & Owen, G. (1987–88) Death and society in twentieth century America. Special Issue: Research in thanatology: A critical appraisal. *Omega, 18*(4), 379–395.

Fulton, R., Markusen, E., Owen, G., & Scheiber, J. (Eds.). (1984). *Death and dying: Challenge and change.* Addison-Wesley, Reading, MA.

Funk, S. C. (1992). Hardiness: A review of theory and research. *Health Psychology, 11*(5), 335–345.

Futterman, E. H., & Hoffman, I. (1983). Mourning the fatally ill child. In J. E. Schowelter (ed.) *The child and death* (pp. 366–381). Columbia University Press, New York.

Gabbard, G. O., & Twemlow, S. W. (1984). *With the eyes of the mind.* Praeger, New York.

Gabbard, G. O., & Twemlow, S. W. (1986). An overview of altered mind/body perception. *Bulletin of the Meninger Clinic, 50*(4), 351–366.

Galambos, N. I. (1992). Parent–adolescent relations. *Current Directions in Psychological Science, 1,* 146–149.

Gallagher, D., Thompson, L., & Peterson, J. (1981–82). Psychosocial factors affecting adaptation to bereavement in the elderly. *International Journal of Aging and Human Development, 14*(2), 79–95.

Gallagher, W. (1996) Every parent's nightmare, *New York Times Review of Books,* June 2, 1996, p. 14.

Gallup Organization. (1986). *Americans volunteer 1985.* Princeton, NJ.

Gallup Organization. (1988). *Giving and volunteering in the United States: Findings from a national survey.* Washington, DC.

Garcia-Preto, N. (1986). Puerto Rican families. *The Family Therapy Networker, 10*(6), 33–34.

Garfield, C. (1979). The dying patient's concern with "life after death." In R. Kastenbaum (Ed.), *Between life and death* (pp. 45–60). Springer, New York. Publishing Inc.

Garfinkel, B. D., Froese, A., & Hood, J. (1982). Suicide attempts in children and adolescents. *American Journal of Psychiatry, 139,* 1257–1261.

Garland, A. F., & Zigler, E. (1993). Adolescent suicide prevention: Current research and social policy implications. *American Psychology, 48,* 169–182.

Garnets, L. D., & Kimmel, D. C. (Eds.). (1993). *Psychological perspectives on lesbian and gay male experiences.* Columbia University Press, New York.

Garrett, L. (1994). *The coming plague.* Farrar, Strauss and Giroux, New York.

Garrison, C. Z., Addy, C. L., McKeown, R. E., & Cuffe, S. P. (1993). Nonsuicidal physically self-damaging acts in adolescents. *Journal of Child and Family Studies, 2*(4), 339–352.

Geddes, G. (1981). *Welcome joy: Death in Puritan New England* (pp. 110–124). U.M.I. Research Press, Ann Arbor, MI.

Genovese, E. D. (1976). *Roll, Jordon, roll: The world the slaves made.* Vintage Books, New York.

Gentile, M., & Fello, M. (1990). Hospice care for the 1990s. *Journal of Home Health Care Practice, 3*(1), 1–15.

Gerber, L. A. (1990). Transformations in self-understanding in surgeons whose treatment efforts were not successful. *American Journal of Psychotherapy, 44*(1), 75–84.

Gerson, R. (1985). *Genograms in family assessment.* Norton, New York.

Gervais, K. (1986). *Redefining death.* Yale University Press, New Haven, CT.

Gesser, G., Wong, P. T. P., & Reker, G. T. (1987–88). Death attitudes across the life span: The development and validation of the death attitude profile (DAP). *Omega, 18,* 113–128.

Gibson, E. J., & Walker, A. S. (1984). Development of knowledge of visual-tactual affordances of substance. *Child Development, 55,* 453–461.

Gilbert, K. (1989). Interactive grief and coping in the marital dyad. *Death Studies, 13,* 605–626.

Ginsberg, H., & Opper, S. (1979). *Piaget's theory of intellectual development* (2nd. ed.). Prentice-Hall, Englewood Cliffs, NJ.

Glaser, B. G., & Strauss, A. L. (1964). The social loss of dying patients. *American Journal of Nursing, 64,* 119–121.

Glaser, B. G., & Strauss, A. L. (1965). *Awareness of dying.* Aldine, Chicago.

Glaser, B. G., & Strauss, A. (1968). *Time for dying.* Aldine, Chicago.

Glick, I., Weiss, R., & Parkes, C. M. (1974). *The first year of bereavement.* Wiley, New York.

Goldberg, E. L. (1981). Depression and suicide ideation in the young adult. *American Journal of Psychiatry, 138,* 35–40.

Goldney, R. D. (1981). Attempted suicide in young women: Correlate of lethality. *British Journal of Psychiatry, 139,* 382–390.

Goldstein, E. B. (1994). *Psychology.* Brooks/Cole, Belmont, CA.

Goleman, D. (1990, February 6). Compassion and comfort in middle age. *New York Times,* pp. C1, C14.

Goodall, J. (1983). Population dynamics during a 15-year period in one community of free-living chimpanzees in the Gombe National Park, Tanzania. *Zeitschrift Psychologie, 61*(1) 1–60.

Gordon, A. K. (1986). The tattered cloak of immortality. In C. A. Corr & J. N. McNeil (Eds.), *Adolescence and Death,* (pp. 16–31). Springer, New York.

Gordon, A. K., & Klass, D. (1979). *The need to know: How to teach children about death.* Prentice Hall, Englewood Cliffs, NJ.

Gould, M. S., & Shaffer, D. (1986). The impact of suicide in television movies: Evidence of imitation. *New England Journal of Medicine, 315,* 690–694.

Gould, R. L. (1972). The phases of adult life: A study in developmental psychology. *American Journal of Psychiatry, 129,* 521–531.

Goy, R. W., & Resko, J. A. (1972). Gonadal hormones and behavior of normal and hermaphroditic non-human female primates. In E. Astwood (Ed.), *Recent Progress in Hormone Research* (pp. 707–733). Academic Press, New York.

Grabmeier, J. (1995, May). Life after near death. *American Health, 38.*

Grabowski, J., & Frantz, T. T. (1992–93). Latinos and Anglos: Cultural experiences of grief intensity. *Omega, 26*(4), 273–285.

Gray, P. (1991). *Psychology.* Worth Publishers, New York.

Green, A. H. (1978). Self-destructive behavior in battered children. *American Journal of Psychiatry, 135,* 579–582.

Greyson, B. A. (1981). *Empirial evidence bearing on the interpretation of NDE among suicide attempters.* Paper presented at the annual meeting of the American Psychological Association, Los Angeles.

Greyson B. A. (1985). A typology of near-death experiences. *American Journal of Psychiatry, 142,* 967–969.

Greyson, B. & Stevenson, I. (1980). The phenomenology of near-death experiences. *American Journal of Psychiatry, 137,* 1193–1196.

Grimes, R. L. (1995). *Marrying and Burying: Rites of Passage in Man's Life,* Westview Press, Boulder, Colorado, p. 262.

Grof, S., & Halifax, J. (1977). *The human encounter with death.* Dutton, New York.

Guillemin, J. (1996). Planning to die. In G. E. Dickinson, M. R. Leming, & A. C. Mermann (Eds.), *Dying, death, and bereavement* (3rd. ed) (pp. 99–103). Dushkin Publishing Group/Brown and Benchmark Publishers, Guilford, CT.

Habenstein, R. W., & Lamers, W. M. (1974). *Funeral customs the world over.* Bulfin Printers, Milwaukee, WI.

Haberlandt, W. (1967). Aportacion a la genetica del suicido. *Folia Clinica International, 17,* 319–322.

Haley, W. E. (1989). Group intervention for dementia family caregivers: A longitudinal perspective. *The Gerontologist, 29*(4), 478–480.

Hall, E. T. (1966). *The hidden dimension.* Doubleday, New York.

Hall, G. S. (1904). *Adolescence.* Appleton, New York.

Hall, G. S. (1922). *Youth: Its education, regimen and hygiene.* Appleton, New York.

Hallam, E. A. (1996). Turning the hourglass: gender relations at the deathbed in early modern Canterbury. *Mortality, 1,*(1), 61–82.

Hallet, J. P. (1967). *Congo Kitabu.* Fawcett World Library, New York.

Hambly, W. D. (1974). Funeral customs. In *World Book Encyclopedia* (Vol. 9, pp. 117–124). World Book, Chicago.

Hammen, C. L. (1985). Predicting depression: A cognitive-behavioral perspective. In P. C. Kendall (Ed.), *Advances in cognitive-behavioral research and therapy* (Vol. 4, pp. 94–103). Academic Press, Orlando, FL.

Hanson, L. C., & Rodgman, E. (1996). The use of living wills at the end of life. *Archives of Internal Medicine, 156,* 1018–1022.

Harding, E. (1973). *The I and the not I: A study in the development of consciousness.* Bollingen Series, Princeton University Press, Princeton, NJ.

Harlow, H. F., & Suomi, S. J. (1974). Induced depression in monkeys. *Behavioral Biology, 12,* 273–296.

Harris, E. S. (1991). Adolescent bereavement following the death of a parent: An exploratory study. *Child Psychiatry and Human Development, 21*(4), 267–281.

Harris, J. M. (1984). Nonconventional human/companion animal bond. In W. J. Kay (eds), *Pet loss and human bereavement* (pp. 31–36). Iowa University Press, Ames.

Harris, P. L., & Kavanaugh, R. D. (1993). Young children's understanding of pretense. *Monographs of the Society for Research in Child Development, 58* (1, Serial No. 231).

Hart, K., Spirito, A., & Overholser, J. (1988). Attributional style in adolescent suicide attempters. (Eds.), *Clinical Psychology Review, 9,* 335–363.

Harvey, J. H. (1995). *Odyssey of the heart: The search for closeness, intimacy, and love.* W. H. Freeman, New York.

Harvey, J. H. (1996). *Embracing their memory: Loss and the social psychology of storytelling.* Allyn & Bacon, Needham Heights, MA.

Harvey, J. H., Orbuch, T. L., & Weber, A. L. (Eds.). (1992). *Attributions, accounts, and close relationships.* Springer-Verlag, New York.

Harvey, J. H., Weber, A. L., & Orbuch, T. L. (1990). *Interpersonal accounts: A social psychological perspective.* Basil Blackwell, Oxford.

Hastings Center. (1987). *The 1987 guidelines on the termination of life-sustaining treatment and the care of the dying.* Indiana University Press, Bloomington.

Havighurst, R. J. (1969). Suicide and education. In E. S. Schneidman (Ed.), *On the nature of suicide* (pp. 112–147). Jossey-Bass, San Francisco.

Havighurst, R. J. (1972). *Developmental tasks and education.* Longman, New York.

Hazzard, A., Weston, J. Gutterres, C. (1992). After a child's death: Factors related to parental bereavement. *Journal of Developmental and Behavioral Pediatrics, 13*(1), 24–30.

Health and Welfare Canada. (1987). *Suicide in Canada: Report of the National Task Force on Suicide in Canada.* Department of National Health and Welfare, Ottawa.

Heidegger, M. (1962). *Being and time.* (J. Macquarrie & E. Robinson, Trans.). SCM Press LTD, London. (Original work published in 1927).

Heller, J. (1996). *Personal communication.*

Helmrath, T., & Steinitz, E. (1978). Death of an infant: Parental grieving and the failure of social support. *The Journal of Family Practice, 6*(4), 785–790.

Helsing, K. J., Szelo, M., & Comstock, G. W. (1981). Factors associated with mortality after widowhood. *American Journal of Public Health, 71,* 802–809.

Henderson, M. (1990). Beyond the living will. *Gerontologist, 30*(4), 480–485.

Hershberger, S. L., & D'Augelli, A. R. (1995). The impact of victimization on the mental health and suicidality of lesbian, gay and bisexual youths. *Developmental Psychology, 31*(1), 65–74.

Hewstone, M. (1989). *Causal attribution: From cognitive processes to collective beliefs.* Basil Blackwell, Oxford.

Hickrod, L. J. H., & Schmitt, R. L. (1982). A naturalistic study of interaction and frame: The pet as "family member," *Urban Life, 11,* 55–77.

Hill, T. P., & Shirley, D. (1992). *A good death: Taking more control at the end of your life.* Addison-Wesley, New York.

Hinton, J. M. (1965). The physical and mental distress of dying, *Quarterly Journal of Medicine,* (New Series) *32,* 1–21.

Hinton, J. M. (1967). *Dying* Penguin, New York.

Hirayama, K. K. (1990). Death and dying in Japanese culture. In J. K. Parry (Ed.), *Social work practice with the terminally ill: A transcultural perspective* (pp. 159–174). Charles C. Thomas, Springfield, IL.

Hite, R., & Holliman, F. (1980). Human behavior and the process of dying. *Hospice of Mercy Handbook.* Mercy General Hospital, Sacramento, CA.

Hobfall, S. E., & Vaux, A. (1993). Social support: Resources and social context. In L. Goldberger & S. Breznitz (Eds.), *Handbook of stress: Theoretical and clinical aspects* (2nd. ed.) (pp. 685–705). Free Press, New York.

Hocker, W. V. (1988). Parental loss of an adult child. In O. S. Margolis, A. H. Kutscher, E. R. Marcus, H. C. Raether, V. R. Pine, I. B. Seeland, & D. J. Cherico (Eds.), *Grief and the loss of an adult child* (pp. 37–49). Praeger, New York.

Hoffman, M. L. (1977). Empathy, its development and prosocial implications. In C. B. Keasey (Ed.), *Nebraska Symposium on Motivation: Vol. 25* (pp. 169–218). University of Nebraska Press, Lincoln.

Hoffman, M. L. (1981). Is altruism part of human nature? *Journal of Personality and Social Psychology 40,* 121–137.

Hoffman, M. L. (1982). Development of prosocial motivation: Empathy and guilt. In N. Eisenberg (Ed.), *The development of prosocial behavior* (pp. 281–313). Academic Press, New York.

Hogshead, H. P. (1978). The art of delivering bad news. In C. Garfield (Ed.), *Psychosocial care of the dying patient* (pp. 128–132). McGraw-Hill, New York.

Holck, F. H. (1978). Life revisited (parallels in death experiences). *Omega, 9,* 1–12.

Holmes, T. H., & Rahe, R. H. (1967). The social readjustment rating scale. *Journal of Psychosomatic Research, 11,* 213–218.

Horacek, B. J. (1995). A heuristic model of grieving after high-grief deaths. *Death Studies, 19,* 21–31.

Horacek, B. J. (1996a). Newspaper obituary anniversary tributes and continuing grief. *Forum,* 22(1), 1/25.

Horacek, B. J. (1996b). Personal communication.

Hornstein, H. A. (1976). *Cruelty and kindness.* Prentice Hall, Englewood Cliffs, NJ.

Horowitz, M. J. (1986). *Stress response syndromes* (2nd ed.). Jason Aronson, Northvale, NJ.

Horowitz, M. J., Bonanno, G. A., & Holen, A. (1993). Pathological grief: Diagnosis and explanation. *Psychosomatic Medicine, 55(3),* 260–273.

Hostler, S. L. (1978). The development of the child's concept of death. In O. J. Z. Sahler (Ed.), *The child and death* (pp. 116–149). Mosby, St. Louis.

House, J. S., Landis, K. R., & Unberson, D. (1988). Social relationships and health. *Science, 241,* 540–545.

Huber, R., Cox, V. M., & Edelen, W. B. (1992). Right-to-die responses from a random sample of 200. *Hospice Journal, 8*(3), 1–19.

Hudgens, R. W. (1983). Preventing suicide. *New England Journal of Medicine, 30,* 897–898.

Hughes, J. J. (1995). Buddhism and Medical ethics: A bibliographic introduction. *Journal of Buddhist Ethics,* (2) 121-131.

Humphrey D. (1992). *Final exit: The practicalities of self-deliverance and assisted suicide for the dying.* Dell, New York.

Illfeld, F. W. (1977). Current social stressors and symptoms of depression. *American Journal of Psychiatry, 134,* 161–166.

Irion, P. E. (1990–91). Changing patterns of ritual response to death. *Omega,* 22(3), 159–172.

Irish, D. P. (1993). Multiculturalism and the Majority Population. In D. P. Irish, K. F. Lundquist, and V. J. Nelsen (Eds.), *Ethnic variations in dying, death, and grief* (p. 7). Taylor and Francis, Washington, DC.

Irish, D. P., Lundquist, K. F., & Nelsen, V. J. (1993). Conclusions. In D. P. Irish, K. F. Lundquist, & V. J. Nelsen (Eds.), *Ethnic variations in dying, death, and grief* (pp. 181–190). Taylor and Francis, Washington, DC.

Iserson, K. V. (1994). *Death to dust: What happens to dead bodies?* Galen Press, Tucson, AZ.

Jackman, C., McGee, H., & Turner, M. (1993). Maternal views of the management of fetal remains following early miscarriage. *Irish Journal of Psychological Medicine, 10*(2), 93–94.

Jackson, E. N. (1965). *Telling a child about death.* Channel Press, New York.

Jacobs, J. (1971). *Adolescent suicide.* Wiley Interscience, New York.

Jacobs, M. K., & Goodman, C. (1989). Psychology and self-help groups: Predictions on a partnership. *American Psychologist, 44,* 536–545.

Jacobs, T. A., & Wilkes, M. S. (1988). Cremation patterns for patients dying of AIDS in New York City. *New York State Journal of Medicine, 88*(12), 628–632.

Janis, I. L., Mahl, G. F., Kagan, J., & Holt, R. R. (1969). *Personality: Dynamics, development, assessment.* Harcourt, Brace, Jovanovich, New York.

Janoff-Bulman, R. (1985). The aftermath of victimization: Rebuilding shattered assumptions. In C. Figley (Ed.), *Trauma and its wake: The study and treatment of post-traumatic stress disorder* (pp. 16–39). Brunner/Mazel, New York.

Janoff-Bulman, R. (1989a). Assumptive worlds and the stress of traumatic events: Application of the schema construct. *Social Cognition 7,* 113–136.

Janoff-Bulman, R. (1989b). The benefit of illusions, the threat of disillusionment, and the limits of inaccuracy. *Journal of Social and Clinical Psychology, 8,* 158–175.

Jasnow, A. (1985). Grief and the loss of connection. *Psychotherapy Patient, 2*(1), 27–33.

Jaspers, K. (1970). *Philosophy* (Vol. 2). University of Chicago Press, Chicago.

Jemmott, J. B., III, & Magloire, K. (1988). Academic stress, social support and secretory immunoglobin A. *Journal of Personality and Social Psychology, 55,* 803–810.

Jenkins, P. (1988). Serial murder in England, 1940–1985. *Journal of Interpersonal Violence, 16,* 1–15.

Joffe, R. T., & Offord, D. R. (1983). A review: Suicidal behavior in childhood. *Canadian Journal of Psychiatry, 28,* 57–63.

Johnson, R. J., Lund, D. A., & Dimond, M. F. (1986). Stress, self-esteem and coping during bereavement among the elderly. *Social Psychology Quarterly, 49*(3), 273–279.

Jonas, D. T. (1976). Life, death, awareness, and concern: A progression. In A. Toynbee, A. Koestler (Eds.), *Life after death* (pp. 19–44). McGraw-Hill, New York.

Journal of the American Medical Association. (1994). *JAMA Publications Web Site* [On-line]. Available: http://www.ama-assn.org/j. . .5/no_18/abstract.html)

Jung, C. G. (1933). *Modern man in search of a soul.* Harcourt, New York.

Kagan, J. (1976). Emergent themes in human development. *American Scientist, 64,* 186–196.

Kai, I., Ohi, G., Yano, E., & Kobayashi, Y. (1993). Communication between patients and physicians about terminal care: A survey in Japan. *Social Science and Medicine, 36*(9), 1151–1159.

Kail, R. (1990). *The development of memory in children.* W. H. Freeman, New York.

Kalish, R. A. (1977). Dying and preparing for death: A view of families. In H. Feifel (Eds.), *New Meanings of Death* (pp. 215–232). McGraw-Hill, New York.

Kalish, R. A. (1985a). Coping with death. In R. A. Kalish (Ed.), *The final transition* (pp. 21–22). Baywood, Farmingdale, New York.

Kalish, R. A. (1985b). *Death, grief and caring relationships* (2nd ed.). Brooks/Cole, Monterey, CA.

Kalish, R. A. (1985c). The social context of death and dying. In R. H. Binstock & E. Shanas (Eds.), *Handbook of aging and the social sciences* (2nd ed.) (pp. 149–170). Van Nostrand, New York.

Kalish, R. A., & Goldberg, H. (1978). Clergy attitudes toward funeral directors, *Death Education, 2,* 247–260.

Kalish, R. A., & Reynolds, D. K. (1976). *Death and ethnicity: A psychocultural study.* USC Press, Los Angeles.

Kalish, R. A., & Reynolds, D. K. (1985). An overview of death attitudes and expectations. In Richard A. Kalish (Ed.), *The final transition* (pp. 25–49). Baywood, Farmingdale, New York.

Kamerman, J. B. (1988). *Death in the midst of life: Social and cultural influences on death, grief, and mourning.* Prentice Hall, Englewood Cliffs, NJ.

Karasek, R., Baker, D., Marxer, F., Ahlbom, A., & Meorell, T. (1981). Job decision latitude, job demands, and cardiovascular disease: A prospective study of Swedish men. *American Journal of Public Health, 71,* 694–705.

Kason, Y. (1994, Spring). Near-death experiences and kundalini awakening: Exploring the link. *Journal of Near-Death Studies, 12*(3), 143–157.

Kassin, S. (1995). *Psychology.* Houghton Mifflin, Boston.

Kastenbaum, R. (1977). *Death, society and human behavior.* Mosby, St. Louis.

Kastenbaum, R. (1981). *Recent studies of the NDE: A critical appraisal.* Paper presented at the annual meeting of the American Psychological Association, Los Angeles.

Kastenbaum, R. (1985). Dying and death: A lifespan approach. In J. E. Birren, K. W. Schaie (Eds.), *Handbook of the psychology of aging* (2nd ed.) (pp. 619–643). Van Nostrand-Reinhold, New York.

Kastenbaum, R. (1986). *Death, society and human experience* (3rd ed.). Merrill, Columbus, OH.

Kastenbaum, R. (1991). *Death, society and human experience* (4th ed.). Macmillan, New York.

Kastenbaum, R. (1992). *The psychology of death* (2nd ed.). Springer, New York.

Kastenbaum, R. (1993). Reconstructing death. *Omega, 27*(1), 76.

Kastenbaum, R., & Aisenberg, R. (1976). *The psychology of death,* Springer, New York.

Kastenbaum, R., & Normand, C. (1990). Deathbed scenes as imagined by the young and experienced by the old. *Death Studies, 14,* 201–217.

Katan, A. (1961). Some thoughts about the role of verbalization in early childhood. *Psychoanalytic Study of the Child, 16,* 184–188.

Katcher, A. H. (1981). Interactions between people and their pets: Form and function. In B. Fogle (Ed.), *Interrelations between people and pets* (pp. 41–67). Charles C. Thomas, Springfield, IL.

Katcher, A. H. (1984, September–October). Are companion animals good for your health? *Aging,* 2–3.

Katcher, A. H. (1985). Physiologic and behavioral responses to companion animals. *Veterinary Clinics of North America: Small Animal Practice, 15,* 403–410.

Katcher, A. H., & Rosenberg, M. A. (1979). Euthanasia and the management of the client's grief. *Compendium on Continuing Education, 1,* 887–891.

Kay, W. (Ed.). (1984). *Pet loss and human bereavement.* Iowa State University Press, Ames.

Kay, W. (Ed.). (1988). *Euthanasia of the companion animal.* Charles Press, Philadelphia.

Kazdin, A. E., French, N. H., Unis, A. S., Esveldt-Dawson, K., & Sherick, R. B. (1983). Helplessness, depression, and suicidal intent among psychiatrically disturbed inpatient children. *Journal of Consulting and Clinical Psychology, 51,* 504–510.

Kearl, Michael C. (1989). *Endings: The sociology of death and dying.* Oxford University Press, New York.

Kearl, Michael C. (1995). Death and politics: A psychosocial perspective. In H. Wass & R. A. Niemeyer (Eds.), *Dying: Facing the facts* (3rd ed.), pp. 3–24. Taylor and Francis, Washington, DC.

Keilitz, I., Bilzor, J. C., Hafemeister, T. L., & Brown, V. (1989). Decision making in authorizing and withholding life-sustaining medical treatment: From Quinlan to Cruzan. *Mental and Physical Disability Law Reporter, 13(5),* 482–493.

Keith, P. M. (1981–82). Perception of time remaining and distance from death. *Omega, 12,* 307–318.

Kellehear, A., Heaven, P. C., & Jia, G. (1990). Community attitudes toward near-death experiences: A Chinese study. *Journal of Near-Death Studies, 8*(3), 163–173.

Kelley, K., & Byrne, D. (1992). *Exploring human sexuality.* Prentice Hall, Englewood Cliffs, NJ.

Kennedy, A. (1991). *Losing a parent: Passage to a new way of living.* Harper Collins, San Francisco.

Kennedy, E., & Charles, S. C. (1990). *On becoming a counselor: A basic guide for non-professional counselors.* Continuum, New York.

Kenyon, G. M. (1990–91). Dealing with human death: The floating perspective, 1990–91. *Omega, 22*(1), 51–61.

Kessler, B. G. (1987). Bereavement and personal growth. *Journal of Humanistic Psychology, 27,* 228–247.

Kieffer, G. (1994). Kundalini and the near-death experience. *Journal of Near-Death Studies, 12*(3), 159–176.

Kierkegaard, S. (1954). *Fear and trembling and the sickness unto death*. Princeton University Press, Princeton, NJ. (Original work published 1843)

Kimmel, D. C. (1974). *Adulthood and aging: An interdisciplinary developmental view*. Wiley, New York.

Kipling, R. (1936). The power of the dog. In H. Felleman (Ed.), *The best-loved poems of the American people* (p. 641). Garden City Books, Garden City, New York.

Kirkley-Best, E., & Kellner, K. R. (1982). The forgotten grief: A review of the psychology of stillbirth. *American Journal of Orthopsychiatry, 52,* 420–29.

Klass, D. (1988). *Parental grief: Solace and resolution*. Springer, New York.

Klass, D. (1992–93). The inner representation of the dead child and the worldviews of bereaved parents. *Omega, 26*(4), 255–272.

Klass, D. (1995). Spiritual aspects of the resolution of grief. In H. Wass & R. A. Niemeyer (Eds.), *Dying: Facing the facts* (pp. 243–268). Taylor & Francis, Washington, DC.

Klass, D., & Marwit, S. (1988–89). Toward a model of parental grief. *Omega, 19*(1), 31–50.

Klenow, D. J., & Bolin, R. C. (1989–90). Belief in an afterlife: A national survey. *Omega, 20,* 63–74.

Klimen, G. (1987). Clinical epidemiology of suicide. *Journal of Clinical Psychiatry, 48*(12), 33–38.

Kliman, G. (1968). *Psychological emergencies of childhood*. Grune & Stratton, New York.

Knauss, W. A., & Lynn, J. (1995). Controlled trial to improve care for seriously ill hospitalized patients: The study to understand prognoses and preferences for outcomes and risks of treatments. *Journal of the American Medical Association, vol 274 #20, pp. 1591–1598.*

Knight, K. H. & Elfenbein, M. H. (1993). Relationship of death education to the anxiety, fear, and meaning associated with death. *Death Studies, 17*(5), 411–425.

Kobasa, S. C. (1979). Stressful life events, personality and health: An inquiry into hardiness. *Journal of Personality and Social Psychology, 37,* 1–11.

Kobasa, S. C. (1984). How much stress can you survive? *American Health,* 64–67.

Kobasa, S. C., Maddi, S. R., & Kahn, S. (1982). Hardiness and health: A prospective study. *Journal of Personality and Social Psychology, 42,* 168–177.

Kogure, N., & Yamazaki, K. (1990). Attitudes to animal euthanasia in Japan: A brief review of cultural influences. *Anthrozoos, 3*(3), 151–154.

Kohlberg, L. (1976). Moral stages and moralization: Cognitive-developmental approach. In T. Lickona (Ed.), *Moral development and behavior: Theory, research and social issues* (pp. 11–21). Holt, Rinehart & Winston, New York.

Kohn, A. (1990). *The brighter side of human nature: Altruism and empathy in everyday life*. Basic Books, New York.

Kosky, P. (1982). Childhood suicidal behavior. *Journal of child psychology and psychiatry and Allied Disciplines, 24,* 457–467.

Krant, M. (1974). *Dying and dignity: The meaning and control of a personal death.* Thomas, Springfield, IL.

Krueger, D. W. (1983). Childhood parent loss: Developmental impact and adult psychopathology. *American Journal of Psychotherapy, 37*(4), 582–592.

Kubler-Ross, E. (1969). *On death and dying.* Macmillan, New York.

Kubler-Ross. (1975). *Death: The final stage of growth.* Prentice Hall: Englewood Cliffs, NJ.

Kubler-Ross, E. (1987). *AIDS: The ultimate challenge,* Macmillan, New York.

Kurash, C. (1979). *The transition to college: A study of separation/individuation in late adolescence.* Unpublished doctoral dissertation, City University of New York, New York.

Kuypers, J. A., & Bengtson, V. L. (1973). Competence and social breakdown: A social-psychological view of aging. *Human Development, 16*(2), 37–49.

LaBarre, W. (1972). *The ghost dance: The origins of religion.* Dell, New York.

Labott, S. M., & Martin, R. B. (1988). Weeping: Evidence for a cognitive theory. *Motivation and Emotion, 12*(3), 205–216.

Labouvie-Vief, G. (1986). Modes of knowledge and the organization of development. In M. L. Commons, L. Kohlberg, F. A. Richards, & J. Sinott (Eds.), *Beyond formal operations 3: Modes and methods in the study of adult and adolescent thoughts* (pp. 111–130). Praeger, New York.

Lang, L. T. (1990). Aspects of the Cambodian death and dying process. In J. K. Parry (Ed.), *Social work practice with the terminally ill: A transcultural perspective* (pp. 205–211). Thomas, Springfield, IL.

Langford, A. (1984). The feminine approach to healing. *The Laughing Man, 5*(1), 48–52.

La Puma, J., Scheidermayer, D. L., Gulyas, A. E., & Siegler, M. (1988). Talking to comatose patients. *Archives of Neurology, 45,* 20–22.

Langlands, A. (1991). Doctor, what are my chances? *Australian Family Physician, 20*(10), 578–582.

Larkin, J. P., & Hopcroft, B. M. (1993). In-hospital respite as a moderator of caregiver stress. *Health and Social Work, 18*(2) 132–138.

Larson, D. G. (1993). *The helper's journey: Working with people facing grief, loss, and life-threatening illness.* Research Press, Champaign, IL.

Lattanzi-Licht, M., & Connor, S. (1995). Care of the dying: The hospice approach. In H. Wass & R. A. Niemeyer (Eds.), *Dying: Facing the facts* (pp. 143–161). Taylor & Francis, Washington, DC.

Lau, A., Pulliam, L., & Yeung, M. (1994, May 2). *San Francisco General Hospital.* Paper presented to the Society for Pediatric Research, Seattle.

Lawton, M. P., Brody, E. M., & Saperstein, A. R. (1989). A controlled study of respite service for caregivers of Alzheimer's patients. *The Gerontologist, 29*(1), 8–16.

Lazarus, R. S. (1969). *Patterns of adjustment and human effectiveness.* McGraw-Hill, New York.

Leafgren, F., & Elsenrath, D. E. (1986). The role of campus recreation programs in institutions of higher education. In M. J. Barr & M. L. Upcraft (Eds.), *Developing campus recreation and wellness programs* (pp. 11–15). Jossey-Bass, San Francisco.

Leash, R. M. (1994). *Death notification: A practical guide to the process.* Upper Access, Hinesburg, VT.

Leavy, R. L. (1983). Social support and psychological disorder: A review. *Journal of Community Psychology, 11,* 3–21.

Lee, J. R. (1974). *Death and beyond in the Eastern perspective.* Gordon & Brezch, New York.

Lee, P. W. H., Lieh-Mak, F., & Hung, S. L. (1983–84). Death anxiety in leukemic Chinese children. *International Journal of Psychiatry in Medicine, 13,* 281–290.

Lee, S. J. (1990). Grief of young adults. In V. R. Pine, O. S. Margolis, K. Doka, A. H. Kutscher, D. J. Schaefer, M. E. Siegel, & D. J. Cherico (Eds.), *Unrecognized and unsanctioned grief* (pp. 49–52). Thomas, Springfield, IL.

Leenaars, A. A. (1989). Suicide across the adult life span. *Crisis, 10,* 132–151.

Lefton, L. A. (1994). *Psychology* (5th ed.). Allyn & Bacon, Needham Heights, MA.

Leming, M. R., & Dickinson, G. E. (1994). *Understanding dying, death and bereavement* (3rd ed.). Harcourt Brace, New York.

Leming, M. R., & Premchit, S. (1993). Funeral customs in Thailand. In J. D. Morgan (Ed.), *Personal care in an impersonal world* (pp. 25–41). Baywood, New York.

Lendrum, S., & Syme, G. (1992). *Gift of tears: A practical approach to loss and bereavement counseling.* Tavistock/Routledge, New York.

Lerner, M. (1970). When, why, and where people die. In O. Brim, H. Freeman, S. Levine, & N. Scotch (Eds.), *The dying patient* (pp. 5–29). Russell Sage Foundation, New York.

LeShan, L. L., & Worthington, R. E. (1956). Personality as a factor in pathogenesis of cancer: Review of the literature. *British Journal of Medical Psychology, 29,* 29.

Lessa, W. A. (1976). Death customs and rites. In *Chamber's encyclopedia* (Vol. 4, pp. 420–426). International Learning Systems, London.

Lester, D. (1994). Are there unique features of suicide in adults of different ages and developmental stages? *Omega, 29,* 337–348.

Levav, I. (1982). Mortality and psychopathology following the death of an adult child: An epidemiological review. *Israel Journal of Psychiatry and Related Sciences, 19(1),* 23–38.

Levav, I., Lubner, M., & Alder, I. (1988). The bereaved parents of adult children: A case study in grief and the loss of an adult child. In O. S. Margolis, A. H. Kutscher, E. R. Marcus, H. C. Raether, V. R. Pine, I. B. Seeland, & D. J. Cherico (Eds.), *Grief and the loss of an adult child* (pp. 71–82). Praeger, New York.

Le Vieux, J. (1993). Terminal illness and death of father: Case of Celeste, age 5½. In N. B. Webb (Ed.), *Helping bereaved children* (pp. 81–82). Guilford, New York.

Levine, S. (1991, September/October). Conscious dying: It all begins with conscious living. *Utne Reader,* 66–74.

Levinson, B. (1972). *Pets and human development.* Thomas, Springfield, IL.

Levinson, D. J., Darrow, C., Klein, E., Levinson, M., & McKee, B. (1978). *The seasons of a man's life.* Knopf, New York.

Leviton, D. (1977). The scope of death education. *Death Education,* 1, 41-56.

Levy, M. H. (1987–88). Pain control research in the terminally ill. *Omega, 18,* 265-280.

Ley, D. C., & Corless, I. B. (1988). Spirituality and hospice care. Special Issue: Cultural and religious perspectives of death. *Death Studies, 12*(2), 101-110.

Lieberman, M. A. (1965). Psychological correlates of impending death: Some preliminary observations. *Journal of Gerontology, 20,* 181-190.

Lieberman, M. A. (1966). Observations on death and dying. *Gerontologist, 6,* 70-73.

Lifton, R., & Olson, E., (1974). *Living and dying,* Praeger, New York.

Lindemann, E. (1944). Symptomology and management of acute grief. *American Journal of Psychiatry, 101,* 141-148.

Linehan, M. M. (1981). A social-behavioral analysis of suicide and parasuicide: Implications for clinical assessment and treatment. In J. F. Clarkin & H. I. Glazer (Eds.), *Depression: Behavioral and directive intervention strategies* (pp. 229-294). Garland Press, New York.

Liston, E. H. (1975). Education on death and dying: A neglected area in the medical curriculum. *Omega, 6*(3), 193-197.

Littlefield, C. H., & Rushton, J. P. (1986). When a child dies: The sociobiology of bereavement. *Journal of Personality and Social Psychology, 51*(4), 797-802.

Lonetto, R. (1980). *Children's conceptions of death.* Springer, New York.

Lonetto, R., & Templer, D. I. (1986). *Death anxiety.* Hemisphere, Washington, DC.

Lopata, H. Z. (1973). *Widowhood in an American city.* Schenckman, Cambridge, MA.

Lord, J. (1987). Grief following a drunk driving crash. *Death Studies, 11,* 413-435.

Lorenz, K., (1952). *King Solomon's ring.* Methuen, London.

Loughlin, C. A., & Dowrick, P. W. (1993). Psychological needs filled by avian companions. *Anthrozoos, 6*(3), 166-172.

Lundahl, C. R. (1992). Angels in near-death experiences. *Journal of Near-Death Studies, 11*(1), 49-56.

Luptak, M. K., & Boult, C. (1994). A method for increasing elders' use of advance directives. *Gerontologist, 34*(3), 409-412.

Lyons, M. J. (1984). Suicide in later life: Some putative causes with implications for prevention. *Journal of Community Psychology, 12,* 379-388.

Maccoby, E. E., & Jacklin, C. N. (1974). *The psychology of sex differences.* Stanford University Press, Stanford, CA.

Macken, B., Fornatale, P., & Ayers, B. (1980). *The rock music source*. Doubleday, New York.

MacLean, P. D. (1970). The triune brain, emotion and scientific bias. In F. O. Schmitt (Ed.), *The neurosciences: Second study program* (pp. 336–349). Rockefeller University press, New York.

Mahler, M. S., Pine, F., & Bergman, A. (1975). *The psychological birth of the human infant: Symbiosis and individuation*. Basic Books, New York.

Mairs, N. (1994). *Voice lessons: On becoming a (woman) writer*. Beacon Press, Boston.

Makinget, G. M. (1975). *On being human: A systematic view*. Harcourt Brace Jovanovich, San Diego, CA.

Mallnow, V. (1981). *Adolescent separation/individuation and the parent/child relationship*. Unpublished doctoral dissertation, University of Cincinnatti.

Mann, J. J., Stanley, M., McBride, P. A., & McEwen, B. S. (1986). Increased serotonin Z and B–adrenergic receptor binding in the frontal cortices of suicide victims. *Archives of General Psychiatry, 43,* 954–959.

Mant, A. K. (1976). The medical definition of death. In E. S. Schneidman (Ed.), *Death: Current perspectives* (pp. 218–231). Mayfield, Palo Alto, CA.

Marais, E. (1969). *The soul of the ape*. Atheneum, New York.

Maris, R. W. (1981). *Pathways to suicide: A survey of self-destructive behaviors*. Johns Hopkins University Press, Baltimore.

Marrone, R. (1990). *Body of knowledge: An introduction to body/mind psychology*. State University of New York Press, Albany.

Marrone, R. (1995) Rock 'n' roll 'n' death. *Forum, 21*(4), pp. 1 & 22.

Marshall, J. R. (1982). Testamentary rights of body disposition. *Law Notes, 18,* 31–36.

Marshall, V. W., & Levy, J. A. (1990). Aging and dying. In R. H. Binstock and L. George (Eds.), *Handbook of aging and the social sciences,* 3rd. ed. Academic press, San Diego, CA.

Martin, G., Clarke, M., & Pearce, C. (1993). Adolescent suicide: Music preference as an indicator of vulnerability. *Journal of the American Academy of Child and Adolescent Psychiatry, 32*(3), 530-535.

Martinson, I., Davies B., & McClowry, S. (1991). Parental depression following the death of a child. *Death Studies, 15,* 259-267.

Marwit, S. J., & Klass, D. (1995). Grief and the role of the inner–representation of the deceased. *Omega, 30*(4), 283-298.

Marzuk, P. M., Tierney, H., Tardiff, K., Gross, E. M., Morgan, E. B., Hsu, M., & Mann, J. (1988). Increased risk of suicide in persons with AIDS. *Journal of the American Medical Association, 259,* 1333-1337.

Maslach, C. (1981). Understanding burnout: Definitional issues in analyzing a complex phenomenon. In W. S. Paine (Ed.), *Job stress and burnout: Research, theory and intervention perspectives* (pp. 121-138). Sage, Beverly Hills, CA.

Maslow, A. (1943). A theory of motivation. *Psychological Review, 50,* 370-396.

Maslow, A. (1954). *Motivation and personality*. Harper & Row, New York.

Maslow, A. (1971). *The farther reaches of human nature.* Viking Penguin, New York.

Maslow, A. (1973). Theory of human motivation. In R. J. Lowry (Ed.), *Dominance, self-esteem, self-actualization: Germinal papers of A. H. Maslow* (pp. 8-33). Brooks/Cole, Pacific Grove, CA.

Masserman, J. H., Wechkin, S., & Terris, W. (1964). Altruistic behavior in rhesus monkeys. *American Journal of Psychiatry, 121,* 584-585.

Masson, J. A. & McCarthy, S. L. (1995). *When elephants weep: The emotional lives of animals.* Delta/Dell, N.Y.

Mattessich, P., & Hill, R. (1987). Life cycle and family development. In M. B. Sussman & S. K. Steinmetz, (Eds.), *Handbook of marriage and the family* (pp. 437-469). Plenum, New York.

Matthews, K. A., Woodall, K. L., & Stoney, C. M. (1990). Changes in and stability of cardiovascular responses to behavioral stress. *Child Development, 61,* 1134-1144.

May, R. (1958). Contributions of existential psychotherapy. In R. May, E. Angel, & H. F. Ellenberger (Eds.), *Existence: A new dimension in psychiatry and psychology* (pp. 17-29). Basic Books, New York.

May, R. (1985). *My quest for beauty.* Saybrook, Dallas, TX.

Mayer, R. A. (1990). *Embalming: History, theory and practice.* Appleton & Lange, Norwalk, CT.

McAnarney, E. R. (1979). Adolescent and the young adult suicide in the United States—a reflection of social unrest. *Adolescence, 14,* 765-774.

McBride, G. (1995, January/February). Stroke: A prevention and survival kit. *American Health,* 65-68.

McCaffery, M., & Wolff, M. (1992). Pain relief using cutaneous modalities, positioning, and movement. Special issue: Noninvasive approaches to pain management in the terminally ill. *Hospice Journal, 8*(1-2), 121-153.

McCarroll, J. E., Ursano, R. J., Wright, K. M., & Fullerton, C. S. (1993). Handling bodies after violent death: Strategies for coping. *American Journal of Orthopsychiatry, 63,* 209-214.

McCormick, J. (1980). *Ethical issues in death and dying.* Columbia University Press, New York.

McCracken, A. L., & Gerdsen, L. (1991). Sharing the legacy: Hospice care principles for terminally ill elders. *Journal of Gerontological Nursing, 17*(12), 4-8.

McGee, R. (1995). Hospice representative, hospice of Auburn, Auburn, CA. (personal communication).

McGoldrick, M., & Walsh, F. (1991). A time to mourn: Death and the family life cycle. In F. Walsh & M. McGoldrick (Eds.), *Living beyond loss: Death in the family* (pp. 30-49). Norton, New York.

McGrath, L. B. (1994, May). Scared to death. *American Health,* 41.

McIntire, M. S., Angle, C. R., & Struempler, L. J. (1972). The concept of death in midwestern children and youth. *American Journal of Diseases of Children, 123,* 527-532.

McIntosh, D. N., Silver, R. C., & Wortman, C. B. (1993). Religion's role in adjustment to a negative life event: Coping with the loss of a child. *Journal of Personality and Social Psychology, 65*(4), 812-821.

McIntosh, J. L. (1985). Suicide among the elderly: Levels and trends. *Journal of Orthopsychiatry, 35,* 288-293.

McIntosh, J. L., Hubbard, R. W., & Santos, J. F. (1981). Suicide among the elderly: A review of issues with case studies. *Journal of Gerontological Social Work, 4,* 63-74.

McLeavey, B. C., Daly, R. J., Murray, C. M., O'Riordan, J., & Taylor, M. (1987). Interpersonal problem-solving deficits in self-poisoning patients. *Suicide and Life-Threatening Behavior, 17,* 33-49.

McNeil, J. N. (1983). Young mothers' communication about death with their children. *Death Education, 4,* 323-339.

Meichenbaum, D. (1977). *Cognitive-behavior modification: An integrative approach.* Plenum Press, New York.

Meichenbaum, D. (1985). *Stress innoculation training.* Pergamon Press, New York.

Mermann, A. C., Gunn, D. B., & Dickinson, G. E. (1991). Learning to care for the dying: A survey of medical schools and a model course. *Academic Medicine, 66*(1), 35-38.

Middleton, J. (1991). Death customs and rites. In *Encyclopedia Americana* (Vol. 8, pp. 116-126). Grolier, Danbury, CT.

Miles, M. S., & Demi, A. S. (1983–84). Toward a theory of bereavement guilt: Sources of guilt in bereaved parents. *Omega, 14,* 299-314.

Miles, M. S., & Demi, A. S. (1991–92). A comparison of guilt in bereaved parents whose children died by suicide, accident, or chronic disease. *Omega, 24*(3), 203-215.

Milgram, S. (1974). *Obedience to authority: An experimental view.* Harper & Row, New York.

Miller, C. (1995). *Nursing care of older adults.* Lippincott, Philadelphia.

Miller, M. (1978a). Geriatric suicide: The Arizona study. *The Gerontologist, 18,* 488-495.

Miller, M. (1978b). Note: Toward a profile of the older white male suicide. *The Gerontologist, 18,* 80-82.

Miller, M. (1979). *Suicide after sixty: The final alternative.* Springer, New York.

Miller, N. E. (1944). Experimental studies of conflict. In J. M. Hunt (Ed.), *Personality and behavior disorders, Vol. 1* (pp. 26-39). Ronald Press, New York.

Miller, N. E. (1959). Liberalization of basic S–R concepts: Extension to conflict behavior, motivation and social learning. In S. Koch (Ed.), *Psychology: A study of a science, Vol. 2* (pp. 119-137). McGraw-Hill, New York.

Miller, S., & Woodruff, D. (1994, November 14). Why parents kill. *Newsweek,* 31-34.

Minuchin, S., & Fishman, H. (1981). *Techniques of family therapy.* Harvard University Press, Cambridge, MA.

Mischel, W. (1974). Processes in delay of gratification. In L. Berkowitz (Ed.), *Advances in experimental social psychology, Vol. 7,* (pp. 12-36). Academic Press, Orlando, FL.

Mitchell, G. (1979). *Sex differences in non-human primates.* Van Nostrand Reinhold, New York.

Mitchell, R. (1994, May 9). *Newsweek,* 73.

Mitford, J. (1963). *The American way of death.* Fawcett Publications, Greenwich, CT.

Moller, D. W. (1990). *Death without dignity.* Baywood Press, New York.

Moller, D. W. (1996). *Confronting death: Values, institutions and human morality.* Oxford University Press, New York.

Money, J., & Ehrhardt, A. (1972). *Man and woman, boy and girl.* Johns Hopkins University Press, Baltimore.

Montaigne, M. de. (1991). *The essays of Michel de Montaigne,* (M. A. Screech, Trans. & Ed.). Allen Lane, London.

Montgomery, R. J. V., & Borgatta, E. F. (1989). The effects of alternative support strategies on family caregiving. *The Gerontologist, 29*(4), 457-464.

Montgomery, R. J. V., Gonyea, J. G., & Hooyman, N. R. (1985). Caregiving and the experience of subjective and objective burden. *Family Relations, 34*(1), 19-26.

Moody, R. A., Jr. (1975). *Life after life: The investigation of a phenomenon—Survival of bodily death.* G. K. Hall, Boston.

Moody, R. A., Jr. (1980). Commentary on "The reality of death experiences: A personal perspective" by Ernest Rodin. *Journal of Nervous and Mental Disease, 168,* 265.

Moody, R. A., Jr. (1988). *The light beyond.* Bantam, New York.

Mor, V., Greer, D. S., & Kastenbaum, R. (1988). *The hospice experiment.* Johns Hopkins University Press, Baltimore.

Morgan, J. D. (1995). Living our dying and our grieving: Historical and cultural attitudes. In H. Wass & R. A. Niemeyer (Eds.), *Dying: Facing the facts* (pp. 25-42). Taylor & Francis, Washington, DC.

Morris, C. G. (1993). *Psychology: An introduction.* Prentice-Hall, Englewood Cliffs, NJ.

Moss, M., Lesher, E., & Moss, S. (1986–87). Impact of the death of an adult child on elderly parents: Some observations. *Omega, 17*(3), 209-218.

Muller, R. J. (1987). *The marginal self: An existential inquiry into narcissism.* Humanities Press International, Atlantic Highlands, NJ.

Mumma, C. M., & Benoliel, J. Q. (1984–85). Care, cure and hospital dying trajectories. *Omega, 15,* 275-288.

Murley, J. (1995). The NDE connection. *Thanatos, 20*(1), 15-16.

Murphy, N. M. (1992). The physician as artist and guide. *Loss, Grief and Care, 6*(2–3), 15-22.

Murphy, P. A. (1986-87). Parental death in childhood and loneliness in young adults. *Omega, 17*(3), 219-228.

Mydans, S. (1995, September 13). Should dying patients be told? Ethnic pitfall is found. *New York Times,* p. A13 .

Myers, D. G. (1992). *Social psychology* (4th ed.). McGraw-Hill, New York.

Myers, J. E. (1990). *Empowerment for later life.* University of Michigan, ERIC Counseling and Personnel Services Clearinghouse, Ann Arbor.

Nabe, C. M. (1982). Seeing death as door or wall. In R. A. Pacholski & C. A. Corr (Eds.), *Priorities in death education and counseling* (pp. 26-39). Forum for Death Education and Counseling, Arlington, VA.

Nagy, M. H. (1948). The child's theories concerning death. *Journal of Genetic Psychology, 73,* 2-27.

Nahmani, N., Neeman, E., & Nir, C. (1989). Parental bereavement: The motivation to participate in support groups and its consequences. *Social Work with Groups, 12*(2) 89-98.

Nash, M. L. (1980). Dignity of person in the final phase of life: An exploratory study. In R. A. Kalish (Ed.), *Caring relationships: The dying and the bereaved* (pp. 62–70). Baywood, Farmingdale, New York.

National Center for Health Statistics. (1987, August 28). *Monthly vital statistics report,* (Vol. 36, no. 5, DHHS Publication No. PHS 87-1120). U.S. Government Printing Office, Washington, DC.

National Cancer Institute. (1996). *SEER cancer statistics review 1973–1991.* Available: http://imedd.meb.uni-bonn...ancernet/600110.html

National Center for Health Statistics. (1991). Centers for Disease Control and Prevention. Available: http://www.cdc.gov80/nchswww/forms/query.htm

National Center for Health Statistics. (1992). *Vital statistics, mortality data, multiple cause-of-death, 1992.* Available: http: //www.cdc.gov80/nchswww/ mormcd92,htm

National Center for Health Statistics. (1993). Centers for Disease Control and Prevention. Available: http://www.cdc.gov80/nchswww/forms/query.htm

National Center for Health Statistics. (1995a). *Health, United States, 1994* (PHS Publication No. 95-1232). Available: http://www.cdc.gov 80/nckswww/ 95pubs.htm

National Center for Health Statistics. (1995b). *Trends in the health of older americans: United States, 1994* (PHS Publication No. 95-1414). Available: http://www.cdclgov80/nchswww/95pubs.htm

National Center for Health Statistics. (1995c). *Health risk behaviors among our nation's youth* (PHS Publication No. 95-1520). Available: http:// www.cdc.gov.80/nchswww/95pubs.htm

National Center for Health Statistics. (1995d). *Births, marriages, divorces, and deaths for 1994* (Monthly Vital Statistics Report, Vol. 43, No. 12).

National Hospice Organization. (1995). *An analysis of cost savings of the Medicare hospice benefit.* The Organization, Arlington, VA.

National Hospice Organization. (1996). *What is hospice?* The Organization, Arlington, VA.

National Lesbian and Gay health Foundation. (1987). *National lesbian health care survey: Mental health implications.* Unpublished report, The Foundation, Atlanta.

National Task Force on Suicide in Canada. (1987). Available: http: www.mae. carleton.calijeff/guns/canfirearms/stats/ghindex.html

Neaman, J. S., & Silver, C. G. (1983). *Kind words: A thesaurus of euphemisms.* Facts on File Publications, New York.

Nerken, I. R. (1993). Grief and the reflective self: Toward a clearer model of loss resolution and growth. *Death Studies, 17*(1), 1-26.

Neugarten, B. L. (1968). The awareness of middle age. In B. L. Neugarten (Ed.), *Middle age and aging* (pp. 93-98). University of Chicago Press, Chicago.

Neugarten, B. L. (1977). Personality and aging. In J. E. Birren & K. W. Schaie (Eds.), *Handbook of the psychology of aging* (pp. 626-649). Van Nostrand Reinhold, New York.

Newsweek (April 3, 1995). *Floating memorials,* 8.

Ng, S. J. (1994). *Metaphors of the feminine and masculine: Creating a personal mythology.* Wm. C. Brown Communications, Dubuque, IA.

Nichols, J. (1986). Newborn death. In T. A. Rando (Ed.), *Parental loss of a child* (pp. 145-157). Research Press, Champaign, Ill.

Nichols, J. (1990). Perinatal death: Bereavement issues. In V. R. Pine, O. S. Margolis, K. Doka, A. H. Kutscher, D. J. Schaefer, M. E. Siegel, & D. J. Cherico (Eds.) *Unrecognized and unsanctioned grief* (pp. 19-28). Thomas, Springfield, IL.

Nieberg, H., & Fischer, A. (1982). *Pet loss: A thoughtful guide for adults and children.* Harper & Row, New York.

Niemeyer, R. A. (1988). Death anxiety. In H. Wass (Ed.), *Dying: Facing the facts* (pp. 97-137). Hemisphere, Washington, DC.

Niemeyer, R. A., & Chapman, K. M. (1980–81). Self/denial discrepancy and fear of death: The test of an existential hypothesis. *Omega, 11,* 233-239.

Niemeyer, R. A., Bagley, K. J., and Moore, M. K. (1986). Cognitive structure and death anxiety. *Death Studies, 10,* 273-278.

Nixon, J., & Pearn, J. (1977). Emotional sequalae of parents and sibs following the drowning or near-drowning of a child. *Australian and New Zealand Journal of Psychiatry, 11,* 265-268.

Nolen-Hoeksema, S., Parker, L. E., & Larson, J. (1994). Ruminative coping with depressed mood following loss. *Journal of Personality and Social Psychology, 67*(1), 92-104.

Normile, L. B. (1990). Psychological distress in bereavement: A comparative study of adult children who died of cancer versus AIDS. *Dissertation Abstracts International, 50* (7B), 2840.

Norris-Shortle, C., Young, P. A., & Williams, M. A. (1993). Understanding death and grief for children three and younger. *Social Work, 38*(6), 736-742.

Noyes, R., Jr. (1979). Near-death experiences: Their interpretation. In R. Kastenbaum (Ed.), *Between life and death* (pp. 73-88). Springer, New York.

Noyes, R., Jr. (1980). Attitude change following near-death experiences. *Psychiatry, 43,* 234-242.

Noyes, R., Jr., & Kletti, R (1976b). Depersonalization in the face of danger: An interpretation. *Omega 7,* 103-114.

Noyes, R., Jr., & Kletti, R. (1977). Panoramic memory: A response to the threat of death. *Omega, 8,* 181-194.

Nuland, S. B. (1993). *How we die: Reflections on life's final chapter.* Knopf, New York.

Oakes, A. R. (1981). Near-death event and critical care nursing. *Topics in Clinical Nursing, 3,* 61-78.

Oaks, J. & Ezell, G. (1993). *Dying and death: Coping, caring, understanding.* Gorsuch Scarisbrick, Scottsdale, AZ.

O'Bryant, S. L., & Morgan, L. A. (1989). Financial experience and well-being among mature widowed women. *Gerontologist, 29,* 245-251.

Offer, D., Ostrov, J. B., & Baker, L. (1981). *The Adolescent.* Basic Books, New York.

Offer, D., & Sabshin, M. (1984). Adolescence: Empirical perspectives. In D. Offer & M. Sabshin (Eds.), *Normality and the life cycle* (pp. 115-129). Basic Books, New York.

Okura, K. P. (1975). Mobilizing in response to a major disaster. *Community Health Journal, 2*(2), 136-144.

Ome, R. M. (1986). Nurses' views of near-death experiences. *American Journal of Nursing, 86,* 419-420.

Omoto, A. M., & Snyder, M. (1990). Basic research in action: Volunteerism and society's response to AIDS. *Personality and Social Psychology Bulletin, 16,* 152-165.

Orbach, I. (1984). Personality characteristics, life circumstances, and dynamics of suicidal children. *Death Education, 8,* 37-52.

Orbach, I., & Glaubman, H. (1979). The concept of death and suicidal behavior in young children: Three case studies. *Journal of the American Academy of Child Psychiatry, 28,* 668-678.

Orbach, I., Gross, Y., & Glaubman, H. (1981). Some common characteristics of latency-age suicidal children: A tentative model based on case study analyses. *Suicide and Life-Threatening Behavior, 11,* 180-190.

Ornstein, R., & Carstensen, L. (1991). *Psychology: The study of human experience.* Harcourt Brace Jovanovich, New York.

Osterweis, M., Solomon, F., & Green, M. (1984). *Bereavement: Reaction, consequences, and care.* National Academy Press, Washington, DC.

Ouellette, S. C. (1993). Inquiries into hardiness. In L. Goldberger & S. Breznitz (Eds.) (2nd. ed., pp. 77-100). *Handbook of stress: Theoretical and clinical aspects,* Free Press, New York.

Pagel, M. D., Erdly, W. W., & Becker, J. (1987). Social networks: We get by with (and in spite of) a little help from our friends. *Journal of Personality and Social Psychology, 53,* 793-804.

Paglia, C. (1994). *Vamps and tramps.* Random House, New York.

Pal, R. K., & Sharma, G. C. (1985). Gerontology—Viewpoint of Hindu psychology. *Indian Psychological Review, 28*(1), 36-40.

Papadatou, D., and Papadatos, C. (Eds.). (1991). *Children and death.* Hemisphere, Washington, DC.

Parkes, C. M. (1972). *Bereavement: Studies of grief in adult life.* International Universities Press, New York.

Parkes, C. M. (1976). Components of the reaction to loss of limb, spouse, a home. *Journal of Psychosomatic Research, 16,* 343-349.

Parkes, C. M. (1986). *Bereavement: Studies of grief in adult life.* International Universities Press, Madison, CO.

Parkes, C. M. (1988). Bereavement as a psychosocial transition: Processes of adaptation to change. *Journal of Social Issues, 44*(3), 53-65.

Parkes, C. M. (1992). Bereavement and mental health in the elderly. *Reviews in Clinical Gerontology, 2*(1), 45-51.

Parkes, C. M., & Weiss, R. S. (1983). *Recovery from bereavement.* Basic Books, New York.

Parson, Edwin R. (1986). Life after death: Vietnam veterans' struggle for meaning and recovery. *Death Studies, 10*(1), 11-26.

Partridge, E. (1966). *A dictionary of slang and unconventional English.* Macmillan, New York.

Pasricha, S. (1992). Near-death experiences in south India: A systematic survey in Channapatna. *NIMHANS Journal, 10*(2), 111-118.

Patterson, P. R. (1989). The pediatrician coping with the dying child. *Loss, Grief and Care, 3*(3−4), 191-198.

Pattison, E. M. (1977). *The experience of dying.* Prentice-Hall, Englewood Cliffs, NJ.

Paul, N. L. (1986). The paradoxical nature of the grief experience. *Contemporary Family Therapy: An International Journal, 8*(1), 5-19.

Peck, M. S. (1978). *The road less traveled.* Simon & Schuster, New York.

Peck, R. C. (1968). Psychological developments in the second half of life. In B. L. Neugarten (Ed.), *Middle age and aging* (pp. 88-92). Unversity of Chicago Press, Chicago.

Pelletier, K., & Garfield, C. (1976). *Consciousness, East and West.* Harper & Row, New York.

Peppers, L. G. (1987−88). Grief and elective abortion: Breaking the emotional bond. *Omega, 18,* 1-12.

Peppers, L. G., & Knapp, R. J. (1980). *Motherhood and mourning: Perinatal death.* Praeger, New York.

Perkins, H., & Harris, L. (1990). Familial bereavement and health in adult life course perspective. *Journal of Marriage and Family, 52,* 233-241.

Perlberg, M. (1979, April). Trauma at Tenerife: The psychic aftershocks of a jet disaster. *Human Behavior,* 49-50.

Perls, F. S., Hefferline, R. F., & Goodman, P. (1951). *Gestalt therapy.* Julian Press, New York.

Perry, Hosea L. (1993). Mourning and funeral customs of African Americans (1993). In D. P. Irish, K. F. Lundquist, & V. J. Nelsen (Eds.), *Ethnic variations in dying, death, and grief* (pp. 51-65). Taylor & Francis, Washington, DC.

Persky, V. W., Kempthorne-Rawson, J. & Shekelle, R. B. (1987). Personality and risk of cancer: 20-year follow-up of the Western Electric Study. *Psychosomatic Medicine, 49,* 435-449.

Peterson, C., Seligman, M. E. P., & Vaillant, G. E. (1988). Pessimistic explanatory style is a risk factor for physical illness: A thirty-five-year longitudinal study. *Journal of Personality and Social Psychology, 55,* 23-27.

Petzold, H. G. (1982). Gestalt therapy with the dying patient: Integrative work using clay, poetry therapy, and creative media, *Death Education, 6,* 249-264.

Pfeffer, C. R. (1981a). The family system of suicidal children. *American Journal of Psychotherapy, 35,* 330-341.

Pfeffer, C. R. (1981b). Suicidal behavior of children: A review with implications for research and practice. *American Journal of Psychiatry, 138,* 154-159.

Pfeffer, C. R. (1982). Intervention for suicidal children and their parents. *Suicide and Life-Threatening Behavior, 12,* 240-248.

Pfeffer, C. R. (1986). *The suicidal child.* Guilford Press, New York.

Pfeffer, C. R., Plutchik, R., & Mizruchi, M. S. (1983). Suicidal and assaultive behavior in children: Classification, measurement, and intervention. *American Jounal of Psychiatry, 140,* 154-157.

Phillips, D. P., & Carstensen, L. L. (1986). Clustering of teenage suicides after television news stories about suicide. *New England Journal of Medicine, 315,* 685-689.

Piaget, J. (1952). *The origins of intelligence in children.* International University Press, New York.

Piaget, J., & Inhelder, B. (1969). *The psychology of the child.* Basic Books, New York.

Pijawka, K. D., Cuthbertson, B., & Olson, R. S. (1987–88). Coping with extreme hazard events: Emerging themes in natural and technological disaster research. *Omega, 18,* 281-297.

Pilisuk, M., & Parks, S. H. (1988). Caregiving: Where families need help. *Social Work, 33*(5), 436-440.

Pincus, L. (1976). *Death and the family: The importance of mourning.* Pantheon, New York.

Pine, V. (1984). Care of the dead. In R. Fulton, E. Markusen, G. Owen, & J. Scheiber, (Eds.), *Death and dying: Challenge and change* (pp. 116-118). Addison-Wesley, Reading, MA.

Pines, A. M. (1993). Burnout. In L. Goldberger and S. Breznitz (Eds.), *Handbook of stress: Theoretical and clinical aspects* (2nd ed., pp. 386-402). Free Press, New York.

Pines, A. M., & Aronson, E. (1988). *Career burnout: Causes and cures.* Free Press, New York.

Pines, A. M., Aronson, E., & Kafry, D. (1981). *Burnout: From tedium to personal growth.* Free Press, New York.

Pinner, R. W., Teutsch, S. M., Simonsen, L., Klug, L. A., Graber, J. M., Clarke, M. J., & Berkelman, R. L. (1996). Trends in infectious diseases mortality in the United States. *JAMA, 275,* 189-193.

Pollak, J. M. (1979–80). Correlates of death anxiety: A review of empirical studies. *Omega, 10,* 97-121.

Pollio, H. R. (1982). Behavior and existence: An introduction to empirical humanistic psychology. Brooks/Cole, Monterey, CA.

Poon, L. (1995, November 24). Researchers seeking insights into the mysteries of longevity. *San Francisco Chronicle,* p. A10.

Potts, M. K., Burnam, M. A., & Wells, K. B. (1991). Gender differences in depression detection: A comparison of clinician diagnosis and standardized assessment. *Psychological Assessment, 3,* 609-615.

Pouissant, A. (1984). *The grief response following a homicide.* Paper presented at the 92nd Annual Convention of the American Psychological Association, Toronto, Canada.

Powell, M. (1991). The psychosocial impact of sudden infant death syndrome on siblings. *Irish Journal of Psychology, 12*(2), 235-247.

Power, T. (1977). Learning to die. In S. H. Zarit (Ed.). *Readings on aging and death: Contemporary perspectives* (pp. 263-270). Harper & Row, New York.

Pratt, C. C., & Kethley, A. J. (1988). Aging and family caregiving in the future: Implications for education and policy. *Educational Gerontology, 14*(6), 567-576.

Principal says suicide intrigued teens who died. (1996, May 25). *San Francisco Chronicle,* p. A19.

Ptacek, J. T., Smith, R. E., & Zanas, J. (1992). Gender, appraisal, and coping. *Journal of Personality, 60,* 94-103.

Purisman, R., and Maoz, B. (1977). Adjustment and bereavement: Some considerations. *British Journal of Medical Psychology, 50,* 1-9.

Quackenbush, J. E. (1981). Pets, owners, problems and the veterinarian: Applied social work in a veterinary teaching hospital. *The Compendium on Continuing Education, 3,* 764-770.

Quackenbush, J. E. (1984). Pet bereavement in older owners. In R. Anderson, B. L. Hart, & L. A. Hart (Eds.), *The pet connection* (pp. 99-111). Center to Study Human-Animal Relationships and Environments, Minneapolis, MN.

Quackenbush, J. (1985). The death of a pet: How it can affect owners. *Veterinary Clinics of North America: Small Animal Practice, 15,* 395-402.

Quackenbush, J. E., & Glickman, L. (1983). Social work services for bereaved pet owners: A retrospective case study in a veterinary teaching hospital. In A. H. Katcher & A. M. Beck (Eds.), *New perspectives on our lives with companion animals* (pp. 22-41). University of Pennsylvania Press, Philadelphia.

Quackenbush, J. E., & Glickman, L. (1984). Helping people adjust to the death of a pet. *Health and Social Work, 9.*, 42-48.

Quadrel, M. J. (1990) *Elicitation of adolescents' risk perceptions: Qualitative and quantitative dimensions.* Unpublished doctoral dissertation, Carnegie Mellon University.

Quadrel, M.J., Fischoff, B., & Davis, W. (1993). Adolescent (in)vulnerability. *American Psychologist, 48,* 102-116.

Rabin, D. L., & Rabin, L. H. (1970). Consequences of death for physicians, nurses and hospitals. In O. G. Brim (Ed.), *The dying patient* (pp. 30-40). Russell Sage Foundation, New York.

Rachels, J. (1993). Active and passive euthanasia. In L. P. Pojman (Ed.), *Life and death: A reader in moral problems* (pp. 252-258). Jones and Bartlett, Boston.

Raether, H. C. (1985). Immediate and extended postdeath activities. In O. S. Margolis (Ed.), *Loss, grief and bereavement* (pp. 126-139). Praeger, New York.

Rahman, F. (1987). *Health and medicine in the Islamic tradition.* Crossroad Press, New York.

Raimbault, G. (1991). The seriously ill child: Management of family and medical surroundings. In D. Papadatou & C. Papadatos (Eds.), *Children and death* (pp. 177-187). Hemisphere, Washington, DC.

Rajaram, S. S., Garrity, T. F., Stallones, L., & Marx, M. B. (1993). Bereavement: Loss of a pet and loss of a human. *Anthrozoos, 6*(1), 8-16.

Ramafedi, G., Farrow, J. A., & Deisher, R. W. (1993). Risk factors for attempted suicide in gay and bisexual youth. In L. D. Garnets & D. C. Kimmel (Eds.), *Psychological perspectives on lesbian and gay male experiences* (pp. 486-499). Columbia University Press, New York.

Rando, T. A. (1983). An investigation of grief and adaptation in parents whose children have died from cancer. *Journal of Pediatric Psychology, 8*(1), 3-20.

Rando, T. A. (1984). *Grief, dying and death: Clinical interventions for caregivers.* Research Press, Champaign, IL.

Rando, T. A. (1986a). Death of the adult child. In T. A. Rando (Ed.), *Parental loss of a child* (pp. 59-96). Research Press, Champaign, IL.

Rando, T. A. (1986b). *Loss and anticipatory grief.* Lexington Books, Lexington, MA.

Rando, T. A. (1986c). The unique issues and impact of the death of a child. In T A. Rando (Ed.), *Parental loss of a child* (pp. 5-43). Research Press, Champaign, IL.

Rando, T. A. (1993). *Treatment of complicated mourning.* Research Press, Champaign, IL.

Rando, T. A. (1995). Grieving and mourning: Accommodating to loss. In H. Wass & R. A. Niemeyer (Eds.), *Dying: Facing the facts* (pp. 211-243). Taylor & Francis, Washington, DC.

Raphael, B. (1972). Psychosocial aspects of induced abortion: Part 1. *Medical Journal of Australia, 2,* 35-40.

Raphael, B. (1983). *The anatomy of bereavement.* HarperCollins, San Francisco.

Raphael, B. (1995). The death of a child. In J. B. Williamson & E. S. Shneidman (Eds.), *Death: Current perspectives* (pp. 261-275). Mayfield, Mountain View, CA.

Rathus, S. (1993). *Psychology.* Harcourt Brace Jovanovich, New York.

Rauch, J. B., & Kneen, K. K. (1989). Accepting the gift of life: Heart transplant recipients' post-operative adaptive tasks. *Social Work in Health Care, 14*(1), 47-59.

Rawnsley, M. M. (1989). Minimizing burnout: Caring for the caregivers. *Journal of Loss, Grief and Care, 3,* 51-57.

Rawnsley, M. M. (1990). Professional caregivers as survivors: An unsanctioned grief. In V. R. Pine, O. S. Margolis, K. Doka, A. H. Kutscher, D. J. Schaefer, M. E. Siegel, & D. J. Cherico (Eds.), *Unrecognized and unsanctioned grief* (pp. 143-151). Thomas, Springfield, IL.

Rechtschaffen, A. (1976). The psychophysiology of mental activity during sleep. In T. X. Barber (Ed.). *Advances in altered states of consciousness and human potentialities, Vol. 1* (pp. 431-476). Psychological Dimensions, New York.

Redding, R. (1980). Doctors, dyscommunication and death. *Death Education, 3,* 371-385.

Redmond, L. M. (1989). *Surviving: When someone you love was murdered.* Psychological Consultation and Education Services, Clearwater, FL.

Reiser, M. F. (1989). The future of psychoanalysis in academic psychiatry: Plain talk. *Psychoanalytic Quarterly, 58*(2), 185-209.

Rensberger, B. (1978, February 6). The touchy ethical issue of trainee surgeons operating without consent of patients. *New York Times,* p. B12.

Reynolds, J. J. (1995). Disenfranchised expertise: The funeral director as helping professional. *Forum,* vol. xxi, #3, May/June, 1995, pp 3 & 14.

Reynolds, J. J. (1996). Reflections on a funeral service tradition, *Forum, 22*(1), 13-27.

Rhodes, C., & Vedder, C. B. (1983). *An introduction to thanatology: Death and dying in American society.* Thomas: Springfield, IL.

Rhodewalt, F., & Zone, J. B. (1989). Appraisal of life change, depression and illness in hardy and nonhardy women. *Journal of Personality and Social Psychology, 56,* 81-88.

Rice, F. P. (1992). *Intimate relationships, marriages and families.* Mayfield, Mountain View, CA.

Rice, L. N., & Greenberg, L. S. (1992). Humanistic approaches to psychotherapy. In D. K. Freedheim (Ed.), *History of psychotherapy: Century of change* (pp. 197-224). American Psychological Association, Washington, DC.

Richman, J. (1981). Suicide and the family: Affective disturbances and their implications for understanding, diagnosis, and treatment. In M. R. Lamsky (Ed.), *Family therapy and major psychopathology* (pp. 145-160). Grune & Stratton, New York.

Rigdon, I. S., Clayton, B. C. & Dimond, M. (1987). Toward a theory of helpfulness for the elderly bereaved: An invitation to a new life. *Advances in Nursing Science, 9*(2), 32-43.

Riley, M. W., & Foner, A. (1968). *Aging and society, Vol. 1*. Russell Sage Foundation, New York.

Rinear, E. E. (1988). Psychosocial aspects of parental response patterns to a death of a child by homicide. *Journal of Traumatic Stress, 1*, 305–322.

Ring, T. (1996, January). AIDS hitting youth, people of color hard. *Outlines*. Chicago, IL. Available: http//www.suba.com/-outl...uary96/aidsstat.html

Rinpoche, Sogyal. (1992). *The Tibetan book of living and dying*. HarperCollins, New York.

Rioch, D. (1959). The psychopathology of death. In A. Simon (Ed.), *The physiology of emotions* (pp. 177–186). Thomas, Springfield, IL.

Robak, R. W., & Weitzman, S. P. (1995). Grieving the loss of romantic relationships in young adults: An empirical study of disenfranchised grief. *Omega, 30*(4), 269–281.

Robbins, Rosemary A. (1990). Signing an organ donor card: Psychological factors. *Death Studies, 14*(3), 219–229.

Robin, M., & ten Bensel, R. (1984). *Pets and the Family*, Haworth Press, New York.

Robin, M., & ten Bensel, R. (1985). Pets and the socialization of children. Special Issue: Pets and the family. *Marriage and Family Review, 8*(3–4), 63–78.

Rochat, P. (1989). Object manipulation and exploration in 2- to 5-month-old infants. *Developmental Psychology, 25*, 871–884.

Rockwell, D., & O'Brien, W. (1973). Physicians' knowledge and attitudes about suicide. *Journal of the American Medical Association, 225*, 1347–1349.

Rodin, E. A. (1980). The reality of death experiences: A personal perspective. *Journal of Nervous and Mental Disease, 168*, 259–263.

Rodin, J., & Stone, G. (1987). Historical highlights in the emergence of the field. In G. C. Stone, S. M. Weiss, J. D. Matarazzo, N. E. Miller, J. Rodin, C. D. Belar, M. J. Follick, & J. E. Singer (Eds.), *Health psychology: A discipline and a profession* (pp. 513–524). University of Chicago Press, Chicago.

Rogers, C. R. (1951). *Client-centered therapy*. Houghton Mifflin, Boston.

Rogers, C. R. (1959). A theory of therapy, personality, and interpersonal relationship as developed in the client-centered framework. In S. Koch (Ed.), *Psychology: A study of a science, Vol. 3* (pp. 184–256). McGraw-Hill, New York.

Rogers, C. R. (1961). *On becoming a person: A therapist's view of psychotherapy*. Houghton Mifflin, Boston.

Rogers, C. R. (1986). Client-centered therapy. In I. L. Kutash & A. Wolf (Eds.), *Psychotherapist's casebook* (pp. 96–111). Jossey-Bass, San Francisco.

Romero, J. R. (1970). *La vida inutil de Pito Perez*. Editorial Porrua, Mexico City.

Rook, K. S. (1990). Parallels in the study of social support and social strain. *Journal of Social and Clinical Psychology, 9*, 118–132.

Rose, M. R. (1991). *Evolutionary biology of aging*. Oxford University Press, London.

Rose, R. M., Gordon, T. P., & Bernstein, I. S. (1972). Plasma testosterone levels in the male rhesus: Influences of sexual and social stimuli. *Science, 178*, 643–645.

Rosenblatt, P. C. (1983). *Bitter, bitter tears*. University of Minnesota Press, Minneapolis.

Rosenblatt, P. C., & Karis, T. A. (1993). Economics and family bereavement following a fatal farm accident. *Journal of Rural Community Psychology, 12,*(2), 37-51.

Rosenblatt, P. C., & Karis, T. A. (1993–94). Family distancing following a fatal farm accident. *Omega, 28*(3), 183-200.

Rosenbloom, C. A. & Whittington, F. J. (1993). The effects of bereavement on eating behaviors and nutrient intakes in elderly widowed persons. *Journal of Gerontology, 48*(4), S223-S229.

Rosenfeld, L., and M. Prupas. (1984). *Left alive: After a suicide death in the family*. Thomas, Springfield, IL.

Rosenheim, E., & Richer, R. (1985). Informing children about a parent's terminal illness. *Journal of Child Psychology and Psychiatry and Allied Disciplines, 26,* 995-998.

Rosenman, R. H., Swan, G. E., & Carmelli, D. (1988). Definition, assessment and evolution of the Type A behavior pattern. In B. K. Houston & C. R. Snyder (Eds.), *Type A behavior pattern: Research, theory, and intervention* (pp. 8-31). Wiley, New York.

Rosenthal, N. R., (1980, Fall). Adolescent death anxiety: The effect of death education, *Education, 101,* 95-101.

Rosenthal, P. A., & Rosenthal, S. (1984). Suicidal behavior by preschool children. *American Journal of Psychiatry, 141,* 520-525.

Ross, L. M., & Pollio, H. R. (1991). Metaphors of death: A thematic analysis of personal meanings. *Omega, 23*(4), 291-307.

Rowe, J., Clyman, R., Green, D., Mikkelson, C., Haight, J., & Ataide, L. (1978). Follow-up of families who experience a perinatal death. *Pediatrics, 62*(2), 166-170.

Roy, A., DeJong, J., & Linnoila, M. (1989). Cerebrospinal fluid monoamine metabolites and suicide behavior in depressed patients: A 5-year follow-up study. *Archives of General Psychiatry, 46,* 609-612.

Roy, A., & Linnoila, M. (1986). Alcoholism and suicide. In R. Maris (Ed.), *Biology of suicide* (pp. 162-191). Guilford Press, New York.

Rubin, A., Peplau, L. A., & Salovey, P. (1993). *Psychology*. Houghton Mifflin, Boston.

Rubin, S. (1990). Death of the future?: An outcome study of bereaved parents in Israel. *Omega, 20*(4), 323-339.

Rubinstein, C. (1982, June). Wellness is all: A report on *Psychology Today's* survey of beliefs about health. *Psychology Today,* 28-37.

Rubonis, A. V., & Bickman, L. (1991). Psychological impairment in the wake of disaster: The disaster-psychopathology relationship. *Psychological Bulletin, 109,* 384-399.

Ruby, J. (1983). Images of the family: The symbolic implication of animal photography. In A. H. Katcher & A. M. Beck (Eds.), *New perspectives on our lives with companion animals,* (pp. 13-29). University of Pennsylvania Press, Philadelphia.

Ruby, J. (1988–89). Portraying the dead. *Omega, 19*(1), 1-20.

Russell, S. (1996, March 8). Right-to-die ruling raises ethical issues. *San Francisco Chronicle,* p. A8.

Rynearson, E. (1978). Humans and pets and attachments. *British Journal of Psychiatry, 133,* 550-555.

Rynearson, E. (1987). Psychological aspects to unnatural dying. In S. Zisook (Ed.), *Biopsychosocial aspects of bereavement* (pp. 77-93). American Psychiatric Association Press, Washington, DC.

Sabbath, J. C. (1969). The suicidal adolescent: The expendable child. *Journal of the American Academy of Child Psychiatry, 8,* 272-289.

Sabom, M. B. (1982). Recollections of Death: A Medical Investigation. Harper & Row, New York.

Sabom, M. B., & Kreutziger. S. (1977). The experience of near death. *Death Education, 2,* 195-204.

Saluter, A. F. (1992). Marital status and living arrangement, March, 1991. *Current population reports,* Series P-20, #461. U.S. Department of Commerce, Bureau of the Census, Washington, DC.

Sanders, C. (1979–80). A comparison of adult bereavement in the death of a spouse, child, and parent. *Omega, 10*(4), 303-321.

Sanders, C. (1989). *Grief: The mourning after.* Wiley, New York.

Santayana, G. (1944). *Persons and places.* Scribner's, New York.

Sanner, M. (1994). Attitudes toward organ donation and transplantation: A model for understanding reactions to medical procedures after death. *Social Science and Medicine, 38*(8), 1141-1152.

Santrock, J. W. (1985). *Adult development and aging.* William C. Brown, Dubuque, IA.

Sarason, I. G., & Sarason, B. R. (1989). *Abnormal psychology: The problem of maladaptive behavior* (6th ed.). Prentice-Hall, Englewood Cliffs, NJ.

Sartre, J. P. (1966). *Being and nothingness: An essay on phenomenological ontology* (H. Barnes, Trans.). Citadel Press, New York. (Original work published 1943).

Saunders, C. M. (1990) (Ed.) *Hospice and palliative care: An interdisciplinary approach,* Edward Arnold, London.

Savage, J. A. (1989). *Mourning unlived lives: A psychological study of childbearing loss.* Chiron Publications, Wilmette, IL.

Saynor, J. K. (1988). Existential and spiritual concerns of people with AIDS. Special Issue: AIDS. *Journal of Palliative Care, 4*(4), 61-65.

Scarmon, M. (1991–92). *Brotherton v. Cleveland:* Property rights in the human body—Are the goods oft interred with the bones? *University of South Dakota Law Review, 37,* 429-449.

Schachter, S. (1991–92). Adolescent experiences with the death of a peer. *Omega, 24*(1), 1-11.

Schaefer, D., & Lyons, C. (1986). *How do we tell the children? A parent's guide to helping children understand and cope when someone dies.* Newmarket Press, New York.

Schaie, K. W. (1989). Perceptual speed in adulthood: Cross-sectional and longitudinal studies. *Psychology and Aging, 4,* 443-453.

Schaie, K. W., & Hertzog, C. (1983). Fourteen-year cohort-sequential analysis of adult intellectual development. *Developmental Psychology, 19,* 531-543.

Scheier, M. F., & Carver, C. S. (1985). Optimism, coping and health: Assessment and implications of generalized expectancies. *Health Psychology, 4,* 219-247.

Scheier, M. F., & Carver, C. S. (1992). Effects of optimism on psychological and physical well-being: Theoretical overview and empirical update. *Cognitive Theory and Research, 16*(2), 201-228.

Scheier, M. F., Matthews, K. A., Owens, J. F., Magovern, G. J., Lefebvre, R. C., Abbott, R. A., & Carver, C. S. (1989). Dispositional optimism and recovery from coronary artery bypass surgery: The beneficial effects on physical and psychological well-being. *Journal of Personality and Social Psychology, 57,* 1024-1040.

Schell, B. H., & Zinger, J. T. (1985). An investigation of self-actualization, job satisfaction, and job commitment for Ontario funeral directors. *Psychological Reports, 57*(2), 455-464.

Schildkraut, J. J. (1965). The catecholamine hypothesis of affective disorders. A review of supporting evidence. *American Journal of Psychiatry, 122,* 509-522.

Schneider, J. (1984). *Stress, loss and grief.* Aspen Systems Corp., Rockville, MD.

Schneider, J. (1989, Autumn). The transformative power of grief. *Noetic Sciences Review,* 26-31.

Schneider, S., & Kastenbaum, R. (1993). Patterns and meanings of prayer in hospice caregivers: An exploratory study. *Death Studies, 17,* 471-485.

Schulsinger, F., Kety, S. S., Rosenthal, D., & Wender, P. H. (1979). A family study of suicide. In M. Schou & E. Stomgren (Eds.), *Origins, prevention and treatment of affective disorders* (pp. 277-288). Academic Press, New York.

Schulz, R., & Aderman, D. (1974). Clinical research and the stages of dying. *Omega, 5,* 137-143.

Schulz, R., & Aderman, D. (1980). How the medical staff copes with dying patients: A critical review. In R. Kalish (Ed.), *Caring relationships: The dying and the bereaved* (pp. 134-144). Baywood, Farmingdale, NY.

Schwab, R. (1992). Effects of a child's death on the marital relationship: A preliminary study. *Death Studies, 16*(2), 141-154.

Schwartzberg, S. S., & Halgin, R. P. (1991). Treating grieving clients: The importance of cognitive change. *Professional Psychology: Research and Practice, 22*(3), 240-246.

Sdorow, L. M. (1995). *Psychology* (3rd Ed.). Brown & Benchmark, Madison, WI.

Seale, C., & Addington-Hall, J. (1994). Euthanasia: Why people want to die earlier. *Social Science and Medicine, 39*(5), 647-654.

Seamon, J. G., & Kenrick, D. T. (1994). *Psychology.* Prentice Hall, Englewood Cliffs, NJ.

Seeland, I. B. (1990). The hidden side of grief. In V. R. Pine, O. S. Margolis, K. Doka, A. H. Kutscher, D. J. Schaefer, M. E. Siegel, & D. J. Cherico (Eds.), *Unrecognized and unsanctioned grief* (pp. 53-61). Thomas, Springfield, IL.

Selye, H. (1956). *The stress of life.* McGraw-Hill, New York.

Seligman, M. E. P. (1974). Depression and learned helplessness. In R. J. Friedman & M. M. Katz (Eds.), *The psychology of depression: Contemporary theory and research* (pp. 83-126). V.H. Winston, Washington, DC.

Seligman, M. E. P. (1975). *Helplessness: On depression, development and death.* Freeman, San Francisco.

Serdahely, W. J. (1989–90). A pediatric near-death experience: Tunnel variants. *Omega, 20*(1), 55-62.

Serdahely, W. J. (1992). Similarities between near-death experiences and multiple personality disorder. *Journal of Near-Death Studies, 11*(1), 19-38.

Service Industries Annual Receipts. (1990). *Statistical abstract of the United States 1990* (110th ed.). U.S. Government Printing Office, Washington, DC.

Shaffer, D. (1974). Suicide in childhood and early adolescence. *Journal of Child Psychology and Psychiatry, 15,* 275-291.

Shane, E., & Shane, M. (1990). Object loss and self object loss: A consideration of self psychology's contribution to understanding mourning and the failure to mourn. *Annual of Psychoanalysis, 18,* 115-131.

Shanfield, S., Benjamin, G., & Swain, B. (1988). The family under stress: The death of adult children. In O. S. Margolis, K. Doka, A. H. Kutscher, D. J. Schaefer, M. E. Siegel, & D. J. Cherico (Eds.), *Grief and loss of an adult child* (pp. 3-7). Praeger, New York.

Shanfield, S. & Swain, B. (1984). Death of adult children in traffic accidents. *Journal of Nervous and Mental Disease, 172*(9), 533-538.

Shapiro, J., Larsen, K., & Jacokes, D. (1991). The psychosocial morbidity and mortality conference: Parallel process in resident training. *Family Systems Medicine, 9*(4), 397-407.

Sheehy, G. (1976). *Passages: Predictable crises of adult life.* Dutton, New York.

Shekelle, R. B., Raynor, W. J., Ostfeld, A. M., Garron, D. C., Bieliauskas, L. A., Liv, S. C., Maliza, C., & Oolesby, P. (1981). Psychological depression and 17-year risk of death from cancer. *Psychosomatic Medicine, 43,* 117-125.

Sheras, P. L. (1983). Suicide in adolescence. In C. E. Walker & C. M. Roberts (Eds.), *Handbook of clinical child psychology* (pp. 26-38). Wiley, New York.

Sherman, R., & Fredman, N. (1986). *Handbook of structural techniques in marriage and family therapy.* Brunner/Mazel, New York.

Shibles, W. (1974). *Death: An interdisciplinary analysis.* Language Press, Whitewater, WI.

Shneidman, E. S. (1973). *Deaths of man.* Quadrangle/New York Times Book Co., New York.

Shneidman, E. S. (1980). *Voices of death*. Harper & Row, New York.

Shneidman, E. S. (1985). *Definition of suicide*. Wiley, New York.

Shneidman, E. S., & Faberow, N. L. (1970). Attempted and completed suicide. In E. S. Shneidman, N. L. Faberow, & R. E. Litman (Eds.), *The psychology of suicide* (pp. 96-100). Science House, New York.

Shore, J. H., Vollmer, W. M., & Tatum, E. L. (1989). Community patterns of posttraumatic stress disorders. *Journal of Nervous and Mental Disease, 177,* 681-685.

Shuchter, S. R. (1986). *Dimensions of grief: Adjusting to the death of a spouse.* Jossey-Bass, San Francisco.

Siefken, S. (1993, Spring). The Hispanic perspective on death and dying: A combination of respect, empathy, and spirituality. *Pride Institute Journal of Long-Term Home-Health Care, 12*(2), 26-28.

Siegel, J. M. (1990). Stressful life events and use of physician services among the elderly. *Journal of Personality and Social Psychology, 58,* 1081-1086.

Siegel, R. K. (1980). The psychology of life and death. *American Psychologist, 35*(10), 911-931.

Siggins, L. (1966). Mourning: A critical survey of the literature. *International Journal of Psychoanalysis, 47,* 14-25.

Silver, R. L., & Wortman, C. B. (1980). Coping with undesirable life events. In J. Garber & M. E. P. Seligman (Eds.), *Human helplessness: Theory and applications* (pp. 220-231). Academic Press, New York.

Silverman, P. R., Nickman, S., & Worden, J. W. (1992). Detachment revisited: The child's reconstruction of a dead parrent. *American Journal of Orthopsychiatry, 62*(4), 494-503.

Silverman, P. R., & Worden, J. W. (1992). Children's understanding of funeral ritual. *Omega, 25*(4), 319-331.

Simpson, M. A., (1979). Social and psychological aspects of dying. In H. Wass (Ed.), *Dying: Facing the facts* (pp. 108-124). Hemisphere, Washington, DC.

Sims, A. M. (1991). Who am I now? A sibling shares her survival. In J. D. Morgan (Ed.), *The dying and the bereaved teenager* (pp. 33-38). Charles Press, Philadelphia.

Singer, J. (1973). *Boundaries of the soul: The practice of Jung's psychology.* Anchor/Doubleday, Garden City, NY.

Singh, B. S., & Raphael, B. (1981). Post-disaster morbidity of the bereavement. *Journal of Nervous and Mental Disease, 169*(4), 208-212.

Slater, J., & Depue, R. A. (1981). The contribution of environmental events and social support to serious suicide attempts in primary depressive disorder. *Journal of Abnormal Psychology, 40,* 275-285.

Smart, L. S. (1993–94). Parental bereavement in Anglo-American history. *Omega, 28*(1), 49-61.

Smith, D. C., & Maher, M. F. (1993). Achieving a healthy death: The dying person's attitudinal contributions. *Hospice Journal, 9*(1), 21-32.

Smith, R. E. (1993). *Psychology*. West, Minneapolis/St. Paul, MN.

Smith, R. L., & Stevens-Smith, P. (1992). *Basic techniques in marriage and family counseling and therapy*. ERIC Clearinghouse on Counseling and Personnel Services, Ann Arbor, MI. Office of Educational Research and Improvement (ED), Washington, DC. (EDO-CG-92-1).

Smith, T. W., & Pope, M. K. (1990). Cynical hostility as a health risk: Current status and future directions. Special issue: Type A behavior. *Journal of Social Behavior and Personality, 5,* 77-88.

Solzhenitsyn, A. (1969). *Cancer ward*. Dial Press, New York.

Sommer, D. R. (1989). The spiritual needs of dying children. Special Issue: The death of a child: II. Issues. *Comprehensive Pediatric Nursing, 12* (2–3), 225-233.

Sontag, S. (1989). *AIDS and its metaphors*. Collins, Toronto.

Sood, B., Weller, E. B., & Weller, R. A. (1992). Somatic complaints in grieving children. *Comprehensive Mental Health Care, 2*(1), 17-25.

Soros, G. (1995, Winter). Reflections on death in America. *Open Society News*. (The Soros Foundation, New York). pp. 2-3.

Soto, A. R., & Villa, J. (1990). Una platica: Mexican-American approaches to death and dying. In J. K. Parry (Ed.), *Social work practice with the terminally ill: A transcultural perspective* (pp. 113-127). Thomas, Springfield, IL.

Speece, M. W. (1983). *Very young children's experiences with and reactions to death*. Unpublished master's thesis, Wayne State University, Detroit, MI.

Speece, M. W. (1995). The search for a mature concept of death: Progress on its specification and definition. *Forum, 21*(6), 1-23.

Speece, M. W., Brent, S. B. (1992, May–June). The acquisition of a mature understanding of three components of the concept of death. *Death Studies, 16*(3), 211-229.

Spirito, A., Brown, L., Overholser, J., & Fritz, G. (1989). Attempted suicide in adolescence: A review and critique of the literature. *Clinical Psychology Review, 9,* 335-363.

Stambrook, M., & Parker, K. C. H. (1987, April). The development of the concept of death in children: A review of the literature. *Merrill-Palmer Quarterly, 33,* 133-157.

Statistical Abstracts of the United States. (1990). U.S. Bureau of the Census. Available: http://www.census.gov

Stephens, J. B. (1985). Suicidal women and their relationships with husbands, boyfriends, and lovers. *Suicide and Life-Threatening Behavior, 15,* 77-89.

Stephenson, D., & Leroux, J. A. (1994). Portrait of a creatively gifted child facing cancer. *Creativity Research Journal, 7*(1), 71-77.

Stern, J. (1985). Pet attachment as a delayed mourning process. *Journal of Psychology and Judaism, 9*(2), 114-119.

Stevenson, I., Cook, C. W., & McClean-Rice, N. (1989–90). Are persons reporting "near-death experiences" really near death? A study of medical records. *Omega, 20,* 45-54.

Stewart, C. S., Thrush, J. C., Paulus, G., & Hafner, P. (1985). The elderly's adjustment to the loss of a companion animal: People-pet dependency. *Death Studies, 9,* 383-393.

Stillion, J. M. (1995). Premature exits: Understanding suicide. In L. A. DeSpelder & A. L. Strickland (Eds.), *The path ahead,* (pp. 182-197). Mayfield, Mountain View, CA.

Stillion, J. M., & McDowell, E. E. (1995). Examining suicide from a life-span perspective. In J. B. Williamsom & E. S. Shneidman (Eds.), *Death: Current perspectives* (4th ed., pp. 345-368). Mayfield, Mountain View, CA.

Stillion, J. M., McDowell, E. E., & May, J. H. (1989). *Suicide across the life span: Premature exits.* Hemisphere, Washington, DC.

Stoddard, J. B., & Henry, J. P. (1985). Affectional bonding and the impact of bereavement. *Advances, 2* (2), 19-28.

Stroebe, M. S. (1994). The broken heart phenomenon: An examination of the mortality of bereavement. *Journal of Community and Applied Social Psychology, 4*(1), 47-61.

Stroebe, M. S., Stroebe, W., & Hansson, R. (1988). Bereavement research: A historical introduction. *Journal of Social Issues, 44,* 1-18.

Stroebe, W., & Stroebe, M. S. (1987). *Bereavement and health: The psychological and physical consequences of partner loss.* Cambridge University Press, Cambridge.

Stone, R., Cafferata, G. L., & Sangl, J. (1987). Caregivers of the frail elderly: A national profile. *The Gerontologist, 27*(5), 616-626.

Stotland, E. (1969). *The psychology of hope.* Jossey-Bass, San Francisco.

Stuart, R. (1989). *Helping couples change.* Guildford Press, New York.

Suarez, E. (1990, August). Anger and heart disease—Is there a link? *Healthline,* 2-4.

Suarez, E. C., & Williams, R. B. (1989). Situational determinants of cardiovascular and emotional reactivity in high- and low-hostile men. *Psychosomatic Medicine, 51,* 404-418.

Sudnow, D. (1967). *Passing on: The social organization of dying.* Prentice-Hall, Englewood Cliffs, NJ.

Sullaway, M. E., & Morell, M. A. (1990). Marital relationships and Type A behavior assessed using the structured interview, Jenkins activity survey, and Framingham Type A scale. *Journal of Behavioral Medicine, 13,* 419-436.

Sullivan, K., & Sullivan, A. (1980). Adolescent/parent separation. *Developmental Psychology, 16,* 93-99.

Sullivan, T. D. (1993). Active and passive euthanasia: An impertinent distinction? In L. P. Pojman (Ed.), *Life and death: A reader in moral problems* (pp. 259-264). Jones and Bartlett, Boston.

Suomi, S. J. (1983). Models of depression in primates. *Psychological Medicine, 13,* 465-468.

Sutherland, C. (1990, Fall). Changes in religious beliefs, attitudes, and practices following near-death experiences: An Australian study. *Journal of Near-Death Studies, 9*(1), 21-31.

Svare, B., & Gandelman, R. (1975). Aggressive behavior of juvenile mice: Influence of androgen and olfactory stimuli. *Developmental Psychobiology, 8,* 405-415.

Sweeting, H. N., & Gilhooly, M. L. (1991–92). Doctor, am I dead? A review of social death in modern societies. *Omega, 24*(4), 251-269.

Takanishi, R. (1993). The opportunities of adolescence—Research interventions and policy. *American Psychologist, 48,* 85-87.

Tart, C. (1989). *Open mind, discriminating mind: Reflections of human possibilities.* Harper & Row, New York.

Taylor, S. (1983). Adjustment to threatening events: A theory of cognitive adaptation. *American Psychologist, 38,* 1161-1173.

Taylor, S. E., Wood, J. V., & Lichtman, R. R. (1983). It could be worse: Selective evaluation as a response to victimization. *Journal of Social Issues, 39*(2), 19-40.

Teleki, G. (1973). Group response to the accidental death of a chimpanzee in Gombe National Park, Tanzania. *Folia Primatologica, 20,* 81-94.

Thatcher, R. W., Walker, R. A., & Giudice, S. (1986). Human cerebral hemispheres develop at different rates and different ages. *Science, 236,* 1110-1113.

Theut, S. K., Moss, H. A., & Zaslow, M. J. (1992). Perinatal loss and maternal attitudes toward the subsequent child. *Infant Mental Health Journal, 13*(2), 157-166.

Thomas, C. B., & Duszynski, K. R. (1974). Closeness to parents and family constellation in a prospective study of five disease states: Suicide, mental illness, malignant tumor, hypertension and coronary heart disease. *Johns Hopkins Medical Journal, 134,* 251-269.

Thomas, V., & Striegel, P. (1995). Stress and grief of a perinatal loss: Integrating qualitative and quantitative methods. *Omega, 30*(4), 299-311.

Thompson, J. N., & Abraham, T. K. (1986). Male genital self-mutilation. *Medical Aspects of Human Sexuality, 20*(5), 148.

Thorson, J. A., & Powell, F. C. (1991). Medical students' attitudes towards aging and death: A cross-sequential study. *Medical Education, 25*(1), 32-37.

Thrush, J. C., & Paulus, G. S. (1970). The concept of death in popular music: A social-psychological perspective. *Popular Music and Society, 1,* 219-228.

Tillich, P. (1952). *The courage to be.* Yale University Press, New Haven, CT.

Tishler, C. L., McKenry, P. C., & Morgan, K. C. (1981). Adolescent suicide attempts: Some significant factors. *Suicide and Life-Threatening Behavior, 11,* 86-92.

Tolle, S. W., Cooney, T. G., & Hickam, D. H. (1989). A program to teach residents humanistic skills for notifying survivors of a patient's death. *Academic Medicine, 64*(9), 505-506.

Tolstoy, L. (1960). *The Death of Ivan Ilych and other stories,* New American Library, New York. (Original work published in 1886).

Tomer, A. (1994). Death anxiety in adult life—Theoretical perspectives. In R. A. Niemeyer (Ed.), *Death anxiety handbook: Research, instrumentation and application* (pp. 3-28). Taylor & Francis, Washington, DC.

Tooley, M. (1984). *Abortion and infanticide*. Oxford University Press, Oxford.

Topol, P., & Retnikoff, M. (1982). Perceived peer and family relationships, hopelessness, locus of control as factors in adolescent suicide attempts. *Suicide and Life-Threatening Behavior, 12,* 141-150.

Torrens, P. R. (1985). *Hospice programs and public policy.* American Hospital Publishing, Chicago.

Toscani, F. (1990). Overcoming professional opposition. *Journal of Palliative Care, 6*(4), 40-42.

Toufexis, A. (1994, April 18). When is crib death a cover for murder? *Time,* 16.

Toufexis, A. (1994, July 4) Killing the psychic pain: A Dutch court says doctors can assist suicides of depressed but physically healthy patients. *Time, 144*(1), 61.

Toufexis, A., & Castronoro, V. (1983, April 18). Turning illness into a way of life. *Time,* 69.

Troll, L. E. (1985). *Early and middle adulthood* (2nd. ed.). Brooks/Cole, Monterey, CA.

Tross, S., & Hirsch, D. A. (1988). Psychological distress and neuropsychological complications of HIV infection and AIDs. *American Psychologist, 43*(11), 929-934.

Tsomo, K. L. (1993, Summer). Opportunity or obstacle: Buddhist views of organ donation. *Tricycle,* 30-35.

Turner, Juan L. (1993). Personal reflections on the African American experience. In D. P. Irish, K. F. Lundquist, & V. J. Nelsen (Eds.), *Ethnic variations in dying, death, and grief* (pp. 201-202). Taylor & Francis, Washington, DC.

Turner, R. H. (1970). *Family interaction.* Wiley, New York.

Turner, R. J., & Avison, W. R. (1989). Gender and depression: Assessing exposure and vulnerability to life events in a chronically strained population. *Journal of Nervous and Mental Disease, 177,* 443-455.

Uhlenhuth, E. (1973, February 7) Free therapy said to be helpful to Chicago train wreck victim. *Psychiatric News, 8*(3), pp. 1-27.

Umberson, D., & Chen, M. D. (1994). Effects of a parent's death on adult children: Relationship salience and reaction to loss. *American Sociological Review, 59*(1), 152-168.

Unger, R. K. (1979). *Female and male psychological perspectives.* Harper & Row, New York.

U.S. Congress, Office of Technology Assessment. (1987). *Life-sustaining technologies and the elderly.* U.S. Government Printing Office, Washington, DC.

U.S. Department of Labor. (1980, March). *Occupational outlook handbook* (Bulletin No. 2075). Bureau of Labor Statistics, Washington, DC.

U.S. Department of Labor. (1996). *Census of fatal occupational injuries: 1994.* Bureau of Labor Statistics and Research, San Francisco. Available: http://www.dir.ca.gov/dir..._day_bul_94/Work_fat

U.S. Select Committee on Aging. (1988). *Exploding the myths: Caregiving in America*. (Comm. Pub. 100-665). U.S. Government Printing Office, Washington, DC. (ED 300 718).

U.S. Select Committee on Aging. (1994, March 30). *Home care and community-based services: Overcoming barriers to access* (Report No. 103-16). Available: gopher;//ftp.senate.gov:7...mmittee_publications

Vasquez, M. (1993). Personal reflections on the Hispanic experience. In D. P. Irish, K. F. Lundquist, and V. J. Nelsen (Eds.), *Ethnic variations in dying, death, and grief* (pp. 203-205). Taylor & Francis, Washington, DC.

Vernon, G. M. (1970). *Sociology of death: An analysis of death-related behaviors*. Ronald Press, New York.

Videka-Sherman, L., & Lieberman, M. (1985). The effects of self-help and psychotherapy intervention on child loss: The limits of recovery. *American Journal of Orthopsychiatry, 55*(1), 70-82.

Vinokur, A. D., & van Ryn, M. (1993). Social support and undermining in close relationships: Their independent effects on the mental health of unemployed persons. *Journal of Personality and Social Psychology, 65,* 350-359.

Viorst, J. (1986). *Necessary losses*. Fawcett, New York.

Vogel G., Foulkes, D., & Trosman, H. (1966). Ego functions and dreaming during sleep onset. *Archives of General Psychology, 14,* 238-248.

Vogt, T., Mullooly, J., Ernst, D., Pope, C., & Hollis, J. (1992). Social networks as predictors of ischemic heart disease, cancer, stroke and hypertension: Incidence, survival and mortality. *Journal of Clinical Epedemiology, 45,* 659-666.

Waldman, S. (1990). The health care giver: Unmasking grief. In V. R. Pine, O. S. Margolis, K. Doka, A. H. Kutscher, D. J. Schaefer, M. E. Siegel, & D. J. Cherico (Eds.), *Unrecognized and unsanctioned grief* (pp. 152-157). Thomas, Springfield, IL.

Waldman, S. (1993). Surviving a fate worse than death: The plight of the homebound elderly. *Loss, Grief and Care, 6*(4), 67-71.

Walker, W. L. (1980). Intentional self-injury in school-age children. *Journal of Adolescence, 3,* 217-228.

Walter, T. (1995). Natural death and the noble savage. *Omega, 30*(4), 237-248.

Walter, T. (1996). A new model of grief: Bereavement and biography. *Mortality, 1*(1), 7-25.

Wang, J. J., & Kaufman, A. S. (1993). Changes in fluid and crystallized intelligence across the 20- to 90-year range in the K-BIT. *Journal of Psychoeducational Assessment, 11,* 29-37.

Ward, R. (1980). Age and acceptance of euthanasia. *Journal of Gerontology, 35,* 421-431.

Warner, R., Carmen, G., & Christiana, N. M. (1989). The spiritual needs of persons with AIDS. *Family and Community Health, 12*(2), 43-51.

Warren, L. W., & Tomlinson-Keasey, C. (1987). The context of suicide. *American Journal of Orthopsychiatry, 57,* 41-48.

Wass, H. (1979). Death and the elderly. In H. Wass (Ed.), *Dying: Facing the facts* (pp. 182-203). Hemisphere, Washington, DC.

Wass, H. (1990). Death education and grief/suicide intervention in the public schools. *Death Studies, 14,* 253-268.

Wass, H. (1995). Death in the lives of children. In H. Wass & R. A. Niemeyer (Eds.), *Dying: Facing the facts* (pp. 269-301). Taylor & Francis, Washington, DC.

Wass, H., Miller, D. M., & Redditt, C. A. (1991). Adolescents and destructive themes in rock music: A follow-up. *Omega, 23,* 199-206.

Wass, H., Miller, M. D., & Stevenson, R. G. (1989). Factors affecting adolescents' behavior and attitudes toward destructive rock lyrics. *Death Studies, 13*(3), 287-303.

Wass, H., Raup, J. L., & Sisler, H. H. (1989). Adolescents and death on television: A follow-up study. *Death Studies, 13*(2), 161-173.

Wass, H., Raup, J. L., Cerullo, K., & Martel, L. G. (1988−89). Adolescents' interest in and views of destructive themes in rock music. *Omega, 19*(3), 177-186.

Waterman, C. K., Beubel, M. E., & Waterman, A. S. (1970). Relationship between resolution of the identity crisis and outcomes of previous psychosocial crises. *Proceedings of the Annual Convention of the American Psychological Association, 5* (Pt. 1), 467-468.

Watson, N. L., Weinstein, M. (1993). Pet ownership in relation to depression, anxiety, and anger in working women. *Anthrozoos, 6*(2), 135-138.

Watts, A. (1987). *The early writing of Alan Watts* (J. Snelling, Ed.). Celestial Arts, Berkeley, CA.

Webb, N. B. (1993). *Helping bereaved children: A handbook for practitioners.* Guildford Press, New York.

Weiner, N. (1994). *Hutu and Tutsi of Rwanda and Barundi.* Available: http://www.backgroundbriefing.com/hutututs.html

Weisman, A. D. (1972). *On dying and denying: A psychiatric study of terminality.* McGraw-Hill, New York.

Weisman, A. D. (1974). *The realization of death.* Aronson, New York.

Weisman, A. D. (1991). Bereavement and companion animals. *Omega, 22,* 241-248.

Weiss, M. (1993). Bedside manners: Paradoxes of physician behavior in grand rounds. *Culture, Medicine and Psychiatry, 17*(2), 235-253.

Weiss, R. (1984). Reactions to particular types of bereavement. In M. Osterwiess, (Ed.), *Bereavement: Reactions, consequences and care* (pp. 71-96). National Academy Press, Washington, DC.

Weissbourd, R. (1996). *The vulnerable child: What really hurts America's children and what we can do about it.* Addison-Wesley, Reading, MA.

Weissman, S. I. (1977). Why the Uniform Anatomical Gifts Act has failed. *Trusts and Estates, 116,* 264-267, 281-282.

Weiten, W. (1994). *Psychology: Themes and variations.* Brooks/Cole, Pacific Grove, CA.

Welford, J. M. (1992, September/October). American death and burial custom derivation from medieval European cultures. *Forum,* 6-9.

Wentzy, J. (1995). *Political funerals*. Available: http: //www.actupny.org/diva/polfunsyn.html

West, M. (1994). Psychological issues in hospice music therapy. *Music Therapy Perspectives, 12*(2), 117–124.

Wetzel, R. D. (1976). Hopelessness, depression, and suicide intent. *Archives of General Psychiatry, 33,* 1069–1073.

Whalen, William J., (1990, September). How different religions pay their final respects. *U.S. Catholic,* pp. 29–35.

White, J. L. (1984). *The psychology of blacks: An Afro-American perspective.* Prentice-Hall, Englewood Cliffs, NJ.

Whitis, P. R. (1968). The legacy of a child's suicide. *Family Process, 7*(2), 159–68.

Wiebe, D. J. (1991). Hardiness and stress moderation: A test of proposed mechanisms. *Journal of Personality and Social Psychology, 60,* 89–99.

Wiesel, E. (1966). *The gates of the forest* (F. Frenaye, Trans.). Holt, Rinehart & Winston, New York.

William, J. L. (1992). Don't discuss it: Reconciling illness, dying, and death in a medical school anatomy laboratory. *Family Systems Medicine, 10*(1), 65–78.

Williams, G. (1993). For legalizing euthanasia, A rejoinder. In Louis P. Pojman (Ed.), *Life and death: A reader in moral problems* (pp. 244–251). Jones and Bartlett, Boston.

Williams, M. D. (1974). *Community in a black Pentecostal church: An anthropological study.* Waveland Press, Prospect Heights, IL.

Winnicott, D. (1965). *The maturational process and the facilitating environment.* International Universities Press, New York.

Wisendale, S. K., & Allison, M. D. (1988). An analysis of 1987 state family leave legislation: Implications for caregivers of the elderly. *The Gerontologist, 28*(6), 779–785.

Wispe, L. (Ed.). (1978). *Alltruism, sympathy and helping.* Academic Press, New York.

Wolf, S. S. (1995). Legal perspectives on planning for death. In H. Wass & R. A. Niemeyer (Eds.), *Dying: Facing the facts.* (pp. 163–184). Taylor & Francis, Washington, DC.

Wolff, C. T., Friedman, S. B., Hofer, M. A., & Mason, J. W. (1964). Relationship between psychological defense and mean urinary 17-hydroxycorticosteroid excretion rate: A study of parents of fatally ill children. *Psychosomatic Medicine, 26,* 576–591.

Wolinsky, F. D., & Johnson, R. J. (1992). Widowhood, health status, and the use of health services by older adults: A cross-sectional and prospective approach. *Journal of Gerontology, 47*(1), S8–S16.

Worden, J. W. (1991). *Grief counseling and grief therapy: A handbook for the mental health practitioner.* Springer, New York.

World Health Organization. (1996). *Global Programme on AIDS.* Available: http://www.otago.ac.nz/qrd/aids/who/stats –WHO-12.31.93

Worsnop, R. L. (1995). Assisted-suicide controversy. *Congressional Quarterly Researcher.* U.S. Congress, Washington, DC.

Wortman, C. B., & Silver, R. C. (1987). Coping with irrevocable loss. In Gr. R. VandenBos & B. K. Bryant (Eds.), *Catacylsms, crises, and catastrophes: Psychology in action* (pp. 189-235). American Psychological Association, Washington, DC.

Wortman, C. B., & Silver, R. C. (1989). The myths of coping with loss. *Journal of Consulting and Clinical Psychology, 57,* 349-357.

Wrenn, R. L. (1991a). College management of student death: A survey. *Death Studies, 15,* 395-402.

Wrenn, R. L. (1991b). College student death: Postvention issues for educators and counselors. In D. Papadatou & C. Papadatou (Eds.), *Children and death* (pp. 53-64). Hemisphere, New York.

Wrenn, R. L. (1992, Spring). Educating the educators. *Thanatos, 33-35.*

Wrenn, R. L. (1994). A death at school: Issues and interventions. *Counseling and Human Development, 26*(7), 1-7.

Yalom, I. (1980). *Existential psychotherapy.* Basic Books, New York.

Yates, B. T., Fullerton, C. S., Goodrich, W., & Heinssen, R. K. (1989). Grandparent deaths and severe maternal reaction in the etiology of adolescent psychopathology. *Journal of Nervous and Mental Disease, 177*(11), 675-680.

Yoder, L. (1986). The funeral meal: A significant funerary ritual. *Journal of Religion and Health, 25*(2), 149-160.

Young, T. J. (1992). Procedures and problems in conducting a psychological autopsy. *International Journal of Offender Therapy and Comparative Criminology, 36*(1), 43-52.

Younoszai, B. (1993). Mexican American perspectives related to death. In D. P. Irish, K. F. Lundquist, and V. J. Nelsen (Eds.), *Ethnic variations in dying, death, and grief* (pp. 67–78). Taylor & Francis, Washington, DC.

Zabrucky, K., Moore, D., & Schultz, Jr., N. R. (1987). Evaluation of comprehension in young and old adults. *Developmental Psychology, 22,* 39-43.

Zahn-Waxler, C., & Radke-Yarrow, M. (1982). The development of altruism: Alternative research strategies. In N. Eisenberg (Ed.), *The development of prosocial behavior* (p. 126). Academic Press, New York.

Zautra, A. J., Okun, M. A., Robinson, S. E., Lee, D., & Emmanual, J. (1989). Life stress and lymphocyte alterations among patients with rheumatoid arthritis. *Health Psychology, 8,* 1-14.

Zeligs, R. (1974). *Children's experiences with death.* Thomas, Springfield, Il.

Zeltzer, L., LeBaron, S., & Zeltzer, P. (1984). The adolescent with cancer. In R. W. Blum (Ed.), *Chronic illness and disabilities in childhood and adolescence* (pp. 16-21). Grune & Stratton, Orlando, FL.

Zhang, Y., & Wang, X. (1994). 56 cases of disturbance in small articulations of the lumbar vertebrae treated by puncturing the effective points—A new system of acupuncture. *Journal of Traditional Chinese Medicine, 2,* 14.

Zisook, S. (Ed.). (1987). *Biopsychosocial aspects of bereavement.* American Psychiatric Press, Washington, DC.

Zisook, S., & Shuchter, S. R. (1986). The first four years of widowhood. *Psychiatric Annals, 16*(5), 288-294.

Zisook, S., Shuchter, S. R., & Sledge, P. (1993). Aging and bereavement. *Journal of Geriatric Psychiatry and Neurology, 6*(3), 137-143.

Zysk, K. G. (1991). *Asceticism and healing in ancient India: Medicine in the Buddhist monastery.* Oxford University Press, Oxford.

Subject Index

Page numbers in *italic* indicate boxed materials

Name Index

Page numbers in *italic* indicate boxed materials